C

Primer Plus

Fifth Edition

Stephen Prata

800 East 96th St., Indianapolis, Indiana, 46240 USA

C Primer Plus

International Standard Book Number: 0-672-32696-5

Library of Congress Catalog Card Number: 2004095068

Printed in the United States of America

First Printing: November 2004

12   14

Trademarks

Warning and Disclaimer

Bulk Sales

Sams Publishing offers excellent discounts on this book when ordered in quantity for bulk purchases or special sales. For more information, please contact

U.S. Corporate and Government Sales

1-800-382-3419

corpsales@pearsontechgroup.com

For sales outside of the U.S., please contact

International Sales

international@pearsoned.com

ASSOCIATE PUBLISHER
Michael Stephens

ACQUISITIONS EDITOR
Loretta Yates

MANAGING EDITOR
Charlotte Clapp

DEVELOPMENT EDITOR
Songlin Qiu

PROJECT EDITOR
George E. Nedeff

COPY EDITOR
Bart Reed

INDEXER
Chris Barrick

PROOFREADER
Paula Lowell

TECHNICAL EDITOR
Greg Perry

PUBLISHING COORDINATOR
Cindy Teeters

MULTIMEDIA DEVELOPER
Dan Scherf

BOOK DESIGNER
Gary Adair

PAGE LAYOUT
Bronkella Publishing

CONTENTS AT A GLANCE

TABLE OF CONTENTS

PREFACE

C was a relatively little-known language when the first edition of *C Primer Plus* was written in 1984. Since then, the language has boomed, and many people have learned C with the help of this book. In fact, over 500,000 people have purchased *C Primer Plus* throughout its various editions.

As the language has grown from the early informal K&R standard through the 1990 ISO/ANSI standard to the 1999 ISO/ANSI standard, so has this book matured through this, the fifth edition. As with all the editions, my aim has been to create an introduction to C that is instructive, clear, and helpful.

Approach and Goals

My goal is for this book to serve as a friendly, easy-to-use, self-study guide. To accomplish that objective, *C Primer Plus* employs the following strategies:

- Programming concepts are explained, along with details of the C language; the book does *not* assume that you are a professional programmer.

- Many short, easily typed examples illustrate just one or two concepts at a time, because learning by doing is one of the most effective ways to master new information.

- Figures and illustrations clarify concepts that are difficult to grasp in words alone.

- Highlight boxes summarize the main features of C for easy reference and review.

- Review questions and programming exercises at the end of each chapter allow you to test and improve your understanding of C.

To gain the greatest benefit, you should take as active a role as possible in studying the topics in this book. Don't just read the examples, enter them into your system, and try them. C is a very portable language, but you may find differences between how a program works on your system and how it works on ours. Experiment—change part of a program to see what the effect is. Modify a program to do something slightly different. Ignore the occasional warnings and see what happens when you do the wrong thing. Try the questions and exercises. The more you do yourself, the more you will learn and remember.

I hope that you'll find this newest edition an enjoyable and effective introduction to the C language.

ABOUT THE AUTHOR

Stephen Prata teaches astronomy, physics, and programming at the College of Marin in Kentfield, California. He received his B.S. from the California Institute of Technology and his Ph.D. from the University of California, Berkeley. His association with computers began with the computer modeling of star clusters. Stephen has authored or coauthored over a dozen books, including *C++ Primer Plus* and *Unix Primer Plus*.

DEDICATION

With love to Vicky and Bill Prata, who, for more than 69 years, have been showing
how rewarding a marriage can be. —SP

ACKNOWLEDGMENTS

I wish to thank Loretta Yates of Sams Publishing for getting this project underway and Songlin
Qiu of Sams Publishing for seeing it through. Also, thank you Ron Liechty of Metrowerks and
Greg Comeau of Comeau Computing for your help with new C99 features and your noteworthy commitment to customer service.

WE WANT TO HEAR FROM YOU!

As the reader of this book, *you* are our most important critic and commentator. We value your opinion and want to know what we're doing right, what we could do better, what areas you'd like to see us publish in, and any other words of wisdom you're willing to pass our way.

As an associate publisher for Sams Publishing, I welcome your comments. You can email or write me directly to let me know what you did or didn't like about this book—as well as what we can do to make our books better.

Please note that I cannot help you with technical problems related to the topic of this book. We do have a User Services group, however, where I will forward specific technical questions related to the book.

When you write, please be sure to include this book's title and author as well as your name, email address, and phone number. I will carefully review your comments and share them with the author and editors who worked on the book.

Email: feedback@samspublishing.com

Mail: Michael Stephens
          Associate Publisher
          Sams Publishing
          800 East 96th Street
          Indianapolis, IN 46240 USA

For more information about this book or another Sams Publishing title, visit our Web site at www.samspublishing.com. Type the ISBN (0672326965) or the title of a book in the Search field to find the page you're looking for.

CHAPTER 1

GETTING READY

You will learn about the following in this chapter:

- C's history and features
- The steps needed to write programs

- A bit about compilers and linkers
- C standards

Welcome to the world of C—a vigorous, professional programming language popular with amateur and commercial programmers alike. This chapter prepares you for learning and using this powerful and popular language, and it introduces you to the kinds of environments in which you will most likely develop your C-legs.

First, we look at C's origin and examine some of its features, both strengths and drawbacks. Then we look at the origins of programming and examine some general principles for programming. Finally, we discuss how to run C programs on some common systems.

Whence C?

Dennis Ritchie of Bell Labs created C in 1972 as he and Ken Thompson worked on designing the Unix operating system. C didn't spring full-grown from Ritchie's head, however. It came from Thompson's B language, which came from... but that's another story. The important point is that C was created as a tool for working programmers, so its chief goal is to be a useful language.

Most languages aim to be useful, but they often have other concerns. The main goal for Pascal, for instance, was to provide a sound basis for teaching good programming principles. BASIC, on the other hand, was developed to resemble English so that it could be learned easily by students unfamiliar with computers. These are important goals, but they are not always compatible with pragmatic, workaday usefulness. C's development as a language designed for programmers, however, has made it one of the modern-day languages of choice.

Why C?

During the past three decades, C has become one of the most important and popular programming languages. It has grown because people try it and like it. In the past decade, many have moved from C to the more ambitious C++ language, but C is still an important language in its own right, as well a migration path to C++. As you learn C, you will recognize its many virtues (see Figure 1.1). Let's preview a few of them now.

FIGURE 1.1
The virtues of C.

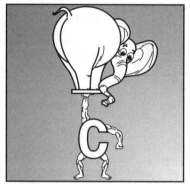
Powerful control structures

Fast

Compact code — small programs

Portable to other computers

Design Features

C is a modern language incorporating the control features found desirable by the theory and practice of computer science. Its design makes it natural for top-down planning, structured programming, and modular design. The result is a more reliable, understandable program.

Efficiency

C is an efficient language. Its design takes advantage of the capabilities of current computers. C programs tend to be compact and to run quickly. In fact, C exhibits some of the fine control usually associated with an assembly language. (An *assembly language* is a mnemonic representation of the set of internal instructions used by a particular central processing unit design; different CPU families have different assembly languages.) If you choose, you can fine-tune your programs for maximum speed or most efficient use of memory.

Portability

C is a portable language, which means that C programs written on one system can be run on other systems with little or no modification. If modifications are necessary, they can often be made by simply changing a few entries in a header file accompanying the main program. Most languages are meant to be portable, but anyone who has converted an IBM PC BASIC program to Apple BASIC (and they are close cousins) or has tried to run an IBM mainframe FORTRAN program on a Unix system knows that porting is troublesome at best. C is a leader in portability. C compilers (programs that convert your C code into the instructions a computer uses internally) are available for about 40 systems, running from 8-bit microprocessors to Cray supercomputers. Note, however, that the portions of a program written specifically to access particular hardware devices, such as a display monitor, or special features of an operating system, such as Windows XP or OS X, typically are not portable.

Because of C's close ties with Unix, Unix systems typically come with a C compiler as part of the packages. Linux installations also usually include a C compiler. Several C compilers are available for personal computers, including PCs running various versions of Windows, and Macintoshes. So whether you are using a home computer, a professional workstation, or a mainframe, the chances are good that you can get a C compiler for your particular system.

Power and Flexibility

C is powerful and flexible (two favorite words in computer literature). For example, most of the powerful, flexible Unix operating system is written in C. Many compilers and interpreters for other languages—such as FORTRAN, Perl, Python, Pascal, LISP, Logo, and BASIC—have been written in C. As a result, when you use FORTRAN on a Unix machine, ultimately a C program has done the work of producing the final executable program. C programs have been used for solving physics and engineering problems and even for animating special effects for movies such as *Gladiator*.

Programmer Oriented

C is oriented to fulfill the needs of programmers. It gives you access to hardware, and it enables you to manipulate individual bits in memory. It has a rich selection of operators that allows you to express yourself succinctly. C is less strict than, say, Pascal in limiting what you can do. This flexibility is both an advantage and a danger. The advantage is that many tasks, such as converting forms of data, are much simpler in C. The danger is that with C, you can make mistakes that are impossible in some languages. C gives you more freedom, but it also puts more responsibility on you.

Also, most C implementations have a large library of useful C functions. These functions deal with many needs that a programmer commonly faces.

Shortcomings

C does have some faults. Often, as with people, faults and virtues are opposite sides of the same feature. For example, we've mentioned that C's freedom of expression also requires added responsibility. C's use of pointers (something you can look forward to learning about in this book), in particular, means that you can make programming errors that are very difficult to trace. As one computer preliterate once commented, the price of liberty is eternal vigilance.

C's conciseness combined with its wealth of operators make it possible to prepare code that is extremely difficult to follow. You aren't compelled to write obscure code, but the opportunity is there. After all, what other language has a yearly Obfuscated Code contest?

There are more virtues and, undoubtedly, a few more faults. Rather than delve further into the matter, let's move on to a new topic.

Whither C?

By the early 1980s, C was already a dominant language in the minicomputer world of Unix systems. Since then, it has spread to personal computers (microcomputers) and to mainframes (the big guys). See Figure 1.2. Many software houses use C as the preferred language for producing word processing programs, spreadsheets, compilers, and other products. These companies know that C produces compact and efficient programs. More important, they know that these programs will be easy to modify and easy to adapt to new models of computers.

FIGURE 1.2

Where C is used.

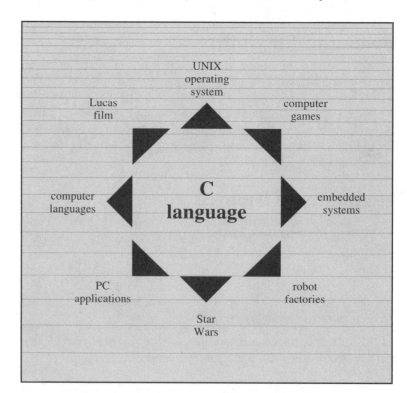

What's good for companies and C veterans is good for other users, too. More and more computer users have turned to C to secure its advantages for themselves. You don't have to be a computer professional to use C.

In the 1990s, many software houses began turning to the C++ language for large programming projects. C++ grafts object-oriented programming tools to the C language. (*Object-oriented programming* is a philosophy that attempts to mold the language to fit a problem instead of molding the problem to fit the language.) C++ is nearly a superset of C, meaning that any C program is, or nearly is, a valid C++ program, too. By learning C, you also learn much of C++.

Despite the popularity of newer languages, such as C++ and Java, C remains a core skill in the software business, typically ranking in the top 10 of desired skills. In particular, C has become popular for programming embedded systems. That is, it's used to program the increasingly common microprocessors found in automobiles, cameras, DVD players, and other modern conveniences. Also, C has been making inroads in FORTRAN's long dominance of scientific programming. Finally, as befits a language created to develop an operating system, it plays a strong role in the development of Linux. Thus, the first decade of the twenty-first century finds C still going strong.

In short, C is one of the most important programming languages and will continue to be so. If you want a job writing software, one of the first questions you should be able to answer yes to is "Oh say, can you C?"

What Computers Do

Now that you are about to learn how to program in C, you probably should know a little about how computers work. This knowledge will help you understand the connection between writing a program in C and what eventually takes place when you run that program.

Modern computers have several components. The *central processing unit*, or *CPU*, does most of the computing work. The *random access memory*, or *RAM*, serves as a workspace to hold programs and files. The permanent memory, typically a hard disk, remembers those programs and files, even if the computer is turned off. And various peripherals—such as the keyboard, mouse, and monitor—provide for communication between the computer and you. The CPU processes your programs, so let's concentrate on its role.

The life of a CPU, at least in this simplistic account, is quite simple. It fetches an instruction from memory and executes it. It fetches the next instruction from memory and executes it, and so on. (A gigahertz CPU can do this about a billion times a second, so the CPU can lead its boring life at a tremendous pace.) The CPU has its own small workspace, consisting of several *registers*, each of which can hold a number. One register holds the memory address of the next instruction, and the CPU uses this information to fetch the next instruction. After it fetches an instruction, the CPU stores the instruction in another register and updates the first register to the address of the next instruction. The CPU has a limited repertoire of instructions (known as the *instruction set*) that it understands. Also, these instructions are rather specific; many of them ask the computer to move a number from one location to another—for example, from a memory location to a register.

A couple interesting points go along with this account. First, everything stored in a computer is stored as a number. Numbers are stored as numbers. Characters, such as the alphabetical characters you use in a text document, are stored as numbers; each character has a numeric code. The instructions that a computer loads into its registers are stored as numbers; each instruction in the instruction set has a numeric code. Second, computer programs ultimately have to be expressed in this numeric instruction code, or what is called *machine language*.

One consequence of how computers work is that if you want a computer to do something, you have to feed a particular list of instructions (a program) telling it exactly what to do and how to do it. You have to create the program in a language that the computer understands directly (machine language). This is a detailed, tedious, exacting task. Something as simple as adding two numbers together would have to be broken down into several steps, perhaps something like the following:

1. Copy the number in memory location 2000 to register 1.

2. Copy the number in memory location 2004 to register 2.

3. Add the contents of register 2 to the contents of register 1, leaving the answer in register 1.

4. Copy the contents of register 1 to memory location 2008.

And you would have to represent each of these instructions with a numeric code!

If writing a program in this manner sounds like something you'd like to do, you'll be sad to learn that the golden age of machine-language programming is long past. But if you prefer something a little more enjoyable, open your heart to high-level programming languages.

High-level Computer Languages and Compilers

High-level programming languages, such as C, simplify your programming life in several ways. First, you don't have to express your instructions in a numeric code. Second, the instructions you use are much closer to how you might think about a problem than they are to the detailed approach a computer uses. Rather than worry about the precise steps a particular CPU would have to take to accomplish a particular task, you can express your desires on a more abstract level. To add two numbers, for example, you might write the following:

```
total = mine + yours;
```

Seeing code like this, you have a good idea what it does; looking at the machine-language equivalent of several instructions expressed in numeric code is much less enlightening.

Unfortunately, the opposite is true for a computer; to it, the high-level instruction is incomprehensible gibberish. This is where compilers enter the picture. The *compiler* is a program that translates the high-level language program into the detailed set of machine language instructions the computer requires. You do the high-level thinking; the compiler takes care of the tedious details.

The compiler approach has another benefit. In general, each computer design has its own unique machine language. So a program written in the machine language for, say, an Intel Pentium CPU means nothing to a Motorola PowerPC CPU. But you can match a compiler to a particular machine language. Therefore, with the right compiler or set of compilers, you can convert the same high-level language program to a variety of different machine-language programs. You solve a programming problem once, and then you let your compilers translate the solution to a variety of machine languages.

In short, high-level languages, such as C, Java, and Pascal, describe actions in a more abstract form and aren't tied to a particular CPU or instruction set. Also, high-level languages are easier to learn and much easier to program in than are machine languages.

Using C: Seven Steps

C, as you've seen, is a compiled language. If you are accustomed to using a compiled language, such as Pascal or FORTRAN, you will be familiar with the basic steps in putting together a C program. However, if your background is in an interpreted language, such as BASIC, or in a graphical interface–oriented language, such as Visual Basic, or if you have no background at all, you need to learn how to compile. We'll look at that process soon, and you'll see that it is straightforward and sensible. First, to give you an overview of programming, let's break down the act of writing a C program into seven steps (see Figure 1.3). Note that this is an idealization. In practice, particularly for larger projects, you would go back and forth, using what you learned at a later step to refine an earlier step.

FIGURE 1.3
The seven steps of
programming.

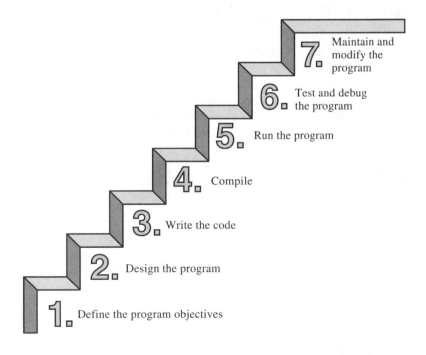

7. Maintain and modify the program

6. Test and debug the program

5. Run the program

4. Compile

3. Write the code

2. Design the program

1. Define the program objectives

Step 1: Define the Program Objectives

Naturally enough, you should start with a clear idea of what you want the program to do. Think in terms of the information your program needs, the feats of calculation and manipulation the program needs to do, and the information the program should report back to you. At this level of planning, you should be thinking in general terms, not in terms of some specific computer language.

Step 2: Design the Program

After you have a conceptual picture of what your program ought to do, you should decide how the program will go about it. What should the user interface be like? How should the program be organized? Who will the target user be? How much time do you have to complete the program?

You also need to decide how to represent the data in the program and, possibly, in auxiliary files, as well as which methods to use to process the data. When you first learn programming in C, the choices will be simple, but as you deal with more complex situations, you'll find that these decisions require more thought. Choosing a good way to represent the information can often make designing the program and processing the data much easier.

Again, you should be thinking in general terms, not about specific code, but some of your decisions may be based on general characteristics of the language. For example, a C programmer has more options in data representation than, say, a Pascal programmer.

Step 3: Write the Code

Now that you have a clear design for your program, you can begin to implement it by writing the code. That is, you translate your program design into the C language. Here is where you really have to put your knowledge of C to work. You can sketch your ideas on paper, but eventually you have to get your code into the computer. The mechanics of this process depend on your programming environment. We'll present the details for some common environments soon. In general, you use a text editor to create what is called a *source code* file. This file contains the C rendition of your program design. Listing 1.1 shows an example of C source code.

LISTING 1.1   Example of C Source Code

```c
#include <stdio.h>
int main(void)
{
    int dogs;

    printf("How many dogs do you have?\n");
    scanf("%d", &dogs);
    printf("So you have %d dog(s)!\n", dogs);

    return 0;
}
```

As part of this step, you should document your work. The simplest way is to use C's comment facility to incorporate explanations into your source code. Chapter 2, "Introducing C," will explain more about using comments in your code.

Step 4: Compile

The next step is to compile the source code. Again, the details depend on your programming environment, and we'll look at some common environments shortly. For now, let's start with a more conceptual view of what happens.

Recall that the compiler is a program whose job is to convert source code into executable code. *Executable code* is code in the native language, or *machine language*, of your computer. This language consists of detailed instructions expressed in a numeric code. As you read earlier, different computers have different machine languages, and a C compiler translates C into a particular machine language. C compilers also incorporate code from C libraries into the final program; the libraries contain a fund of standard routines, such as `printf()` and `scanf()`, for your use. (More accurately, a program called a *linker* brings in the library routines, but the compiler runs the linker for you on most systems.) The end result is an executable file containing code that the computer understands and that you can run.

The compiler also checks that your program is valid C. If the compiler finds errors, it reports them to you and doesn't produce an executable file. Understanding a particular compiler's complaints is another skill you will pick up.

Step 5: Run the Program

Traditionally, the executable file is a program you can run. To run the program in many common environments, including MS-DOS, Unix, Linux consoles, just type the name of the executable file. Other environments, such as VMS on a VAX, might require a run command or some other mechanism. *Integrated development environments* (IDEs), such as those provided for Windows and Macintosh environments, allow you to edit and execute your C program from within the IDE by selecting choices from a menu or by pressing special keys. The resulting program also can be run directly from the operating system by clicking or double-clicking the filename or icon.

Step 6: Test and Debug the Program

The fact that your program runs is a good sign, but it's possible that it could run incorrectly. Consequently, you should check to see that your program does what it is supposed to do. You'll find that some of your programs have mistakes—*bugs*, in computer jargon. *Debugging* is the process of finding and fixing program errors. Making mistakes is a natural part of learning. It seems inherent to programming, so when you combine learning and programming, you had best prepare yourself to be reminded often of your fallibility. As you become a more powerful and subtle programmer, your errors, too, will become more powerful and subtle.

You have many opportunities to err. You can make a basic design error. You can implement good ideas incorrectly. You can overlook unexpected input that messes up your program. You can use C incorrectly. You can make typing errors. You can put parentheses in the wrong place, and so on. You'll find your own items to add to this list.

Fortunately, the situation isn't hopeless, although there might be times when you think it is. The compiler catches many kinds of errors, and there are things you can do to help yourself track down the ones that the compiler doesn't catch. This book will give you debugging advice as you go along.

Step 7: Maintain and Modify the Program

When you create a program for yourself or for someone else, that program could see extensive use. If it does, you'll probably find reasons to make changes in it. Perhaps there is a minor bug that shows up only when someone enters a name beginning with Zz, or you might think of a better way to do something in the program. You could add a clever new feature. You might adapt the program so that it runs on a different computer system. All these tasks are greatly simplified if you document the program clearly and if you follow sound design practices.

Commentary

Programming is not usually as linear as the process just described. Sometimes you have to go back and forth between steps. For instance, when you are writing code, you might find that your plan was impractical. You may see a better way of doing things or, after you see how a program runs, you might feel motivated to change the design. Documenting your work helps you move back and forth between levels.

Most learners tend to neglect steps 1 and 2 (defining program objectives and designing the program) and go directly to step 3 (writing the program). The first programs you write are simple enough that you can visualize the whole process in your head. If you make a mistake, it's easy to find. As your programs grow longer and more complex, mental visualizations begin to fail, and errors get harder to find. Eventually, those who neglect the planning steps are condemned to hours of lost time, confusion, and frustration as they produce ugly, dysfunctional, and abstruse programs. The larger and more complex the job is, the more planning it requires.

The moral here is that you should develop the habit of planning before coding. Use the ancient but honorable pen-and-pencil technology to jot down the objectives of your program and to outline the design. If you do so, you eventually will reap substantial dividends in time saved and satisfaction gained.

Programming Mechanics

The exact steps you must follow to produce a program depend on your computer environment. Because C is portable, it's available in many environments, including Unix, Linux, MS-DOS (yes, some people still use it), Windows, and Macintosh OS. There's not enough space in this book to cover all environments, particularly because particular products evolve, die, and are replaced.

First, however, let's look at some aspects shared by many C environments, including the five we just mentioned. You don't really need to know what follows to run a C program, but it is good background. It can also help you understand why you have to go through some particular steps to get a C program.

When you write a program in the C language, you store what you write in a text file called a *source code file*. Most C systems, including the ones we mentioned, require that the name of the file end in .c (for example, wordcount.c and budget.c). The part of the name before the period is called the *basename*, and the part after the period is called the *extension*. Therefore, budget is a basename and c is the extension. The combination budget.c is the filename. The name should also satisfy the requirements of the particular computer operating system. For example, MS-DOS is an operating systems for IBM PCs and clones. It requires that the basename be no more than eight characters long, so the wordcount.c filename mentioned earlier would not be a valid DOS filename. Some Unix systems place a 14-character limit on the whole name, including the extension; other Unix systems allow longer names, up to 255 characters. Linux, Windows, and the Macintosh OS also allow long names.

So that we'll have something concrete to refer to, let's assume we have a source file called concrete.c containing the C source code in Listing 1.2.

LISTING 1.2   The concrete.c Program

```
#include <stdio.h>
int main(void)
{
    printf("Concrete contains gravel and cement.\n");

    return 0;
}
```

Don't worry about the details of the source code file shown in Listing 1.2; you'll learn about them in Chapter 2.

Object Code Files, Executable Files, and Libraries

The basic strategy in C programming is to use programs that convert your source code file to an executable file, which is a file containing ready-to-run machine language code. C implementations do this in two steps: compiling and linking. The compiler converts your source code to an intermediate code, and the linker combines this with other code to produce the executable file. C uses this two-part approach to facilitate the modularization of programs. You can compile individual modules separately and then use the linker to combine the compiled modules later. That way, if you need to change one module, you don't have to recompile the other ones. Also, the linker combines your program with precompiled library code.

There are several choices for the form of the intermediate files. The most prevalent choice, and the one taken by the implementations described here, is to convert the source code to machine language code, placing the result in an *object code file*, or *object file* for short. (This assumes that your source code consists of a single file.) Although the object file contains machine language code, it is not ready to run. The object file contains the translation of your source code, but it is not yet a complete program.

The first element missing from the object code file is something called *startup code*, which is code that acts as an interface between your program and the operating system. For example, you can run an IBM PC compatible under DOS or under Linux. The hardware is the same in either case, so the same object code would work with both, but you would need different startup code for DOS than you would for Linux because these systems handle programs differently from one another.

The second missing element is the code for library routines. Nearly all C programs make use of routines (called *functions*) that are part of the standard C library. For example, `concrete.c` uses the function `printf()`. The object code file does not contain the code for this function; it merely contains instructions saying to use the `printf()` function. The actual code is stored in another file, called a *library*. A library file contains object code for many functions.

The role of the linker is to bring together these three elements—your object code, the standard startup code for your system, and the library code—and put them together into a single file, the executable file. For library code, the linker extracts only the code needed for the functions you use from the library (see Figure 1.4).

FIGURE 1.4
Compiler and linker.

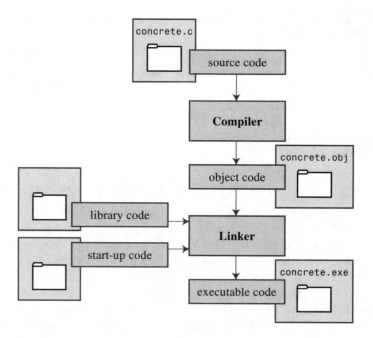

In short, an object file and an executable file both consist of machine language instructions. However, the object file contains the machine language translation only for the code you used, but the executable file also has machine code for the library routines you use and for the startup code.

On some systems, you must run the compile and link programs separately. On other systems, the compiler starts the linker automatically, so you have to give only the compile command.

Now let's look at some specific systems.

Unix System

Because C's popularity began on Unix systems, we will start there.

Editing on a Unix System

Unix C does not have its own editor. Instead, you use one of the general-purpose Unix editors, such as emacs, jove, vi, or an X Window System text editor.

Your two main responsibilities are typing the program correctly and choosing a name for the file that will store the program. As discussed, the name should end with `.c`. Note that Unix distinguishes between uppercase and lowercase. Therefore, `budget.c`, `BUDGET.c`, and `Budget.c` are three distinct and valid names for C source files, but `BUDGET.C` is not a valid name because it uses an uppercase `C` instead of a lowercase `c`.

Using the vi editor, we prepared the following program and stored it in a file called `inform.c`.

```
#include <stdio.h>
int main(void)
{
    printf("A .c is used to end a C program filename.\n");

    return 0;
}
```

This text is the source code, and `inform.c` is the source file. The important point here is that the source file is the beginning of a process, not the end.

Compiling on a Unix System

Our program, although undeniably brilliant, is still gibberish to a computer. A computer doesn't understand things such as `#include` and `printf`. (At this point, you probably don't either, but you will soon learn, whereas the computer won't.) As we discussed earlier, we need the help of a compiler to translate our code (source code) to the computer's code (machine code). The result of these efforts will be the executable file, which contains all the machine code that the computer needs to get the job done.

The Unix C compiler is called *cc*. To compile the `inform.c` program, you need to type the following:

```
cc inform.c
```

After a few seconds, the Unix prompt will return, telling you that the deed is done. You might get warnings and error messages if you failed to write the program properly, but let's assume you did everything right. (If the compiler complains about the word `void`, your system has not yet updated to an ANSI C compiler. We'll talk more about standards soon. Meanwhile, just delete the word `void` from the example.) If you use the `ls` command to list your files, you will find that there is a new file called `a.out` (see Figure 1.5). This is the executable file containing the translation (or compilation) of the program. To run it, just type

`a.out`

and wisdom pours forth:

`A .c is used to end a C program filename.`

If you want to keep the executable file (`a.out`), you should rename it. Otherwise, the file is replaced by a new `a.out` the next time you compile a program.

FIGURE 1.5
Preparing a C program using Unix.

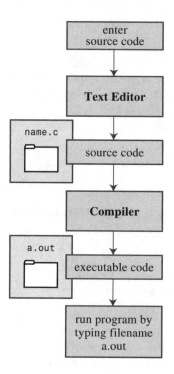

What about the object code? The cc compiler creates an object code file having the same base-name as the source code, but with an `.o` extension. In our example, the object code file is called `inform.o`, but you won't find it, because the linker removes it once the executable program has been completed. However, if the original program used more than one source code file, the object code files would be saved. When we discuss multiple-file programs later in the text, you will see that this is a fine idea.

Linux System

Linux is a popular open-source, Unix-like operating system that runs on a variety of platforms, including IBM compatibles and Macintoshes. Preparing C programs on Linux is much the same as for Unix systems, except that you would use the public domain C compiler, called *gcc*, that's provided by GNU. The compile command would look like this:

```
gcc inform.c
```

Note that installing gcc may be optional when installing Linux, so you (or someone) might have to install gcc if it wasn't installed earlier. Typically, the installation makes cc an alias for gcc, so you can use cc in the command line instead of gcc if you like.

You can obtain further information about gcc, including information about new releases, at http://www.gnu.org/software/gcc/gcc.html.

Integrated Development Environments (Windows)

C compilers are not part of the standard Windows package, so you may need to obtain and install a C compiler. Quite a few vendors, including Microsoft, Borland, Metrowerks, and Digital Mars, offer Windows-based integrated development environments, or *IDEs*. (These days, most are combined C and C++ compilers.) All have fast, integrated environments for putting together C programs. The key point is that each of these programs has a built-in editor you can use to write a C program. Each provides menus that enable you to name and save your source code file, as well as menus that allow you to compile and run your program without leaving the IDE. Each dumps you back into the editor if the compiler finds any errors, and each identifies the offending lines and matches them to the appropriate error messages.

The Windows IDEs can be a little intimidating at first because they offer a variety of *targets*—that is, a variety of environments in which the program will be used. For example, they might give you a choice of 16-bit Windows programs, 32-bit Windows programs, dynamic link library files (DLLs), and so on. Many of the targets involve bringing in support for the Windows graphical interface. To manage these (and other) choices, you typically create a *project* to which you then add the names of the source code files you'll be using. The precise steps depend on the product you use. Typically, you first use the File menu or Project menu to create a project. What's important is choosing the correct form of project. The examples in this book are generic examples designed to run in a simple command-line environment. The various Windows IDEs provide one or more choices to match this undemanding assumption. Microsoft Visual C 7.1, for example, offers the Win32 Console Application option. For Metrowerks CodeWarrior 9.0, choose Win32 C Stationery and then select C Console App or the WinSIOUX C App (the latter has a nicer user interface). For other systems, look for an option using terms such as DOS EXE, Console, or Character Mode executable. These modes will run your executable program in a console-like window. After you have the correct project type, use the IDE menu to open a new source code file. For most products, you can do this by using the File menu. You may have to take additional steps to add the source file to the project.

Because the Windows IDEs typically handle both C and C++, you need to indicate that you want a C program. With some products, such as Metrowerks CodeWarrior, you use the project type to indicate that you want to use C. With other products, such as Microsoft Visual C++, you use the .c file extension to indicate that you want to use C rather than C++. However, most C programs also work as C++ programs. Reference Section IX, "Differences Between C and C++," compares C and C++.

One problem you might encounter is that the window showing the program execution vanishes when the program terminates. If that is the case for you, you can make the program pause until you press the Enter key. To do that, add the following line to the end of the program, just before the `return` statement:

```
getchar();
```

This line reads a keystroke, so the program will pause until you press the Enter key. Sometimes, depending on how the program functions, there might already be a keystroke waiting. In that case, you'll have to use `getchar()` twice:

```
getchar();
getchar();
```

For example, if the last thing the program did was ask you to enter your weight, you would have typed your weight and then pressed the Enter key to enter the data. The program would read the weight, the first `getchar()` would read the Enter key, and the second `getchar()` would cause the program to pause until you press Enter again. If this doesn't make a lot of sense to you now, it will after you learn more about C input.

Although the various IDEs have many broad principles in common, the details vary from product to product and, within a product line, from version to version. You'll have to do some experimenting to learn how your compiler works. You might even have to read the manual or try an online tutorial.

DOS Compilers for the IBM PC

For many, running DOS on a PC is out of fashion these days, but it is still an option for those with limited computer resources and a modest budget and for those who prefer a simpler operating system without the bells, whistles, and distractions of a windowing environment. Many Windows IDEs additionally provide command-line tools, allowing you to program in the DOS command-line environment. The Comeau C/C++ compiler that is available on many systems, including several Unix and Linux variants, has a command-line DOS version. Also, there are freeware and shareware C compilers that work under DOS. For example, there is a DOS-based version of the GNU gcc compiler.

Source code files should be text files, not word processor files. (Word processor files contain a lot of additional information about fonts and formatting.) You should use a text editor, such as Windows Notepad, or the EDIT program that comes with some versions of DOS. You can use a word processor, if you use the Save As feature to save the file in text mode. The file should have a `.c` extension. Some word processors automatically add a `.txt` extension to text files. If this happens to you, you need to change the filename, replacing `txt` with `c`.

C compilers for the PC typically, but not always, produce intermediate object code files having an `.obj` extension. Unlike Unix compilers, C compilers typically don't remove these files when done. Some compilers produce assembly language files with `.asm` extensions or use some special format of their own.

Some compilers run the linker automatically after compiling; others might require that you run the linker manually. Linking results in the executable file, which appends the `.EXE` extension to the original source code basename. For example, compiling and linking a source code file called `concrete.c` produces a file called `concrete.exe`. Some compilers provide an option to create an executable named `concrete.com` instead. In either case, you can run the program by typing the basename at the command line:

```
C>concrete
```

C on the Macintosh

The best known Macintosh C/C++ compiler is the Metrowerks CodeWarrior compiler. (The Windows and Macintosh versions of CodeWarrior have very similar interfaces.) It provides a project-based IDE similar to what you would find in a Windows compiler. Start by choosing New Project from the File menu. You'll be given a choice of project types. For recent CodeWarrior versions, use the Std C Console choice. (Different releases of Code Warrior take different navigation routes to this choice.) You might also have to choose between a 68KB version (for the Motorola 680×0 series of processors), a PPC version (for the PowerPC processors), or a Carbon version (for OS X).

The new project has a small source code file as part of the initial project. You can try compiling and running that program to see whether you have your system set up properly.

Language Standards

Currently, many C implementations are available. Ideally, when you write a C program, it should work the same on any implementation, providing it doesn't use machine-specific programming. For this to be true in practice, different implementations need to conform to a recognized standard.

At first, there was no official standard for C. Instead, the first edition of *The C Programming Language* by Brian Kernighan and Dennis Ritchie (1978) became the accepted standard, usually referred to as *K&R C* or *classic C*. In particular, the "C Reference Manual" in that book's appendix acted as the guide to C implementations. Compilers, for example, would claim to offer a full K&R implementation. However, although this appendix defined the C language, it did not define the C library. More than most languages, C depends on its library, so there is need for a library standard, too. In the absence of any official standard, the library supplied with the Unix implementation became a de facto standard.

The First ANSI/ISO C Standard

As C evolved and became more widely used on a greater variety of systems, the C community realized it needed a more comprehensive, up-to-date, and rigorous standard. To meet this need, the American National Standards Institute (ANSI) established a committee (X3J11) in 1983 to develop a new standard, which was adopted formally in 1989. This new standard (ANSI C) defines both the language and a standard C library. The International Organization for Standardization adopted a C standard (ISO C) in 1990. ISO C and ANSI C are essentially the same standard. The final version of the ANSI/ISO standard is often referred to as *C89* (because that's when ANSI approval came) or *C90* (because that's when ISO approval came). Also, because the ANSI version came out first, people often used the term *ANSI C*.

The committee had several guiding principles. Perhaps the most interesting was this: Keep the spirit of C. The committee listed the following ideas as expressing part of that spirit:

- Trust the programmer.

- Don't prevent the programmer from doing what needs to be done.

- Keep the language small and simple.

- Provide only one way to do an operation.

- Make it fast, even if it is not guaranteed to be portable.

By the last point, the committee meant that an implementation should define a particular operation in terms of what works best for the target computer instead of trying to impose an abstract, uniform definition. You'll encounter examples of this philosophy as you learn the language.

The C99 Standard

In 1994, work began on revising the standard, an effort that resulted in the C99 standard. A joint ANSI/ISO committee, known then as the *C9X* committee, endorsed the original principles of the C90 standard, including keeping the language small and simple. The committee's intent was not to add new features to the language except as needed to meet the new goals. One of these main goals was to support international programming by, for example, providing ways to deal with international character sets. A second goal was to "codify existing practice to address evident deficiencies." Thus, when meeting the need of moving C to 64-bit processors, the committee based the additions to the standard on the experiences of those who dealt with this problem in real life. A third goal was to improve the suitability of C for doing critical numeric calculations for scientific and engineering projects.

These three points—internationalization, correction of deficiencies, and improvement of computational usefulness—were the main change-oriented goals. The remaining plans for change were more conservative in nature—for example, minimizing incompatibilities with C90 and with C++ and keeping the language conceptually simple. In the committee's words, "...the committee is content to let C++ be the *big* and ambitious language."

The upshot is that C99 changes preserve the essential nature of C, and C remains a lean, clean, efficient language. This book points out many of the C99 changes. Because most compilers at this time don't fully implement all the C99 changes, you may find that some of them are not available on your system. Or you may find that some C99 features are available only if you alter the compiler settings.

Note

This book will use the terms *ISO/ANSI C* to mean features common to both standards and *C99* to refer to new features. Occasionally, it will refer to *C90* (for example, when discussing when a feature was first added to C).

How This Book Is Organized

There are many ways to organize information. One of the most direct approaches is to present everything about topic A, everything about topic B, and so on. This is particularly useful for a reference so you can find all the information about a given topic in one place. But usually it's not the best sequence for learning a subject. For instance, if you began learning English by first learning all the nouns, your ability to express ideas would be severely limited. Sure, you could point to objects and shout their names, but you'd be much better equipped to express yourself if you learned just a few nouns, verbs, adjectives, and so on, along with a few rules about how those parts relate to one another.

To provide you with a more balanced intake of information, this book uses a spiral approach of introducing several topics in earlier chapters and returning later to discuss them more fully. For example, understanding functions is essential to understanding C. Consequently, several of the early chapters include some discussion of functions so that when you reach the full discussion in Chapter 9, "Functions," you'll already have achieved some ease about using functions. Similarly, early chapters preview strings and loops so that you can begin using these useful tools in your programs before learning about them in detail.

Conventions Used in This Book

We are almost ready to begin studying the C language itself. This section covers some of the conventions we use in presenting material.

Typeface

For text representing programs and computer input and output, we use a type font that resembles what you might see on a screen or on printed output. We have already used it a few times. In case it slipped your notice, the font looks like the following:

```c
#include <stdio.h>
int main(void)
{
    printf("Concrete contains gravel and cement.\n");

    return 0;
}
```

The same monospace type is for code-related terms used in the text, such as `main()`, and for filenames, such as `stdio.h`. The book uses italicized monospace for placeholder terms for which you are expected to substitute specific terms, as in the following model of a declaration:

```
type_name variable_name;
```

Here, for instance, you might replace *type_name* with `int` and *variable_name* with `zebra_count`.

Program Output

Output from the computer is printed in the same format, with the exception that user input is shown in boldface type. For instance, the following is program output from an example in Chapter 14, "Structures and Other Data Forms":

```
Please enter the book title.
Press [enter] at the start of a line to stop.

My Life as a Budgie
Now enter the author.
```

Mack Zackles

The lines printed in normal computer font are program output, and the boldface line is user input.

There are many ways you and a computer can communicate with each other. However, we will assume that you type in commands by using a keyboard and that you read the response on a screen.

Special Keystrokes

Usually, you send a line of instructions by pressing a key labeled Enter, c/r, Return, or some variation of these. We refer to this key in the text as the *Enter key*. Normally, the book takes it for granted that you press the Enter key at the end of each line of input. However, to clarify particular points, a few examples explicitly show the Enter key, using the symbol [enter] to represent it. The brackets mean that you press a single key rather than type the word *enter*.

We also refer to control characters, such as Ctrl+D. This notation means to press the D key while you are pressing the key labeled Ctrl (or perhaps Control).

Systems Used in Preparing This Book

Some aspects of C, such as the amount of space used to store a number, depend on the system. When we give examples and refer to "our system," we speak of a Pentium PC running under Windows XP Professional and using Metrowerks CodeWarrior Development Studio 9.2, Microsoft Visual C++ 7.1 (the version that comes with Microsoft Visual Studio .NET 2003), or gcc 3.3.3. At the time of this writing, C99 support is incomplete, and none of these compilers support all the C99 features. But, between them, these compilers cover much of the new standard. Most of the examples have also been tested using Metrowerks CodeWarrior Development Studio 9.2 on a Macintosh G4.

The book occasionally refers to running programs on a Unix system, too. The one used is Berkeley's BSD 4.3 version of Unix running on a VAX 11/750 computer. Also, several programs were tested on a Pentium PC running Linux and using gcc 3.3.1 and Comeau 4.3.3.

The sample code; for the complete programs described in this book is available on the Sams website, at www.samspublishing.com. Enter this book's ISBN (without the hyphens) in the Search box and click Search. When the book's title is displayed, click the title to go to a page where you can download the code. You also can find solutions to selected programming exercises at this site.

Your System—What You Need

You need to have a C compiler or access to one. C runs on an enormous variety of computer systems, so you have many choices. Do make sure that you use a C compiler designed for your particular system. Some of the examples in this book require support for the new C99 standard, but most of the examples will work with a C90 compiler. If the compiler you use is pre-ANSI/ISO, you will have to make adjustments, probably often enough to encourage you to seek something newer.

Most compiler vendors offer special pricing to students and educators, so if you fall into that category, check the vendor websites.

Special Elements

The book includes several special elements that highlight particular points: Sidebars, Tips, Cautions, and Notes. The following illustrates their appearances and uses:

Sidebar

A sidebar provides a deeper discussion or additional background to help illuminate a topic.

Tip

Tips present short, helpful guides to particular programming situations.

Caution

A caution alerts you to potential pitfalls.

Note

The notes provide a catchall category for comments that don't fall into one of the other categories.

Summary

C is a powerful, concise programming language. It is popular because it offers useful programming tools and good control over hardware and because C programs are easier than most to transport from one system to another.

C is a compiled language. C compilers and linkers are programs that convert C language source code into executable code.

Programming in C can be taxing, difficult, and frustrating, but it can also be intriguing, exciting, and satisfying. We hope you find it as enjoyable and fascinating as we do.

Review Questions

You'll find answers to the review questions in Appendix A, "Answers to Review Questions."

1. What does *portability* mean in the context of programming?

2. Explain the difference between a source code file, object code file, and executable file.

3. What are the seven major steps in programming?

4. What does a compiler do?

5. What does a linker do?

Programming Exercise

We don't expect you to write C code yet, so this exercise concentrates on the earlier stages of the programming process.

1. You have just been employed by MacroMuscle, Inc. (Software for Hard Bodies). The company is entering the European market and wants a program that converts inches to centimeters (1 inch = 2.54 cm). The company wants the program set up so that it prompts the user to enter an inch value. Your assignment is to define the program objectives and to design the program (steps 1 and 2 of the programming process).

## CHAPTER 2

INTRODUCING C

You will learn about the following in this chapter:

- Operator:
  =

- Functions:
  `main()`, `printf()`

- Putting together a simple C program

- Creating integer-valued variables, assigning them values, and displaying those values onscreen

- The newline character

- How to include comments in your programs, create programs containing more than one function, and find program errors

- What keywords are

W hat does a C program look like? If you skim through this book, you'll see many examples. Quite likely, you'll find that C looks a little peculiar, sprinkled with symbols such as `{`, `cp->tort`, and `*ptr++`. As you read through this book, however, you will find that the appearance of these and other characteristic C symbols grows less strange, more familiar, and perhaps even welcome! In this chapter, we begin by presenting a simple sample program and explaining what it does. At the same time, we highlight some of C's basic features.

A Simple Example of C

Let's take a look at a simple C program. This program, shown in Listing 2.1, serves to point out some of the basic features of programming in C. Before you read the upcoming line-by-line explanation of the program, read through Listing 2.1 to see whether you can figure out for yourself what it will do.

LISTING 2.1   The `first.c` Program

```c
#include <stdio.h>
int main(void)                    /* a simple program          */
{
    int num;                      /* define a variable called num */
    num = 1;                      /* assign a value to num      */

    printf("I am a simple "); /* use the printf() function     */
    printf("computer.\n");
    printf("My favorite number is %d because it is first.\n",num);

    return 0;
}
```

If you think this program will print something on your screen, you're right! Exactly what will be printed might not be apparent, so run the program and see the results. First, use your favorite editor (or your compiler's favorite editor) to create a file containing the text from Listing 2.1. Give the file a name that ends in `.c` and that satisfies your local system's name requirements. You can use `first.c`, for example. Now compile and run the program. (Check Chapter 1, "Getting Ready," for some general guidelines to this process.) If all went well, the output should look like the following:

```
I am a simple computer.
My favorite number is 1 because it is first.
```

All in all, this result is not too surprising, but what happened to the `\n`s and the `%d` in the program? And some of the lines in the program do look strange. It's time for an explanation.

The Example Explained

We'll take two passes through the program's source code. The first pass ("Pass 1: Quick Synopsis") highlights the meaning of each line to help you get a general feel for what's going on. The second pass ("Pass 2: Program Details") explores specific implications and details to help you gain a deeper understanding.

Figure 2.1 summarizes the parts of a C program; it includes more elements than our first example uses.

Pass 1: Quick Synopsis

This section presents each line from the program followed by a short description; the next section (Pass 2) explores the topics raised here more fully.

```
#include <stdio.h>      ←include another file
```

This line tells the compiler to include the information found in the file **stdio.h**, which is a standard part of all C compiler packages; this file provides support for keyboard input and for displaying output.

```
int main(void)        ←a function name
```

FIGURE 2.1

Anatomy of a C program.

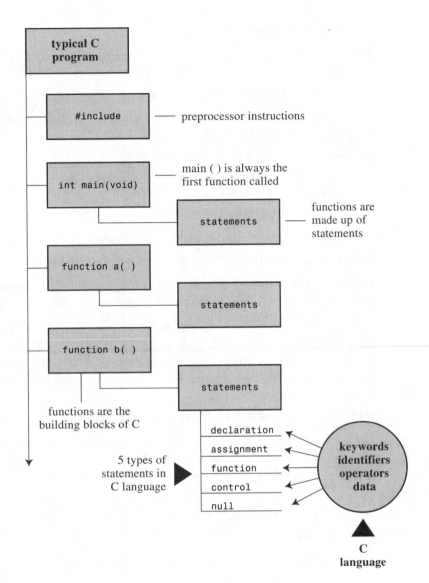

C programs consist of one or more *functions*, the basic modules of a C program. This program consists of one function called `main`. The parentheses identify `main()` as a function name. The `int` indicates that the `main()` function returns an integer, and the `void` indicates that `main()` doesn't take any arguments. These are matters we'll go into later. Right now, just accept both `int` and `void` as part of the standard ISO/ANSI C way for defining `main()`. (If you have a pre-ISO/ANSI C compiler, omit `void`; you may want to get something more recent to avoid incompatibilities.)

```
/* a simple program */    ←a comment
```

The symbols `/*` and `*/` enclose comments, remarks that help clarify a program. They are intended for the reader only and are ignored by the compiler.

```
{          ←beginning of the body of the function
```

This opening brace marks the start of the statements that make up the function. The function definition is ended with a closing brace (`}`).

```
int num;        ←a declaration statement
```

This statement announces that you are using a variable called `num` and that `num` will be an `int` (integer) type.

```
num = 1;    ←an assignment statement
```

The statement `num = 1;` assigns the value 1 to the variable called `num`.

```
printf("I am a simple ");    ←a function call statement
```

The first statement using `printf()` displays the phrase `I am a simple` on your screen, leaving the cursor on the same line. Here `printf()` is part of the standard C library. It's termed a *function*, and using a function in the program is termed *calling a function*.

```
printf("computer.\n");    ←another function call statement
```

The next call to the `printf()` function tacks on `computer` to the end of the last phrase printed. The `\n` is code telling the computer to start a new line—that is, to move the cursor to the beginning of the next line.

```
printf("My favorite number is %d because it is first.\n", num);
```

The last use of `printf()` prints the value of `num` (which is 1) embedded in the phrase in quotes. The `%d` instructs the computer where and in what form to print the value of `num`.

```
return 0;    ←a return statement
```

A C function can furnish, or *return*, a number to the agency that used it. For the present, just regard this line as part of the ISO/ANSI C requirement for a properly written `main()` function.

```
}    ←the end
```

As promised, the program ends with a closing brace.

Pass 2: Program Details

Now that you have an overview of Listing 2.1, we'll take a closer look. Once again, we'll examine the individual lines from the program, this time using each line of code as a starting point for going deeper into the details behind the code and as a basis for developing a more general perspective of C programming features.

#include Directives and Header Files

```
#include <stdio.h>
```

This is the line that begins the program. The effect of #include <stdio.h> is the same as if you had typed the entire contents of the stdio.h file into your file at the point where the #include line appears. In effect, it's a cut-and-paste operation. include files provide a convenient way to share information that is common to many programs.

The #include statement is an example of a C *preprocessor directive*. In general, C compilers perform some preparatory work on source code before compiling; this is termed *preprocessing*.

The stdio.h file is supplied as part of all C compiler packages. It contains information about input and output functions, such as printf(), for the compiler to use. The name stands for *standard input/output header*. C people call a collection of information that goes at the top of a file a *header*, and C implementations typically come with several header files.

For the most part, header files contain information used by the compiler to build the final executable program. For example, they may define constants or indicate the names of functions and how they should be used. But the actual code for a function is in a library file of precompiled code, not in a header file. The linker component of the compiler takes care of finding the library code you need. In short, header files help guide the compiler in putting your program together correctly.

ISO/ANSI C has standardized which header files must be supplied. Some programs need to include stdio.h, and some don't. The documentation for a particular C implementation should include a description of the functions in the C library. These function descriptions identify which header files are needed. For example, the description for printf() says to use stdio.h. Omitting the proper header file might not affect a particular program, but it is best not to rely on that. Each time this book uses library functions, it will use the include files specified by the ISO/ANSI standard for those functions.

Why Input and Output Are Not Built In

Perhaps you are wondering why something as basic as input and output information isn't included automatically. One answer is that not all programs use this I/O (input/output) package, and part of the C philosophy is to avoid carrying unnecessary weight. This principle of economic use of resources makes C popular for embedded programming—for example, writing code for a chip that controls an automotive fuel system. Incidentally, the #include line is not even a C language statement! The # symbol in column 1 identifies the line as one to be handled by the C preprocessor before the compiler takes over. You will encounter more examples of preprocessor instructions later, and Chapter 16, "The C Preprocessor and the C Library," discusses this topic more fully.

The main() Function

```
int main(void)
```

This next line from the program proclaims a function by the name of main. True, main is a rather plain name, but it is the only choice available. A C program (with some exceptions we won't worry about) always begins execution with the function called `main()`. You are free to choose names for other functions you use, but `main()` must be there to start things. What about the parentheses? They identify `main()` as a function. You will learn more about functions soon. For now, just remember that functions are the basic modules of a C program.

The `int` is the `main()` function's return type. That means that the kind of value `main()` can return is an integer. Return where? To the operating system—we'll come back to this question in Chapter 6, "C Control Statements: Looping."

The parentheses following a function name generally enclose information being passed along to the function. For this simple example, nothing is being passed along, so the parentheses contain the word `void`. (Chapter 11, "Character Strings and String Functions," introduces a second format that allows information to be passed to `main()` from the operating system.)

If you browse through ancient C code, you'll often see programs starting off with the following format:

```
main()
```

The C90 standard grudgingly tolerated this form, but the C99 standard doesn't. So even if your current compiler lets you do this, don't.

The following is another form you may see:

```
void main()
```

Some compilers allow this, but none of the standards have ever listed it as an option. Therefore, compilers don't have to accept this form, and several don't. Again, stick to the standard form, and you won't run into problems if you move a program from one compiler to another.

Comments

```
/* a simple program */
```

The parts of the program enclosed in the `/* */` symbols are comments. Using comments makes it easier for someone (including yourself) to understand your program. One nice feature of C comments is that they can be placed anywhere, even on the same line as the material they explain. A longer comment can be placed on its own line or even spread over more than one line. Everything between the opening `/*` and the closing `*/` is ignored by the compiler. The following are some valid and invalid comment forms:

```
/* This is a C comment. */
/* This comment is spread over
   two lines. */
/*
  You can do this, too.
*/
/* But this is invalid because there is no end marker.
```

C99 adds a second style of comments, one popularized by C++ and Java. The new style uses the symbols // to create comments that are confined to a single line:

```
// Here is a comment confined to one line.
int rigue;      // Such comments can go here, too.
```

Because the end of the line marks the end of the comment, this style needs comment markers just at the beginning of the comment.

The newer form is a response to a potential problem with the old form. Suppose you have the following code:

```
/*
I hope this works.
*/
x = 100;
y = 200;
/* Now for something else. */
```

Next, suppose you decide to remove the fourth line and accidentally delete the third line (the */), too. The code then becomes

```
/*
I hope this works.
y = 200;
/* Now for something else. */
```

Now the compiler pairs the /* in the first line with the */ in the fourth line, making all four lines into one comment, including the line that was supposed to be part of the code. Because the // form doesn't extend over more than one line, it can't lead to this "disappearing code" problem.

Some compilers may not support this C99 feature; others may require changing a compiler setting to enable C99 features.

This book, operating on the theory that needless consistency can be boring, uses both kinds of comments.

Braces, Bodies, and Blocks

```
{
...
}
```

In Listing 2.1, braces delimited the main() function. In general, all C functions use braces to mark the beginning as well as the end of the body of a function. Their presence is mandatory, so don't leave them out. Only braces ({ }) work for this purpose, not parentheses (( )) and not brackets ([ ]).

Braces can also be used to gather statements within a function into a unit or block. If you are familiar with Pascal, ADA, Modula-2, or Algol, you will recognize the braces as being similar to begin and end in those languages.

Declarations

```
int num;
```

This line from the program is termed a *declaration statement*. The declaration statement is one of C's most important features. This particular example declares two things. First, somewhere in the function, you have a *variable* called num. Second, the int proclaims num as an integer—that is, a number without a decimal point or fractional part. (int is an example of a *data type*.) The compiler uses this information to arrange for suitable storage space in memory for the num variable. The semicolon at the end of the line identifies the line as a C *statement* or instruction. The semicolon is part of the statement, not just a separator between statements as it is in Pascal.

The word int is a C *keyword* identifying one of the basic C data types. Keywords are the words used to express a language, and you can't usurp them for other purposes. For instance, you can't use int as the name of a function or a variable. These keyword restrictions don't apply outside the language, however, so it is okay to name a cat or favorite child int. (Local custom or law may void this option in some locales.)

The word num in this example is an *identifier*—that is, a name you select for a variable, a function, or some other entity. So the declaration connects a particular identifier with a particular location in computer memory, and it also establishes the type of information, or data type, to be stored at that location.

In C, *all* variables must be declared *before* they are used. This means that you have to provide lists of all the variables you use in a program and that you have to show which data type each variable is. Declaring variables is considered a good programming technique, and, in C, it is mandatory.

Traditionally, C has required that variables be declared at the beginning of a block with no other kind of statement allowed to come before any of the declarations. That is, the body of main() might look like the following:

```
int main()     // traditional rules
{
    int doors;
    int dogs;
    doors = 5;
    dogs = 3;
    // other statements
}
```

C99, following the practice of C++, now lets you place declarations about anywhere in a block. However, you still must declare a variable before its first use. So if your compiler supports this feature, your code can look like the following:

```
int main()          // C99 rules
{
// some statements
    int doors;
    doors = 5;      // first use of doors
```

```
// more statements
    int dogs;
    dogs = 3;          // first use of dogs
    // other statements
}
```

For greater compatibility with older systems, this book will stick to the original convention. (Some newer compilers support C99 features only if you turn them on.)

At this point, you probably have three questions. First, what are data types? Second, what choices do you have in selecting a name? Third, why do you have to declare variables at all? Let's look at some answers.

Data Types

C deals with several kinds (or types) of data: integers, characters, and floating point, for example. Declaring a variable to be an integer or a character type makes it possible for the computer to store, fetch, and interpret the data properly. You'll investigate the variety of available types in the next chapter.

Name Choice

You should use meaningful names for variables (such as sheep_count instead of x3 if your program counts sheep.). If the name doesn't suffice, use comments to explain what the variables represent. Documenting a program in this manner is one of the basic techniques of good programming.

The number of characters you can use varies among implementations. The C99 standard calls for up to 63 characters, except for external identifiers (see Chapter 12, "Storage Classes, Linkage, and Memory Management"), for which only 31 characters need to be recognized. This is a substantial increase from the C90 requirement of 31 characters and six characters, respectively, and older C compilers often stopped at eight characters max. Actually, you can use more than the maximum number of characters, but the compiler won't pay attention to the extra characters. Therefore, on a system with an eight-character limit, shakespeare and shakespencil would be considered the same name because they have the same first eight characters. (If you want an example based on the 63-character limit, you'll have to concoct it yourself.)

The characters at your disposal are lowercase letters, uppercase letters, digits, and the underscore (_). The first character must be a letter or an underscore. The following are some examples:

Valid Names	Invalid Names
wiggles	$Z]**
cat2	2cat
Hot_Tub	Hot-Tub
taxRate	tax rate
_kcab	don't

Operating systems and the C library often use identifiers with one or two initial underscore characters, such as in `_kcab`, so it is better to avoid that usage yourself. The standard labels beginning with one or two underscore characters, such as library identifiers, are *reserved*. This means that although it is not a syntax error to use them, it could lead to name conflicts.

C names are *case sensitive*, meaning an uppercase letter is considered distinct from the corresponding lowercase letter. Therefore, `stars` is different from `Stars` and `STARS`.

To make C more international, C99 makes an extensive set of characters available for use by the Universal Character Names (or *UCN*) mechanism. Reference Section VII, "Expanded Character Support," in Appendix B discusses this addition.

Four Good Reasons to Declare Variables

Some older languages, such as the original forms of FORTRAN and BASIC, allow you to use variables without declaring them. So why can't you take this easy-going approach in C? Here are some reasons:

- Putting all the variables in one place makes it easier for a reader to grasp what the program is about. This is particularly true if you give your variables meaningful names (such as `taxrate` instead of `r`). If the name doesn't suffice, use comments to explain what the variables represent. Documenting a program in this manner is one of the basic techniques of good programming.

- Thinking about which variables to declare encourages you to do some planning before plunging into writing a program. What information does the program need to get started? What exactly do I want the program to produce as output? What is the best way to represent the data?

- Declaring variables helps prevent one of programming's more subtle and hard-to-find bugs—that of the misspelled variable name. For example, suppose that in some language that lacks declarations, you made the statement

```
RADIUS1 = 20.4;
```

and that elsewhere in the program you mistyped

```
CIRCUM = 6.28 * RADIUSl;
```

You unwittingly replaced the numeral 1 with the letter *l*. That other language would create a new variable called `RADIUSl` and use whatever value it had (perhaps zero, perhaps garbage). `CIRCUM` would be given the wrong value, and you might have a heck of a time trying to find out why. This can't happen in C (unless you were silly enough to declare two such similar variable names) because the compiler will complain when the undeclared `RADIUSl` shows up.

- Your C program will not compile if you don't declare your variables. If the preceding reasons fail to move you, you should give this one serious thought.

Given that you need to declare your variables, where do they go? As mentioned before, C prior to C99 required that the declarations go at the beginning of a block. A good reason for following this practice is that grouping the declarations together makes it easier to see what the program is doing. Of course, there's also a good reason to spread your declarations around, as C99 now allows. The idea is to declare variables just before you're ready to give them a value. That makes it harder to forget to give them a value. As a practical matter, many compilers don't yet support the C99 rule.

Assignment

```
num = 1;
```

The next program line is an *assignment statement*, one of the basic operations in C. This particular example means "assign the value 1 to the variable num." The earlier `int num;` line set aside space in computer memory for the variable num, and the assignment line stores a value in that location. You can assign num a different value later, if you want; that is why num is termed a *variable*. Note that the assignment statement assigns a value from the right side to the left side. Also, the statement is completed with a semicolon, as shown in Figure 2.2.

FIGURE 2.2

The assignment statement is one of the basic C operations.

num = 1;

assignment operator

The `printf()` Function

```
printf("I am a simple ");
printf("computer.\n");
printf("My favorite number is %d because it is first.\n", num);
```

These lines all use a standard C function called `printf()`. The parentheses signify that `printf` is a function name. The material enclosed in the parentheses is information passed from the `main()` function to the `printf()` function. For example, the first line passes the phrase I am a simple to the `printf()` function. Such information is called the *argument* or, more fully, the *actual argument* of a function (see Figure 2.3). What does the function `printf()` do with this argument? It looks at whatever lies between the double quotation marks and prints that text onscreen.

FIGURE 2.3

The `printf()` function with an argument.

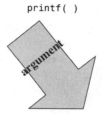

printf( )

argument

printf("That's mere contrariness!\n");

This first `printf()` line is an example of how you *call* or *invoke* a function in C. You need type only the name of the function, placing the desired argument(s) within the parentheses. When the program reaches this line, control is turned over to the named function (`printf()` in this case). When the function is finished with whatever it does, control is returned to the original (the *calling*) function—`main()`, in this example.

What about this next `printf()` line? It has the characters \n included in the quotes, and they didn't get printed! What's going on? The \n symbol means to start a new line. The \n combination (typed as two characters) represents a single character called the *newline character*. To `printf()`, it means "start a new line at the far-left margin." In other words, printing the newline character performs the same function as pressing the Enter key of a typical keyboard. Why not just use the Enter key when typing the `printf()` argument? Because that would be interpreted as an immediate command to your editor, not as an instruction to be stored in your source code. In other words, when you press the Enter key, the editor quits the current line on which you are working and starts a new one. The newline character, however, affects how the output of the program is displayed.

The newline character is an example of an *escape sequence*. An escape sequence is used to represent difficult- or impossible-to-type characters. Other examples are \t for Tab and \b for Backspace. In each case, the escape sequence begins with the backslash character, \. We'll return to this subject in Chapter 3, "Data and C."

Well, that explains why the three `printf()` statements produced only two lines: The first print instruction didn't have a newline character in it, but the second and third did.

The final `printf()` line brings up another oddity: What happened to the %d when the line was printed? As you will recall, the output for this line was

My favorite number is 1 because it is first.

Aha! The digit 1 was substituted for the symbol group %d when the line was printed, and 1 was the value of the variable num. The %d is a placeholder to show where the value of num is to be printed. This line is similar to the following BASIC statement:

PRINT "My favorite number is "; num; " because it is first."

The C version does a little more than this, actually. The `%` alerts the program that a variable is to be printed at that location, and the `d` tells it to print the variable as a decimal (base 10) integer. The `printf()` function allows several choices for the format of printed variables, including hexadecimal (base 16) integers and numbers with decimal points. Indeed, the `f` in `printf()` is a reminder that this is a *formatting* print function. Each type of data has its own specifier; as the book introduces new types, it will also introduce the appropriate specifiers.

Return Statement

```
return 0;
```

This return statement is the final statement of the program. The `int` in `int main(void)` means that the `main()` function is supposed to return an integer. The C standard requires that `main()` behave that way. C functions that return values do so with a return statement, which consists of the keyword `return`, followed by the returned value, followed by a semicolon. If you leave out the return statement for `main()`, most compilers will chide you for the omission, but will still compile the program. At this point, you can regard the return statement in `main()` as something required for logical consistency, but it has a practical use with some operating systems, including DOS and Unix. Chapter 11 will deal further with this topic.

The Structure of a Simple Program

Now that you've seen a specific example, you are ready for a few general rules about C programs. A *program* consists of a collection of one or more functions, one of which must be called `main()`. The description of a *function* consists of a header and a body. The *header* contains preprocessor statements, such as `#include`, and the function name. You can recognize a function name by the parentheses, which may be empty. The *body* is enclosed by braces (`{}`) and consists of a series of statements, each terminated by a semicolon (see Figure 2.4). The example in this chapter had a *declaration statement*, announcing the name and type of variable being used. Then it had an *assignment statement* giving the variable a value. Next, there were three *print statements*, each calling the `printf()` function. The print statements are examples of *function call statements*. Finally, `main()` ends with a *return statement*.

In short, a simple standard C program should use the following format:

```
#include <stdio.h>
int main(void)
{
    statements
    return 0;
}
```

FIGURE 2.4

A function has a header
and a body.

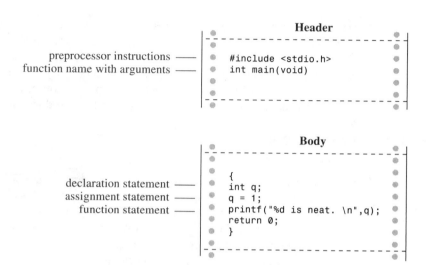

preprocessor instructions ——
function name with arguments ——

declaration statement ——
assignment statement ——
function statement ——

Header

```
#include <stdio.h>
int main(void)
```

Body

```
{
    int q;
    q = 1;
    printf("%d is neat. \n",q);
    return 0;
}
```

Tips on Making Your Programs Readable

Making your programs readable is good programming practice. A readable program is much easier to understand, and that makes it easier to correct or modify. The act of making a program readable also helps clarify your own concept of what the program does.

You've already seen two techniques for improving readability: Choose meaningful variable names and use comments. Note that these two techniques complement each other. If you give a variable the name `width`, you don't need a comment saying that this variable represents a width, but a variable called `video_routine_4` begs for an explanation of what video routine 4 does.

Another technique involves using blank lines to separate one conceptual section of a function from another. For example, the simple sample program has a blank line separating the declaration section from the action section. C doesn't require the blank line, but it enhances readability.

A fourth technique is to use one line per statement. Again, this is a readability convention, not a C requirement. C has a *free-form* format. You can place several statements on one line or spread one statement over several. The following is legitimate, but ugly, code:

```
int main(  void  ) { int four; four
=
4
;
printf(
        "%d\n",
four); return 0;}
```

The semicolons tell the compiler where one statement ends and the next begins, but the program logic is much clearer if you follow the conventions used in this chapter's example (see Figure 2.5).

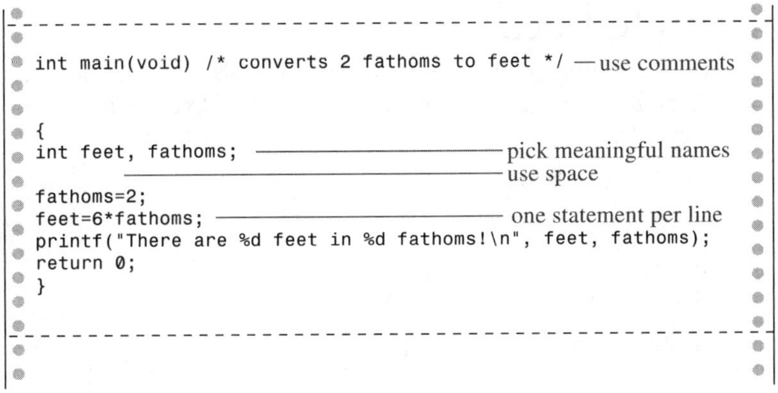

FIGURE 2.5
Making your program
readable.

```
int main(void) /* converts 2 fathoms to feet */ ──── use comments

{
int feet, fathoms; ─────────────────────── pick meaningful names
                    ─────────────────────── use space
fathoms=2;
feet=6*fathoms; ────────────────────────── one statement per line
printf("There are %d feet in %d fathoms!\n", feet, fathoms);
return 0;
}
```

Taking Another Step in Using C

The first sample program was pretty easy, and the next example, shown in Listing 2.2, isn't much harder.

LISTING 2.2   The `fathm_ft.c` Program

```c
// fathm_ft.c -- converts 2 fathoms to feet
#include <stdio.h>
int main(void)
{
    int feet, fathoms;

    fathoms = 2;
    feet = 6 * fathoms;
    printf("There are %d feet in %d fathoms!\n", feet, fathoms);
    printf("Yes, I said %d feet!\n", 6 * fathoms);

    return 0;
}
```

What's new? The code provides a program description, declares multiple variables, does some multiplication, and prints the values of two variables. Let's examine these points in more detail.

Documentation

First, the program begins with a comment (using the new comment style) identifying the filename and the purpose of the program. This kind of program documentation takes but a moment to do and is helpful later when you browse through several files or print them.

Multiple Declarations

Next, the program declares two variables instead of just one in a single declaration statement. To do this, separate the two variables (`feet` and `fathoms`) by a comma in the declaration statement. That is,

```
int feet, fathoms;
```

and

```
int feet;
int fathoms;
```

are equivalent.

Multiplication

Third, the program makes a calculation. It harnesses the tremendous computational power of a computer system to multiply 2 by 6. In C, as in many languages, `*` is the symbol for multiplication. Therefore, the statement

```
feet = 6 * fathoms;
```

means "look up the value of the variable `fathoms`, multiply it by 6, and assign the result of this calculation to the variable `feet`."

Printing Multiple Values

Finally, the program makes fancier use of `printf()`. If you compile and run the example, the output should look like this:

```
There are 12 feet in 2 fathoms!
Yes, I said 12 feet!
```

This time, the code made *two* substitutions in the first use of `printf()`. The first `%d` in the quotes was replaced by the value of the first variable (`feet`) in the list following the quoted segment, and the second `%d` was replaced by the value of the second variable (`fathoms`) in the list. Note that the list of variables to be printed comes at the tail end of the statement after the quoted part. Also note that each item is separated from the others by a comma.

The second use of `printf()` illustrates that the value printed doesn't have to be a variable; it just has to be something, such as `6 * fathoms`, that reduces to a value of the right type.

This program is limited in scope, but it could form the nucleus of a program for converting fathoms to feet. All that is needed is a way to assign additional values to `feet` interactively; we will explain how to do that in later chapters.

While You're at It—Multiple Functions

So far, these programs have used the standard `printf()` function. Listing 2.3 shows you how to incorporate a function of your own—besides `main()`—into a program.

LISTING 2.3   The `two_func.c` Program

```
/* two_func.c -- a program using two functions in one file */
#include <stdio.h>
void butler(void);        /* ISO/ANSI C function prototyping */
int main(void)
{
    printf("I will summon the butler function.\n");
    butler();
    printf("Yes. Bring me some tea and writeable CD-ROMS.\n");

    return 0;
}

void butler(void)           /* start of function definition */
{
    printf("You rang, sir?\n");
}
```

The output looks like the following:

```
I will summon the butler function.
You rang, sir?
Yes. Bring me some tea and writeable CD-ROMS.
```

The `butler()` function appears three times in this program. The first appearance is in the *prototype*, which informs the compiler about the functions to be used. The second appearance is in `main()` in the form of a *function call*. Finally, the program presents the *function definition*, which is the source code for the function itself. Let's look at each of these three appearances in turn.

The C90 standard added prototypes, and older compilers might not recognize them. (We'll tell you what to do when using such compilers in a moment.) A prototype is a form of declaration that tells the compiler that you are using a particular function. It also specifies properties of the function. For example, the first `void` in the prototype for the `butler()` function indicates that `butler()` does not have a return value. (In general, a function can return a value to the calling function for its use, but `butler()` doesn't.) The second `void`—the one in `butler(void)`—means that the `butler()` function has no arguments. Therefore, when the compiler reaches the point in `main()` where `butler()` is used, it can check to see whether `butler()` is used correctly. Note that `void` is used to mean "empty," not "invalid."

Older C supported a more limited form of function declaration in which you just specified the return type but omitted describing the arguments:

```
void butler();
```

Older C code uses function declarations like the preceding one instead of function prototypes. The C90 and C99 standards recognize this older form but indicate it will be phased out in time, so don't use it. If you inherit some legacy C code, you may want to convert the old-style declarations to prototypes. Later chapters in this book return to prototyping, function declarations, and return values.

Next, you invoke `butler()` in `main()` simply by giving its name, including parentheses. When `butler()` finishes its work, the program moves to the next statement in `main()`.

Finally, the function `butler()` is defined in the same manner as `main()`, with a function header and the body enclosed in braces. The header repeats the information given in the prototype: `butler()` takes no arguments and has no return value. For older compilers, omit the second `void`.

One point to note is that it is the location of the `butler()` call in `main()`—not the location of the `butler()` definition in the file—that determines when the `butler()` function is executed. You could, for example, put the `butler()` definition above the `main()` definition in this program, and the program would still run the same, with the `butler()` function executed between the two calls to `printf()` in `main()`. Remember, all C programs begin execution with `main()`, no matter where `main()` is located in the program files. However, C practice is to list `main()` first because it normally provides the basic framework for a program.

The C standard recommends that you provide function prototypes for all functions you use. The standard `include` files take care of this task for the standard library functions. For example, under standard C, the `stdio.h` file has a function prototype for `printf()`. The final example in Chapter 6 will show you how to extend prototyping to non-`void` functions, and Chapter 9 covers functions fully.

Introducing Debugging

Now that you can write a simple C program, you are in a position to make simple errors. Program errors often are called *bugs*, and finding and fixing the errors is called *debugging*. Listing 2.4 presents a program with some bugs. See how many you can spot.

LISTING 2.4   The `nogood.c` Program

```
/*  nogood.c -- a program with errors */
#include <stdio.h>
int main(void)
(
    int n, int n2, int n3;

/* this program has several errors
    n = 5;
    n2 = n * n;
    n3 = n2 * n2;
    printf("n = %d, n squared = %d, n cubed = %d\n", n, n2, n3)

    return 0;
)
```

Syntax Errors

Listing 2.4 contains several syntax errors. You commit a *syntax error* when you don't follow C's rules. It's analogous to a grammatical error in English. For instance, consider the following sentence: *Bugs frustrate be can.* This sentence uses valid English words but doesn't follow the rules for word order, and it doesn't have quite the right words, anyway. C syntax errors use valid C symbols in the wrong places.

So what syntax errors did `nogood.c` make? First, it uses parentheses instead of braces to mark the body of the function—it uses a valid C symbol in the wrong place. Second, the declaration should have been

```
int n, n2, n3;
```

or perhaps

```
int n;
int n2;
int n3;
```

Next, the example omits the `*/` symbol pair necessary to complete a comment. (Alternatively, you could replace `/*` with the new `//` form.) Finally, it omits the mandatory semicolon that should terminate the `printf()` statement.

How do you detect syntax errors? First, before compiling, you can look through the source code and see whether you spot anything obvious. Second, you can examine errors found by the compiler because part of its job is to detect syntax errors. When you compile this program, the compiler reports back any errors it finds, identifying the nature and location of each error.

However, the compiler can get confused. A true syntax error in one location might cause the compiler to mistakenly think it has found other errors. For instance, because the example does not declare `n2` and `n3` correctly, the compiler might think it has found further errors whenever those variables are used. In fact, rather than trying to correct all the reported errors at once, you should correct just the first one or two and then recompile; some of the other errors may go away. Continue in this way until the program works. Another common compiler trick is reporting the error a line late. For instance, the compiler may not deduce that a semicolon is missing until it tries to compile the next line. So if the compiler complains of a missing semi-colon on a line that has one, check the line before.

Semantic Errors

Semantic errors are errors in meaning. For example, consider the following sentence: *Furry inflation thinks greenly.* The syntax is fine because adjectives, nouns, verbs, and adverbs are in the right places, but the sentence doesn't mean anything. In C, you commit a semantic error when you follow the rules of C correctly but to an incorrect end. The example has one such error:

```
n3 = n2 * n2;
```

Here, `n3` is supposed to represent the cube of `n`, but the code sets it up to be the fourth power of `n`.

The compiler does not detect semantic errors, because they don't violate C rules. The compiler has no way of divining your true intentions. That leaves it to you to find these kinds of errors. One way is to compare what a program does to what you expected it to do. For instance, suppose you fix the syntax errors in the example so that it now reads as shown in Listing 2.5.

LISTING 2.5   The `stillbad.c` Program

```
/* stillbad.c -- a program with its syntax errors fixed */
#include <stdio.h>
int main(void)
{
    int n, n2, n3;

/* this program has a semantic error */
    n = 5;
    n2 = n * n;
    n3 = n2 * n2;
    printf("n = %d, n squared = %d, n cubed = %d\n", n, n2, n3);

    return 0;
}
```

Its output is

```
n = 5, n squared = 25, n cubed = 625
```

If you are cube-wise, you'll notice that 625 is the wrong value. The next stage is to track down how you wound up with this answer. For this example, you probably can spot the error by inspection. In general, however, you need to take a more systematic approach. One method is to pretend you are the computer and to follow the program steps one by one. Let's try that method now.

The body of the program starts by declaring three variables: n, n2, and n3. You can simulate this situation by drawing three boxes and labeling them with the variable names (see Figure 2.6). Next, the program assigns 5 to n. Simulate that by writing 5 into the n box. Next, the program multiplies n by n and assigns the result to n2, so look in the n box, see that the value is 5, multiply 5 by 5 to get 25, and place 25 in box n2. To duplicate the next C statement (n3 = n2 * n2;), look in n2 and find 25. You multiply 25 by 25, get 625, and place it in n3. Aha! You are squaring n2 instead of multiplying it by n.

Well, perhaps this procedure is overkill for this example, but going through a program step-by-step in this fashion is often the best way to see what's happening.

Program State

By tracing the program step-by-step manually, keeping track of each variable, you monitor the program state. The *program state* is simply the set of values of all the variables at a given point in program execution. It is a snapshot of the current state of computation.

FIGURE 2.6

Tracing a program.

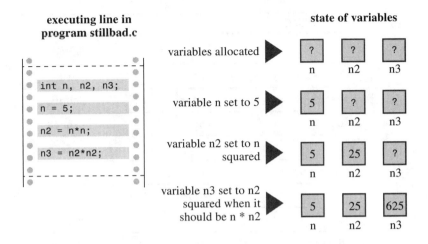

We just discussed one method of tracing the state: executing the program step-by-step yourself. In a program that makes, say, 10,000 iterations, you might not feel up to that task. Still, you can go through a few iterations to see whether your program does what you intend. However, there is always the possibility that you will execute the steps as you intended them to be executed instead of as you actually wrote them, so try to be faithful to the actual code.

Another approach to locating semantic problems is to sprinkle extra `printf()` statements throughout to monitor the values of selected variables at key points in the program. Seeing how the values change can illuminate what's happening. After you have the program working to your satisfaction, you can remove the extra statements and recompile.

A third method for examining the program states is to use a debugger. A *debugger* is a program that enables you to run another program step-by-step and examine the value of that program's variables. Debuggers come in various levels of ease of use and sophistication. The more advanced debuggers show which line of source code is being executed. This is particularly handy for programs with alternative paths of execution because it is easy to see which particular paths are being followed. If your compiler comes with a debugger, take time now to learn how to use it. Try it with Listing 2.4, for example.

Keywords and Reserved Identifiers

Keywords are the vocabulary of C. Because they are special to C, you can't use them as identifiers, for example, or as variable names. Many of these keywords specify various types, such as `int`. Others, such as `if`, are used to control the order in which program statements are executed. In the following list of C keywords, boldface indicates keywords added by the ISO/ANSI C90 standard, and italics indicate new keywords added by the C99 standard.

ISO/ANSI C Keywords			
auto	**enum**	*restrict*	unsigned
break	extern	return	**void**
case	float	short	**volatile**
char	for	**signed**	while
const	goto	sizeof	*_Bool*
continue	if	static	*_Complex*
default	*inline*	struct	*_Imaginary*
do	int	switch	
double	long	typedef	
else	register	union	

If you try to use a keyword, for, say, the name of a variable, the compiler catches that as a syntax error. There are other identifiers, called *reserved identifiers*, that you shouldn't use. They don't cause syntax errors because they are valid names. However, the language already uses them or reserves the right to use them, so it could cause problems if you use these identifiers to mean something else. Reserved identifiers include those beginning with an underscore character and the names of the standard library functions, such as `printf()`.

Key Concepts

Computer programming is a challenging activity. It demands abstract, conceptual thinking combined with careful attention to detail. You'll find that compilers enforce the attention to detail. When you talk to a friend, you might use a few words incorrectly, make a grammatical error or two, perhaps leave some sentences unfinished, but your friend will still understand what you are trying to say. But a compiler doesn't make such allowances; to it, almost right is still wrong.

The compiler won't help you with conceptual matters, such as these, so this book will try to fill that gap by outlining the key concepts in each chapter.

For this chapter, your goal should be to understand what a C program is. You can think of a program as a description you prepare of how you want the computer to behave. The compiler handles the really detailed job of converting your description to the underlying machine language. (As a measure of how much work a compiler does, it can create an executable file of 60KB from your source code file of 1KB; a lot of machine language goes into representing even a simple C program.) Because the compiler has no real intelligence, you have to express your description in the compiler's terms, and these terms are the formal rules set up by the C language standard. (Although restrictive, this still is far better than having to express your description directly in machine language!)

The compiler expects to receive its instructions in a specific format, which we described in detail in this chapter. Your job as a programmer is to express your ideas about how a program should behave within the framework that the compiler—guided by the C standard—can process successfully.

Summary

A C program consists of one or more C functions. Every C program must contain a function called `main()` because it is the function called when the program starts up. A simple function consists of a header followed by an opening brace, followed by the statements constituting the function body, followed by a terminating, or *closing*, brace.

Each C statement is an instruction to the computer and is marked by a terminating semicolon. A declaration statement creates a name for a variable and identifies the type of data to be stored in the variable. The name of a variable is an example of an identifier. An assignment statement assigns a value to a variable or, more generally, to a storage area. A function call statement causes the named function to be executed. When the called function is done, the program returns to the next statement after the function call.

The `printf()` function can be used to print phrases and the values of variables.

The *syntax* of a language is the set of rules that governs the way in which valid statements in that language are put together. The *semantics* of a statement is its meaning. The compiler helps you detect syntax errors, but semantic errors show up in a program's behavior only after it is compiled. Detecting semantic errors may involve tracing the program state—that is, the values of all variables—after each program step.

Finally, *keywords* are the vocabulary of the C language.

Review Questions

You'll find answers to the review questions in Appendix A, "Answers to the Review Questions."

1. What are the basic modules of a C program called?

2. What is a syntax error? Give an example of one in English and one in C.

3. What is a semantic error? Give an example of one in English and one in C.

4. Indiana Sloth has prepared the following program and brought it to you for approval. Please help him out.

```
include studio.h
int main{void} /* this prints the number of weeks in a year /*
(
int s

s := 56;
print(There are s weeks in a year.);
return 0;
```

5. Assuming that each of the following examples is part of a complete program, what will each one print?

a. `printf("Baa Baa Black Sheep.");`
   `printf("Have you any wool?\n");`

b. `printf("Begone!\nO creature of lard!");`

c. `printf("What?\nNo/nBonzo?\n");`

d. `int num;`

   `num = 2;`
   `printf("%d + %d = %d", num, num, num + num);`

6. Which of the following are C keywords? `main`, `int`, `function`, `char`, `=`

7. How would you print the values of `words` and `lines` in the form `There were 3020 words and 350 lines.`? Here, `3020` and `350` represent values for the two variables.

8. Consider the following program:

```
#include <stdio.h>
int main(void)
{
   int a, b;

    a = 5;
    b = 2;      /* line 7 */
    b = a;      /* line 8 */
    a = b;      /* line 9 */
    printf("%d %d\n", b, a);
    return 0;
}
```

What is the program state after line 7? Line 8? Line 9?

Programming Exercises

Reading about C isn't enough. You should try writing one or two simple programs to see whether writing a program goes as smoothly as it looks in this chapter. A few suggestions follow, but you should also try to think up some problems yourself. You'll find answers to selected programming exercises on the publisher's website: www.samspublishing.com.

1. Write a program that uses one `printf()` call to print your first name and last name on one line, uses a second `printf()` call to print your first and last names on two separate lines, and uses a pair of `printf()` calls to print your first and last names on one line. The output should look like this (but using your name):

   ```
   Anton Bruckner     ←First print statement

   Anton              ←Second print statement

   Bruckner           ←Still the second print statement

   Anton Bruckner     ←Third and fourth print statements
   ```

2. Write a program to print your name and address.

3. Write a program that converts your age in years to days and displays both values. At this point, don't worry about fractional years and leap years.

4. Write a program that produces the following output:

   ```
   For he's a jolly good fellow!
   For he's a jolly good fellow!
   For he's a jolly good fellow!
   Which nobody can deny!
   ```

   Have the program use two user-defined functions in addition to `main()`: one that prints the "jolly good" message once, and one that prints the final line once.

5. Write a program that creates an integer variable called `toes`. Have the program set `toes` to `10`. Also have the program calculate what twice `toes` is and what `toes` squared is. The program should print all three values, identifying them.

6. Write a program that produces the following output:

   ```
   Smile!Smile!Smile!
   Smile!Smile!
   Smile!
   ```

   Have the program define a function that displays the string `Smile!` once, and have the program use the function as often as needed.

7. Write a program that calls a function named `one_three()`. This function should display the word `one` on one line, call the function `two()`, and then display the word `three` on

one line. The function `two()` should display the word `two` on one line. The `main()` function should display the phrase `starting now:` before calling `one_three()` and display `done!` after calling it. Thus, the output should look like the following:

```
starting now:
one
two
three
done!
```

CHAPTER 3

DATA AND C

You will learn about the following in this chapter:

- Keywords:
  int, short, long, unsigned, char,
  float, double, _Bool, _Complex,
  _Imaginary

- Operator:
  sizeof

- Function:
  scanf()

- The basic data types that C uses

- The distinctions between integer types and floating-point types

- Writing constants and declaring variables of those types

- How to use the printf() and scanf() functions to read and write values of different types

Programs work with data. You feed numbers, letters, and words to the computer, and you expect it to do something with the data. For example, you might want the computer to calculate an interest payment or display a sorted list of vintners. In this chapter, you do more than just read about data; you practice manipulating data, which is much more fun.

This chapter explores the two great families of data types: integer and floating point. C offers several varieties of these types. This chapter tells you what the types are, how to declare them, and how and when to use them. Also, you discover the differences between constants and variables, and as a bonus, your first interactive program is coming up shortly.

A Sample Program

Once again, you begin with a sample program. As before, you'll find some unfamiliar wrinkles that we'll soon iron out for you. The program's general intent should be clear, so try compiling and running the source code shown in Listing 3.1. To save time, you can omit typing the comments.

LISTING 3.1   The `rhodium.c` Program

```c
/* rhodium.c  -- your weight in rhodium        */
#include <stdio.h>
int main(void)
{
    float weight;     /* user weight           */
    float value;      /* rhodium equivalent    */

    printf("Are you worth your weight in rhodium?\n");
    printf("Let's check it out.\n");
    printf("Please enter your weight in pounds: ");

/* get input from the user                      */
    scanf("%f", &weight);
/* assume rhodium is $770 per ounce             */
/* 14.5833 converts pounds avd. to ounces troy */
    value = 770.0 * weight * 14.5833;
    printf("Your weight in rhodium is worth $%.2f.\n", value);
    printf("You are easily worth that! If rhodium prices drop,\n");
    printf("eat more to maintain your value.\n");

    return 0;
}
```

Errors and Warnings

If you type this program incorrectly and, say, omit a semicolon, the compiler gives you a syntax error message. Even if you type it correctly, however, the compiler may give you a warning similar to "Warning—conversion from 'double' to 'float,' possible loss of data." An error message means you did something wrong and prevents the program from being compiled. A *warning*, however, means you've done something that is valid code but possibly is not what you meant to do. A warning does not stop compilation. This particular warning pertains to how C handles values such as 770.0. It's not a problem for this example, and the chapter explains the warning later.

When you type this program, you might want to change the **770.0** to the current price of the precious metal rhodium. Don't, however, fiddle with the **14.5833**, which represents the number of ounces in a pound. (That's ounces troy, used for precious metals, and pounds avoirdupois, used for people—precious and otherwise.)

Note that "entering" your weight means to type your weight and then press the Enter or Return key. (Don't just type your weight and wait.) Pressing Enter informs the computer that you have finished typing your response. The program expects you to enter a number, such as **150**, not words, such as **too much**. Entering letters rather than digits causes problems that require an **if** statement (Chapter 7, "C Control Statements: Branching and Jumps") to defeat, so please be polite and enter a number. Here is some sample output:

```
Are you worth your weight in rhodium?
Let's check it out.
Please enter your weight in pounds: 150
Your weight in rhodium is worth $1684371.12.
You are easily worth that! If rhodium prices drop,
eat more to maintain your value.
```

What's New in This Program?

There are several new elements of C in this program:

- Notice that the code uses a new kind of variable declaration. The previous examples just used an integer variable type (int), but this one adds a floating-point variable type (float) so that you can handle a wider variety of data. The float type can hold numbers with decimal points.

- The program demonstrates some new ways of writing constants. You now have numbers with decimal points.

- To print this new kind of variable, use the %f specifier in the printf() code to handle a floating-point value. Use the .2 modifier to the %f specifier to fine-tune the appearance of the output so that it displays two places to the right of the decimal.

- To provide keyboard input to the program, use the scanf() function. The %f instructs scanf() to read a floating-point number from the keyboard, and the &weight tells scanf() to assign the input value to the variable named weight. The scanf() function uses the & notation to indicate where it can find the weight variable. The next chapter discusses & further; meanwhile, trust us that you need it here.

- Perhaps the most outstanding new feature is that this program is interactive. The computer asks you for information and then uses the number you enter. An interactive program is more interesting to use than the noninteractive types. More important, the interactive approach makes programs more flexible. For example, the sample program can be used for any reasonable weight, not just for 150 pounds. You don't have to rewrite the program every time you want to try it on a new person. The scanf() and printf() functions make this interactivity possible. The scanf() function reads data from the keyboard and delivers that data to the program, and printf() reads data from a program and delivers that data to your screen. Together, these two functions enable you to establish a two-way communication with your computer (see Figure 3.1), and that makes using a computer much more fun.

This chapter explains the first two items in this list of new features: variables and constants of various data types. Chapter 4, "Character Strings and Formatted Input/Output," covers the last three items, but this chapter will continue to make limited use of scanf() and printf().

FIGURE 3.1

The scanf() and printf() functions at work.

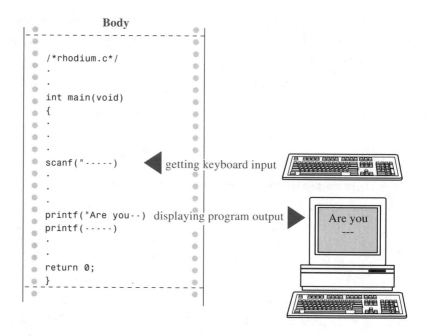

```
                              Body
/*rhodium.c*/
.
.

int main(void)
{
.
.
.
scanf("-----)              getting keyboard input
.
.
.
printf("Are you--)  displaying program output
printf(-----)
.
.
return 0;
}
```

Are you

Data Variables and Constants

A computer, under the guidance of a program, can do many things. It can add numbers, sort names, command the obedience of a speaker or video screen, calculate cometary orbits, prepare a mailing list, dial phone numbers, draw stick figures, draw conclusions, or anything else your imagination can create. To do these tasks, the program needs to work with *data*, the numbers and characters that bear the information you use. Some types of data are preset before a program is used and keep their values unchanged throughout the life of the program. These are *constants*. Other types of data may change or be assigned values as the program runs; these are *variables*. In the sample program, weight is a variable and 14.5833 is a constant. What about 770.0? True, the price of rhodium isn't a constant in real life, but this program treats it as a constant. The difference between a variable and a constant is that a variable can have its value assigned or changed while the program is running, and a constant can't.

Data: Data-Type Keywords

Beyond the distinction between variable and constant is the distinction between different *types* of data. Some types of data are numbers. Some are letters or, more generally, characters. The computer needs a way to identify and use these different kinds. C does this by recognizing several fundamental *data types*. If a datum is a constant, the compiler can usually tell its type just by the way it looks: 42 is an integer, and 42.100 is floating point. A variable, however, needs to have its type announced in a declaration statement. You'll learn the details of declaring variables as you move along. First, though, take a look at the fundamental types recognized by C. K&R C recognized seven keywords relating to types. The C90 standard added two to the list. The C99 standard adds yet another three (see Table 3.1).

TABLE 3.1   C Data Keywords

Original K&R Keywords	C90 Keywords	C99 Keywords
int	signed	_Bool
long	void	_Complex
short		_Imaginary
unsigned		
char		
float		
double		

The `int` keyword provides the basic class of integers used in C. The next three keywords (`long`, `short`, and `unsigned`) and the ANSI addition `signed` are used to provide variations of the basic type. Next, the `char` keyword designates the type used for letters of the alphabet and for other characters, such as #, $, %, and *. The `char` type also can be used to represent small integers. Next, `float`, `double`, and the combination `long double` are used to represent numbers with decimal points. The `_Bool` type is for Boolean values (`true` and `false`), and `_Complex` and `_Imaginary` represent complex and imaginary numbers, respectively.

The types created with these keywords can be divided into two families on the basis of how they are stored in the computer: *integer* types and *floating-point* types.

Bits, Bytes, and Words

The terms *bit*, *byte*, and *word* can be used to describe units of computer data or to describe units of computer memory. We'll concentrate on the second usage here.

The smallest unit of memory is called a *bit*. It can hold one of two values: 0 or 1. (Or you can say that the bit is set to "off" or "on.") You can't store much information in one bit, but a computer has a tremendous stock of them. The bit is the basic building block of computer memory.

The *byte* is the usual unit of computer memory. For nearly all machines, a byte is 8 bits, and that is the standard definition, at least when used to measure storage. (The C language, however, has a different definition, as discussed in the "Using Characters: Type `char`" section later in this chapter.) Because each bit can be either 0 or 1, there are 256 (that's 2 times itself 8 times) possible bit patterns of 0s and 1s that can fit in an 8-bit byte. These patterns can be used, for example, to represent the integers from 0 to 255 or to represent a set of characters. Representation can be accomplished with binary code, which uses (conveniently enough) just 0s and 1s to represent numbers. (Chapter 15, "Bit Fiddling," discusses binary code, but you can read through the introductory material of that chapter now if you like.)

A *word* is the natural unit of memory for a given computer design. For 8-bit microcomputers, such as the original Apples, a word is just 8 bits. Early IBM compatibles using the 80286 processor are 16-bit machines. This means that they have a word size of 16 bits. Machines such as the Pentium-based PCs and the Macintosh PowerPCs have 32-bit words. More powerful computers can have 64-bit words or even larger.

Integer Versus Floating-Point Types

Integer types? Floating-point types? If you find these terms disturbingly unfamiliar, relax. We are about to give you a brief rundown of their meanings. If you are unfamiliar with bits, bytes, and words, you might want to read the nearby sidebar about them first. Do you have to learn all the details? Not really, not any more than you have to learn the principles of internal combustion engines to drive a car, but knowing a little about what goes on inside a computer or engine can help you occasionally.

For a human, the difference between integers and floating-point numbers is reflected in the way they can be written. For a computer, the difference is reflected in the way they are stored. Let's look at each of the two classes in turn.

The Integer

An *integer* is a number with no fractional part. In C, an integer is never written with a decimal point. Examples are 2, –23, and 2456. Numbers such as 3.14, 0.22, and 2.000 are not integers. Integers are stored as binary numbers. The integer 7, for example, is written 111 in binary. Therefore, to store this number in an 8-bit byte, just set the first 5 bits to 0 and the last 3 bits to 1 (see Figure 3.2).

FIGURE 3.2
Storing the integer 7 using a binary code.

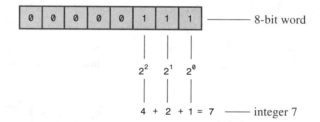

The Floating-Point Number

A *floating-point* number more or less corresponds to what mathematicians call a *real number*. Real numbers include the numbers between the integers. Some floating-point numbers are 2.75, 3.16E7, 7.00, and 2e–8. Notice that adding a decimal point makes a value a floating-point value. So 7 is an integer type but 7.00 is a floating-point type. Obviously, there is more than one way to write a floating-point number. We will discuss the e-notation more fully later, but, in brief, the notation 3.16E7 means to multiply 3.16 by 10 to the 7th power; that is, by 1 followed by 7 zeros. The 7 would be termed the *exponent* of 10.

The key point here is that the scheme used to store a floating-point number is different from the one used to store an integer. Floating-point representation involves breaking up a number into a fractional part and an exponent part and storing the parts separately. Therefore, the 7.00 in this list would not be stored in the same manner as the integer 7, even though both have the same value. The decimal analogy would be to write 7.0 as 0.7E1. Here, 0.7 is the fractional part, and the 1 is the exponent part. Figure 3.3 shows another example of floating-point storage. A computer, of course, would use binary numbers and powers of two instead of powers of 10 for internal storage. You'll find more on this topic in Chapter 15. Now, let's concentrate on the practical differences:

- An integer has no fractional part; a floating-point number can have a fractional part.

- Floating-point numbers can represent a much larger range of values than integers can. See Table 3.3 near the end of this chapter.

- For some arithmetic operations, such as subtracting one large number from another, floating-point numbers are subject to greater loss of precision.

- Because there is an infinite number of real numbers in any range—for example, in the range between 1.0 and 2.0—computer floating-point numbers can't represent all the values in the range. Instead, floating-point values are often approximations of a true value. For example, 7.0 might be stored as a 6.99999 `float` value—more about precision later.

- Floating-point operations are normally slower than integer operations. However, microprocessors developed specifically to handle floating-point operations are now available, and they have closed the gap.

FIGURE 3.3
Storing the number pi in floating-point format (decimal version).

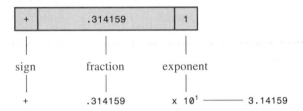

Basic C Data Types

Now let's look at the specifics of the basic data types used by C. For each type, we describe how to declare a variable, how to represent a constant, and what a typical use would be. Some older C compilers do not support all these types, so check your documentation to see which ones you have available.

The `int` Type

C offers many integer types, and you might wonder why one type isn't enough. The answer is that C gives the programmer the option of matching a type to a particular use. In particular, the C integer types vary in the range of values offered and in whether negative numbers can be used. The `int` type is the basic choice, but should you need other choices to meet the requirements of a particular task or machine, they are available.

The `int` type is a signed integer. That means it must be an integer and it can be positive, negative, or zero. The range in possible values depends on the computer system. Typically, an `int` uses one machine word for storage. Therefore, older IBM PC compatibles, which have a 16-bit word, use 16 bits to store an `int`. This allows a range in values from –32768 to 32767. Current personal computers typically have 32-bit integers and fit an `int` to that size. See Table 3.3 near the end of this chapter for examples. Now the personal computer industry is moving toward 64-bit processors that naturally will use even larger integers. ISO/ANSI C specifies that the minimum range for type `int` should be from −32767 to 32767. Typically, systems represent signed integers by using the value of a particular bit to indicate the sign. Chapter 15 discusses common methods.

Declaring an `int` Variable

As you saw in Chapter 2, "Introducing C," the keyword `int` is used to declare the basic integer variable. First comes `int`, and then the chosen name of the variable, and then a semicolon. To declare more than one variable, you can declare each variable separately, or you can follow the `int` with a list of names in which each name is separated from the next by a comma. The following are valid declarations:

```
int erns;
int hogs, cows, goats;
```

You could have used a separate declaration for each variable, or you could have declared all four variables in the same statement. The effect is the same: Associate names and arrange storage space for four `int`-sized variables.

These declarations create variables but don't supply values for them. How do variables get values? You've seen two ways that they can pick up values in the program. First, there is assignment:

```
cows = 112;
```

Second, a variable can pick up a value from a function—from `scanf()`, for example. Now let's look at a third way.

Initializing a Variable

To *initialize* a variable means to assign it a starting, or *initial*, value. In C, this can be done as part of the declaration. Just follow the variable name with the assignment operator (=) and the value you want the variable to have. Here are some examples:

```
int hogs = 21;
int cows = 32, goats = 14;
int dogs, cats = 94;        /* valid, but poor, form */
```

In the last line, only `cats` is initialized. A quick reading might lead you to think that `dogs` is also initialized to 94, so it is best to avoid putting initialized and noninitialized variables in the same declaration statement.

In short, these declarations create and label the storage for the variables and assign starting values to each (see Figure 3.4).

FIGURE 3.4
Defining and initializing a
variable.

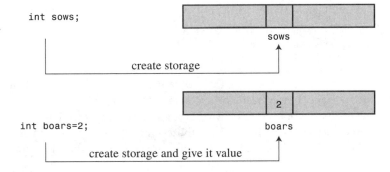

Type int Constants

The various integers (**21**, **32**, **14**, and **94**) in the last example are *integer constants*. When you write a number without a decimal point and without an exponent, C recognizes it as an integer. Therefore, **22** and **–44** are integer constants, but **22.0** and **2.2E1** are not. C treats most integer constants as type **int**. Very large integers can be treated differently; see the later discussion of the **long int** type in the section "**long** Constants and **long long** Constants."

Printing int Values

You can use the **printf()** function to print **int** types. As you saw in Chapter 2, the **%d** notation is used to indicate just where in a line the integer is to be printed. The **%d** is called a *format specifier* because it indicates the form that **printf()** uses to display a value. Each **%d** in the format string must be matched by a corresponding **int** value in the list of items to be printed. That value can be an **int** variable, an **int** constant, or any other expression having an **int** value. It's your job to make sure the number of format specifiers matches the number of values; the compiler won't catch mistakes of that kind. Listing 3.2 presents a simple program that initializes a variable and prints the value of the variable, the value of a constant, and the value of a simple expression. It also shows what can happen if you are not careful.

LISTING 3.2   The print1.c Program

```
/* print1.c-displays some properties of printf() */
#include <stdio.h>
int main(void)
{
    int ten = 10;
    int two = 2;

    printf("Doing it right: ");
    printf("%d minus %d is %d\n", ten, 2, ten - two );
    printf("Doing it wrong: ");
    printf("%d minus %d is %d\n", ten );  // forgot 2 arguments

    return 0;
}
```

Compiling and running the program produced this output on one system:

```
Doing it right: 10 minus 2 is 8
Doing it wrong: 10 minus 10 is 2
```

For the first line of output, the first %d represents the int variable ten, the second %d represents the int constant 2, and the third %d represents the value of the int expression ten - two. The second time, however, the program used ten to provide a value for the first %d and used whatever values happened to be lying around in memory for the next two! (The numbers you get could very well be different from those shown here. Not only might the memory contents be different, but different compilers will manage memory locations differently.)

You might be annoyed that the compiler doesn't catch such an obvious error. Blame the unusual design of printf(). Most functions take a specific number of arguments, and the compiler can check to see whether you've used the correct number. However, printf() can have one, two, three, or more arguments, and that keeps the compiler from using its usual methods for error checking. Remember, check to see that the number of format specifiers you give to printf() matches the number of values to be displayed.

Octal and Hexadecimal

Normally, C assumes that integer constants are decimal, or base 10, numbers. However, octal (base 8) and hexadecimal (base 16) numbers are popular with many programmers. Because 8 and 16 are powers of 2, and 10 is not, these number systems occasionally offer a more convenient way for expressing computer-related values. For example, the number 65536, which often pops up in 16-bit machines, is just 10000 in hexadecimal. Also, each digit in a hexadecimal number corresponds to exactly 4 bits. For example, the hexadecimal digit 3 is 0011 and the hexadecimal digit 5 is 0101. So the hexadecimal value 35 is the bit pattern 0011 0101, and the hexadecimal value 53 is 0101 0011. This correspondence makes it easy to go back and forth between hexadecimal and binary (base 2) notation. But how can the computer tell whether 10000 is meant to be a decimal, hexadecimal, or octal value? In C, special prefixes indicate which number base you are using. A prefix of 0x or 0X (zero-ex) means that you are specifying a hexadecimal value, so 16 is written as 0x10, or 0X10, in hexadecimal. Similarly, a 0 (zero) prefix means that you are writing in octal. For example, the decimal value 16 is written as 020 in octal. Chapter 15 discusses these alternative number bases more fully.

Be aware that this option of using different number systems is provided as a service for your convenience. It doesn't affect how the number is stored. That is, you can write 16 or 020 or 0x10, and the number is stored exactly the same way in each case—in the binary code used internally by computers.

Displaying Octal and Hexadecimal

Just as C enables you write a number in any one of three number systems, it also enables you to display a number in any of these three systems. To display an integer in octal notation instead of decimal, use %o instead of %d. To display an integer in hexadecimal, use %x. If you want to display the C prefixes, you can use specifiers %#o, %#x, and %#X to generate the 0, 0x, and 0X prefixes, respectively. Listing 3.3 shows a short example. (Recall that you may have to insert a `getchar();` statement in the code for some IDEs to keep the program execution window from closing immediately.)

LISTING 3.3   The `bases.c` Program

```
/* bases.c--prints 100 in decimal, octal, and hex */
#include <stdio.h>
int main(void)
{
    int x = 100;

    printf("dec = %d; octal = %o; hex = %x\n", x, x, x);
    printf("dec = %d; octal = %#o; hex = %#x\n", x, x, x);

    return 0;
}
```

Compiling and running this program produces this output:

```
dec = 100; octal = 144; hex = 64
dec = 100; octal = 0144; hex = 0x64
```

You see the same value displayed in three different number systems. The `printf()` function makes the conversions. Note that the `0` and the `0x` prefixes are not displayed in the output unless you include the `#` as part of the specifier.

Other Integer Types

When you are just learning the language, the `int` type will probably meet most of your integer needs. To be complete, however, we'll cover the other forms now. If you like, you can skim this section and jump to the discussion of the `char` type in the "Using Characters: Type `char`" section, returning here when you have a need.

C offers three adjective keywords to modify the basic integer type: `short`, `long`, and `unsigned`. Here are some points to keep in mind:

- The type `short int` or, more briefly, `short` may use less storage than `int`, thus saving space when only small numbers are needed. Like `int`, `short` is a signed type.

- The type `long int`, or `long`, may use more storage than `int`, thus enabling you to express larger integer values. Like `int`, `long` is a signed type.

- The type `long long int`, or `long long` (both introduced in the C99 standard), may use more storage than `long`, thus enabling you to express even larger integer values. Like `int`, `long long` is a signed type.

- The type `unsigned int`, or `unsigned`, is used for variables that have only nonnegative values. This type shifts the range of numbers that can be stored. For example, a 16-bit `unsigned int` allows a range from `0` to `65535` in value instead of from `-32768` to `32767`. The bit used to indicate the sign of signed numbers now becomes another binary digit, allowing the larger number.

- The types `unsigned long int`, or `unsigned long`, and `unsigned short int`, or `unsigned short`, are recognized as valid by the C90 standard. To this list, C99 adds `unsigned long long int`, or `unsigned long long`.

- The keyword `signed` can be used with any of the signed types to make your intent explicit. For example, `short`, `short int`, `signed short`, and `signed short int` are all names for the same type.

Declaring Other Integer Types

Other integer types are declared in the same manner as the `int` type. The following list shows several examples. Not all older C compilers recognize the last three, and the final example is new with the C99 standard.

```
long int estine;
long johns;
short int erns;
short ribs;
unsigned int s_count;
unsigned players;
unsigned long headcount;
unsigned short yesvotes;
long long ago;
```

Why Multiple Integer Types?

Why do we say that `long` and `short` types "may" use more or less storage than `int`? Because C guarantees only that `short` is no longer than `int` and that `long` is no shorter than `int`. The idea is to fit the types to the machine. On an IBM PC running Windows 3.1, for example, an `int` and a `short` are both 16 bits, and a `long` is 32 bits. On a Windows XP machine or a Macintosh PowerPC, however, a `short` is 16 bits, and both `int` and `long` are 32 bits. The natural word size on a Pentium chip or a PowerPC G3 or G4 chip is 32 bits. Because this allows integers in excess of 2 billion (see Table 3.3), the implementers of C on these processor/operating system combinations did not see a necessity for anything larger; therefore, `long` is the same as `int`. For many uses, integers of that size are not needed, so a space-saving `short` was created. The original IBM PC, on the other hand, has only a 16-bit word, which means that a larger `long` was needed.

Now that 64-bit processors, such as the IBM Itanium, AMD Opteron, and PowerPC G5, are beginning to become more common, there's a need for 64-bit integers, and that's the motivation for the `long long` type.

The most common practice today is to set up `long long` as 64 bits, `long` as 32 bits, `short` as 16 bits, and `int` to either 16 bits or 32 bits, depending on the machine's natural word size. In principle, however, these four types could represent four distinct sizes.

The C standard provides guidelines specifying the minimum allowable size for each basic data type. The minimum range for both `short` and `int` is –32,767 to 32,767, corresponding to a 16-bit unit, and the minimum range for `long` is –2,147,483,647 to 2,147,483,647, corresponding to a 32-bit unit. (Note: For legibility, we've used commas, but C code doesn't allow that option.) For `unsigned short` and `unsigned int`, the minimum range is 0 to 65,535, and for `unsigned long`, the minimum range is 0 to 4,294,967,295. The `long long` type is intended to support 64-bit needs. Its minimum range is a substantial −9,223,372,036,854,775,807 to 9,223,372,036,854,775,807, and the minimum range for `unsigned long long` is 0 to 18,446,744,073,709,551,615. (For those of you writing checks, that's eighteen quintillion, four hundred and forty-six quadrillion, seven hundred forty-four trillion, seventy-three billion, seven hundred nine million, five hundred fifty-one thousand, six hundred fifteen in U.S. notation, but who's counting?)

When do you use the various `int` types? First, consider `unsigned` types. It is natural to use them for counting because you don't need negative numbers, and the unsigned types enable you to reach higher positive numbers than the signed types.

Use the `long` type if you need to use numbers that `long` can handle and that `int` cannot. However, on systems for which `long` is bigger than `int`, using `long` can slow down calculations, so don't use `long` if it is not essential. One further point: If you are writing code on a machine for which `int` and `long` are the same size, and you do need 32-bit integers, you should use `long` instead of `int` so that the program will function correctly if transferred to a 16-bit machine.

Similarly, use `long long` if you need 64-bit integer values. Some computers already use 64-bit processors, and 64-bit processing in servers, workstations, and even desktops may soon become common.

Use `short` to save storage space if, say, you need a 16-bit value on a system where `int` is 32-bit. Usually, saving storage space is important only if your program uses arrays of integers that are large in relation to a system's available memory. Another reason to use `short` is that it may correspond in size to hardware registers used by particular components in a computer.

Integer Overflow

What happens if an integer tries to get too big for its type? Let's set an integer to its largest possible value, add to it, and see what happens. Try both signed and unsigned types. (The `printf()` function uses the `%u` specifier to display `unsigned int values`.)

```
/* toobig.c-exceeds maximum int size on our system */
#include <stdio.h>
int main(void)
{
    int i = 2147483647;
    unsigned int j = 4294967295;

    printf("%d %d %d\n", i, i+1, i+2);
    printf("%u %u %u\n", j, j+1, j+2);

    return 0;
}
```

Here is the result for our system:

```
2147483647 -2147483648 -2147483647
4294967295 0 1
```

The unsigned integer j is acting like a car's odometer. When it reaches its maximum value, it starts over at the beginning. The integer i acts similarly. The main difference is that the unsigned int variable j, like an odometer, begins at 0, but the int variable i begins at –2147483648. Notice that you are not informed that i has exceeded (overflowed) its maximum value. You would have to include your own programming to keep tabs on that.

The behavior described here is mandated by the rules of C for unsigned types. The standard doesn't define how signed types should behave. The behavior shown here is typical, but you could encounter something different

long Constants and long long Constants

Normally, when you use a number such as 2345 in your program code, it is stored as an int type. What if you use a number such as 1000000 on a system in which int will not hold such a large number? Then the compiler treats it as a long int, assuming that type is large enough. If the number is larger than the long maximum, C treats it as unsigned long. If that is still insufficient, C treats the value as long long or unsigned long long, if those types are available.

Octal and hexadecimal constants are treated as type int unless the value is too large. Then the compiler tries unsigned int. If that doesn't work, it tries, in order, long, unsigned long, long long, and unsigned long long.

Sometimes you might want the compiler to store a small number as a long integer. Programming that involves explicit use of memory addresses on an IBM PC, for instance, can create such a need. Also, some standard C functions require type long values. To cause a small constant to be treated as type long, you can append an l (lowercase L) or L as a suffix. The second form is better because it looks less like the digit 1. Therefore, a system with a 16-bit int and a 32-bit long treats the integer 7 as 16 bits and the integer 7L as 32 bits. The l and L suffixes can also be used with octal and hex integers, as in 020L and 0x10L.

Similarly, on those systems supporting the long long type, you can use an ll or LL suffix to indicate a long long value, as in 3LL. Add a u or U to the suffix for unsigned long long, as in 5ull or 10LLU or 6LLU or 9Ull.

Printing short, long, long long, and unsigned Types

To print an unsigned int number, use the %u notation. To print a long value, use the %ld format specifier. If int and long are the same size on your system, just %d will suffice, but your program will not work properly when transferred to a system on which the two types are different, so use the %ld specifier for long. You can use the l prefix for x and o, too. Therefore, you would use %lx to print a long integer in hexadecimal format and %lo to print in octal format. Note that although C allows both uppercase and lowercase letters for constant suffixes, these format specifiers use just lowercase.

C has several additional `printf()` formats. First, you can use an h prefix for `short` types. Therefore, `%hd` displays a `short` integer in decimal form, and `%ho` displays a `short` integer in octal form. Both the h and l prefixes can be used with u for unsigned types. For instance, you would use the `%lu` notation for printing unsigned `long` types. Listing 3.4 provides an example. Systems supporting the `long long` types use `%lld` and `%llu` for the signed and unsigned versions. Chapter 4 provides a fuller discussion of format specifiers.

LISTING 3.4   The `print2.c` Program

```
/* print2.c-more printf() properties */
#include <stdio.h>
int main(void)
{
    unsigned int un = 3000000000; /* system with 32-bit int */
    short end = 200;              /* and 16-bit short       */
    long big = 65537;
    long long verybig = 12345678908642;

    printf("un = %u and not %d\n", un, un);
    printf("end = %hd and %d\n", end, end);
    printf("big = %ld and not %hd\n", big, big);
    printf("verybig= %lld and not %ld\n", verybig, verybig);

    return 0;
}
```

Here is the output on one system:

```
un = 3000000000 and not -1294967296
end = 200 and 200
big = 65537 and not 1
verybig= 12345678908642 and not 1942899938
```

This example points out that using the wrong specification can produce unexpected results. First, note that using the `%d` specifier for the unsigned variable un produces a negative number! The reason for this is that the unsigned value 3000000000 and the signed value −129496296 have exactly the same internal representation in memory on our system. (Chapter 15 explains this property in more detail.) So if you tell `printf()` that the number is unsigned, it prints one value, and if you tell it that the same number is signed, it prints the other value. This behavior shows up with values larger than the maximum signed value. Smaller positive values, such as 96, are stored and displayed the same for both signed and unsigned types.

Next, note that the `short` variable end is displayed the same whether you tell `printf()` that end is a `short` (the `%hd` specifier) or an `int` (the `%d` specifier). That's because C automatically expands a type `short` value to a type `int` value when it's passed as an argument to a function. This may raise two questions in your mind: Why does this conversion take place, and what's the use of the h modifier? The answer to the first question is that the `int` type is intended to be the integer size that the computer handles most efficiently. So, on a computer for which `short` and `int` are different sizes, it may be faster to pass the value as an `int`. The answer to the second question is that you can use the h modifier to show how a longer integer would look if truncated to the size of **short**. The third line of output illustrates this point. When the value 65537 is written in binary format as a 32-bit number, it looks like 00000000000000010000000000000001. Using the **%hd** specifier persuaded **printf()** to look at just the last 16 bits; therefore, it displayed the value as 1. Similarly, the final output line shows the full value of **verybig** and then the value stored in the last 32 bits, as viewed through the **%ld** specifier.

Earlier you saw that it is your responsibility to make sure the number of specifiers matches the number of values to be displayed. Here you see that it is also your responsibility to use the correct specifier for the type of value to be displayed.

Match the Type printf() Specifiers

Remember to check to see that you have one format specifier for each value being displayed in a **printf()** statement. And also check that the type of each format specifier matches the type of the corresponding display value.

Using Characters: Type char

The **char** type is used for storing characters such as letters and punctuation marks, but technically it is an integer type. Why? Because the **char** type actually stores integers, not characters. To handle characters, the computer uses a numerical code in which certain integers represent certain characters. The most commonly used code in the U.S. is the ASCII code given in the table on the inside front cover. It is the code this book assumes. In it, for example, the integer value **65** represents an uppercase *A*. So to store the letter *A*, you actually need to store the integer **65**. (Many IBM mainframes use a different code, called EBCDIC, but the principle is the same. Computer systems outside the U.S. may use entirely different codes.)

The standard ASCII code runs numerically from 0 to 127. This range is small enough that 7 bits can hold it. The **char** type is typically defined as an 8-bit unit of memory, so it is more than large enough to encompass the standard ASCII code. Many systems, such as the IBM PC and the Apple Macintosh, offer extended ASCII codes (different for the two systems) that still stay within an 8-bit limit. More generally, C guarantees that the **char** type is large enough to store the basic character set for the system on which C is implemented.

Many character sets have many more than 127 or even 255 values. For example, there is the Japanese kanji character set. The commercial Unicode initiative has created a system to represent a variety of characters sets worldwide and currently has over 96,000 characters. The International Organization for Standardization (ISO) and the International Electrotechnical Commission (IEC) has developed a standard called ISO/IEC 10646 for character sets. Fortunately, the Unicode standard has been kept compatible with the more extensive ISO/IEC 10646 standard.

A platform that uses one of these sets as its basic character set could use a 16-bit or even a 32-bit **char** representation. The C language defines a byte to be the number of bits used by type **char**, so as far as C documentation goes, a byte would be 16 or 32 bits, rather than 8 bits on such systems.

Declaring Type char Variables

As you might expect, char variables are declared in the same manner as other variables. Here are some examples:

```
char response;
char itable, latan;
```

This code would create three char variables: response, itable, and latan.

Character Constants and Initialization

Suppose you want to initialize a character constant to the letter *A*. Computer languages are supposed to make things easy, so you shouldn't have to memorize the ASCII code, and you don't. You can assign the character A to grade with the following initialization:

```
char grade = 'A';
```

A single letter contained between single quotes is a C *character constant*. When the compiler sees 'A', it converts the 'A' to the proper code value. The single quotes are essential. Here's another example:

```
char broiled;          /* declare a char variable          */
broiled = 'T';         /* OK                               */
broiled = T;           /* NO! Thinks T is a variable       */
broiled = "T";         /* NO! Thinks "T" is a string       */
```

If you omit the quotes, the compiler thinks that T is the name of a variable. If you use double quotes, it thinks you are using a string. We'll discuss strings in Chapter 4.

Because characters are really stored as numeric values, you can also use the numerical code to assign values:

```
char grade = 65;   /* ok for ASCII, but poor style */
```

In this example, 65 is type int, but, because the value is smaller than the maximum char size, it can be assigned to grade without any problems. Because 65 is the ASCII code for the letter *A*, this example assigns the value A to grade. Note, however, that this example assumes that the system is using ASCII code. Using 'A' instead of 65 produces code that works on any system. Therefore, it's much better to use character constants than numeric code values.

Somewhat oddly, C treats character constants as type int rather than type char. For example, on an ASCII system with a 32-bit int and an 8-bit char, the code

```
char grade = 'B';
```

represents 'B' as the numerical value 66 stored in a 32-bit unit, but grade winds up with 66 stored in an 8-bit unit. This characteristic of character constants makes it possible to define a character constant such as 'FATE', with four separate 8-bit ASCII codes stored in a 32-bit unit. However, attempting to assign such a character constant to a char variable results in only the last 8 bits being used, so the variable gets the value 'E'.

Nonprinting Characters

The single-quote technique is fine for characters, digits, and punctuation marks, but if you look through the table on the inside front cover of this book, you'll see that some of the ASCII characters are nonprinting. For example, some represent actions such as backspacing or going to the next line or making the terminal bell ring (or speaker beep). How can these be represented? C offers three ways.

The first way we have already mentioned—just use the ASCII code. For example, the ASCII value for the beep character is 7, so you can do this:

```
char beep = 7;
```

The second way to represent certain awkward characters in C is to use special symbol sequences. These are called *escape sequences*. Table 3.2 shows the escape sequences and their meanings.

TABLE 3.2   Escape Sequences

Sequence	Meaning
\a	Alert (ANSI C).
\b	Backspace.
\f	Form feed.
\n	Newline.
\r	Carriage return.
\t	Horizontal tab.
\v	Vertical tab.
\\	Backslash (\).
\'	Single quote (').
\"	Double quote (").
\?	Question mark (?).
\0oo	Octal value. (o represents an octal digit.)
\xhh	Hexadecimal value. (h represents a hexadecimal digit.)

Escape sequences must be enclosed in single quotes when assigned to a character variable. For example, you could make the statement

```
char nerf = '\n';
```

and then print the variable **nerf** to advance the printer or screen one line.

Now take a closer look at what each escape sequence does. The alert character (\a), added by C90, produces an audible or visible alert. The nature of the alert depends on the hardware, with the beep being the most common. (With some systems, the alert character has no effect.) The ANSI standard states that the alert character shall not change the active position. By *active position*, the standard means the location on the display device (screen, teletype, printer, and so on) at which the next character would otherwise appear. In short, the active position is a generalization of the screen cursor with which you are probably accustomed. Using the alert character in a program displayed on a screen should produce a beep without moving the screen cursor.

Next, the \b, \f, \n, \r, \t, and \v escape sequences are common output device control characters. They are best described in terms of how they affect the active position. A backspace (\b) moves the active position back one space on the current line. A form feed character (\f) advances the active position to the start of the next page. A newline character (\n) sets the active position to the beginning of the next line. A carriage return (\r) moves the active position to the beginning of the current line. A horizontal tab character (\t) moves the active position to the next horizontal tab stop (typically, these are found at character positions 1, 9, 17, 25, and so on). A vertical tab (\v) moves the active position to the next vertical tab position.

These escape sequence characters do not necessarily work with all display devices. For example, the form feed and vertical tab characters produce odd symbols on a PC screen instead of any cursor movement, but they work as described if sent to a printer instead of to the screen.

The next three escape sequences (\\, \', and \") enable you to use \, ', and " as character constants. (Because these symbols are used to define character constants as part of a `printf()` command, the situation could get confusing if you use them literally.) Suppose you want to print the following line:

```
Gramps sez, "a \ is a backslash."
```

Then use this code:

```
printf("Gramps sez, \"a \\ is a backslash.\"\n");
```

The final two forms (\0oo and \xhh) are special representations of the ASCII code. To represent a character by its octal ASCII code, precede it with a backslash (\) and enclose the whole thing in single quotes. For example, if your compiler doesn't recognize the alert character (\a), you could use the ASCII code instead:

```
beep = '\007';
```

You can omit the leading zeros, so '\07' or even '\7' will do. This notation causes numbers to be interpreted as octal, even if there is no initial 0.

Beginning with C90, C provides a third option—using a hexadecimal form for character constants. In this case, the backslash is followed by an x or X and one to three hexadecimal digits. For example, the Ctrl+P character has an ASCII hex code of 10 (16, in decimal), so it can be expressed as '\x10' or '\X010'. Figure 3.5 shows some representative integer types.

FIGURE 3.5
Writing constants with the int family.

Examples of Integer Constants			
type	hexadecimal	octal	decimal
char	\0x41	\0101	N.A.
int	0x41	0101	65
unsigned int	0x41u	0101u	65u
long	0x41L	0101L	65L
unsigned long	0x41UL	0101UL	65UL
long long	0x41LL	0101LL	65LL
unsigned long long	0x41ULL	0101ULL	65ULL

When you use ASCII code, note the difference between numbers and number characters. For example, the character 4 is represented by ASCII code value 52. The notation '4' represents the symbol 4, not the numerical value 4.

At this point, you may have three questions:

- *Why aren't the escape sequences enclosed in single quotes in the last example* (printf("Gramps sez, \"a \\ is a backslash\"\"n");)? When a character, be it an escape sequence or not, is part of a string of characters enclosed in double quotes, don't enclose it in single quotes. Notice that none of the other characters in this example (G, r, a, m, p, s, and so on) are marked off by single quotes. A string of characters enclosed in double quotes is called a *character string*. (Chapter 4 explores strings.) Similarly, printf("Hello!\007\n"); will print Hello! and beep, but printf("Hello!7\n"); will print Hello!7. Digits that are not part of an escape sequence are treated as ordinary characters to be printed.

- *When should I use the ASCII code, and when should I use the escape sequences?* If you have a choice between using one of the special escape sequences, say '\f', or an equivalent ASCII code, say '\014', use the '\f'. First, the representation is more mnemonic. Second, it is more portable. If you have a system that doesn't use ASCII code, the '\f' will still work.

- *If I need to use numeric code, why use, say, '\032' instead of 032?*—First, using '\032' instead of 032 makes it clear to someone reading the code that you intend to represent a character code. Second, an escape sequence such as \032 can be embedded in part of a C string, the way \007 was in the first point.

Printing Characters

The printf() function uses %c to indicate that a character should be printed. Recall that a character variable is stored as a 1-byte integer value. Therefore, if you print the value of a char variable with the usual %d specifier, you get an integer. The %c format specifier tells printf() to display the character that has that integer as its code value. Listing 3.5 shows a char variable both ways.

LISTING 3.5   The charcode.c Program

```
/* charcode.c-displays code number for a character */
#include <stdio.h>
int main(void)
{
    char ch;

    printf("Please enter a character.\n");
    scanf("%c", &ch);    /* user inputs character */
    printf("The code for %c is %d.\n", ch, ch);

    return 0;
}
```

Here is a sample run:

```
Please enter a character.
C
The code for C is 67.
```

When you use the program, remember to press the Enter or Return key after typing the character. The `scanf()` function then fetches the character you typed, and the ampersand (`&`) causes the character to be assigned to the variable `ch`. The `printf()` function then prints the value of `ch` twice, first as a character (prompted by the `%c` code) and then as a decimal integer (prompted by the `%d` code). Note that the `printf()` specifiers determine how data is displayed, not how it is stored (see Figure 3.6).

FIGURE 3.6
Data display versus data storage.

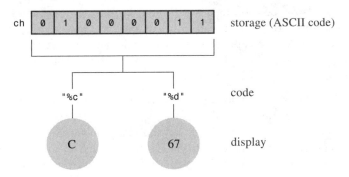

Signed or Unsigned?

Some C implementations make `char` a signed type. This means a `char` can hold values typically in the range –128 through 127. Other implementations make `char` an unsigned type, which provides a range of 0 through 255. Your compiler manual should tell you which type your `char` is, or you can check the `limits.h` header file, discussed in the next chapter.

With C90, C enables you to use the keywords `signed` and `unsigned` with `char`. Then, regardless of what your default `char` is, `signed char` would be signed, and `unsigned char` would be unsigned. These versions of `char` are useful if you're using the type to handle small integers. For character use, just use the standard `char` type without modifiers.

The _Bool Type

The _Bool type is a C99 addition that's used to represent Boolean values—that is, the logical values true and false. Because C uses the value 1 for true and 0 for false, the _Bool type really is just an integer type, but one that, in principle, only requires 1 bit of memory, because that is enough to cover the full range from 0 to 1.

Programs use Boolean values to choose which code to execute next. Code execution is covered more fully in Chapter 6, "C Control Statements: Looping," and Chapter 7, "C Control Statements: Branching and Jumps," so let's defer further discussion until then.

Portable Types: inttypes.h

Are there even more integer types? No, but there are more names that you can use for the existing types. You might think you've seen more than an adequate number of names, but the primary names do have a problem. Knowing that a variable is an int doesn't tell you how many bits it is unless you check the documentation for your system. To get around this problem, C99 provides an alternative set of names that describes exactly what you get. For example, the name int16_t indicates a 16-bit signed integer type and the name uint32_t indicates a 32-bit unsigned integer type.

To make these names available to a program, include the inttypes.h header file. (Note that at the time this edition was prepared, some compilers don't yet support this feature.) That file uses the typedef facility (first described briefly in Chapter 5, "Operators, Expressions, and Statements") to create new type names. For example, it will make uint32_t a synonym or alias for a standard type with the desired characteristics—perhaps unsigned int on one system and unsigned long on another. Your compiler will provide a header file consistent with the computer system you are using. These new designations are called *exact width types*. Note that, unlike int, uint32_t is not a keyword, so the compiler won't recognize it unless you include the inttypes.h header file.

One possible problem with attempting to provide exact width types is that a particular system might not support some of the choices, so there is no guarantee that there will be, say, an int8_t type (8-bit signed). To get around that problem, the C99 standard defines a second set of names that promises the type is at least big enough to meet the specification and that no other type that can do the job is smaller. These types are called *minimum width types*. For example, int_least8_t will be an alias for the smallest available type that can hold an 8-bit signed integer value. If the smallest type on a particular system were 8 bits, the int8_t type would not be defined. However, the int_least8_t type would be available, perhaps implemented as a 16-bit integer.

Of course, some programmers are more concerned with speed than with space. For them, C99 defines a set of types that will allow the fastest computations. These are called the *fastest minimum width* types. For example, the int_fast8_t will be defined as an alternative name for the integer type on your system that allows the fastest calculations for 8-bit signed values.

Finally, for some programmers, only the biggest possible integer type on a system will do; `intmax_t` stands for that type, a type that can hold any valid signed integer value. Similarly, `uintmax_t` stands for the largest available unsigned type. Incidentally, these types could be bigger than `long long` and `unsigned long` because C implementations are permitted to define types beyond the required ones.

C99 not only provides these new, portable type names, it also has to assist with input and output. For example, `printf()` requires specific specifiers for particular types. So what do you do to display an `int32_t` value when it might require a `%d` specifier for one definition and an `%ld` for another? The C99 standard provides some string macros (introduced in Chapter 4) to be used to display the portable types. For example, the `inttypes.h` header file will define `PRId16` as a string representing the appropriate specifier (`hd` or `d`, for instance) for a 16-bit signed value. Listing 3.6 shows a brief example illustrating how to use a portable type and its associated specifier.

LISTING 3.6   The `altnames.c` Program

```
/* altnames.c -- portable names for integer types */
#include <stdio.h>
#include <inttypes.h> // supports portable types
int main(void)
{
    int16_t me16;     // me16 a 16-bit signed variable

    me16 = 4593;
    printf("First, assume int16_t is short: ");
    printf("me16 = %hd\n", me16);
    printf("Next, let's not make any assumptions.\n");
    printf("Instead, use a \"macro\" from inttypes.h: ");
    printf("me16 = %" PRId16 "\n", me16);

    return 0;
}
```

In the final `printf()` argument, the `PRId16` is replaced by its `inttypes.h` definition of `"hd"`, making the line this:

```
printf("me16 = %" "hd" "\n", me16);
```

But C combines consecutive quoted strings into a single quoted string, making the line this:

```
printf("me16 = %hd\n", me16);
```

Here's the output; note that the example also uses the `\"` escape sequence to display double quotation marks:

```
First, assume int16_t is short: me16 = 4593
Next, let's not make any assumptions.
Instead, use a "macro" from inttypes.h: me16 = 4593
```

Reference Section VI, "Expanded Integer Types," provides a complete rundown of the `inttypes.h` header file additions and also lists all the specifier macros.

Types `float`, `double`, and `long double`

The various integer types serve well for most software development projects. However, financial and mathematically oriented programs often make use of *floating-point* numbers. In C, such numbers are called type `float`, `double`, or `long double`. They correspond to the `real` types of FORTRAN and Pascal. The floating-point approach, as already mentioned, enables you to represent a much greater range of numbers, including decimal fractions. Floating-point number representation is similar to *scientific notation*, a system used by scientists to express very large and very small numbers. Let's take a look.

In scientific notation, numbers are represented as decimal numbers times powers of 10. Here are some examples.

Number	Scientific Notation	Exponential Notation
1,000,000,000	$= 1.0 \times 10^9$	$= 1.0e9$
123,000	$= 1.23 \times 10^5$	$= 1.23e5$
322.56	$= 3.2256 \times 10^2$	$= 3.2256e2$
0.000056	$= 5.6 \times 10^{-5}$	$= 5.6e-5$

The first column shows the usual notation, the second column scientific notation, and the third column exponential notation, or *e-notation*, which is the way scientific notation is usually written for and by computers, with the *e* followed by the power of 10. Figure 3.7 shows more floating-point representations.

The C standard provides that a `float` has to be able to represent at least six significant figures and allow a range of at least 10^{-37} to 10^{+37}. The first requirement means, for example, that a `float` has to represent accurately at least the first six digits in a number such as 33.333333. The second requirement is handy if you like to use numbers such as the mass of the sun (2.0e30 kilograms), the charge of a proton (1.6e-19 coulombs), or the national debt. Often, systems use 32 bits to store a floating-point number. Eight bits are used to give the exponent its value and sign, and 24 bits are used to represent the nonexponent part, called the *mantissa* or *significand*, and its sign.

FIGURE 3.7
Some floating-point
numbers.

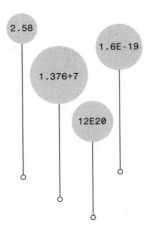

C also has a **double** (for double precision) floating-point type. The **double** type has the same minimum range requirements as **float**, but it extends the minimum number of significant figures that can be represented to 10. Typical **double** representations use 64 bits instead of 32. Some systems use all 32 additional bits for the nonexponent part. This increases the number of significant figures and reduces round-off errors. Other systems use some of the bits to accommodate a larger exponent; this increases the range of numbers that can be accommodated. Either approach leads to at least 13 significant figures, more than meeting the minimum standard.

C allows for a third floating-point type: **long double**. The intent is to provide for even more precision than **double**. However, C guarantees only that **long double** is at least as precise as **double**.

Declaring Floating-Point Variables

Floating-point variables are declared and initialized in the same manner as their integer cousins. Here are some examples:

```
float noah, jonah;
double trouble;
float planck = 6.63e-34;
long double gnp;
```

Floating-Point Constants

There are many choices open to you when you write a floating-point constant. The basic form of a floating-point constant is a signed series of digits, including a decimal point, followed by an *e* or *E*, followed by a signed exponent indicating the power of 10 used. Here are two valid floating-point constants:

-1.56E+12

2.87e-3

You can leave out positive signs. You can do without a decimal point (2E5) or an exponential part (19.28), but not both simultaneously. You can omit a fractional part (3.E16) or an integer part (.45E–6), but not both (that wouldn't leave much!). Here are some more valid floating-point constants:

3.14159

.2

4e16

.8E-5

100.

Don't use spaces in a floating-point constant.

Wrong: 1.56 E+12

By default, the compiler assumes floating-point constants are `double` precision. Suppose, for example, that `some` is a `float` variable and that you have the following statement:

```
some = 4.0 * 2.0;
```

Then `4.0` and `2.0` are stored as `double`, using (typically) 64 bits for each. The product is calculated using double precision arithmetic, and only then is the answer trimmed to regular `float` size. This ensures greater precision for your calculations, but it can slow down a program.

C enables you to override this default by using an `f` or `F` suffix to make the compiler treat a floating-point constant as type `float`; examples are `2.3f` and `9.11E9F`. An `l` or `L` suffix makes a number type `long double`; examples are `54.31` and `4.32e4L`. Note that `L` is less likely to be mistaken for 1 (one) than is `l`. If the floating-point number has no suffix, it is type `double`.

C99 has added a new format for expressing floating-point constants. It uses a hexadecimal prefix (`0x` or `0X`) with hexadecimal digits, a `p` or `P` instead of `e` or `E`, and an exponent that is a power of 2 instead of a power of 10. Here's what such a number might look like:

```
0xa.1fp10
```

The `a` is 10, the `.1f` is 1/16th plus 15/256th, and the `p10` is 2^{10}, or 1024, making the complete value 10364.0 in base 10 notation.

Not all C compilers have added support for this C99 feature.

Printing Floating-Point Values

The `printf()` function uses the `%f` format specifier to print type `float` and `double` numbers using decimal notation, and it uses `%e` to print them in exponential notation. If your system supports the C99 hexadecimal format for floating-point numbers, you can use `a` or `A` instead of `e` or `E`. The `long double` type requires the `%Lf`, `%Le`, and `%La` specifiers to print that type. Note that both `float` and `double` use the `%f`, `%e`, or `%a` specifier for output. That's because C automatically expands type `float` values to type `double` when they are passed as arguments to any function, such as `printf()`, that doesn't explicitly prototype the argument type. Listing 3.7 illustrates these behaviors.

LISTING 3.7   The `showf_pt.c` Program

```
/* showf_pt.c -- displays float value in two ways */
#include <stdio.h>
int main(void)
{
    float aboat = 32000.0;
    double abet = 2.14e9;
    long double dip = 5.32e-5;

    printf("%f can be written %e\n", aboat, aboat);
    printf("%f can be written %e\n", abet, abet);
    printf("%f can be written %e\n", dip, dip);

    return 0;
}
```

This is the output:

```
32000.000000 can be written 3.200000e+04
2140000000.000000 can be written 2.140000e+09
0.000053 can be written 5.320000e-05
```

This example illustrates the default output. The next chapter discusses how to control the appearance of this output by setting field widths and the number of places to the right of the decimal.

Floating-Point Overflow and Underflow

Suppose the biggest possible `float` value on your system is about 3.4E38 and you do this:

```
float toobig = 3.4E38 * 100.0f;
printf("%e\n", toobig);
```

What happens? This is an example of *overflow*—when a calculation leads to a number too large to be expressed. The behavior for this case used to be undefined, but now C specifies that `toobig` gets assigned a special value that stands for *infinity* and that `printf()` displays either `inf` or `infinity` (or some variation on that theme) for the value.

What about dividing very small numbers? Here the situation is more involved. Recall that a `float` number is stored as an exponent and as a value part, or *mantissa*. There will be a number that has the smallest possible exponent and also the smallest value that still uses all the bits available to represent the mantissa. This will be the smallest number that still is represented to the full precision available to a `float` value. Now divide it by 2. Normally, this reduces the exponent, but the exponent already is as small as it can get. So, instead, the computer moves the bits in the mantissa over, vacating the first position and losing the last binary digit. An analogy would be taking a base 10 value with four significant digits, such as 0.1234E-10, dividing by 10, and getting 0.0123E-10. You get an answer, but you've lost a digit in the process. This situation is called *underflow*, and C refers to floating-point values that have lost the full precision of the type as *subnormal*. So dividing the smallest positive normal floating-point value by 2 results in a subnormal value. If you divide by a large enough value, you lose all the digits and are left with 0. The C library now provides functions that let you check whether your computations are producing subnormal values.

There's another special floating-point value that can show up: NaN, or not-a-number. For example, you give the `asin()` function a value, and it returns the angle that has that value as its sine. But the value of a sine can't be greater than 1, so the function is undefined for values in excess of 1. In such cases, the function returns the NaN value, which `printf()` displays as nan, NaN, or something similar.

Floating-Point Round-off Errors

Take a number, add 1 to it, and subtract the original number. What do you get? You get 1. A floating-point calculation, such as the following, may give another answer:

```
/* floaterr.c--demonstrates round-off error */
#include <stdio.h>
int main(void)
{
    float a,b;

    b = 2.0e20 + 1.0;
    a = b - 2.0e20;
    printf("%f \n", a);

    return 0;
}
```

The output is this:

```
0.000000      ←older gcc on Linux
-13584010575872.000000      ←Turbo C 1.5
4008175468544.000000     ←CodeWarrior 9.0, MSVC++ 7.1
```

The reason for these odd results is that the computer doesn't keep track of enough decimal places to do the operation correctly. The number 2.0e20 is 2 followed by 20 zeros and, by adding 1, you are trying to change the 21st digit. To do this correctly, the program would need to be able to store a 21-digit number. A `float` number is typically just six or seven digits scaled to bigger or smaller numbers with an exponent. The attempt is doomed. On the other hand, if you used 2.0e4 instead of 2.0e20, you would get the correct answer because you are trying to change the fifth digit, and `float` numbers are precise enough for that.

Complex and Imaginary Types

Many computations in science and engineering use complex and imaginary numbers. C99 supports these numbers, with some reservations. A free-standing implementation, such as that used for embedded processors, doesn't need to have these types. (A VCR chip probably doesn't need complex numbers to do its job.) Also, more generally, the imaginary types are optional.

In brief, there are three complex types, called `float _Complex`, `double _Complex`, and `long double _Complex`. A `float _Complex` variable, for example, would contain two `float` values, one representing the real part of a complex number and one representing the imaginary part. Similarly, there are three imaginary types, called `float _Imaginary`, `double _Imaginary`, and `long double _Imaginary`.

Including the `complex.h` header file lets you substitute the word `complex` for `_Complex` and the word `imaginary` for `_Imaginary`, and it allows you to use the symbol `I` to represent the square root of −1.

Beyond the Basic Types

That finishes the list of fundamental data types. For some of you, the list must seem long. Others of you might be thinking that more types are needed. What about a character string type? C doesn't have one, but it can still deal quite well with strings. You will take a first look at strings in Chapter 4.

C does have other types derived from the basic types. These types include arrays, pointers, structures, and unions. Although they are subject matter for later chapters, we have already smuggled some pointers into this chapter's examples. (A *pointer* points to the location of a variable or other data object. The `&` prefix used with the `scanf()` function creates a pointer telling `scanf()` where to place information.)

Summary: The Basic Data Types

Keywords:

The basic data types are set up using 11 keywords: `int`, `long`, `short`, `unsigned`, `char`, `float`, `double`, `signed`, `_Bool`, `_Complex`, and `_Imaginary`.

Signed Integers:

These can have positive or negative values:

- `int`—The basic integer type for a given system. C guarantees at least 16 bits for `int`.
- `short` or `short int`—The largest `short` integer is no larger than the largest `int` and may be smaller. C guarantees at least 16 bits for `short`.
- `long` or `long int`—Can hold an integer at least as large as the largest `int` and possibly larger. C guarantees at least 32 bits for `long`.
- `long long` or `long long int`—This type can hold an integer at least as large as the largest `long` and possibly larger. The `long long` type is least 64 bits.

Typically, `long` will be bigger than `short`, and `int` will be the same as one of the two. For example, DOS-based systems for the PC provide 16-bit `short` and `int` and 32-bit `long`, and Windows 95–based systems provide 16-bit `short` and 32-bit `int` and `long`.

You can, if you like, use the keyword `signed` with any of the signed types, making the fact that they are signed explicit.

Unsigned Integers:

These have zero or positive values only. This extends the range of the largest possible positive number. Use the keyword `unsigned` before the desired type: `unsigned int`, `unsigned long`, `unsigned short`. A lone `unsigned` is the same as `unsigned int`.

Characters:

These are typographic symbols such as A, &, and +. By definition, the char type uses 1 byte of memory to represent a character. Historically, this character byte has most often been 8 bits, but it can be 16 bits or larger, if needed to represent the base character set.

- **char**—The keyword for this type. Some implementations use a signed char, but others use an unsigned char. C enables you to use the keywords signed and unsigned to specify which form you want.

Boolean:

Boolean values represent true and false; C uses 1 for true and 0 for false.

- **_Bool**—The keyword for this type. It is an unsigned int and need only be large enough to accommodate the range 0 through 1.

Real Floating Point:

These can have positive or negative values:

- **float**—The basic floating-point type for the system; it can represent at least six significant figures accurately.
- **double**—A (possibly) larger unit for holding floating-point numbers. It may allow more significant figures (at least 10, typically more) and perhaps larger exponents than float.
- **long double**—A (possibly) even larger unit for holding floating-point numbers. It may allow more significant figures and perhaps larger exponents than double.

Complex and Imaginary Floating Point:

The imaginary types are optional. The real and imaginary components are based on the corresponding real types:

- float _Complex
- double _Complex
- long double _Complex
- float _Imaginary
- double _Imaginary
- long double _Imaginary

Summary: How to Declare a Simple Variable

1. Choose the type you need.
2. Choose a name for the variable using the allowed characters.
3. Use the following format for a declaration statement:

   type-specifier variable-name;

   The *type-specifier* is formed from one or more of the type keywords; here are examples of declarations:

   int erest;
   unsigned short cash;.

4. You can declare more than one variable of the same type by separating the variable names with commas. Here's an example:

   char ch, init, ans;.

5. You can initialize a variable in a declaration statement:

   float mass = 6.0E24;

Type Sizes

Tables 3.3 and 3.4 show type sizes for some common C environments. (In some environments, you have a choice.) What is your system like? Try running the program in Listing 3.8 to find out.

TABLE 3.3 Integer Type Sizes (Bits) for Representative Systems

Type	Macintosh Metrowerks CW (Default)	Linux on a PC	IBM PC Windows XP and Windows NT	ANSI C Minimum
char	8	8	8	8
int	32	32	32	16
short	16	16	16	16
long	32	32	32	32
long long	64	64	64	64

TABLE 3.4 Floating-point Facts for Representative Systems

Type	Macintosh Metrowerks CW (Default)	Linux on a PC	IBM PC Windows XP and Windows NT	ANSI C Minimum
float	6 digits	6 digits	6 digits	6 digits
	–37 to 38	–37 to 38	–37 to 38	–37 to 37
double	18 digits	15 digits	15 digits	10 digits
	–4931 to 4932	–307 to 308	–307 to 308	–37 to 37
long double	18 digits	18 digits	18 digits	10 digits
	–4931 to 4932	–4931 to 4932	–4931 to 4932	–37 to 37

For each type, the top row is the number of significant digits and the second row is the exponent range (base 10).

LISTING 3.8 The `typesize.c` Program

```
/* typesize.c -- prints out type sizes */
#include <stdio.h>
int main(void)
{
```

```
/* c99 provides a %zd specifier for sizes */
    printf("Type int has a size of %u bytes.\n", sizeof(int));
    printf("Type char has a size of %u bytes.\n", sizeof(char));
    printf("Type long has a size of %u bytes.\n", sizeof(long));
    printf("Type double has a size of %u bytes.\n",
            sizeof(double));
    return 0;
}
```

C has a built-in operator called `sizeof` that gives sizes in bytes. (Some compilers require `%lu` instead of `%u` for printing `sizeof` quantities. That's because C leaves some latitude as to the actual unsigned integer type that `sizeof` uses to report its findings. C99 provides a `%zd` specifier for this type, and you should use it if your compiler supports it.) The output from Listing 3.8 is as follows:

```
Type int has a size of 4 bytes.
Type char has a size of 1 bytes.
Type long has a size of 4 bytes.
Type double has a size of 8 bytes.
```

This program found the size of only four types, but you can easily modify it to find the size of any other type that interests you. Note that the size of `char` is necessarily 1 byte because C defines the size of 1 byte in terms of `char`. So, on a system with a 16-bit `char` and a 64-bit `double`, `sizeof` will report `double` as having a size of 4 bytes. You can check the `limits.h` and `float.h` header files for more detailed information on type limits. (The next chapter discusses these two files further.)

Incidentally, notice in the last line how the `printf()` statement is spread over two lines. You can do this as long as the break does not occur in the quoted section or in the middle of a word.

Using Data Types

When you develop a program, note the variables you need and which type they should be. Most likely, you can use `int` or possibly `float` for the numbers and `char` for the characters. Declare them at the beginning of the function that uses them. Choose a name for the variable that suggests its meaning. When you initialize a variable, match the constant type to the variable type. Here's an example:

```
int apples = 3;         /* RIGHT     */
int oranges = 3.0;      /* POOR FORM */
```

C is more forgiving about type mismatches than, say, Pascal. C compilers allow the second initialization, but they might complain, particularly if you have activated a higher warning level. It is best not to develop sloppy habits.

When you initialize a variable of one numeric type to a value of a different type, C converts the value to match the variable. This means you may lose some data. For example, consider the following initializations:

```
int cost = 12.99;        /* initializing an int to a double  */
float pi = 3.1415926536; /* initializing a float to a double */
```

The first declaration assigns 12 to cost; when converting floating-point values to integers, C simply throws away the decimal part (*truncation*) instead of rounding. The second declaration loses some precision, because a float is guaranteed to represent only the first six digits accurately. Compilers may issue a warning (but don't have to) if you make such initializations. You might have run into this when compiling Listing 3.1.

Many programmers and organizations have systematic conventions for assigning variable names in which the name indicates the type of variable. For example, you could use an i_ prefix to indicate type int and us_ to indicate unsigned short, so i_smart would be instantly recognizable as a type int variable and us_verysmart would be an unsigned short variable.

Arguments and Pitfalls

It's worth repeating and amplifying a caution made earlier in this chapter about using printf(). The items of information passed to a function, as you may recall, are termed *arguments*. For instance, the function call printf("Hello, pal.") has one argument: "Hello, pal.". A series of characters in quotes, such as "Hello, pal.", is called a *string*. We'll discuss strings in Chapter 4. For now, the important point is that one string, even one containing several words and punctuation marks, counts as one argument.

Similarly, the function call scanf("%d", &weight) has two arguments: "%d" and &weight. C uses commas to separate arguments to a function. The printf() and scanf() functions are unusual in that they aren't limited to a particular number of arguments. For example, we've used calls to printf() with one, two, and even three arguments. For a program to work properly, it needs to know how many arguments there are. The printf() and scanf() functions use the first argument to indicate how many additional arguments are coming. The trick is that each format specification in the initial string indicates an additional argument. For instance, the following statement has two format specifiers, %d and %d:

```
printf("%d cats ate %d cans of tuna\n", cats, cans);
```

This tells the program to expect two more arguments, and indeed, there are two more—cats and cans.

Your responsibility as a programmer is to make sure that the number of format specifications matches the number of additional arguments and that the specifier type matches the value type. C now has a function-prototyping mechanism that checks whether a function call has the correct number and correct kind of arguments, but it doesn't work with printf() and scanf() because they take a variable number of arguments. What happens if you don't live up to the programmer's burden? Suppose, for example, you write a program like that in Listing 3.9.

LISTING 3.9   The `badcount.c` Program

```
/* badcount.c -- incorrect argument counts */
#include <stdio.h>
int main(void)
{
    int f = 4;
    int g = 5;
    float h = 5.0f;

    printf("%d\n", f, g);     /* too many arguments   */
    printf("%d %d\n",f);      /* too few arguments    */
    printf("%d %f\n", h, g); /* wrong kind of values */

    return 0;
}
```

Here's the output from Microsoft Visual C++ 7.1 (Windows XP):

```
4
4 34603777
0 0.000000
```

Next, here's the output from Digital Mars (Windows XP):

```
4
4 4239476
0 0.000000
```

And the following is the output from Metrowerks CodeWarrior Development Studio 9 (Macintosh OS X):

```
4
4 3327456
1075052544 0.000000
```

Note that using `%d` to display a `float` value doesn't convert the `float` value to the nearest `int`; instead, it displays what appears to be garbage. Similarly, using `%f` to display an `int` value doesn't convert an integer value to a floating-point value. Also, the results you get for too few arguments or the wrong kind of argument differ from platform to platform.

None of the compilers we tried raised any objections to this code. Nor were there any complaints when we ran the program. It is true that some compilers might catch this sort of error, but the C standard doesn't require them to. Therefore, the computer may not catch this kind of error, and because the program may otherwise run correctly, you might not notice the errors, either. If a program doesn't print the expected number of values or if it prints unexpected values, check to see whether you've used the correct number of `printf()` arguments. (Incidentally, the Unix syntax-checking program lint, which is much pickier than the Unix compiler, does mention erroneous `printf()` arguments.)

One More Example: Escape Sequences

Let's run one more printing example, one that makes use of some of C's special escape sequences for characters. In particular, the program in Listing 3.10 shows how the backspace (\b), tab (\t), and carriage return (\r) work. These concepts date from when computers used teletype machines for output, and they don't always translate successfully to contemporary graphical interfaces. For example, Listing 3.10 doesn't work as described on some Macintosh implementations.

LISTING 3.10   The escape.c Program

```
/* escape.c -- uses escape characters */
#include <stdio.h>
int main(void)
{
    float salary;

    printf("\aEnter your desired monthly salary:");/* 1 */
    printf(" $_____\b\b\b\b\b\b\b");             /* 2 */
    scanf("%f", &salary);
    printf("\n\t$%.2f a month is $%.2f a year.", salary,
              salary * 12.0);                      /* 3 */
    printf("\rGee!\n");                            /* 4 */

    return 0;
}
```

What Happens When the Program Runs

Let's walk through this program step by step as it would work under an ANSI C implementation. The first printf() statement (the one numbered 1) sounds the alert signal (prompted by the \a) and then prints the following:

```
Enter your desired monthly salary:
```

Because there is no \n at the end of the string, the cursor is left positioned after the colon.

The second printf() statement picks up where the first one stops, so after it is finished, the screen looks as follows:

```
Enter your desired monthly salary: $_____
```

The space between the colon and the dollar sign is there because the string in the second printf() statement starts with a space. The effect of the seven backspace characters is to move the cursor seven positions to the left. This backs the cursor over the seven underscore characters, placing the cursor directly after the dollar sign. Usually, backspacing does not erase the characters that are backed over, but some implementations may use destructive backspacing, negating the point of this little exercise.

At this point, you type your response, say **2000.00**. Now the line looks like this:

```
Enter your desired monthly salary: $2000.00
```

The characters you type replace the underscore characters, and when you press Enter (or Return) to enter your response, the cursor moves to the beginning of the next line.

The third `printf()` statement output begins with `\n\t`. The newline character moves the cursor to the beginning of the next line. The tab character moves the cursor to the next tab stop on that line, typically, but not necessarily, to column 9. Then the rest of the string is printed. After this statement, the screen looks like this:

```
Enter your desired monthly salary: $2000.00
        $2000.00 a month is $24000.00 a year.
```

Because the `printf()` statement doesn't use the newline character, the cursor remains just after the final period.

The fourth `printf()` statement begins with `\r`. This positions the cursor at the beginning of the current line. Then `Gee!` is displayed there, and the `\n` moves the cursor to the next line. Here is the final appearance of the screen:

```
Enter your desired monthly salary: $2000.00
Gee!    $2000.00 a month is $24000.00 a year.
```

Flushing the Output

When does `printf()` actually send output to the screen? Initially, `printf()` statements send output to an intermediate storage area called a *buffer*. Every now and then, the material in the buffer is sent to the screen. The standard C rules for when output is sent from the buffer to the screen are clear: It is sent when the buffer gets full, when a newline character is encountered, or when there is impending input. (Sending the output from the buffer to the screen or file is called *flushing the buffer*.) For instance, the first two `printf()` statements don't fill the buffer and don't contain a newline, but they are immediately followed by a `scanf()` statement asking for input. That forces the `printf()` output to be sent to the screen.

You may encounter an older implementation for which `scanf()` doesn't force a flush, which would result in the program looking for your input without having yet displayed the prompt onscreen. In that case, you can use a newline character to flush the buffer. The code can be changed to look like this:

```
printf("Enter your desired monthly salary:\n");
scanf("%f", &salary);
```

This code works whether or not impending input flushes the buffer. However, it also puts the cursor on the next line, preventing you from entering data on the same line as the prompting string. Another solution is to use the `fflush()` function described in Chapter 13, "File Input/Output."

Key Concepts

C has an amazing number of numeric types. This reflects the intent of C to avoid putting obstacles in the path of the programmer. Instead of mandating, say, that one kind of integer is enough, C tries to give the programmer the options of choosing a particular variety (signed or unsigned) and size that best meet the needs of a particular program.

Floating-point numbers are fundamentally different from integers on a computer. They are stored and processed differently. Two 32-bit memory units could hold identical bit patterns, but if one were interpreted as a `float` and the other as a `long`, they would represent totally different and unrelated values. For example, on a PC, if you take the bit pattern that represents the `float` number 256.0 and interpret it as a `long` value, you get 113246208. C does allow you to write an expression with mixed data types, but it will make automatic conversions so that the actual calculation uses just one data type.

In computer memory, characters are represented by a numeric code. The ASCII code is the most common in the U.S., but C supports the use of other codes. A character constant is the symbolic representation for the numeric code used on a computer system—it consists of a character enclosed in single quotes, such as `'A'`.

Summary

C has a variety of data types. The basic types fall into two categories: integer types and floating-point types. The two distinguishing features for integer types are the amount of storage allotted to a type and whether it is signed or unsigned. The smallest integer type is `char`, which can be either signed or unsigned, depending on the implementation. You can use `signed char` and `unsigned char` to explicitly specify which you want, but that's usually done when you are using the type to hold small integers rather than character codes. The other integer types include the `short`, `int`, `long`, and `long long` type. C guarantees that each of these types is at least as large as the preceding type. Each of them is a signed type, but you can use the `unsigned` keyword to create the corresponding unsigned types: `unsigned short`, `unsigned int`, `unsigned long`, and `unsigned long long`. Or you can add the `signed` modifier to explicitly state that the type is signed. Finally, there is the `_Bool` type, an unsigned type able to hold the values `0` and `1`, representing `false` and `true`.

The three floating-point types are `float`, `double`, and, new with ANSI C, `long double`. Each is at least as large as the preceding type. Optionally, an implementation can support complex and imaginary types by using the keywords `_Complex` and `_Imaginary` in conjunction with the floating-type keywords. For example, there would be a `double _Complex` type and a `float _Imaginary` type.

Integers can be expressed in decimal, octal, or hexadecimal form. A leading `0` indicates an octal number, and a leading `0x` or `0X` indicates a hexadecimal number. For example, `32`, `040`, and `0x20` are decimal, octal, and hexadecimal representations of the same value. An `l` or `L` suffix indicates a `long` value, and an `ll` or `LL` indicates a `long long` value.

Character constants are represented by placing the character in single quotes: `'Q'`, `'8'`, and `'$'`, for example. C escape sequences, such as `'\n'`, represent certain nonprinting characters. You can use the form `'\007'` to represent a character by its ASCII code.

Floating-point numbers can be written with a fixed decimal point, as in `9393.912`, or in exponential notation, as in `7.38E10`.

The `printf()` function enables you to print various types of values by using conversion specifiers, which, in their simplest form, consist of a percent sign and a letter indicating the type, as in `%d` or `%f`.

Review Questions

You'll find answers to the review questions in Appendix A, "Answers to the Review Questions."

1. Which data type would you use for each of the following kinds of data?

   a. The population of East Simpleton

   b. The cost of a movie on DVD

   c. The most common letter in this chapter

   d. The number of times that the letter occurs in this chapter

2. Why would you use a type `long` variable instead of type `int`?

3. What portable types might you use to get a 32-bit signed integer, and what would the rationale be for each choice?

4. Identify the type and meaning, if any, of each of the following constants:

   a. `'\b'`

   b. `1066`

   c. `99.44`

   d. `0XAA`

   e. `2.0e30`

5. Dottie Cawm has concocted an error-laden program. Help her find the mistakes.

```
include <stdio.h>
main
(
float g; h;
float tax, rate;

g = e21;
tax = rate*g;
)
```

6. Identify the data type (as used in declaration statements) and the `printf()` format specifier for each of the following constants:

Constant	Type	Specifier
a. 12		
b. 0X3		
c. 'C'		
d. 2.34E07		
e. '\040'		
f. 7.0		
g. 6L		
h. 6.0f		

7. Identify the data type (as used in declaration statements) and the `printf()` format specifier for each of the following constants (assume a 16-bit `int`):

Constant	Type	Specifier
a. 012		
b. 2.9e05L		
c. 's'		
d. 100000		
e. '\n'		
f. 20.0f		
g. 0x44		

8. Suppose a program begins with these declarations:

```
int imate = 2;
long shot = 53456;
char grade = 'A';
float log = 2.71828;
```

Fill in the proper type specifiers in the following `printf()` statements:

```
printf("The odds against the %__ were %__ to 1.\n", imate, shot);
printf("A score of %__ is not an %__ grade.\n", log, grade);
```

9. Suppose that ch is a type char variable. Show how to assign the carriage-return character to ch by using an escape sequence, a decimal value, an octal character constant, and a hex character constant. (Assume ASCII code values.)

10. Correct this silly program. (The / in C means division.)

```
void main(int) / this program is perfect /
{
cows, legs integer;
printf("How many cow legs did you count?\n");
scanf("%c", legs);
cows = legs / 4;
printf("That implies there are %f cows.\n", cows)
}
```

11. Identify what each of the following escape sequences represents:

    a. \n

    b. \\

    c. \"

    d. \t

Programming Exercises

1. Find out what your system does with integer overflow, floating-point overflow, and floating-point underflow by using the experimental approach; that is, write programs having these problems.

2. Write a program that asks you to enter an ASCII code value, such as 66, and then prints the character having that ASCII code.

3. Write a program that sounds an alert and then prints the following text:

   Startled by the sudden sound, Sally shouted, "By the Great Pumpkin, what was that!"

4. Write a program that reads in a floating-point number and prints it first in decimal-point notation and then in exponential notation. Have the output use the following format (the actual number of digits displayed for the exponent depends on the system):

   The input is 21.290000 or 2.129000e+001.

5. There are approximately 3.156×10^7 seconds in a year. Write a program that requests your age in years and then displays the equivalent number of seconds.

6. The mass of a single molecule of water is about 3.0×10^{-23} grams. A quart of water is about 950 grams. Write a program that requests an amount of water, in quarts, and displays the number of water molecules in that amount.

7. There are 2.54 centimeters to the inch. Write a program that asks you to enter your height in inches and then displays your height in centimeters. Or, if you prefer, ask for the height in centimeters and convert that to inches.

## CHAPTER 4

CHARACTER STRINGS AND FORMATTED INPUT/OUTPUT

You will learn about the following in this chapter:

- Function:
  strlen()

- Keywords:
  const

- Character strings

- How character strings are created and stored

- How you can use scanf() and printf() to read and display character strings

- How to use the strlen() function to measure string lengths

- The C preprocessor's #define directive and ANSI C's const modifier for creating symbolic constants

This chapter concentrates on input and output. You'll add personality to your programs by making them interactive and using character strings. You will also take a more detailed look at those two handy C input/output functions, printf() and scanf(). With these two functions, you have the program tools you need to communicate with users and to format output to meet your needs and tastes. Finally, you'll take a quick look at an important C facility, the C preprocessor, and learn how to define and use symbolic constants.

Introductory Program

By now, you probably expect a sample program at the beginning of each chapter, so Listing 4.1 is a program that engages in a dialog with the user. To add a little variety, the code uses the new C99 comment style.

LISTING 4.1   The `talkback.c` Program

```c
// talkback.c -- nosy, informative program
#include <stdio.h>
#include <string.h>       // for strlen() prototype
#define DENSITY 62.4      // human density in lbs per cu ft
int main()
{
    float weight, volume;
    int size, letters;
    char name[40];          // name is an array of 40 chars

    printf("Hi! What's your first name?\n");
    scanf("%s", name);
    printf("%s, what's your weight in pounds?\n", name);
    scanf("%f", &weight);
    size = sizeof name;
    letters = strlen(name);
    volume = weight / DENSITY;
    printf("Well, %s, your volume is %2.2f cubic feet.\n",
           name, volume);
    printf("Also, your first name has %d letters,\n",
           letters);
    printf("and we have %d bytes to store it in.\n", size);

    return 0;
}
```

Running `talkback.c` produces results such as the following:

```
Hi! What's your first name?
Sharla
Sharla, what's your weight in pounds?
139
Well, Sharla, your volume is 2.23 cubic feet.
Also, your first name has 6 letters,
and we have 40 bytes to store it in.
```

Here are the main new features of this program:

- It uses an *array* to hold a *character string*. Here, someone's name is read into the array, which, in this case, is a series of 40 consecutive bytes in memory, each able to hold a single character value.

- It uses the `%s` *conversion specification* to handle the input and output of the string. Note that `name`, unlike `weight`, does not use the `&` prefix when used with `scanf()`. (As you'll see later, both `&weight` and `name` are addresses.)

- It uses the C preprocessor to define the symbolic constant `DENSITY` to represent the value `62.4`.

- It uses the C function `strlen()` to find the length of a string.

The C approach might seem a little complex compared with the input/output of, say, BASIC. However, this complexity buys a finer control of I/O and greater program efficiency, and it's surprisingly easy once you get used to it.

Let's investigate these new ideas.

Character Strings: An Introduction

A *character string* is a series of one or more characters. Here is an example of a string:

```
"Zing went the strings of my heart!"
```

The double quotation marks are not part of the string. They inform the compiler that they enclose a string, just as single quotation marks identify a character.

Type char Arrays and the Null Character

C has no special variable type for strings. Instead, strings are stored in an array of type char. Characters in a string are stored in adjacent memory cells, one character per cell, and an array consists of adjacent memory locations, so placing a string in an array is quite natural (see Figure 4.1).

FIGURE 4.1
A string in an array.

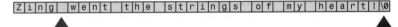

each cell is one byte   null character

Note that Figure 4.1 shows the character \0 in the last array position. This is the *null character*, and C uses it to mark the end of a string. The null character is not the digit zero; it is the nonprinting character whose ASCII code value (or equivalent) is 0. Strings in C are always stored with this terminating null character. The presence of the null character means that the array must have at least one more cell than the number of characters to be stored.

Now just what is an array? You can think of an array as several memory cells in a row. If you prefer more formal language, an array is an ordered sequence of data elements of one type. This example creates an array of 40 memory cells, or *elements*, each of which can store one char-type value by using this declaration:

```
char name[40];
```

The brackets after name identify it as an array. The 40 within the brackets indicates the number of elements in the array. The char identifies the type of each element (see Figure 4.2).

Using a character string is beginning to sound complicated! You have to create an array, place the characters of a string into an array, one by one, and remember to add \0 at the end. Fortunately, the computer can take care of most of the details itself.

FIGURE 4.2
Declaring a variable versus declaring an array.

allocate 1 byte
char ch;

type char

ch

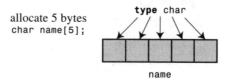

allocate 5 bytes
char name[5];

type char

name

Using Strings

Try the program in Listing 4.2 to see how easy it really is to use strings.

LISTING 4.2   The praise1.c Program

```c
/* praise1.c -- uses an assortment of strings */
#include <stdio.h>
#define PRAISE "What a super marvelous name!"
int main(void)
{
    char name[40];

    printf("What's your name?\n");
    scanf("%s", name);
    printf("Hello, %s. %s\n", name, PRAISE);

    return 0;
}
```

The %s tells printf() to print a string. The %s appears twice because the program prints two strings: the one stored in the name array and the one represented by PRAISE. Running praise1.c should produce an output similar to this:

```
What's your name?
Hilary Bubbles
Hello, Hilary. What a super marvelous name!
```

You do not have to put the null character into the name array yourself. That task is done for you by scanf() when it reads the input. Nor do you include a null character in the *character string constant* PRAISE. We'll explain the #define statement soon; for now, simply note that the double quotation marks that enclose the text following PRAISE identify the text as a string. The compiler takes care of putting in the null character.

Note (and this is important) that `scanf()` just reads Hilary Bubble's first name. After `scanf()` starts to read input, it stops reading at the first *whitespace* (blank, tab, or newline) it encounters. Therefore, it stops scanning for `name` when it reaches the blank between `Hilary` and `Bubbles`. In general, `scanf()` is used with `%s` to read only a single word, not a whole phrase, as a string. C has other input-reading functions, such as `gets()`, for handling general strings. Later chapters will explore string functions more fully.

Strings Versus Characters

The string constant `"x"` is not the same as the character constant `'x'`. One difference is that `'x'` is a basic type (`char`), but `"x"` is a derived type, an array of `char`. A second difference is that `"x"` really consists of two characters, `'x'` and `'\0'`, the null character (see Figure 4.3).

FIGURE 4.3

The character `'x'` and the string `"x"`.

The `strlen()` Function

The previous chapter unleashed the `sizeof` operator, which gives the size of things in bytes. The `strlen()` function gives the length of a string in characters. Because it takes one byte to hold one character, you might suppose that both would give the same result when applied to a string, but they don't. Add a few lines to the example, as shown in Listing 4.3, and see why.

LISTING 4.3   The `praise2.c` Program

```
/* praise2.c */
#include <stdio.h>
#include <string.h>       /* provides strlen() prototype */
#define PRAISE "What a super marvelous name!"
int main(void)
{
    char name[40];

    printf("What's your name?\n");
    scanf("%s", name);
    printf("Hello, %s. %s\n", name, PRAISE);
    printf("Your name of %d letters occupies %d memory cells.\n",
        strlen(name), sizeof name);
    printf("The phrase of praise has %d letters ",
        strlen(PRAISE));
    printf("and occupies %d memory cells.\n", sizeof PRAISE);

    return 0;
}
```

If you are using a pre-ANSI C compiler, you might have to remove the following line:

```
#include <string.h>
```

The `string.h` file contains function prototypes for several string-related functions, including `strlen()`. Chapter 11, "Character Strings and String Functions," discusses this header file more fully. (By the way, some pre-ANSI Unix systems use `strings.h` instead of `string.h` to contain declarations for string functions.)

More generally, C divides the C function library into families of related functions and provides a header file for each family. For example, `printf()` and `scanf()` belong to a family of standard input and output functions and use the `stdio.h` header file. The `strlen()` function joins several other string-related functions, such as functions to copy strings and to search through strings, in a family served by the `string.h` header.

Notice that Listing 4.3 uses two methods to handle long `printf()` statements. The first method spreads one `printf()` statement over two lines. (You can break a line between arguments to `printf()` but not in the middle of a string—that is, not between the quotation marks.) The second method uses two `printf()` statements to print just one line. The newline character (\n) appears only in the second statement. Running the program could produce the following interchange:

```
What's your name?
Morgan Buttercup
Hello, Morgan. What a super marvelous name!
Your name of 6 letters occupies 40 memory cells.
The phrase of praise has 28 letters and occupies 29 memory cells.
```

See what happens. The array `name` has 40 memory cells, and that is what the `sizeof` operator reports. Only the first six cells are needed to hold `Morgan`, however, and that is what `strlen()` reports. The seventh cell in the array `name` contains the null character, and its presence tells `strlen()` when to stop counting. Figure 4.4 illustrates this concept.

FIGURE 4.4

The `strlen()` function knows when to stop.

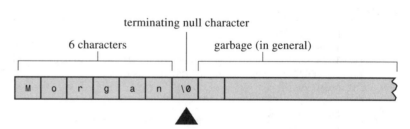

When you get to `PRAISE`, you find that `strlen()` again gives you the exact number of characters (including spaces and punctuation) in the string. The `sizeof` operator gives you a number one larger because it also counts the invisible null character used to end the string. You didn't tell the computer how much memory to set aside to store the phrase. It had to count the number of characters between the double quotes itself.

One other point: The preceding chapter used `sizeof` with parentheses, but this example doesn't. Whether you use parentheses depends on whether you want the size of a type or the size of a particular quantity. Parentheses are required for types but are optional for particular quantities. That is, you would use `sizeof(char)` or `sizeof(float)` but can use `sizeof name` or `sizeof 6.28`. However, it is all right to use parentheses in these cases, too, as in `sizeof (6.28)`.

The last example used `strlen()` and `sizeof` for the rather trivial purpose of satisfying a user's potential curiosity. Actually, however, `strlen()` and `sizeof` are important programming tools. For example, `strlen()` is useful in all sorts of character-string programs, as you'll see in Chapter 11.

Let's move on to the `#define` statement.

Constants and the C Preprocessor

Sometimes you need to use a constant in a program. For example, you could give the circumference of a circle as follows:

```
circumference = 3.14159 * diameter;
```

Here, the constant 3.14159 represents the world-famous constant pi (Π). To use a constant, just type in the actual value, as in the example. However, there are good reasons to use a *symbolic constant* instead. That is, you could use a statement such as the following and have the computer substitute in the actual value later:

```
circumference = pi * diameter;
```

Why is it better to use a symbolic constant? First, a name tells you more than a number does. Compare the following two statements:

```
owed = 0.015 * housevalue;
owed = taxrate * housevalue;
```

If you read through a long program, the meaning of the second version is plainer.

Also, suppose you have used a constant in several places, and it becomes necessary to change its value. After all, tax rates do change. Then you only need to alter the definition of the symbolic constant, rather than find and change every occurrence of the constant in the program.

Okay, how do you set up a symbolic constant? One way is to declare a variable and set it equal to the desired constant. You could write this:

```
float taxrate;
taxrate = 0.015;
```

This provides a symbolic name, but `taxrate` is a variable, so your program might change its value accidentally. Fortunately, C has a couple better ideas.

The original better idea is the C preprocessor. In Chapter 2, "Introducing C," you saw how the preprocessor uses #include to incorporate information from another file. The preprocessor also lets you define constants. Just add a line like the following at the top of the file containing your program:

```
#define TAXRATE 0.015
```

When your program is compiled, the value `0.015` will be substituted everywhere you have used `TAXRATE`. This is called a *compile-time substitution*. By the time you run the program, all the substitutions have already been made (see Figure 4.5). Such defined constants are often termed *manifest constants*.

FIGURE 4.5

What you type versus what is compiled.

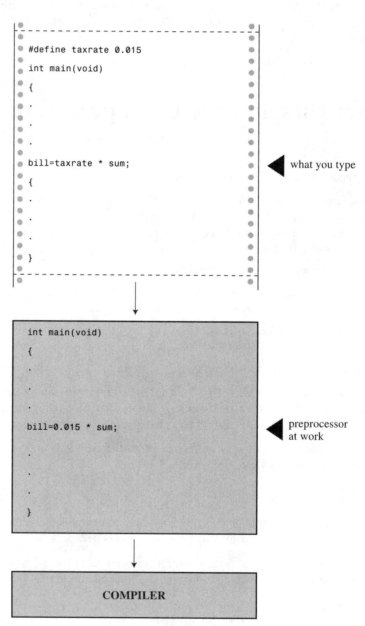

Note the format. First comes #define. Next comes the symbolic name (TAXRATE) for the constant and then the value (0.015) for the constant. (Note that this construction does not use the = sign.) So the general form is as follows:

#define NAME value

You would substitute the symbolic name of your choice for *NAME* and the appropriate value for *value*. No semicolon is used because this is a substitution mechanism, not a C statement. Why is TAXRATE capitalized? It is a sensible C tradition to type constants in uppercase. Then, when you encounter one in the depths of a program, you know immediately that it is a constant, not a variable. Capitalizing constants is just another technique to make programs more readable. Your programs will still work if you don't capitalize the constants, but capitalizing them is a good habit to cultivate.

Other, less common, naming conventions include prefixing a name with a c_ or k_ to indicate a constant, producing names such as c_level or k_line.

The names you use for symbolic constants must satisfy the same rules that the names of variables do. You can use uppercase and lowercase letters, digits, and the underscore character. The first character cannot be a digit. Listing 4.4 shows a simple example.

LISTING 4.4   The pizza.c Program

```c
/* pizza.c -- uses defined constants in a pizza context */
#include <stdio.h>
#define PI 3.14159
int main(void)
{
    float area, circum, radius;

    printf("What is the radius of your pizza?\n");
    scanf("%f", &radius);
    area = PI * radius * radius;
    circum = 2.0 * PI *radius;
    printf("Your basic pizza parameters are as follows:\n");
    printf("circumference = %1.2f, area = %1.2f\n", circum,
           area);
    return 0;
}
```

The %1.2f in the printf() statement causes the printout to be rounded to two decimal places. Of course, this program may not reflect your major pizza concerns, but it does fill a small niche in the world of pizza programs. Here is a sample run:

```
What is the radius of your pizza?
6.0
Your basic pizza parameters are as follows:
circumference = 37.70, area = 113.10
```

The `#define` statement can be used for character and string constants, too. Just use single quotes for the former and double quotes for the latter. The following examples are valid:

```
#define BEEP '\a'
#define TEE 'T'
#define ESC '\033'
#define OOPS "Now you have done it!"
```

Remember that everything following the symbolic name is substituted for it. Don't make this common error:

```
/* the following is wrong */
#define TOES = 20
```

If you do this, TOES is replaced by = 20, not just 20. In that case, a statement such as

```
digits = fingers + TOES;
```

is converted to the following misrepresentation:

```
digits = fingers + = 20;
```

The const Modifier

C90 added a second way to create symbolic constants—using the const keyword to convert a declaration for a variable into a declaration for a constant:

```
const int MONTHS = 12;    // MONTHS a symbolic constant for 12
```

This makes MONTHS into a read-only value. That is, you can display MONTHS and use it in calculations, but you cannot alter the value of MONTHS. This newer approach is more flexible than using `#define`; Chapter 12, "Storage Classes, Linkage, and Memory Management," discusses this and other uses of const.

Actually, C has yet a third way to create symbolic constants, and that is the enum facility discussed in Chapter 14, "Structures and Other Data Forms."

Manifest Constants on the Job

The C header files `limits.h` and `float.h` supply detailed information about the size limits of integer types and floating types, respectively. Each file defines a series of manifest constants that apply to your implementation. For instance, the `limits.h` file contains lines similar to the following:

```
#define INT_MAX    +32767
#define INT_MIN    -32768
```

These constants represent the largest and smallest possible values for the int type. If your system uses a 32-bit int, the file would provide different values for these symbolic constants. The file defines minimum and maximum values for all the integer types. If you include the `limits.h` file, you can use code such as the following:

```
printf("Maximum int value on this system = %d\n", INT_MAX);
```

If your system uses a 4-byte `int`, the `limits.h` file that comes with that system would provide definitions for `INT_MAX` and `INT_MIN` that match the limits of a 4-byte `int`. Table 4.1 lists some of the constants found in `limits.h`.

TABLE 4.1 Some Symbolic Constants from `limits.h`

Symbolic Constant	Represents
CHAR_BIT	Number of bits in a `char`
CHAR_MAX	Maximum `char` value
CHAR_MIN	Minimum `char` value
SCHAR_MAX	Maximum `signed char` value
SCHAR_MIN	Minimum `signed char` value
UCHAR_MAX	Maximum `unsigned char` value
SHRT_MAX	Maximum `short` value
SHRT_MIN	Minimum `short` value
USHRT_MAX	Maximum `unsigned short` value
INT_MAX	Maximum `int` value
INT_MIN	Minimum `int` value
UINT_MAX	Maximum `unsigned int` value
LONG_MAX	Maximum `long` value
LONG_MIN	Minimum `long` value
ULONG_MAX	Maximum `unsigned long` value
LLONG_MAX	Maximum `long long` value
LLONG_MIN	Minimum `long long` value
ULLONG_MAX	Maximum `unsigned long long` value

Similarly, the `float.h` file defines constants such as `FLT_DIG` and `DBL_DIG`, which represent the number of significant figures supported by the `float` type and the `double` type. Table 4.2 lists some of the constants found in `float.h`. (You can use a text editor to open and inspect the `float.h` header file your system uses.) This example relates to the `float` type. Equivalent constants are defined for types `double` and `long double`, with `DBL` and `LDBL` substituted for `FLT` in the name. (The table assumes the system represents floating-point numbers in terms of powers of 2.)

TABLE 4.2   Some Symbolic Constants from `float.h`

Symbolic Constant	Represents
FLT_MANT_DIG	Number of bits in the mantissa of a `float`
FLT_DIG	Minimum number of significant decimal digits for a `float`
FLT_MIN_10_EXP	Minimum base-10 negative exponent for a `float` with a full set of significant figures
FLT_MAX_10_EXP	Maximum base-10 positive exponent for a `float`
FLT_MIN	Minimum value for a positive `float` retaining full precision
FLT_MAX	Maximum value for a positive `float`
FLT_EPSILON	Difference between 1.00 and the least float value greater than 1.00

Listing 4.5 illustrates using data from `float.h` and `limits.h`. (Note that many current compilers do not yet fully support the C99 standard and may not accept the `LLONG_MIN` identifier.)

LISTING 4.5   The `defines.c` Program

```
// defines.c -- uses defined constants from limit.h and float.
#include <stdio.h>
#include <limits.h>      // integer limits
#include <float.h>       // floating-point limits
int main(void)
{
    printf("Some number limits for this system:\n");
    printf("Biggest int: %d\n", INT_MAX);
    printf("Smallest long long: %lld\n", LLONG_MIN);
    printf("One byte = %d bits on this system.\n", CHAR_BIT);
    printf("Largest double: %e\n", DBL_MAX);
    printf("Smallest normal float: %e\n", FLT_MIN);
    printf("float precision = %d digits\n", FLT_DIG);
    printf("float epsilon = %e\n", FLT_EPSILON);

    return 0;
}
```

Here is the sample output:

```
Some number limits for this system:
Biggest int: 2147483647
Smallest long long: -9223372036854775808
One byte = 8 bits on this system.
Largest double: 1.797693e+308
Smallest normal float: 1.175494e-38
float precision = 6 digits
float epsilon = 1.192093e-07
```

The C preprocessor is a useful, helpful tool, so take advantage of it when you can. We'll show you more applications as you move along through this book.

Exploring and Exploiting `printf()` and `scanf()`

The functions `printf()` and `scanf()` enable you to communicate with a program. They are called *input/output functions*, or *I/O functions* for short. They are not the only I/O functions you can use with C, but they are the most versatile. Historically, these functions, like all other functions in the C library, were not part of the definition of C. C originally left the implementation of I/O up to the compiler writers; this made it possible to better match I/O to specific machines. In the interests of compatibility, various implementations all came with versions of `scanf()` and `printf()`. However, there were occasional discrepancies between implementations. The C90 and C99 standards describe standard versions of these functions, and we'll follow that standard.

Although `printf()` is an output function and `scanf()` is an input function, both work much the same, each using a control string and a list of arguments. We will show you how these work, first with `printf()` and then with `scanf()`.

The `printf()` Function

The instructions you give `printf()` when you ask it to print a variable depend on the variable type. For example, we have used the `%d` notation when printing an integer and the `%c` notation when printing a character. These notations are called *conversion specifications* because they specify how the data is to be converted into displayable form. We'll list the conversion specifications that the ANSI C standard provides for `printf()` and then show how to use the more common ones. Table 4.3 presents the conversion specifiers and the type of output they cause to be printed.

TABLE 4.3 Conversion Specifiers and the Resulting Printed Output

Conversion Specification	Output
%a	Floating-point number, hexadecimal digits and p-notation (C99).
%A	Floating-point number, hexadecimal digits and P-notation (C99).
%c	Single character.
%d	Signed decimal integer.
%e	Floating-point number, e-notation.
%E	Floating-point number, e-notation.

TABLE 4.3   Continued

Conversion Specification	Output
%f	Floating-point number, decimal notation.
%g	Use %f or %e, depending on the value. The %e style is used if the exponent is less than –4 or greater than or equal to the precision.
%G	Use %f or %E, depending on the value. The %E style is used if the exponent is less than –4 or greater than or equal to the precision.
%i	Signed decimal integer (same as %d).
%o	Unsigned octal integer.
%p	A pointer.
%s	Character string.
%u	Unsigned decimal integer.
%x	Unsigned hexadecimal integer, using hex digits 0f.
%X	Unsigned hexadecimal integer, using hex digits 0F.
%%	Prints a percent sign.

Using `printf()`

Listing 4.6 contains a program that uses some of the conversion specifications.

LISTING 4.6   The `printout.c` Program

```c
/* printout.c -- uses conversion specifiers */
#include <stdio.h>
#define PI 3.141593
int main(void)
{
    int number = 5;
    float espresso = 13.5;
    int cost = 3100;

    printf("The %d CEOs drank %f cups of espresso.\n", number,
           espresso);
    printf("The value of pi is %f.\n", PI);
    printf("Farewell! thou art too dear for my possessing,\n");
    printf("%c%d\n", '$', 2 * cost);

    return 0;
}
```

The output, of course, is

```
The 5 CEOs drank 13.500000 cups of espresso.
The value of pi is 3.141593.
Farewell! thou art too dear for my possessing,
$6200
```

This is the format for using `printf()`:

```
printf(Control-string, item1, item2,...);
```

Item1, *item2*, and so on, are the items to be printed. They can be variables or constants, or even expressions that are evaluated first before the value is printed. *Control-string* is a character string describing how the items are to be printed. As mentioned in Chapter 3, "Data and C," the control string should contain a conversion specifier for each item to be printed. For example, consider the following statement:

```
printf("The %d CEOs drank %f cups of espresso.\n", number,
    espresso);
```

Control-string is the phrase enclosed in double quotes. It contains two conversion specifiers corresponding to `number` and `espresso`—the two items to be displayed. Figure 4.6 shows another example of a `printf()` statement.

FIGURE 4.6
Arguments for `printf()`.

Here is another line from the example:

```
printf("The value of pi is %f.\n", PI);
```

This time, the list of items has just one member—the symbolic constant `PI`.

As you can see in Figure 4.7, *Control-string* contains two distinct forms of information:

- Characters that are actually printed
- Conversion specifications

Caution

Don't forget to use one conversion specification for each item in the list following *Control-string*. Woe unto you should you forget this basic requirement! Don't do the following:

```
printf("The score was Squids %d, Slugs %d.\n", score1);
```

Here, there is no value for the second `%d`. The result of this faux pas depends on your system, but at best you will get nonsense.

FIGURE 4.7

Anatomy of a control string.

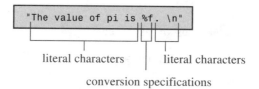

literal characters   literal characters

conversion specifications

If you want to print only a phrase, you don't need any conversion specifications. If you just want to print data, you can dispense with the running commentary. Each of the following statements from Listing 4.6 is quite acceptable:

```
printf("Farewell! thou art too dear for my possessing,\n");
printf("%c%d\n", '$', 2 * cost);
```

In the second statement, note that the first item on the print list was a character constant rather than a variable and that the second item is a multiplication. This illustrates that `printf()` uses values, be they variables, constants, or expressions.

Because the `printf()` function uses the `%` symbol to identify the conversion specifications, there is a slight problem if you want to print the `%` sign itself. If you simply use a lone `%` sign, the compiler thinks you have bungled a conversion specification. The way out is simple—just use two `%` symbols, as shown here:

```
pc = 2*6;
printf("Only %d%% of Sally's gribbles were edible.\n", pc);
```

The following output would result:

```
Only 12% of Sally's gribbles were edible.
```

Conversion Specification Modifiers for `printf()`

You can modify a basic conversion specification by inserting modifiers between the `%` and the defining conversion character. Tables 4.4 and 4.5 list the characters you can place there legally. If you use more than one modifier, they should be in the same order as they appear in Table 4.4. Not all combinations are possible. The table reflects the C99 additions; your implementation may not yet support all the options shown here.

TABLE 4.4 The `printf()` Modifiers

Modifier	Meaning
flag	The five flags (`-`, `+`, space, `#`, and `0`) are described in Table 4.5. Zero or more flags may be present.
	Example: `"%-10d"`
digit(s)	The minimum field width. A wider field will be used if the printed number or string won't fit in the field.
	Example: `"%4d"`

Modifier	Meaning
.digit(s)	Precision. For `%e`, `%E`, and `%f` conversions, the number of digits to be printed to the right of the decimal. For `%g` and `%G` conversions, the maximum number of significant digits. For `%s` conversions, the maximum number of characters to be printed. For integer conversions, the minimum number of digits to appear; leading zeros are used if necessary to meet this minimum. Using only `.` implies a following zero, so `%.f` is the same as `%.0f`. Example: `"%5.2f"` prints a `float` in a field five characters wide with two digits after the decimal point.
h	Used with an integer conversion specifier to indicate a `short int` or `unsigned short int` value. Examples: `"%hu"`, `"%hx"`, and `"%6.4hd"`
hh	Used with an integer conversion specifier to indicate a `signed char` or `unsigned char` value. Examples: `"%hhu"`, `"%hhx"`, and `"%6.4hhd"`
j	Used with an integer conversion specifier to indicate an `intmax_t` or `uintmax_t` value. Examples: `"%jd"` and `"%8jX"`
l	Used with an integer conversion specifier to indicate a `long int` or `unsigned long int`. Examples: `"%ld"` and `"%8lu"`
ll	Used with an integer conversion specifier to indicate a `long long int` or `unsigned long long int`. (C99) Examples: `"%lld"` and `"%8llu"`
L	Used with a floating-point conversion specifier to indicate a `long double` value. Examples: `"%Lf"` and `"%10.4Le"`
t	Used with an integer conversion specifier to indicate a `ptrdiff_t` value. This is the type corresponding to the difference between two pointers. (C99) Examples: `"%td"` and `"%12ti"`
z	Used with an integer conversion specifier to indicate a `size_t` value. This is the type returned by `sizeof`. (C99) Examples: `"%zd"` and `"%12zx"`

Conversion of `float` Arguments

There are conversion specifiers to print the floating types `double` and `long double`. However, there is no specifier for `float`. The reason is that `float` values were automatically converted to type `double` before being used in an expression or as an argument under K&R C. ANSI C, in general, does not automatically convert `float` to `double`. To protect the enormous number of existing programs that assume `float` arguments are converted to `double`, however, all `float` arguments to `printf()`—as well as to any other C function not using an explicit prototype—are still automatically converted to `double`. Therefore, under either K&R C or ANSI C, no special conversion specifier is needed for displaying type `float`.

TABLE 4.5   The `printf()` Flags

Flag	Meaning
-	The item is left-justified; that is, it is printed beginning at the left of the field.
	Example: `"%-20s"`
+	Signed values are displayed with a plus sign, if positive, and with a minus sign, if negative.
	Example: `"%+6.2f"`
space	Signed values are displayed with a leading space (but no sign) if positive and with a minus sign if negative. A + flag overrides a space.
	Example: `"% 6.2f"`
#	Use an alternative form for the conversion specification. Produces an initial 0 for the %o form and an initial 0x or 0X for the %x or %X form, respectively. For all floating-point forms, # guarantees that a decimal-point character is printed, even if no digits follow. For %g and %G forms, it prevents trailing zeros from being removed.
	Examples: `"%#o"`, `"%#8.0f"`, and `"%+#10.3E"`
0	For numeric forms, pad the field width with leading zeros instead of with spaces. This flag is ignored if a - flag is present or if, for an integer form, a precision is specified.
	Examples: `"%010d"` and `"%08.3f"`

Examples Using Modifiers and Flags

Let's put these modifiers to work, beginning with a look at the effect of the field width modifier on printing an integer. Consider the program in Listing 4.7.

LISTING 4.7   The `width.c` Program

```
/* width.c -- field widths */
#include <stdio.h>
#define PAGES 931
int main(void)
{
    printf("*%d*\n", PAGES);
    printf("*%2d*\n", PAGES);
    printf("*%10d*\n", PAGES);
    printf("*%-10d*\n", PAGES);

    return 0;
}
```

Listing 4.7 prints the same quantity four times using four different conversion specifications. It uses an asterisk (*) to show you where each field begins and ends. The output looks as follows:

```
*931*
*931*
*       931*
*931       *
```

The first conversion specification is %d with no modifiers. It produces a field with the same width as the integer being printed. This is the default option; that is, it's what's printed if you don't give further instructions. The second conversion specification is %2d. This should produce a field width of 2, but because the integer is three digits long, the field is expanded automatically to fit the number. The next conversion specification is %10d. This produces a field 10 spaces wide, and, indeed, there are seven blanks and three digits between the asterisks, with the number tucked into the right end of the field. The final specification is %-10d. It also produces a field 10 spaces wide, and the - puts the number at the left end, just as advertised. After you get used to it, this system is easy to use and gives you nice control over the appearance of your output. Try altering the value for PAGES to see how different numbers of digits are printed.

Now look at some floating-point formats. Enter, compile, and run the program in Listing 4.8.

LISTING 4.8   The `floats.c` Program

```
// floats.c -- some floating-point combinations
#include <stdio.h>

int main(void)
{
    const double RENT = 3852.99;  // const-style constant

    printf("*%f*\n", RENT);
    printf("*%e*\n", RENT);
    printf("*%4.2f*\n", RENT);
    printf("*%3.1f*\n", RENT);
```

LISTING 4.8   Continued

```
    printf("*%10.3f*\n", RENT);
    printf("*%10.3e*\n", RENT);
    printf("*%+4.2f*\n", RENT);
    printf("*%010.2f*\n", RENT);

    return 0;
}
```

This time, the program uses the keyword **const** to create a symbolic constant. The output is

```
*3852.990000*
*3.852990e+03*
*3852.99*
*3853.0*
*   3852.990*
* 3.853e+03*
*+3852.99*
*0003852.99*
```

The example begins with the default version, **%f**. In this case, there are two defaults—the field width and the number of digits to the right of the decimal. The second default is six digits, and the field width is whatever it takes to hold the number.

Next is the default for **%e**. It prints one digit to the left of the decimal point and six places to the right. We're getting a lot of digits! The cure is to specify the number of decimal places to the right of the decimal, and the next four examples in this segment do that. Notice how the fourth and the sixth examples cause the output to be rounded off.

Finally, the + flag causes the result to be printed with its algebraic sign, which is a plus sign in this case, and the **0** flag produces leading zeros to pad the result to the full field width. Note that in the specifier **%010**, the first **0** is a flag, and the remaining digits (**10**) specify the field width.

You can modify the **RENT** value to see how variously sized values are printed. Listing 4.9 demonstrates a few more combinations.

LISTING 4.9   The `flags.c` Program

```
/* flags.c -- illustrates some formatting flags */
#include <stdio.h>
int main(void)
{
    printf("%x %X %#x\n", 31, 31, 31);
    printf("**%d**% d**% d**\n", 42, 42, -42);
    printf("**%5d**%5.3d**%05d**%05.3d**\n", 6, 6, 6, 6);

    return 0;
}
```

The output looks as follows:

```
1f 1F 0x1f
**42** 42**-42**
**    6** 006**00006**  006**
```

First, 1f is the hex equivalent of 31. The x specifier yields 1f, and the X specifier yields 1F. Using the # flag provides an initial 0x.

The second line of output illustrates how using a space in the specifier produces a leading space for positive values, but not for negative values. This can produce a pleasing output because positive and negative values with the same number of significant digits are printed with the same field widths.

The third line illustrates how using a precision specifier (%5.3d) with an integer form produces enough leading zeros to pad the number to the minimum value of digits (three, in this case). Using the 0 flag, however, pads the number with enough leading zeros to fill the whole field width. Finally, if you provide both the 0 flag and the precision specifier, the 0 flag is ignored.

Now let's examine some of the string options. Consider the example in Listing 4.10.

LISTING 4.10   The strings.c Program

```c
/* strings.c -- string formatting */
#include <stdio.h>
#define BLURB "Authentic imitation!"
int main(void)
{
    printf("/%2s/\n", BLURB);
    printf("/%24s/\n", BLURB);
    printf("/%24.5s/\n", BLURB);
    printf("/%-24.5s/\n", BLURB);

    return 0;
}
```

Here is the output:

```
/Authentic imitation!/
/    Authentic imitation!/
/                   Authe/
/Authe                   /
```

Notice how the field is expanded to contain all the specified characters. Also notice how the precision specification limits the number of characters printed. The .5 in the format specifier tells printf() to print just five characters. Again, the - modifier left-justifies the text.

Using What You Just Learned

Okay, you've seen some examples. Now how would you set up a statement to print something having the following form?

```
The NAME family just may be $XXX.XX dollars richer!
```

Here, `NAME` and `XXX.XX` represent values that will be supplied by variables in the program—say, `name[40]` and `cash`.

One solution is

```
printf("The %s family just may be $%.2f richer!\n",name,cash);
```

What Does a Conversion Specification Convert?

Let's take a closer look at what a conversion specification converts. It converts a value stored in the computer in some binary format to a series of characters (a string) to be displayed. For example, the number 76 may be stored internally as binary 01001100. The `%d` conversion specifier converts this to the characters 7 and 6, displaying 76. The `%x` conversion converts the same value (`01001100`) to the hexadecimal representation 4c. The `%c` converts the same value to the character representation L.

The term *conversion* is probably somewhat misleading because it might suggest that the original value is replaced with a converted value. Conversion specifications are really translation specifications; `%d` means "translate the given value to a decimal integer text representation and print the representation."

Mismatched Conversions

Naturally, you should match the conversion specification to the type of value being printed. Often, you have choices. For instance, if you want to print a type `int` value, you can use `%d` or `%x` or `%o`. All these specifiers assume that you are printing a type `int` value; they merely provide different representations of the value. Similarly, you can use `%f`, `%e`, or `%g` to represent a type `double` value.

What if you mismatch the conversion specification to the type? You've seen in the preceding chapter that mismatches can cause problems. This is a very important point to keep in mind, so Listing 4.11 shows some more examples of mismatches within the integer family.

LISTING 4.11   The `intconv.c` Program

```
/* intconv.c -- some mismatched integer conversions */
#include <stdio.h>
#define PAGES 336
#define WORDS 65618
int main(void)
{
    short num = PAGES;
    short mnum = -PAGES;

    printf("num as short and unsigned short:  %hd %hu\n", num,
            num);
    printf("-num as short and unsigned short: %hd %hu\n", mnum,
            mnum);
    printf("num as int and char: %d %c\n", num, num);
    printf("WORDS as int, short, and char: %d %hd %c\n",
            WORDS, WORDS, WORDS);
    return 0;
}
```

Our system produces the following results:

```
num as short and unsigned short:  336 336
-num as short and unsigned short: -336 65200
num as int and char: 336 P
WORDS as int, short, and char: 65618 82 R
```

Looking at the first line, you can see that both `%hd` and `%hu` produce **336** as output for the variable num; no problem there. The `%u` (unsigned) version of mnum came out as **65200**, however, not as the **336** you might have expected. This results from the way that signed `short int` values are represented on our reference system. First, they are 2 bytes in size. Second, the system uses a method called the *two's complement* to represent signed integers. In this method, the numbers 0 to 32767 represent themselves, and the numbers 32768 to 65535 represent negative numbers, with 65535 being –1, 65534 being –2, and so forth. Therefore, –**336** is represented by **65536** - **336**, or **65200**. So 65200 represents –336 when interpreted as a signed `int` and represents 65200 when interpreted as an unsigned `int`. Be wary! One number can be interpreted as two different values. Not all systems use this method to represent negative integers. Nonetheless, there is a moral: Don't expect a `%u` conversion to simply strip the sign from a number.

The second line shows what happens if you try to convert a value greater than 255 to a character. On this system, a `short int` is 2 bytes and a `char` is 1 byte. When `printf()` prints 336 using `%c`, it looks at only 1 byte out of the 2 used to hold 336. This truncation (see Figure 4.8) amounts to dividing the integer by 256 and keeping just the remainder. In this case, the remainder is 80, which is the ASCII value for the character *P*. More technically, you can say that the number is interpreted *modulo 256*, which means using the remainder when the number is divided by 256.

FIGURE 4.8
Reading 336 as a character.

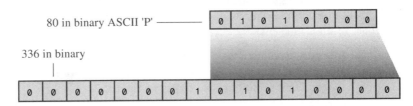

Finally, we tried printing an integer (65618) larger than the maximum `short int` (32767) allowed on our system. Again, the computer does its modulo thing. The number 65618, because of its size, is stored as a 4-byte `int` value on our system. When we print it using `%hd` specification, `printf()` uses only the last 2 bytes. This corresponds to using the remainder after dividing by 65536. In this case, the remainder is 82. A remainder between 32767 and 65536 would be printed as a negative number because of the way negative numbers are stored. Systems with different integer sizes would have the same general behavior, but with different numerical values.

When you start mixing integer and floating types, the results are more bizarre. Consider, for example, Listing 4.12.

LISTING 4.12   The `floatcnv.c` Program

```
/* floatcnv.c -- mismatched floating-point conversions */
#include <stdio.h>
int main(void)
{
    float n1 = 3.0;
    double n2 = 3.0;
    long n3 = 2000000000;
    long n4 = 1234567890;

    printf("%.1e %.1e %.1e %.1e\n", n1, n2, n3, n4);
    printf("%ld %ld\n", n3, n4);
    printf("%ld %ld %ld %ld\n", n1, n2, n3, n4);

    return 0;
}
```

On our system, Listing 4.12 produces the following output:

```
3.0e+00 3.0e+00 3.1e+46 1.7e+266
2000000000 1234567890
0 1074266112 0 1074266112
```

The first line of output shows that using a `%e` specifier does not convert an integer to a floating-point number. Consider, for example, what happens when you try to print n3 (type `long`) using the `%e` specifier. First, the `%e` specifier causes `printf()` to expect a type `double` value, which is an 8-byte value on this system. When `printf()` looks at n3, which is a 4-byte value on this system, it also looks at the adjacent 4 bytes. Therefore, it looks at an 8-byte unit in which the actual n3 is embedded. Second, it interprets the bits in this unit as a floating-point number. Some bits, for example, would be interpreted as an exponent. So even if n3 had the correct number of bits, they would be interpreted differently under `%e` than under `%ld`. The net result is nonsense.

The first line also illustrates what we mentioned earlier—that `float` is converted to `double` when used as arguments to `printf()`. On this system, `float` is 4 bytes, but n1 was expanded to 8 bytes so that `printf()` would display it correctly.

The second line of output shows that `printf()` can print n3 and n4 correctly if the correct specifier is used.

The third line of output shows that even the correct specifier can produce phony results if the `printf()` statement has mismatches elsewhere. As you might expect, trying to print a floating-point value with an `%ld` specifier fails, but here, trying to print a type `long` using `%ld` fails! The problem lies in how C passes information to a function. The exact details of this failure are implementation dependent, but the sidebar "Passing Arguments" discusses a representative system.

Passing Arguments

The mechanics of argument passing depend on the implementation. This is how argument passing works on our system. The function call looks as follows:

```
printf("%ld %ld %ld %ld\n", n1, n2, n3, n4);
```

This call tells the computer to hand over the values of the variables n1, n2, n3, and n4 to the computer. It does so by placing them in an area of memory called the *stack*. When the computer puts these values on the stack, it is guided by the types of the variables, not by the conversion specifiers. Consequently, for n1, it places 8 bytes on the stack (`float` is converted to `double`). Similarly, it places 8 more bytes for n2, followed by 4 bytes each for n3 and n4. Then control shifts to the `printf()` function. This function reads the values off the stack but, when it does so, it reads them according to the conversion specifiers. The `%ld` specifier indicates that `printf()` should read 4 bytes, so `printf()` reads the first 4 bytes in the stack as its first value. This is just the first half of n1, and it is interpreted as a `long` integer. The next `%ld` specifier reads 4 more bytes; this is just the second half of n1 and is interpreted as a second `long` integer (see Figure 4.9). Similarly, the third and fourth instances of `%ld` cause the first and second halves of n2 to be read and to be interpreted as two more `long` integers, so although we have the correct specifiers for n3 and n4, `printf()` is reading the wrong bytes.

FIGURE 4.9

Passing arguments.

```
float n1;   /* passed as type double */
double n2;
long n3, n4;
...
printf("%ld %ld %ld %ld\n", n1, n2, n3, n4);
```

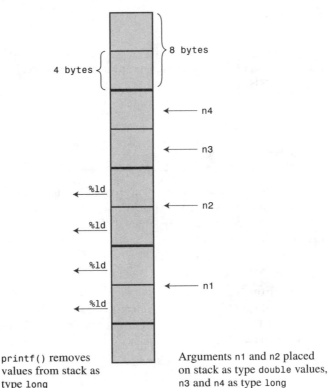

printf() removes values from stack as type long

Arguments n1 and n2 placed on stack as type double values, n3 and n4 as type long

The Return Value of `printf()`

As mentioned in Chapter 2, a C function generally has a return value. This is a value that the function computes and returns to the calling program. For example, the C library contains a `sqrt()` function that takes a number as an argument and returns its square root. The return value can be assigned to a variable, can be used in a computation, can be passed as an argument—in short, it can be used like any other value. The `printf()` function also has a return value; it returns the number of characters it printed. If there is an output error, `printf()` returns a negative value. (Some ancient versions of `printf()` have different return values.)

The return value for `printf()` is incidental to its main purpose of printing output, and it usually isn't used. One reason you might use the return value is to check for output errors. This is more commonly done when writing to a file rather than to a screen. If a full floppy disk prevented writing from taking place, you could then have the program take some appropriate action, such as beeping the terminal for 30 seconds. However, you have to know about the `if` statement before doing that sort of thing. The simple example in Listing 4.13 shows how you can determine the return value.

LISTING 4.13   The `prntval.c` Program

```
/* prntval.c -- finding printf()'s return value */
#include <stdio.h>
int main(void)
{
    int bph2o = 212;
    int rv;

    rv = printf("%d F is water's boiling point.\n", bph2o);
    printf("The printf() function printed %d characters.\n",
            rv);
    return 0;
}
```

The output is as follows:

```
212 F is water's boiling point.
The printf() function printed 32 characters.
```

First, the program used the form `rv = printf(...);` to assign the return value to `rv`. This statement therefore performs two tasks: printing information and assigning a value to a variable. Second, note that the count includes all the printed characters, including the spaces and the unseen newline character.

Printing Long Strings

Occasionally, `printf()` statements are too long to put on one line. Because C ignores whitespace (spaces, tabs, newlines) except when used to separate elements, you can spread a statement over several lines, as long as you put your line breaks between elements. For example, Listing 4.13 used two lines for a statement.

```
printf("The printf() function printed %d characters.\n",
        rv);
```

The line is broken between the comma element and rv. To show a reader that the line was being continued, the example indents the rv. C ignores the extra spaces.

However, you cannot break a quoted string in the middle. Suppose you try something like the following:

```
printf("The printf() function printed %d
        characters.\n", rv);
```

C will complain that you have an illegal character in a string constant. You can use \n in a string to symbolize the newline character, but you can't have the actual newline character generated by the Enter (or Return) key in a string.

If you do have to split a string, you have three choices, as shown in Listing 4.14.

LISTING 4.14   The longstrg.c Program

```
/* longstrg.c -- printing long strings */
#include <stdio.h>
int main(void)
{
    printf("Here's one way to print a ");
    printf("long string.\n");
    printf("Here's another way to print a \
long string.\n");
    printf("Here's the newest way to print a "
            "long string.\n");      /* ANSI C */
    return 0;
}
```

Here is the output:

```
Here's one way to print a long string.
Here's another way to print a long string.
Here's the newest way to print a long string.
```

Method 1 is to use more than one printf() statement. Because the first string printed doesn't end with a \n character, the second string continues where the first ends.

Method 2 is to terminate the end of the first line with a backslash/return combination. This causes the text onscreen to start a new line without a newline character being included in the string. The effect is to continue the string over to the next line. However, the next line has to start at the far left, as shown. If you indent that line, say, five spaces, those five spaces become part of the string.

Method 3, new with ANSI C, is string concatenation. If you follow one quoted string constant with another, separated only by whitespace, C treats the combination as a single string, so the following three forms are equivalent:

```
printf("Hello, young lovers, wherever you are.");
printf("Hello, young "    "lovers" ", wherever you are.");
printf("Hello, young lovers"
        ", wherever you are.");
```

With all these methods, you should include any required spaces in the strings: `"young"` `"lovers"` becomes `"younglovers"`, but the combination `"young "` `"lovers"` is `"young lovers"`.

Using `scanf()`

Now let's go from output to input and examine the `scanf()` function. The C library contains several input functions, and `scanf()` is the most general of them, because it can read a variety of formats. Of course, input from the keyboard is text because the keys generate text characters: letters, digits, and punctuation. When you want to enter, say, the integer 2004, you type the characters `2` `0` `0` and `4`. If you want to store that as a numerical value rather than as a string, your program has to convert the string character-by-character to a numerical value; that is what `scanf()` does! It converts string input into various forms: integers, floating-point numbers, characters, and C strings. It is the inverse of `printf()`, which converts integers, floating-point numbers, characters, and C strings to text that is to be displayed onscreen.

Like `printf()`, `scanf()` uses a control string followed by a list of arguments. The control string indicates the destination data types for the input stream of characters. The chief difference is in the argument list. The `printf()` function uses variable names, constants, and expressions. The `scanf()` function uses pointers to variables. Fortunately, you don't have to know anything about pointers to use the function. Just remember these simple rules:

- If you use `scanf()` to read a value for one of the basic variable types we've discussed, precede the variable name with an `&`.

- If you use `scanf()` to read a string into a character array, don't use an `&`.

Listing 4.15 presents a short program illustrating these rules.

LISTING 4.15   The `input.c` Program

```
// input.c -- when to use &
#include <stdio.h>
int main(void)
{
    int age;            // variable
    float assets;       // variable
    char pet[30];       // string

    printf("Enter your age, assets, and favorite pet.\n");
    scanf("%d %f", &age, &assets); // use the & here
```

LISTING 4.15 Continued

```
    scanf("%s", pet);                  // no & for char array
    printf("%d $%.2f %s\n", age, assets, pet);

    return 0;
}
```

Here is a sample exchange:

```
Enter your age, assets, and favorite pet.
38
92360.88 llama
38 $92360.88 llama
```

The scanf() function uses whitespace (newlines, tabs, and spaces) to decide how to divide the input into separate fields. It matches up consecutive conversion specifications to consecutive fields, skipping over the whitespace in between. Note how the input is spread over two lines. You could just as well have used one or five lines, as long as you had at least one newline, space, or tab between each entry. The only exception to this is the %c specification, which reads the very next character, even if that character is whitespace. We'll return to this topic in a moment.

The scanf() function uses pretty much the same set of conversion-specification characters as printf() does. The main difference is that printf() uses %f, %e, %E, %g, and %G for both type float and type double, whereas scanf() uses them just for type float, requiring the l modifier for double. Table 4.6 lists the main conversion specifiers as described in the C99 standard.

TABLE 4.6 ANSI C Conversion Specifiers for scanf()

Conversion Specifier	Meaning
%c	Interpret input as a character.
%d	Interpret input as a signed decimal integer.
%e, %f, %g, %a	Interpret input as a floating-point number (%a is C99).
%E, %F, %G, %A	Interpret input as a floating-point number (%A is C99).
%i	Interpret input as a signed decimal integer.
%o	Interpret input as a signed octal integer.
%p	Interpret input as a pointer (an address).
%s	Interpret input as a string. Input begins with the first non-whitespace character and includes everything up to the next whitespace character.
%u	Interpret input as an unsigned decimal integer.
%x, %X	Interpret input as a signed hexadecimal integer.

You also can use modifiers in the conversion specifiers shown in Table 4.6. The modifiers go between the percent sign and the conversion letter. If you use more than one in a specifier, they should appear in the same order as shown in Table 4.7.

TABLE 4.7   Conversion Modifiers for `scanf()`

Modifier	Meaning
*	Suppress assignment (see text).
	Example: `"%*d"`
digit(s)	Maximum field width. Input stops when the maximum field width is reached or when the first whitespace character is encountered, whichever comes first.
	Example: `"%10s"`
hh	Read an integer as a `signed char` or `unsigned char`.
	Examples: `"%hhd"` `"%hhu"`
ll	Read an integer as a `long long` or unsigned `long long` (C99).
	Examples: `"%lld"` `"%llu"`
h, l, or L	`"%hd"` and `"%hi"` indicate that the value will be stored in a `short int`. `"%ho"`, `"%hx"`, and `"%hu"` indicate that the value will be stored in an `unsigned short int`. `"%ld"` and `"%li"` indicate that the value will be stored in a `long`. `"%lo"`, `"%lx"`, and `"%lu"` indicate that the value will be stored in `unsigned long`. `"%le"`, `"%lf"`, and `"%lg"` indicate that the value will be stored in type `double`. Using L instead of l with e, f, and g indicates that the value will be stored in type `long double`. In the absence of these modifiers, d, i, o, and x indicate type `int`, and e, f, and g indicate type `float`.

As you can see, using conversion specifiers can be involved, and these tables have omitted some of the features. The omitted features primarily facilitate reading selected data from highly formatted sources, such as punched cards or other data records. Because this book uses `scanf()` primarily as a convenient means for feeding data to a program interactively, it won't discuss the more esoteric features.

The `scanf()` View of Input

Let's look in more detail at how `scanf()` reads input. Suppose you use a `%d` specifier to read an integer. The `scanf()` function begins reading input a character at a time. It skips over whitespace characters (spaces, tabs, and newlines) until it finds a non-whitespace character. Because it is attempting to read an integer, `scanf()` expects to find a digit character or, perhaps, a sign (+ or -). If it finds a digit or a sign, it saves the sign and then reads the next character. If that is a digit, it saves the digit and reads the next character. `scanf()` continues reading and saving characters until it encounters a nondigit. It then concludes that it has reached the end of the integer. scanf() places the nondigit back in the input. This means that the next time the program goes to read input, it starts at the previously rejected, nondigit character. Finally, scanf() computes the numerical value corresponding to the digits it read and places that value in the specified variable.

If you use a field width, scanf() halts at the field end or at the first whitespace, whichever comes first.

What if the first non-whitespace character is, say, an A instead of a digit? Then scanf() stops right there and places the A (or whatever) back in the input. No value is assigned to the specified variable, and the next time the program reads input, it starts at the A again. If your program has only %d specifiers, scanf() will never get past that A. Also, if you use a scanf() statement with several specifiers, ANSI C requires the function to stop reading input at the first failure.

Reading input using the other numeric specifiers works much the same as the %d case. The main difference is that scanf() may recognize more characters as being part of the number. For instance, the %x specifier requires that scanf() recognize the hexadecimal digits a–f and A–F. Floating-point specifiers require scanf() to recognize decimal points, e-notation, and the new p-notation.

If you use an %s specifier, any character other than whitespace is acceptable, so scanf() skips whitespace to the first non-whitespace character and then saves up non-whitespace characters until hitting whitespace again. This means that %s results in scanf() reading a single word—that is, a string with no whitespace in it. If you use a field width, scanf() stops at the end of the field or at the first whitespace. You can't use the field width to make scanf() read more than one word for one %s specifier. A final point: When scanf() places the string in the designated array, it adds the terminating '\0' to make the array contents a C string.

If you use a %c specifier, all input characters are fair game. If the next input character is a space or a newline, a space or a newline is assigned to the indicated variable; whitespace is not skipped.

Actually, scanf() is not the most commonly used input function in C. It is featured here because of its versatility (it can read all the different data types), but C has several other input functions, such as getchar() and gets(), that are better suited for specific tasks, such as reading single characters or reading strings containing spaces. We will cover some of these functions in Chapter 7, "C Control Statements: Branching and Jumps," Chapter 11, "Character Strings and String Functions," and Chapter 13, "File Input/Output." In the meantime, if you need an integer or decimal fraction or a character or a string, you can use scanf().

Regular Characters in the Format String

The scanf() function does enable you to place ordinary characters in the format string. Ordinary characters other than the space character must be matched exactly by the input string. For example, suppose you accidentally place a comma between two specifiers:

```
scanf("%d,%d", &n, &m);
```

The `scanf()` function interprets this to mean that you will type a number, type a comma, and then type a second number. That is, you would have to enter two integers as follows:

```
88,121
```

Because the comma comes immediately after the `%d` in the format string, you would have to type it immediately after the `88`. However, because `scanf()` skips over whitespace preceding an integer, you could type a space or newline after the comma when entering the input. That is,

```
88, 121
```

and

```
88,
121
```

also would be accepted.

A space in the format string means to skip over any whitespace before the next input item. For instance, the statement

```
scanf("%d ,%d", &n, &m);
```

would accept any of the following input lines:

```
88,121
88  ,121
88 ,   121
```

Note that the concept of "any whitespace" includes the special cases of no whitespace.

Except for `%c`, the specifiers automatically skip over whitespace preceding an input value, so `scanf("%d%d", &n, &m)` behaves the same as `scanf("%d %d", &n, &m)`. For `%c`, adding a space character to the format string does make a difference. For example, if `%c` is preceded by a space in the format string, `scanf()` does skip to the first non-whitespace character. That is, the command `scanf("%c", &ch)` reads the first character encountered in input, and `scanf(" %c", &ch)` reads the first non-whitespace character encountered.

The `scanf()` Return Value

The `scanf()` function returns the number of items that it successfully reads. If it reads no items, which happens if you type a nonnumeric string when it expects a number, `scanf()` returns the value `0`. It returns `EOF` when it detects the condition known as "end of file." (`EOF` is a special value defined in the `stdio.h` file. Typically, a `#define` directive gives `EOF` the value `-1`.) We'll discuss end of file in Chapter 6, "C Control Statements: Looping," and make use of `scanf()`'s return value later in the book. After you learn about `if` statements and `while` statements, you can use the `scanf()` return value to detect and handle mismatched input.

The * Modifier with `printf()` and `scanf()`

Both `printf()` and `scanf()` can use the * modifier to modify the meaning of a specifier, but they do so in dissimilar fashions. First, let's see what the * modifier can do for `printf()`.

Suppose that you don't want to commit yourself to a field width in advance but rather you want the program to specify it. You can do this by using * instead of a number for the field width, but you also have to use an argument to tell what the field width should be. That is, if you have the conversion specifier %*d, the argument list should include a value for * *and* a value for d. The technique also can be used with floating-point values to specify the precision as well as the field width. Listing 4.16 is a short example showing how this works.

LISTING 4.16   The varwid.c Program

```c
/* varwid.c -- uses variable-width output field */
#include <stdio.h>
int main(void)
{
    unsigned width, precision;
    int number = 256;
    double weight = 242.5;

    printf("What field width?\n");
    scanf("%d", &width);
    printf("The number is :%*d:\n", width, number);
    printf("Now enter a width and a precision:\n");
    scanf("%d %d", &width, &precision);
    printf("Weight = %*.*f\n", width, precision, weight);
    printf("Done!\n");

    return 0;
}
```

The variable width provides the field width, and number is the number to be printed. Because the * precedes the d in the specifier, width comes before number in printf()'s argument list. Similarly, width and precision provide the formatting information for printing weight. Here is a sample run:

```
What field width?
6
The number is :   256:
Now enter a width and a precision:
8 3
Weight =  242.500
Done!
```

Here, the reply to the first question was 6, so 6 was the field width used. Similarly, the second reply produced a width of 8 with 3 digits to the right of the decimal. More generally, a program could decide on values for these variables after looking at the value of weight.

The * serves quite a different purpose for scanf(). When placed between the % and the specifier letter, it causes that function to skip over corresponding input. Listing 4.17 provides an example.

LISTING 4.17   The `skip2.c` Program

```
/* skip2.c -- skips over first two integers of input */
#include <stdio.h>
int main(void)
{
    int n;

    printf("Please enter three integers:\n");
    scanf("%*d %*d %d", &n);
    printf("The last integer was %d\n", n);

    return 0;
}
```

The `scanf()` instruction in Listing 4.17 says, "Skip two integers and copy the third into n." Here is a sample run:

```
Please enter three integers:
2004 2005 2006
The last integer was 2006
```

This skipping facility is useful if, for example, a program needs to read a particular column of a file that has data arranged in uniform columns.

Usage Tips for `printf()`

Specifying fixed field widths is useful when you want to print columns of data. Because the default field width is just the width of the number, the repeated use of, say,

```
printf("%d %d %d\n", val1, val2, val3);
```

produces ragged columns if the numbers in a column have different sizes. For example, the output could look like the following:

```
   12      234     1222
    4        5       23
22334     2322    10001
```

(This assumes that the value of the variables has been changed between `print` statements.)

The output can be cleaned up by using a sufficiently large fixed field width. For example, using

```
printf("%9d %9d %9d\n", val1, val2, val3);
```

yields the following:

```
   12      234     1222
    4        5       23
22334     2322    10001
```

Leaving a blank between one conversion specification and the next ensures that one number never runs into the next, even if it overflows its own field. This is so because the regular characters in the control string, including spaces, are printed.

On the other hand, if a number is to be embedded in a phrase, it is often convenient to specify a field as small or smaller than the expected number width. This makes the number fit in without unnecessary blanks. For example,

```
printf("Count Beppo ran %.2f miles in 3 hours.\n", distance);
```

might produce

```
Count Beppo ran 10.22 miles in 3 hours.
```

Changing the conversion specification to `%10.2f` would give you the following:

```
Count Beppo ran      10.22 miles in 3 hours.
```

Key Concepts

The C `char` type represents a single character. To represent a sequence of characters, C uses the character string. One form of string is the character constant, in which the characters are enclosed in double quotation marks; `"Good luck, my friend"` is an example. You can store a string in a character array, which consists of adjacent bytes in memory. Character strings, whether expressed as a character constant or stored in a character array, are terminated by a hidden character called the *null* character.

It's a good idea to represent numerical constants in a program symbolically, either by using `#define` or the keyword `const`. Symbolic constants make a program more readable and easier to maintain and modify.

The standard C input and output functions `scanf()` and `printf()` use a system in which you have to match type specifiers in the first argument to values in the subsequent arguments. Matching, say, an `int` specifier such as `%d` to a `float` value produces odd results. You have to exert care to match the number and type of specifiers to the rest of the function arguments. For `scanf()`, remember to prefix variables' names with the address operator (`&`).

Whitespace characters (tabs, spaces, and newlines) play a critical role in how `scanf()` views input. Except when in the `%c` mode (which reads just the next character), `scanf()` skips over whitespace characters to the first non-whitespace character when reading input. It then keeps reading characters either until encountering whitespace or until encountering a character that doesn't fit the type being read. Let's consider what happens if we feed the identical input line to several different `scanf()` input modes. Start with the following input line:

```
 -13.45e12#  0
```

First, suppose we use the `%d` mode; `scanf()` would read the three characters (`-13`) and stop at the period, leaving the period as the next input character. `scanf()` then would convert the character sequence `-13` into the corresponding integer value and store that value in the destination `int` variable. Next, reading the same line in the `%f` mode, `scanf()` would read the `-13.45E12` characters and stop at the `#` symbol, leaving it as the next input character. It then would convert the character sequence `-13.45E12` into the corresponding floating-point value and store that value in the destination `float` variable. Reading the same line in the `%s` mode, scanf() would read –13.45E12#, stopping at the space, leaving it as the next input character. It then would store the character codes for these 10 characters into the destination character array, appending a null character at the end. Finally, reading the same line using the %c specifier, scanf() would read and store the first character, in this case a space.

Summary

A string is a series of characters treated as a unit. In C, strings are represented by a series of characters terminated by the null character, which is the character whose ASCII code is 0. Strings can be stored in character arrays. An array is a series of items, or elements, all of the same type. To declare an array called name that has 30 elements of type char, do the following:

```
char name[30];
```

Be sure to allot a number of elements sufficient to hold the entire string, including the null character.

String constants are represented by enclosing the string in double quotes: "This is an example of a string".

The strlen() function (declared in the string.h header file) can be used to find the length of a string (not counting the terminating null character). The scanf() function, when used with the %s specifier, can be used to read in single-word strings.

The C preprocessor searches a source code program for preprocessor directives, which begin with the # symbol, and acts upon them before the program is compiled. The #include directive causes the processor to add the contents of another file to your file at the location of the directive. The #define directive lets you establish manifest constants—that is, symbolic representations for constants. The limits.h and float.h header files use #define to define a set of constants representing various properties of integer and floating-point types. You also can use the const modifier to create symbolic constants.

The printf() and scanf() functions provide versatile support for input and output. Each uses a control string containing embedded conversion specifiers to indicate the number and type of data items to be read or printed. Also, you can use the conversion specifiers to control the appearance of the output: field widths, decimal places, and placement within a field.

Review Questions

You'll find answers to the review questions in Appendix A, "Answers to Review Questions."

1. Run Listing 4.1 again, but this time give your first and last name when it asks you for your first name. What happens? Why?

2. Assuming that each of the following examples is part of a complete program, what will each one print?

   a.
   ```
   printf("He sold the painting for $%2.2f.\n", 2.345e2);
   ```

   b.
   ```
   printf("%c%c%c\n", 'H', 105, '\41');
   ```

   c.
   ```
   #define Q "His Hamlet was funny without being vulgar."
       printf("%s\nhas %d characters.\n", Q, strlen(Q));
   ```

   d.
   ```
   printf("Is %2.2e the same as %2.2f?\n", 1201.0, 1201.0);
   ```

3. In Question 2c, what changes could you make so that string Q is printed out enclosed in double quotation marks?

4. It's find the error time!
   ```
   define B booboo
   define X 10
   main(int)
   {
       int age;
       char name;

       printf("Please enter your first name.");
       scanf("%s", name);
       printf("All right, %c, what's your age?\n", name);
       scanf("%f", age);
       xp = age + X;
       printf("That's a %s! You must be at least %d.\n", B, xp);
       rerun 0;
   }
   ```

5. Suppose a program starts as follows:
   ```
   #define BOOK "War and Peace"
   int main(void)
   {
       float cost =12.99;
       float percent = 80.0;
   ```

   Construct a printf() statement that uses BOOK, cost, and percent to print the following:
   ```
   This copy of "War and Peace" sells for $12.99.
   That is 80% of list.
   ```

6. What conversion specification would you use to print each of the following?

    a. A decimal integer with a field width equal to the number of digits

    b. A hexadecimal integer in the form 8A in a field width of 4

    c. A floating-point number in the form 232.346 with a field width of 10

    d. A floating-point number in the form 2.33e+002 with a field width of 12

    e. A string left-justified in a field of width 30

7. Which conversion specification would you use to print each of the following?

    a. An `unsigned long` integer in a field width of 15

    b. A hexadecimal integer in the form 0x8a in a field width of 4

    c. A floating-point number in the form 2.33E+02 that is left-justified in a field width of 12

    d. A floating-point number in the form +232.346 in a field width of 10

    e. The first eight characters of a string in a field eight characters wide

8. What conversion specification would you use to print each of the following?

    a. A decimal integer having a minimum of four digits in a field width of 6

    b. An octal integer in a field whose width will be given in the argument list

    c. A character in a field width of 2

    d. A floating-point number in the form +3.13 in a field width equal to the number of characters in the number

    e. The first five characters in a string left-justified in a field of width 7

9. For each of the following input lines, provide a `scanf()` statement to read it. Also declare any variables or arrays used in the statement.

    a. 101

    b. 22.32 8.34E–09

    c. linguini

    d. catch 22

    e. catch 22 (but skip over catch)

10. What is whitespace?

11. Suppose that you would rather use parentheses than braces in your programs. How well would the following work?

```
#define ( {
#define ) }
```

Programming Exercises

1. Write a program that asks for your first name, your last name, and then prints the names in the format *last, first*.

2. Write a program that requests your first name and does the following with it:

   a. Prints it enclosed in double quotation marks

   b. Prints it in a field 20 characters wide, with the whole field in quotes

   c. Prints it at the left end of a field 20 characters wide, with the whole field enclosed in quotes

   d. Prints it in a field three characters wider than the name

3. Write a program that reads in a floating-point number and prints it first in decimal-point notation and then in exponential notation. Have the output use the following formats (the number of digits shown in the exponent may be different for your system):

   a. The input is `21.3` or `2.1e+001`.

   b. The input is `+21.290` or `2.129E+001`.

4. Write a program that requests your height in inches and your name, and then displays the information in the following form:

   `Dabney, you are 6.208 feet tall`

   Use type `float`, and use `/` for division. If you prefer, request the height in centimeters and display it in meters.

5. Write a program that requests the user's first name and then the user's last name. Have it print the entered names on one line and the number of letters in each name on the following line. Align each letter count with the end of the corresponding name, as in the following:

   ```
   Melissa Honeybee
         7        8
   ```

   Next, have it print the same information, but with the counts aligned with the beginning of each name.

   ```
   Melissa Honeybee
   7       8
   ```

6. Write a program that sets a type `double` variable to 1.0/3.0 and a type `float` variable to 1.0/3.0. Display each result three times—once showing four digits to the right of the decimal, once showing 12 digits to the right of the decimal, and once showing 16 digits to the right of the decimal. Also have the program include `float.h` and display the values of `FLT_DIG` and `DBL_DIG`. Are the displayed values of 1.0/3.0 consistent with these values?

7. Write a program that asks the user to enter the number of miles traveled and the number of gallons of gasoline consumed. It should then calculate and display the miles-per-gallon value, showing one place to the right of the decimal. Next, using the fact that one gallon is about 3.785 liters and one mile is about 1.609 kilometers, it should convert the mile-per-gallon value to a liters-per-100-km value, the usual European way of expressing fuel consumption, and display the result, showing one place to the right of the decimal. (Note that the U.S. scheme measures the amount of fuel per distance, whereas the European scheme measures the distance per amount of fuel.) Use symbolic constants (using `const` or `#define`) for the two conversion factors.

CHAPTER 5

OPERATORS, EXPRESSIONS, AND STATEMENTS

You will learn about the following in this chapter:

- Keyword:
  while, typedef

- Operators:
  = - * /
  % ++ -- (type)

- C's multitudinous operators, including those used for common arithmetic operations

- Operator precedence and the meanings of the terms *statement* and *expression*

- The handy while loop

- Compound statements, automatic type conversions, and type casts

- How to write functions that use arguments

Now that you've looked at ways to represent data, let's explore ways to process data. C offers a wealth of operations for that purpose. You can do arithmetic, compare values, modify variables, combine relationships logically, and more. Let's start with basic arithmetic—addition, subtraction, multiplication, and division.

Another aspect of processing data is organizing your programs so that they take the right steps in the right order. C has several language features to help you with that task. One of these features is the loop, and in this chapter you get a first look at it. A loop enables you to repeat actions and makes your programs more interesting and powerful.

Introducing Loops

Listing 5.1 shows a sample program that does a little arithmetic to calculate the length in inches of a foot that wears a size 9 (men's) shoe. To enhance your appreciation of loops, this first version illustrates the limitations of programming without using a loop.

LISTING 5.1   The shoes1.c Program

```
/* shoes1.c -- converts a shoe size to inches */
#include <stdio.h>
#define ADJUST 7.64
#define SCALE 0.325
int main(void)
{
    double shoe, foot;

    shoe = 9.0;
    foot = SCALE * shoe + ADJUST;
    printf("Shoe size (men's)    foot length\n");
    printf("%10.1f %15.2f inches\n", shoe, foot);

    return 0;
}
```

Here is a program with multiplication and addition. It takes your shoe size (if you wear a size 9) and tells you how long your foot is in inches. "But," you say, "I could solve this problem by hand more quickly than you could type the program." That's a good point. A one-shot program that does just one shoe size is a waste of time and effort. You could make the program more useful by writing it as an interactive program, but that still barely taps the potential of a computer.

What you need is some way to have a computer do repetitive calculations for a succession of shoe sizes. After all, that's one of the main reasons for using a computer to do arithmetic. C offers several methods for doing repetitive calculations, and we will outline one here. This method, called a *while loop*, will enable you to make a more interesting exploration of operators. Listing 5.2 presents the improved shoe-sizing program.

LISTING 5.2   The shoes2.c Program

```
/* shoes2.c -- calculates foot lengths for several sizes */
#include <stdio.h>
#define ADJUST 7.64
#define SCALE 0.325
int main(void)
{
    double shoe, foot;

    printf("Shoe size (men's)    foot length\n");
    shoe = 3.0;
    while (shoe < 18.5)      /* starting the while loop */
    {                        /* start of block          */
        foot = SCALE*shoe + ADJUST;
        printf("%10.1f %15.2f inches\n", shoe, foot);
        shoe = shoe + 1.0;
    }                        /* end of block            */
    printf("If the shoe fits, wear it.\n");

    return 0;
}
```

Here is a condensed version of `shoes2.c`'s output:

```
Shoe size (men's)      foot length
        3.0            8.62 inches
        4.0            8.94 inches
        ...               ...
       17.0           13.16 inches
       18.0           13.49 inches
If the shoe fits, wear it.
```

(Incidentally, the constants for this conversion were obtained during an incognito visit to a shoe store. The only shoe-sizer left lying around was for men's sizes. Those of you interested in women's sizes will have to make your own visit to a shoe store. Also, the program makes the unrealistic assumption that there is a rational and uniform system of shoe sizes.)

Here is how the `while` loop works. When the program first reaches the `while` statement, it checks to see whether the condition within parentheses is true. In this case, the expression is as follows:

```
shoe < 18.5
```

The `<` symbol means "is less than." The variable `shoe` was initialized to `3.0`, which certainly is less than `18.5`. Therefore, the condition is true and the program proceeds to the next statement, which converts the size to inches. Then it prints the results. The next statement increases `shoe` by 1.0, making it 4.0:

```
shoe = shoe + 1.0;
```

At this point, the program returns to the `while` portion to check the condition. Why at this point? Because the next line is a closing brace (`}`), and the code uses a set of braces (`{}`) to mark the extent of the `while` loop. The statements between the two braces are the ones that are repeated. The section of program between and including the braces is called a *block*. Now back to the program. The value 4 is less than `18.5`, so the whole cycle of embraced commands (the block) following the `while` is repeated. (In computerese, the program is said to "loop" through these statements.) This continues until `shoe` reaches a value of `19.0`. Now the condition

```
shoe < 18.5
```

becomes false because `19.0` is not less than `18.5`. When this happens, control passes to the first statement following the `while` loop. In this case, that is the final `printf()` statement.

You can easily modify this program to do other conversions. For example, change `SCALE` to `1.8` and `ADJUST` to `32.0`, and you have a program that converts Centigrade to Fahrenheit. Change `SCALE` to `0.6214` and `ADJUST` to `0`, and you convert kilometers to miles. If you make these changes, you should change the printed messages, too, to prevent confusion.

The `while` loop provides a convenient, flexible means of controlling a program. Now let's turn to the fundamental operators that you can use in your programs.

Fundamental Operators

C uses *operators* to represent arithmetic operations. For example, the + operator causes the two values flanking it to be added together. If the term *operator* seems odd to you, please keep in mind that those things had to be called something. "Operator" does seem to be a better choice than, say, "those things" or "arithmetical transactors." Now take a look at the operators used for basic arithmetic: =, +, -, *, and /. (C does not have an exponentiating operator. The standard C math library, however, provides the **pow()** function for that purpose. For example, **pow(3.5, 2.2)** returns 3.5 raised to the power of 2.2.)

Assignment Operator: =

In C, the equal sign does not mean "equals." Rather, it is a value-assigning operator. The statement

```
bmw = 2002;
```

assigns the value **2002** to the variable named **bmw**. That is, the item to the left of the = sign is the *name* of a variable, and the item on the right is the *value* assigned to the variable. The = symbol is called the *assignment operator*. Again, don't think of the line as saying, "**bmw** equals **2002**." Instead, read it as "assign the value **2002** to the variable **bmw**." The action goes from right to left for this operator.

Perhaps this distinction between the name of a variable and the value of a variable seems like hair-splitting, but consider the following common type of computer statement:

```
i = i + 1;
```

As mathematics, this statement makes no sense. If you add 1 to a finite number, the result isn't "equal to" the number you started with, but as a computer assignment statement, it is perfectly reasonable. It means "Find the value of the variable named **i**, add **1** to that value, and then assign this new value to the variable **i**" (see Figure 5.1).

FIGURE 5.1

The statement i = i + 1;.

```
i=i+1;
i=22+1;
i=23;
```

A statement such as

```
2002 = bmw;
```

makes no sense in C (and, indeed, is invalid) because **2002** is just a constant. You can't assign a value to a constant; it already *is* its value. When you sit down at the keyboard, therefore, remember that the item to the left of the = sign must be the name of a variable. Actually, the left side must refer to a storage location. The simplest way is to use the name of a variable, but, as you will see later, a "pointer" can be used to point to a location. More generally, C uses the term *modifiable lvalue* to label those entities to which you can assign values. "Modifiable lvalue" is not, perhaps, the most intuitive phrase you've encountered, so let's look at some definitions.

Some Terminology: Data Objects, Lvalues, Rvalues, and Operands

Data object is a general term for a region of data storage that can be used to hold values. The data storage used to hold a variable or an array is a data object, for instance. C uses the term *lvalue* to mean a name or expression that identifies a particular data object. The name of a variable, for instance, is an lvalue, so *object* refers to the actual data storage, but *lvalue* is a label used to identify, or locate, that storage.

Not all objects can have their values changed, so C uses the term *modifiable lvalue* to identify objects whose value can be changed. Therefore, the left side of an assignment operator should be a modifiable lvalue. Indeed, the *l* in *lvalue* comes from *left* because modifiable lvalues can be used on the left side of assignment operators.

The term *rvalue* refers to quantities that can be assigned to modifiable lvalues. For instance, consider the following statement:

bmw = 2002;

Here, bmw is a modifiable lvalue, and 2002 is an rvalue. As you probably guessed, the *r* in *rvalue* comes from *right*. Rvalues can be constants, variables, or any other expression that yields a value.

As long as you are learning the names of things, the proper term for what we have called an "item" (as in "the item to the left of the =") is *operand*. Operands are what operators operate on. For example, you can describe eating a hamburger as applying the "eat" operator to the "hamburger" operand; similarly, you can say that the left operand of the = operator shall be a modifiable lvalue.

The basic C assignment operator is a little flashier than most. Try the short program in Listing 5.3.

LISTING 5.3   The golf.c Program

```
/* golf.c -- golf tournament scorecard */
#include <stdio.h>
int main(void)
{
    int jane, tarzan, cheeta;

    cheeta = tarzan = jane = 68;
    printf("                 cheeta    tarzan    jane\n");
    printf("First round score %4d %8d %8d\n",cheeta,tarzan,jane);

    return 0;
}
```

Many languages would balk at the triple assignment made in this program, but C accepts it routinely. The assignments are made right to left: First, `jane` gets the value 68, and then `tarzan` does, and finally `cheeta` does. Therefore, the output is as follows:

```
                  cheeta   tarzan   jane
First round score   68       68      68
```

Addition Operator: +

The *addition operator* causes the two values on either side of it to be added together. For example, the statement

```
printf("%d", 4 + 20);
```

causes the number 24 to be printed, not the expression

```
4 + 20.
```

The values (operands) to be added can be variables as well as constants. Therefore, the statement

```
income = salary + bribes;
```

causes the computer to look up the values of the two variables on the right, add them, and then assign this total to the variable `income`.

Subtraction Operator: −

The *subtraction operator* causes the number after the − sign to be subtracted from the number before the sign. The statement

```
takehome = 224.00 - 24.00;
```

assigns the value 200.0 to `takehome`.

The + and − operators are termed *binary*, or *dyadic,* operators, meaning that they require *two* operands.

Sign Operators: − and +

The minus sign can also be used to indicate or to change the algebraic sign of a value. For instance, the sequence

```
rocky = -12;
smokey = -rocky;
```

gives `smokey` the value 12.

When the minus sign is used in this way, it is called a ***unary operator***, meaning that it takes just one operand (see Figure 5.2).

The C90 standard adds a unary + operator to C. It doesn't alter the value or sign of its operand; it just enables you to use statements such as

```
dozen = +12;
```

without getting a compiler complaint. Formerly, this construction was not allowed.

FIGURE 5.2
Unary and binary operators.

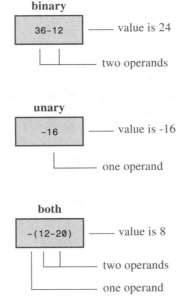

Multiplication Operator: *

Multiplication is indicated by the * symbol. The statement

```
cm = 2.54 * inch;
```

multiplies the variable `inch` by `2.54` and assigns the answer to `cm`.

By any chance, do you want a table of squares? C doesn't have a squaring function, but, as shown in Listing 5.4, you can use multiplication to calculate squares.

LISTING 5.4   The `squares.c` Program

```
/* squares.c -- produces a table of first 20 squares */
#include <stdio.h>
int main(void)
{
    int num = 1;

    while (num < 21)
    {
        printf("%4d %6d\n", num, num * num);
        num = num + 1;
```

LISTING 5.4   Continued

```
        }

        return 0;
}
```

This program prints the first 20 integers and their squares, as you can verify for yourself. Let's look at a more interesting example.

Exponential Growth

You have probably heard the story of the powerful ruler who seeks to reward a scholar who has done him a great service. When the scholar is asked what he would like, he points to a chessboard and says, just one grain of wheat on the first square, two on the second, four on the third, eight on the next, and so on. The ruler, lacking mathematical erudition, is astounded at the modesty of this request, for he had been prepared to offer great riches. The joke, of course, is on the ruler, as the program in Listing 5.5 shows. It calculates how many grains go on each square and keeps a running total. Because you might not be up to date on wheat crops, the program also compares the running total to a rough estimate of the annual wheat crop in the United States.

LISTING 5.5   The wheat.c Program

```
/* wheat.c -- exponential growth */
#include <stdio.h>
#define SQUARES 64      /* squares on a checkerboard   */
#define CROP 1E15       /* US wheat crop in grains     */
int main(void)
{
    double current, total;
    int count = 1;

    printf("square     grains        total      ");
    printf("fraction of \n");
    printf("           added       grains       ");
    printf("US total\n");
    total = current = 1.0; /* start with one grain    */
    printf("%4d %13.2e %12.2e %12.2e\n", count, current,
           total, total/CROP);
    while (count < SQUARES)
    {
        count = count + 1;
        current = 2.0 * current;
                    /* double grains on next square */
        total = total + current;     /* update total */
        printf("%4d %13.2e %12.2e %12.2e\n", count, current,
               total, total/CROP);
    }
    printf("That's all.\n");

    return 0;
}
```

The output begins innocuously enough:

```
square      grains          total       fraction of
            added           grains      US total
   1        1.00e+00        1.00e+00    1.00e-15
   2        2.00e+00        3.00e+00    3.00e-15
   3        4.00e+00        7.00e+00    7.00e-15
   4        8.00e+00        1.50e+01    1.50e-14
   5        1.60e+01        3.10e+01    3.10e-14
   6        3.20e+01        6.30e+01    6.30e-14
   7        6.40e+01        1.27e+02    1.27e-13
   8        1.28e+02        2.55e+02    2.55e-13
   9        2.56e+02        5.11e+02    5.11e-13
  10        5.12e+02        1.02e+03    1.02e-12
```

After ten squares, the scholar has acquired just a little over a thousand grains of wheat, but look what has happened by square 50!

```
  50        5.63e+14        1.13e+15    1.13e+00
```

The haul has exceeded the total U.S. annual output! If you want to see what happens by the 64th square, you will have to run the program yourself.

This example illustrates the phenomenon of exponential growth. The world population growth and our use of energy resources have followed the same pattern.

Division Operator: /

C uses the / symbol to represent division. The value to the left of the / is divided by the value to the right. For example, the following gives **four** the value of **4.0**:

```
four = 12.0/3.0;
```

Division works differently for integer types than it does for floating types. Floating-type division gives a floating-point answer, but integer division yields an integer answer. An integer can't have a fractional part, which makes dividing 5 by 3 awkward, because the answer does have a fractional part. In C, any fraction resulting from integer division is discarded. This process is called *truncation*.

Try the program in Listing 5.6 to see how truncation works and how integer division differs from floating-point division.

LISTING 5.6   The `divide.c` Program

```
/* divide.c -- divisions we have known */
#include <stdio.h>
int main(void)
{
    printf("integer division:  5/4   is %d \n", 5/4);
    printf("integer division:  6/3   is %d \n", 6/3);
    printf("integer division:  7/4   is %d \n", 7/4);
    printf("floating division: 7./4. is %1.2f \n", 7./4.);
    printf("mixed division:    7./4  is %1.2f \n", 7./4);

    return 0;
}
```

Listing 5.6 includes a case of "mixed types" by having a floating-point value divided by an integer. C is a more forgiving language than some and will let you get away with this, but normally you should avoid mixing types. Now for the results:

```
integer division:  5/4   is 1
integer division:  6/3   is 2
integer division:  7/4   is 1
floating division: 7./4. is 1.75
mixed division:    7./4  is 1.75
```

Notice how integer division does not round to the nearest integer, but always truncates (that is, discards the entire fractional part). When you mixed integers with floating point, the answer came out the same as floating point. Actually, the computer is not really capable of dividing a floating-point type by an integer type, so the compiler converts both operands to a single type. In this case, the integer is converted to floating point before division.

Until the C99 standard, C gave language implementers some leeway in deciding how integer division with negative numbers worked. One could take the view that the rounding procedure consists of finding the largest integer smaller than or equal to the floating-point number. Certainly, 3 fits that description when compared to 3.8. But what about –3.8? The largest integer method would suggest rounding to –4 because –4 is less than –3.8. But another way of looking at the rounding process is that it just dumps the fractional part; that interpretation, called *truncating toward zero*, suggests converting –3.8 to –3. Before C99, some implementations used one approach, some the other. But C99 says to truncate toward zero, so –3.8 is converted to –3.

The properties of integer division turn out to be handy for some problems, and you'll see an example fairly soon. First, there is another important matter: What happens when you combine more than one operation into one statement? That is the next topic.

Operator Precedence

Consider the following line of code:

```
butter = 25.0 + 60.0 * n / SCALE;
```

This statement has an addition, a multiplication, and a division operation. Which operation takes place first? Is 25.0 added to 60.0, the result of 85.0 then multiplied by n, and that result then divided by SCALE? Is 60.0 multiplied by n, the result added to 25.0, and that answer then divided by SCALE? Is it some other order? Let's take n to be 6.0 and SCALE to be 2.0. If you work through the statement using these values, you will find that the first approach yields a value of 255. The second approach yields 192.5. A C program must have some other order in mind, because it would give a value of 205.0 for butter.

Clearly, the order of executing the various operations can make a difference, so C needs unambiguous rules for choosing what to do first. C does this by setting up an operator pecking order. Each operator is assigned a *precedence* level. As in ordinary arithmetic, multiplication and division have a higher precedence than addition and subtraction, so they are performed first. What if two operators have the same precedence? If they share an operand, they are executed according to the order in which they occur in the statement. For most operators, the order is from left to right. (The = operator was an exception to this.) Therefore, in the statement

```
butter = 25.0 + 60.0 * n / SCALE;
```

the order of operations is as follows:

60.0 * n	The first * or / in the expression (assuming n is 6 so that 60.0 * n is 360.0)
360.0 / SCALE	Then the second * or / in the expression
25.0 + 180	Finally (because SCALE is 2.0), the first + or - in the expression, to yield 205.0

Many people like to represent the order of evaluation with a type of diagram called an *expression tree*. Figure 5.3 is an example of such a diagram. The diagram shows how the original expression is reduced by steps to a single value.

FIGURE 5.3

Expression trees showing operators, operands, and order of evaluation.

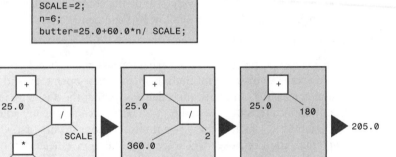

What if you want an addition operation to take place before division? Then you can do as we have done in the following line:

```
flour = (25.0 + 60.0 * n) / SCALE;
```

Whatever is enclosed in parentheses is executed first. Within the parentheses, the usual rules hold. For this example, first the multiplication takes place and then the addition. That completes the expression in the parentheses. Now the result can be divided by SCALE.

Table 5.1 summarizes the rules for the operators used so far. (The inside back cover of this book presents a table covering all operators.)

TABLE 5.1   Operators in Order of Decreasing Precedence

Operators	Associativity
( )	Left to right
+ - (unary)	Right to left
* /	Left to right
+ - (binary)	Left to right
=	Right to left

Notice that the two uses of the minus sign have different precedences, as do the two uses of the plus sign. The associativity column tells you how an operator associates with its operands. For example, the unary minus sign associates with the quantity to its right, and in division the left operand is divided by the right.

Precedence and the Order of Evaluation

Operator precedence provides vital rules for determining the order of evaluation in an expression, but it doesn't necessarily determine the complete order. C leaves some choices up to the implementation. Consider the following statement:

```
y = 6 * 12 + 5 * 20;
```

Precedence dictates the order of evaluation when two operators share an operand. For example, the **12** is an operand for both the ***** and the **+** operators, and precedence says that multiplication comes first. Similarly, precedence says that the **5** is to be multiplied, not added. In short, the multiplications **6 * 12** and **5 * 20** take place before any addition. What precedence does not establish is which of these two multiplications occurs first. C leaves that choice to the implementation because one choice might be more efficient for one kind of hardware, but the other choice might work better on another kind of hardware. In either case, the expression reduces to **72 + 100**, so the choice doesn't affect the final value for this particular example. "But," you say, "multiplication associates from left to right. Doesn't that mean the leftmost multiplication is performed first?" (Well, maybe you don't say that, but somewhere someone does.) The association rule applies for operators that *share* an operand. For instance, in the expression **12 / 3 * 2**, the **/** and ***** operators, which have the same precedence, share the operand **3**. Therefore, the left-to-right rule applies in this case, and the expression reduces to **4 * 2**, or **8**. (Going from right to left would give **12 / 6**, or **2**. Here the choice does matter.) In the previous example, the two ***** operators did not share a common operand, so the left-to-right rule did not apply.

Trying the Rules

Let's try these rules on a more complex example—Listing 5.7.

LISTING 5.7   The `rules.c` Program

```
/* rules.c -- precedence test */
#include <stdio.h>
int main(void)
{
    int top, score;

    top = score = -(2 + 5) * 6 + (4 + 3 * (2 + 3));
    printf("top = %d \n", top);

    return 0;
}
```

What value will this program print? Figure it out, and then run the program or read the following description to check your answer.

First, parentheses have the highest precedence. Whether the parentheses in `-(2 + 5) * 6` or in `(4 + 3 * (2 + 3))` are evaluated first depends on the implementation, as just discussed. Either choice will lead to the same result for this example, so let's take the left one first. The high precedence of parentheses means that in the subexpression `-(2 + 5) * 6`, you evaluate `(2 + 5)` first, getting `7`. Next, you apply the unary minus operator to `7` to get `-7`. Now the expression is

`top = score = -7 * 6 + (4 + 3 * (2 + 3))`

The next step is to evaluate `2 + 3`. The expression becomes

`top = score = -7 * 6 + (4 + 3 * 5)`

Next, because the `*` in the parentheses has priority over `+`, the expression becomes

`top = score = -7 * 6 + (4 + 15)`

and then

`top = score = -7 * 6 + 19`

Multiply `-7` by `6` and get the following expression:

`top = score = -42 + 19`

Then addition makes it

`top = score = -23`

Now `score` is assigned the value `-23`, and, finally, `top` gets the value `-23`. Remember that the `=` operator associates from right to left.

Some Additional Operators

C has about 40 operators, but some are used much more than others. The ones just covered are the most common, but let's add four more useful operators to the list.

The `sizeof` Operator and the `size_t` Type

You saw the `sizeof` operator in Chapter 3, "Data and C." To review, the `sizeof` operator returns the size, in bytes, of its operand. (Recall that a C byte is defined as the size used by the `char` type. In the past, this has most often been 8 bits, but some character sets may use larger bytes.) The operand can be a specific data object, such as the name of a variable, or it can be a type. If it is a type, such as `float`, the operand must be enclosed in parentheses. The example in Listing 5.8 shows both forms.

LISTING 5.8   The `sizeof.c` Program

```
// sizeof.c -- uses sizeof operator
// uses C99 %z modifier -- try %u or %lu if you lack %zd
#include <stdio.h>
int main(void)
{
    int n = 0;
    size_t intsize;

    intsize = sizeof (int);
    printf("n = %d, n has %zd bytes; all ints have %zd bytes.\n",
        n, sizeof n, intsize );

    return 0;
}
```

C says that `sizeof` returns a value of type `size_t`. This is an unsigned integer type, but not a brand-new type. Instead, like the portable types (`int32_t` and so on), it is defined in terms of the standard types. C has a `typedef` mechanism (discussed further in Chapter 14, "Structures and Other Data Forms") that lets you create an alias for an existing type. For example,

```
typedef double real;
```

makes `real` another name for `double`. Now you can declare a variable of type `real`:

```
real deal;    // using a typedef
```

The compiler will see the word `real`, recall that the `typedef` statement made `real` an alias for `double`, and create `deal` as a type `double` variable. Similarly, the C header files system can use `typedef` to make `size_t` a synonym for `unsigned int` on one system or for `unsigned long` on another. Thus, when you use the `size_t` type, the compiler will substitute the standard type that works for your system.

C99 goes a step further and supplies `%zd` as a `printf()` specifier for displaying a `size_t` value. If your system doesn't implement `%zd`, you can try using `%u` or `%lu` instead.

Modulus Operator: `%`

The *modulus operator* is used in integer arithmetic. It gives the *remainder* that results when the integer to its left is divided by the integer to its right. For example, `13 % 5` (read as "13 modulo 5") has the value 3, because 5 goes into 13 twice, with a remainder of 3. Don't bother trying to use this operator with floating-point numbers. It just won't work.

At first glance, this operator might strike you as an esoteric tool for mathematicians, but it is actually rather practical and helpful. One common use is to help you control the flow of a program. Suppose, for example, you are working on a bill-preparing program designed to add in an extra charge every third month. Just have the program evaluate the month number modulo 3 (that is, month % 3) and check to see whether the result is 0. If it is, the program adds in the extra charge. After you learn about if statements in Chapter 7, "C Control Statements: Branching and Jumps," you'll understand this better.

Listing 5.9 shows another use for the % operator. It also shows another way to use a while loop.

LISTING 5.9   The min_sec.c Program

```
// min_sec.c -- converts seconds to minutes and seconds
#include <stdio.h>
#define SEC_PER_MIN 60          // seconds in a minute
int main(void)
{
    int sec, min, left;

    printf("Convert seconds to minutes and seconds!\n");
    printf("Enter the number of seconds (<=0 to quit):\n");
    scanf("%d", &sec);          // read number of seconds
    while (sec > 0)
    {
        min = sec / SEC_PER_MIN;  // truncated number of minutes
        left = sec % SEC_PER_MIN; // number of seconds left over
        printf("%d seconds is %d minutes, %d seconds.\n", sec,
               min, left);
        printf("Enter next value (<=0 to quit):\n");
        scanf("%d", &sec);
    }
    printf("Done!\n");

    return 0;
}
```

Here is some sample output:

```
Convert seconds to minutes and seconds!
Enter the number of seconds (<=0 to quit):
154
154 seconds is 2 minutes, 34 seconds.
Enter next value (<=0 to quit):
567
567 seconds is 9 minutes, 27 seconds.
Enter next value (<=0 to quit):
0
Done!
```

Listing 5.2 used a counter to control a while loop. When the counter exceeded a given size, the loop quit. Listing 5.9, however, uses scanf() to fetch new values for the variable sec. As long as the value is positive, the loop continues. When the user enters a zero or negative value, the loop quits. The important design point in both cases is that each loop cycle revises the value of the variable being tested.

What about negative numbers? Before C99 settled on the "truncate toward zero" rule for integer division, there were a couple of possibilities. But with the rule in place, you get a negative modulus value if the first operand is negative, and you get a positive modulus otherwise:

11 / 5 is 2, and 11 % 5 is 1

11 / -5 is -2, and 11 % -2 is 1

-11 / -5 is 2, and -11 % -5 is -1

-11 / 5 is -2, and -11 % 5 is -1

If your system shows different behavior, it hasn't caught up to the C99 standard. In any case, the standard says, in effect, that if a and b are integer values, you can calculate a%b by subtracting (a/b)*b from a. For example, you can evaluate -11%5 this way:

-11 - (-11/5) * 5 = -11 -(-2)*5 = -11 -(-10) = -1

Increment and Decrement Operators: ++ and --

The *increment operator* performs a simple task; it increments (increases) the value of its operand by 1. This operator comes in two varieties. The first variety has the ++ come before the affected variable; this is the *prefix* mode. The second variety has the ++ after the affected variable; this is the *postfix* mode. The two modes differ with regard to the precise time that the incrementing takes place. We'll explain the similarities first and then return to that difference. The short example in Listing 5.10 shows how the increment operators work.

LISTING 5.10   The add_one.c Program

```
/* add_one.c -- incrementing: prefix and postfix */
#include <stdio.h>
int main(void)
{
    int ultra = 0, super = 0;

    while (super < 5)
    {
        super++;
        ++ultra;
        printf("super = %d, ultra = %d \n", super, ultra);
    }

    return 0;
}
```

Running add_one.c produces this output:

```
super = 1, ultra = 1
super = 2, ultra = 2
super = 3, ultra = 3
```

```
super = 4, ultra = 4
super = 5, ultra = 5
```

The program counted to five twice and simultaneously. You could get the same results by replacing the two increment statements with this:

```
super = super + 1;
ultra = ultra + 1;
```

These are simple enough statements. Why bother creating one, let alone two, abbreviations? One reason is that the compact form makes your programs neater and easier to follow. These operators give your programs an elegant gloss that cannot fail to please the eye. For example, you can rewrite part of shoes2.c (Listing 5.2) this way:

```
shoe = 3.0;
while (shoe < 18.5)
{
    foot = SCALE * size + ADJUST;
    printf("%10.1f %20.2f inches\n", shoe, foot);
    ++shoe;
}
```

However, you still haven't taken full advantage of the increment operator. You can shorten the fragment this way:

```
shoe = 2.0;
while (++shoe < 18.5)
{
    foot = SCALE*shoe + ADJUST;
    printf("%10.1f %20.2f inches\n", shoe, foot);
}
```

Here you have combined the incrementing process and the while comparison into one expression. This type of construction is so common in C that it merits a closer look.

First, how does this construction work? Simply. The value of shoe is increased by 1 and then compared to 18.5. If it is less than 18.5, the statements between the braces are executed once. Then shoe is increased by 1 again, and the cycle is repeated until shoe gets too big. You changed the initial value of shoe from 3.0 to 2.0 to compensate for shoe being incremented before the first evaluation of foot (see Figure 5.4).

FIGURE 5.4

Through the loop once.

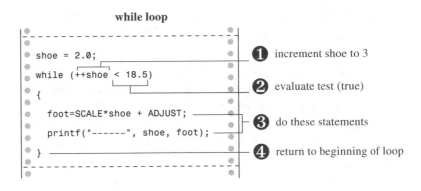

Second, what's so good about this approach? It is more compact. More important, it gathers in one place the two processes that control the loop. The primary process is the test: Do you continue or not? In this case, the test is checking to see whether the shoe size is less than 18.5. The secondary process changes an element of the test; in this case, the shoe size is increased.

Suppose you forgot to change the shoe size. Then shoe would *always* be less than 18.5, and the loop would never end. The computer would churn out line after identical line, caught in a dreaded *infinite loop*. Eventually, you would lose interest in the output and have to kill the program somehow. Having the loop test and the loop change at one place, instead of at separate locations, helps you to remember to update the loop.

A disadvantage is that combining two operations in a single expression can make the code harder to follow and can make it easier to make counting errors.

Another advantage of the increment operator is that it usually produces slightly more efficient machine language code because it is similar to actual machine language instructions. However, as vendors produce better C compilers, this advantage may disappear. A smart compiler can recognize that x = x + 1 can be treated the same as ++x.

Finally, these operators have an additional feature that can be useful in certain delicate situations. To find out what this feature is, try running the program in Listing 5.11.

LISTING 5.11   The post_pre.c Program

```c
/* post_pre.c -- postfix vs prefix */
#include <stdio.h>
int main(void)
{
    int a = 1, b = 1;
    int aplus, plusb;

    aplus = a++;        /* postfix */
    plusb = ++b;        /* prefix  */
    printf("a    aplus    b    plusb \n");
    printf("%1d %5d %5d %5d\n", a, aplus, b, plusb);

    return 0;
}
```

If you and your compiler do everything correctly, you should get this result:

```
a    aplus    b    plusb
2      1      2      2
```

Both a and b were increased by 1, as promised. However, aplus has the value of a *before* a changed, but plusb has the value of b *after* b changed. This is the difference between the prefix form and the postfix form (see Figure 5.5).

```c
aplus = a++;   /* postfix: a is changed after its value is used */
plusb = ++b;   /* prefix: b is changed before its value is used */
```

When one of these increment operators is used by itself, as in a solitary `ego++;` statement, it doesn't matter which form you use. The choice does matter, however, when the operator and its operand are part of a larger expression, as in the assignment statements you just saw. In this kind of situation, you must give some thought to the result you want. For instance, recall that we suggested using the following:

```
while (++shoe < 18.5)
```

FIGURE 5.5

Prefix and postfix.

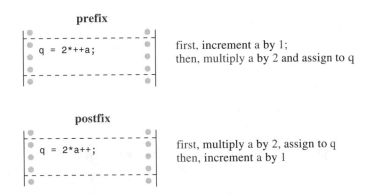

prefix

```
q = 2*++a;
```

first, increment a by 1;
then, multiply a by 2 and assign to q

postfix

```
q = 2*a++;
```

first, multiply a by 2, assign to q
then, increment a by 1

This test condition provides a table up to size 18. If you use `shoe++` instead of `++shoe`, the table will go to size 19 because `shoe` will be increased after the comparison instead of before.

Of course, you could fall back on the less subtle form,

```
shoe = shoe + 1;
```

but then no one will believe you are a true C programmer.

You should pay special attention to the examples of increment operators as you read through this book. Ask yourself if you could have used the prefix and the suffix forms interchangeably or if circumstances dictated a particular choice.

Perhaps an even wiser policy is to avoid code in which it makes a difference whether you use the prefix or postfix form. For example, instead of

```
b = ++i;  // different result for b if i++ is used
```

use

```
++i;     // line 1
b = i;   // same result for b as if i++ used in line 1
```

However, sometimes it's more fun to be a little reckless, so this book will not always follow this sensible advice.

Decrementing: - -

For each form of increment operator, there is a corresponding form of *decrement operator*. Instead of ++, use --:

```
-- count;    /* prefix form of decrement operator  */
count --;    /* postfix form of decrement operator */
```

Listing 5.12 illustrates that computers can be accomplished lyricists.

LISTING 5.12   The `bottles.c` Program

```c
#include <stdio.h>
#define MAX 100
int main(void)
{
    int count = MAX + 1;

    while (--count > 0) {
        printf("%d bottles of spring water on the wall, "
               "%d bottles of spring water!\n", count, count);
        printf("Take one down and pass it around,\n");
        printf("%d bottles of spring water!\n\n", count - 1);
    }

    return 0;
}
```

The output starts like this:

```
100 bottles of spring water on the wall, 100 bottles of spring water!
Take one down and pass it around,
99 bottles of spring water!

99 bottles of spring water on the wall, 99 bottles of spring water!
Take one down and pass it around,
98 bottles of spring water!
```

It goes on a bit and ends this way:

```
1 bottles of spring water on the wall, 1 bottles of spring water!
Take one down and pass it around,
0 bottles of spring water!
```

Apparently the accomplished lyricist has a problem with plurals, but that could be fixed by using the conditional operator of Chapter 7, "C Control Statements: Branching and Jumps."

Incidentally, the > operator stands for "is greater than." Like < ("is less than"), it is a *relational operator*. You will get a longer look at relational operators in Chapter 6, "C Control Statements: Looping."

Precedence

The increment and decrement operators have a very high precedence of association; only parentheses are higher. Therefore, `x*y++` means `(x)*(y++)`, not `(x*y)++`, which is fortunate because the latter is invalid. The increment and decrement operators affect a *variable* (or, more generally, a modifiable lvalue), and the combination `x*y` is not itself a variable, although its parts are.

Don't confuse precedence of these two operators with the order of evaluation. Suppose you have the following:

```
y = 2;
n = 3;
nextnum = (y + n++)*6;
```

What value does `nextnum` get? Substituting in values yields

```
nextnum = (2 + 3)*6 = 5*6 = 30
```

Only after `n` is used is it increased to `4`. Precedence tells us that the `++` is attached only to the `n`, not to `y + n`. It also tells us when the value of `n` is used for evaluating the expression, but the nature of the increment operator determines when the value of `n` is changed.

When `n++` is part of an expression, you can think of it as meaning "use n; then increment it." On the other hand, `++n` means "increment n; then use it."

Don't Be Too Clever

You can get fooled if you try to do too much at once with the increment operators. For example, you might think that you could improve on the `squares.c` program (Listing 5.4) to print integers and their squares by replacing the `while` loop with this one:

```
while (num < 21)
    {
    printf("%10d %10d\n", num, num*num++);
    }
```

This looks reasonable. You print the number `num`, multiply it by itself to get the square, and then increase `num` by 1. In fact, this program may even work on some systems, but not all. The problem is that when `printf()` goes to get the values for printing, it might evaluate the last argument first and increment `num` before getting to the other argument. Therefore, instead of printing

```
5          25
```

it may print

```
6          25
```

It even might work from right to left, using 5 for the rightmost `num` and 6 for the next two, resulting in this output:

```
6          30
```

In C, the compiler can choose which arguments in a function to evaluate first. This freedom increases compiler efficiency, but can cause trouble if you use an increment operator on a function argument.

Another possible source of trouble is a statement like this one:

```
ans = num/2 + 5*(1 + num++);
```

Again, the problem is that the compiler may not do things in the same order you have in mind. You would think that it would find num/2 first and then move on, but it might do the last term first, increase num, and use the new value in num/2. There is no guarantee.

Yet another troublesome case is this:

```
n = 3;
y = n++ + n++;
```

Certainly, n winds up larger by 2 after the statement is executed, but the value for y is ambiguous. A compiler can use the old value of n twice in evaluating y and then increment n twice. This gives y the value 6 and n the value 5, or it can use the old value once, increment n once, use that value for the second n in the expression, and then increment n a second time. This gives y the value 7 and n the value 5. Either choice is allowable. More exactly, the result is undefined, which means the C standard fails to define what the result should be.

You can easily avoid these problems:

- Don't use increment or decrement operators on a variable that is part of more than one argument of a function.

- Don't use increment or decrement operators on a variable that appears more than once in an expression.

On the other hand, C does have some guarantees about when incrementing takes place. We'll return to this subject when we discuss sequence points later this chapter in the section "Side Effects and Sequence Points."

Expressions and Statements

We have been using the terms *expression* and *statement* throughout these first few chapters, and now the time has come to study their meanings more closely. Statements form the basic program steps of C, and most statements are constructed from expressions. This suggests that you look at expressions first.

Expressions

An *expression* consists of a combination of operators and operands. (An operand, recall, is what an operator operates on.) The simplest expression is a lone operand, and you can build in complexity from there. Here are some expressions:

```
4
-6
```

```
4+21
a*(b + c/d)/20
q = 5*2
x = ++q % 3
q > 3
```

As you can see, the operands can be constants, variables, or combinations of the two. Some expressions are combinations of smaller expressions, called *subexpressions*. For example, c/d is a subexpression of the fourth example.

Every Expression Has a Value

An important property of C is that every C expression has a value. To find the value, you perform the operations in the order dictated by operator precedence. The value of the first few expressions we just listed is clear, but what about the ones with = signs? Those expressions simply have the same value that the variable to the left of the = sign receives. Therefore, the expression q=5*2 as a whole has the value 10. What about the expression q > 3? Such relational expressions have the value 1 if true and 0 if false. Here are some expressions and their values:

Expression	Value
-4 + 6	2
c = 3 + 8	11
5 > 3	1
6 + (c = 3 + 8)	17

The last expression looks strange! However, it is perfectly legal (but ill-advised) in C because it is the sum of two subexpressions, each of which has a value.

Statements

Statements are the primary building blocks of a program. A *program* is a series of statements with some necessary punctuation. A statement is a complete instruction to the computer. In C, statements are indicated by a semicolon at the end. Therefore,

```
legs = 4
```

is just an expression (which could be part of a larger expression), but

```
legs = 4;
```

is a statement.

What makes a complete instruction? First, C considers any expression to be a statement if you append a semicolon. (These are called *expression statements*.) Therefore, C won't object to lines such as the following:

```
8;
3 + 4;
```

However, these statements do nothing for your program and can't really be considered sensible statements. More typically, statements change values and call functions:

```
x = 25;
++x;
y = sqrt(x);
```

Although a statement (or, at least, a sensible statement) is a complete instruction, not all complete instructions are statements. Consider the following statement:

```
x = 6 + (y = 5);
```

In it, the subexpression y = 5 is a complete instruction, but it is only part of the statement. Because a complete instruction is not necessarily a statement, a semicolon is needed to identify instructions that truly are statements.

So far you have encountered four kinds of statements. Listing 5.13 gives a short example that uses all four.

LISTING 5.13   The addemup.c Program

```
/* addemup.c -- four kinds of statements */
#include <stdio.h>
int main(void)                   /* finds sum of first 20 integers */
{
    int count, sum;              /* declaration statement           */

    count = 0;                   /* assignment statement            */
    sum = 0;                     /* ditto                           */
    while (count++ < 20)         /* while                           */
        sum = sum + count;       /*      statement                  */
    printf("sum = %d\n", sum);/* function statement                 */

    return 0;
}
```

Let's discuss Listing 5.13. By now, you must be pretty familiar with the declaration statement. Nonetheless, we will remind you that it establishes the names and type of variables and causes memory locations to be set aside for them. Note that a declaration statement is not an expression statement. That is, if you remove the semicolon from a declaration, you get something that is not an expression and that does not have a value:

```
int port                         /* not an expression, has no value */
```

The *assignment statement* is the workhorse of many programs; it assigns a value to a variable. It consists of a variable name followed by the assignment operator (=) followed by an expression followed by a semicolon. Note that this particular while statement includes an assignment statement within it. An assignment statement is an example of an expression statement.

A *function statement* causes the function to do whatever it does. In this example, the printf() function is invoked to print some results. A while statement has three distinct parts (see Figure 5.6). First is the keyword while. Then, in parentheses, is a test condition. Finally, you have the statement that is performed if the test is met. Only one statement is included in the loop. It can be a simple statement, as in this example, in which case no braces are needed to mark it off, or the statement can be a compound statement, like some of the earlier examples, in which case braces are required. You can read about compound statements just ahead.

FIGURE 5.6
Structure of a simple
`while` loop.

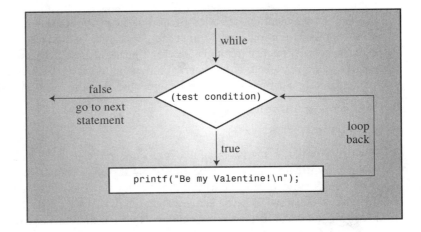

The `while` statement belongs to a class of statements sometimes called *structured statements* because they possess a structure more complex than that of a simple assignment statement. In later chapters, you will encounter many other kinds of structured statements.

Side Effects and Sequence Points

Now for a little more C terminology. A *side effect* is the modification of a data object or file. For instance, the side effect of the statement

```
states = 50;
```

is to set the `states` variable to `50`. Side effect? This looks more like the main intent! From the standpoint of C, however, the main intent is evaluating expressions. Show C the expression **4 + 6**, and C evaluates it to 10. Show it the expression `states = 50`, and C evaluates it to 50. Evaluating that expression has the side effect of changing the `states` variable to `50`. The increment and decrement operators, like the assignment operator, have side effects and are used primarily because of their side effects.

A *sequence point* is a point in program execution at which all side effects are evaluated before going on to the next step. In C, the semicolon in a statement marks a sequence point. That means all changes made by assignment operators, increment operators, and decrement operators in a statement must take place before a program proceeds to the next statement. Some operators that we'll discuss in later chapters have sequence points. Also, the end of any full expression is a sequence point.

What's a full expression? A *full expression* is one that's not a subexpression of a larger expression. Examples of full expressions include the expression in an expression statement and the expression serving as a test condition for a `while` loop.

Sequence points help clarify when postfix incrementation takes place. Consider, for instance, the following code:

```
while (guests++ < 10)
     printf("%d \n", guests);
```

Sometimes C newcomers assume that "use the value and then increment it" means, in this context, to increment `guests` after it's used in the `printf()` statement. However, the `guests++ < 10` expression is a full expression because it is a `while` loop test condition, so the end of this expression is a sequence point. Therefore, C guarantees that the side effect (incrementing `guests`) takes place before the program moves on to `printf()`. Using the postfix form, however, guarantees that `guests` will be incremented after the comparison to `10` is made.

Now consider this statement:

```
y = (4 + x++) + (6 + x++);
```

The expression `4 + x++` is not a full expression, so C does not guarantee that `x` will be incremented immediately after the subexpression `4 + x++` is evaluated. Here, the full expression is the entire assignment statement, and the semicolon marks the sequence point, so all that C guarantees is that `x` will have been incremented twice by the time the program moves to the following statement. C does not specify whether `x` is incremented after each subexpression is evaluated or only after all the expressions have been evaluated, which is why you should avoid statements of this kind.

Compound Statements (Blocks)

A *compound statement* is two or more statements grouped together by enclosing them in braces; it is also called a *block*. The `shoes2.c` program used a block to let the `while` statement encompass several statements. Compare the following program fragments:

```
/* fragment 1 */
index = 0;
while (index++ < 10)
    sam = 10 * index + 2;
printf("sam = %d\n", sam);

/* fragment 2 */
index = 0;
while (index++ < 10)
{
    sam = 10 * index + 2;
    printf("sam = %d\n", sam);
}
```

In fragment 1, only the assignment statement is included in the `while` loop. In the absence of braces, a `while` statement runs from the `while` to the next semicolon. The `printf()` function will be called just once, after the loop has been completed.

In fragment 2, the braces ensure that both statements are part of the `while` loop, and `printf()` is called each time the loop is executed. The entire compound statement is considered to be the single statement in terms of the structure of a `while` statement (see Figure 5.7).

FIGURE 5.7

A while loop with a compound statement.

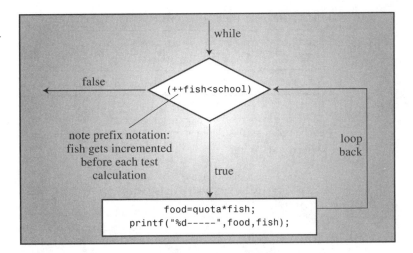

Style Tips

Look again at the two while fragments and notice how an indentation marks off the body of each loop. The indentation makes no difference to the compiler; it uses the braces and its knowledge of the structure of while loops to decide how to interpret your instructions. The indentation is there so you can see at a glance how the program is organized.

The example shows one popular style for positioning the braces for a block, or compound, statement. Another very common style is this:

```
while (index++ < 10) {
    sam = 10*index + 2;
    printf("sam = %d \n", sam);
}
```

This style highlights the attachment of the block to the while loop. The other style emphasizes that the statements form a block. Again, as far as the compiler is concerned, both forms are identical.

To sum up, use indentation as a tool to point out the structure of a program to the reader.

Summary: Expressions and Statements

Expressions:

An *expression* is a combination of operators and operands. The simplest expression is just a constant or a variable with no operator, such as 22 or beebop. More complex examples are 55 + 22 and vap = 2 * (vip + (vup = 4)).

Statements:

A *statement* is a command to the computer. There are simple statements and compound statements. *Simple statements* terminate in a semicolon, as in these examples:

Declaration statement:	`int toes;`
Assignment statement:	`toes = 12;`

Function call statement:	`printf("%d\n", toes);`
Structured statement:	`while (toes < 20)` `    toes = toes + 2;`
NULL statement:	`; /* does nothing */`

Compound statements, or *blocks*, consist of one or more statements (which themselves can be compound statements) enclosed in braces. The following `while` statement contains an example:

```
while (years < 100)
{
    wisdom = wisdom * 1.05;
    printf("%d %d\n", years, wisdom);
    years = years + 1;
}
```

Type Conversions

Statements and expressions should normally use variables and constants of just one type. If, however, you mix types, C doesn't stop dead in its tracks the way, say, Pascal does. Instead, it uses a set of rules to make type conversions automatically. This can be a convenience, but it can also be a danger, especially if you are mixing types inadvertently. (The lint program, found on many Unix systems, checks for type "clashes." Many non-Unix C compilers report possible type problems if you select a higher error level.) It is a good idea to have at least some knowledge of the type conversion rules.

The basic rules are

1. When appearing in an expression, `char` and `short`, both `signed` and `unsigned`, are automatically converted to `int` or, if necessary, to `unsigned int`. (If `short` is the same size as `int`, `unsigned short` is larger than `int`; in that case, `unsigned short` is converted to `unsigned int`.) Under K&R C, but not under current C, `float` is automatically converted to `double`. Because they are conversions to larger types, they are called *promotions*.

2. In any operation involving two types, both values are converted to the higher ranking of the two types.

3. The ranking of types, from highest to lowest, is `long double`, `double`, `float`, `unsigned long long`, `long long`, `unsigned long`, `long`, `unsigned int`, and `int`. One possible exception is when `long` and `int` are the same size, in which case `unsigned int` outranks `long`. The `short` and `char` types don't appear in this list because they would have been already promoted to `int` or perhaps `unsigned int`.

4. In an assignment statement, the final result of the calculations is converted to the type of the variable being assigned a value. This process can result in promotion, as described in rule 1, or *demotion*, in which a value is converted to a lower-ranking type.

5. When passed as function arguments, char and short are converted to int, and float is converted to double. This automatic promotion can be overridden by function prototyping, as discussed in Chapter 9, "Functions."

Promotion is usually a smooth, uneventful process, but demotion can lead to real trouble. The reason is simple: The lower-ranking type may not be big enough to hold the complete number. An 8-bit char variable can hold the integer 101 but not the integer 22334. When floating types are demoted to integer types, they are truncated, or rounded toward zero. That means 23.12 and 23.99 both are truncated to 23 and that -23.5 is truncated to -23. Listing 5.14 illustrates the working of these rules.

LISTING 5.14   The convert.c Program

```
/* convert.c -- automatic type conversions */
#include <stdio.h>
int main(void)
{
    char ch;
    int i;
    float fl;

    fl = i = ch = 'C';                                     /* line 9  */
    printf("ch = %c, i = %d, fl = %2.2f\n", ch, i, fl);   /* line 10 */
    ch = ch + 1;                                           /* line 11 */
    i = fl + 2 * ch;                                       /* line 12 */
    fl = 2.0 * ch + i;                                     /* line 13 */
    printf("ch = %c, i = %d, fl = %2.2f\n", ch, i, fl);   /* line 14 */
    ch = 5212205.17;                                       /* line 15 */
    printf("Now ch = %c\n", ch);

    return 0;
}
```

Running convert.c produces the following output:

```
ch = C, i = 67, fl = 67.00
ch = D, i = 203, fl = 339.00
Now ch = -
```

On this system, which has an 8-bit char and a 32-bit int, here is what happened:

- **Lines 9 and 10**—The character 'C' is stored as a 1-byte ASCII value in ch. The integer variable i receives the integer conversion of 'C', which is 67 stored as 4 bytes. Finally, fl receives the floating conversion of 67, which is 67.00.

- **Lines 11 and 14**—The character variable 'C' is converted to the integer 67, which is then added to the 1. The resulting 4-byte integer 68 is truncated to 1 byte and stored in ch. When printed using the %c specifier, 68 is interpreted as the ASCII code for 'D'.

- **Lines 12 and 14**—The value of ch is converted to a 4-byte integer (68) for the multiplication by 2. The resulting integer (136) is converted to floating point in order to be added to fl. The result (203.00f) is converted to int and stored in i.

- **Lines 13 and 14**—The value of ch (`'D'`, or **68**) is converted to floating point for multiplication by **2.0**. The value of i (**203**) is converted to floating point for the addition, and the result (**339.00**) is stored in fl.

- **Lines 15 and 16**—Here the example tries a case of demotion, setting ch equal to a rather large number. After truncation takes place, ch winds up with the ASCII code for the hyphen character.

The Cast Operator

You should usually steer clear of automatic type conversions, especially of demotions, but sometimes it is convenient to make conversions, provided you exercise care. The type conversions we've discussed so far are done automatically. However, it is possible for you to demand the precise type conversion that you want or else document that you know you're making a type conversion. The method for doing this is called a *cast* and consists of preceding the quantity with the name of the desired type in parentheses. The parentheses and type name together constitute a *cast operator*. This is the general form of a cast operator:

`(type)`

The actual type desired, such as **long**, is substituted for the word *type*.

Consider the next two code lines, in which mice is an int variable. The second line contains two casts to type int.

```
mice = 1.6 + 1.7;
mice = (int) 1.6 + (int) 1.7;
```

The first example uses automatic conversion. First, **1.6** and **1.7** are added to yield **3.3**. This number is then converted through truncation to the integer **3** to match the **int** variable. In the second example, **1.6** is converted to an integer (**1**) before addition, as is **1.7**, so that mice is assigned the value 1+1, or **2**. Neither form is intrinsically more correct than the other; you have to consider the context of the programming problem to see which makes more sense.

Normally, you shouldn't mix types (that is why some languages don't allow it), but there are occasions when it is useful. The C philosophy is to avoid putting barriers in your way and to give you the responsibility of not abusing that freedom.

Summary: Operating in C

Here are the operators we have discussed so far:

Assignment Operator:

=	Assigns the value at its right to the variable at its left.

Arithmetic Operators:

+	Adds the value at its right to the value at its left.
-	Subtracts the value at its right from the value at its left.

–	As a unary operator, changes the sign of the value at its right.
*	Multiplies the value at its left by the value at its right.
/	Divides the value at its left by the value at its right. The answer is truncated if both operands are integers.
%	Yields the remainder when the value at its left is divided by the value to its right (integers only).
++	Adds 1 to the value of the variable to its right (prefix mode) or to the value of the variable to its left (postfix mode).
--	Like ++, but subtracts 1.

Miscellaneous Operators:

sizeof	Yields the size, in bytes, of the operand to its right. The operand can be a type specifier in parentheses, as in sizeof (float), or it can be the name of a particular variable, array, and so forth, as in sizeof foo.
(type)	As the cast operator, converts the following value to the type specified by the enclosed keyword(s). For example, (float) 9 converts the integer 9 to the floating-point number 9.0.

Function with Arguments

By now, you're familiar with using function arguments. The next step along the road to function mastery is learning how to write your own functions that use arguments. Let's preview that skill now. (At this point, you might want to review the **butler()** function example near the end of Chapter 2, "Introducing C"; it shows how to write a function without an argument.) Listing 5.15 includes a **pound()** function that prints a specified number of pound signs (#). The example also illustrates some points about type conversion.

LISTING 5.15   The pound.c Program

```
/* pound.c -- defines a function with an argument    */
#include <stdio.h>
void pound(int n);    /* ANSI prototype               */

int main(void)
{
    int times = 5;
    char ch = '!';    /* ASCII code is 33              */
    float f = 6.0;

    pound(times);    /* int argument                 */
    pound(ch);       /* char automatically -> int    */
```

LISTING 5.15   Continued

```
        pound((int) f);  /* cast forces f -> int        */

        return 0;
}

void pound(int n)    /* ANSI-style function header  */
{                    /* says takes one int argument */
    while (n-- > 0)
        printf("#");
    printf("\n");
}
```

Running the program produces this output:

```
#####
################################
######
```

First, let's examine the function heading:

```
void pound(int n)
```

If the function took no arguments, the parentheses in the function heading would contain the keyword `void`. Because the function takes one type `int` argument, the parentheses contain a declaration of an `int` variable called n. You can use any name consistent with C's naming rules.

Declaring an argument creates a variable called the *formal argument* or the *formal parameter*. In this case, the formal parameter is the `int` variable called n. Making a function call such as `pound(10)` acts to assign the value `10` to n. In this program, the call `pound(times)` assigns the value of `times` (5) to n. We say that the function call *passes* a value, and this value is called the *actual argument* or the *actual parameter*, so the function call `pound(10)` passes the actual argument `10` to the function, where `10` is assigned to the formal parameter (the variable n). That is, the value of the `times` variable in `main()` is copied to the new variable n in `pound()`.

Arguments versus Parameters

Although the terms *argument* and *parameter* often have been used interchangeably, the C99 documentation has decided to use the term *argument* for actual argument or actual parameter and the term *parameter* for formal parameter or formal argument. With this convention, we can say that parameters are variables and that arguments are values provided by a function call and assigned to the corresponding parameters.

Variable names are private to the function. This means that a name defined in one function doesn't conflict with the same name defined elsewhere. If you used `times` instead of n in `pound()`, that would create a variable distinct from the `times` in `main()`. That is, you would have two variables with the same name, but the program keeps track of which is which.

Now let's look at the function calls. The first one is `pound(times)`, and, as we said, it causes the `times` value of 5 to be assigned to n. This causes the function to print five pound signs and a newline. The second call is **pound(ch)**. Here, **ch** is type **char**. It is initialized to the **!** character, which, on ASCII systems, means that **ch** has the numerical value 33. The automatic promotion of **char** to **int** converts this, on this system, from 33 stored in 1 byte to 33 stored in 4 bytes, so the value 33 is now in the correct form to be used as an argument to this function. The last call, **pound ((int) f)**, uses a type cast to convert the type **float** variable **f** to the proper type for this argument.

Suppose you omit the type cast. With modern C, the program will make the type cast automatically for you. That's because of the ANSI prototype near the top of the file:

```
void pound(int n);       /* ANSI prototype                    */
```

A *prototype* is a function declaration that describes a function's return value and its arguments. This prototype says two things about the **pound()** function:

- The function has no return value.

- The function takes one argument, which is a type **int** value.

Because the compiler sees this prototype before **pound()** is used in **main()**, the compiler knows what sort of argument **pound()** should have, and it inserts a type cast if one is needed to make the actual argument agree in type with the prototype. For example, the call **pound(3.859)** will be converted to **pound(3)**.

A Sample Program

Listing 5.16 is a useful program (for a narrowly defined subgrouping of humanity) that illustrates several of the ideas in this chapter. It looks long, but all the calculations are done in six lines near the end. The bulk of the program relays information between the computer and the user. We've tried using enough comments to make it nearly self-explanatory. Read through it, and when you are done, we'll clear up a few points.

LISTING 5.16   The running.c Program

```
// running.c -- A useful program for runners
#include <stdio.h>
const int S_PER_M = 60;       // seconds in a minute
const int S_PER_H = 3600;     // seconds in an hour
const double M_PER_K = 0.62137; // miles in a kilometer
int main(void)
{
    double distk, distm;  // distance run in km and in miles
    double rate;          // average speed in mph
    int min, sec;         // minutes and seconds of running time
    int time;             // running time in seconds only
    double mtime;         // time in seconds for one mile
    int mmin, msec;       // minutes and seconds for one mile

    printf("This program converts your time for a metric race\n");
    printf("to a time for running a mile and to your average\n");
```

LISTING 5.16   Continued

```
    printf("speed in miles per hour.\n");
    printf("Please enter, in kilometers, the distance run.\n");
    scanf("%lf", &distk);  // %lf for type double
    printf("Next enter the time in minutes and seconds.\n");
    printf("Begin by entering the minutes.\n");
    scanf("%d", &min);
    printf("Now enter the seconds.\n");
    scanf("%d", &sec);
// converts time to pure seconds
    time = S_PER_M * min + sec;
// converts kilometers to miles
    distm = M_PER_K * distk;
// miles per sec x sec per hour = mph
    rate = distm / time * S_PER_H;
// time/distance = time per mile
    mtime = (double) time / distm;
    mmin = (int) mtime / S_PER_M; // find whole minutes
    msec = (int) mtime % S_PER_M; // find remaining seconds
    printf("You ran %1.2f km (%1.2f miles) in %d min, %d sec.\n",
        distk, distm, min, sec);
    printf("That pace corresponds to running a mile in %d min, ",
        mmin);
    printf("%d sec.\nYour average speed was %1.2f mph.\n",msec,
        rate);

    return 0;
}
```

Listing 5.16 uses the same approach used earlier in min_sec to convert the final time to minutes and seconds, but it also makes type conversions. Why? Because you need integer arguments for the seconds-to-minutes part of the program, but the metric-to-mile conversion involves floating-point numbers. We have used the cast operator to make these conversions explicit.

To tell the truth, it should be possible to write the program using just automatic conversions. In fact, we did so, using mtime of type int to force the time calculation to be converted to integer form. However, that version failed to run on one of the 11 systems we tried. That compiler (an ancient and obsolete version) failed to follow the C rules. Using type casts makes your intent clearer not only to the reader, but perhaps to the compiler as well.

Here's some sample output:

```
This program converts your time for a metric race
to a time for running a mile and to your average
speed in miles per hour.
Please enter, in kilometers, the distance run.
10.0
Next enter the time in minutes and seconds.
Begin by entering the minutes.
36
Now enter the seconds.
23
```

```
You ran 10.00 km (6.21 miles) in 36 min, 23 sec.
That pace corresponds to running a mile in 5 min, 51 sec.
Your average speed was 10.25 mph.
```

Key Concepts

C uses operators to provide a variety of services. Each operator can be characterized by the number of operands it requires, its precedence, and its associativity. The last two qualities determine which operator is applied first when the two share an operand. Operators are combined with values to produce expressions, and every C expression has a value. If you are not aware of operator precedence and associativity, you may construct expressions that are illegal or that have values different from what you intend; that would not enhance your reputation as a programmer.

C allows you to write expressions combining different numerical types. But arithmetic operations require operands to be of the same type, so C makes automatic conversions. However, it's good programming practice not to rely upon automatic conversions. Instead, make your choice of types explicit either by choosing variables of the correct type or by using typecasts. That way, you won't fall prey to automatic conversions that you did not expect.

Summary

C has many operators, such as the assignment and arithmetic operators discussed in this chapter. In general, an *operator* operates on one or more operands to produce a value. Operators that take one operand, such as the minus sign and `sizeof`, are termed *unary operators*. Operators requiring two operands, such as the addition and the multiplication operators, are called *binary operators*.

Expressions are combinations of operators and operands. In C, every expression has a value, including assignment expressions and comparison expressions. Rules of *operator precedence* help determine how terms are grouped when expressions are evaluated. When two operators share an operand, the one of higher precedence is applied first. If the operators have equal precedence, the associativity (left-right or right-left) determines which operator is applied first.

Statements are complete instructions to the computer and are indicated in C by a terminating semicolon. So far, you have worked with declaration statements, assignment statements, function call statements, and control statements. Statements included within a pair of braces constitute a *compound statement*, or *block*. One particular control statement is the `while` loop, which repeats statements as long as a test condition remains true.

In C, many *type conversions* take place automatically. The `char` and `short` types are promoted to type `int` whenever they appear in expressions or as function arguments. The `float` type is promoted to type `double` when used as a function argument. Under K&R C (but not ANSI C), `float` is also promoted to `double` when used in an expression. When a value of one type is assigned to a variable of a second type, the value is converted to the same type as the variable.

When larger types are converted to smaller types (`long` to `short` or `double` to `float`, for example), there might be a loss of data. In cases of mixed arithmetic, smaller types are converted to larger types following the rules outlined in this chapter.

When you define a function that takes an argument, you declare a *variable*, or *formal argument*, in the function definition. Then the value passed in a function call is assigned to this variable, which can now be used in the function.

Review Questions

1. Assume all variables are of type `int`. Find the value of each of the following variables:

   a. `x = (2 + 3) * 6;`

   b. `x = (12 + 6)/2*3;`

   c. `y = x = (2 + 3)/4;`

   d. `y = 3 + 2*(x = 7/2);`

2. Assume all variables are of type `int`. Find the value of each of the following variables:

   a. `x = (int) 3.8 + 3.3;`

   b. `x = (2 + 3) * 10.5;`

   c. `x = 3 / 5 * 22.0;`

   d. `x = 22.0 * 3 / 5;`

3. You suspect that there are some errors in the next program. Can you find them?

```
int main(void)
{
  int i = 1,
  float n;
  printf("Watch out! Here come a bunch of fractions!\n");
  while (i < 30)
    n = 1/i;
    printf(" %f", n);
  printf("That's all, folks!\n");
  return;
}
```

4. Here's an alternative design for Listing 5.9. It appears to simplify the code by replacing the two `scanf()` statements in Listing 5.9 with a single `scanf()` statement. What makes this design inferior to the original?

```
#include <stdio.h>
#define S_TO_M 60
int main(void)
{
  int sec, min, left;
```

```
   printf("This program converts seconds to minutes and ");
   printf("seconds.\n");
   printf("Just enter the number of seconds.\n");
   printf("Enter 0 to end the program.\n");
   while (sec > 0) {
     scanf("%d", &sec);
     min = sec/S_TO_M;
     left = sec % S_TO_M;
     printf("%d sec is %d min, %d sec. \n", sec, min, left);
     printf("Next input?\n");
     }
   printf("Bye!\n");
   return 0;
}
```

5. What will this program print?

```
#include <stdio.h>
#define FORMAT "%s! C is cool!\n"
int main(void)
{
      int num = 10;

      printf(FORMAT,FORMAT);
      printf("%d\n", ++num);
      printf("%d\n", num++);
      printf("%d\n", num--);
      printf("%d\n", num);
      return 0;
}
```

6. What will the following program print?

```
#include <stdio.h>
int main(void)
{
      char c1, c2;
      int diff;
      float num;

      c1 = 'S';
      c2 = 'O';
      diff = c1 - c2;
      num = diff;
      printf("%c%c%c:%d %3.2f\n", c1, c2, c1, diff, num);
      return 0;
}
```

7. What will this program print?

```
#include <stdio.h>
#define TEN 10
int main(void)
{
      int n = 0;
```

```
        while (n++ < TEN)
            printf("%5d", n);
        printf("\n");
        return 0;
    }
```

8. Modify the last program so that it prints the letters *a* through *g* instead.

9. If the following fragments were part of a complete program, what would they print?

    a.

    ```
    int x = 0;
    while (++x < 3)
        printf("%4d", x);
    ```

    b.

    ```
    int x = 100;

    while (x++ < 103)
        printf("%4d\n",x);
        printf("%4d\n",x);
    ```

    c.

    ```
    char ch = 's';

    while (ch < 'w')
    {
        printf("%c", ch);
        ch++;
    }
    printf("%c\n",ch);
    ```

10. What will the following program print?

    ```
    #define MESG "COMPUTER BYTES DOG"
    #include <stdio.h>
    int main(void)
    {
        int n = 0;

        while ( n < 5 )
            printf("%s\n", MESG);
            n++;
        printf("That's all.\n");
        return 0;
    }
    ```

11. Construct statements that do the following (or, in other terms, have the following side effects):

    a. Increase the variable x by `10`.

    b. Increase the variable x by `1`.

    c. Assign twice the sum of a and b to c.

    d. Assign a plus twice b to c.

12. Construct statements that do the following:

    a. Decrease the variable x by `1`.

    b. Assigns to m the remainder of n divided by k.

    c. Divide q by b minus a and assign the result to p.

    d. Assign to x the result of dividing the sum of a and b by the product of c and d.

Programming Exercises

1. Write a program that converts time in minutes to time in hours and minutes. Use `#define` or `const` to create a symbolic constant for 60. Use a `while` loop to allow the user to enter values repeatedly and terminate the loop if a value for the time of 0 or less is entered.

2. Write a program that asks for an integer and then prints all the integers from (and including) that value up to (and including) a value larger by 10. (That is, if the input is 5, the output runs from 5 to 15.) Be sure to separate each output value by a space or tab or newline.

3. Write a program that asks the user to enter the number of days and then converts that value to weeks and days. For example, it would convert 18 days to 2 weeks, 4 days. Display results in the following format:

   ```
   18 days are 2 weeks, 4 days.
   ```

   Use a `while` loop to allow the user to repeatedly enter day values; terminate the loop when the user enters a nonpositive value, such as `0` or `-20`.

4. Write a program that asks the user to enter a height in centimeters and then displays the height in centimeters and in feet and inches. Fractional centimeters and inches should be allowed, and the program should allow the user to continue entering heights until a nonpositive value is entered. A sample run should look like this:

   ```
   Enter a height in centimeters: 182
   182.0 cm = 5 feet, 11.7 inches
   Enter a height in centimeters (<=0 to quit): 168
   168.0 cm = 5 feet, 6.1 inches
   Enter a height in centimeters (<=0 to quit): 0
   bye
   ```

5. Change the program `addemup.c` (Listing 5.13), which found the sum of the first 20 integers. (If you prefer, you can think of `addemup.c` as a program that calculates how much money you get in 20 days if you receive $1 the first day, $2 the second day, $3 the third day, and so on.) Modify the program so that you can tell it interactively how far the calculation should proceed. That is, replace the **20** with a variable that is read in.

6. Now modify the program of Programming Exercise 5 so that it computes the sum of the squares of the integers. (If you prefer, how much money you receive if you get $1 the first day, $4 the second day, $9 the third day, and so on. This looks like a much better deal!) C doesn't have a squaring function, but you can use the fact that the square of **n** is **n * n**.

7. Write a program that requests a type `float` number and prints the value of the number cubed. Use a function of your own design to cube the value and print it. The `main()` program should pass the entered value to this function.

8. Write a program that requests the user to enter a Fahrenheit temperature. The program should read the temperature as a type `double` number and pass it as an argument to a user-supplied function called `Temperatures()`. This function should calculate the Celsius equivalent and the Kelvin equivalent and display all three temperatures with a precision of two places to the right of the decimal. It should identify each value with the temperature scale it represents. Here is the formula for converting Fahrenheit to Celsius:

    Fahrenheit = 1.8 * Celsius + 32.0

    The Kelvin scale, commonly used in science, is a scale in which 0 represents absolute zero, the lower limit to possible temperatures. Here is the formula for converting Celsius to Kelvin:

    Kelvin = Celsius + 273.16

    The `Temperatures()` function should use `const` to create symbolic representations of the three constants that appear in the conversions. The `main()` function should use a loop to allow the user to enter temperatures repeatedly, stopping when a `q` or other non-numeric value is entered.

CHAPTER 6

C CONTROL STATEMENTS: LOOPING

You will learn about the following in this chapter:

- Keywords:
  for
  while
  do while

- Operators:
  < > >=
  <= != == +=
  *= -= /= %=

- Functions:
  fabs()

- C's three loop structures—while, for, and do while

- Using relational operators to construct expressions to control these loops

- Several other operators

- Arrays, which are often used with loops

- Writing functions that have return values

Powerful, intelligent, versatile, and useful! Most of us wouldn't mind being described that way. With C, there's at least the chance of having our programs described that way. The trick is controlling the flow of a program. According to computer science (which is the science of computers and not science by computers…yet), a good language should provide these three forms of program flow:

- Executing a sequence of statements

- Repeating a sequence of statements until some condition is met (looping)

- Using a test to decide between alternative sequences (branching)

The first form you know well; all the previous programs have consisted of a sequence of statements. The while loop is one example of the second form. This chapter takes a closer look at the while loop along with two other loop structures—for and do while. The final form, choosing between different possible courses of action, makes a program much more "intelligent" and increases the usefulness of a computer enormously. Sadly, you'll have to wait a chapter before being entrusted with such power. The chapter also introduces arrays because they give you something to do with your new knowledge of loops. In addition, the chapter continues your education about functions. Let's begin by reviewing the while loop.

Revisiting the while Loop

You are already somewhat familiar with the while loop, but let's review it with a program that sums integers entered from the keyboard (see Listing 6.1). This example makes use of the return value of scanf() to terminate input.

LISTING 6.1   The summing.c Program

```c
/* summing.c -- sums integers entered interactively */
#include <stdio.h>
int main(void)
{
    long num;
    long sum = 0L;      /* initialize sum to zero    */
    int status;

    printf("Please enter an integer to be summed ");
    printf("(q to quit): ");
    status = scanf("%ld", &num);
    while (status == 1) /* == means "is equal to"    */
    {
        sum = sum + num;
        printf("Please enter next integer (q to quit): ");
        status = scanf("%ld", &num);
    }
    printf("Those integers sum to %ld.\n", sum);

    return 0;
}
```

Listing 6.1 uses type long to allow for larger numbers. For consistency, the program initializes sum to 0L (type long zero) rather than to 0 (type int zero), even though C's automatic conversions enable you to use a plain 0.

Here is a sample run:

```
Please enter an integer to be summed (q to quit): 44
Please enter next integer (q to quit): 33
Please enter next integer (q to quit): 88
Please enter next integer (q to quit): 121
Please enter next integer (q to quit): q
Those integers sum to 286.
```

Program Comments

Let's look at the while loop first. The test condition for this loop is the following expression:

```
status == 1
```

The == operator is C's *equality operator*; that is, this expression tests whether status is equal to 1. Don't confuse it with status = 1, which assigns 1 to status. With the status == 1 test condition, the loop repeats as long as status is 1. For each cycle, the loop adds the current value of num to sum, so that sum maintains a running total. When status gets a value other than 1, the loop terminates, and the program reports the final value of sum.

For the program to work properly, it should get a new value for num on each loop cycle, and it should reset status on each cycle. The program accomplishes this by using two distinct features of scanf(). First, it uses scanf() to attempt to read a new value for num. Second, it uses the scanf() return value to report on the success of that attempt. Recall from Chapter 4, "Character Strings and Formatted Input/Output," that scanf() returns the number of items successfully read. If scanf() succeeds in reading an integer, it places the integer into num and returns the value 1, which is assigned to status. (Note that the input value goes to num, not to status.) This updates both num and the value of status, and the while loop goes through another cycle. If you respond with nonnumeric input, such as q, scanf() fails to find an integer to read, so its return value and status will be 0. That terminates the loop. The input character q, because it isn't a number, is placed back into the input queue; it does not get read. (Actually, any nonnumeric input, not just q, terminates the loop, but asking the user to enter q is a simpler instruction than asking the user to enter nonnumeric input.)

If scanf() runs into a problem before attempting to convert the value (for example, by detecting the end of the file or by encountering a hardware problem), it returns the special value EOF, which typically is defined as -1. This value, too, will cause the loop to terminate.

This dual use of scanf() gets around a troublesome aspect of interactive input to a loop: How do you tell the loop when to stop? Suppose, for instance, that scanf() did not have a return value. Then, the only thing that would change on each loop is the value of num. You could use the value of num to terminate the loop, using, say, num > 0 (num greater than 0) or num != 0 (num not equal to 0) as a test condition, but this prevents you from entering certain values, such as –3 or 0, as input. Instead, you could add new code to the loop, such as asking "Do you wish to continue? <y/n>" at each cycle, and then test to see whether the user entered y. This is a bit clunky and slows down input. Using the return value of scanf() avoids these problems.

Now let's take a closer look at the program structure. You can summarize it as follows:

```
initialize sum to 0
prompt user
read input
while the input is an integer,
    add the input to sum,
    prompt user,
    then read next input
after input completes, print sum
```

This, incidentally, is an example of *pseudocode*, which is the art of expressing a program in simple English that parallels the forms of a computer language. Pseudocode is useful for working out the logic of a program. After the logic seems right, you can translate the pseudocode to the actual programming code. One advantage of pseudocode is that it enables you to concentrate on the logic and organization of a program and spares you from simultaneously worrying about how to express the ideas in a computer language. Here, for example, you can use indentation to indicate a block of code and not worry about C syntax requiring braces. Another advantage is that pseudocode is not tied to a particular language, so the same pseudocode can be translated into different computer languages.

Anyway, because the `while` loop is an entry-condition loop, the program must get the input and check the value of **status** *before* it goes to the body of the loop. That is why the program has a `scanf()` before the `while`. For the loop to continue, you need a read statement inside the loop so that it can find out the status of the next input. That is why the program also has a `scanf()` statement at the end of the `while` loop; it readies the loop for its next iteration. You can think of the following as a standard format for a loop:

```
get first value to be tested
while the test is successful
    process value
    get next value
```

C-Style Reading Loop

Listing 6.1 could be written in Pascal, BASIC, or FORTRAN along the same design displayed in the pseudocode. C, however, offers a shortcut. The construction

```
status = scanf("%ld", &num);
while (status == 1)
{
        /* loop actions */
        status = scanf("%ld", &num);
}
```

can be replaced by the following:

```
while (scanf("%ld", &num) == 1)
{
        /* loop actions */
}
```

The second form uses `scanf()` in two different ways simultaneously. First, the function call, if successful, places a value in **num**. Second, the function's return value (which is **1** or **0** and not the value of **num**) controls the loop. Because the loop condition is tested at each iteration, `scanf()` is called at each iteration, providing a new **num** and a new test. In other words, C's syntax features let you replace the standard loop format with the following condensed version:

```
while getting and testing the value succeeds
    process the value
```

Now let's take a more formal look at the `while` statement.

The `while` Statement

This is the general form of the `while` loop:

```
while (expression)
    statement
```

The *statement* part can be a simple statement with a terminating semicolon, or it can be a compound statement enclosed in braces.

So far, the examples have used relational expressions for the expression part; that is, *expression* has been a comparison of values. More generally, you can use any expression. If *expression* is true (or, more generally, nonzero), the statement is executed once and then the expression is tested again. This cycle of test and execution is repeated until *expression* becomes false (zero). Each cycle is called an *iteration* (see Figure 6.1).

FIGURE 6.1
Structure of the `while` loop.

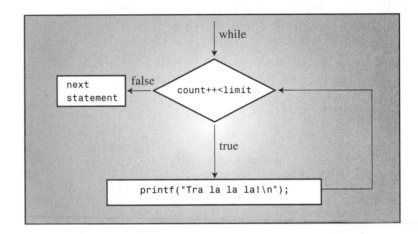

Terminating a `while` Loop

Here is a *crucial* point about `while` loops: When you construct a `while` loop, it must include something that changes the value of the test expression so that the expression eventually becomes false. Otherwise, the loop never terminates. (Actually, you can use `break` and an `if` statement to terminate a loop, but you haven't learned about them yet.) Consider this example:

```
index = 1;
while (index < 5)
    printf("Good morning!\n");
```

The preceding fragment prints its cheerful message indefinitely. Why? Because nothing within the loop changes the value of `index` from its initial value of `1`. Now consider this:

```
index = 1;
while (--index < 5)
    printf("Good morning!\n");
```

This last fragment isn't much better. It changes the value of `index`, but in the wrong direction! At least this version will terminate eventually when `index` drops below the most negative number that the system can handle and becomes the largest possible positive value. (The `toobig.c` program in Chapter 3, "Data and C," illustrates how adding 1 to the largest positive number typically produces a negative number; similarly, subtracting 1 from the most negative number typically yields a positive value.)

When a Loop Terminates

It is important to realize that the decision to terminate the loop or to continue takes place only when the test condition is evaluated. For example, consider the program shown in Listing 6.2.

LISTING 6.2   The when.c Program

```
// when.c -- when a loop quits
#include <stdio.h>
int main(void)
{
    int n = 5;

    while (n < 7)                       // line 7
    {
        printf("n = %d\n", n);
        n++;                            // line 10
        printf("Now n = %d\n", n);      // line 11
    }
    printf("The loop has finished.\n");

    return 0;
}
```

Running Listing 6.2 produces the following output:

```
n = 5
Now n = 6
n = 6
Now n = 7
The loop has finished.
```

The variable n first acquires the value 7 on line 10 during the second cycle of the loop. However, the program doesn't quit then. Instead, it completes the loop (line 11) and quits the loop only when the test condition on line 7 is evaluated for the third time. (The variable n was 5 for the first test and 6 for the second test.)

while: An Entry-Condition Loop

The while loop is a *conditional* loop using an entry condition. It is called "conditional" because the execution of the statement portion depends on the condition described by the test expression, such as (index < 5). The expression is an *entry condition* because the condition must be met before the body of the loop is entered. In a situation such as the following, the body of the loop is never entered because the condition is false to begin with:

```
index = 10;
while (index++ < 5)
    printf("Have a fair day or better.\n");
```

Change the first line to

```
index = 3;
```

and the loop will execute.

Syntax Points

One point to keep in mind when using `while` is that only the single statement, simple or compound, following the test condition is part of the loop. Indentation is an aid to the reader, not the computer. Listing 6.3 shows what can happen if you forget this.

LISTING 6.3   The `while1.c` Program

```
/* while1.c -- watch your braces       */
/* bad coding creates an infinite loop */
#include <stdio.h>
int main(void)
{
    int n = 0;

    while (n < 3)
        printf("n is %d\n", n);
        n++;
    printf("That's all this program does\n");

    return 0;
}
```

Listing 6.3 produces the following output:

```
n is 0
n is 0
n is 0
n is 0
n is 0
```

(...and so on, until you kill the program.)

Although this example indents the `n++;` statement, it doesn't enclose it and the preceding statement within braces. Therefore, only the single print statement immediately following the test condition is part of the loop. The variable n is never updated, the condition n < 3 remains eternally true, and you get a loop that goes on printing `n is 0` until you kill the program. This is an example of an *infinite loop*, one that does not quit without outside intervention.

Always remember that the `while` statement itself, even if it uses compound statements, counts syntactically as a single statement. The statement runs from the `while` to the first semicolon or, in the case of using a compound statement, to the terminating brace.

Be careful where you place your semicolons. For instance, consider the program in Listing 6.4.

LISTING 6.4   The `while2.c` Program

```
/* while2.c -- watch your semicolons */
#include <stdio.h>
int main(void)
{
    int n = 0;

    while (n++ < 3);               /* line 7 */
        printf("n is %d\n", n);    /* line 8 */
    printf("That's all this program does.\n");

    return 0;
}
```

Listing 6.4 produces the following output:

```
n is 4
That's all this program does.
```

As we said earlier, the loop ends with the first statement, simple or compound, following the test condition. Because there is a semicolon immediately after the test condition on line 7, the loop ends there, because a lone semicolon counts as a statement. The print statement on line 8 is not part of the loop, so n is incremented on each loop, but it is printed only after the loop is exited.

In this example, the test condition is followed with the *null statement*, one that does nothing. In C, the lone semicolon represents the null statement. Occasionally, programmers intentionally use the `while` statement with a null statement because all the work gets done in the test. For example, suppose you want to skip over input to the first character that isn't whitespace or a digit. You can use a loop like this:

```
while (scanf("%d", &num) == 1)
    ;    /* skip integer input */
```

As long as `scanf()` reads an integer, it returns 1, and the loop continues. Note that, for clarity, you put the semicolon (the null statement) on the line below instead of on the same line. This makes it easier to see the null statement when you read a program and also reminds you that the null statement is there deliberately. Even better, use the `continue` statement discussed in the next chapter.

Which Is Bigger: Using Relational Operators and Expressions

Because `while` loops often rely on test expressions that make comparisons, comparison expressions merit a closer look. Such expressions are termed *relational expressions*, and the operators that appear in them are called *relational operators*. You have used several already, and Table 6.1 gives a complete list of C relational operators. This table pretty much covers all the possibilities for numerical relationships. (Numbers, even complex ones, are less complex than humans.)

TABLE 6.1   Relational Operators

Operator	Meaning
<	Is less than
<=	Is less than or equal to
==	Is equal to
>=	Is greater than or equal to
>	Is greater than
!=	Is not equal to

The relational operators are used to form the relational expressions used in `while` statements and in other C statements that we'll discuss later. These statements check to see whether the expression is true or false. Here are three unrelated statements containing examples of relational expressions. The meaning, we hope, is clear.

```c
while (number < 6)
{
    printf("Your number is too small.\n");
    scanf("%d", &number);
}

while (ch != '$')
{
    count++;
    scanf("%c", &ch);
}

while (scanf("%f", &num) == 1)
    sum = sum + num;
```

Note in the second example that the relational expressions can be used with characters, too. The machine character code (which we have been assuming is ASCII) is used for the comparison. However, you can't use the relational operators to compare strings. Chapter 11, "Character Strings and String Functions," will show you what to use for strings.

The relational operators can be used with floating-point numbers, too. Beware, though: You should limit yourself to using only < and > in floating-point comparisons. The reason is that round-off errors can prevent two numbers from being equal, even though logically they should be. For example, certainly the product of 3 and 1/3 is 1.0. If you express 1/3 as a six-place decimal fraction, however, the product is .999999, which is not quite equal to 1. The `fabs()` function, declared in the `math.h` header file, can be handy for floating-point tests. This function returns the absolute value of a floating-point value—that is, the value without the algebraic sign. For example, you could test whether a number is close to a desired result with something like Listing 6.5.

LISTING 6.5   The `cmpflt.c` Program

```
// cmpflt.c -- floating-point comparisons
#include <math.h>
#include <stdio.h>
int main(void)
{
    const double ANSWER = 3.14159;
    double response;

    printf("What is the value of pi?\n");
    scanf("%lf", &response);
    while (fabs(response - ANSWER) > 0.0001)
    {
        printf("Try again!\n");
        scanf("%lf", &response);
    }
    printf("Close enough!\n");

    return 0;
}
```

This loop continues to elicit a response until the user gets within 0.0001 of the correct value:

```
What is the value of pi?
3.14
Try again!
3.1416
Close enough!
```

Each relational expression is judged to be true or false (but never maybe). This raises an interesting question.

What Is Truth?

You can answer this age-old question, at least as far as C is concerned. Recall that an expression in C always has a value. This is true even for relational expressions, as the example in Listing 6.6 shows. In it, you print the values of two relational expressions—one true and one false.

LISTING 6.6   The `t_and_f.c` Program

```
/* t_and_f.c -- true and false values in C */
#include <stdio.h>
int main(void)
{
    int true_val, false_val;

    true_val = (10 > 2);    /* value of a true relationship  */
    false_val = (10 == 2);  /* value of a false relationship */
    printf("true = %d; false = %d \n", true_val, false_val);

    return 0;
}
```

Listing 6.6 assigns the values of two relational expressions to two variables. Being straightforward, it assigns `true_val` the value of a true expression, and `false_val` the value of a false expression. Running the program produces the following simple output:

```
true = 1; false = 0
```

Aha! For C, a true expression has the value 1, and a false expression has the value 0. Indeed, some C programs use the following construction for loops that are meant to run forever because 1 always is true:

```
while (1)
{
    ...
}
```

What Else Is True?

If you can use a 1 or a 0 as a `while` statement test expression, can you use other numbers? If so, what happens? Let's experiment by trying the program in Listing 6.7.

LISTING 6.7   The `truth.c` Program

```
// truth.c -- what values are true?
#include <stdio.h>
int main(void)
{
    int n = 3;

    while (n)
        printf("%2d is true\n", n--);
    printf("%2d is false\n", n);

    n = -3;
    while (n)
        printf("%2d is true\n", n++);
    printf("%2d is false\n", n);

    return 0;
}
```

Here are the results:

```
 3 is true
 2 is true
 1 is true
 0 is false
-3 is true
-2 is true
-1 is true
 0 is false
```

The first loop executes when n is 3, 2, and 1, but terminates when n is 0. Similarly, the second loop executes when n is -3, -2, and -1, but terminates when n is 0. More generally, *all* nonzero values are regarded as true, and only 0 is recognized as false. C has a very tolerant notion of truth!

Alternatively, you can say that a while loop executes as long as its test condition evaluates to nonzero. This puts test conditions on a numeric basis instead of a true/false basis. Keep in mind that relational expressions evaluate to 1 if true and to 0 if false, so such expressions really are numeric.

Many C programmers make use of this property of test conditions. For example, the phrase while (goats != 0) can be replaced by while (goats) because the expression (goats != 0) and the expression (goats) both become 0, or false, only when goats has the value 0. The first form probably is clearer to those just learning the language, but the second form is the idiom most often used by C programmers. You should try to become sufficiently familiar with the while (goats) form so that it seems natural to you.

Troubles with Truth

C's tolerant notion of truth can lead to trouble. For example, let's make one subtle change to the program from Listing 6.1, producing the program shown in Listing 6.8.

LISTING 6.8   The trouble.c Program

```
// trouble.c -- misuse of =
// will cause infinite loop
#include <stdio.h>
int main(void)
{
    long num;
    long sum = 0L;
    int status;

    printf("Please enter an integer to be summed ");
    printf("(q to quit): ");
    status = scanf("%ld", &num);
    while (status = 1)
    {
        sum = sum + num;
        printf("Please enter next integer (q to quit): ");
        status = scanf("%ld", &num);
    }
    printf("Those integers sum to %ld.\n", sum);

    return 0;
}
```

Listing 6.8 produces output like the following:

```
Please enter an integer to be summed (q to quit): 20
Please enter next integer (q to quit): 5
```

```
Please enter next integer (q to quit): 30
Please enter next integer (q to quit): q
Please enter next integer (q to quit):
Please enter next integer (q to quit):
Please enter next integer (q to quit):
Please enter next integer (q to quit):
```

(…and so on until you kill the program—so perhaps you shouldn't actually try running this example.)

This troublesome example made a change in the `while` test condition, replacing `status == 1` with `status = 1`. The second statement is an assignment statement, so it gives `status` the value `1`. Furthermore, the value of an assignment statement is the value of the left side, so `status = 1` has the same numerical value of `1`. So for all practical purposes, the `while` loop is the same as using `while (1)`; that is, it is a loop that never quits. You enter q, and `status` is set to `0`, but the loop test resets `status` to `1` and starts another cycle.

You might wonder why, because the program keeps looping, the user doesn't get a chance to type in any more input after entering q. When `scanf()` fails to read the specified form of input, it leaves the nonconforming input in place to be read the next time. When `scanf()` tries to read the q as an integer and fails, it leaves the q there. During the next loop cycle, `scanf()` attempts to read where it left off the last time—at the q. Once again, `scanf()` fails to read the q as an integer, so not only does this example set up an infinite loop, it also creates a loop of infinite failure, a daunting concept. It is fortunate that computers, as yet, lack feelings. Following stupid instructions eternally is no better or worse to a computer than successfully predicting the stock market for the next 10 years.

Don't use = for ==. Some computer languages (BASIC, for example) do use the same symbol for both the assignment operator and the relational equality operator, but the two operations are quite different (see Figure 6.2). The assignment operator assigns a value to the left variable. The relational equality operator, however, checks to see whether the left and right sides are already equal. It doesn't change the value of the left-hand variable, if one is present. Here's an example:

```
canoes = 5        ←Assigns the value 5 to canoes

canoes == 5       ←Checks to see whether canoes has the value 5
```

Be careful about using the correct operator. A compiler will let you use the wrong form, yielding results other than what you expect. (However, so many people have misused = so often that most compilers today will issue a warning to the effect that perhaps you didn't mean to use this.) If one of the values being compared is a constant, you can put it on the left side of the comparison to help catch errors:

```
5 = canoes        ←syntax error

5 == canoes       ←Checks to see whether canoes has the value 5
```

The point is that it is illegal to assign to a constant, so the compiler will tag the use of the assignment operator as a syntax error. Many practitioners put the constant first when constructing expressions that test for equality.

FIGURE 6.2
The relational operator ==
and the assignment
operator =.

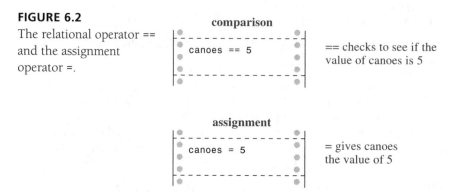

To sum up, the relational operators are used to form relational expressions. Relational expressions have the value 1 if true and 0 if false. Statements (such as `while` and `if`) that normally use relational expressions as tests can use any expression as a test, with nonzero values recognized as "true" and zero values as "false."

The New `_Bool` Type

Variables intended to represent true/false values traditionally have been represented by type `int` in C. C99 adds the `_Bool` type specifically for variables of this sort. The type is named after George Boole, the English mathematician who developed a system of algebra to represent and solve problems in logic. In programming, variables representing true or false have come to be known as *Boolean variables*, so `_Bool` is the C type name for a Boolean variable. A `_Bool` variable can only have a value of 1 (true) or 0 (false). If you try to assign a nonzero numeric value to a `_Bool` variable, the variable is set to 1, reflecting that C considers any nonzero value to be true.

Listing 6.9 fixes the test condition in Listing 6.8 and replaces the `int` variable `status` with the `_Bool` variable `input_is_good`. It's a common practice to give Boolean variables names that suggest true or false values.

LISTING 6.9   The `boolean.c` Program

```
// boolean.c -- using a _Bool variable
#include <stdio.h>
int main(void)
{
    long num;
    long sum = 0L;
    _Bool input_is_good;
```

LISTING 6.9   Continued

```
    printf("Please enter an integer to be summed ");
    printf("(q to quit): ");
    input_is_good = (scanf("%ld", &num) == 1);
    while (input_is_good)
    {
        sum = sum + num;
        printf("Please enter next integer (q to quit): ");
        input_is_good = (scanf("%ld", &num) == 1);
    }
    printf("Those integers sum to %ld.\n", sum);

    return 0;
}
```

Note how the code assigns the result of a comparison to the variable:

```
input_is_good = (scanf("%ld", &num) == 1);
```

This makes sense, because the == operator returns either a value of 1 or 0. Incidentally, the parentheses enclosing the == expression are not needed because the == operator has higher precedence than =; however, they may make the code easier to read. Also note how the choice of name for the variable makes the while loop test easy to understand:

```
while (input_is_good)
```

C99 also provides for a stdbool.h header file. This header file makes bool an alias for _Bool and defines true and false as symbolic constants for the values 1 and 0. Including this header file allows you to write code that is compatible with C++, which defines bool, true, and false as keywords.

If your system does not yet support the _Bool type, you can replace _Bool with int, and the example will work the same.

Precedence of Relational Operators

The precedence of the relational operators is less than that of the arithmetic operators, including + and -, and greater than that of assignment operators. This means, for example, that

```
x > y + 2
```

means the same as

```
x > (y + 2)
```

It also means that

```
x = y > 2
```

means

```
x = (y > 2)
```

In other words, x is assigned 1 if y is greater than 2 and is 0 otherwise; x is not assigned the value of y.

The relational operators have a greater precedence than the assignment operator. Therefore,

```
x_bigger = x > y;
```

means

```
x_bigger = (x > y);
```

The relational operators are themselves organized into two different precedences.

Higher precedence group: <   <=   >   >=

Lower precedence group: ==   !=

Like most other operators, the relational operators associate from left to right. Therefore,

```
ex != wye == zee
```

is the same as

```
(ex != wye) == zee
```

First, C checks to see whether **ex** and **wye** are unequal. Then, the resulting value of **1** or **0** (true or false) is compared to the value of **zee**. We don't anticipate using this sort of construction, but we feel it is our duty to point out such sidelights.

Table 6.2 shows the priorities of the operators introduced so far, and Reference Section II, "C Operators," has a complete precedence ranking of all operators.

TABLE 6.2   Operator Precedence

Operators (From High to Low Precedence)	Associativity
( )	L–R
- + ++ -- sizeof (*type*) (all unary)	R–L
* / %	L–R
+ -	L–R
< > <= >=	L–R
== !=	L–R
=	R–L

Summary: The while Statement

Keyword:

while

General Comments:

The while statement creates a loop that repeats until the test expression becomes false, or zero. The while statement is an entry-condition loop; that is, the decision to go through one more pass of the loop is made before the loop is traversed. Therefore, it is possible that the loop is never traversed. The statement part of the form can be a simple statement or a compound statement.

Form:

```
while (expression)
      statement
```

The *statement* portion is repeated until the *expression* becomes false or 0.

Examples:

```
while (n++ < 100)
   printf(" %d %d\n",n, 2 * n + 1); /* single statement */

while (fargo < 1000)
{                               /* compound statement */
   fargo = fargo + step;
   step = 2 * step;
}
```

Summary: Relational Operators and Expressions

Relational Operators:

Each relational operator compares the value at its left to the value at its right.

<	Is less than
<=	Is less than or equal to
==	Is equal to
>=	Is greater than or equal to
>	Is greater than
!=	Is unequal to

Relational Expressions:

A simple relational expression consists of a relational operator with an operand on each side. If the relation is true, the relational expression has the value 1. If the relation is false, the relational expression has the value 0.

Examples:

5 > 2 is true and has the value 1.

(2 + a) == a is false and has the value 0.

Indefinite Loops and Counting Loops

Some of the `while` loop examples have been *indefinite* loops. That means you don't know in advance how many times the loop will be executed before the expression becomes false. For example, when Listing 6.1 used an interactive loop to sum integers, you didn't know before-hand how many integers would be entered. Other examples, however, have been *counting* loops. They execute a predetermined number of repetitions. Listing 6.10 is a short example of a `while` counting loop.

LISTING 6.10   The `sweetie1.c` Program

```
// sweetie1.c -- a counting loop
#include <stdio.h>
int main(void)
{
    const int NUMBER = 22;
    int count = 1;                      // initialization

    while (count <= NUMBER)             // test
    {
        printf("Be my Valentine!\n");   // action
        count++;                        // update count
    }

    return 0;
}
```

Although the form used in Listing 6.10 works fine, it is not the best choice for this situation because the actions defining the loop are not all gathered together. Let's elaborate on that point.

Three actions are involved in setting up a loop that is to be repeated a fixed number of times:

1. A counter must be initialized.

2. The counter is compared with some limiting value.

3. The counter is incremented each time the loop is traversed.

The `while` loop condition takes care of the comparison. The increment operator takes care of the incrementing. In Listing 6.10, the incrementing is done at the end of the loop. This choice makes it possible to omit the incrementing accidentally. So it would be better to combine the test and update actions into one expression by using `count++ <= NUMBER`, but the initializa-tion of the counter is still done outside the loop, making it possible to forget to initialize a counter. Experience teaches us that what might happen *will* happen eventually, so let's look at a control statement that avoids these problems.

The `for` Loop

The `for` loop gathers all three actions (initializing, testing, and updating) into one place. By using a `for` loop, you can replace the preceding program with the one shown in Listing 6.11.

LISTING 6.11   The `sweetie2.c` Program

```
// sweetie2.c -- a counting loop using for
#include <stdio.h>
int main(void)
{
    const int NUMBER = 22;
    int count;

    for (count = 1; count <= NUMBER; count++)
        printf("Be my Valentine!\n");

    return 0;
}
```

The parentheses following the keyword `for` contain three expressions separated by two semi-colons. The first expression is the initialization. It is done just once, when the `for` loop first starts. The second expression is the test condition; it is evaluated before each potential execution of a loop. When the expression is false (when **count** is greater than **NUMBER**), the loop is terminated. The third expression, the change or update, is evaluated at the end of each loop. Listing 6.10 uses it to increment the value of **count**, but it needn't be restricted to that use. The `for` statement is completed by following it with a single simple or compound statement. Each of the three control expressions is a full expression, so any side effects in a control expression, such as incrementing a variable, take place before the program evaluates another expression. Figure 6.3 summarizes the structure of a `for` loop.

To show another example, Listing 6.12 uses the `for` loop in a program that prints a table of cubes.

LISTING 6.12   The `for_cube.c` Program

```
/* for_cube.c -- using a for loop to make a table of cubes */
#include <stdio.h>
int main(void)
{
    int num;

    printf("    n    n cubed\n");
    for (num = 1; num <= 6; num++)
        printf("%5d %5d\n", num, num*num*num);

    return 0;
}
```

FIGURE 6.3

Structure of a `for` loop.

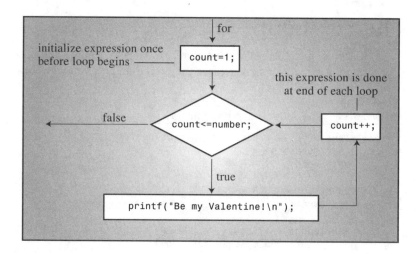

Listing 6.12 prints the integers 1 through 6 and their cubes.

```
n    n cubed
1      1
2      8
3     27
4     64
5    125
6    216
```

The first line of the `for` loop tells us immediately all the information about the loop parameters: the starting value of `num`, the final value of `num`, and the amount that `num` increases on each looping.

Using `for` for Flexibility

Although the `for` loop looks similar to the FORTRAN `DO` loop, the Pascal `FOR` loop, and the BASIC `FOR...NEXT` loop, it is much more flexible than any of them. This flexibility stems from how the three expressions in a `for` specification can be used. The examples so far have used the first expression to initialize a counter, the second expression to express the limit for the counter, and the third expression to increase the value of the counter by 1. When used this way, the C `for` statement is very much like the others we have mentioned. However, there are many more possibilities; here are nine variations:

- You can use the decrement operator to count down instead of up:

```
/* for_down.c */
#include <stdio.h>
int main(void)
{
    int secs;
```

```
    for (secs = 5; secs > 0; secs--)
        printf("%d seconds!\n", secs);
    printf("We have ignition!\n");
    return 0;
}
```

Here is the output:

```
5 seconds!
4 seconds!
3 seconds!
2 seconds!
1 seconds!
We have ignition!
```

- You can count by twos, tens, and so on, if you want:

```
/* for_13s.c */
#include <stdio.h>
int main(void)
{
    int n;          /* count by 13s */

    for (n = 2;  n < 60; n = n + 13)
        printf("%d \n", n);
    return 0;
}
```

This would increase n by 13 during each cycle, printing the following:

```
 2
15
28
41
54
```

- You can count by characters instead of by numbers:

```
/* for_char.c */
#include <stdio.h>
int main(void)
{
    char ch;

    for (ch = 'a'; ch <= 'z'; ch++)
        printf("The ASCII value for %c is %d.\n", ch, ch);
    return 0;
}
```

Here's the abridged output:

```
The ASCII value for a is 97.
The ASCII value for b is 98.
...
The ASCII value for x is 120.
The ASCII value for y is 121.
The ASCII value for z is 122.
```

The program works because characters are stored as integers, so this loop really counts by integers anyway.

- You can test some condition other than the number of iterations. In the `for_cube` program, you can replace

```
for (num = 1; num <= 6; num++)
```

with

```
for (num = 1; num*num*num <= 216; num++)
```

You would use this test condition if you were more concerned with limiting the size of the cube than with limiting the number of iterations.

- You can let a quantity increase geometrically instead of arithmetically; that is, instead of adding a fixed amount each time, you can multiply by a fixed amount:

```
/* for_geo.c */
#include <stdio.h>
int main(void)
{
    double debt;

    for (debt = 100.0; debt < 150.0; debt = debt * 1.1)
        printf("Your debt is now $%.2f.\n", debt);
    return 0;
}
```

This program fragment multiplies `debt` by 1.1 for each cycle, increasing it by 10% each time. The output looks like this:

```
Your debt is now $100.00.
Your debt is now $110.00.
Your debt is now $121.00.
Your debt is now $133.10.
Your debt is now $146.41.
```

- You can use any legal expression you want for the third expression. Whatever you put in will be updated for each iteration.

```
/* for_wild.c */
#include <stdio.h>
int main(void)
{
    int x;
    int y = 55;

    for (x = 1; y <= 75; y = (++x * 5) + 50)
        printf("%10d %10d\n", x, y);
    return 0;
}
```

This loop prints the values of x and of the algebraic expression ++x * 5 + 50. The output looks like this:

```
1              55
2              60
3              65
4              70
5              75
```

Notice that the test involves y, not x. Each of the three expressions in the for loop control can use different variables. (Note that although this example is valid, it does not show good style. The program would have been clearer if we hadn't mixed the updating process with an algebraic calculation.)

- You can even leave one or more expressions blank (but don't omit the semicolons). Just be sure to include within the loop itself some statement that eventually causes the loop to terminate.

```c
/* for_none.c */
#include <stdio.h>
int main(void)
{
    int ans, n;

    ans = 2;
    for (n = 3; ans <= 25; )
        ans = ans * n;
    printf("n = %d; ans = %d.\n", n, ans);
    return 0;
}
```

Here is the output:

```
n = 3; ans = 54.
```

The loop keeps the value of n at 3. The variable ans starts with the value 2, and then increases to 6 and 18 and obtains a final value of 54. (The value 18 is less than 25, so the for loop goes through one more iteration, multiplying 18 by 3 to get 54.) Incidentally, an empty middle control expression is considered to be true, so the following loop goes on forever:

```c
for (; ; )
    printf("I want some action\n");
```

- The first expression need not initialize a variable. It could, instead, be a printf() statement of some sort. Just remember that the first expression is evaluated or executed only once, before any other parts of the loop are executed.

```c
/* for_show.c */
#include <stdio.h>
int main(void)
{
    int num = 0;
```

```
    for (printf("Keep entering numbers!\n"); num != 6;   )
        scanf("%d", &num);
    printf("That's the one I want!\n");
    return 0;
}
```

This fragment prints the first message once and then keeps accepting numbers until you enter 6:

```
Keep entering numbers!
3
5
8
6
That's the one I want!
```

- The parameters of the loop expressions can be altered by actions within the loop. For example, suppose you have the loop set up like this:

```
for (n = 1; n < 10000; n = n + delta)
```

If after a few iterations your program decides that **delta** is too small or too large, an **if** statement (Chapter 7, "C Control Statements: Branching and Jumps") inside the loop can change the size of **delta**. In an interactive program, **delta** can be changed by the user as the loop runs. This sort of adjustment is a bit on the dangerous side; for example, setting **delta** to **0** gets you (and the loop) nowhere.

In short, the freedom you have in selecting the expressions that control a **for** loop makes this loop able to do much more than just perform a fixed number of iterations. The usefulness of the **for** loop is enhanced further by the operators we will discuss shortly.

Summary: The for Statement

Keyword:

for

General Comments:

The **for** statement uses three control expressions, separated by semicolons, to control a looping process. The **initialize** expression is executed once, before any of the loop statements are executed. Then the **test** expression is evaluated and, if it is true (or nonzero), the loop is cycled through once. Then the **update** expression is evaluated, and it is time to check the **test** expression again. The **for** statement is an entry-condition loop—the decision to go through one more pass of the loop is made before the loop is traversed. Therefore, it is possible that the loop is never traversed. The **statement** part of the form can be a simple statement or a compound statement.

Form:

for (*initialize* ; *test* ; *update*)
    statement

The loop is repeated until **test** becomes false or zero.

Example:

```
for (n = 0;  n < 10 ; n++)
    printf(" %d %d\n", n, 2 * n + 1);
```

More Assignment Operators: +=, -=, *=, /=, %=

C has several assignment operators. The most basic one, of course, is =, which simply assigns the value of the expression at its right to the variable at its left. The other assignment operators update variables. Each is used with a variable name to its left and an expression to its right. The variable is assigned a new value equal to its old value adjusted by the value of the expression at the right. The exact adjustment depends on the operator. For example,

scores += 20 is the same as scores = scores + 20.

dimes -= 2 is the same as dimes = dimes - 2.

bunnies *= 2 is the same as bunnies = bunnies * 2.

time /= 2.73 is the same as time = time / 2.73.

reduce %= 3 is the same as reduce = reduce % 3.

The preceding list uses simple numbers on the right, but these operators also work with more elaborate expressions, such as the following:

x *= 3 * y + 12 is the same as x = x * (3 * y + 12).

The assignment operators we've just discussed have the same low priority that = does—that is, less than that of + or *. This low priority is reflected in the last example in which 12 is added to 3 * y before the result is multiplied by x.

You are not required to use these forms. They are, however, more compact, and they may produce more efficient machine code than the longer form. The combination assignment operators are particularly useful when you are trying to squeeze something complex into a for loop specification.

The Comma Operator

The comma operator extends the flexibility of the for loop by enabling you to include more than one initialization or update expression in a single for loop specification. For example, Listing 6.13 shows a program that prints first-class postage rates. (At the time of this writing, the rate is 37 cents for the first ounce and 23 cents for each additional ounce. You can check www.usps.gov for the current rates.)

LISTING 6.13   The postage.c Program

```
// postage.c -- first-class postage rates
#include <stdio.h>
int main(void)
{
```

LISTING 6.13 *Continued*

```
        const int FIRST_OZ = 37;
        const int NEXT_OZ = 23;
        int ounces, cost;

        printf(" ounces  cost\n");
        for (ounces=1, cost=FIRST_OZ; ounces <= 16; ounces++,
             cost += NEXT_OZ)
            printf("%5d    $%4.2f\n", ounces, cost/100.0);

        return 0;
}
```

The first five lines of the output look like this:

```
ounces  cost
     1   $0.37
     2   $0.60
     3   $0.83
     4   $1.06
```

The program uses the comma operator in the initialize and the update expressions. Its presence in the first expression causes `ounces` and `cost` to be initialized. Its second occurrence causes `ounces` to be increased by 1 and `cost` to be increased by 23 (the value of `NEXT_OZ`) for each iteration. All the calculations are done in the `for` loop specifications (see Figure 6.4).

FIGURE 6.4

The comma operator and the `for` loop.

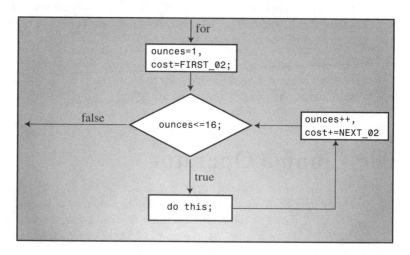

The comma operator is not restricted to `for` loops, but that's where it is most often used. The operator has two further properties. First, it guarantees that the expressions it separates are evaluated in a left-to-right order. (In other words, the comma is a sequence point, so all side effects to the left of the comma take place before the program moves to the right of the comma.) Therefore, ounces is initialized before cost. The order is not important for this example, but it would be important if the expression for cost contained ounces. Suppose, for instance, that you had this expression:

```
ounces++, cost = ounces * FIRST_OZ
```

This would increment ounces and then use the new value for ounces in the second subexpression. The comma being a sequence point guarantees that the side effects of the left subexpression occur before the right subexpression is evaluated.

Second, the value of the whole comma expression is the value of the right-hand member. The effect of the statement

```
x = (y = 3, (z = ++y + 2) + 5);
```

is to first assign 3 to y, increment y to 4, and then add 2 to 4 and assign the resulting value of 6 to z, next add 5 to z, and finally assign the resulting value of 11 to x. Why anyone would do this is beyond the scope of this book. On the other hand, suppose you get careless and use comma notation in writing a number:

```
houseprice = 249,500;
```

This is not a syntax error. Instead, C interprets this as a comma expression, with houseprice = 249 being the left subexpression and 500 the right subexpression. Therefore, the value of the whole comma expression is the value of the right-hand expression, and the left substatement assigns the value 249 to the houseprice variable. Therefore, the effect is the same as the following code:

```
houseprice = 249;
500;
```

Remember that any expression becomes a statement with the addition of a semicolon, so 500; is a statement that does nothing.

On the other hand, the statement

```
houseprice = (249,500);
```

assigns 500, the value of the right subexpression, to houseprice.

The comma also is used as a separator, so the commas in

```
char ch, date;
```

and

```
printf("%d %d\n", chimps, chumps);
```

are separators, not comma operators.

Summary: The New Operators

Assignment Operators:

Each of these operators updates the variable at its left by the value at its right, using the indicated operation:

+=	Adds the right-hand quantity to the left-hand variable
-=	Subtracts the right-hand quantity from the left-hand variable
*=	Multiplies the left-hand variable by the right-hand quantity
/=	Divides the left-hand variable by the right-hand quantity
%=	Gives the remainder obtained from dividing the left-hand variable by the right-hand quantity

Example:

```
rabbits *= 1.6;
```

is the same as

```
rabbits = rabbits * 1.6;
```

These combination assignment operators have the same low precedence as the regular assignment operator, lower than arithmetic operators. Therefore, a statement such as

```
contents *= old_rate + 1.2;
```

has the same final effect as this:

```
contents = contents * (old_rate + 1.2);
```

The Comma Operator:

The comma operator links two expressions into one and guarantees that the leftmost expression is evaluated first. It is typically used to include more information in a `for` loop control expression. The value of the whole expression is the value of the right-hand expression.

Example:

```
for (step = 2, fargo = 0; fargo < 1000; step *= 2)
     fargo += step;
```

Zeno Meets the `for` Loop

Let's see how the `for` loop and the comma operator can help solve an old paradox. The Greek philosopher Zeno once argued that an arrow will never reach its target. First, he said, the arrow covers half the distance to the target. Then it has to cover half of the remaining distance. Then it still has half of what's left to cover, ad infinitum. Because the journey has an infinite number of parts, Zeno argued, it would take the arrow an infinite amount of time to reach its journey's end. We doubt, however, that Zeno would have volunteered to be a target on the strength of this argument.

Let's take a quantitative approach and suppose that it takes the arrow 1 second to travel the first half. Then it would take 1/2 second to travel half of what was left, 1/4 second to travel half of what was left next, and so on. You can represent the total time by the following infinite series:

```
1 + 1/2 + 1/4 + 1/8 + 1/16 +....
```

The short program in Listing 6.14 finds the sum of the first few terms.

LISTING 6.14   The zeno.c Program

```
/* zeno.c -- series sum */
#include <stdio.h>

int main(void)
{
    int t_ct;          // term count
    double time, x;
    int limit;

    printf("Enter the number of terms you want: ");
    scanf("%d", &limit);
    for (time=0, x=1, t_ct=1; t_ct <= limit; t_ct++, x *= 2.0)
    {
        time += 1.0/x;
        printf("time = %f when terms = %d.\n", time, t_ct);
    }

    return 0;
}
```

Here is the output for 15 terms:

```
Enter the number of terms you want: 15
time = 1.000000 when terms = 1.
time = 1.500000 when terms = 2.
time = 1.750000 when terms = 3.
time = 1.875000 when terms = 4.
time = 1.937500 when terms = 5.
time = 1.968750 when terms = 6.
time = 1.984375 when terms = 7.
time = 1.992188 when terms = 8.
time = 1.996094 when terms = 9.
time = 1.998047 when terms = 10.
time = 1.999023 when terms = 11.
time = 1.999512 when terms = 12.
time = 1.999756 when terms = 13.
time = 1.999878 when terms = 14.
time = 1.999939 when terms = 15.
```

You can see that although you keep adding more terms, the total seems to level out. Indeed, mathematicians have proven that the total approaches 2.0 as the number of terms approaches infinity, just as this program suggests. Here's one demonstration. Suppose you let S represent the sum:

```
S = 1 + 1/2 + 1/4 + 1/8 + ...
```

Here the ellipses mean "and so on." Then dividing by 2 gives

```
S/2 = 1/2 + 1/4 + 1/8 + 1/16 + ...
```

Subtracting the second expression from the first gives

```
S - S/2 = 1 +1/2 -1/2 + 1/4 -1/4 +...
```

Except for the initial value of 1, each other value occurs in pairs, one positive and one negative, so those terms cancel each other, leaving

```
S/2 = 1.
```

Then, multiplying both sides by 2 gives

```
S = 2.
```

One possible moral to draw from this is that before doing an involved calculation, check to see whether mathematicians have an easier way to do it.

What about the program itself? It shows that you can use more than one comma operator in an expression. You initialized `time`, `x`, and `count`. After you set up the conditions for the loop, the program itself is extremely brief.

An Exit-Condition Loop: `do while`

The `while` loop and the `for` loop are both entry-condition loops. The test condition is checked *before* each iteration of the loop, so it is possible for the statements in the loop to never execute. C also has an *exit-condition* loop, in which the condition is checked after each iteration of the loop, guaranteeing that statements are executed at least once. This variety is called a `do while` loop. Listing 6.15 shows an example.

LISTING 6.15 The do_while.c Program

```c
/* do_while.c -- exit condition loop */
#include <stdio.h>
int main(void)
{
    const int secret_code = 13;
    int code_entered;

    do
    {
        printf("To enter the triskaidekaphobia therapy club,\n");
        printf("please enter the secret code number: ");
        scanf("%d", &code_entered);
    } while (code_entered != secret_code);
    printf("Congratulations! You are cured!\n");

    return 0;
}
```

The program in Listing 6.15 reads input values until the user enters **13**. The following is a sample run:

```
To enter the triskaidekaphobia therapy club,
please enter the secret code number: 12
To enter the triskaidekaphobia therapy club,
please enter the secret code number: 14
To enter the triskaidekaphobia therapy club,
please enter the secret code number: 13
Congratulations! You are cured!
```

An equivalent program using a `while` loop would be a little longer, as shown in Listing 6.16.

LISTING 6.16   The entry.c Program

```c
/* entry.c -- entry condition loop */
#include <stdio.h>
int main(void)
{
    const int secret_code = 13;
    int code_entered;

    printf("To enter the triskaidekaphobia therapy club,\n");
    printf("please enter the secret code number: ");
    scanf("%d", &code_entered);
    while (code_entered != secret_code)
    {
        printf("To enter the triskaidekaphobia therapy club,\n");
        printf("please enter the secret code number: ");
        scanf("%d", &code_entered);
    }
    printf("Congratulations! You are cured!\n");

    return 0;
}
```

Here is the general form of the `do while` loop:

```
do
    statement
while ( expression );
```

The statement can be simple or compound. Note that the `do while` loop itself counts as a statement and, therefore, requires a terminating semicolon. Also, see Figure 6.5.

A `do while` loop is always executed at least once because the test is made after the body of the loop has been executed. A `for` loop or a `while` loop, on the other hand, can be executed zero times because the test is made before execution. You should restrict the use of `do while` loops to cases that require at least one iteration. For example, a password program could include a loop along these pseudocode lines:

```
do
{
    prompt for password
    read user input
} while (input not equal to password);
```

Avoid a `do while` structure of the type shown in the following pseudocode:

```
do
{
    ask user if he or she wants to continue
    some clever stuff
} while (answer is yes);
```

Here, after the user answers "no," some clever stuff gets done anyway because the test comes too late.

FIGURE 6.5

Structure of a `do while` loop.

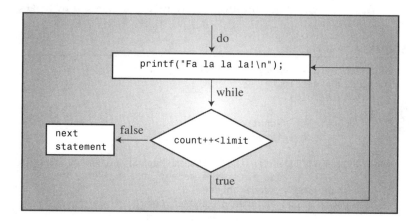

Summary: The do while Statement

Keywords:

do while

General Comments:

The `do while` statement creates a loop that repeats until the test *expression* becomes false or zero. The `do while` statement is an exit-condition loop—the decision to go through one more pass of the loop is made after the loop has been traversed. Therefore, the loop must be executed at least once. The *statement* part of the form can be a simple statement or a compound statement.

Form:

```
do
    statement
while (expression);
```

The *statement* portion is repeated until the *expression* becomes false or zero.

Example:

```
do
    scanf("%d", &number);
while (number != 20);
```

Which Loop?

When you decide you need a loop, which one should you use? First, decide whether you need an entry-condition loop or an exit-condition loop. Your answer should usually be an entry-condition loop. There are several reasons computer scientists consider an entry-condition loop to be superior. One is the general principle that it is better to look before you leap (or loop) than after. A second is that a program is easier to read if the loop test is found at the beginning of the loop. Finally, in many uses, it is important that the loop be skipped entirely if the test is not initially met.

Assume that you need an entry-condition loop. Should it be a `for` or a `while`? This is partly a matter of taste, because what you can do with one, you can do with the other. To make a `for` loop like a `while`, you can omit the first and third expressions. For example,

```
for ( ;test; )
```

is the same as

```
while (test)
```

To make a `while` like a `for`, preface it with an initialization and include update statements. For example,

```
initialize;
while (test)
{
  body;
  update;
}
```

is the same as

```
for (initialize; test; update)
   body;
```

In terms of prevailing style, a `for` loop is appropriate when the loop involves initializing and updating a variable, and a `while` loop is better when the conditions are otherwise. A `while` loop is natural for the following condition:

```
while (scanf("%ld", &num) == 1)
```

The `for` loop is a more natural choice for loops involving counting with an index:

```
for (count = 1; count <= 100; count++)
```

Nested Loops

A *nested loop* is one loop inside another loop. A common use for nested loops is to display data in rows and columns. One loop can handle, say, all the columns in a row, and the second loop handles the rows. Listing 6.17 shows a simple example.

LISTING 6.17   The rows1.c Program

```
/* rows1.c -- uses nested loops */
#include <stdio.h>
#define ROWS  6
#define CHARS 10
int main(void)
{
    int row;
    char ch;

    for (row = 0; row < ROWS; row++)            /* line 10 */
    {
        for (ch = 'A'; ch < ('A' + CHARS); ch++)  /* line 12 */
            printf("%c", ch);
        printf("\n");
    }

    return 0;
}
```

Running the program produces this output:

```
ABCDEFGHIJ
ABCDEFGHIJ
ABCDEFGHIJ
ABCDEFGHIJ
ABCDEFGHIJ
ABCDEFGHIJ
```

Program Discussion

The `for` loop beginning on line 10 is called an *outer* loop, and the loop beginning on line 12 is called an *inner* loop because it is inside the other loop. The outer loop starts with `row` having a value of `0` and terminates when `row` reaches `6`. Therefore, the outer loop goes through six cycles, with `row` having the values `0` through `5`. The first statement in each cycle is the inner `for` loop. This loop goes through 10 cycles, printing the characters `A` through `J` on the same line. The second statement of the outer loop is `printf("\n");`. This statement starts a new line so that the next time the inner loop is run, the output is on a new line.

Note that, with a nested loop, the inner loop runs through its full range of iterations for each single iteration of the outer loop. In the last example, the inner loop prints 10 characters to a row, and the outer loop creates six rows.

A Nested Variation

In the preceding example, the inner loop did the same thing for each cycle of the outer loop. You can make the inner loop behave differently each cycle by making part of the inner loop depend on the outer loop. Listing 6.18, for example, alters the last program slightly by making the starting character of the inner loop depend on the cycle number of the outer loop. It also uses the new comment style and `const` instead of `#define` to help you get comfortable with both approaches.

LISTING 6.18   The `rows2.c` Program

```
// rows2.c -- using dependent nested loops
#include <stdio.h>
int main(void)
{
    const int ROWS = 6;
    const int CHARS = 6;
    int row;
    char ch;

    for (row = 0; row < ROWS; row++)
    {
        for (ch = ('A' + row);  ch < ('A' + CHARS); ch++)
            printf("%c", ch);
        printf("\n");
    }

    return 0;
}
```

Here's the output this time:

```
ABCDEF
BCDEF
CDEF
DEF
EF
F
```

Because `row` is added to `'A'` during each cycle of the outer loop, `ch` is initialized in each row to one character later in the alphabet. The test condition, however, is unaltered, so each row still ends on `F`. This results in one fewer character being printed in each row.

Introducing Arrays

Arrays are important features in many programs. They enable you to store several items of related information in a convenient fashion. We will devote all of Chapter 10, "Arrays and Pointers," to arrays, but because arrays are often used with loops, we want to introduce them now.

An *array* is a series of values of the same type, such as 10 chars or 15 ints, stored sequentially. The whole array bears a single name, and the individual items, or *elements*, are accessed by using an integer index. For example, the declaration

```
float debts[20];
```

announces that `debts` is an array with 20 elements, each of which can hold a type `float` value. The first element of the array is called `debts[0]`, the second element is called `debts[1]`, and so on, up to `debts[19]`. Note that the numbering of array elements starts with 0, not 1. Each element can be assigned a `float` value. For example, you can have the following:

```
debts[5] = 32.54;
debts[6] = 1.2e+21;
```

In fact, you can use an array element the same way you would use a variable of the same type. For example, you can read a value into a particular element:

```
scanf("%f", &debts[4]);  // read a value into the 5th element
```

One potential pitfall is that, in the interest of speed of execution, C doesn't check to see whether you use a correct subscript. Each of the following, for example, is bad code:

```
debts[20] = 88.32;   // no such array element
debts[33] = 828.12;  // no such array element
```

However, the compiler doesn't look for such errors. When the program runs, these statements would place data in locations possibly used for other data, potentially corrupting the output of the program or even causing it to abort.

An array can be of any data type.

```
int nannies[22];    /* an array to hold 22 integers       */
char actors[26];    /* an array to hold 26 characters      */
long big[500];      /* an array to hold 500 long integers  */
```

Earlier, for example, we talked about strings, which are a special case of what can be stored in a `char` array. (A `char` array, in general, is one whose elements are assigned `char` values.) The contents of a `char` array form a string if the array contains the null character, `\0`, which marks the end of the string (see Figure 6.6).

FIGURE 6.6
Character arrays and strings.

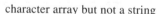

character array but not a string

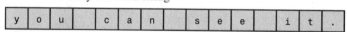

character array and a string

null character

The numbers used to identify the array elements are called *subscripts*, *indices*, or *offsets*. The subscripts must be integers, and, as mentioned, the subscripting begins with 0. The array elements are stored next to each other in memory, as shown in Figure 6.7.

FIGURE 6.7
The char and int arrays in memory.

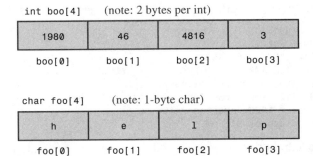

Using a for Loop with an Array

There are many, many uses for arrays. Listing 6.19 is a relatively simple one. It's a program that reads in 10 golf scores that will be processed later. By using an array, you avoid inventing 10 different variable names, one for each score. Also, you can use a for loop to do the reading. The program goes on to report the sum of the scores and their average and a handicap, which is the difference between the average and a standard score, or par.

LISTING 6.19   The scores_in.c Program

```
// scores_in.c -- uses loops for array processing
#include <stdio.h>
#define SIZE 10
#define PAR 72
int main(void)
{
    int index, score[SIZE];
    int sum = 0;
    float average;

    printf("Enter %d golf scores:\n", SIZE);
    for (index = 0; index < SIZE; index++)
        scanf("%d", &score[index]);  // read in the ten scores
    printf("The scores read in are as follows:\n");
    for (index = 0; index < SIZE; index++)
        printf("%5d", score[index]); // verify input
    printf("\n");
    for (index = 0; index < SIZE; index++)
        sum += score[index];         // add them up
    average = (float) sum / SIZE;    // time-honored method
    printf("Sum of scores = %d, average = %.2f\n", sum, average);
    printf("That's a handicap of %.0f.\n", average - PAR);

    return 0;
}
```

Let's see if Listing 6.19 works; then we can make a few comments. Here is the output:

```
Enter 10 scores:
Enter 10 golf scores:
102  98  112  108  105  103
99  101  96  102 100
The scores read in are as follows:
   102    98  112  108  105  103   99  101   96  102
Sum of scores = 1026, average = 102.60
That's a handicap of 31.
```

It works, so let's check out some of the details. First, note that although the example shows 11 numbers typed, only 10 were read because the reading loop reads just 10 values. Because scanf() skips over whitespace, you can type all 10 numbers on one line, place each number on its own line, or, as in this case, use a mixture of newlines and spaces to separate the input. (Because input is buffered, the numbers are sent to the program only when you press the Enter key.)

Next, using arrays and loops is much more convenient than using 10 separate scanf() statements and 10 separate printf() statements to read in and verify the 10 scores. The for loop offers a simple and direct way to use the array subscripts. Notice that an element of an int array is handled like an int variable. To read the int variable fue, you would use scanf("%d", &fue). Listing 6.19 is reading the int element score[index], so it uses scanf("%d", &score[index]).

This example illustrates several style points. First, it's a good idea to use a #define directive to create a manifest constant (SIZE) to specify the size of the array. You use this constant in defining the array and in setting the loop limits. If you later need to expand the program to handle 20 scores, simply redefine SIZE to be 20. You don't have to change every part of the program that uses the array size. C99 allows you to use const values for specifying an array size, but C90 didn't; #define works with both.

Second, the idiom

```
for (index = 0; index < SIZE; index++)
```

is a handy one for processing an array of size SIZE. It's important to get the right array limits. The first element has index 0, and the loop starts by setting index to 0. Because the numbering starts with 0, the element index for the last element is SIZE - 1. That is, the tenth element is score[9]. Using the test condition index < SIZE accomplishes this, making the last value of index used in the loop SIZE - 1.

Third, a good practice is to have a program repeat or "echo" the values it has just read in. This helps ensure that the program is processing the data you think it is.

Finally, note that Listing 6.19 uses three separate for loops. You might wonder if this is really necessary. Could you have combined some of the operations in one loop? The answer is yes, you could have done so. That would have made the program more compact. However, you should be swayed by the principle of *modularity*. The idea behind this term is that a program should be broken into separate units, with each unit having one task to perform. This makes a program easier to read. Perhaps even more important, modularity makes it much easier to update or modify a program if different parts of the program are not intermingled. When you know enough about functions, you could make each unit into a function, enhancing the modularity of the program.

A Loop Example Using a Function Return Value

The last example in this chapter uses a function that calculates the result of raising a number to an integer power. (For the serious number-cruncher, the `math.h` library provides a more powerful power function called `pow()` that allows floating-point exponents.) The three main tasks in this exercise are devising the algorithm for calculating the answer, expressing the algorithm in a function that returns the answer, and providing a convenient way of testing the function.

First, let's look at an algorithm. Keep the function simple by restricting it to positive integer powers. Then, if you want to raise n to the p power, you have to multiply n times itself p times. This is a natural task for a loop. You can set the variable pow to 1 and then repeatedly multiply it by n:

```
for(i = 1; i <= p; i++)
    pow *= n;
```

Recall that the `*=` operator multiplies the left side by the right side. After the first loop cycle, pow is 1 times n, or n. After the second cycle, pow is its previous value (n) times n, or n squared, and so on. The for loop is natural in this context because the loop is executed a predetermined (after p is known) number of times.

Now that you have an algorithm, you should decide which data types to use. The exponent p, being an integer, should be type int. To allow ample range in values for n and its power, make n and pow type double.

Next, let's consider how to put the function together. You need to give the function two values, and the function should give back one. To get information to the function, you can use two arguments, one double and one int, specifying which number to raise to what power. How do you arrange for the function to return a value to the calling program? To write a function with a return value, do the following:

1. When you define a function, state the type of value it returns.

2. Use the keyword return to indicate the value to be returned.

For example, you can do this:

```
double power(double n, int p)   // returns a double
{
    double pow = 1;
    int i;
```

```
    for (i = 1; i <= p; i++)
        pow *= n;

    return pow;                    // return the value of pow
}
```

To declare the function type, preface the function name with the type, just as you do when declaring a variable. The keyword `return` causes the function to return the following value to the calling function. Here you return the value of a variable, but you can return the value of expressions, too. For instance, the following is a valid statement:

```
return 2 * x + b;
```

The function would compute the value of the expression and return it. In the calling function, the return value can be assigned to another variable, can be used as a value in an expression, can be used as an argument to another function—as in `printf("%f", power(6.28, 3))`—or can be ignored.

Now let's use the function in a program. To test the function, it would be convenient to be able to feed several values to the function to see how it reacts. This suggests setting up an input loop. The natural choice is the `while` loop. You can use `scanf()` to read in two values at a time. If successful in reading two values, `scanf()` returns the value 2, so you can control the loop by comparing the `scanf()` return value to 2. One more point: To use the `power()` function in your program, you need to declare it, just as you declare variables that the program uses. Listing 6.20 shows the program.

LISTING 6.20   The `power.c` Program

```
// power.c -- raises numbers to integer powers
#include <stdio.h>
double power(double n, int p); // ANSI prototype
int main(void)
{
    double x, xpow;
    int exp;

    printf("Enter a number and the positive integer power");
    printf(" to which\nthe number will be raised. Enter q");
    printf(" to quit.\n");
    while (scanf("%lf%d", &x, &exp) == 2)
    {
        xpow = power(x,exp);      // function call
        printf("%.3g to the power %d is %.5g\n", x, exp, xpow);
        printf("Enter next pair of numbers or q to quit.\n");
    }
    printf("Hope you enjoyed this power trip -- bye!\n");

    return 0;
}

double power(double n, int p)  // function definition
```

LISTING 6.20   Continued

```
{
    double pow = 1;
    int i;

    for (i = 1; i <= p; i++)
        pow *= n;

    return pow;                    // return the value of pow
}
```

Here is a sample run:

```
Enter a number and the positive integer power to which
the number will be raised. Enter q to quit.
1.2 12
1.2 to the power 12 is 8.9161
Enter next pair of numbers or q to quit.
2
16
2 to the power 16 is 65536
Enter next pair of numbers or q to quit.
q
Hope you enjoyed this power trip -- bye!
```

Program Discussion

The `main()` program is an example of a *driver*, a short program designed to test a function.

The `while` loop is a generalization of a form we've used before. Entering `1.2 12` causes `scanf()` to read two values successfully and to return `2`, and the loop continues. Because `scanf()` skips over whitespace, input can be spread over more than one line, as the sample output shows, but entering `q` produces a return value of `0` because `q` can't be read using the `%1f` specifier. This causes `scanf()` to return `0`, thus terminating the loop. Similarly, entering `2.8 q` would produce a `scanf()` return value of `1`; that, too, would terminate the loop.

Now let's look at the function-related matters. The `power()` function appears three times in this program. The first appearance is this:

```
double power(double n, int p); // ANSI prototype
```

This statement announces, or *declares*, that the program will be using a function called `power()`. The initial keyword `double` indicates that the `power()` function returns a type `double` value. The compiler needs to know what kind of value `power()` returns so that it will know how many bytes of data to expect and how to interpret them; this is why you have to declare the function. The `double n, int p` within the parentheses means that `power()` takes two arguments. The first should be a type `double` value, and the second should be type `int`.

The second appearance is this:

```
xpow = power(x,exp);           // function call
```

Here the program calls the function, passing it two values. The function calculates x to the exp power and returns the result to the calling program, where the return value is assigned to the variable xpow.

The third appearance is in the head of the function definition:

```
double power(double n, int p)  // function definition
```

Here power() takes two parameters, a double and an int, represented by the variables n and p. Note that power() is not followed by a semicolon when it appears in a function definition, but is followed by a semicolon when in a function declaration. After the function heading comes the code that specifies what power() does.

Recall that the function uses a for loop to calculate the value of n to the p power and assign it to pow. The following line makes the value of pow the function return value:

```
return pow;                      // return the value of pow
```

Using Functions with Return Values

Declaring the function, calling the function, defining the function, using the return keyword—these are the basic elements in defining and using a function with a return value.

At this point, you might have some questions. For example, if you are supposed to declare functions before you use their return values, how come you used the return value of scanf() without declaring scanf()? Why do you have to declare power() separately when your definition of it says it is type double?

Let's take the second question first. The compiler needs to know what type power() is when it first encounters power() in the program. At this point, the compiler has not yet encountered the definition of power(), so it doesn't know that the definition says the return type is double. To help out the compiler, you preview what is to come by using a *forward declaration*. This declaration informs the compiler that power() is defined elsewhere and that it will return type double. If you place the power() function definition ahead of main() in the file, you can omit the forward declaration because the compiler will know all about power() before reaching main(). However, that is not standard C style. Because main() usually provides the overall framework for a program, it's best to show main() first. Also, functions often are kept in separate files, so a forward declaration is essential.

Next, why didn't you declare scanf()? Well, you did. The stdio.h header file has function declarations for scanf(), printf(), and several other I/O functions. The scanf() declaration states that it returns type int.

Key Concepts

The loop is a powerful programming tool. You should pay particular attention to three aspects when setting up a loop:

- Clearly defining the condition that causes the loop to terminate
- Making sure the values used in the loop test are initialized before the first use
- Making sure the loop does something to update the test each cycle

C handles test conditions by evaluating them numerically. A result of **0** is false, and any other value is true. Expressions using the relational operators often are used as tests, and they are a bit more specific. Relational expressions evaluate to **1** if true and to **0** if false, which is consistent with the values allowed for the new **_Bool** type.

Arrays consist of adjacent memory locations all of the same type. You need to keep in mind that array element numbering starts with 0 so that the subscript of the last element is always one less than the number of elements. C doesn't check to see if you use valid subscript values, so the responsibility is yours.

Employing a function involves three separate steps:

1. Declare the function with a function prototype.
2. Use the function from within a program with a function call.
3. Define the function.

The prototype allows the compiler to see whether you've used the function correctly, and the definition sets down how the function works. The prototype and definition are examples of the contemporary programming practice of separating a program element into an interface and an implementation. The interface describes how a feature is used, which is what a prototype does, and the implementation sets forth the particular actions taken, which is what the definition does.

Summary

The main topic of this chapter has been program control. C offers you many aids for structuring your programs. The `while` and the `for` statements provide entry-condition loops. The `for` statements are particularly suited for loops that involve initialization and updating. The comma operator enables you to initialize and update more than one variable in a `for` loop. For the less common occasion when an exit-condition loop is needed, C has the `do while` statement.

A typical `while` loop design looks like this:

```
get first value
while (value meets test)
{
```

```
        process the value
        get next value
}
```

A `for` loop doing the same thing would look like this:

```
for (get first value; value meets test; get next value)
    process the value
```

All these loops use a test condition to determine whether another loop cycle is to be executed. In general, the loop continues if the test expression evaluates to a nonzero value; otherwise, it terminates. Often, the test condition is a relational expression, which is an expression formed by using a relational operator. Such an expression has a value of 1 if the relation is true and a value of 0 otherwise. Variables of the `_Bool` type, introduced by C99, can only hold the value 1 or 0, signifying true or false.

In addition to relational operators, this chapter looked at several of C's arithmetic assignment operators, such as `+=` and `*=`. These operators modify the value of the left-hand operand by performing an arithmetic operation on it.

Arrays were the next subject. Arrays are declared using brackets to indicate the number of elements. The first element of an array is numbered 0; the second is numbered 1, and so forth. For example, the declaration

```
double hippos[20];
```

creates an array of 20 elements, and the individual elements range from `hippos[0]` through `hippos[19]`. The subscripts used to number arrays can be manipulated conveniently by using loops.

Finally, the chapter showed how to write and use a function with a return value.

Review Questions

1. Find the value of `quack` after each line.

   ```
   int quack = 2)|
   quack += 5;
   quack *= 10;
   quack -= 6;
   quack /= 8;
   quack %= 3;
   ```

2. Given that `value` is an `int`, what output would the following loop produce?

   ```
   for ( value = 36; value > 0; value /= 21;
           printf("%3d", value);
   ```
                                        ↑ I think.
                                        2

   What problems would there be if `value` were `double` instead of `int`?

3. Represent each of the following test conditions:

   a. x is greater than 5.

   b. scanf() attempts to read a single double (called x) and fails.

   c. x has the value 5.

4. Represent each of the following test conditions:

   a. scanf() succeeds in reading a single integer.

   b. x is not 5.

   c. x is 20 or greater.

5. You suspect that the following program is not perfect. What errors can you find?

```
#include <stdio.h>
int main(void)
{                                       /* line 3   */
    int i, j, list(10);                 /* line 4   */

    for (i = 1, i <= 10,   i++)         /* line 6   */
    {                                   /* line 7   */
        list[i] = 2*i + 3;              /* line 8   */
        for (j = 1, j > = i, j++)       /* line 9   */
            printf(" %d", list[j]);     /* line 10  */
        printf("\n");                   /* line 11  */
    }                                   /* line 12  */
}
```

6. Use nested loops to write a program that produces this pattern:

```
$$$$$$$$
$$$$$$$$
$$$$$$$$
$$$$$$$$
```

7. What will each of the following programs print?

   a.

```
#include <stdio.h>
int main(void)
{
    int i = 0;

    while (++i < 4)
        printf("Hi! ");
    do
        printf("Bye! ");
    while (i++ < 8);
    return 0;
}
```

b.

```c
#include <stdio.h>
int main(void)
{
        int i;
        char ch;

        for (i = 0, ch = 'A'; i < 4; i++, ch += 2 * i)
                printf("%c", ch);
        return 0;
}
```

8. Given the input `"Go west, young man!"`, what would each of the following programs produce for output? (The ! follows the space character in the ASCII sequence.)

a.

```c
#include <stdio.h>
int main(void)
{
    char ch;

    scanf("%c", &ch);
    while ( ch != 'g' )
    {
        printf("%c", ch);
        scanf("%c", &ch);
    }
    return 0;
}
```

b.

```c
#include <stdio.h>
int main(void)
{
    char ch;

    scanf("%c", &ch);
    while ( ch != 'g' )
    {
        printf("%c", ++ch);
        scanf("%c", &ch);
    }
    return 0;
}
```

c.

```
#include <stdio.h>
int main(void)
{
    char ch;

    do {
        scanf("%c", &ch);
        printf("%c", ch);
    } while ( ch != 'g' );
    return 0;
}
```

d.

```
#include <stdio.h>
int main(void)
{
    char ch;

    scanf("%c", &ch);
    for ( ch = '$'; ch != 'g'; scanf("%c", &ch) )
        putchar(ch);
    return 0;
}
```

9. What will the following program print?

```
#include <stdio.h>
int main(void)
{
    int n, m;

    n = 30;
    while (++n <= 33)
        printf("%d|",n);

    n = 30;
    do
        printf("%d|",n);
    while (++n <= 33);

    printf("\n***\n");

    for (n = 1; n*n < 200; n += 4)
        printf("%d\n", n);

    printf("\n***\n");

    for (n = 2, m = 6; n < m; n *= 2, m+= 2)
        printf("%d %d\n", n, m);
```

```
        printf("\n***\n");

        for (n = 5; n > 0; n--)
        {
              for (m = 0; m <= n; m++)
                  printf("=");
              printf("\n");
        }
        return 0;
}
```

10. Consider the following declaration:

    `double mint[10];`

    a. What is the array name?

    b. How many elements does the array have?

    c. What kind of value can be stored in each element?

    d. Which of the following is a correct usage of `scanf()` with this array?

        i. `scanf("%lf", mint[2])`

        ii. `scanf("%lf", &mint[2])`

        iii. `scanf("%lf", &mint)`

11. Mr. Noah likes counting by twos, so he's written the following program to create an array and to fill it with the integers 2, 4, 6, 8, and so on. What, if anything, is wrong with this program?

```
#include <stdio.h>
#define SIZE 8
int main(void)
{
  int by_twos[SIZE];
  int index;

  for (index = 1; index <= SIZE; index++)
      by_twos[index] = 2 * index;
  for (index = 1; index <= SIZE; index++)
      printf("%d ", by_twos);
  printf("\n");
  return 0;
}
```

12. You want to write a function that returns a `long` value. What should your definition of the function include?

13. Define a function that takes an `int` argument and that returns, as a `long`, the square of that value.

14. What will the following program print?

```c
#include <stdio.h>
int main(void)
{
    int k;

    for(k = 1, printf("%d: Hi!\n", k); printf("k = %d\n",k),
        k*k < 26; k+=2, printf("Now k is %d\n", k) )
            printf("k is %d in the loop\n",k);
    return 0;
}
```

Programming Exercises

1. Write a program that creates an array with 26 elements and stores the 26 lowercase letters in it. Also have it show the array contents.

2. Use nested loops to produce the following pattern:

```
$
$$
$$$
$$$$
$$$$$
```

3. Use nested loops to produce the following pattern:

```
F
FE
FED
FEDC
FEDCB
FEDCBA
```

Note: If your system doesn't use ASCII or some other code that encodes letters in numeric order, you can use the following to initialize a character array to the letters of the alphabet:

```c
char lets[26] = "ABCDEFGHIJKLMNOPQRSTUVWXYZ";
```

Then you can use the array index to select individual letters; for example, lets[0] is 'A', and so on.

4. Have a program request the user to enter an uppercase letter. Use nested loops to produce a pyramid pattern like this:

```
    A
   ABA
  ABCBA
 ABCDCDA
ABCDEDCBA
```

The pattern should extend to the character entered. For example, the preceding pattern would result from an input value of E. Hint: Use an outer loop to handle the rows. Use three inner loops in a row, one to handle the spaces, one for printing letters in ascending order, and one for printing letters in descending order. If your system doesn't use ASCII or a similar system that represents letters in strict number order, see the suggestion in programming exercise 3.

5. Write a program that prints a table with each line giving an integer, its square, and its cube. Ask the user to input the lower and upper limits for the table. Use a `for` loop.

6. Write a program that reads a single word into a character array and then prints the word backward. Hint: Use `strlen()` (Chapter 4) to compute the index of the last character in the array.

7. Write a program that requests two floating-point numbers and prints the value of their difference divided by their product. Have the program loop through pairs of input values until the user enters nonnumeric input.

8. Modify exercise 7 so that it uses a function to return the value of the calculation.

9. Write a program that requests lower and upper integer limits, calculates the sum of all the integer squares from the square of the lower limit to the square of the upper limit, and displays the answer. The program should then continue to prompt for limits and display answers until the user enters an upper limit that is equal to or less than the lower limit. A sample run should look something like this:

```
Enter lower and upper integer limits: 5 9
The sums of the squares from 25 to 81 is 255
Enter next set of limits: 3 25
The sums of the squares from 9 to 625 is 5520
Enter next set of limits: 5 5
Done
```

10. Write a program that reads eight integers into an array and then prints them in reverse order.

11. Consider these two infinite series:

```
1.0 + 1.0/2.0 + 1.0/3.0 + 1.0/4.0 + ...
1.0 - 1.0/2.0 + 1.0/3.0 - 1.0/4.0 + ...
```

Write a program that evaluates running totals of these two series up to some limit of number of terms. Have the user enter the limit interactively. Look at the running totals after 20 terms, 100 terms, 500 terms. Does either series appear to be converging to some value? Hint: -1 times itself an odd number of times is -1, and -1 times itself an even number of times is 1.

12. Write a program that creates an eight-element array of `int`s and sets the elements to the first eight powers of 2 and then prints the values. Use a `for` loop to set the values, and, for variety, use a `do while` loop to display the values.

13. Write a program that creates two eight-element arrays of doubles and uses a loop to let the user enter values for the eight elements of the first array. Have the program set the elements of the second array to the cumulative totals of the elements of the first array. For example, the fourth element of the second array should equal the sum of the first four elements of the first array, and the fifth element of the second array should equal the sum of the first five elements of the first array. (It's possible to do this with nested loops, but by using the fact that the fifth element of the second array equals the fourth element of the second array plus the fifth element of the first array, you can avoid nesting and just use a single loop for this task.) Finally, use loops to display the contents of the two arrays, with the first array displayed on one line and with each element of the second array displayed below the corresponding element of the first array.

14. Write a program that reads in a line of input and then prints the line in reverse order. You can store the input in an array of char; assume that the line is no longer than 255 characters. Recall that you can use scanf() with the %c specifier to read a character at a time from input and that the newline character (\n) is generated when you press the Enter key.

15. Daphne invests $100 at 10% simple interest. (That is, every year, the investment earns an interest equal to 10% of the original investment.) Deirdre invests $100 at 5% interest compounded annually. (That is, interest is 5% of the current balance, including previous addition of interest.) Write a program that finds how many years it takes for the value of Deirdre's investment to exceed the value of Daphne's investment. Also show the two values at that time.

16. Chuckie Lucky won a million dollars, which he places in an account that earns 8% a year. On the last day of each year, Chuckie withdraws $100,000. Write a program that finds out how many years it takes for Chuckie to empty his account.

CHAPTER 7

C CONTROL STATEMENTS: BRANCHING AND JUMPS

You will learn about the following in this chapter:

- Keywords
  if, else, switch, continue
  break, case, default, goto

- Operators
  && || ?:

- Functions
  getchar(), putchar(), the
  ctype.h family

- How to use the if and if else
  statements and how to nest them

- Using logical operators to combine
  relational expressions into more
  involved test expressions

- C's conditional operator

- The switch statement

- The break, continue, and goto
  jumps

- Using C's character I/O functions—
  getchar() and putchar()

- The family of character-analysis
  functions provided by the ctype.h
  header file

As you grow more comfortable with C, you will probably want to tackle more complex tasks. When you do, you'll need ways to control and organize these projects. C has the tools to meet these needs. You've already learned to use loops to program repetitive tasks. In this chapter, you'll learn about branching structures such as if and switch, which allow a program to base its actions on conditions it checks. Also, you are introduced to C's logical operators, which enable you to test for more than one relationship in a while or if condition, and you look at C's jump statements, which shift the program flow to another part of a program. By the end of this chapter, you'll have all the basic information you need to design a program that behaves the way you want.

The if Statement

Let's start with a simple example of an if statement, shown in Listing 7.1. This program reads in a list of daily low temperatures (in Celsius) and reports the total number of entries and the percentage that were below freezing (that is, below zero degrees Celsius). It uses scanf() in a loop to read in the values. Once during each loop cycle, it increments a counter to keep track of the number of entries. An if statement identifies temperatures below freezing and keeps track of the number of below-freezing days separately.

LISTING 7.1   The colddays.c Program

```
// colddays.c -- finds percentage of days below freezing
#include <stdio.h>
int main(void)
{
    const int FREEZING = 0;
    float temperature;
    int cold_days = 0;
    int all_days = 0;

    printf("Enter the list of daily low temperatures.\n");
    printf("Use Celsius, and enter q to quit.\n");
    while (scanf("%f", &temperature) == 1)
    {
        all_days++;
        if (temperature < FREEZING)
            cold_days++;
    }
    if (all_days != 0)
        printf("%d days total: %.1f%% were below freezing.\n",
                all_days, 100.0 * (float) cold_days / all_days);
    if (all_days == 0)
        printf("No data entered!\n");

    return 0;
}
```

Here is a sample run:

```
Enter the list of daily low temperatures.
Use Celsius, and enter q to quit.
12 5 -2.5 0 6 8 -3 -10 5 10 q
10 days total: 30.0% were below freezing.
```

The while loop test condition uses the return value of scanf() to terminate the loop when scanf() encounters nonnumeric input. By using float instead of int for temperature, the program is able to accept input such as -2.5 as well as 8.

Here is the new statement in the while block:

```
if (temperature < FREEZING)
    cold_days++;
```

This `if` statement instructs the computer to increase `cold_days` by 1 *if* the value just read (`temperature`) is less than zero. What happens if `temperature` is not less than zero? Then the `cold_days++;` statement is skipped, and the `while` loop moves on to read the next temperature value.

The program uses the `if` statement two more times to control the output. If there is data, the program prints the results. If there is no data, the program reports that fact. (Soon you'll see a more elegant way to handle this part of the program.)

To avoid integer division, the example uses the cast to `float` when the percentage is being calculated. You don't really need the type cast because in the expression `100.0 * cold_days / all_days`, the subexpression `100.0 * cold_days` is evaluated first and is forced into floating point by the automatic type conversion rules. Using the type cast documents your intent, however, and helps protect the program against misguided revisions.

The `if` statement is called a *branching statement* or *selection statement* because it provides a junction where the program has to select which of two paths to follow. The general form is this:

```
if (expression)
    statement
```

If *expression* evaluates to true (nonzero), *statement* is executed. Otherwise, it is skipped. As with a `while` loop, *statement* can be either a single statement or a single block (also termed a compound statement). The structure is very similar to that of a `while` statement. The chief difference is that in an `if` statement, the test and (possibly) the execution are done just once, but in the `while` loop, the test and execution can be repeated several times.

Normally, *expression* is a relational expression; that is, it compares the magnitude of two quantities, as in the expressions `x > y` and `c == 6`. If *expression* is true (`x` is greater than `y`, or `c` does equal `6`), the statement is executed. Otherwise, the statement is ignored. More generally, any expression can be used, and an expression with a `0` value is taken to be false.

The statement portion can be a simple statement, as in the example, or it can be a compound statement or block, marked off by braces:

```
if (score > big)
    printf("Jackpot!\n");  // simple statement

if (joe > ron)
{                          // compound statement
    joecash++;
    printf("You lose, Ron.\n");
}
```

Note that the entire `if` structure counts as a single statement, even when it uses a compound statement.

Adding `else` to the `if` Statement

The simple form of an `if` statement gives you the choice of executing a statement (possibly compound) or skipping it. C also enables you to choose between two statements by using the `if else` form. Let's use the `if else` form to fix an awkward segment from Listing 7.1.

```
if (all_days != 0)
    printf("%d days total: %.1f%% were below freezing.\n",
           all_days, 100.0 * (float) cold_days / all_days);
if (all_days == 0)
    printf("No data entered!\n");
```

If the program finds that `all_days` is not equal to `0`, it should know that `days` must be `0` without retesting, and it does. With `if else`, you can take advantage of that knowledge by rewriting the fragment this way:

```
if (all_days!= 0)
    printf("%d days total: %.1f%% were below freezing.\n",
           all_days, 100.0 * (float) cold_days / all_days);
else
    printf("No data entered!\n");
```

Only one test is made. If the `if` test expression is true, the temperature data is printed. If it's false, the warning message is printed.

Note the general form of the `if else` statement:

```
if (expression)
    statement1
else
    statement2
```

If *expression* is true (nonzero), *statement1* is executed. If *expression* is false or zero, the single statement following the `else` is executed. The statements can be simple or compound. C doesn't require indentation, but it is the standard style. Indentation shows at a glance the statements that depend on a test for execution.

If you want more than one statement between the `if` and the `else`, you must use braces to create a single block. The following construction violates C syntax, because the compiler expects just one statement (single or compound) between the `if` and the `else`:

```
if (x > 0)
    printf("Incrementing x:\n");
    x++;
else              // will generate an error
    printf("x <= 0 \n");
```

The compiler sees the `printf()` statement as part of the `if` statement, and it sees the `x++;` statement as a separate statement, not as part of the `if` statement. It then sees the `else` as being unattached to an `if`, which is an error. Instead, use this:

```
if (x > 0)
{
```

```
    printf("Incrementing x:\n");
    x++;
}
else
    printf("x <= 0 \n");
```

The `if` statement enables you to choose whether to do one action. The `if else` statement enables you to choose between two actions. Figure 7.1 compares the two statements.

FIGURE 7.1

`if` versus `if else`.

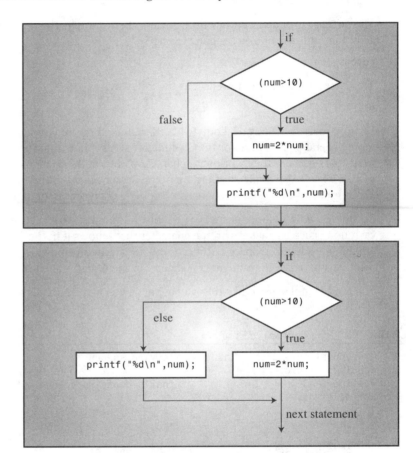

Another Example: Introducing `getchar()` and `putchar()`

Most of the examples have used numeric input. To give you practice with other types, let's look at a character-oriented example. You already know how to use `scanf()` and `printf()` with the `%c` specifier to read and write characters; but now you'll meet a pair of C functions specifically designed for character-oriented I/O—`getchar()` and `putchar()`.

The `getchar()` function takes no arguments, and it returns the next character from input. For example, the following statement reads the next input character and assigns its value to the variable `ch`:

```
ch = getchar();
```

This statement has the same effect as the following statement:

```
scanf("%c", &ch);
```

The `putchar()` function prints its argument. For example, the next statement prints as a character the value previously assigned to `ch`:

```
putchar(ch);
```

This statement has the same effect as the following:

```
printf("%c", ch);
```

Because these functions deal only with characters, they are faster and more compact than the more general `scanf()` and `printf()` functions. Also, note that they don't need format specifiers; that's because they work with characters only. Both functions are typically defined in the `stdio.h` file. (Also, typically, they are preprocessor *macros* rather than true functions; we'll talk about function-like macros in Chapter 16, "The C Preprocessor and the C Library.")

Let's see how these functions work by writing a program that repeats an input line but replaces each non-space character with the character that follows it in the ASCII code sequence. Spaces will be reproduced as spaces. You can state the desired response as, "If the character is a space, print it; otherwise, print the next character in the ASCII sequence."

The C code looks much like this statement, as you can see in Listing 7.2.

LISTING 7.2   The `cypher1.c` Program

```
/* cypher1.c -- alters input, preserving spaces */
#include <stdio.h>
#define SPACE ' '              /* that's quote-space-quote */
int main(void)
{
    char ch;

    ch = getchar();            /* read a character         */
    while (ch != '\n')         /* while not end of line    */
    {
        if (ch == SPACE)       /* leave the space          */
            putchar(ch);       /* character unchanged      */
        else
            putchar(ch + 1);   /* change other characters  */
        ch = getchar();        /* get next character       */
    }
    putchar(ch);               /* print the newline        */

    return 0;
}
```

Here is a sample run:

CALL ME HAL.
DBMM NF IBM/

Compare this loop to the one from Listing 7.1. Listing 7.1 uses the status returned by `scanf()` instead of the value of the input item to determine when to terminate the loop. Listing 7.2, however, uses the value of the input item itself to decide when to terminate the loop. This difference results in a slightly different loop structure, with one read statement before the loop and one read statement at the end of each loop. C's flexible syntax, however, enables you to emulate Listing 7.1 by combining reading and testing into a single expression. That is, you can replace a loop of the form

```
ch = getchar();          /* read a character        */
while (ch != '\n')       /* while not end of line   */
{
    ...                  /* process character       */
    ch = getchar();      /* get next character      */
}
```

with one that looks like this:

```
while ((ch = getchar()) != '\n')
{
    ...                              /* process character        */
}
```

The critical line is

```
while ((ch = getchar()) != '\n')
```

It demonstrates a characteristic C programming style—combining two actions in one expression. C's free-formatting facility can help to make the separate components of the line clearer:

```
while (
        (ch = getchar())              // assign a value to ch
                    != '\n')          // compare ch to \n
```

The actions are assigning a value to `ch` and comparing this value to the newline character. The parentheses around `ch = getchar()` make it the left operand of the `!=` operator. To evaluate this expression, the computer must first call the `getchar()` function and then assign its return value to `ch`. Because the value of an assignment expression is the value of the left member, the value of `ch = getchar()` is just the new value of `ch`. Therefore, after `ch` is read, the test condition boils down to `ch != '\n'` (that is, to `ch` *not* being the newline character).

This particular idiom is very common in C programming, so you should be familiar with it. You also should make sure you remember to use parentheses to group the subexpressions properly.

All the parentheses are necessary. Suppose that you mistakenly used this:

```
while (ch = getchar() != '\n')
```

The != operator has higher precedence than =, so the first expression to be evaluated is
getchar() != '\n'. Because this is a relational expression, its value is 1 or 0 (true or false).
Then this value is assigned to ch. Omitting the parentheses means that ch is assigned 0 or 1
rather than the return value of getchar(); this is not desirable.

The statement

```
putchar(ch + 1);    /* change other characters  */
```

illustrates once again that characters really are stored as integers. In the expression ch + 1, ch
is expanded to type int for the calculation, and the resulting int is passed to putchar(),
which takes an int argument but only uses the final byte to determine which character to display.

The ctype.h Family of Character Functions

Notice that the output for Listing 7.2 shows a period being converted to a slash; that's because
the ASCII code for the slash character is one greater than the code for the period character. But
if the point of the program is to convert only letters, it would be nice to leave all non-letters,
not just spaces, unaltered. The logical operators, discussed later in this chapter, provide a way
to test whether a character is not a space, not a comma, and so on, but it would be rather cum-
bersome to list all the possibilities. Fortunately, ANSI C has a standard set of functions for analyzing characters; the ctype.h header file contains the prototypes. These functions take a
character as an argument and return nonzero (true) if the character belongs to a particular category and zero (false) otherwise. For example, the isalpha() function returns a nonzero value
if its argument is a letter. Listing 7.3 generalizes Listing 7.2 by using this function; it also
incorporates the shortened loop structure we just discussed.

LISTING 7.3   The cypher2.c Program

```
// cypher2.c -- alters input, preserving non-letters
#include <stdio.h>
#include <ctype.h>              // for isalpha()
int main(void)
{
    char ch;

    while ((ch = getchar()) != '\n')
    {
        if (isalpha(ch))        // if a letter,
            putchar(ch + 1);    // change it
        else                    // otherwise,
            putchar(ch);        // print as is
    }
    putchar(ch);                // print the newline

    return 0;
}
```

Here is a sample run; note how both lowercase and uppercase letters are enciphered, but spaces and punctuation are not:

Look! It's a programmer!
Mppl! Ju't b qsphsbnnfs!

Tables 7.1 and 7.2 list several functions provided when you include the `ctype.h` header file. Some mention a locale; this refers to C's facility for specifying a locale that modifies or extends basic C usage. (For example, many nations use a comma instead of a decimal point when writing decimal fractions, and a particular locale could specify that C use the comma in the same way for floating-point output, thus displaying `123.45` as `123,45`.) Note that the mapping functions don't modify the original argument; instead, they return the modified value. That is,

```
tolower(ch);        // no effect on ch
```

doesn't change `ch`. To change `ch`, do this:

```
ch = tolower(ch);   // convert ch to lowercase
```

TABLE 7.1   The `ctype.h` Character-Testing Functions

Name	True If the Argument Is
isalnum()	Alphanumeric (alphabetic or numeric)
isalpha()	Alphabetic
isblank()	A standard blank character (space, horizontal tab, or newline) or any additional locale-specific character so specified
iscntrl()	A control character, such as Ctrl+B
isdigit()	A digit
isgraph()	Any printing character other than a space
islower()	A lowercase character
isprint()	A printing character
ispunct()	A punctuation character (any printing character other than a space or an alphanumeric character)
isspace()	A whitespace character (a space, newline, formfeed, carriage return, vertical tab, horizontal tab, or, possibly, other locale-defined character)
isupper()	An uppercase character
isxdigit()	A hexadecimal-digit character

TABLE 7.2   The `ctype.h` Character-Mapping Functions

Name	Action
`tolower()`	If the argument is an uppercase character, this function returns the lowercase version; otherwise, it just returns the original argument.
`toupper()`	If the argument is a lowercase character, this function returns the uppercase version; otherwise, it just returns the original argument.

Multiple Choice `else if`

Life often offers us more than two choices. You can extend the `if else` structure with `else if` to accommodate this fact. Let's look at a particular example. Utility companies often have charges that depend on the amount of energy the customer uses. Here are the rates one company charges for electricity, based on kilowatt-hours (kWh):

First 360 kWh: $0.12589 per kWh

Next 320 kWh: $0.17901 per kWh

Over 680 kWh: $0.20971 per kWh

If you worry about your energy management, you might want to prepare a program to calculate your energy costs. The program in Listing 7.4 is a first step in that direction.

LISTING 7.4   The `electric.c` Program

```
/* electric.c -- calculates electric bill */
#include <stdio.h>
#define RATE1   0.12589      /* rate for first 360 kwh       */
#define RATE2   0.17901      /* rate for next 320 kwh        */
#define RATE3   0.20971      /* rate for over 680 kwh        */
#define BREAK1  360.0        /* first breakpoint for rates   */
#define BREAK2  680.0        /* second breakpoint for rates  */
#define BASE1   (RATE1 * BREAK1)
                             /* cost for 360 kwh             */
#define BASE2   (BASE1 + (RATE2 * (BREAK2 - BREAK1)))
                             /* cost for 680 kwh             */
int main(void)
{
    double kwh;              /* kilowatt-hours used          */
    double bill;             /* charges                      */

    printf("Please enter the kwh used.\n");
    scanf("%lf", &kwh);      /* %lf for type double          */
    if (kwh <= BREAK1)
        bill = RATE1 * kwh;
    else if (kwh <= BREAK2)  /* kwh between 360 and 680      */
```

LISTING 7.4   Continued

```
          bill = BASE1 + (RATE2 * (kwh - BREAK1));
     else                        /* kwh above 680              */
          bill = BASE2 + (RATE3 * (kwh - BREAK2));
     printf("The charge for %.1f kwh is $%1.2f.\n", kwh, bill);

     return 0;
}
```

Here's some sample output:

```
Please enter the kwh used.
580
The charge for 580.0 kwh is $84.70.
```

Listing 7.4 uses symbolic constants for the rates so that the constants are conveniently gathered in one place. If the power company changes its rates (it's possible), having the rates in one place makes them easy to update. The listing also expresses the rate breakpoints symbolically. They, too, are subject to change. BASE1 and BASE2 are expressed in terms of the rates and breakpoints. Then, if the rates or breakpoints change, the bases are updated automatically. You may recall that the preprocessor does not do calculations. Where BASE1 appears in the program, it will be replaced by 0.12589 * 360.0. Don't worry; the compiler does evaluate this expression to its numerical value (45.3204) so that the final program code uses 45.3204 rather than a calculation.

The flow of the program is straightforward. The program selects one of three formulas, depending on the value of kwh. Figure 7.2 illustrates this flow. You should pay particular attention to the fact that the only way the program can reach the first else is if kwh is equal to or greater than 360. Therefore, the else if (kwh <= BREAK2) line really is equivalent to demanding that kwh be between 360 and 680, as the program comment notes. Similarly, the final else can be reached only if kwh exceeds 680. Finally, note that BASE1 and BASE2 represent the total charges for the first 360 and 680 kilowatt-hours, respectively. Therefore, you need add on only the additional charges for electricity in excess of those amounts.

Actually, the else if is a variation on what you already knew. For example, the core of the program is just another way of writing

```
if (kwh <=BREAK1)
    bill = RATE1 * kwh;
else
    if (kwh <=BREAK2)
        bill = BASE1 + RATE2 * (kwh - BREAK1);
    else
        bill = BASE2 + RATE3 * (kwh - BREAK2);
```

That is, the program consists of an if else statement for which the statement part of the else is another if else statement. The second if else statement is said to be *nested* inside the first. Recall that the entire if else structure counts as a single statement, which is why we didn't have to enclose the nested if else in braces. However, using braces would clarify the intent of this particular format.

FIGURE 7.2

Program flow for Listing
7.4, `electric.c`.

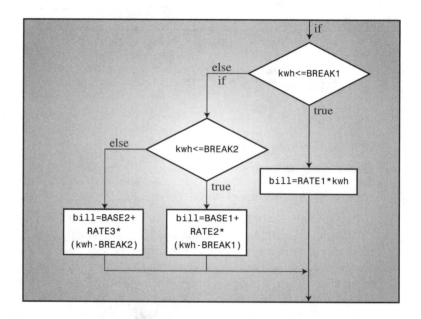

These two forms are perfectly equivalent. The only differences are in where you put spaces and newlines, and these differences are ignored by the compiler. Nonetheless, the first form is better because it shows more clearly that you are making a three-way choice. This form makes it easier to skim the program and see what the choices are. Save the nested forms of indentation for when they are needed—for example, when you must test two separate quantities. An example of such a situation is having a 10% surcharge for kilowatt-hours in excess of 680 during the summer only.

You can string together as many **else if** statements as you need (within compiler limits, of course), as illustrated by this fragment:

```
if (score < 1000)
    bonus = 0;
else if (score < 1500)
    bonus = 1;
else if (score < 2000)
    bonus = 2;
else if (score < 2500)
    bonus = 4;
else
    bonus = 6;
```

(This might be part of a game program, in which **bonus** represents how many additional photon bombs or food pellets you get for the next round.)

Speaking of compiler limits, the C99 standard requires that a compiler support a minimum of 127 levels of nesting.

Pairing `else` with `if`

When you have a lot of `if`s and `else`s, how does the computer decide which `if` goes with which `else`? For example, consider the following program fragment:

```
if (number > 6)
    if (number < 12)
        printf("You're close!\n");
else
    printf("Sorry, you lose a turn!\n");
```

When is `Sorry, you lose a turn!` printed? When `number` is less than or equal to **6**, or when `number` is greater than 12? In other words, does the `else` go with the first `if` or the second? The answer is, the `else` goes with the second `if`. That is, you would get these responses:

Number	Response
5	None
10	You're close!
15	Sorry, you lose a turn!

The rule is that an `else` goes with the most recent `if` unless braces indicate otherwise (see Figure 7.3).

FIGURE 7.3

The rule for `if else` pairings.

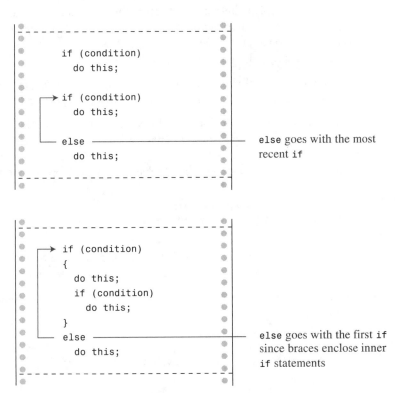

```
          if (condition)
              do this;

        ┌→ if (condition)
        │      do this;
        │
        └─ else ─────────────────── else goes with the most
               do this;              recent if
```

```
        ┌→ if (condition)
        │  {
        │      do this;
        │      if (condition)
        │          do this;
        │  }
        └─ else ─────────────────── else goes with the first if
               do this;             since braces enclose inner
                                    if statements
```

The indentation of the first example makes it look as though the `else` goes with the first `if`, but remember that the compiler ignores indentation. If you really want the `else` to go with the first `if`, you could write the fragment this way:

```
if (number > 6)
{
    if (number < 12)
        printf("You're close!\n");
}
else
    printf("Sorry, you lose a turn!\n");
```

Now you would get these responses:

Number	Response
5	Sorry, you lose a turn!
10	You're close!
15	None

More Nested `ifs`

You've already seen that the `if...else if...else` sequence is a form of nested `if`, one that selects from a series of alternatives. Another kind of nested `if` is used when choosing a particular selection leads to an additional choice. For example, a program could use an `if else` to select between males and females. Each branch within the `if else` could then contain another `if else` to distinguish between different income groups.

Let's apply this form of nested `if` to the following problem. Given an integer, print all the integers that divide into it evenly; if there are no divisors, report that the number is prime.

This problem requires some forethought before you whip out the code. First, you need an overall design for the program. For convenience, the program should use a loop to enable you to input numbers to be tested. That way, you don't have to run the program again each time you want to examine a new number. We've already developed a model for this kind of loop:

```
prompt user
while the scanf() return value is 1
    analyze the number and report results
    prompt user
```

Recall that by using `scanf()` in the loop test condition, the program attempts both to read a number and to check to see whether the loop should be terminated.

Next, you need a plan for finding divisors. Perhaps the most obvious approach is something like this:

```
for (div = 2; div < num; div++)
  if (num % div == 0)
        printf("%d is divisible by %d\n", num, div);
```

The loop checks all the numbers between 2 and num to see whether they divide evenly into num. Unfortunately, this approach is wasteful of computer time. You can do much better. Consider, for example, finding the divisors of 144. You find that 144 % 2 is 0, meaning 2 goes into 144 evenly. If you then actually divide 2 into 144, you get 72, which also is a divisor, so you can get two divisors instead of one divisor out of a successful num % div test. The real payoff, however, comes in changing the limits of the loop test. To see how this works, look at the pairs of divisors you get as the loop continues: 2,72, 3,48, 4,36, 6,24, 8,18, 9,16, 12,12, 16,9, 18,8, and so on. Ah! After you get past the 12,12 pair, you start getting the same divisors (in reverse order) that you already found. Instead of running the loop to 143, you can stop after reaching 12. That saves a lot of cycles!

Generalizing this discovery, you see that you have to test only up to the square root of num instead of to num. For numbers such as 9, this is not a big savings, but the difference is enormous for a number such as 10,000. Instead of messing with square roots, however, you can express the test condition as follows:

```
for (div = 2; (div * div) <= num; div++)
    if (num % div == 0)
        printf("%d is divisible by %d and %d.\n",
               num, div, num / div);
```

If num is 144, the loop runs through div = 12. If num is 145, the loop runs through div = 13.

There are two reasons for using this test rather than a square root test. First, integer multiplication is much faster than extracting a square root. Second, the square root function hasn't been formally introduced yet.

We need to address just two more problems, and then you'll be ready to program. First, what if the test number is a perfect square? Reporting that 144 is divisible by 12 and 12 is a little clumsy, but you can use a nested if statement to test whether div equals num / div. If so, the program will print just one divisor instead of two.

```
for (div = 2; (div * div) <= num; div++)
{
    if (num % div == 0)
    {
        if (div * div != num)
            printf("%d is divisible by %d and %d.\n",
                num, div, num / div);
        else
            printf("%d is divisible by %d.\n", num, div);
    }
}
```

Note

Technically, the if else statement counts as a single statement, so the braces around it are not needed. The outer if is a single statement also, so the braces around it are not needed. However, when statements get long, the braces make it easier to see what is happening, and they offer protection if later you add another statement to an if or to the loop.

Second, how do you know if a number is prime? If num is prime, program flow never gets inside the if statement. To solve this problem, you can set a variable to some value, say 1, outside the loop and reset the variable to 0 inside the if statement. Then, after the loop is completed, you can check to see whether the variable is still 1. If it is, the if statement was never entered, and the number is prime. Such a variable is often called a *flag*.

Traditionally, C has used the int type for flags, but the new _Bool type matches the requirements perfectly. Furthermore, by including the stdbool.h header file, you can use bool instead of the keyword _Bool for the type and use the identifiers true and false instead of 1 and 0.

Listing 7.5 incorporates all these ideas. To extend the range, the program uses type long instead of type int. (If your system doesn't support the _Bool type, you can use the int type for isPrime and use 1 and 0 instead of true and false.)

LISTING 7.5   The divisors.c Program

```c
// divisors.c -- nested ifs display divisors of a number
#include <stdio.h>
#include <stdbool.h>
int main(void)
{
    unsigned long num;        // number to be checked
    unsigned long div;        // potential divisors
    bool isPrime;             // prime flag

    printf("Please enter an integer for analysis; ");
    printf("Enter q to quit.\n");
    while (scanf("%lu", &num) == 1)
    {
        for (div = 2, isPrime= true; (div * div) <= num; div++)
        {
            if (num % div == 0)
            {
                if ((div * div) != num)
                    printf("%lu is divisible by %lu and %lu.\n",
                            num, div, num / div);
                else
                    printf("%lu is divisible by %lu.\n",
                            num, div);
                isPrime= false; // number is not prime
            }
        }
        if (isPrime)
            printf("%lu is prime.\n", num);
        printf("Please enter another integer for analysis; ");
        printf("Enter q to quit.\n");
    }
    printf("Bye.\n");

    return 0;
}
```

Note that the program uses the comma operator in the `for` loop control expression to enable you to initialize `isPrime` to `true` for each new input number.

Here's a sample run:

```
Please enter an integer for analysis; Enter q to quit.
36
36 is divisible by 2 and 18.
36 is divisible by 3 and 12.
36 is divisible by 4 and 9.
36 is divisible by 6.
Please enter another integer for analysis; Enter q to quit.
149
149 is prime.
Please enter another integer for analysis; Enter q to quit.
30077
30077 is divisible by 19 and 1583.
Please enter another integer for analysis; Enter q to quit.
q
```

The program will identify 1 as prime, which, technically, it isn't. The logical operators, coming up in the next section, would let you exclude 1 from the prime list.

Summary: Using `if` Statements for Making Choices

Keywords:

`if, else`

General Comments:

In each of the following forms, the statement can be either a simple statement or a compound statement. A true expression means one with a nonzero value.

Form 1:

```
if (expression)
    statement
```

The *statement* is executed if the *expression* is true.

Form 2:

```
if (expression)
    statement1
  else
    statement2
```

If the *expression* is true, *statement1* is executed. Otherwise, *statement2* is executed.

Form 3:

```
if (expression1)
    statement1
else if (expression2)
    statement2
  else
    statement3
```

If *expression1* is true, *statement1* is executed. If *expression1* is false but *expression2* is true, *statement2* is executed. Otherwise, if both expressions are false, *statement3* is executed.

Example:

```
if (legs == 4)
    printf("It might be a horse.\n");
else if (legs > 4)
    printf("It is not a horse.\n");
else    /* case of legs < 4 */
{
    legs++;
    printf("Now it has one more leg.\n");
}
```

Let's Get Logical

You've seen how `if` and `while` statements often use relational expressions as tests. Sometimes you will find it useful to combine two or more relational expressions. For example, suppose you want a program that counts how many times the characters other than single or double quotes appear in an input sentence. You can use logical operators to meet this need, and you can use the period character (`.`) to identify the end of a sentence. Listing 7.6 presents a short program illustrating this method.

LISTING 7.6   The chcount.c Program

```
// chcount.c  -- use the logical AND operator
#include <stdio.h>
#define PERIOD '.'
int main(void)
{
    int ch;
    int charcount = 0;

    while ((ch = getchar()) != PERIOD)
    {
        if (ch != '"' && ch != '\'')
            charcount++;
    }
    printf("There are %d non-quote characters.\n", charcount);

    return 0;
}
```

The following is a sample run:

I didn't read the "I'm a Programming Fool" best seller.
There are 50 non-quote characters.

The action begins as the program reads a character and checks to see whether it is a period, because the period marks the end of a sentence. Next comes something new, a statement using the logical AND operator, `&&`. You can translate the `if` statement as, "If the character is not a double quote AND if it is not a single quote, increase `charcount` by 1."

Both conditions must be true if the whole expression is to be true. The logical operators have a lower precedence than the relational operators, so it is not necessary to use additional parentheses to group the subexpressions.

C has three logical operators:

Operator	Meaning
`&&`	and
`||`	or
`!`	not

Suppose `exp1` and `exp2` are two simple relational expressions, such as `cat > rat` and `debt == 1000`. Then you can state the following:

* `exp1 && exp2` is true only if both `exp1` and `exp2` are true.

* `exp1 || exp2` is true if either `exp1` or `exp2` is true or if both are true.

* `!exp1` is true if `exp1` is false, and it's false if `exp1` is true.

Here are some concrete examples:

`5 > 2 && 4 > 7` is false because only one subexpression is true.
`5 > 2 || 4 > 7` is true because at least one of the subexpressions is true.
`!(4 > 7)` is true because 4 is not greater than 7.

The last expression, incidentally, is equivalent to the following:

`4 <= 7`

If you are unfamiliar or uncomfortable with logical operators, remember that

`(practice && time) == perfection`

Alternate Spellings: The `iso646.h` Header File

C was developed in the U.S. on systems using the standard U.S. keyboards. But in the wider world, not all keyboards have the same symbols as U.S. keyboards do. Therefore, the C99 standard has added alternative spellings for the logical operators. They are defined in the `iso646.h` header file. If you use this header file, you can use **and** instead of `&&`, **or** instead of `||`, and **not** instead of `!`. For example, you can rewrite

```
if (ch != '"' && ch != '\'')
    charcount++;
```

this way:

```
if (ch != '"' and ch != '\'')
    charcount++;
```

Table 7.3 lists your choices; they are pretty easy to remember. In fact, you might wonder why C didn't simply use the new terms. The answer probably is that C historically has tried to keep the number of keywords small. Reference Section VII, "Universal Character Names," lists additional alternative spellings for some operators you haven't met yet.

TABLE 7.3   Alternative Representations of Logical Operators

Traditional	iso646.h
&&	and
||	or
!	not

Precedence

The ! operator has a very high precedence—higher than multiplication, the same as the increment operators, and just below that of parentheses. The && operator has higher precedence than ||, and both rank below the relational operators and above assignment in precedence. Therefore, the expression

```
a > b && b > c || b > d
```

would be interpreted as

```
((a > b) && (b > c)) || (b > d)
```

That is, b is between a and c, or b is greater than d.

Many programmers would use parentheses, as in the second version, even though they are not needed. That way, the meaning is clear even if the reader doesn't quite remember the precedence of the logical operators.

Order of Evaluation

Aside from those cases in which two operators share an operand, C ordinarily does not guarantee which parts of a complex expression are evaluated first. For example, in the following statement, the expression 5 + 3 might be evaluated before 9 + 6, or it might be evaluated afterward:

```
apples = (5 + 3) * (9 + 6);
```

This ambiguity was left in the language so that compiler designers could make the most efficient choice for a particular system. One exception to this rule (or lack of rule) is the treatment of logical operators. C guarantees that logical expressions are evaluated from left to right. The && and || operators are sequence points, so all side effects take place before a program moves from one operand to the next. Furthermore, it guarantees that as soon as an element is found that invalidates the expression as a whole, the evaluation stops. These guarantees make it possible to use constructions such as the following:

```
while ((c = getchar()) != ' ' && c != '\n')
```

This construction sets up a loop that reads characters up to the first space or newline character. The first subexpression gives a value to c, which then is used in the second subexpression. Without the order guarantee, the computer might try to test the second expression before finding out what value c has.

Here is another example:

```
if (number != 0 && 12/number == 2)
    printf("The number is 5 or 6.\n");
```

If `number` has the value `0`, the first subexpression is false, and the relational expression is not evaluated any further. This spares the computer the trauma of trying to divide by zero. Many languages do not have this feature. After seeing that `number` is 0, they still plunge ahead to check the next condition.

Finally, consider this example:

```
while ( x++ < 10 && x + y < 20)
```

The fact that the && operator is a sequence point guarantees that x is incremented before the expression on the right is evaluated.

Summary: Logical Operators and Expressions

Logical Operators:

Logical operators normally take relational expressions as operands. The ! operator takes one operand. The rest take two—one to the left, one to the right.

Operator	Meaning
&&	and
||	or
!	not

Logical Expressions:

expression1 && expression2 is true if and only if both expressions are true. expression1 || expression2 is true if either one or both expressions are true. !expression is true if the expression is false, and vice versa.

Order of Evaluation:

Logical expressions are evaluated from left to right. Evaluation stops as soon as something is discovered that renders the expression false.

Examples:

`6 > 2 && 3 == 3`	True.
`! (6 > 2 && 3 == 3)`	False.
`x != 0 && (20 / x) < 5`	The second expression is evaluated only if x is nonzero.

Ranges

You can use the `&&` operator to test for ranges. For example, to test for **score** being in the range 90 to 100, you can do this:

```
if (range >= 90 && range <= 100)
    printf("Good show!\n");
```

It's important to avoid imitating common mathematical notation, as in the following:

```
if (90 <= range <= 100)      // NO! Don't do it!
    printf("Good show!\n");
```

The problem is that the code is a semantic error, not a syntax error, so the compiler will not catch it (although it might issue a warning). Because the order of evaluation for the `<=` operator is left-to-right, the test expression is interpreted as follows:

```
(90 <= range) <= 100
```

The subexpression `90 <= range` either has the value `1` (for true) or `0` (for false). Either value is less than 100, so the whole expression is always true, regardless of the value of `range`. So use `&&` for testing for ranges.

A lot of code uses range tests to see whether a character is, say, a lowercase letter. For instance, suppose ch is a `char` variable:

```
if (ch >= 'a' && ch <= 'z')
    printf("That's a lowercase character.\n");
```

This works for character codes such as ASCII, in which the codes for consecutive letters are consecutive numbers. However, this is not true for some codes, including EBCDIC. The more portable way of doing this test is to use the `islower()` function from the `ctype.h` family (refer to Table 7.1):

```
if (islower(ch))
    printf("That's a lowercase character.\n");
```

The `islower()` function works regardless of the particular character code used. (However, some ancient implementations lack the `ctype.h` family.)

A Word-Count Program

Now you have the tools to make a word-counting program (that is, a program that reads input and reports the number of words it finds). You may as well count characters and lines while you are at it. Let's see what such a program involves.

First, the program should read input character-by-character, and it should have some way of knowing when to stop. Second, it should be able to recognize and count the following units: characters, lines, and words. Here's a pseudocode representation:

```
read a character
while there is more input
    increment character count
    if a line has been read, increment line count
    if a word has been read, increment word count
    read next character
```

You already have a model for the input loop:

```
while ((ch = getchar()) != STOP)
{
    ...
}
```

Here, **STOP** represents some value for **ch** that signals the end of the input. The examples so far have used the newline character and a period for this purpose, but neither is satisfactory for a general word-counting program. For the present, choose a character (such as |) that is not common in text. In Chapter 8, "Character Input/Output and Input Validation," we'll present a better solution that also allows the program to be used with text files as well as keyboard input.

Now let's consider the body of the loop. Because the program uses **getchar()** for input, it can count characters by incrementing a counter during each loop cycle. To count lines, the program can check for newline characters. If a character is a newline, the program should increment the line count. One question to decide is what to do if the **STOP** character comes in the middle of a line. Should that count as a line or not? One answer is to count it as a partial line—that is, a line with characters but no newline. You can identify this case by keeping track of the previous character read. If the last character read before the **STOP** character isn't a newline, you have a partial line.

The trickiest part is identifying words. First, you have to define what you mean by a word. Let's take a relatively simple approach and define a word as a sequence of characters that contains no whitespace (that is, no spaces, tabs, or newlines). Therefore, "glymxck" and "r2d2" are words. A word starts when the program first encounters non-whitespace, and then it ends when the next whitespace character shows up. Here is the most straightforward test expression for detecting non-whitespace:

```
c != ' ' && c != '\n' && c != '\t'    /* true if c is not whitespace */
```

And the most straightforward test for detecting whitespace is

```
c == ' ' || c == '\n' || c == '\t'    /* true if c is whitespace */
```

However, it is simpler to use the **ctype.h** function **isspace()**, which returns true if its argument is a whitespace character. So **isspace(c)** is true if **c** is whitespace, and **!isspace(c)** is true if **c** isn't whitespace.

To keep track of whether a character is in a word, you can set a flag (call it `inword`) to 1 when the first character in a word is read. You can also increment the word count at that point. Then, as long as `inword` remains 1 (or true), subsequent non-whitespace characters don't mark the beginning of a word. At the next whitespace character, you must reset the flag to 0 (or false) and then the program will be ready to find the next word. Let's put that into pseudocode:

```
if c is not whitespace and inword is false
    set inword to true and count the word
if c is whitespace and inword is true
    set inword to false
```

This approach sets `inword` to 1 (true) at the beginning of each word and to 0 (false) at the end of each word. Words are counted only at the time the flag setting is changed from 0 to 1. If you have the `_Bool` type available, you can include the `stdbool.h` header file and use `bool` for the `inword` type and `true` and `false` for the values. Otherwise, use the `int` type and 1 and 0 as the values.

If you do use a Boolean variable, the usual idiom is to use the value of the variable itself as a test condition. That is, use

```
if (inword)
```

instead of

```
if (inword == true)
```

and use

```
if (!inword)
```

instead of

```
if (inword == false)
```

The reasoning is that the expression `inword == true` evaluates to `true` if `inword` is `true` and to `false` if `inword` is `false`, so you may as well just use `inword` as the test. Similarly, `!inword` has the same value as the expression `inword == false` (not true is `false`, and not false is `true`).

Listing 7.7 translates these ideas (identifying lines, identifying partial lines, and identifying words) into C.

LISTING 7.7   The `wordcnt.c` Program

```
// wordcnt.c -- counts characters, words, lines
#include <stdio.h>
#include <ctype.h>          // for isspace()
#include <stdbool.h>        // for bool, true, false
#define STOP '|'
int main(void)
{
    char c;                 // read in character
```

LISTING 7.7 *Continued*

```
    char prev;              // previous character read
    long n_chars = 0L;      // number of characters
    int n_lines = 0;        // number of lines
    int n_words = 0;        // number of words
    int p_lines = 0;        // number of partial lines
    bool inword = false;    // == true if c is in a word

    printf("Enter text to be analyzed (| to terminate):\n");
    prev = '\n';            // used to identify complete lines
    while ((c = getchar()) != STOP)
    {
        n_chars++;          // count characters
        if (c == '\n')
            n_lines++;      // count lines
        if (!isspace(c) && !inword)
        {
            inword = true;  // starting a new word
            n_words++;      // count word
        }
        if (isspace(c) && inword)
            inword = false; // reached end of word
        prev = c;           // save character value
    }

    if (prev != '\n')
        p_lines = 1;
    printf("characters = %ld, words = %d, lines = %d, ",
           n_chars, n_words, n_lines);
    printf("partial lines = %d\n", p_lines);

    return 0;
}
```

Here is a sample run:

```
Enter text to be analyzed (| to terminate):
Reason is a
powerful servant but
an inadequate master.
|
characters = 55, words = 9, lines = 3, partial lines = 0
```

The program uses logical operators to translate the pseudocode to C. For example,

```
if c is not whitespace and inword is false
```

gets translated into the following:

```
if (!isspace(c) && !inword)
```

Note that !inword is equivalent to inword == false. The entire test condition certainly is more readable than testing for each whitespace character individually:

```
if (c != ' ' && c != '\n' && c != '\t' && !inword)
```

Either form says, "If c is *not* whitespace *and* if you are *not* in a word." If both conditions are met, you must be starting a new word, and n_words is incremented. If you are in the middle of a word, the first condition holds, but inword will be true, and n_words is not incremented. When you reach the next whitespace character, inword is set equal to false again. Check the coding to see whether the program gets confused when there are several spaces between one word and the next. Chapter 8 shows how to modify this program to count words in a file.

The Conditional Operator: ?:

C offers a shorthand way to express one form of the if else statement. It is called a *conditional expression* and uses the ?: conditional operator. This is a two-part operator that has three operands. Recall that operators with one operand are called *unary* operators and that operators with two operands are called *binary* operators. In that tradition, operators with three operands are called *ternary* operators, and the conditional operator is C's only example in that category. Here is an example that yields the absolute value of a number:

```
x = (y < 0) ? -y : y;
```

Everything between the = and the semicolon is the conditional expression. The meaning of the statement, is "If y is less than zero, x = -y; otherwise, x = y." In if else terms, the meaning can be expressed as follows:

```
if (y < 0)
    x = -y;
else
    x = y;
```

The following is the general form of the conditional expression:

```
expression1 ? expression2 : expression3
```

If *expression1* is true (nonzero), the whole conditional expression has the same value as *expression2*. If *expression1* is false (zero), the whole conditional expression has the same value as *expression3*.

You can use the conditional expression when you have a variable to which you want to assign one of two possible values. A typical example is setting a variable equal to the maximum of two values:

```
max = (a > b) ? a : b;
```

This sets max to a if it is greater than b, and to b otherwise.

Usually, an if else statement can accomplish the same thing as the conditional operator. The conditional operator version, however, is more compact and, depending on the compiler, may result in more compact program code.

Let's look at a paint program example, shown in Listing 7.8. The program calculates how many cans of paint are needed to paint a given number of square feet. The basic algorithm is simple: Divide the square footage by the number of square feet covered per can. However, suppose the answer is 1.7 cans. Stores sell whole cans, not fractional cans, so you would have to buy two cans. Therefore, the program should round up to the next integer when a fractional paint can is involved. The conditional operator is used to handle that situation, and it's also used to print *cans* or *can*, as appropriate.

LISTING 7.8   The paint.c Program

```
/* paint.c -- uses conditional operator */
#include <stdio.h>
#define COVERAGE 200        /* square feet per paint can */
int main(void)
{
    int sq_feet;
    int cans;

    printf("Enter number of square feet to be painted:\n");
    while (scanf("%d", &sq_feet) == 1)
    {
        cans = sq_feet / COVERAGE;
        cans += ((sq_feet % COVERAGE == 0)) ? 0 : 1;
        printf("You need %d %s of paint.\n", cans,
                cans == 1 ? "can" : "cans");
        printf("Enter next value (q to quit):\n");
    }

    return 0;
}
```

Here's a sample run:

```
Enter number of square feet to be painted:
200
You need 1 can of paint.
Enter next value (q to quit):
215
You need 2 cans of paint.
Enter next value (q to quit):
q
```

Because the program is using type int, the division is truncated; that is, 215/200 becomes 1. Therefore, cans is rounded down to the integer part. If sq_feet % COVERAGE is 0, COVERAGE divides evenly into sq_feet and cans is left unchanged. Otherwise, there is a remainder, so 1 is added. This is accomplished with the following statement:

```
cans += ((sq_feet % COVERAGE == 0)) ? 0 : 1;
```

It adds the value of the expression to the right of += to cans. The expression to the right is a conditional expression having the value 0 or 1, depending on whether COVERAGE divides evenly into sq_feet.

The final argument to the printf() function is also a conditional expression:

```
cans == 1 ? "can" : "cans");
```

If the value of cans is 1, the string "can" is used. Otherwise, "cans" is used. This demonstrates that the conditional operator can use strings for its second and third operands.

Summary: The Conditional Operator

The Conditional Operator:

?:

General Comments:

This operator takes three operands, each of which is an expression. They are arranged as follows:

expression1 ? *expression2* : *expression3*

The value of the whole expression equals the value of *expression2* if *expression1* is true. Otherwise, it equals the value of *expression3*.

Examples:

(5 > 3) ? 1 : 2 has the value 1.

(3 > 5) ? 1 : 2 has the value 2.

(a > b) ? a : b has the value of the larger of a or b.

Loop Aids: continue and break

Normally, after the body of a loop has been entered, a program executes all the statements in the body before doing the next loop test. The continue and break statements enable you to skip part of a loop or even terminate it, depending on tests made in the body of the loop.

The continue Statement

This statement can be used in the three loop forms. When encountered, it causes the rest of an iteration to be skipped and the next iteration to be started. If the continue statement is inside nested structures, it affects only the innermost structure containing it. Let's try continue in the short program in Listing 7.9.

LISTING 7.9   The skippart.c Program

```
/* skippart.c  -- uses continue to skip part of loop */
#include <stdio.h>
int main(void)
{
    const float MIN = 0.0f;
    const float MAX = 100.0f;

    float score;
    float total = 0.0f;
    int n = 0;
    float min = MAX;
    float max = MIN;
```

LISTING 7.9   Continued

```
    printf("Enter the first score (q to quit): ");
    while (scanf("%f", &score) == 1)
    {
        if (score < MIN || score > MAX)
        {
            printf("%0.1f is an invalid value. Try again: ",
                    score);
            continue;
        }
        printf("Accepting %0.1f:\n", score);
        min = (score < min)? score: min;
        max = (score > max)? score: max;
        total += score;
        n++;
        printf("Enter next score (q to quit): ");
    }
    if (n > 0)
    {
        printf("Average of %d scores is %0.1f.\n", n, total / n);
        printf("Low = %0.1f, high = %0.1f\n", min, max);
    }
    else
        printf("No valid scores were entered.\n");
    return 0;
}
```

In Listing 7.9, the `while` loop reads input until you enter nonnumeric data. The `if` statement within the loop screens out invalid score values. If, say, you enter 188, the program tells you `188 is an invalid value`. Then the `continue` statement causes the program to skip over the rest of the loop, which is devoted to processing valid input. Instead, the program starts the next loop cycle by attempting to read the next input value.

Note that there are two ways you could have avoided using `continue`. One way is omitting the `continue` and making the remaining part of the loop an `else` block:

```
if (score < 0 || score > 100)
    /* printf() statement */
else
{
    /* statements */
}
```

Alternatively, you could have used this format instead:

```
if (score >= 0 && score <= 100)
{
    /* statements */
}
```

An advantage of using `continue` in this case is that you can eliminate one level of indentation in the main group of statements. Being concise can enhance readability when the statements are long or are deeply nested already.

Another use for `continue` is as a placeholder. For example, the following loop reads and discards input up to, and including, the end of a line:

```
while (getchar() != '\n')
    ;
```

Such a technique is handy when a program has already read some input from a line and needs to skip to the beginning of the next line. The problem is that the lone semicolon is hard to spot. The code is much more readable if you use `continue`:

```
while (getchar() != '\n')
    continue;
```

Don't use `continue` if it complicates rather than simplifies the code. Consider the following fragment, for example:

```
while ((ch = getchar() ) != '\n')
{
    if (ch == '\t')
        continue;
    putchar(ch);
}
```

This loop skips over the tabs and quits only when a newline character is encountered. The loop could have been expressed more economically as this:

```
while ((ch = getchar()) != '\n')
        if (ch != '\t')
            putchar(ch);
```

Often, as in this case, reversing an `if` test eliminates the need for a `continue`.

You've seen that the `continue` statement causes the remaining body of a loop to be skipped. Where exactly does the loop resume? For the `while` and `do while` loops, the next action taken after the `continue` statement is to evaluate the loop test expression. Consider the following loop, for example:

```
count = 0;
while (count < 10)
{
    ch = getchar();
    if (ch == '\n')
        continue;
    putchar(ch);
    count++;
}
```

It reads 10 characters (excluding newlines, because the `count++;` statement gets skipped when `ch` is a newline) and echoes them, except for newlines. When the `continue` statement is executed, the next expression evaluated is the loop test condition.

For a `for` loop, the next actions are to evaluate the update expression and then the loop test expression. Consider the following loop, for example:

```
for (count = 0; count < 10; count++)
{
```

```
    ch = getchar();
    if (ch == '\n')
        continue;
    putchar(ch);
}
```

In this case, when the continue statement is executed, first count is incremented and then it's compared to 10. Therefore, this loop behaves slightly differently from the while example. As before, only non-newline characters are displayed. However, this time, newline characters are included in the count, so it reads 10 characters, including newlines.

The break Statement

A break statement in a loop causes the program to break free of the loop that encloses it and to proceed to the next stage of the program. In Listing 7.9, replacing continue with break would cause the loop to quit when, say, 188 is entered, instead of just skipping to the next loop cycle. Figure 7.4 compares break and continue. If the break statement is inside nested loops, it affects only the innermost loop containing it.

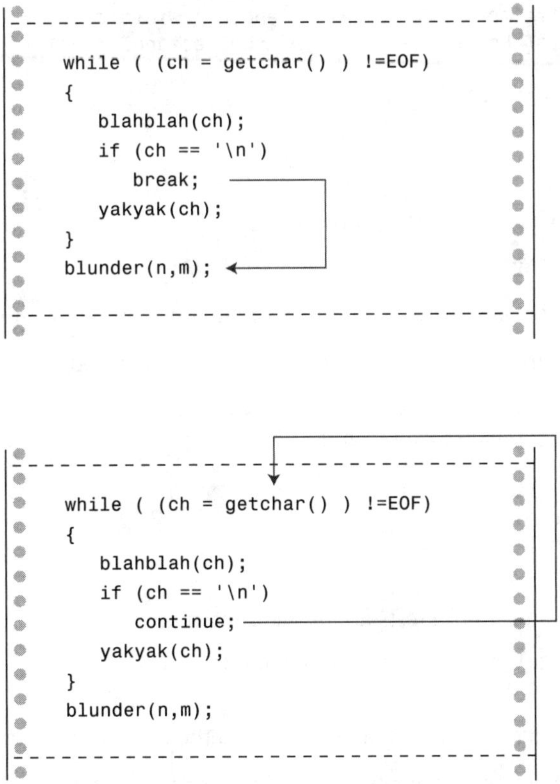

FIGURE 7.4

Comparing break and continue.

Sometimes **break** is used to leave a loop when there are two separate reasons to leave. Listing 7.10 uses a loop that calculates the area of a rectangle. The loop terminates if you respond with nonnumeric input for the rectangle's length or width.

LISTING 7.10   The `break.c` Program

```
/* break.c -- uses break to exit a loop */
#include <stdio.h>
int main(void)
{
    float length, width;

    printf("Enter the length of the rectangle:\n");
    while (scanf("%f", &length) == 1)
    {
        printf("Length = %0.2f:\n", length);
        printf("Enter its width:\n");
        if (scanf("%f", &width) != 1)
            break;
        printf("Width = %0.2f:\n", width);
        printf("Area = %0.2f:\n", length * width);
        printf("Enter the length of the rectangle:\n");
    }
    printf("Done.\n");

    return 0;
}
```

You could have controlled the loop this way:

```
while (scanf("%f %f", &length, &width) == 2)
```

However, using **break** makes it simple to echo each input value individually.

As with **continue**, don't use **break** when it complicates code. For example, consider the following loop:

```
while ((ch = getchar()) != '\n')
{
    if (ch == '\t')
        break;
    putchar(ch);
}
```

The logic is clearer if both tests are in the same place:

```
while ((ch = getchar() ) != '\n' && ch != '\t')
    putchar(ch);
```

The **break** statement is an essential adjunct to the **switch** statement, which is coming up next.

A **break** statement takes execution directly to the first statement following the loop; unlike the case for **continue** in a **for** loop, the update part of the control section is skipped. A **break** in a nested loop just takes the program out of the inner loop; to get out of the outer loop requires a second `break`:

```
int p, q;

scanf("%d", &p);
while ( p > 0)
{
    printf("%d\n", p);
    scanf("%d", &q);
    while( q > 0)
    {
        printf("%d\n",p*q);
        if (q > 100)
            break;            // break from inner loop
        scanf("%d", &q);
    }
    if (q > 100)
        break;                // break from outer loop
    scanf("%d", &p);
}
```

Multiple Choice: `switch` and `break`

The conditional operator and the `if else` construction make it easy to write programs that choose between two alternatives. Sometimes, however, a program needs to choose one of several alternatives. You can do this by using `if else if...else`. However, in many cases, it is more convenient to use the C `switch` statement. Listing 7.11 shows how the `switch` statement works. This program reads in a letter and then responds by printing an animal name that begins with that letter.

LISTING 7.11   The `animals.c` Program

```
/* animals.c -- uses a switch statement */
#include <stdio.h>
#include <ctype.h>
int main(void)
{
    char ch;

    printf("Give me a letter of the alphabet, and I will give ");
    printf("an animal name\nbeginning with that letter.\n");
    printf("Please type in a letter; type # to end my act.\n");
    while ((ch = getchar()) != '#')
    {
        if('\n' == ch)
            continue;
        if (islower(ch))      /* lowercase only          */
            switch (ch)
            {
```

LISTING 7.11   Continued

```
                    case 'a' :
                            printf("argali, a wild sheep of Asia\n");
                            break;
                    case 'b' :
                            printf("babirusa, a wild pig of Malay\n");
                            break;
                    case 'c' :
                            printf("coati, racoonlike mammal\n");
                            break;
                    case 'd' :
                            printf("desman, aquatic, molelike critter\n");
                            break;
                    case 'e' :
                            printf("echidna, the spiny anteater\n");
                            break;
                    case 'f' :
                            printf("fisher, brownish marten\n");
                            break;
                    default :
                            printf("That's a stumper!\n");
            }                       /* end of switch            */
        else
            printf("I recognize only lowercase letters.\n");
        while (getchar() != '\n')
                continue;           /* skip rest of input line */
        printf("Please type another letter or a #.\n");
    }                               /* while loop end           */
    printf("Bye!\n");

    return 0;
}
```

We got a little lazy and stopped at *f*, but we could have continued in the same manner. Let's look at a sample run before explaining the program further:

```
Give me a letter of the alphabet, and I will give an animal name
beginning with that letter.
Please type in a letter; type # to end my act.
a [enter]
argali, a wild sheep of Asia
Please type another letter or a #.
dab [enter]
desman, aquatic, molelike critter
Please type another letter or a #.
r [enter]
That's a stumper!
Please type another letter or a #.
Q [enter]
I recognize only lowercase letters.
Please type another letter or a #.
# [enter]
Bye!
```

The program's two main features are its use of the **switch** statement and its handling of input. We'll look first at how **switch** works.

Using the `switch` Statement

The expression in the parentheses following the word `switch` is evaluated. In this case, it has whatever value you last entered for `ch`. Then the program scans the list of *labels* (here, `case 'a' :`, `case 'b' :`, and so on) until it finds one matching that value. The program then jumps to that line. What if there is no match? If there is a line labeled `default :`, the program jumps there. Otherwise, the program proceeds to the statement following the `switch`.

What about the `break` statement? It causes the program to break out of the `switch` and skip to the next statement after the `switch` (see Figure 7.5). Without the `break` statement, every statement from the matched label to the end of the `switch` would be processed. For example, if you removed all the `break` statements from the program and then ran the program using the letter *d*, you would get this exchange:

```
Give me a letter of the alphabet, and I will give an animal name
beginning with that letter.
Please type in a letter; type # to end my act.
d [enter]
desman, aquatic, molelike critter
echidna, the spiny anteater
fisher, a brownish marten
That's a stumper!
Please type another letter or a #.
# [enter]
Bye!
```

All the statements from `case 'd' :` to the end of the `switch` were executed.

Incidentally, a `break` statement works with loops and with `switch`, but `continue` works just with loops. However, `continue` can be used as part of a `switch` statement if the statement is in a loop. In that situation, as with other loops, `continue` causes the program to skip over the rest of the loop, including other parts of the `switch`.

If you are familiar with Pascal, you will recognize the `switch` statement as being similar to the Pascal `case` statement. The most important difference is that the `switch` statement requires the use of a `break` if you want only the labeled statement to be processed. Also, you can't use a range as a C case.

The `switch` test expression in the parentheses should be one with an integer value (including type `char`). The `case` labels must be integer-type (including `char`) constants or integer constant expressions (expressions containing only integer constants). You can't use a variable for a `case` label. Here, then, is the structure of a `switch`:

```
switch (integer expression)
{
    case constant1:
            statements        ←optional
    case constant2:
            statements        ←optional
    default :                 ←optional
            statements        ←optional
}
```

FIGURE 7.5
Program flow in
`switch`es, with and without `break`s.

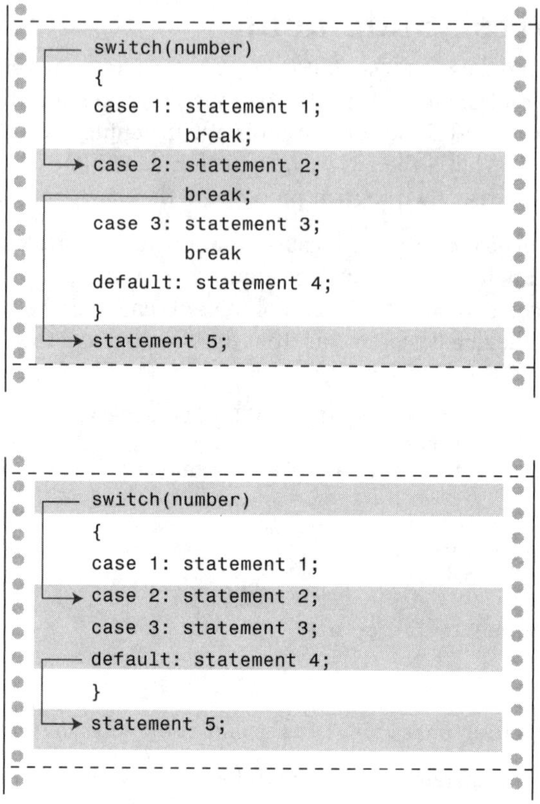

Reading Only the First Character of a Line

The other new feature incorporated into `animals.c` is how it reads input. As you might have noticed in the sample run, when `dab` was entered, only the first character was processed. This behavior is often desirable in interactive programs looking for single-character responses. The following code produced this behavior:

```
while (getchar() != '\n')
    continue;          /* skip rest of input line */
```

This loop reads characters from input up to and including the newline character generated by the Enter key. Note that the function return value is not assigned to `ch`, so the characters are merely read and discarded. Because the last character discarded is the newline character, the next character to be read is the first character of the next line. It gets read by `getchar()` and assigned to `ch` in the outer `while` loop.

Suppose a user starts out by pressing Enter so that the first character encountered is a newline. The following code takes care of that possibility:

```
if (ch == '\n')
    continue;
```

Multiple Labels

You can use multiple case labels for a given statement, as shown in Listing 7.12.

LISTING 7.12   The vowels.c Program

```
/* vowels.c -- uses multiple labels */
#include <stdio.h>
int main(void)
{
    char ch;
    int a_ct, e_ct, i_ct, o_ct, u_ct;

    a_ct = e_ct = i_ct = o_ct = u_ct = 0;

    printf("Enter some text; enter # to quit.\n");
    while ((ch = getchar()) != '#')
    {
        switch (ch)
        {
            case 'a' :
            case 'A' :  a_ct++;
                        break;
            case 'e' :
            case 'E' :  e_ct++;
                        break;
            case 'i' :
            case 'I' :  i_ct++;
                        break;
            case 'o' :
            case 'O' :  o_ct++;
                        break;
            case 'u' :
            case 'U' :  u_ct++;
                        break;
            default :   break;
        }                           /* end of switch  */
    }                               /* while loop end */
    printf("number of vowels:   A    E    I    O    U\n");
    printf("                 %4d %4d %4d %4d %4d\n",
        a_ct, e_ct, i_ct, o_ct, u_ct);

    return 0;
}
```

If ch is, say, the letter i, the switch statement goes to the location labeled case 'i' :.
Because there is no break associated with that label, program flow goes to the next statement,
which is i_ct++;. If ch is I, program flow goes directly to that statement. In essence, both
labels refer to the same statement.

Strictly speaking, the break statement for case 'U' isn't needed, because in its absence, program flow goes to the next statement in the switch, which is the break for the default case.

So the `case 'U'` break could be dropped, thus shortening the code. On the other hand, if other cases might be added later (you might want to count the letter *y* as a sometimes vowel), having the `break` already in place protects you from forgetting to add one.

Here's a sample run:

```
Enter some text; enter # to quit.
I see under the overseer.#
number of vowels:   A    E    I    O    U
                    0    7    1    1    1
```

In this particular case, you can avoid multiple labels by using the `toupper()` function from the `ctype.h` family (refer to Table 7.2) to convert all letters to uppercase before testing:

```c
while ((ch = getchar()) != '#')
{
    ch = toupper(ch);
    switch (ch)
    {
      case 'A' :   a_ct++;
                   break;
      case 'E' :   e_ct++;
                   break;
      case 'I' :   i_ct++;
                   break;
      case 'O' :   o_ct++;
                   break;
      case 'U' :   u_ct++;
                   break;
      default :    break;
    }                              /* end of switch */
}                                  /* while loop end */
```

Or, if you want to leave `ch` unchanged, use the function this way:

```c
switch(toupper(ch))
```

Summary: Multiple Choice with `switch`

Keyword:

`switch`

General Comments:

Program control jumps to the `case` label bearing the value of *expression*. Program flow then proceeds through all the remaining statements unless redirected again with a `break` statement. Both *expression* and `case` labels must have integer values (type `char` is included), and the labels must be constants or expressions formed solely from constants. If no `case` label matches the expression value, control goes to the statement labeled `default`, if present. Otherwise, control passes to the next statement following the `switch` statement.

Form:

```c
switch (expression)
{
```

```
        case label1 : statement1 /* use break to skip to end */
        case label2 : statement2
        default     : statement3
    }
```

There can be more than two labeled statements, and the `default` case is optional.

Example:

```
switch (choice)
    {
    case 1  :
    case 2  : printf("Darn tootin'!\n");  break;
    case 3  : printf("Quite right!\n");
    case 4  : printf("Good show!\n"); break;
    default : printf("Have a nice day.\n");
    }
```

If `choice` has the integer value 1 or 2, the first message is printed. If it is 3, the second and third messages are printed. (Flow continues to the following statement because there is no `break` statement after `case 3`.) If it is 4, the third message is printed. Other values print only the last message.

switch and if else

When should you use a `switch` and when should you use the `if else` construction? Often you don't have a choice. You can't use a `switch` if your choice is based on evaluating a float variable or expression. Nor can you conveniently use a `switch` if a variable must fall into a certain range. It is simple to write the following:

```
if (integer < 1000 && integer > 2)
```

Unhappily, covering this range with a `switch` would involve setting up `case` labels for each integer from 3 to 999. However, if you can use a `switch`, your program often runs a little faster and takes less code.

The goto Statement

The `goto` statement, bulwark of the older versions of BASIC and FORTRAN, is available in C. However, C, unlike those two languages, can get along quite well without it. Kernighan and Ritchie refer to the `goto` statement as "infinitely abusable" and suggest that it "be used sparingly, if at all." First, we will show you how to use `goto`. Then, we will show why you usually don't need to.

The `goto` statement has two parts—the `goto` and a label name. The label is named following the same convention used in naming a variable, as in this example:

```
goto part2;
```

For the preceding statement to work, the function must contain another statement bearing the `part2` label. This is done by beginning a statement with the label name followed by a colon:

```
part2: printf("Refined analysis:\n");
```

Avoiding `goto`

In principle, you never need to use the `goto` statement in a C program, but if you have a background in older versions of FORTRAN or BASIC, both of which require its use, you might have developed programming habits that depend on using `goto`. To help you get over that dependence, we will outline some familiar `goto` situations and then show you a more C-like approach:

- Handling an `if` situation that requires more than one statement:

```
if (size > 12)
    goto a;
goto b;
a: cost = cost * 1.05;
   flag = 2;
b: bill = cost * flag;
```

In old-style BASIC and FORTRAN, only the single statement immediately following the `if` condition is attached to the `if`. No provision is made for blocks or compound statements. We have translated that pattern into the equivalent C. The standard C approach of using a compound statement or block is much easier to follow:

```
if (size > 12)
{
    cost = cost * 1.05;
    flag = 2;
}
bill = cost * flag;
```

- Choosing from two alternatives:

```
if (ibex > 14)
    goto a;
sheds = 2;
goto b;
a: sheds= 3;
b: help = 2 * sheds;
```

Having the `if else` structure available allows C to express this choice more cleanly:

```
if (ibex > 14)
    sheds = 3;
else
    sheds = 2;
help = 2 * sheds;
```

Indeed, newer versions of BASIC and FORTRAN have incorporated `else` into their syntax.

- Setting up an indefinite loop:

```
readin: scanf("%d", &score);
if (score < 0)
    goto stage2;
```

```
lots of statements;
goto readin;
stage2: more stuff;
```

Use a `while` loop instead:

```
scanf("%d", &score);
while (score <= 0)
{
    lots of statements;
    scanf("%d", &score);
}
more stuff;
```

- Skipping to the end of a loop and starting the next cycle. Use `continue` instead.

- Leaving a loop. Use `break` instead. Actually, `break` and `continue` are specialized forms of `goto`. The advantages of using them are that their names tell you what they are supposed to do and that, because they don't use labels, there is no danger of putting a label in the wrong place.

- Leaping madly about to different parts of a program. In a word, *don't!*

There is one use of `goto` tolerated by many C practitioners—getting out of a nested set of loops if trouble shows up (a single `break` gets you out of the innermost loop only):

```
while (funct > 0)
    {
    for (i = 1, i <= 100; i++)
        {
        for (j = 1; j <= 50; j++)
            {
            statements galore;
            if (bit trouble)
                goto help;
            statements;
            }
        more statements;
        }
    yet more statements;
    }
and more statements;
help : bail out;
```

As you can see from the other examples, the alternative forms are clearer than the `goto` forms. This difference grows even greater when you mix several of these situations. Which `goto`s are helping `if`s, which are simulating `if else`s, which are controlling loops, which are just there because you have programmed yourself into a corner? By using `goto`s excessively, you create a labyrinth of program flow. If you aren't familiar with `goto`s, keep it that way. If you are used to using them, try to train yourself not to. Ironically, C, which doesn't need a `goto`, has a better `goto` than most languages because it enables you to use descriptive words for labels instead of numbers.

Summary: Program Jumps

Keywords:

break, continue, goto

General Comments:

These three instructions cause program flow to jump from one location of a program to another location.

The break Command:

The break command can be used with any of the three loop forms and with the switch statement. It causes program control to skip the rest of the loop or the switch containing it and to resume with the next command following the loop or switch.

Example:

```
switch (number)
{
    case 4:  printf("That's a good choice.\n");
             break;
    case 5:  printf("That's a fair choice.\n");
             break;
    default: printf("That's a poor choice.\n");
}
```

The continue Command:

The continue command can be used with any of the three loop forms but not with a switch. It causes program control to skip the remaining statements in a loop. For a while or for loop, the next loop cycle is started. For a do while loop, the exit condition is tested and then, if necessary, the next loop cycle is started.

Example:

```
while ((ch = getchar())  != '\n')
{
    if (ch == ' ')
        continue;
    putchar(ch);
    chcount++;
}
```

This fragment echoes and counts non-space characters.

The goto Command:

A goto statement causes program control to jump to a statement bearing the indicated label. A colon is used to separate a labeled statement from its label. Label names follow the rules for variable names. The labeled statement can come either before or after the goto.

Form:

```
goto label;
    .
    .
    .
label : statement
```

Example:

```
top : ch = getchar();
       .
       .
       .
if (ch != 'y')
        goto top;
```

Key Concepts

One aspect of intelligence is the ability to adjust one's responses to the circumstances. Therefore, selection statements are the foundation for developing programs that behave intelligently. In C, the `if`, `if else`, and `switch` statements, along with the conditional operator (`?:`), implement selection.

The `if` and `if else` statements use a test condition to determine which statements are executed. Any nonzero value is treated as `true`, whereas zero is treated as `false`. Typically, tests involve relational expressions, which compare two values, and logical expressions, which use logical operators to combine or modify other expressions.

One general principle to keep in mind is that if you want to test for two conditions, you should use a logical operator together with two complete test expressions. For instance, the following two attempts are faulty:

```
if (a < x < z)              // wrong --no logical operator
...
if (ch != 'q' && != 'Q') // wrong -- missing a complete test
...
```

Remember, the correct way is to join two relational expressions with a logical operator:

```
if (a < x && x < z)         // use && to combine two expressions
...
if (ch != 'q' && ch != 'Q')  // use && to combine two expressions
```

The control statements presented in these last two chapters will enable you to tackle programs that are much more powerful and ambitious than those you worked with before. As proof, just compare some of the examples in these chapters to those of the earlier chapters.

Summary

This chapter has presented quite a few topics to review, so let's get to it. The `if` statement uses a test condition to control whether a program executes the single simple statement or block following the test condition. Execution occurs if the test expression has a nonzero value and doesn't occur if the value is zero. The `if else` statement enables you to select from two alternatives. If the test condition is nonzero, the statement before the `else` is executed. If the test expression evaluates to zero, the statement following the `else` is executed. By using another `if` statement to immediately follow the `else`, you can set up a structure that chooses between a series of alternatives.

The test condition is often a *relational expression*—that is, an expression formed by using one of the relational operators, such as < or ==. By using C's logical operators, you can combine relational expressions to create more complex tests.

The *conditional operator* (`? :`) creates an expression that, in many cases, provides a more compact alternative to an `if else` statement.

The `ctype.h` family of character functions, such as `isspace()` and `isalpha()`, offers convenient tools for creating test expressions based on classifying characters.

The `switch` statement enables you to select from a series of statements labeled with integer values. If the integer value of the test condition following the `switch` keyword matches a label, execution goes to the statement bearing that label. Execution then proceeds through the statements following the labeled statement unless you use a `break` statement.

Finally, `break`, `continue`, and `goto` are jump statements that cause program flow to jump to another location in the program. A `break` statement causes the program to jump to the next statement following the end of the loop or `switch` containing the `break`. The `continue` statement causes the program to skip the rest of the containing loop and to start the next cycle.

Review Questions

1. Determine which expressions are `true` and which are `false`.

    a. `100 > 3 && 'a'>'c'`

    b. `100 > 3 || 'a'>'c'`

    c. `!(100>3)`

2. Construct an expression to express the following conditions:

    a. `number` is equal to or greater than 90 but smaller than 100.

    b. `ch` is not a `q` or a `k` character.

    c. `number` is between 1 and 9 (including the end values) but is not a 5.

    d. `number` is not between 1 and 9.

3. The following program has unnecessarily complex relational expressions as well as some outright errors. Simplify and correct it.

```
#include <stdio.h>
int main(void)                                    /* 1  */
{                                                 /* 2  */
    int weight, height;  /* weight in lbs, height in inches */
                                                  /* 4  */
    scanf("%d , weight, height);                  /* 5  */
```

```
    if (weight < 100 && height > 64)                /* 6  */
        if (height >= 72)                           /* 7  */
            printf("You are very tall for your weight.\n");
        else if (height < 72 &&  > 64)              /* 9  */
            printf("You are tall for your weight.\n");  /* 10 */
    else if (weight > 300 && ! (weight <= 300)      /* 11 */
            && height < 48)                         /* 12 */
        if (!(height >= 48) )                       /* 13 */
            printf(" You are quite short for your weight.\n");
    else                                            /* 15 */
        printf("Your weight is ideal.\n");          /* 16 */
                                                    /* 17 */

    return 0;
}
```

4. What is the numerical value of each of the following expressions?

   a. 5 > 2

   b. 3 + 4 > 2 && 3 < 2

   c. x >= y || y > x

   d. d = 5 + (6 > 2)

   e. 'X' > 'T' ? 10 : 5

   f. x > y ? y > x : x > y

5. What will the following program print?

```
#include <stdio.h>
int main(void)
{
    int num;
    for (num = 1; num <= 11; num++)
    {
        if (num % 3 == 0)
            putchar('$');
        else
            putchar('*');
            putchar('#');
        putchar('%');
    }
    putchar('\n');
    return 0;
}
```

6. What will the following program print?

```
#include <stdio.h>
int main(void)
{
    int i = 0;
    while ( i < 3) {
```

```
            switch(i++) {
                case 0 : printf("fat ");
                case 1 : printf("hat ");
                case 2 : printf("cat ");
                default: printf("Oh no!");
            }
            putchar('\n');
        }
        return 0;
    }
```

7. What's wrong with this program?

```
#include <stdio.h>
int main(void)
{
   char ch;
   int lc = 0;     /* lowercase char count */
   int uc = 0;     /* uppercase char count */
   int oc = 0;     /* other char count     */

   while ((ch = getchar()) != '#')
   {
       if ('a' <= ch >= 'z')
           lc++;
       else if (!(ch < 'A') || !(ch > 'Z'))
           uc++;
       oc++;
   }
   printf(%d lowercase, %d uppercase, %d other, lc, uc, oc);
   return 0;
}
```

8. What will the following program print?

```
/* retire.c    */
#include <stdio.h>
int main(void)
{
   int age = 20;

   while (age++ <= 65)
   {
      if (( age % 20) == 0) /* is age divisible by 20? */
          printf("You are %d. Here is a raise.\n", age);
      if (age = 65)
          printf("You are %d. Here is your gold watch.\n", age);
   }
   return 0;
}
```

9. What will the following program print when given this input?

```
q
c
g
b
```

```c
#include <stdio.h>
int main(void)
{
   char ch;

   while ((ch = getchar()) != '#')
   {
        if (ch == '\n')
            continue;
        printf("Step 1\n");
        if (ch == 'c')
            continue;q
        else if (ch == 'b')
            break;
        else if (ch == 'g')
            goto laststep;
        printf("Step 2\n");
   laststep:   printf("Step 3\n");
   }
   printf("Done\n");
   return 0;
}
```

10. Rewrite the program in question 9 so that it exhibits the same behavior but does not use a continue or a goto.

Programming Exercises

1. Write a program that reads input until encountering the # character and then reports the number of spaces read, the number of newline characters read, and the number of all other characters read.

2. Write a program that reads input until encountering #. Have the program print each input character and its ASCII decimal code. Print eight character-code pairs per line. Suggestion: Use a character count and the modulus operator (%) to print a newline character for every eight cycles of the loop.

3. Write a program that reads integers until 0 is entered. After input terminates, the program should report the total number of even integers (excluding the 0) entered, the average value of the even integers, the total number of odd integers entered, and the average value of the odd integers.

4. Using if else statements, write a program that reads input up to #, replaces each period with an exclamation mark, replaces each exclamation mark initially present with two exclamation marks, and reports at the end the number of substitutions it has made.

5. Redo exercise 3 using a `switch`.

6. Write a program that reads input up to # and reports the number of times that the sequence `ei` occurs.

> ### Note
>
> The program will have to "remember" the preceding character as well as the current character. Test it with input such as "Receive your eieio award."

7. Write a program that requests the hours worked in a week and then prints the gross pay, the taxes, and the net pay. Assume the following:

   a. Basic pay rate = $10.00/hr

   b. Overtime (in excess of 40 hours) = time and a half

   c. Tax rate: 15% of the first $300

   20% of the next $150

   25% of the rest

   Use `#define` constants, and don't worry if the example does not conform to current tax law.

8. Modify assumption a. in exercise 7 so that the program presents a menu of pay rates from which to choose. Use a `switch` to select the pay rate. The beginning of a run should look something like this:

```
******************************************************************
Enter the number corresponding to the desired pay rate or action:
1) $8.75/hr                        2) $9.33/hr
3) $10.00/hr                       4) $11.20/hr
5) quit
******************************************************************
```

   If choices 1 through 4 are selected, the program should request the hours worked. The program should recycle until 5 is entered. If something other than choices 1 through 5 is entered, the program should remind the user what the proper choices are and then recycle. Use `#defined` constants for the various earning rates and tax rates.

9. Write a program that accepts an integer as input and then displays all the prime numbers smaller than or equal to that number.

10. The 1988 United States Federal Tax Schedule was the simplest in recent times. It had four categories, and each category had two rates. Here is a summary (dollar amounts are taxable income):

Category	Tax
Single	15% of first $17,850 plus 28% of excess
Head of Household	15% of first $23,900 plus 28% of excess
Married, Joint	15% of first $29,750 plus 28% of excess
Married, Separate	15% of first $14,875 plus 28% of excess

For example, a single wage earner with a taxable income of $20,000 dollars owes $0.15 \times$ $17,850 + 0.28 \times (\$20,000–\$17,850)$. Write a program that lets the user specify the tax category and the taxable income and that then calculates the tax. Use a loop so that the user can enter several tax cases.

11. The ABC Mail Order Grocery sells artichokes for $1.25 per pound, beets for $0.65 per pound, and carrots for $0.89 per pound. It gives a 5% discount for orders of $100 or more prior to adding shipping costs. It charges $3.50 shipping and handling for any order of 5 pounds or under, $10.00 shipping and handling for orders over 5 pounds and under 20 pounds, and $8.00 plus $0.10 per pound for shipments of 20 pounds or more. Write a program that uses a **switch** statement in a loop such that a response of **a** lets the user enter the pounds of artichokes desired, **b** the pounds of beets, **c** the pounds of carrots, and **q** allows the user to exit the ordering process. The program then should compute the total charges, the discount, if any, the shipping charges, and the grand total. The program then should display all the purchase information: the cost per pound, the pounds ordered, and the cost for that order for each vegetable, the total cost of the order, the discount (if there is one), the shipping charge, and the grand total of all the charges.

CHAPTER 8

CHARACTER INPUT/OUTPUT AND INPUT VALIDATION

You will learn about the following in this chapter:

- More about input, output, and the differences between buffered and unbuffered input

- How to simulate the end-of-file condition from the keyboard

- How to use redirection to connect your programs to files

- Making the user interface friendlier

*I*n the computing world, we use the words *input* and *output* in several ways. We speak of input and output devices, such as keyboards, disk drives, and laser printers. We talk about the data used for input and output. We discuss the functions that perform input and output. This chapter concentrates on the functions used for input and output (or *I/O*, for short).

I/O functions transport information to and from your program; `printf()`, `scanf()`, `getchar()`, and `putchar()` are examples. You've seen these functions in previous chapters, and now you'll be able to look at their conceptual basis. Along the way, you'll see how to improve the program-user interface.

Originally, input/output functions were not part of the definition of C. Their development was left to C implementations. In practice, the Unix implementation of C has served as a model for these functions. The ANSI C library, recognizing past practice, contains a large number of these Unix I/O functions, including the ones we've used. Because such standard functions must work in a wide variety of computer environments, they seldom take advantage of features peculiar to a particular system. Therefore, many C vendors supply additional I/O functions that do make use of special features, such as the Intel microprocessor I/O ports or the Macintosh ROM routines. Other functions or families of functions tap into particular operating systems that support, for example, specific graphical interfaces, such as those provided by Windows or Macintosh OS. These specialized, nonstandard functions enable you to write programs that use a particular computer more effectively. Unfortunately, they often can't be used on other computer systems. Consequently, we'll concentrate on the standard I/O functions available on all systems, because they enable you to write portable programs that can be moved easily from one system to another. They also generalize to programs using files for input and output.

One important task many programs face is that of validating input; that is, determining whether the user has entered input that matches the expectations of a program. This chapter illustrates some of the problems and solutions associated with input validation.

Single-Character I/O: `getchar()` and `putchar()`

As you saw in Chapter 7, "C Control Statements: Branching and Jumps," `getchar()` and `putchar()` perform input and output one character at a time. That method might strike you as a rather silly way of doing things. After all, you can easily read groupings larger than a single character, but this method does suit the capability of a computer. Furthermore, this approach is the heart of most programs that deal with text—that is, with ordinary words. To remind yourself of how these functions work, examine Listing 8.1, a very simple example. All it does is fetch characters from keyboard input and send them to the screen. This process is called *echoing the input*. It uses a `while` loop that terminates when the # character is encountered.

LISTING 8.1   The `echo.c` Program

```
/* echo.c -- repeats input */
#include <stdio.h>
int main(void)
{
    char ch;

    while ((ch = getchar()) != '#')
        putchar(ch);

    return 0;
}
```

ANSI C associates the `stdio.h` header file with using `getchar()` and `putchar()`, which is why we have included that file in the program. (Typically, `getchar()` and `putchar()` are not true functions, but are defined using preprocessor macros, a topic we'll cover in Chapter 16, "The C Preprocessor and the C Library.") Using this program produces exchanges like this:

Hello, there. I would[enter]
Hello, there. I would
like a #3 bag of potatoes.[enter]
like a

After watching this program run, you might wonder why you must type a whole line before the input is echoed. You might also wonder if there is a better way to terminate input. Using a particular character, such as #, to terminate input prevents you from using that character in the text. To answer these questions, let's look at how C programs handle keyboard input. In particular, let's examine buffering and the concept of a standard input file.

Buffers

When you run the previous program on some systems, the text you input is echoed immediately. That is, a sample run would look like this:

```
HHeelllloo,,  tthheerree..  II  wwoouulldd[enter]

lliikkee  aa  #
```

The preceding behavior is the exception. On most systems, nothing happens until you press Enter, as in the first example. The immediate echoing of input characters is an instance of *unbuffered* (or *direct*) input, meaning that the characters you type are immediately made available to the waiting program. The delayed echoing, on the other hand, illustrates *buffered* input, in which the characters you type are collected and stored in an area of temporary storage called a *buffer*. Pressing Enter causes the block of characters you typed to be made available to your program. Figure 8.1 compares these two kinds of input.

Why have buffers? First, it is less time-consuming to transmit several characters as a block than to send them one by one. Second, if you mistype, you can use your keyboard correction features to fix your mistake. When you finally press Enter, you can transmit the corrected version.

Unbuffered input, on the other hand, is desirable for some interactive programs. In a game, for instance, you would like each command to take place as soon as you press a key. Therefore, both buffered and unbuffered input have their uses.

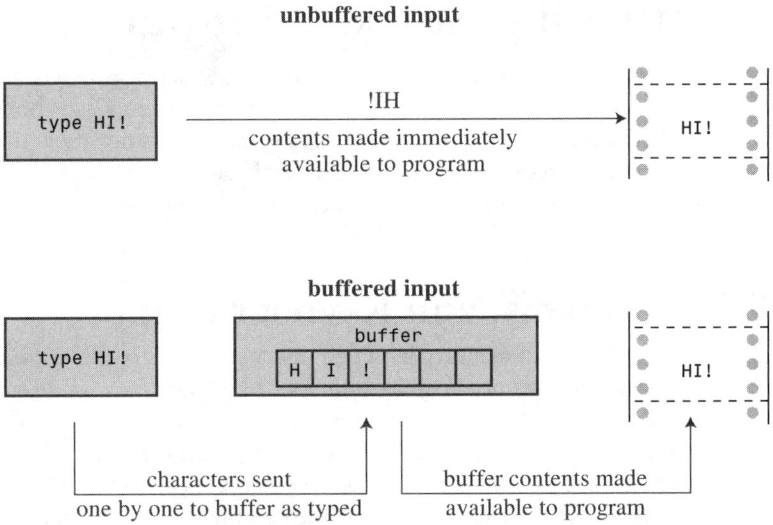

FIGURE 8.1

Buffered versus unbuffered input.

Buffering comes in two varieties: *fully buffered* I/O and *line-buffered* I/O. For fully buffered input, the buffer is flushed (the contents are sent to their destination) when it is full. This kind of buffering usually occurs with file input. The buffer size depends on the system, but 512 bytes and 4096 bytes are common values. With line-buffered I/O, the buffer is flushed whenever a newline character shows up. Keyboard input is normally line buffered, so that pressing Enter flushes the buffer.

Which kind of input do you have: buffered or unbuffered? ANSI C specifies that input should be buffered, but K&R originally left the choice open to the compiler writer. You can find out by running the `echo.c` program and seeing which behavior results.

The reason ANSI C settled on buffered input as the standard is that some computer designs don't permit unbuffered input. If your particular computer does allow unbuffered input, most likely your C compiler offers unbuffered input as an option. Many compilers for IBM PC compatibles, for example, supply a special family of functions, supported by the `conio.h` header file, for unbuffered input. These functions include `getche()` for echoed unbuffered input and `getch()` for unechoed unbuffered input. (*Echoed input* means the character you type shows onscreen, and *unechoed input* means the keystrokes don't show.) Unix systems use a different approach, for Unix itself controls buffering. With Unix, you use the `ioctl()` function (part of the Unix library but not part of standard C) to specify the type of input you want, and `getchar()` behaves accordingly. In ANSI C, the `setbuf()` and `setvbuf()` functions (see Chapter 13, "File Input/Output") supply some control over buffering, but the inherent limitations of some systems can restrict the effectiveness of these functions. In short, there is no standard ANSI way of invoking unbuffered input; the means depend on the computer system. In this book, with apologies to our unbuffered friends, we assume you are using buffered input.

Terminating Keyboard Input

The `echo.c` program halts when # is entered, which is convenient as long as you exclude that character from normal input. As you've seen, however, # can show up in normal input. Ideally, you'd like a terminating character that normally does not show up in text. Such a character won't pop up accidentally in the middle of some input, stopping the program before you want it to stop. C has an answer to this need, but, to understand it, you need to know how C handles files.

Files, Streams, and Keyboard Input

A *file* is an area of memory in which information is stored. Normally, a file is kept in some sort of permanent memory, such as a floppy disk, a hard disk, or a tape. You are doubtless aware of the importance of files to computer systems. For example, your C programs are kept in files, and the programs used to compile your programs are kept in files. This last example points out that some programs need to be able to access particular files. When you compile a program stored in a file called `echo.c`, the compiler opens the `echo.c` file and reads its contents. When the compiler finishes, it closes the file. Other programs, such as word processors, not only open, read, and close files, they also write to them.

C, being powerful, flexible, and so on, has many library functions for opening, reading, writing, and closing files. On one level, it can deal with files by using the basic file tools of the host operating system. This is called *low-level I/O*. Because of the many differences among computer systems, it is impossible to create a standard library of universal low-level I/O functions, and ANSI C does not attempt to do so; however, C also deals with files on a second level called the *standard I/O package*. This involves creating a standard model and a standard set of I/O functions for dealing with files. At this higher level, differences between systems are handled by specific C implementations so that you deal with a uniform interface.

What sort of differences are we talking about? Different systems, for example, store files differently. Some store the file contents in one place and information about the file elsewhere. Some build a description of the file into the file itself. In dealing with text, some systems use a single newline character to mark the end of a line. Others might use the combination of the carriage return and linefeed characters to represent the end of a line. Some systems measure file sizes to the nearest byte; some measure in blocks of bytes.

When you use the standard I/O package, you are shielded from these differences. Therefore, to check for a newline, you can use `if (ch == '\n')`. If the system actually uses the carriage-return/linefeed combination, the I/O functions automatically translate back and forth between the two representations.

Conceptually, the C program deals with a stream instead of directly with a file. A *stream* is an idealized flow of data to which the actual input or output is mapped. That means various kinds of input with differing properties are represented by streams with more uniform properties. The process of opening a file then becomes one of associating a stream with the file, and reading and writing take place via the stream.

Chapter 13 discusses files in greater detail. For this chapter, simply note that C treats input and output devices the same as it treats regular files on storage devices. In particular, the keyboard and the display device are treated as files opened automatically by every C program. Keyboard input is represented by a stream called `stdin`, and output to the screen (or teletype or other output device) is represented by a stream called `stdout`. The `getchar()`, `putchar()`, `printf()`, and `scanf()` functions are all members of the standard I/O package, and they deal with these two streams.

One implication of all this is that you can use the same techniques with keyboard input as you do with files. For example, a program reading a file needs a way to detect the end of the file so that it knows where to stop reading. Therefore, C input functions come equipped with a built-in, end-of-file detector. Because keyboard input is treated like a file, you should be able to use that end-of-file detector to terminate keyboard input, too. Let's see how this is done, beginning with files.

The End of File

A computer operating system needs some way to tell where each file begins and ends. One method to detect the end of a file is to place a special character in the file to mark the end. This is the method once used, for example, in CP/M, IBM-DOS, and MS-DOS text files. Today, these operating systems may use an embedded Ctrl+Z character to mark the ends of files. At one time, this was the sole means these operating systems used, but there are other options now, such as keeping track of the file size. So a modern text file may or may not have an embedded Ctrl+Z, but if it does, the operating system will treat it as an end-of-file marker. Figure 8.2 illustrates this approach.

FIGURE 8.2

A file with an end-of-file marker.

prose:

    Ishphat the robot
    slid open the hatch
    and shouted his challenge.

prose in a file:

```
Ishphat the robot\nslid open the hatch\nand shouted his challenge.\n^Z
```

A second approach is for the operating system to store information on the size of the file. If a file has 3000 bytes and a program has read 3000 bytes, the program has reached the end. MS-DOS and its relatives use this approach for binary files because this method allows the files to hold all characters, including Ctrl+Z. Newer versions of DOS also use this approach for text files. Unix uses this approach for all files.

C handles this variety of methods by having the `getchar()` function return a special value when the end of a file is reached, regardless of how the operating system actually detects the end of file. The name given to this value is `EOF` (end of file). Therefore, the return value for `getchar()` when it detects an end of file is `EOF`. The `scanf()` function also returns `EOF` on detecting the end of a file. Typically, `EOF` is defined in the `stdio.h` file as follows:

```
#define EOF (-1)
```

Why `-1`? Normally, `getchar()` returns a value in the range `0` through `127`, because those are values corresponding to the standard character set, but it might return values from `0` through `255` if the system recognizes an extended character set. In either case, the value `-1` does not correspond to any character, so it can be used to signal the end of a file.

Some systems may define `EOF` to be a value other than `-1`, but the definition is always different from a return value produced by a legitimate input character. If you include the `stdio.h` file and use the `EOF` symbol, you don't have to worry about the numeric definition. The important point is that `EOF` represents a value that signals the end of a file was detected; it is not a symbol actually found in the file.

Okay, how can you use `EOF` in a program? Compare the return value of `getchar()` with `EOF`. If they are different, you have not yet reached the end of a file. In other words, you can use an expression like this:

```
while ((ch = getchar()) != EOF)
```

What if you are reading keyboard input and not a file? Most systems (but not all) have a way to simulate an end-of-file condition from the keyboard. Knowing that, you can rewrite the basic read and echo program, as shown in Listing 8.2.

LISTING 8.2   The echo_eof.c Program

```c
/* echo_eof.c -- repeats input to end of file */
#include <stdio.h>
int main(void)
{
    int ch;

    while ((ch = getchar()) != EOF)
        putchar(ch);

    return 0;
}
```

Note these points:

- You don't have to define EOF because stdio.h takes care of that.

- You don't have to worry about the actual value of EOF, because the #define statement in stdio.h enables you to use the symbolic representation EOF. You shouldn't write code that assumes EOF has a particular value.

- The variable ch is changed from type char to type int because char variables may be represented by unsigned integers in the range 0 to 255, but EOF may have the numeric value -1. That is an impossible value for an unsigned char variable, but not for an int. Fortunately, getchar() is actually type int itself, so it can read the EOF character. Implementations that use a signed char type may get by with declaring ch as type char, but it is better to use the more general form.

- The fact that ch is an integer doesn't faze putchar(). It still prints the character equivalent.

- To use this program on keyboard input, you need a way to type the EOF character. No, you can't just type the letters *E O F*, and you can't just type –1. (Typing -1 would transmit two characters: a hyphen and the digit 1.) Instead, you have to find out what your system requires. On most Unix systems, for example, pressing Ctrl+D at the beginning of a line causes the end-of-file signal to be transmitted. Many micro-computing systems recognize Ctrl+Z at the beginning of a line as an end-of-file signal; some interpret a Ctrl+Z anywhere as an end-of-file signal.

Here is a buffered example of running echo_eof.c on a Unix system:

She walks in beauty, like the night
She walks in beauty, like the night
  Of cloudless climes and starry skies...
  Of cloudless climes and starry skies...
                    Lord Byron
                    Lord Byron
[Ctrl+D]

Each time you press Enter, the characters stored in the buffer are processed, and a copy of the line is printed. This continues until you simulate the end of file, Unix-style. On a PC, you would press Ctrl+Z instead.

Let's stop for a moment and think about the possibilities for `echo_eof.c`. It copies onto the screen whatever input you feed it. Suppose you could somehow feed a file to it. Then it would print the contents of the file onscreen, stopping when it reached the end of the file, on finding an `EOF` signal. Suppose, instead, that you could find a way to direct the program's output to a file. Then you could enter data from the keyboard and use `echo_eof.c` to store what you type in a file. Suppose you could do both simultaneously: Direct input from one file into `echo_eof.c` and send the output to another file. Then you could use `echo_eof.c` to copy files. This little program has the potential to look at the contents of files, to create new files, and to make copies of files—pretty good for such a short program! The key is to control the flow of input and output, and that is the next topic.

Simulated EOF and Graphical Interfaces

The concept of simulated EOF arose in a command-line environment using a text interface. In such an environment, the user interacts with a program through keystrokes, and the operating system generates the EOF signal. Some practices don't translate particularly well to graphical interfaces, such as Windows and the Macintosh, with more complex user interfaces that incorporate mouse movement and button clicks. The program behavior on encountering a simulated EOF depends on the compiler and project type. For example, a Ctrl+Z may terminate input or it may terminate the entire program, depending on the particular settings.

Redirection and Files

Input and output involve functions, data, and devices. Consider, for instance, the `echo_eof.c` program. It uses the input function `getchar()`. The input device (we have assumed) is a keyboard, and the input data stream consists of individual characters. Suppose you want to keep the same input function and the same kind of data, but want to change where the program looks for data. A good question to ask is, "How does a program know where to look for its input?"

By default, a C program using the standard I/O package looks to the standard input as its source for input. This is the stream identified earlier as `stdin`. It is whatever has been set up as the usual way for reading data into the computer. It could be an old-fashioned device, such as magnetic tape, punched cards, or a teletype, or (as we will continue to assume) your keyboard, or some upcoming technology, such as voice input. A modern computer is a suggestible tool, however, and you can influence it to look elsewhere for input. In particular, you can tell a program to seek its input from a file instead of from a keyboard.

There are two ways to get a program to work with files. One way is to explicitly use special functions that open files, close files, read files, write in files, and so forth. That method we'll save for Chapter 13. The second way is to use a program designed to work with a keyboard and screen, but to *redirect* input and output along different channels—to and from files, for example. In other words, you reassign the `stdin` stream to a file. The `getchar()` program continues to get its data from the stream, not really caring from where the stream gets its data. This approach (redirection) is more limited in some respects than the first, but it is much simpler to use, and it allows you to gain familiarity with common file-processing techniques.

One major problem with redirection is that it is associated with the operating system, not C. However, the many C environments, including Unix, Linux, and MS-DOS (2.0 and later), feature redirection, and some C implementations simulate it on systems lacking the feature. We'll look at the Unix, Linux, and DOS versions.

Unix, Linux, and DOS Redirection

Unix, Linux, and current DOS versions enable you to redirect both input and output. Redirecting input enables your program to use a file instead of the keyboard for input, and redirecting output enables it to use a file instead of the screen for output.

Redirecting Input

Suppose you have compiled the `echo_eof.c` program and placed the executable version in a file called `echo_eof` (or `echo_eof.exe` on DOS systems). To run the program, type the executable file's name:

```
echo_eof
```

The program runs as described earlier, taking its input from the keyboard. Now suppose you want to use the program on a text file called `words`. A *text file* is one containing text—that is, data stored as human-readable characters. It could be an essay or a program in C, for example. A file containing machine language instructions, such as the file holding the executable version of a program, is not a text file. Because the program works with characters, it should be used with text files. All you need to do is enter this command instead of the previous one:

```
echo_eof < words
```

The `<` symbol is a Unix and Linux (and DOS) redirection operator. It causes the `words` file to be associated with the `stdin` stream, channeling the file contents into the `echo_eof` program. The `echo_eof` program itself doesn't know (or care) that the input is coming from a file instead of the keyboard. All it knows is that a stream of characters is being fed to it, so it reads them and prints them one character at a time until the end of file shows up. Because C puts files and I/O devices on the same footing, the file is now the I/O *device*. Try it!

Redirection Sidelights

With Unix, Linux, and DOS, the spaces on either side of the < are optional. Some systems, such as AmigaDOS, support redirection but don't allow a space between the redirection symbol and the filename.

Here is a sample run for one particular `words` file; the `$` is one of the standard Unix and Linux prompts. On a DOS system, you would see the DOS prompt, perhaps an `A>` or `C>`.

```
$ echo_eof < words
The world is too much with us: late and soon,
Getting and spending, we lay waste our powers:
Little we see in Nature that is ours;
We have given our hearts away, a sordid boon!
$
```

Well, that time we got our words' worth.

Redirecting Output

Now suppose you want to have `echo_eof` send your keyboard input to a file called `mywords`. Then you can enter the following and begin typing:

```
echo_eof > mywords
```

The > is a second redirection operator. It causes a new file called `mywords` to be created for your use, and then it redirects the output of `echo_eof` (that is, a copy of the characters you type) to that file. The redirection reassigns `stdout` from the display device (your screen) to the `mywords` file instead. If you already have a file with the name `mywords`, normally it would be erased and then replaced by the new one. (Many operating systems, however, give you the option of protecting existing files by making them read-only.) All that appears on your screen are the letters as you type them, and the copies go to the file instead. To end the program, press Ctrl+D (Unix) or Ctrl+Z (DOS) at the beginning of a line. Try it. If you can't think of anything to type, just imitate the next example. In it, we use the $ Unix prompt. Remember to end each line by pressing Enter to send the buffer contents to the program.

```
$ echo_eof > mywords
You should have no problem recalling which redirection
operator does what. Just remember that each operator points
in the direction the information flows. Think of it as
a funnel.
[Ctrl+D]
$
```

After the Ctrl+D or Ctrl+Z is processed, the program terminates and your system prompt returns. Did the program work? The Unix `ls` command or DOS `dir` command, which lists filenames, should show you that the file `mywords` now exists. You can use the Unix and Linux `cat` or DOS `type` command to check the contents, or you can use `echo_eof` again, this time redirecting the file to the program:

```
$ echo_eof < mywords
You should have no problem recalling which redirection
operator does what. Just remember that each operator points
in the direction the information flows. Think of it as a
funnel.
$
```

Combined Redirection

Now suppose you want to make a copy of the file `mywords` and call it `savewords`. Just issue this next command,

```
echo_eof < mywords > savewords
```

and the deed is done. The following command would have worked as well, because the order of redirection operations doesn't matter:

```
echo_eof > savewords < mywords
```

Beware: Don't use the same file for both input and output to the same command.

```
echo_eof < mywords > mywords....<--WRONG
```

The reason is that > `mywords` causes the original `mywords` to be truncated to zero length before it is ever used as input.

In brief, here are the rules governing the use of the two redirection operators (< and >) with Unix, Linux, or DOS:

- A redirection operator connects an *executable* program (including standard operating system commands) with a data file. It cannot be used to connect one data file to another, nor can it be used to connect one program to another program.

- Input cannot be taken from more than one file, nor can output be directed to more than one file by using these operators.

- Normally, spaces between the names and operators are optional, except occasionally when some characters with special meaning to the Unix shell or Linux shell or DOS are used. We could, for example, have used `echo_eof<words`.

You have already seen several proper examples. Here are some wrong examples, with `addup` and `count` as executable programs and `fish` and `beets` as text files:

`fish > beets`	← Violates the first rule
`addup < count`	← Violates the first rule
`addup < fish < beets`	← Violates the second rule
`count > beets fish`	← Violates the second rule

Unix, Linux, and DOS also feature the >> operator, which enables you to add data to the end of an existing file, and the pipe operator (|), which enables you to connect the output of one program to the input of a second program. See a Unix book, such as *UNIX Primer Plus, Third Edition* (Wilson, Pierce, and Wessler; Sams Publishing), for more information on all these operators.

Comments

Redirection enables you to use keyboard-input programs with files. For this to work, the program has to test for the end of file. For example, Chapter 7 presents a word-counting program that counts words up to the first | character. Change `ch` from type `char` to type `int`, and replace `'|'` with `EOF` in the loop test, and you can use the program to count words in text files.

Redirection is a command-line concept, because you indicate it by typing special symbols on the command line. If you are not using a command-line environment, you might still be able to try the technique. First, some integrated environments have menu options that let you indicate redirection. Second, for Windows systems, you can open a DOS window and run the executable file from the command line. Microsoft Visual C++ 7.1, by default, puts the executable file in a subfolder called `Debug`. The filename will have the same base name as the project name and use the `.exe` extension. For Codewarrior, use the Win 32 Console App mode; it will name the executable file `Cproj Debug.exe` by default (where `Cproj` would be replaced by your project name), and place it in the project folder.

If redirection doesn't work for you, you can try having the program open a file directly. Listing 8.3 shows an example with minimal explanation. You'll have to wait until Chapter 13 for the details.

LISTING 8.3   The `file_eof.c` Program

```
// file_eof.c --open a file and display it
#include <stdio.h>
#include <stdlib.h>  // for exit()
int main()
{
    int ch;
    FILE * fp;
    char fname[50];         // to hold the file name

    printf("Enter the name of the file: ");
    scanf("%s", fname);
    fp = fopen(fname, "r"); // open file for reading
    if (fp == NULL)         // attempt failed
    {
        printf("Failed to open file. Bye\n");
        exit(1);            // quit program
    }
// getc(fp) gets a character from the open file
    while ((ch = getc(fp)) != EOF)
        putchar(ch);
    fclose(fp);             // close the file

    return 0;
}
```

Summary: How to Redirect Input and Output

With most C systems, you can use redirection, either for all programs through the operating system or else just for C programs, courtesy of the C compiler. In the following, let `prog` be the name of the executable program and let `file1` and `file2` be names of files.

Redirecting Output to a File: `>prog >file1`

Redirecting Input from a File: `<`

```
prog <file2
```

Combined Redirection:

```
prog <file2 >file1
prog >file1 <file2
```

Both forms use `file2` for input and `file1` for output.

Spacing:

Some systems require a space to the left of the redirection operator and no space to the right. Other systems (Unix, for example) accept either spaces or no spaces on either side.

Creating a Friendlier User Interface

Most of us have on occasion written programs that are awkward to use. Fortunately, C gives you the tools to make input a smoother, more pleasant process. Unfortunately, learning these tools could, at first, lead to new problems. The goal in this section is to guide you through some of these problems to a friendlier user interface, one that eases interactive data entry and smoothes over the effects of faulty input.

Working with Buffered Input

Buffered input is often a convenience to the user, providing an opportunity to edit input before sending it on to a program, but it can be bothersome to the programmer when character input is used. The problem, as you've seen in some earlier examples, is that buffered input requires you to press the Enter key to transmit your input. This act also transmits a newline character that the program must handle. Let's examine this and other problems with a guessing program. You pick a number, and the computer tries to guess it. The computer uses a plodding method, but we are concentrating on I/O, not algorithms. See Listing 8.4 for the starting version of the program.

LISTING 8.4   The guess.c Program

```
/* guess.c -- an inefficient and faulty number-guesser */
#include <stdio.h>
int main(void)
{
    int guess = 1;

    printf("Pick an integer from 1 to 100. I will try to guess ");
    printf("it.\nRespond with a y if my guess is right and with");
    printf("\nan n if it is wrong.\n");
    printf("Uh...is your number %d?\n", guess);
    while (getchar() != 'y')      /* get response, compare to y */
        printf("Well, then, is it %d?\n", ++guess);
    printf("I knew I could do it!\n");

    return 0;
}
```

Here's a sample run:

```
Pick an integer from 1 to 100. I will try to guess it.
Respond with a y if my guess is right and with
an n if it is wrong.
Uh...is your number 1?
n
Well, then, is it 2?
Well, then, is it 3?
n
Well, then, is it 4?
Well, then, is it 5?
y
I knew I could do it!
```

Out of consideration for the program's pathetic guessing algorithm, we chose a small number. Note that the program makes two guesses every time you enter n. What's happening is that the program reads the n response as a denial that the number is 1 and then reads the newline character as a denial that the number is 2.

One solution is to use a `while` loop to discard the rest of the input line, including the newline character. This has the additional merit of treating responses such as no and no way the same as a simple n. The version in Listing 8.4 treats no as two responses. Here is a revised loop that fixes the problem:

```
while (getchar() != 'y')    /* get response, compare to y */
{
    printf("Well, then, is it %d?\n", ++guess);
    while (getchar() != '\n')
        continue;            /* skip rest of input line    */
}
```

Using this loop produces responses such as the following:

```
Pick an integer from 1 to 100. I will try to guess it.
Respond with a y if my guess is right and with
an n if it is wrong.
Uh...is your number 1?
n
Well, then, is it 2?
no
Well, then, is it 3?
no sir
Well, then, is it 4?
forget it
Well, then, is it 5?
y
I knew I could do it!
```

That takes care of the problems with the newline character. However, as a purist, you might not like f being treated as meaning the same as n. To eliminate that defect, you can use an `if` statement to screen out other responses. First, add a `char` variable to store the response:

```
char response;
```

Then change the loop to this:

```
while ((response = getchar()) != 'y')      /* get response */
{
    if (response == 'n')
        printf("Well, then, is it %d?\n", ++guess);
    else
        printf("Sorry, I understand only y or n.\n");
    while (getchar() != '\n')
        continue;                   /* skip rest of input line */
}
```

Now the program's response looks like this:

```
Pick an integer from 1 to 100. I will try to guess it.
```

```
Respond with a y if my guess is right and with
an n if it is wrong.
Uh...is your number 1?
n
Well, then, is it 2?
no
Well, then, is it 3?
no sir
Well, then, is it 4?
forget it
Sorry, I understand only y or n.
n
Well, then, is it 5?
y
I knew I could do it!
```

When you write interactive programs, you should try to anticipate ways in which users might fail to follow instructions. Then you should design your program to handle user failures gracefully. Tell them when they are wrong, and give them another chance.

You should, of course, provide clear instructions to the user, but no matter how clear you make them, someone will always misinterpret them and then blame you for poor instructions.

Mixing Numeric and Character Input

Suppose your program requires both character input using `getchar()` and numeric input using `scanf()`. Each of these functions does its job well, but the two don't mix together well. That's because `getchar()` reads every character, including spaces, tabs, and newlines, whereas `scanf()`, when reading numbers, skips over spaces, tabs, and newlines.

To illustrate the sort of problem this causes, Listing 8.5 presents a program that reads in a character and two numbers as input. It then prints the character using the number of rows and columns specified in the input.

LISTING 8.5   The `showchar1.c` Program

```c
/* showchar1.c -- program with a BIG I/O problem */
#include <stdio.h>
void display(char cr, int lines, int width);
int main(void)
{
    int ch;              /* character to be printed     */
    int rows, cols;      /* number of rows and columns */
    printf("Enter a character and two integers:\n");
    while ((ch = getchar()) != '\n')
    {
        scanf("%d %d", &rows, &cols);
        display(ch, rows, cols);
        printf("Enter another character and two integers;\n");
        printf("Enter a newline to quit.\n");
    }
    printf("Bye.\n");
```

LISTING 8.5   Continued

```
      return 0;
}

void display(char cr, int lines, int width)
{
    int row, col;

    for (row = 1; row <= lines; row++)
    {
        for (col = 1; col <= width; col++)
            putchar(cr);
        putchar('\n');  /* end line and start a new one */
    }
}
```

Note that the program reads a character as type `int` to enable the `EOF` test. However, it passes the character as type `char` to the `display()` function. Because `char` is smaller than `int`, some compilers will warn about the conversion. In this case, you can ignore the warning.

The program is set up so that `main()` gets the data, and the `display()` function does the printing. Let's look at a sample run to see what the problem is:

```
Enter a character and two integers:
c 2 3
ccc
ccc
Enter another character and two integers;
Enter a newline to quit.
Bye.
```

The program starts off fine. You enter `c 2 3`, and it prints two rows of three *c* characters, as expected. Then the program prompts you to enter a second set of data and quits before you have a chance to respond! What's wrong? It's that newline character again, this time the one immediately following the `3` on the first input line. The `scanf()` function leaves it in the input queue. Unlike `scanf()`, `getchar()` doesn't skip over newline characters, so this newline character is read by `getchar()` during the next cycle of the loop before you have a chance to enter anything else. Then it's assigned to `ch`, and `ch` being the newline character is the condition that terminates the loop.

To clear up this problem, the program has to skip over any newlines or spaces between the last number typed for one cycle of input and the character typed at the beginning of the next line. Also, it would be nice if the program could be terminated at the `scanf()` stage in addition to the `getchar()` test. The next version, shown in Listing 8.6, accomplishes this.

LISTING 8.6   The `showchar2.c` Program

```
/* showchar2.c -- prints characters in rows and columns */
#include <stdio.h>
void display(char cr, int lines, int width);
int main(void)
```

LISTING 8.6   *Continued*

```
{
    int ch;              /* character to be printed     */
    int rows, cols;      /* number of rows and columns  */

    printf("Enter a character and two integers:\n");
    while ((ch = getchar()) != '\n')
    {
        if (scanf("%d %d",&rows, &cols) != 2)
            break;
        display(ch, rows, cols);
        while (getchar() !=  '\n')
            continue;
        printf("Enter another character and two integers;\n");
        printf("Enter a newline to quit.\n");
    }
    printf("Bye.\n");

    return 0;
}

void display(char cr, int lines, int width)
{
    int row, col;

    for (row = 1; row <= lines; row++)
    {
        for (col = 1; col <= width; col++)
            putchar(cr);
        putchar('\n');  /* end line and start a new one */
    }
}
```

The `while` statement causes the program to dispose of all characters following the `scanf()` input, including the newline. This prepares the loop to read the first character at the beginning of the next line. This means you can enter data fairly freely:

```
Enter a character and two integers:
c 1 2
cc
Enter another character and two integers;
Enter a newline to quit.
! 3 6
!!!!!!
!!!!!!
!!!!!!
Enter another character and two integers;
Enter a newline to quit.

Bye.
```

By using an `if` statement with a `break`, you terminate the program if the return value of `scanf()` is not 2. This occurs if one or both input values are not integers or if end-of-file is encountered.

Input Validation

In practice, program users don't always follow instructions, and you can get a mismatch between what a program expects as input and what it actually gets. Such conditions can cause a program to fail. However, often you can anticipate likely input errors, and, with some extra programming effort, have a program detect and work around them.

Suppose, for example, that you're writing a program that prompts the user to enter a nonnegative integer. Another kind of error is to enter values that are not valid for the particular task the program is doing.

Suppose, for instance, that you had a loop that processes nonnegative numbers. One kind of error the user can make is to enter a negative number. You can use a relational expression to test for that:

```
int n;
scanf("%d", &n);        // get first value
while (n >= 0)          // detect out-of-range value
{
    // process n
    scanf("%d", &n);    // get next value
}
```

Another potential pitfall is that the user might enter the wrong type of value, such as the character **q**. One way to detect this kind of misuse is to check the return value of **scanf()**. This function, as you'll recall, returns the number of items it successfully reads; therefore, the expression

```
scanf("%d", &n) == 1
```

is true only if the user inputs an integer. This suggests the following revision of the code:

```
int n;
while (scanf("%d", &n) == 1 && n >= 0)
{
    // process n
}
```

In words, the **while** loop condition is "while input is an integer and the integer is positive."

The last example terminates input if the user enters the wrong type of value. You can, however, choose to make the program a little more user friendly and give the user the opportunity to try to enter the correct type of value. In that case, you need to dispose of the input that caused the problem in the first place; if **scanf()** doesn't succeed in reading input, it leaves it in the input queue. Here the fact that input really is a stream of characters comes in handy, because you can use **getchar()** to read the input character-by-character. You could even incorporate all these ideas into a function such as the following:

```
int get_int(void)
{
    int input;
    char ch;
```

```
    while (scanf("%d", &input) != 1)
    {
        while ((ch = getchar()) != '\n')
            putchar(ch);    // dispose of bad input
        printf(" is not an integer.\nPlease enter an ");
        printf("integer value, such as 25, -178, or 3: ");
    }
    return input;
}
```

This function attempts to read an int value into the variable input. If it fails to do so, the
function enters the body of the outer while loop. The inner while loop then reads the offending input character-by-character. Note that this function chooses to discard all the remaining
input on the line. Other possible choices are to discard just the next character or word. Then
the function prompts the user to try again. The outer loop keeps going until the user successfully enters an integer, causing scanf() to return the value 1.

After the user clears the hurdle of entering integers, the program can check to see whether the
values are valid. Consider an example that requires the user to enter a lower limit and an
upper limit defining a range of values. In this case, you probably would want the program to
check that the first value isn't greater than the second (usually ranges assume that the first
value is the smaller one). It may also need to check that the values are within acceptable limits.
For example, the archive search may not work with year values less than 1958 or greater
than 2004. This checking, too, can be accomplished with a function.

Here's one possibility; the following function assumes that the stdbool.h header file has been
included. If you don't have _Bool on your system, you can substitute int for bool, 1 for true,
and 0 for false. Note that the function returns true if the input is invalid; hence the name
bad_limits():

```
bool bad_limits(int begin, int end, int low, int high)
{
    bool not_good = false;
    if (begin > end)
    {
        printf("%d isn't smaller than %d.\n", begin, end);
        not_good = true;
    }
    if (begin < low || end < low)
    {
        printf("Values must be %d or greater.\n", low);
        not_good = true;
    }
    if (begin > high || end > high)
    {
        printf("Values must be %d or less.\n", high);
        not_good = true;
    }

        return not_good;
}
```

Listing 8.7 uses these two functions to feed integers to an arithmetic function that calculates the sum of the squares of all the integers in a specified range. The program limits the upper and lower bounds of the range to 1000 and –1000, respectively.

LISTING 8.7   The `checking.c` Program

```c
/* checking.c -- validating input */
#include <stdio.h>
#include <stdbool.h>
// validate that input is an integer
int get_int(void);
// validate that range limits are valid
bool bad_limits(int begin, int end, int low, int high);
// calculate the sum of the squares of the integers
// a through b
double sum_squares(int a, int b);
int main(void)
{
    const int MIN = -1000;   // lower limit to range
    const int MAX = +1000;   // upper limit to range
    int start;               // start of range
    int stop;                // end of range
    double answer;

    printf("This program computes the sum of the squares of "
           "integers in a range.\nThe lower bound should not "
           "be less than -1000 and\nthe upper bound should not "
           "be more than +1000.\nEnter the limits (enter 0 for "
           "both limits to quit):\nlower limit: ");
    start = get_int();
    printf("upper limit: ");
    stop = get_int();
    while (start !=0 || stop != 0)
    {
        if (bad_limits(start, stop, MIN, MAX))
            printf("Please try again.\n");
        else
        {
            answer = sum_squares(start, stop);
            printf("The sum of the squares of the integers ");
            printf("from %d to %d is %g\n", start, stop, answer);
        }
        printf("Enter the limits (enter 0 for both "
               "limits to quit):\n");
        printf("lower limit: ");
        start = get_int();
        printf("upper limit: ");
        stop = get_int();
    }
    printf("Done.\n");

    return 0;
```

LISTING 8.7 Continued

```
    }

    int get_int(void)
    {
        int input;
        char ch;

        while (scanf("%d", &input) != 1)
        {
            while ((ch = getchar()) != '\n')
                putchar(ch);  // dispose of bad input
            printf(" is not an integer.\nPlease enter an ");
            printf("integer value, such as 25, -178, or 3: ");
        }

        return input;
    }

    double sum_squares(int a, int b)
    {
        double total = 0;
        int i;

        for (i = a; i <= b; i++)
            total += i * i;

        return total;
    }

    bool bad_limits(int begin, int end, int low, int high)
    {
        bool not_good = false;

        if (begin > end)
        {
            printf("%d isn't smaller than %d.\n", begin, end);
            not_good = true;
        }
        if (begin < low || end < low)
        {
            printf("Values must be %d or greater.\n", low);
            not_good = true;
        }
        if (begin > high || end > high)
        {
            printf("Values must be %d or less.\n", high);
            not_good = true;
        }

        return not_good;
    }
```

Here's a sample run:

```
This program computes the sum of the squares of integers in a range.
The lower bound should not be less than -1000 and
the upper bound should not be more than +1000.
Enter the limits (enter 0 for both limits to quit):
lower limit: low
low is not an integer.
Please enter an integer value, such as 25, -178, or 3: 3
upper limit: a big number
a big number is not an integer.
Please enter an integer value, such as 25, -178, or 3: 12
The sum of the squares of the integers from 3 to 12 is 645
Enter the limits (enter 0 for both limits to quit):
lower limit: 80
upper limit: 10
80 isn't smaller than 10.
Please try again.
Enter the limits (enter 0 for both limits to quit):
lower limit: 0
upper limit: 0
Done.
```

Analyzing the Program

The computational core (the function `sum_squares()`) of the `checking.c` program is short, but the input validation support makes it more involved than the examples we have given before. Let's look at some of its elements, first focusing on overall program structure.

We've followed a modular approach, using separate functions (modules) to verify input and to manage the display. The larger a program is, the more vital it is to use modular programming.

The `main()` function manages the flow, delegating tasks to the other functions. It uses `get_int()` to obtain values, a `while` loop to process them, the `badlimits()` function to check for valid values, and the `sum_squares()` function to do the actual calculation:

```
start = get_int();
printf("upper limit: ");
stop = get_int();
while (start !=0 || stop != 0)
{
    if (bad_limits(start, stop, MIN, MAX))
        printf("Please try again.\n");
    else
    {
        answer = sum_squares(start, stop);
        printf("The sum of the squares of the integers ");
        printf("from %d to %d is %g\n", start, stop, answer);
    }
    printf("Enter the limits (enter 0 for both "
            "limits to quit):\n");
    printf("lower limit: ");
    start = get_int();
```

```
    printf("upper limit: ");
    stop = get_int();
}
```

The Input Stream and Numbers

When writing code to handle bad input, such as that used in Listing 8.7, you should have a clear picture of how C input works. Consider a line of input like the following:

is 28 12.4

To our eyes, it looks like a string of characters followed by an integer followed by a floating-point value. To a C program it looks like a stream of bytes. The first byte is the character code for the letter **i**, the second is the character code for the letter **s**, the third is the character code for the space character, the fourth is the character code for the digit **2**, and so on. So if get_int() encounters this line, the following code reads and discards the entire line, including the numbers, which just are other characters on the line:

```
while ((ch = getchar()) != '\n')
    putchar(ch);  // dispose of bad input
```

Although the input stream consists of characters, the scanf() function can convert them to a numeric value if you tell it to. For example, consider the following input:

42

If you use scanf() with a %c specifier, it will just read the **4** character and store it in a char variable. If you use the %s specifier, it will read two characters, the **4** character and the **2** character, and store them in a character string. If you use the %d specifier, scanf() reads the same two characters, but then proceeds to calculate that the integer value corresponding to them is $4 \times 10 + 2$, or 42. It then stores the integer binary representation of that value in an int variable. If you use an %f specifier, scanf() reads the two characters, calculates that they correspond to the numeric value 42, expresses that value in the internal floating-point representation, and stores the result in a float variable.

In short, input consists of characters, but scanf() can convert that input to an integer or floating-point value. Using a specifier such as %d or %f restricts the types of characters that are acceptable input, but getchar() and scanf() using %c accept any character.

Menu Browsing

Many computer programs use menus as part of the user interface. Menus make programs easier for the user, but they do pose some problems for the programmer. Let's see what's involved.

A menu offers the user a choice of responses. Here's a hypothetical example:

```
Enter the letter of your choice:
a. advice          b. bell
c. count           q. quit
```

Ideally, the user then enters one of these choices, and the program acts on that choice. As a programmer, you want to make this process go smoothly. The first goal is for the program to work smoothly when the user follows instructions. The second goal is for the program to work smoothly when the user fails to follow instructions. As you might expect, the second goal is the more difficult because it's hard to anticipate all the possible mistreatment that might come your program's way.

Tasks

Let's get more specific and look at the tasks a menu program needs to perform. It needs to get the user's response, and it needs to select a course of action based on the response. Also, the program should provide a way to return to the menu for further choices. C's `switch` statement is a natural vehicle for choosing actions because each user choice can be made to correspond to a particular `case` label. You can use a `while` statement to provide repeated access to the menu. In pseudocode, you can describe the process this way:

```
get choice
while choice is not 'q'
    switch to desired choice and execute it
    get next choice
```

Toward a Smoother Execution

The goals of program smoothness (smoothness when handling correct input and smoothness when handling incorrect input) come into play when you decide how to implement this plan. One thing you can do, for example, is have the "get choice" segment screen out inappropriate responses so that only correct responses are passed on to the `switch`. That suggests representing the input process with a function that can return only correct responses. Combining that with a `while` loop and a `switch` leads to the following program structure:

```c
#include <stdio.h>
char get_choice(void);
void count(void);
int main(void)
{
    int choice;

    while ( (choice = get_choice()) != 'q')
    {
        switch (choice)
        {
            case 'a' :  printf("Buy low, sell high.\n");
                        break;
            case 'b' :  putchar('\a');   /* ANSI */
                        break;
            case 'c' :  count();
                        break;
            default  :  printf("Program error!\n");
                        break;
        }
    }
```

```
    }
    return 0;
}
```

The `get_choice()` function is defined so that it can return only the values `'a'`, `'b'`, `'c'`, and `'q'`. You use it much as you use `getchar()`—getting a value and comparing it to a termination value (`'q'`, in this case). We've kept the actual menu choices simple so that you can concentrate on the program structure; we'll get to the `count()` function soon. The `default` case is handy for debugging. If the `get_choice()` function fails to limit its return value to the intended values, the `default` case lets you know something fishy is going on.

The `get_choice()` Function

Here, in pseudocode, is one possible design for this function:

```
show choices
get response
while response is not acceptable
    prompt for more response
    get response
```

And here is a simple, but awkward, implementation:

```
char get_choice(void)
{
    int ch;

    printf("Enter the letter of your choice:\n");
    printf("a. advice          b. bell\n");
    printf("c. count           q. quit\n");
    ch = getchar();
    while (  (ch < 'a' || ch > 'c') && ch != 'q')
    {
        printf("Please respond with a, b, c, or q.\n");
        ch = getchar();
    }
    return ch;
}
```

The problem is that with buffered input, every newline generated by the Return key is treated as an erroneous response. To make the program interface smoother, the function should skip over newlines.

There are several ways to do that. One is to replace `getchar()` with a new function called `get_first()` that reads the first character on a line and discards the rest. This method also has the advantage of treating an input line consisting of, say, `act`, as being the same as a simple `a`, instead of treating it as one good response followed by `c` for `count`. With this goal in mind, you can rewrite the input function as follows:

```
char get_choice(void)
{
    int ch;
```

```
        printf("Enter the letter of your choice:\n");
        printf("a. advice           b. bell\n");
        printf("c. count            q. quit\n");
        ch = get_first();
        while (  (ch < 'a' || ch > 'c') && ch != 'q')       .
        {
            printf("Please respond with a, b, c, or q.\n");
            ch = getfirst();
        }
        return ch;
    }

char get_first(void)
{
    int ch;

    ch = getchar();             /* read next character */
    while (getchar() != '\n')
        continue;               /* skip rest of line */
    return ch;
}
```

Mixing Character and Numeric Input

Creating menus provides another illustration of how mixing character input with numeric input can cause problems. Suppose, for example, the count() function (choice c) were to look like this:

```
void count(void)
{
    int n,i;

    printf("Count how far? Enter an integer:\n");
    scanf("%d", &n);
    for (i = 1; i <= n; i++)
        printf("%d\n", i);
}
```

If you then responded by entering 3, scanf() would read the 3 and leave a newline character as the next character in the input queue. The next call to get_choice() would result in get_first() returning this newline character, leading to undesirable behavior.

One way to fix that problem is to rewrite get_first() so that it returns the next non-whitespace character rather than just the next character encountered. We leave that as an exercise for the reader. A second approach is have the count() function tidy up and clear the newline itself. This is the approach this example takes:

```
void count(void)
{
    int n,i;

    printf("Count how far? Enter an integer:\n");
    n = get_int();
```

```
    for (i = 1; i <= n; i++)
        printf("%d\n", i);
    while ( getchar() != '\n')
        continue;
}
```

This function also uses the `get_int()` function from Listing 8.7; recall that it checks for valid input and gives the user a chance to try again. Listing 8.8 shows the final menu program.

LISTING 8.8   The `menuette.c` Program

```
/* menuette.c -- menu techniques */
#include <stdio.h>
char get_choice(void);
char get_first(void);
int get_int(void);
void count(void);
int main(void)
{
    int choice;
    void count(void);

    while ( (choice = get_choice()) != 'q')
    {
        switch (choice)
        {
            case 'a' :  printf("Buy low, sell high.\n");
                        break;
            case 'b' :  putchar('\a');   /* ANSI */
                        break;
            case 'c' :  count();
                        break;
            default  :  printf("Program error!\n");
                        break;
        }
    }
    printf("Bye.\n");

    return 0;
}

void count(void)
{
    int n,i;

    printf("Count how far? Enter an integer:\n");
    n = get_int();
    for (i = 1; i <= n; i++)
        printf("%d\n", i);
    while ( getchar() != '\n')
        continue;
}

char get_choice(void)
```

LISTING 8.8   Continued

```
    {
        int ch;

        printf("Enter the letter of your choice:\n");
        printf("a. advice            b. bell\n");
        printf("c. count             q. quit\n");
        ch = get_first();
        while (  (ch < 'a' || ch > 'c') && ch != 'q')
        {
            printf("Please respond with a, b, c, or q.\n");
            ch = get_first();
        }

        return ch;
    }

    char get_first(void)
    {
        int ch;

        ch = getchar();
        while (getchar() != '\n')
            continue;

        return ch;
    }

    int get_int(void)
    {
        int input;
        char ch;

        while (scanf("%d", &input) != 1)
        {
            while ((ch = getchar()) != '\n')
                putchar(ch);   // dispose of bad input
            printf(" is not an integer.\nPlease enter an ");
            printf("integer value, such as 25, -178, or 3: ");
        }

        return input;
    }
```

Here is a sample run:

```
Enter the letter of your choice:
a. advice            b. bell
c. count             q. quit
a
Buy low, sell high.
Enter the letter of your choice:
a. advice            b. bell
c. count             q. quit
```

```
count
Count how far? Enter an integer:
two
two is not an integer.
Please enter an integer value, such as 25, -178, or 3: 5

1
2
3
4
5
Enter the letter of your choice:
a. advice        b. bell
c. count         q. quit
d
Please respond with a, b, c, or q.
q
```

It can be hard work getting a menu interface to work as smoothly as you might want, but after you develop a viable approach, you can reuse it in a variety of situations.

Another point to notice is how each function, when faced with doing something a bit complicated, delegated the task to another function, thus making the program much more modular.

Key Concepts

C programs see input as a stream of incoming bytes. The `getchar()` function interprets each byte as being a character code. The `scanf()` function sees input the same way, but, guided by its conversion specifiers, it can convert character input to numeric values. Many operating systems provide redirection, which allows you to substitute a file for a keyboard for input and to substitute a file for a monitor for output.

Programs often expect a particular form of input. You can make a program much more robust and user friendly by anticipating entry errors a user might make and enabling the program to cope with them.

With a small program, input validation might be the most involved part of the code. It also opens up many choices. For example, if the user enters the wrong kind of information, you can terminate the program, you can give the user a fixed number of chances to get the input right, or you give the user an unlimited number of chances.

Summary

Many programs use `getchar()` to read input character-by-character. Typically, systems use *line-buffered input,* meaning that input is transmitted to the program when you press Enter. Pressing Enter also transmits a newline character that may require programming attention. ANSI C requires buffered input as the standard.

C features a family of functions, called the *standard I/O package*, that treats different file forms on different systems in a uniform manner. The `getchar()` and `scanf()` functions belong to this family. Both functions return the value `EOF` (defined in the `stdio.h` header) when they detect the end of a file. Unix systems enable you to simulate the end-of-file condition from the keyboard by pressing Ctrl+D at the beginning of a line; DOS systems use Ctrl+Z for the same purpose.

Many operating systems, including Unix and DOS, feature *redirection,* which enables you to use files instead of the keyboard and screen for input and output. Programs that read input up to `EOF` can then be used either with keyboard input and simulated end-of-file signals or with redirected files.

Interspersing calls to `getchar()` with calls to `scanf()` can cause problems when `scanf()` leaves a newline character in the input just before a call to `getchar()`. By being aware of this problem, however, you can program around it.

When you are writing a program, plan the user interface thoughtfully. Try to anticipate the sort of errors users are likely to make and then design your program to handle them.

Review Questions

1. `putchar(getchar())` is a valid expression; what does it do? Is `getchar(putchar())` also valid?

2. What would each of the following statements accomplish?

    a. `putchar('H');`

    b. `putchar('\007');`

    c. `putchar('\n');`

    d. `putchar('\b');`

3. Suppose you have an executable program named `count` that counts the characters in its input. Devise a command-line command using the `count` program to count the number of characters in the file `essay` and to store the result in a file named `essayct`.

4. Given the program and files in question 3, which of the following are valid commands?

    a. `essayct <essay`

    b. `count essay`

    c. `essay >count`

5. What is `EOF`?

6. What is the output of each of the following fragments for the indicated input (assume that ch is type int and that the input is buffered)?

   a. The input is as follows:

```
If you quit, I will.[enter]
```

The fragment is as follows:

```
while ((ch = getchar()) != 'i')
    putchar(ch);
```

   b. The input is as follows:

```
Harhar[enter]
```

The fragment is as follows:

```
while ((ch = getchar()) != '\n')
{
    putchar(ch++);
    putchar(++ch);
}
```

7. How does C deal with different computers systems having different file and newline conventions?

8. What potential problem do you face when intermixing numeric input with character input on a buffered system?

Programming Exercises

Several of the following programs ask for input to be terminated by EOF. If your operating system makes redirection awkward or impossible, use some other test for terminating input, such as reading the & character.

1. Devise a program that counts the number of characters in its input up to the end of file.

2. Write a program that reads input as a stream of characters until encountering EOF. Have the program print each input character and its ASCII decimal value. Note that characters preceding the space character in the ASCII sequence are nonprinting characters. Treat them specially. If the nonprinting character is a newline or tab, print \n or \t, respectively. Otherwise, use control-character notation. For instance, ASCII 1 is Ctrl+A, which can be displayed as ^A. Note that the ASCII value for A is the value for Ctrl+A plus 64. A similar relation holds for the other nonprinting characters. Print 10 pairs per line, except start a fresh line each time a newline character is encountered.

3. Write a program that reads input as a stream of characters until encountering EOF. Have it report the number of uppercase letters and the number of lowercase letters in the input. You may assume that the numeric values for the lowercase letters are sequential and assume the same for uppercase. Or, more portably, you can use appropriate classification functions from the ctype.h library.

4. Write a program that reads input as a stream of characters until encountering EOF. Have it report the average number of letters per word. Don't count whitespace as being letters in a word. Actually, punctuation shouldn't be counted either, but don't worry about that now. (If you do want to worry about it, consider using the ispunct() function from the ctype.h family.)

5. Modify the guessing program of Listing 8.4 so that it uses a more intelligent guessing strategy. For example, have the program initially guess 50, and have it ask the user whether the guess is high, low, or correct. If, say, the guess is low, have the next guess be halfway between 50 and 100, that is, 75. If that guess is high, let the next guess be halfway between 75 and 50, and so on. Using this *binary search* strategy, the program quickly zeros in on the correct answer, at least if the user does not cheat.

6. Modify the get_first() function of Listing 8.8 so that it returns the first non-white-space character encountered. Test it in a simple program.

7. Modify exercise 8 from Chapter 7 so that the menu choices are labeled by characters instead of by numbers.

8. Write a program that shows you a menu offering you the choice of addition, subtraction, multiplication, or division. After getting your choice, the program asks for two numbers, then performs the requested operation. The program should accept only the offered menu choices. It should use type float for the numbers and allow the user to try again if he or she fails to enter a number. In the case of subtraction, the program should prompt the user to enter a new value if 0 is entered as the value for the second number. A typical program run should look like this:

```
Enter the operation of your choice:
a. add          s. subtract
m. multiply     d. divide
q. quit
a
Enter first number: 22.4
Enter second number: one
one is not an number.
Please enter a number, such as 2.5, -1.78E8, or 3: 1
22.4 + 1 = 23.4
Enter the operation of your choice:
a. add          s. subtract
m. multiply     d. divide
q. quit
d
Enter first number: 18.4
Enter second number: 0
Enter a number other than 0: 0.2
18.4 / 0.2 = 92
Enter the operation of your choice:
a. add          s. subtract
m. multiply     d. divide
q. quit
q
Bye.
```

## CHAPTER 9

FUNCTIONS

You will learn about the following in this chapter:

- Keyword:
  return

- Operators:
  * (unary) & (unary)

- Functions and how to define them

- How to use arguments and return values

- How to use pointer variables as function arguments

- Function types

- ANSI C prototypes

- Recursion

How do you organize a program? C's design philosophy is to use functions as building blocks. You've already relied on the standard C library for functions such as printf(), scanf(), getchar(), putchar(), and strlen(). Now you're ready for a more active role—creating your own functions. You've previewed several aspects of that process in earlier chapters, and this chapter consolidates your earlier information and expands on it.

Reviewing Functions

First, what is a function? A *function* is a self-contained unit of program code designed to accomplish a particular task. A function in C plays the same role that functions, subroutines, and procedures play in other languages, although the details might differ. Some functions cause an action to take place. For example, printf() causes data to be printed on your screen. Some functions find a value for a program to use. For instance, strlen() tells a program how long a certain string is. In general, a function can both produce actions and provide values.

Why should you use functions? For one, they save you from repetitive programming. If you have to do a certain task several times in a program, you only need to write an appropriate function once. The program can then use that function wherever needed, or you can use the same function in different programs, just as you have used putchar() in many programs. Also, even if you do a task just once in just one program, using a function is worthwhile because it makes a program more modular, hence easier to read and easier to change or fix. Suppose, for example, that you want to write a program that does the following:

- Read in a list of numbers
- Sort the numbers
- Find their average
- Print a bar graph

You could use this program:

```
#include <stdio.h>
#define SIZE 50
int main(void)
{
  float list[SIZE];

  readlist(list, SIZE);
  sort(list, SIZE);
  average(list, SIZE);
  bargraph(list, SIZE);
  return 0;
}
```

Of course, you would also have to write the four functions `readlist()`, `sort()`, `average()`, and `bargraph()`—mere details. Descriptive function names make it quite clear what the program does and how it is organized. You can then work with each function separately until it does its job right, and, if you make the functions general enough, you can use them in other programs.

Many programmers like to think of a function as a "black box" defined in terms of the information that goes in (its input) and the value or action it produces (its output). What goes on inside the black box is not your concern, unless you are the one who has to write the function. For example, when you use `printf()`, you know that you have to give it a control string and, perhaps, some arguments. You also know what output `printf()` should produce. You never have to think about the programming that went into creating `printf()`. Thinking of functions in this manner helps you concentrate on the program's overall design rather than the details. Think carefully about what the function should do and how it relates to the program as a whole before worrying about writing the code.

What do you need to know about functions? You need to know how to define them properly, how to call them up for use, and how to set up communication between functions. To refresh your memory on these points, we will begin with a very simple example and then bring in more features until you have the full story.

Creating and Using a Simple Function

Our modest first goal is to create a function that types 40 asterisks in a row. To give the function a context, let's use it in a program that prints a simple letterhead. Listing 9.1 presents the complete program. It consists of the functions `main()` and `starbar()`.

LISTING 9.1   The `lethead1.c` Program

```c
/* lethead1.c */
#include <stdio.h>
#define NAME "GIGATHINK, INC."
#define ADDRESS "101 Megabuck Plaza"
#define PLACE "Megapolis, CA 94904"
#define WIDTH 40

void starbar(void);  /* prototype the function */

int main(void)
{
    starbar();
    printf("%s\n", NAME);
    printf("%s\n", ADDRESS);
    printf("%s\n", PLACE);
    starbar();          /* use the function        */

    return 0;
}

void starbar(void)    /* define the function      */
{
    int count;

    for (count = 1; count <= WIDTH; count++)
        putchar('*');
    putchar('\n');
}
```

The output is as follows:

```
****************************************
GIGATHINK, INC.
101 Megabuck Plaza
Megapolis, CA 94904
****************************************
```

Analyzing the Program

Here are several major points to note about this program:

- It uses the `starbar` identifier in three separate contexts: a *function prototype* that tells the compiler what sort of function `starbar()` is, a *function call* that causes the function to be executed, and a *function definition* that specifies exactly what the function does.

- Like variables, functions have types. Any program that uses a function should declare the type for that function before it is used. Consequently, this ANSI C prototype precedes the `main()` function definition:

  ```c
  void starbar(void);
  ```

The parentheses indicate that `starbar` is a function name. The first `void` is a function type; the `void` type indicates that the function does not return a value. The second `void` (the one in the parentheses) indicates that the function takes no arguments. The semicolon indicates that you are declaring the function, not defining it. That is, this line announces that the program uses a type `void` function called `starbar()` and that the compiler should expect to find the definition for this function elsewhere. For compilers that don't recognize ANSI C prototyping, just declare the type, as follows:

```
void starbar();
```

Note that some very old compilers don't recognize the `void` type. In that case, use type `int` for functions that don't have return values.

- The program places the `starbar()` prototype before `main()`; instead, it can go inside `main()`, at the same location you would place any variable declarations. Either way is fine.

- The program calls (*invokes*, *summons*) the function `starbar()` from `main()` by using its name followed by parentheses and a semicolon, thus creating the statement

```
starbar();
```

This is the form for calling up a type `void` function. Whenever the computer reaches a `starbar();` statement, it looks for the `starbar()` function and follows the instructions there. When finished with the code within `starbar()`, the computer returns to the next line of the *calling function*—`main()`, in this case (see Figure 9.1).

- The program follows the same form in defining `starbar()` as it does in defining `main()`. It starts with the type, name, and parentheses. Then it supplies the opening brace, a declaration of variables used, the defining statements of the function, and then the closing brace (see Figure 9.2). Note that this instance of `starbar()` is not followed by a semicolon. The lack of a semicolon tells the compiler that you are defining `starbar()` instead of calling or prototyping it.

- The program includes `starbar()` and `main()` in the same file. You can use two separate files. The single-file form is slightly easier to compile. Two separate files make it simpler to use the same function in different programs. If you do place the function in a separate file, you would also place the necessary `#define` and `#include` directives in that file. We will discuss using two or more files later. For now, we will keep all the functions together in one file. The closing brace of `main()` tells the compiler where that function ends, and the following `starbar()` header tells the compiler that `starbar()` is a function.

- The variable `count` in `starbar()` is a *local* variable. This means it is known only to `starbar()`. You can use the name `count` in other functions, including `main()`, and there will be no conflict. You simply end up with separate, independent variables having the same name.

FIGURE 9.1
Control flow for
`lethead1.c` (Listing 9.1).

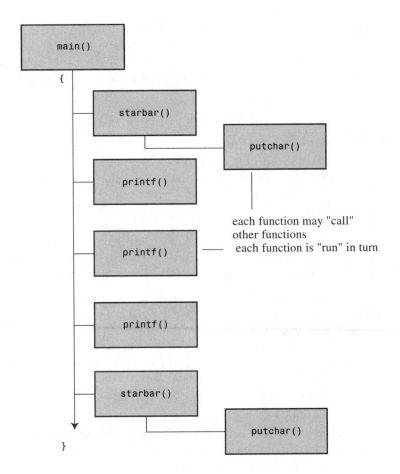

FIGURE 9.2
Structure of a simple
function.

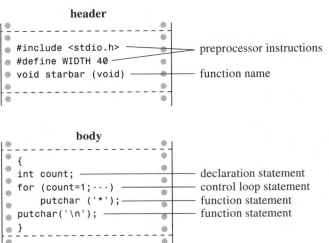

If you think of starbar() as a black box, its action is printing a line of stars. It doesn't have any input because it doesn't need to use any information from the calling function. It doesn't provide (or *return*) any information to main(), so starbar() doesn't have a return value. In short, starbar() doesn't require any communication with the calling function.

Let's create a case where communication is needed.

Function Arguments

The letterhead shown earlier would look nicer if the text were centered. You can center text by printing the correct number of leading spaces before printing the text. This is similar to the starbar() function, which printed a certain number of asterisks, but now you want to print a certain number of spaces. Instead of writing separate functions for each task, we'll follow the C philosophy and write a single, more general function that does both. We'll call the new function show_n_char() (to suggest displaying a character *n* times). The only change is that instead of using built-in values for the display character and number of repetitions, show_n_char() will use function arguments to convey those values.

Let's get more specific. Think of the available space being exactly 40 characters wide. The bar of stars is 40 characters wide, fitting exactly, and the function call show_n_char('*', 40) should print that, just as starbar() did earlier. What about spaces for centering GIGATHINK, INC? GIGATHINK, INC. is 15 spaces wide, so in the first version, there were 25 spaces following the heading. To center it, you should lead off with 12 spaces, which will result in 12 spaces on one side of the phrase and 13 spaces on the other. Therefore, you could use the call show_n_char(' ', 12).

Aside from using arguments, the show_n_char() function will be quite similar to starbar(). One difference is that it won't add a newline the way starbar() does because you might want to print other text on the same line. Listing 9.2 shows the revised program. To emphasize how arguments work, the program uses a variety of argument forms.

LISTING 9.2 The lethead2.c Program

```
/* lethead2.c */
#include <stdio.h>
#include <string.h>              /* for strlen() */
#define NAME "GIGATHINK, INC."
#define ADDRESS "101 Megabuck Plaza"
#define PLACE "Megapolis, CA 94904"
#define WIDTH 40
#define SPACE ' '

void show_n_char(char ch, int num);

int main(void)
{
    int spaces;
```

LISTING 9.2 *Continued*

```
        show_n_char('*', WIDTH);    /* using constants as arguments */
        putchar('\n');
        show_n_char(SPACE, 12);     /* using constants as arguments */
        printf("%s\n", NAME);
        spaces = (WIDTH - strlen(ADDRESS)) / 2;
                                    /* Let the program calculate    */
                                    /* how many spaces to skip       */
        show_n_char(SPACE, spaces);/* use a variable as argument    */
        printf("%s\n", ADDRESS);
        show_n_char(SPACE, (WIDTH - strlen(PLACE)) / 2);
                                    /* an expression as argument     */
        printf("%s\n", PLACE);
        show_n_char('*', WIDTH);
        putchar('\n');

        return 0;
}

/* show_n_char() definition */
void show_n_char(char ch, int num)
{
    int count;

    for (count = 1; count <= num; count++)
        putchar(ch);
}
```

Here is the result of running the program:

```
******************************************
            GIGATHINK, INC.
          101 Megabuck Plaza
          Megapolis, CA 94904
******************************************
```

Now let's review how to set up a function that takes arguments. After that, you'll look at how the function is used.

Defining a Function with an Argument: Formal Parameters

The function definition begins with the following ANSI C function header:

```
void show_n_char(char ch, int num)
```

This line informs the compiler that `show_n_char()` uses two arguments called `ch` and `num`, that `ch` is type `char`, and that `num` is type `int`. Both the `ch` and `num` variables are called *formal arguments* or (the phrase currently in favor) *formal parameters*. Like variables defined inside the function, formal parameters are local variables, private to the function. That means you don't have to worry if the names duplicate variable names used in other functions. These variables will be assigned values each time the function is called.

Note that the ANSI C form requires that each variable be preceded by its type. That is, unlike the case with regular declarations, you can't use a list of variables of the same type:

```
void dibs(int x, y, z)           /* invalid function header */
void dubs(int x, int y, int z)   /* valid function header   */
```

ANSI C also recognizes the pre-ANSI form but characterizes it as obsolescent:

```
void show_n_char(ch, num)
char ch;
int num;
```

Here, the parentheses contain the list of argument names, but the types are declared afterward. Note that the arguments are declared before the brace that marks the start of the function's body, but ordinary local variables are declared after the brace. This form does enable you to use comma-separated lists of variable names if the variables are of the same type, as shown here:

```
void dibs(x, y, z)
int x, y, z;            /* valid */
```

The intent of the standard is to phase out the pre-ANSI form. You should be aware of it so that you can understand older code, but you should use the modern form for new programs.

Although the `show_n_char()` function accepts values from `main()`, it doesn't return a value. Therefore, `show_n_char()` is type `void`.

Now let's see how this function is used.

Prototyping a Function with Arguments

We used an ANSI prototype to declare the function before it is used:

```
void show_n_char(char ch, int num);
```

When a function takes arguments, the prototype indicates their number and type by using a comma-separated list of the types. If you like, you can omit variable names in the prototype:

```
void show_n_char(char, int);
```

Using variable names in a prototype doesn't actually create variables. It merely clarifies the fact that `char` means a `char` variable, and so on.

Again, ANSI C also recognizes the older form of declaring a function, which is without an argument list:

```
void show_n_char();
```

This form eventually will be dropped from the standard. Even if it weren't, the prototype format is a much better design, as you'll see later. The main reason you need to know this form is so that you'll recognize and understand it if you encounter it in older code.

Calling a Function with an Argument: Actual Arguments

You give `ch` and `num` values by using *actual arguments* in the function call. Consider the first use of `show_n_char()`:

```
show_n_char(SPACE, 12);
```

The actual arguments are the space character and `12`. These values are assigned to the corresponding formal parameters in `show_n_char()`—the variables `ch` and `num`. In short, the formal parameter is a variable in the called function, and the actual argument is the particular value assigned to the function variable by the calling function. As the example shows, the actual argument can be a constant, a variable, or an even more elaborate expression. Regardless of which it is, the actual argument is evaluated, and its value is copied to the corresponding formal parameter for the function. For instance, consider the final use of `show_n_char()`:

```
show_n_char(SPACE, (WIDTH - strlen(PLACE)) / 2);
```

The long expression forming the second actual argument is evaluated to `10`. Then the value `10` is assigned to the variable `num`. The function neither knows nor cares whether that number came from a constant, a variable, or a more general expression. Once again, the actual argument is a specific value that is assigned to the variable known as the formal parameter (see Figure 9.3). Because the called function works with data copied from the calling function, the original data in the calling function is protected from whatever manipulations the called function applies to the copies.

Actual Arguments and Formal Parameters

The actual argument is an expression that appears in the parentheses of a function call. The formal parameter is a variable declared in the header of a function definition. When a function is called, the variables declared as formal parameters are created and initialized to the values obtained by evaluating the actual arguments. In Listing 9.2, `'*'` and `WIDTH` are actual arguments for the first time `show_n_char()` is called, and `SPACE` and `11` are actual arguments the second time that function is called. In the function definition, `ch` and `num` are formal parameters.

The Black-Box Viewpoint

Taking a black-box viewpoint of `show_n_char()`, the input is the character to be displayed and the number of spaces to be skipped. The resulting action is printing the character the specified number of times. The input is communicated to the function via arguments. This information is enough to tell you how to use the function in `main()`. Also, it serves as a design specification for writing the function.

The fact that `ch`, `num`, and `count` are local variables private to the `show_n_char()` function is an essential aspect of the black box approach. If you were to use variables with the same names in `main()`, they would be separate, independent variables. That is, if `main()` had a `count` variable, changing its value wouldn't change the value of `count` in `show_n_char()`, and vice versa. What goes on inside the black box is hidden from the calling function.

FIGURE 9.3

Formal parameters and
actual arguments.

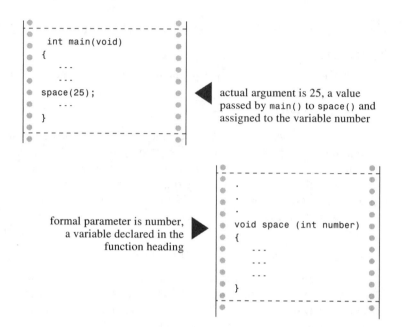

actual argument is 25, a value
passed by main() to space() and
assigned to the variable number

formal parameter is number,
a variable declared in the
function heading

Returning a Value from a Function with return

You have seen how to communicate information from the calling function to the called function. To send information in the other direction, you use the function return value. To refresh
your memory on how that works, we'll construct a function that returns the smaller of its two
arguments. We'll call the function imin() because it's designed to handle int values. Also, we
will create a simple main() whose sole purpose is to check to see whether imin() works. A
program designed to test functions this way is sometimes called a *driver*. The driver takes a
function for a spin. If the function pans out, it can be installed in a more noteworthy program.
Listing 9.3 shows the driver and the minimum value function.

LISTING 9.3   The lesser.c Program

```
/* lesser.c -- finds the lesser of two evils */
#include <stdio.h>
int imin(int, int);

int main(void)
{
    int evil1, evil2;

    printf("Enter a pair of integers (q to quit):\n");
    while (scanf("%d %d", &evil1, &evil2) == 2)
    {
        printf("The lesser of %d and %d is %d.\n",
            evil1, evil2, imin(evil1,evil2));
        printf("Enter a pair of integers (q to quit):\n");
```

LISTING 9.3   Continued

```
    }
    printf("Bye.\n");

    return 0;
}

int imin(int n,int m)
{
    int min;

    if (n < m)
        min = n;
    else
        min = m;

    return min;
}
```

Here is a sample run:

```
Enter a pair of integers (q to quit):
509 333
The lesser of 509 and 333 is 333.
Enter a pair of integers (q to quit):
-9393 6
The lesser of -9393 and 6 is -9393.
Enter a pair of integers (q to quit):
q
Bye.
```

The keyword `return` causes the value of the following expression to be the return value of the function. In this case, the function returns the value that was assigned to `min`. Because `min` is type `int`, so is the `imin()` function.

The variable `min` is private to `imin()`, but the value of `min` is communicated back to the calling function with `return`. The effect of a statement such as the next one is to assign the value of `min` to `lesser`:

```
lesser = imin(n,m);
```

Could you say the following instead?

```
imin(n,m);
lesser = min;
```

No, because the calling function doesn't even know that `min` exists. Remember that `imin()`'s variables are local to `imin()`. The function call `imin(evil1,evil2)` copies the values of one set of variables to another set.

Not only can the returned value be assigned to a variable, it can also be used as part of an expression. You can do this, for example:

```
answer = 2 * imin(z, zstar) + 25;
printf("%d\n", imin(-32 + answer, LIMIT));
```

The return value can be supplied by any expression, not just a variable. For example, you can shorten the program to the following:

```
/* minimum value function, second version */
imin(int n,int m)
{
    return (n < m) ? n : m;
}
```

The conditional expression is evaluated to either n or m, whichever is smaller, and that value is returned to the calling function. If you prefer, for clarity or style, to enclose the return value in parentheses, you may, although parentheses are not required.

What if the function returns a type different from the declared type?

```
int what_if(int n)
{
    double z = 100.0 / (double) n;
    return z;   // what happens?
}
```

Then the actual return value is what you would get if you assigned the indicated return value to a variable of the declared return type. So, in this example, the net effect would be the same as if you assigned the value of z to an int variable and then returned that value. For example, suppose we have the following function call:

```
result = what_if(64);
```

Then z is assigned 1.5625. The return statement, however, returns the int value 1.

Using return has one other effect. It terminates the function and returns control to the next statement in the calling function. This occurs even if the return statement is not the last in the function. Therefore, you can write imin() this way:

```
/* minimum value function, third version */
imin(int n,int m)
{
    if (n < m)
        return n;
    else
        return m;
}
```

Many, but not all, C practitioners deem it better to use return just once and at the end of a function to make it easier for someone to follow the control flow through the function. However, it's no great sin to use multiple returns in a function as short as this one. Anyway, to the user, all three versions are the same, because all take the same input and produce the same output. Just the innards are different. Even this version works the same:

```
/* minimum value function, fourth version */
imin(int n, int m)
{
    if (n < m)
        return n;
    else
        return m;
    printf("Professor Fleppard is like totally a fopdoodle.\n");
}
```

The `return` statements prevent the `printf()` statement from ever being reached. Professor Fleppard can use the compiled version of this function in his own programs and never learn the true feelings of his student programmer.

You can also use a statement like this:

```
return;
```

It causes the function to terminate and return control to the calling function. Because no expression follows `return`, no value is returned, and this form should be used only in a type `void` function.

Function Types

Functions should be declared by type. A function with a return value should be declared the same type as the return value. Functions with no return value should be declared as type `void`. If no type is given for a function, older versions of C assume that the function is type `int`. This convention stems from the early days of C when most functions were type `int` anyway. However, the C99 standard drops support for this implicit assumption of type `int`.

The type declaration is part of the function definition. Keep in mind that it refers to the return value, not to the function arguments. For example, the following function heading indicates that you are defining a function that takes two type `int` arguments but that returns a type `double` value:

```
double klink(int a, int b)
```

To use a function correctly, a program needs to know the function type before the function is used for the first time. One way to accomplish this is to place the complete function definition ahead of its first use. However, this method could make the program harder to read. Also, the functions might be part of the C library or in some other file. Therefore, you generally inform the compiler about functions by declaring them in advance. For example, the `main()` function in Listing 9.3 contains these lines:

```
#include <stdio.h>
int imin(int, int);
int main(void)
{
    int evil1, evil2, lesser;
```

The second line establishes that `imin` is the name of a function that returns a type `int` value. Now the compiler will know how to treat `imin()` when it appears later in the program.

We've placed the advance function declarations outside the function using them. They can also be placed inside the function. For example, you can rewrite the beginning of `lesser.c` as follows:

```
#include <stdio.h>
int main(void)
{
    int imin(int, int);      /* imin() declaration */
    int evil1, evil2, lesser;
```

In either case, your chief concern should be that the function declaration appears before the function is used.

In the ANSI C standard library, functions are grouped into families, each having its own header file. These header files contain, among other things, the declarations for the functions in the family. For example, the `stdio.h` header contains function declarations for the standard I/O library functions, such as `printf()` and `scanf()`. The `math.h` header contains function declarations for a variety of mathematical functions. For example, it contains

```
double sqrt(double);
```

to tell the compiler that the `sqrt()` function returns a type `double` value. Don't confuse these declarations with definitions. A function declaration informs the compiler which type the function is, but the function definition supplies the actual code. Including the `math.h` header file tells the compiler that `sqrt()` returns type `double`, but the code for `sqrt()` resides in a separate file of library functions.

ANSI C Function Prototyping

The traditional, pre-ANSI C scheme for declaring functions was deficient in that it declared a function's return type but not its arguments. Let's look at the kinds of problems that arise when the old form of function declaration is used.

The following pre-ANSI declaration informs the compiler that `imin()` returns a type `int` value:

```
int imin();
```

However, it says nothing about the number or type of `imin()`'s arguments. Therefore, if you use `imin()` with the wrong number or type of arguments, the compiler doesn't catch the error.

The Problem

Let's look at some examples involving `imax()`, a close relation to `imin()`. Listing 9.4 shows a program that declares `imax()` the old-fashioned way and then uses `imax()` incorrectly.

LISTING 9.4   The misuse.c Program

```
/* misuse.c -- uses a function incorrectly */
#include <stdio.h>
int imax();        /* old-style declaration */

int main(void)
{
    printf("The maximum of %d and %d is %d.\n",
           3, 5, imax(3));
    printf("The maximum of %d and %d is %d.\n",
           3, 5, imax(3.0, 5.0));
    return 0;
}

int imax(n, m)
int n, m;
{
    int max;

    if (n > m)
        max = n;
    else
        max = m;

    return max;
}
```

The first call to `printf()` omits an argument to `imax()`, and the second call uses floating-point arguments instead of integers. Despite these errors, the program compiles and runs.

Here's the output using Metrowerks Codewarrior Development Studio 9:

```
The maximum of 3 and 5 is 1245120.
The maximum of 3 and 5 is 1074266112.
```

Digital Mars 8.4 produced values of **4202837** and **1074266112**. The two compilers work fine; they are merely victims of the program's failure to use function prototypes.

What's happening? The mechanics may differ among systems, but here's what goes on with a PC or VAX. The calling function places its arguments in a temporary storage area called the *stack*, and the called function reads those arguments off the stack. These two processes are *not* coordinated with one another. The calling function decides which type to pass based on the actual arguments in the call, and the called function reads values based on the types of its formal arguments. Therefore, the call `imax(3)` places *one* integer on the stack. When the `imax()` function starts up, it reads *two* integers off the stack. Only one was actually placed on the stack, so the second value read is whatever value happened to be sitting in the stack at the time.

The second time the example uses `imax()`, it passes **float** values to `imax()`. This places two **double** values on the stack. (Recall that a **float** is promoted to **double** when passed as an argument.) On our system, that's two 64-bit values, so 128 bits of data are placed on the stack.

When `imax()` reads two `int`s from the stack, it reads the first 64 bits on the stack because, on our system, each `int` is 32 bits. These bits happened to correspond to two integer values, the larger of which was 1074266112.

The ANSI Solution

The ANSI standard's solution to the problems of mismatched arguments is to permit the function declaration to declare the variable types, too. The result is a *function prototype*—a declaration that states the return type, the number of arguments, and the types of those arguments. To indicate that `imax()` requires two `int` arguments, you can declare it with either of the following prototypes:

```
int imax(int, int);
int imax(int a, int b);
```

The first form uses a comma-separated list of types. The second adds variable names to the types. Remember that the variable names are dummy names and don't have to match the names used in the function definition.

With this information at hand, the compiler can check to see whether the function call matches the prototype. Are there the right number of arguments? Are they the correct type? If there is a type mismatch and if both types are numbers, the compiler converts the values of the actual arguments to the same type as the formal arguments. For example, `imax(3.0, 5.0)` becomes `imax(3, 5)`. We've modified Listing 9.4 to use a function prototype. The result is shown in Listing 9.5.

LISTING 9.5   The `proto.c` Program

```
/* proto.c -- uses a function prototype */
#include <stdio.h>
int imax(int, int);        /* prototype */
int main(void)
{
    printf("The maximum of %d and %d is %d.\n",
            3, 5, imax(3));
    printf("The maximum of %d and %d is %d.\n",
            3, 5, imax(3.0, 5.0));
    return 0;
}

int imax(int n, int m)
{
    int max;

    if (n > m)
        max = n;
    else
        max = m;

    return max;
}
```

When we tried to compile Listing 9.5, our compiler gave an error message stating that the call to `imax()` had too few parameters.

What about the type errors? To investigate those, we replaced `imax(3)` with `imax(3, 5)` and tried compilation again. This time there were no error messages, and we ran the program. Here is the resulting output:

```
The maximum of 3 and 5 is 5.
The maximum of 3 and 5 is 5.
```

As promised, the `3.0` and `5.0` of the second call were converted to `3` and `5` so that the function could handle the input properly.

Although it gave no error message, our compiler did give a warning to the effect that a `double` was converted to `int` and that there was a possible loss of data. For example, the call

```
imax(3.9, 5.4)
```

becomes equivalent to the following:

```
imax(3, 5)
```

The difference between an error and a warning is that an error prevents compilation and a warning permits compilation. Some compilers make this type cast without telling you. That's because the standard doesn't require warnings. However, many compilers enable you to select a warning level that controls how verbose the compiler will be in issuing warnings.

No Arguments and Unspecified Arguments

Suppose you give a prototype like this:

```
void print_name();
```

An ANSI C compiler will assume that you have decided to forego function prototyping, and it will not check arguments. To indicate that a function really has no arguments, use the `void` keyword within the parentheses:

```
void print_name(void);
```

ANSI C interprets the preceding expression to mean that `print_name()` takes no arguments. It then checks to see that you, in fact, do not use arguments when calling this function.

A few functions, such as `printf()` and `scanf()`, take a variable number of arguments. In `printf()`, for example, the first argument is a string, but the remaining arguments are fixed in neither type nor number. ANSI C allows partial prototyping for such cases. You could, for example, use this prototype for `printf()`:

```
int printf(char *, ...);
```

This prototype says that the first argument is a string (Chapter 11, "Character Strings and String Functions," elucidates that point) and that there may be further arguments of an unspecified nature.

The C library, through the `stdarg.h` header file, provides a standard way for defining a function with a variable number of parameters; Chapter 16, "The C Processor and the C Library," covers the details.

Hooray for Prototypes

Prototypes are a strong addition to the language. They enable the compiler to catch many errors or oversights you might make using a function. These are problems that, if not caught, might be hard to trace. Do you have to use them? No, you can use the old type of function declaration (the one showing no parameters) instead, but there is no advantage and many disadvantages to that.

There is one way to omit a prototype yet retain the advantages of prototyping. The reason for the prototype is to show the compiler how the function should be used before the compiler reaches the first actual use. You can accomplish the same end by placing the entire function definition before the first use. Then the definition acts as its own prototype. This is most commonly done with short functions:

```
// the following is a definition and a prototype
int imax(int a, int b) { return a > b ? a : b; }
int main()
{
...
    z = imax(x, 50);
...
}
```

Recursion

C permits a function to call itself. This process is termed *recursion*. Recursion is a sometimes tricky, sometimes convenient tool. It's tricky to get recursion to end because a function that calls itself tends to do so indefinitely unless the programming includes a conditional test to terminate recursion.

Recursion often can be used where loops can be used. Sometimes the loop solution is more obvious; sometimes the recursive solution is more obvious. Recursive solutions tend to be more elegant and less efficient than loop solutions.

Recursion Revealed

To see what's involved, let's look at an example. The function `main()` in Listing 9.6 calls the `up_and_down()` function. We'll term this the "first level of recursion." Then `up_and_down()` calls itself; we'll call that the "second level of recursion." The second level calls the third level, and so on. This example is set up to go four levels. To provide an inside look at what is happening, the program not only displays the value of the variable n, it also displays &n, which is the memory address at which the variable n is stored. (This chapter discusses the & operator more fully later. The `printf()` function uses the %p specifier for addresses.)

LISTING 9.6   The `recur.c` Program

```c
/* recur.c -- recursion illustration */
#include <stdio.h>
void up_and_down(int);

int main(void)
{
    up_and_down(1);
    return 0;
}

void up_and_down(int n)
{
    printf("Level %d: n location %p\n", n, &n); /* 1 */
    if (n < 4)
        up_and_down(n+1);
    printf("LEVEL %d: n location %p\n", n, &n); /* 2 */

}
```

The output looks like this:

```
Level 1: n location 0x0012ff48
Level 2: n location 0x0012ff3c
Level 3: n location 0x0012ff30
Level 4: n location 0x0012ff24
LEVEL 4: n location 0x0012ff24
LEVEL 3: n location 0x0012ff30
LEVEL 2: n location 0x0012ff3c
LEVEL 1: n location 0x0012ff48
```

Let's trace through the program to see how recursion works. First, `main()` calls `up_and_down()` with an argument of 1. As a result, the formal parameter n in `up_and_down()` has the value 1, so print statement #1 prints `Level 1`. Then, because n is less than 4, `up_and_down()` (Level 1) calls `up_and_down()` (Level 2) with an actual argument of n + 1, or 2. This causes n in the Level 2 call to be assigned the value 2, so print statement #1 prints `Level 2`. Similarly, the next two calls lead to printing `Level 3` and `Level 4`.

When Level 4 is reached, n is 4, so the `if` test fails. The `up_and_down()` function is not called again. Instead, the Level 4 call proceeds to print statement #2, which prints `LEVEL 4`, because n is 4. Then it reaches the `return` statement. At this point, the Level 4 call ends, and control passes back to the function that called it (the Level 3 call). The last statement executed in the Level 3 call was the call to Level 4 in the `if` statement. Therefore, Level 3 resumes with the following statement, which is print statement #2. This causes `LEVEL 3` to be printed. Then Level 3 ends, passing control to Level 2, which prints `LEVEL 2`, and so on.

Note that each level of recursion uses its own private n variable. You can tell this is so by looking at the address values. (Of course, different systems, in general, will report different addresses, possibly in a different format. The critical point is that the address on the `Level 1` line is the same as the address on the `LEVEL 1` line, and so on.)

If you find this a bit confusing, think about when you have a chain of function calls, with fun1() calling fun2(), fun2() calling fun3(), and fun3() calling fun4(). When fun4() finishes, it passes control back to fun3(). When fun3() finishes, it passes control back to fun2(). And when fun2() finishes, it passes control back to fun1(). The recursive case works the same, except that fun1(), fun2(), fun3(), and fun4() are all the same function.

Recursion Fundamentals

Recursion can be confusing at first, so let's look at a few basic points that will help you understand the process.

First, each level of function call has its own variables. That is, the n of Level 1 is a different variable from the n of Level 2, so the program created four separate variables, each called n, but each having a distinct value. When the program finally returned to the first-level call of up_and_down(), the original n still had the value 1 it started with (see Figure 9.4).

FIGURE 9.4

Recursion variables.

variables:	n	n	n	n
after level 1 call	1			
after level 2 call	1	2		
after level 3 call	1	2	3	
after level 4 call	1	2	3	4
after return from level 4	1	2	3	
after return from level 3	1	2		
after return from level 2	1			
after return from level 1				
	(all gone)			

Second, each function call is balanced with a return. When program flow reaches the return at the end of the last recursion level, control passes to the previous recursion level. The program does not jump all the way back to the original call in main(). Instead, the program must move back through each recursion level, returning from one level of up_and_down() to the level of up_and_down() that called it.

Third, statements in a recursive function that come before the recursive call are executed in the same order that the functions are called. For example, in Listing 9.6, print statement #1 comes before the recursive call. It was executed four times in the order of the recursive calls: Level 1, Level 2, Level 3, and Level 4.

Fourth, statements in a recursive function that come after the recursive call are executed in the opposite order from which the functions are called. For example, print statement #2 comes after the recursive call, and it was executed in the order: Level 4, Level 3, Level 2, Level 1. This feature of recursion is useful for programming problems involving reversals of order. You'll see an example soon.

Fifth, although each level of recursion has its own set of variables, the code itself is not duplicated. The code is a sequence of instructions, and a function call is a command to go to the beginning of that set of instructions. A recursive call, then, returns the program to the beginning of that instruction set. Aside from recursive calls creating new variables on each call, they are much like a loop. Indeed, sometimes recursion can be used instead of loops, and vice versa.

Finally, it's vital that a recursive function contain something to halt the sequence of recursive calls. Typically, a recursive function uses an `if` test, or equivalent, to terminate recursion when a function parameter reaches a particular value. For this to work, each call needs to use a different value for the parameter. For example, in the last example, `up_and_down(n)` calls `up_and_down(n+1)`. Eventually, the actual argument reaches the value `4`, causing the `if (n < 4)` test to fail.

Tail Recursion

In the simplest form of recursion, the recursive call is at the end of the function, just before the `return` statement. This is called *tail recursion*, or *end recursion*, because the recursive call comes at the end. Tail recursion is the simplest form because it acts like a loop.

Let's look at both a loop version and a tail recursion version of a function to calculate factorials. The *factorial* of an integer is the product of the integers from 1 through that number. For example, 3 factorial (written `3!`) is `1*2*3`. Also, `0!` is taken to be 1, and factorials are not defined for negative numbers. Listing 9.7 presents one function that uses a `for` loop to calculate factorials and a second that uses recursion.

LISTING 9.7   The `factor.c` Program

```
// factor.c -- uses loops and recursion to calculate factorials
#include <stdio.h>
long fact(int n);
long rfact(int n);
int main(void)
{
    int num;

    printf("This program calculates factorials.\n");
    printf("Enter a value in the range 0-12 (q to quit):\n");
    while (scanf("%d", &num) == 1)
    {
        if (num < 0)
            printf("No negative numbers, please.\n");
        else if (num > 12)
            printf("Keep input under 13.\n");
        else
        {
            printf("loop: %d factorial = %ld\n",
                    num, fact(num));
```

LISTING 9.7 *Continued*

```
            printf("recursion: %d factorial = %ld\n",
                    num, rfact(num));
        }
        printf("Enter a value in the range 0-12 (q to quit):\n");
    }
    printf("Bye.\n");

    return 0;
}

long fact(int n)      // loop-based function
{
    long ans;

    for (ans = 1; n > 1; n--)
        ans *= n;

    return ans;
}

long rfact(int n)     // recursive version
{
    long ans;

    if (n > 0)
        ans= n * rfact(n-1);
    else
        ans = 1;

    return ans;
}
```

The test driver program limits input to the integers 0–12. It turns out that **12!** is slightly under half a billion, which makes **13!** much larger than long on our system. To go beyond **12!**, you would have to use a type with greater range, such as **double** or **long long**.

Here's a sample run:

```
This program calculates factorials.
Enter a value in the range 0-12 (q to quit):
5
loop: 5 factorial = 120
recursion: 5 factorial = 120
Enter a value in the range 0-12 (q to quit):
10
loop: 10 factorial = 3628800
recursion: 10 factorial = 3628800
Enter a value in the range 0-12 (q to quit):
q
Bye.
```

The loop version initializes **ans** to 1 and then multiplies it by the integers from n down to **2**. Technically, you should multiply by **1**, but that doesn't change the value.

Now consider the recursive version. The key is that n! = n × (n-1)!. This follows because (n-1)! is the product of all the positive integers through n-1. Therefore, multiplying by n gives the product through n. This suggests a recursive approach. If you call the function `rfact()`, `rfact(n)` is n * `rfact(n-1)`. You can thus evaluate `rfact(n)` by having it call `rfact(n-1)`, as in Listing 9.7. Of course, you have to end the recursion at some point, and you can do this by setting the return value to **1** when n is **0**.

The recursive version of Listing 9.7 produces the same output as the loop version. Note that although the recursive call to `rfact()` is not the last line in the function, it is the last statement executed when n > **0**, so it is tail recursion.

Given that you can use either a loop or recursion to code a function, which should you use? Normally, the loop is the better choice. First, because each recursive call gets its own set of variables, recursion uses more memory; each recursive call places a new set of variables on the stack. Second, recursion is slower because each function call takes time. So why show this example? Because tail recursion is the simplest form of recursion to understand, and recursion is worth understanding because in some cases, there is no simple loop alternative.

Recursion and Reversal

Now let's look at a problem in which recursion's ability to reverse order is handy. (This is a case for which recursion is simpler than using a loop.) The problem is this: Write a function that prints the binary equivalent of an integer. Binary notation represents numbers in terms of powers of 2. Just as 234 in decimal means $2 \times 10^2 + 3 \times 10^1 + 4 \times 10^0$, so 101 in binary means $1 \times 2^2 + 0 \times 2^1 + 1 \times 2^0$. Binary numbers use only the digits 0 and 1.

You need a method, or *algorithm*. How can you, say, find the binary equivalent of 5? Well, odd numbers must have a binary representation ending in 1. Even numbers end in 0, so you can determine whether the last digit is a 1 or a 0 by evaluating 5 % **2**. If the result is 1, 5 is odd, and the last digit is 1. In general, if n is a number, the final digit is n % **2**, so the first digit you find is the last digit you want to print. This suggests using a recursive function in which n % **2** is calculated before the recursive call but in which it is printed after the recursive call. That way, the first value calculated is the last value printed.

To get the next digit, divide the original number by 2. This is the binary equivalent of moving the decimal point one place to the left so that you can examine the next binary digit. If this value is even, the next binary digit is 0. If it is odd, the binary digit is 1. For example, 5/2 is 2 (integer division), so the next digit is 0. This gives 01 so far. Now repeat the process. Divide 2 by 2 to get 1. Evaluate 1 % **2** to get 1, so the next digit is 1. This gives 101. When do you stop? You stop when the result of dividing by 2 is less than 2 because as long as it is 2 or greater, there is one more binary digit. Each division by 2 lops off one more binary digit until you reach the end. (If this seems confusing to you, try working through the decimal analogy. The remainder of 628 divided by 10 is 8, so 8 is the last digit. Integer division by 10 yields 62, and the remainder from dividing 62 by 10 is 2, so that's the next digit, and so on.) Listing 9.8 implements this approach.

LISTING 9.8 The binary.c Program

```c
/* binary.c -- prints integer in binary form */
#include <stdio.h>
void to_binary(unsigned long n);

int main(void)
{
    unsigned long number;
    printf("Enter an integer (q to quit):\n");
    while (scanf("%ul", &number) == 1)
    {
        printf("Binary equivalent: ");
        to_binary(number);
        putchar('\n');
        printf("Enter an integer (q to quit):\n");
    }
    printf("Done.\n");

    return 0;
}

void to_binary(unsigned long n)    /* recursive function */
{
    int r;

    r = n % 2;
    if (n >= 2)
        to_binary(n / 2);
    putchar('0' + r);

    return;
}
```

In Listing 9.8, the expression `'0'` + r evaluates to the character `'0'`, if r is `0`, and to the character `'1'`, if r is `1`. This assumes that the numeric code for the `'1'` character is one greater than the code for the `'0'` character. Both the ASCII and the EBCDIC codes satisfy that assumption. More generally, you could use the following approach:

```c
putchar( r ? '1' : '0');
```

Here's a sample run:

```
Enter an integer (q to quit):
9
Binary equivalent: 1001
Enter an integer (q to quit):
255
Binary equivalent: 11111111
Enter an integer (q to quit):
1024
Binary equivalent: 10000000000
Enter an integer (q to quit):
q
done.
```

Could you use this algorithm for calculating a binary representation without using recursion? Yes, you could. But because the algorithm calculates the final digit first, you'd have to store all the digits somewhere (in an array, for example) before displaying the result. Chapter 15, "Bit Fiddling," shows an example of a nonrecursive approach.

Recursion Pros and Cons

Recursion has its good points and bad points. One good point is that recursion offers the simplest solution to some programming problems. One bad point is that some recursive algorithms can rapidly exhaust a computer's memory resources. Also, recursion can be difficult to document and maintain. Let's look at an example that illustrates both the good and bad aspects.

Fibonacci numbers can be defined as follows: The first Fibonacci number is 1, the second Fibonacci number is 1, and each subsequent Fibonacci number is the sum of the preceding two. Therefore, the first few numbers in the sequence are 1, 1, 2, 3, 5, 8, 13. Fibonacci numbers are among the most beloved in mathematics; there even is a journal devoted to them. But let's not get into that. Instead, let's create a function that, given a positive integer n, returns the corresponding Fibonacci number.

First, the recursive strength: Recursion supplies a simple definition. If we name the function `Fibonacci()`, `Fibonacci(n)` should return 1 if n is 1 or 2, and it should return the sum `Fibonacci(n-1) + Fibonacci(n-2)` otherwise:

```
long Fibonacci(int n)
{
    if (n > 2)
        return Fibonacci(n-1) + Fibonacci(n-2);
    else
        return 1;
}
```

The recursive C function merely restates the recursive mathematical definition. (To keep matters simple, the function doesn't deal with values of n less than 1.) This function uses *double recursion*; that is, the function calls itself twice. And that leads to a weakness.

To see the nature of that weakness, suppose you use the function call `Fibonacci(40)`. That would be the first level of recursion, and it allocates a variable called n. It then evokes `Fibonacci()` twice, creating two more variables called n at the second level of recursion. Each of those two calls generates two more calls, requiring four more variables called n at the third level of recursion, for a total of seven variables. Each level requires twice the number of variables as the preceding level, and the number of variables grows exponentially! As you saw in the grains-of-wheat example in Chapter 5, "Operators, Expressions, and Statements," exponential growth rapidly leads to large values. In this case, exponential growth soon leads to the computer requiring an enormous amount of memory, most likely causing the program to crash.

Well, this is an extreme example, but it does illustrate the need for caution when using recursion, particularly when efficiency is important.

All C Functions Are Created Equal

Each C function in a program is on equal footing with the others. Each can call any other function or be called by any other function. This makes the C function somewhat different from Pascal and Modula-2 procedures because those procedures can be nested within other procedures. Procedures in one nest are ignorant of procedures in another nest.

Isn't the function `main()` special? Yes, it is a little special in that when a program of several functions is put together, execution starts with the first statement in `main()`, but that is the limit of its preference. Even `main()` can be called by itself recursively or by other functions, although this is rarely done.

Compiling Programs with Two or More Source Code Files

The simplest approach to using several functions is to place them in the same file. Then just compile that file as you would a single-function file. Other approaches are more system dependent, as the next few sections illustrate.

Unix

This assumes the Unix system has the standard Unix C compiler `cc` installed. Suppose that `file1.c` and `file2.c` are two files containing C functions. Then the following command will compile both files and produce an executable file called `a.out`:

```
cc file1.c file2.c
```

In addition, two object files called `file1.o` and `file2.o` are produced. If you later change `file1.c` but not `file2.c`, you can compile the first and combine it with the object code version of the second file by using this command:

```
cc file1.c file2.o
```

Unix has a `make` command that automates management of multifile programs, but that's beyond the scope of this book.

Linux

This assumes the Linux system has the GNU C compiler gcc installed. Suppose that `file1.c` and `file2.c` are two files containing C functions. Then the following command will compile both files and produce an executable file called `a.out`:

```
gcc file1.c file2.c
```

In addition, two object files called `file1.o` and `file2.o` are produced. If you later change `file1.c` but not `file2.c`, you can compile the first and combine it with the object code version of the second file by using this command:

```
gcc file1.c file2.o
```

DOS Command-Line Compilers

Most DOS command-line compilers work similarly to the Unix `cc` command. One difference is that object files wind up with an `.obj` extension instead of an `.o` extension. Some compilers produce intermediate files in assembly language or in some other special code, instead of object code files.

Windows and Macintosh Compilers

Windows and Macintosh compilers are *project oriented*. A *project* describes the resources a particular program uses. The resources include your source code files. If you've been using one of these compilers, you've probably had to create projects to run one-file programs. For multiple-file programs, find the menu command that lets you add a source code file to a project. You should make sure all your source code files (the ones with the `.c` extension) are listed as part of the project. Be careful, however, not to place your header files (the ones with the `.h` extension) in a project. The idea is that the project manages which source code files are used, and `#include` directives in the source code files manage which header files get used.

Using Header Files

If you put `main()` in one file and your function definitions in a second file, the first file still needs the function prototypes. Rather than type them in each time you use the function file, you can store the function prototypes in a header file. That is what the standard C library does, placing I/O function prototypes in `stdio.h` and math function prototypes in `math.h`, for example. You can do the same for your function files.

Also, you will often use the C preprocessor to define constants used in a program. Such definitions hold only for the file containing the `#define` directives. If you place the functions of a program into separate files, you also have to make the `#define` directives available to each file. The most direct way is to retype the directives for each file, but this is time-consuming and increases the possibility for error. Also, it poses a maintenance problem: If you revise a `#define` value, you have to remember to do so for each file. A better solution is to place the `#define` directives in a header file and then use the `#include` directive in each source code file.

So it's good programming practice to place function prototypes and defined constants in a header file. Let's examine an example. Suppose you manage a chain of four hotels. Each hotel charges a different room rate, but all the rooms in a given hotel go for the same rate. For people who book multiple nights, the second night goes for 95% of the first night, the third night goes for 95% of the second night, and so on. (Don't worry about the economics of such a policy.) You want a program that enables you to specify the hotel and the number of nights and gives you the total charge. You'd like the program to have a menu that enables you to continue entering data until you choose to quit.

Listings 9.9, 9.10, and 9.11 show what you might come up with. The first listing contains the `main()` function, which provides the overall organization for the program. The second listing contains the supporting functions, which we assume are kept in a separate file. Finally, Listing 9.11 shows a header file that contains the defined constants and function prototypes for all the program's source files. Recall that in the Unix and DOS environments, the double quotes in the directive `#include "hotels.h"` indicate that the `include` file is in the current working directory (typically the directory containing the source code).

LISTING 9.9   The `usehotel.c` Control Module

```
/* usehotel.c -- room rate program */
/* compile with  Listing 9.10      */
#include <stdio.h>
#include "hotel.h" /* defines constants, declares functions */

int main(void)
{
    int nights;
    double hotel_rate;
    int code;

    while ((code = menu()) != QUIT)
    {
        switch(code)
        {
        case 1 : hotel_rate = HOTEL1;
                 break;
        case 2 : hotel_rate = HOTEL2;
                 break;
        case 3 : hotel_rate = HOTEL3;
                 break;
        case 4 : hotel_rate = HOTEL4;
                 break;
        default: hotel_rate = 0.0;
                 printf("Oops!\n");
                 break;
        }
        nights = getnights();
        showprice(hotel_rate, nights);
    }
    printf("Thank you and goodbye.");

    return 0;
}
```

LISTING 9.10   The `hotel.c` Function Support Module

```
/* hotel.c -- hotel management functions */
#include <stdio.h>
#include "hotel.h"
int menu(void)
{
```

LISTING 9.10   Continued

```
      int code, status;

      printf("\n%s%s\n", STARS, STARS);
      printf("Enter the number of the desired hotel:\n");
      printf("1) Fairfield Arms        2) Hotel Olympic\n");
      printf("3) Chertworthy Plaza      4) The Stockton\n");
      printf("5) quit\n");
      printf("%s%s\n", STARS, STARS);
      while ((status = scanf("%d", &code)) != 1  ||
             (code < 1 || code > 5))
   {
         if (status != 1)
             scanf("%*s");
         printf("Enter an integer from 1 to 5, please.\n");
      }

      return code;
   }

int getnights(void)
{
      int nights;

      printf("How many nights are needed? ");
      while (scanf("%d", &nights) != 1)
      {
          scanf("%*s");
          printf("Please enter an integer, such as 2.\n");
      }

      return nights;
   }

void showprice(double rate, int nights)
{
      int n;
      double total = 0.0;
      double factor = 1.0;

      for (n = 1; n <= nights; n++, factor *= DISCOUNT)
          total += rate * factor;
      printf("The total cost will be $%0.2f.\n", total);
   }
```

LISTING 9.11   The hotel.h Header File

```
/* hotel.h -- constants and declarations for hotel.c */
#define QUIT      5
#define HOTEL1    80.00
#define HOTEL2    125.00
#define HOTEL3    155.00
```

LISTING 9.11   Continued

```
#define HOTEL4   200.00
#define DISCOUNT   0.95
#define STARS "********************************"

// shows list of choices
int menu(void);

// returns number of nights desired
int getnights(void);

// calculates price from rate, nights
// and displays result
void showprice(double rate, int nights);
```

Here's a sample run:

```
**********************************************************************
Enter the number of the desired hotel:
1) Fairfield Arms          2) Hotel Olympic
3) Chertworthy Plaza       4) The Stockton
5) quit
**********************************************************************
3
How many nights are needed? 1
The total cost will be $155.00.

**********************************************************************
Enter the number of the desired hotel:
1) Fairfield Arms          2) Hotel Olympic
3) Chertworthy Plaza       4) The Stockton
5) quit
**********************************************************************
4
How many nights are needed? 3
The total cost will be $570.50.

**********************************************************************
Enter the number of the desired hotel:
1) Fairfield Arms          2) Hotel Olympic
3) Chertworthy Plaza       4) The Stockton
5) quit
**********************************************************************
5
Thank you and goodbye.
```

Incidentally, the program itself has some interesting features. In particular, the `menu()` and `getnights()` functions skip over nonnumeric data by testing the return value of `scanf()` and by using the `scanf("%*s")` call to skip to the next whitespace. Note how the following excerpt from `menu()` checks for both nonnumeric input and out-of-limits numerical input:

```
while ((status = scanf("%d", &code)) != 1  ||
       (code < 1 || code > 5))
```

This code fragment uses C's guarantee that logical expressions are evaluated from left to right and that evaluation ceases the moment the statement is clearly false. In this instance, the values of `code` are checked only after it is determined that `scanf()` succeeded in reading an integer value.

Assigning separate tasks to separate functions encourages this sort of refinement. A first pass at `menu()` or `getnights()` might use a simple `scanf()` without the data-verification features that have been added. Then, after the basic version works, you can begin improving each module.

Finding Addresses: The & Operator

One of the most important C concepts (and sometimes one of the most perplexing) is the *pointer*, which is a variable used to store an address. You've already seen that `scanf()` uses addresses for arguments. More generally, any C function that modifies a value in the calling function without using a `return` value uses addresses. We'll cover functions using addresses next, beginning with the unary `&` operator. (The next chapter continues the exploration and exploitation of pointers.)

The unary `&` operator gives you the address where a variable is stored. If `pooh` is the name of a variable, `&pooh` is the address of the variable. You can think of the address as a location in memory. Suppose you have the following statement:

```
pooh = 24;
```

Suppose that the address where `pooh` is stored is `0B76`. (PC addresses often are given as hexadecimal values.) Then the statement

```
printf("%d %p\n", pooh, &pooh);
```

would produce this (`%p` is the specifier for addresses):

```
24 0B76
```

Listing 9.12 uses this operator to see where variables of the same name—but in different functions—are kept.

LISTING 9.12   The `loccheck.c` Program

```
/* loccheck.c  -- checks to see where variables are stored  */
#include <stdio.h>
void mikado(int);                       /* declare function  */
int main(void)
{
    int pooh = 2, bah = 5;              /* local to main()   */

    printf("In main(), pooh = %d and &pooh = %p\n",
           pooh, &pooh);
    printf("In main(), bah = %d and &bah = %p\n",
           bah, &bah);
```

LISTING 9.12   Continued

```
    mikado(pooh);

    return 0;
}

void mikado(int bah)                    /* define function    */
{
    int pooh = 10;                      /* local to mikado() */

    printf("In mikado(), pooh = %d and &pooh = %p\n",
            pooh, &pooh);
    printf("In mikado(), bah = %d and &bah = %p\n",
            bah, &bah);
}
```

Listing 9.12 uses the ANSI C %p format for printing the addresses. Our system produced the following output for this little exercise:

```
In main(), pooh = 2 and &pooh = 0x0012ff48
In main(), bah = 5 and &bah = 0x0012ff44
In mikado(), pooh = 10 and &pooh = 0x0012ff34
In mikado(), bah = 2 and &bah = 0x0012ff40
```

The way that %p represents addresses varies between implementations. However, many implementations, such as one used for this example, display the address in hexadecimal form.

What does this output show? First, the two poohs have different addresses. The same is true for the two bahs. So, as promised, the computer considers them to be four separate variables. Second, the call mikado(pooh) did convey the value (2) of the actual argument (pooh of main()) to the formal argument (bah of mikado()). Note that just the value was transferred. The two variables involved (pooh of main() and bah of mikado()) retain their distinct identities.

We raise the second point because it is not true for all languages. In FORTRAN, for example, the subroutine affects the original variable in the calling routine. The subroutine's variable might have a different name, but the address is the same. C doesn't do this. Each function uses its own variables. This is preferable because it prevents the original variable from being altered mysteriously by some side effect of the called function. However, it can make for some difficulties, too, as the next section shows.

Altering Variables in the Calling Function

Sometimes you want one function to make changes in the variables of a different function. For example, a common task in sorting problems is interchanging the values of two variables. Suppose you have two variables called x and y and you want to swap their values. The simple sequence

```
x = y;
y = x;
```

does not work because by the time the second line is reached, the original value of x has already been replaced by the original y value. An additional line is needed to temporarily store the original value of x.

```
temp = x;
x = y;
y = temp;
```

Now that the method works, you can put it into a function and construct a driver to test it. To make clear which variables belong to main() and which belong to the interchange() function, Listing 9.13 uses x and y for the first, and u and v for the second.

LISTING 9.13   The swap1.c Program

```
/* swap1.c -- first attempt at a swapping function */
#include <stdio.h>
void interchange(int u, int v); /* declare function */

int main(void)
{
    int x = 5, y = 10;

    printf("Originally x = %d and y = %d.\n", x , y);
    interchange(x, y);
    printf("Now x = %d and y = %d.\n", x, y);

    return 0;
}

void interchange(int u, int v)   /* define function   */
{
    int temp;

    temp = u;
    u = v;
    v = temp;
}
```

Running the program gives these results:

```
Originally x = 5 and y = 10.
Now x = 5 and y = 10.
```

Oops! The values didn't get switched! Let's put some print statements into interchange() to see what has gone wrong (see Listing 9.14).

LISTING 9.14   The swap2.c Program

```
/* swap2.c -- researching swap1.c */
#include <stdio.h>
void interchange(int u, int v);
```

LISTING 9.14 Continued

```
int main(void)
{
    int x = 5, y = 10;

    printf("Originally x = %d and y = %d.\n", x , y);
    interchange(x, y);
    printf("Now x = %d and y = %d.\n", x, y);

    return 0;
}

void interchange(int u, int v)
{
    int temp;

    printf("Originally u = %d and v = %d.\n", u , v);
    temp = u;
    u = v;
    v = temp;
    printf("Now u = %d and v = %d.\n", u, v);
}
```

Here is the new output:

```
Originally x = 5 and y = 10.
Originally u = 5 and v = 10.
Now u = 10 and v = 5.
Now x = 5 and y = 10.
```

Nothing is wrong with `interchange()`; it does swap the values of u and v. The problem is in communicating the results to `main()`. As we pointed out, `interchange()` uses different variables from `main()`, so interchanging the values of u and v has no effect on x and y! Can you somehow use `return`? Well, you could finish `interchange()` with the line

```
return(u);
```

and then change the call in `main()` to this:

```
x = interchange(x,y);
```

This change gives x its new value, but it leaves y in the cold. With `return`, you can send just one value back to the calling function, but you need to communicate two values. It can be done! All you have to do is use pointers.

Pointers: A First Look

Pointers? What are they? Basically, a *pointer* is a variable (or, more generally, a data object) whose value is a memory address. Just as a `char` variable has a character as a value and an `int` variable has an integer as a value, the pointer variable has an address as a value. Pointers have many uses in C; in this chapter, you'll see how and why they are used as function parameters.

If you give a particular pointer variable the name `ptr`, you can have statements such as the following:

```
ptr = &pooh;  /* assigns pooh's address to ptr */
```

We say that `ptr` "points to" `pooh`. The difference between `ptr` and `&pooh` is that `ptr` is a variable, and `&pooh` is a constant. If you want, you can make `ptr` point elsewhere:

```
ptr = &bah;  /* make ptr point to bah instead of to pooh */
```

Now the value of `ptr` is the address of `bah`.

To create a pointer variable, you need to be able to declare its type. Suppose you want to declare `ptr` so that it can hold the address of an `int`. To make this declaration, you need to use a new operator. Let's examine that operator now.

The Indirection Operator: *

Suppose you know that `ptr` points to `bah`, as shown here:

```
ptr = &bah;
```

Then you can use the *indirection* operator * (also called the *dereferencing* operator) to find the value stored in `bah` (don't confuse this unary indirection operator with the binary * operator of multiplication):

```
val = *ptr;  /* finding the value ptr points to */
```

The statements `ptr = &bah;` and `val = *ptr;` taken together amount to the following statement:

```
val = bah;
```

Using the address and indirection operators is a rather indirect way of accomplishing this result, hence the name "indirection operator."

Summary: Pointer-Related Operators

The Address Operator:

&

General Comments:

When followed by a variable name, & gives the address of that variable.

Example:

&nurse is the address of the variable nurse.

The Indirection Operator:

*

General Comments:

When followed by a pointer name or an address, * gives the value stored at the pointed-to address.

Example:

```
nurse = 22;
ptr = &nurse;  /* pointer to nurse */
val = *ptr;    /* assigns value at location ptr to val */
```

The net effect is to assign the value 22 to `val`.

Declaring Pointers

You already know how to declare int variables and other fundamental types. How do you declare a pointer variable? You might guess that the form is like this:

```
pointer ptr;      /* not the way to declare a pointer */
```

Why not? Because it is not enough to say that a variable is a pointer. You also have to specify the kind of variable to which the pointer points. The reason is that different variable types take up different amounts of storage, and some pointer operations require knowledge of that storage size. Also, the program has to know what kind of data is stored at the address. A long and a float might use the same amount of storage, but they store numbers quite differently. Here's how pointers are declared:

```
int * pi;         /* pi is a pointer to an integer variable  */
char * pc;        /* pc is a pointer to a character variable */
float * pf, * pg; /* pf, pg are pointers to float variables  */
```

The type specification identifies the type of variable pointed to, and the asterisk (*) identifies the variable itself as a pointer. The declaration int * pi; says that pi is a pointer and that *pi is type int (see Figure 9.5).

FIGURE 9.5

Declaring and using pointers.

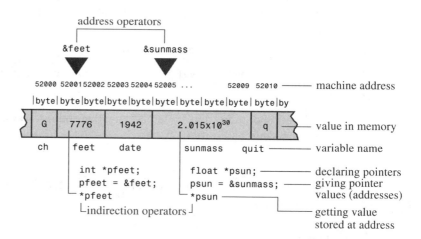

The space between the * and the pointer name is optional. Often, programmers use the space in a declaration and omit it when dereferencing a variable.

The value (*pc) of what pc points to is of type char. What of pc itself? We describe it as being of type "pointer to char." The value of pc is an address, and it is represented internally as an unsigned integer on most systems. However, you shouldn't think of a pointer as an integer type. There are things you can do with integers that you can't do with pointers, and vice versa. For example, you can multiply one integer by another, but you can't multiply one pointer by another. So a pointer really is a new type, not an integer type. Therefore, as mentioned before, ANSI C provides the %p form specifically for pointers.

Using Pointers to Communicate Between Functions

We have touched only the surface of the rich and fascinating world of pointers, but our concern here is using pointers to solve our communication problem. Listing 9.15 shows a program that uses pointers to make the `interchange()` function work. Let's look at it, run it, and then try to understand how it works.

LISTING 9.15   The `swap3.c` Program

```
/* swap3.c -- using pointers to make swapping work */
#include <stdio.h>
void interchange(int * u, int * v);

int main(void)
{
    int x = 5, y = 10;

    printf("Originally x = %d and y = %d.\n", x, y);
    interchange(&x, &y);  /* send addresses to function  */
    printf("Now x = %d and y = %d.\n", x, y);

    return 0;
}

void interchange(int * u, int * v)
{
    int temp;

    temp = *u;       /* temp gets value that u points to */
    *u = *v;
    *v = temp;
}
```

After all this build-up, does Listing 9.15 really work?

```
Originally x = 5 and y = 10.
Now x = 10 and y = 5.
```

Yes, it works.

Now, let's see how Listing 9.15 works. First, the function call looks like this:

```
interchange(&x, &y);
```

Instead of transmitting the *values* of x and y, the function transmits their *addresses*. That means the formal arguments u and v, appearing in the prototype and in the definition of `interchange()`, will have addresses as their values. Therefore, they should be declared as pointers. Because x and y are integers, u and v are pointers to integers, so declare them as follows:

```
void interchange (int * u, int * v)
```

Next, the body of the function declares

```
int temp;
```

to provide the needed temporary storage. To store the value of x in temp, use

```
temp = *u;
```

Remember, u has the value &x, so u points to x. This means that *u gives you the value of x, which is what we want. Don't write

```
temp = u;    /* NO */
```

because that would assign temp the address of x rather than its value, and we are trying to interchange values, not addresses.

Similarly, to assign the value of y to x, use

```
*u = *v;
```

which ultimately has this effect:

```
x = y;
```

Let's summarize what this example does. We want a function that alters the values x and y. By passing the function the addresses of x and y, we give interchange() access to those variables. Using pointers and the * operator, the function can examine the values stored at those locations and change them.

You can omit the variable names in the ANSI prototype. Then the prototype declaration looks like this:

```
void interchange(int *, int *);
```

In general, you can communicate two kinds of information about a variable to a function. If you use a call of the form

```
function1(x);
```

you transmit the value of x. If you use a call of the form

```
function2(&x);
```

you transmit the address of x. The first form requires that the function definition includes a formal argument of the same type as x:

```
int function1(int num)
```

The second form requires the function definition to include a formal parameter that is a pointer to the right type:

```
int function2(int * ptr)
```

Use the first form if the function needs a value for some calculation or action. Use the second form if the function needs to alter variables in the calling function. You have been doing this all along with the scanf() function. When you want to read in a value for a variable (num, for example), you use `scanf("%d", &num)`. That function reads a value and then uses the address you give it to store the value.

Pointers enable you to get around the fact that the variables of `interchange()` are local. They let that function reach out into `main()` and alter what is stored there.

Pascal and Modula-2 users might recognize the first form as being the same as Pascal's value parameter and the second form as being similar (but not identical) to Pascal's variable parameter. BASIC users might find the whole setup a bit unsettling. If this section seems strange to you, be assured that a little practice will make at least some uses of pointers seem simple, normal, and convenient (see Figure 9.6).

Variables: Names, Addresses, and Values

The preceding discussion of pointers has hinged on the relationships between the names, addresses, and values of variables. Let's discuss these matters further.

When you write a program, you think of a variable as having two attributes: a name and a value. (There are other attributes, including type, but that's another matter.) After the program has been compiled and loaded, the computer also thinks of the same variable as having two attributes: an address and a value. An address is the computer's version of a name.

In many languages, the address is the computer's business, concealed from the programmer. In C, however, you can access the address through the `&` operator.

For example, `&barn` is the address of the variable `barn`.

You can get the value from the name just by using the name.

For example, `printf("%d\n", barn)` prints the value of `barn`.

You can get the value from the address by using the `*` operator.

Given `pbarn = &barn;`, `*pbarn` is the value stored at address `&barn`.

In short, a regular variable makes the value the primary quantity and the address a derived quantity, via the `&` operator. A pointer variable makes the address the primary quantity and the value a derived quantity via the `*` operator.

Although you can print an address to satisfy your curiosity, that is not the main use for the `&` operator. More important, using `&`, `*`, and pointers enables you to manipulate addresses and their contents symbolically, as in `swap3.c` (Listing 9.15).

FIGURE 9.6

Names, addresses, and values in a byte-addressable system, such as the IBM PC.

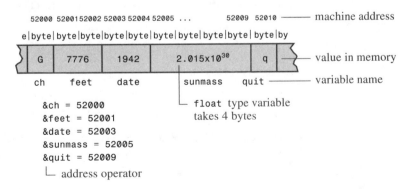

Summary: Functions

Form:

A typical ANSI C function definition has this form:

```
name(parameter declaration list)
function body
```

The argument declaration list is a comma-separated list of variable declarations. Variables other than the function parameters are declared within the body, which is bounded by braces.

Example:

```
int diff(int x, int y)     // ANSI C
{                          // begin function body
    int z;                 // declare local variable

    z = x - y;

    return z;              // return a value
}                          // end function body
```

Communicating Values:

Arguments are used to convey values from the calling function to the function. If variables a and b have the values 5 and 2, the call

```
c = diff(a,b);
```

transmits 5 and 2 to the variables x and y. The values 5 and 2 are called *actual arguments*, and the diff() variables x and y are called *formal parameters*. The keyword return communicates one value from the function to the calling function. In this example, c receives the value of z, which is 3. A function ordinarily has no effect on the variables in a calling function. To directly affect variables in the calling function, use pointers as arguments. This might be necessary if you want to communicate more than one value back to the calling function.

Function Return Type:

The function return type indicates the type of value the function returns. If the returned value is of a type different from the declared return type, the value is type cast to the declared type.

Example:

```
int main(void)
{
    double q, x, duff();   /*  declare in calling function   */
    int n;


...
    q = duff(x,n);


...
 }
double duff(u, k)          /* declare in function definition */
double u;
int k;
{
    double tor;
...
    return tor;            /* returns a double value         */
}
```

Key Concepts

If you want to program successfully and efficiently in C, you need to understand functions. It's useful, even essential, to organize larger programs into several functions. If you follow the practice of giving one function one task, your programs will be easier to understand and debug. Make sure that you understand how functions communicate information to one another—that is, that you understand how function arguments and return values work. Also, be aware how function parameters and other local variables are private to a function; thus, declaring two variables of the same name in different functions creates two distinct variables. Also, one function does not have direct access to variables declared in another function. This limited access helps preserve data integrity. However, if you do need one function to access another function's data, you can use pointer function arguments.

Summary

Use functions as building blocks for larger programs. Each function should have a single, well-defined purpose. Use arguments to communicate values to a function, and use the keyword `return` to communicate back a value. If the function returns a value not of type `int`, you must specify the function type in the function definition and in the declaration section of the calling function. If you want the function to affect variables in the calling function, use addresses and pointers.

ANSI C offers *function prototyping*, a powerful C enhancement that allows compilers to verify that the proper number and types of arguments are used in a function call.

A C function can call itself; this is called *recursion*. Some programming problems lend themselves to recursive solutions, but recursion can be inefficient in its use of memory and time.

Review Questions

1. What is the difference between an actual argument and a formal parameter?

2. Write ANSI C function headings for the following functions described. Note we are asking just for the headings, not the body.

    a. `donut()` takes an `int` argument and prints that number of `0`s.

    b. `gear()` takes two `int` arguments and returns type `int`.

    c. `stuff_it()` takes a `double` and the address of a `double` variable and stores the first value in the given location.

3. Write ANSI C function headings for the following functions described. Note that you need write only the headings, not the body.

    a. `n_to_char()` takes an `int` argument and returns a `char`.

    b. `digits()` takes a `double` argument and an `int` argument and returns an `int`.

    c. `random()` takes no argument and returns an `int`.

4. Devise a function that returns the sum of two integers.

5. What changes, if any, would you need to make to have the function of question 4 add two `double` numbers instead?

6. Devise a function called `alter()` that takes two `int` variables, x and y, and changes their values to their sum and their difference, respectively.

7. Is anything wrong with this function definition?

```
void salami(num)
{
    int num, count;

    for (count = 1; count <= num; num++)
        printf(" O salami mio!\n");
}
```

8. Write a function that returns the largest of three integer arguments.

9. Given the following output:

```
Please choose one of the following:
1) copy files            2) move files
3) remove files          4) quit
Enter the number of your choice:
```

    a. Write a function that displays a menu of four numbered choices and asks you to choose one. (The output should look like the preceding.)

    b. Write a function that has two `int` arguments: a lower limit and an upper limit. The function should read an integer from input. If the integer is outside the limits, the function should print a menu again (using the function from part "a" of this question) to reprompt the user and then get a new value. When an integer in the proper limits is entered, the function should return that value to the calling function.

    c. Write a minimal program using the functions from parts "a" and "b" of this question. By *minimal*, we mean it need not actually perform the actions promised by the menu; it should just show the choices and get a valid response.

Programming Exercises

1. Devise a function called `min(x,y)` that returns the smaller of two `double` values. Test the function with a simple driver.

2. Devise a function `chline(ch,i,j)` that prints the requested character in columns `i` through `j`. Test it in a simple driver.

3. Write a function that takes three arguments: a character and two integers. The character is to be printed. The first integer specifies the number of times that the character is to be printed on a line, and the second integer specifies the number of lines that are to be printed. Write a program that makes use of this function.

4. The harmonic mean of two numbers is obtained by taking the inverses of the two numbers, averaging them, and taking the inverse of the result. Write a function that takes two `double` arguments and returns the harmonic mean of the two numbers.

5. Write and test a function called `larger_of()` that replaces the contents of two `double` variables with the maximum of the two values. For example, `larger_of(x,y)` would reset both `x` and `y` to the larger of the two.

6. Write a program that reads characters from the standard input to end-of-file. For each character, have the program report whether it is a letter. If it is a letter, also report its numerical location in the alphabet. For example, c and C would both be letter 3. Incorporate a function that takes a character as an argument and returns the numerical location if the character is a letter and that returns –1 otherwise.

7. Chapter 6, "C Control Statements: Looping," (Listing 6.20) shows a `power()` function that returned the result of raising a type `double` number to a positive integer value. Improve the function so that it correctly handles negative powers. Also, build into the function that 0 to any power is 0 and that any number to the 0 power is 1. Use a loop. Test the function in a program.

8. Redo exercise 7, but this time use a recursive function.

9. Generalize the `to_binary()` function of Listing 9.8 to a `to_base_n()` function that takes a second argument in the range 2–10. It then should print the number that is its first argument to the number base given by the second argument. For example, `to_base_n(129,8)` would display `201`, the base-8 equivalent of `129`. Test the function in a complete program.

10. Write and test a `Fibonacci()` function that uses a loop instead of recursion to calculate Fibonacci numbers.

CHAPTER 10

ARRAYS AND POINTERS

You will learn about the following in this chapter:

- Keyword:
  static
- Operators:
  & * (unary)
- How to create and initialize arrays

- Pointers (building on the basics you already know) and see how they relate to arrays
- Writing functions that process arrays
- Two-dimensional arrays

People turn to computers for tasks such as tracking monthly expenses, daily rainfall, quarterly sales, and weekly weights. Enterprises turn to computers to manage payrolls, inventory, and customer transactions. As a programmer, you inevitably have to deal with large quantities of related data. Often, arrays offer the best way to handle such data in an efficient, convenient manner. Chapter 6, "C Control Statements: Looping," introduced arrays, and this chapter takes a more thorough look. In particular, it examines how to write array-processing functions. Such functions enable you to extend the advantages of modular programming to arrays. In doing so, you can see the intimate relationship between arrays and pointers.

Arrays

Recall that an *array* is composed of a series of elements of one data type. You use *declarations* to tell the compiler when you want an array. An *array declaration* tells the compiler how many elements the array contains and what the type is for these elements. Armed with this information, the compiler can set up the array properly. Array elements can have the same types as ordinary variables. Consider the following example of array declarations:

```
/* some array declarations */
int main(void)
{
    float candy[365];    /* array of 365 floats */
    char code[12];       /* array of 12 chars   */
    int states[50];      /* array of 50 ints    */
    ...
}
```

The brackets ([ ]) identify candy and the rest as arrays, and the number enclosed in the brackets indicates the number of elements in the array.

To access elements in an array, you identify an individual element by using its subscript number, also called its *index*. The numbering starts with 0. Hence, candy[0] is the first element of the candy array, and candy[364] is the 365th and last element.

This is rather old hat; let's learn something new.

Initialization

Arrays are often used to store data needed for a program. For example, a 12-element array can store the number of days in each month. In cases such as these, it's convenient to initialize the array at the beginning of a program. Let's see how it is done.

You know you can initialize single-valued variables (sometimes called *scalar* variables) in a declaration with expressions such as

```
int fix = 1;
float flax = PI * 2;
```

where, one hopes, PI was defined earlier as a macro. C extends initialization to arrays with a new syntax, as shown next:

```
int main(void)
{
    int powers[8] = {1,2,4,6,8,16,32,64}; /* ANSI only */
    ...
}
```

As you can see, you initialize an array by using a comma-separated list of values enclosed in braces. You can use spaces between the values and the commas, if you want. The first element (powers[0]) is assigned the value 1, and so on. (If your compiler rejects this form of initialization as a syntax error, you may be suffering from a pre-ANSI compiler. Prefixing the array declaration with the keyword static should solve the problem. Chapter 12, "Storage Classes, Linkage, and Memory Management," discusses the meaning of this keyword.)

Listing 10.1 presents a short program that prints the number of days per month.

LISTING 10.1   The day_mon1.c Program

```
/* day_mon1.c -- prints the days for each month */
#include <stdio.h>
#define MONTHS 12

int main(void)
{
    int days[MONTHS] = {31,28,31,30,31,30,31,31,30,31,30,31};
    int index;
```

LISTING 10.1   Continued

```
    for (index = 0; index < MONTHS; index++)
        printf("Month %d has %2d days.\n", index +1,
                days[index]);

    return 0;
}
```

The output looks like this:

```
Month  1 has 31 days.
Month  2 has 28 days.
Month  3 has 31 days.
Month  4 has 30 days.
Month  5 has 31 days.
Month  6 has 30 days.
Month  7 has 31 days.
Month  8 has 31 days.
Month  9 has 30 days.
Month 10 has 31 days.
Month 11 has 30 days.
Month 12 has 31 days.
```

Not quite a superb program, but it's wrong only one month in every four years. The program initializes days[] with a list of comma-separated values enclosed in braces.

Note that this example used the symbolic constant MONTHS to represent the array size. This is a common and recommended practice. For example, if the world switched to a 13-month calendar, you just have to modify the #define statement and don't have to track down every place in the program that uses the array size.

Using const with Arrays

Sometimes you might use an array that's intended to be a read-only array. That is, the program will retrieve values from the array, but it won't try to write new values into the array. In such cases, you can, and should, use the const keyword when you declare and initialize the array. Therefore, a better choice for Listing 10.1 would be

```
const int days[MONTHS] = {31,28,31,30,31,30,31,31,30,31,30,31};
```

This makes the program treat each element in the array as a constant. Just as with regular variables, you should use the declaration to initialize const data because once it's declared const, you can't assign values later. Now that you know about this, we can use const in subsequent examples.

What if you fail to initialize an array? Listing 10.2 shows what happens.

LISTING 10.2   The no_data.c Program

```
/* no_data.c -- uninitialized array */
#include <stdio.h>
#define SIZE 4
```

LISTING 10.2   Continued

```c
int main(void)
{
    int no_data[SIZE];  /* uninitialized array */
    int i;

    printf("%2s%14s\n",
           "i", "no_data[i]");
    for (i = 0; i < SIZE; i++)
        printf("%2d%14d\n", i, no_data[i]);

    return 0;
}
```

Here is some sample output (your results may vary):

```
i    no_data[i]
0            16
1       4204937
2       4219854
3    2147348480
```

The array members are like ordinary variables—if you don't initialize them, they might have any value. The compiler just uses whatever values were already present at those memory locations, which is why your results may vary from these.

Storage Class Caveat

Arrays, like other variables, can be created using different *storage classes*. Chapter 12 investigates this topic, but for now, you should be aware that the current chapter describes arrays that belong to the automatic storage class. That means they are declared inside of a function and without using the keyword static. All the variables and arrays used in this book, so far, are of the automatic kind.

The reason for mentioning storage classes at this point is that occasionally the different storage classes have different properties, so you can't generalize everything in this chapter to other storage classes. In particular, variables and arrays of some of the other storage classes have their contents set to 0 if they are not initialized.

The number of items in the list should match the size of the array. But what if you count wrong? Let's try the last example again, as shown in Listing 10.3, with a list that is two too short.

LISTING 10.3   The somedata.c Program

```c
/* some_data.c -- partially initialized array */
#include <stdio.h>
#define SIZE 4
int main(void)
{
```

LISTING 10.3   Continued

```
        int some_data[SIZE] = {1492, 1066};
        int i;

        printf("%2s%14s\n",
                "i", "some_data[i]");
        for (i = 0; i < SIZE; i++)
            printf("%2d%14d\n", i, some_data[i]);

        return 0;
}
```

This time the output looks like this:

```
i    some_data[i]
0           1492
1           1066
2              0
3              0
```

As you can see, the compiler had no problem. When it ran out of values from the list, it initialized the remaining elements to **0**. That is, if you don't initialize an array at all, its elements, like uninitialized ordinary variables, get garbage values, but if you partially initialize an array, the remaining elements are set to **0**.

The compiler is not so forgiving if you have too many list values. This overgenerosity is considered an error. However, there is no need to subject yourself to the ridicule of your compiler. Instead, you can let the compiler match the array size to the list by omitting the size from the braces (see Listing 10.4).

LISTING 10.4   The day_mon2.c Program

```
/* day_mon2.c -- letting the compiler count elements */
#include <stdio.h>
int main(void)
{
    const int days[] = {31,28,31,30,31,30,31,31,30,31};
    int index;

    for (index = 0; index < sizeof days / sizeof days[0]; index++)
        printf("Month %2d has %d days.\n", index +1,
                days[index]);

    return 0;
}
```

There are two main points to note in Listing 10.4:

- When you use empty brackets to initialize an array, the compiler counts the number of items in the list and makes the array that large.

- Notice what we did in the `for` loop control statement. Lacking faith (justifiably) in our ability to count correctly, we let the computer give us the size of the array. The `sizeof` operator gives the size, in bytes, of the object, or *type*, following it. So `sizeof days` is the size, in bytes, of the whole array, and `sizeof days[0]` is the size, in bytes, of one element. Dividing the size of the entire array by the size of one element tells us how many elements are in the array.

Here is the result of running this program:

```
Month  1 has 31 days.
Month  2 has 28 days.
Month  3 has 31 days.
Month  4 has 30 days.
Month  5 has 31 days.
Month  6 has 30 days.
Month  7 has 31 days.
Month  8 has 31 days.
Month  9 has 30 days.
Month 10 has 31 days.
```

Oops! We put in just 10 values, but our method of letting the program find the array size kept us from trying to print past the end of the array. This points out a potential disadvantage of automatic counting: Errors in the number of elements could pass unnoticed.

There is one more short method of initializing arrays. Because it works only for character strings, however, we will save it for the next chapter.

Designated Initializers (C99)

C99 has added a new capability—*designated initializers*. This feature allows you to pick and choose which elements are initialized. Suppose, for example, that you just want to initialize the last element in an array. With traditional C initialization syntax, you also have to initialize every element preceding the last one:

```
int arr[6] = {0,0,0,0,0,212};  // traditional syntax
```

With C99, you can use an index in brackets in the initialization list to specify a particular element:

```
int arr[6] = {[5] = 212}; // initialize arr[5] to 212
```

As with regular initialization, after you initialize at least one element, the uninitialized elements are set to `0`. Listing 10.5 shows a more involved example.

LISTING 10.5   The `designate.c` Program

```
// designate.c -- use designated initializers
#include <stdio.h>
#define MONTHS 12
int main(void)
{
```

LISTING 10.5   Continued

```
    int days[MONTHS] = {31,28, [4] = 31,30,31, [1] = 29};
    int i;

    for (i = 0; i < MONTHS; i++)
        printf("%2d  %d\n", i + 1, days[i]);

    return 0;
}
```

Here's the output if the compiler supports this C99 feature:

```
 1  31
 2  29
 3  0
 4  0
 5  31
 6  30
 7  31
 8  0
 9  0
10  0
11  0
12  0
```

The output reveals a couple important features of designated initializers. First, if the code follows a designated initializer with further values, as in the sequence [4] = 31,30,31, these further values are used to initialize the subsequent elements. That is, after initializing days[4] to 31, the code initializes days[5] and days[6] to 30 and 31, respectively. Second, if the code initializes a particular element to a value more than once, the last initialization is the one that takes effect. For example, in Listing 10.5, the start of the initialization list initializes days[1] to 28, but that is overridden by the [1] = 29 designated initialization later.

Assigning Array Values

After an array has been declared, you can *assign* values to array members by using an array index, or *subscript*. For example, the following fragment assigns even numbers to an array:

```
/* array assignment */
#include <stdio.h>
#define SIZE 50
int main(void)
{
    int counter, evens[SIZE];

    for (counter = 0; counter < SIZE; counter++)
        evens[counter] = 2 * counter;
    ...
}
```

Note that the code uses a loop to assign values element by element. C doesn't let you assign one array to another as a unit. Nor can you use the list-in-braces form except when initializing. The following code fragment shows some forms of assignment that are not allowed:

```
/* nonvalid array assignment */
#define SIZE 5
int main(void)
{
    int oxen[SIZE] = {5,3,2,8};      /* ok here        */
    int yaks[SIZE];

    yaks = oxen;                     /* not allowed   */
    yaks[SIZE] = oxen[SIZE];         /* invalid       */
    yaks[SIZE] = {5,3,2,8};          /* doesn't work */
```

Array Bounds

You have to make sure you use array indices that are within bounds; that is, you have to make sure they have values valid for the array. For instance, suppose you make the following declaration:

```
int doofi[20];
```

Then it's your responsibility to make sure the program uses indices only in the range 0 through 19, because the compiler won't check for you.

Consider the program in Listing 10.6. It creates an array with four elements and then carelessly uses index values ranging from −1 to 6.

LISTING 10.6   The bounds.c Program

```
// bounds.c -- exceed the bounds of an array
#include <stdio.h>
#define SIZE 4
int main(void)
{
    int value1 = 44;
    int arr[SIZE];
    int value2 = 88;
    int i;

    printf("value1 = %d, value2 = %d\n", value1, value2);
    for (i = -1; i <= SIZE; i++)
        arr[i] = 2 * i + 1;

    for (i = -1; i < 7; i++)
        printf("%2d  %d\n", i , arr[i]);
    printf("value1 = %d, value2 = %d\n", value1, value2);

    return 0;
}
```

The compiler doesn't check to see whether the indices are valid. The result of using a bad index is, in the language of the C standard, undefined. That means when you run the program, it might seem to work, it might work oddly, or it might abort. Here is the output using Digital Mars 8.4:

```
value1 = 44, value2 = 88
-1   -1
 0   1
 1   3
 2   5
 3   7
 4   9
 5   5
 6   1245120
value1 = -1, value2 = 9
```

Note that this compiler appears to have stored `value2` just after the array and `value1` just ahead of it. (Other compilers might store the data in a different order in memory.) In this case, `arr[-1]` corresponded to the same memory location as `value1`, and `arr[4]` corresponded to the same memory location as `value2`. Therefore, using out-of-bounds array indices resulted in the program altering the value of other variables. Another compiler might produce different results, including a program that aborts.

You might wonder why C allows nasty things like that to happen. It goes back to the C philosophy of trusting the programmer. Not checking bounds allows a C program to run faster. The compiler can't necessarily catch all index errors because the value of an index might not be determined until after the resulting program begins execution. Therefore, to be safe, the compiler would have to add extra code to check the value of each index during runtime, and that would slow things down. So C trusts the programmer to do the coding correctly and rewards the programmer with a faster program. Of course, not all programmers deserve that trust, and then problems can arise.

One simple thing to remember is that array numbering begins with 0. One simple habit to develop is to use a symbolic constant in the array declaration and in other places the array size is used:

```c
#define SIZE 4
int main(void)
{
    int arr[SIZE];
    for (i = 0; i < SIZE; i++)
    ....
```

This helps ensure that you use the same array size consistently throughout the program.

Specifying an Array Size

So far, the examples have used integer constants when declaring arrays:

```c
#define SIZE 4
int main(void)
```

```
{
    int arr[SIZE];      // symbolic integer constant
    double lots[144];   // literal integer constant
    ...
```

What else is allowed? Until the C99 standard, the answer has been that you have to use a *constant integer expression* between the brackets when declaring an array. A constant integer expression is one formed from integer constants. For this purpose, a `sizeof` expression is considered an integer constant, but (unlike the case in C++) a `const` value isn't. Also, the value of the expression must be greater than 0:

```
int n = 5;
int m = 8;
float a1[5];                 // yes
float a2[5*2 + 1];           // yes
float a3[sizeof(int) + 1];   // yes
float a4[-4];                // no, size must be > 0
float a5[0];                 // no, size must be > 0
float a6[2.5];               // no, size must be an integer
float a7[(int)2.5];          // yes, typecast float to int constant
float a8[n];                 // not allowed before C99
float a9[m];                 // not allowed before C99
```

As the comments indicate, C compilers following the C90 standard would not allow the last two declarations. C99, however, does allow them, but they create a new breed of array, something called a *variable-length array*, or *VLA* for short.

C99 introduced variable-length arrays primarily to allow C to become a better language for numerical computing. For example, VLAs make it easier to convert existing libraries of FORTRAN numerical calculation routines to C. VLAs have some restrictions; for example, you can't initialize a VLA in its declaration. This chapter will return to VLAs later, after you've learned enough to understand more about the limitations of the classic C array.

Multidimensional Arrays

Tempest Cloud, a weather person who takes her subject "cirrusly," wants to analyze five years of monthly rainfall data. One of her first decisions is how to represent the data. One choice is to use 60 variables, one for each data item. (We mentioned this choice once before, and it is as senseless now as it was then.) Using an array with 60 elements would be an improvement, but it would be even nicer still if she could keep each year's data separate. She could use five arrays, each with 12 elements, but that is clumsy and could get really awkward if Tempest decides to study 50 years' worth of rainfall instead of five. She needs something better.

The better approach is to use an array of arrays. The master array would have five elements, one for each year. Each of those elements, in turn, would be a 12-element array, one for each month. Here is how to declare such an array:

```
float rain[5][12];  // array of 5 arrays of 12 floats
```

One way to view this declaration is to first look at the inner portion (the part in bold):

```
float rain[5][12];          // rain is an array of 5 somethings
```

It tells us that `rain` is an array with five elements. But what is each of those elements? Now look at the remaining part of the declaration (now in bold):

```
float rain[5] [12];  // an array of 12 floats
```

This tells us that each element is of type `float[12]`; that is, each of the five elements of `rain` is, in itself, an array of 12 `float` values.

Pursuing this logic, `rain[0]`, being the first element of `rain`, is an array of 12 `float` values. So are `rain[1]`, `rain[2]`, and so on. If `rain[0]` is an array, its first element is `rain[0][0]`, its second element is `rain[0][1]`, and so on. In short, `rain` is a five-element array of 12-element arrays of `float`, `rain[0]` is an array of 12 `floats`, and `rain[0][0]` is a `float`. To access, say, the value in row 2, column 3, use `rain[2][3]`. (Remember, array counting starts at 0, so row 2 is the third row.)

You can also visualize this `rain` array as a two-dimensional array consisting of five rows, each of 12 columns, as shown in Figure 10.1. By changing the second subscript, you move along a row, month by month. By changing the first subscript, you move vertically along a column, year by year.

FIGURE 10.1

Two-dimensional array.

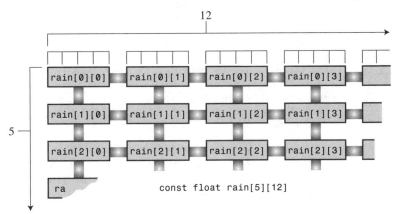

The two-dimensional view is merely a convenient way of visualizing an array with two indices. Internally, such an array is stored sequentially, beginning with the first 12-element array, followed by the second 12-element array, and so on.

Let's use this two-dimensional array in a weather program. The program goal is to find the total rainfall for each year, the average yearly rainfall, and the average rainfall for each month. To find the total rainfall for a year, you have to add all the data in a given row. To find the average rainfall for a given month, you have to add all the data in a given column. The two-dimensional array makes it easy to visualize and execute these activities. Listing 10.7 shows the program.

LISTING 10.7 The rain.c Program

```c
/* rain.c  -- finds yearly totals, yearly average, and monthly
                   average for several years of rainfall data */
#include <stdio.h>
#define MONTHS 12    // number of months in a year
#define YEARS   5    // number of years of data
int main(void)
{
 // initializing rainfall data for 2000 - 2004
    const float rain[YEARS][MONTHS] =
    {
        {4.3,4.3,4.3,3.0,2.0,1.2,0.2,0.2,0.4,2.4,3.5,6.6},
        {8.5,8.2,1.2,1.6,2.4,0.0,5.2,0.9,0.3,0.9,1.4,7.3},
        {9.1,8.5,6.7,4.3,2.1,0.8,0.2,0.2,1.1,2.3,6.1,8.4},
        {7.2,9.9,8.4,3.3,1.2,0.8,0.4,0.0,0.6,1.7,4.3,6.2},
        {7.6,5.6,3.8,2.8,3.8,0.2,0.0,0.0,0.0,1.3,2.6,5.2}
    };
    int year, month;
    float subtot, total;

    printf(" YEAR    RAINFALL  (inches)\n");
    for (year = 0, total = 0; year < YEARS; year++)
    {             // for each year, sum rainfall for each month
        for (month = 0, subtot = 0; month < MONTHS; month++)
            subtot += rain[year][month];
        printf("%5d %15.1f\n", 2000 + year, subtot);
        total += subtot; // total for all years
     }
    printf("\nThe yearly average is %.1f inches.\n\n",
            total/YEARS);
    printf("MONTHLY AVERAGES:\n\n");
    printf(" Jan Feb Mar Apr May Jun Jul Aug Sep Oct ");
    printf(" Nov  Dec\n");

    for (month = 0; month < MONTHS; month++)
    {             // for each month, sum rainfall over years
        for (year = 0, subtot =0; year < YEARS; year++)
            subtot += rain[year][month];
        printf("%4.1f ", subtot/YEARS);
    }
    printf("\n");

    return 0;
}
```

Here is the output:

```
   YEAR     RAINFALL  (inches)
   2000             32.4
   2001             37.9
   2002             49.8
   2003             44.0
   2004             32.9
```

```
The yearly average is 39.4 inches.

MONTHLY AVERAGES:

Jan Feb Mar Apr May Jun Jul Aug Sep Oct Nov Dec
7.3 7.3 4.9 3.0 2.3 0.6 1.2 0.3 0.5 1.7 3.6 6.7
```

As you study this program, concentrate on the initialization and on the computation scheme. The initialization is the more involved of the two, so let's look at the simpler part (the computation) first.

To find the total for a given year, keep `year` constant and let `month` go over its full range. This is the inner `for` loop of the first part of the program. Then repeat the process for the next value of `year`. This is the outer loop of the first part of the program. A nested loop structure like this one is natural for handling a two-dimensional array. One loop handles the first subscript, and the other loop handles the second subscript.

The second part of the program has the same structure, but now it changes `year` with the inner loop and `month` with the outer. Remember, each time the outer loop cycles once, the inner loop cycles its full allotment. Therefore, this arrangement cycles through all the years before changing months. You get a five-year average for the first month, and so on.

Initializing a Two-Dimensional Array

Initializing a two-dimensional array builds on the technique for initializing a one-dimensional array. First, recall that initializing a one-dimensional array looks like this:

```
sometype ar1[5] = {val1, val2, val3, val4, val5};
```

Here `val1`, `val2`, and so on are each a value appropriate for `sometype`. For example, if `sometype` were `int`, `val1` might be `7`, or if `sometype` were `double`, `val1` might be `11.34`. But `rain` is a five-element array for which each element is of type array-of-12-`float`. So, for `rain`, `val1` would be a value appropriate for initializing a one-dimensional array of `float`, such as the following:

```
{4.3,4.3,4.3,3.0,2.0,1.2,0.2,0.2,0.4,2.4,3.5,6.6}
```

That is, if `sometype` is array-of-12-`double`, `val1` is a list of 12 `double` values. Therefore, we need a comma-separated list of five of these things to initialize a two-dimensional array, such as `rain`:

```
const float rain[YEARS][MONTHS] =
{
    {4.3,4.3,4.3,3.0,2.0,1.2,0.2,0.2,0.4,2.4,3.5,6.6},
    {8.5,8.2,1.2,1.6,2.4,0.0,5.2,0.9,0.3,0.9,1.4,7.3},
    {9.1,8.5,6.7,4.3,2.1,0.8,0.2,0.2,1.1,2.3,6.1,8.4},
    {7.2,9.9,8.4,3.3,1.2,0.8,0.4,0.0,0.6,1.7,4.3,6.2},
    {7.6,5.6,3.8,2.8,3.8,0.2,0.0,0.0,0.0,1.3,2.6,5.2}
};
```

This initialization uses five embraced lists of numbers, all enclosed by one outer set of braces. The data in the first interior set of braces is assigned to the first row of the array, the data in the second interior set goes to the second row, and so on. The rules we discussed about mismatches between data and array sizes apply to each row. That is, if the first inner set of braces encloses 10 numbers, only the first 10 elements of the first row are affected. The last two elements in that row are then initialized by default to zero. If there are too many numbers, it is an error; the numbers do not get shoved into the next row.

You could omit the interior braces and just retain the two outermost braces. As long as you have the right number of entries, the effect is the same. If you are short of entries, however, the array is filled sequentially, row by row, until the data runs out. Then the remaining elements are initialized to **0**. Figure 10.2 shows both ways of initializing an array.

FIGURE 10.2
Two methods of initializing an array.

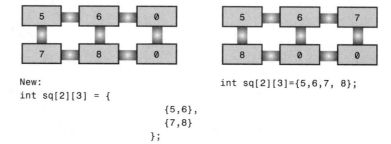

```
New:
int sq[2][3] = {
                  {5,6},
                  {7,8}
               };
```

```
int sq[2][3]={5,6,7, 8};
```

Because the **rain** array holds data that should not be modified, the program uses the **const** modifier when declaring the array.

More Dimensions

Everything we have said about two-dimensional arrays can be generalized to three-dimensional arrays and further. You can declare a three-dimensional array this way:

```
int box[10][20][30];
```

You can visualize a one-dimensional array as a row of data, a two-dimensional array as a table of data, and a three-dimensional array as a stack of data tables. For example, you can visualize the **box** array as 10 two-dimensional arrays (each 20×30) stacked atop each other.

The other way to think of **box** is as an array of arrays of arrays. That is, it is a 10-element array, each element of which is a 20-element array. Each 20-element array then has elements that are 30-element arrays. Or, you can simply think of arrays in terms of the number of indices needed.

Typically, you would use three nested loops to process a three-dimensional array, four nested loops to process a four-dimensional array, and so on. We'll stick to two dimensions in our examples.

Pointers and Arrays

Pointers, as you might recall from Chapter 9, "Functions," provide a symbolic way to use addresses. Because the hardware instructions of computing machines rely heavily on addresses, pointers enable you to express yourself in a way that is close to how the machine expresses itself. This correspondence makes programs with pointers efficient. In particular, pointers offer an efficient way to deal with arrays. Indeed, as you will see, array notation is simply a disguised use of pointers.

An example of this disguised use is that an array name is also the address of the first element of the array. That is, if `flizny` is an array, the following is true:

```
flizny == &flizny[0];    // name of array is the address of the first element
```

Both `flizny` and `&flizny[0]` represent the memory address of that first element. (Recall that `&` is the address operator.) Both are *constants* because they remain fixed for the duration of the program. However, they can be assigned as values to a pointer *variable*, and you can change the value of a variable, as Listing 10.8 shows. Notice what happens to the value of a pointer when you add a number to it. (Recall that the `%p` specifier for pointers typically displays hexadecimal values.)

LISTING 10.8   The `pnt_add.c` Program

```c
// pnt_add.c -- pointer addition
#include <stdio.h>
#define SIZE 4
int main(void)
{
    short dates [SIZE];
    short * pti;
    short index;
    double bills[SIZE];
    double * ptf;

    pti = dates;    // assign address of array to pointer
    ptf = bills;
    printf("%23s %10s\n", "short", "double");
    for (index = 0; index < SIZE; index ++)
        printf("pointers + %d: %10p %10p\n",
                index, pti + index, ptf + index);

    return 0;
}
```

Here is the output:

```
                 short     double
pointers + 0: 0x0064fd20 0x0064fd28
pointers + 1: 0x0064fd22 0x0064fd30
pointers + 2: 0x0064fd24 0x0064fd38
pointers + 3: 0x0064fd26 0x0064fd40
```

The second line prints the beginning addresses of the two arrays, and the next line gives the result of adding 1 to the address, and so on. Keep in mind that the addresses are in hexadecimal, so 30 is 1 more than 2f and 8 more than 28. What?

```
0x0064fd20 + 1 is 0x0064fd22?
0x0064fd30 + 1 is 0x0064fd38?
```

Pretty dumb? Like a fox! Our system is addressed by individual bytes, but type short uses 2 bytes and type double uses 8 bytes. What is happening here is that when you say "add 1 to a pointer," C adds one *storage unit*. For arrays, that means the address is increased to the address of the next *element*, not just the next byte (see Figure 10.3). This is one reason why you have to declare the sort of object to which a pointer points. The address is not enough because the computer needs to know how many bytes are used to store the object. (This is true even for pointers to scalar variables; otherwise, the *pt operation to fetch the value wouldn't work correctly.)

FIGURE 10.3

An array and pointer addition.

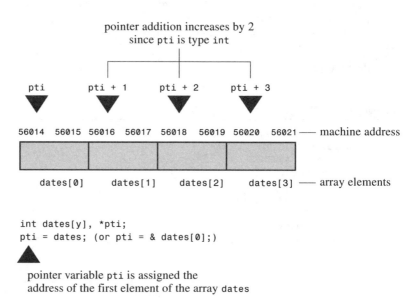

Now we can define more clearly what is meant by pointer-to-int, pointer-to-float, or pointer-to–any other data object:

- The value of a pointer is the address of the object to which it points. How the address is represented internally is hardware dependent. Many computers, including PCs and Macintoshes, are *byte addressable*, meaning that each byte in memory is numbered sequentially. Here, the address of a large object, such as type double variable, typically is the address of the first byte of the object.

- Applying the * operator to a pointer yields the value stored in the pointed-to object.

- Adding 1 to the pointer increases its value by the size, in bytes, of the pointed-to type.

As a result of C's cleverness, you have the following equalities:

```
dates +2 == &date[2]        /* same address */
*(dates + 2) == dates[2]    /* same value   */
```

These relationships sum up the close connection between arrays and pointers. They mean that you can use a pointer to identify an individual element of an array and to obtain its value. In essence, you have two different notations for the same thing. Indeed, the C language standard describes array notation in terms of pointers. That is, it defines `ar[n]` to mean `*(ar + n)`. You can think of the second expression as meaning, "Go to memory location `ar`, move over `n` units, and retrieve the value there."

Incidentally, don't confuse `*(dates+2)` with `*dates+2`. The indirection operator (`*`) binds more tightly (that is, has higher precedence) than +, so the latter means (`*dates`)+2:

```
*(dates +2)       /* value of the 3rd element of dates       */
*dates +2         /* 2 added to the value of the 1st element */
```

The relationship between arrays and pointers means that you can often use either approach when writing a program. Listing 10.9, for instance, produces the same output as Listing 10.1 when compiled and run.

LISTING 10.9 The day_mon3.c Program

```c
/* day_mon3.c -- uses pointer notation */
#include <stdio.h>
#define MONTHS 12

int main(void)
{
    int days[MONTHS] = {31,28,31,30,31,30,31,31,30,31,30,31};
    int index;

    for (index = 0; index < MONTHS; index++)
        printf("Month %2d has %d days.\n", index +1,
                *(days + index));    // same as days[index]

    return 0;
}
```

Here, `days` is the address of the first element of the array, `days + index` is the address of element `days[index]`, and `*(days + index)` is the value of that element, just as `days[index]` is. The loop references each element of the array, in turn, and prints the contents of what it finds.

Is there an advantage to writing the program this way? Not really. The point to Listing 10.9 is that pointer notation and array notation are two equivalent methods. This example shows that you can use pointer notation with arrays. The reverse is also true; you can use array notation with pointers. This turns out to be important when you have a function with an array as an argument.

Functions, Arrays, and Pointers

Suppose you want to write a function that operates on an array. For example, suppose you want a function that returns the sum of the elements of an array. Suppose `marbles` is the name of an array of `int`. What would the function call look like? A reasonable guess would be this:

```
total = sum(marbles); // possible function call
```

What would the prototype be? Remember, the name of an array is the address of its first element, so the actual argument `marbles`, being the address of an `int`, should be assigned to a formal parameter that is a pointer-to-`int`:

```
int sum(int * ar);  // corresponding prototype
```

What information does `sum()` get from this argument? It gets the address of the first element of the array, and it learns that it will find an `int` at that location. Note that this information says nothing about the number of elements in the array. We're left with a couple choices of how to proceed with the function definition. The first choice is to code a fixed array size into the function:

```
int sum(int *ar)      // corresponding definition
{
    int i;
    int total = 0;

    for( i = 0; i < 10; i++)    // assume 10 elements
        total += ar[i];    // ar[i] the same as *(ar + i)
    return total;
}
```

Here, we make use of the fact that just as you can use pointer notation with array names, you can use array notation with a pointer. Also, recall that the `+=` operator adds the value of the operand on its right to the operand on its left. Therefore, `total` is a running sum of the array elements.

This function definition is limited; it will work only with arrays of 10 elements. A more flexible approach is to pass the array size as a second argument:

```
int sum(int * ar, int n)  // more general approach
{
    int i;
    int total = 0;

    for( i = 0; i < n; i++)    // use n elements
        total += ar[i];    // ar[i] the same as *(ar + i)
    return total;
}
```

Here, the first parameter tells the function where to find the array and the type of data in the array, and the second parameter tells the function how many elements are present.

There's one more thing to tell about function parameters. In the context of a function prototype or function definition header, and *only* in that context, you can substitute `int ar[]` for `int * ar`:

```
int sum (int ar[], int n);
```

The form `int * ar` always means that `ar` is type pointer-to-int. The form `int ar[]` also means that `ar` is type pointer-to-int, but *only* when used to declare formal parameters. The idea is that the second form reminds the reader that not only does `ar` point to an `int`, it points to an `int` that's an element of an array.

Declaring Array Parameters

Because the name of an array is the address of the first element, an actual argument of an array name requires that the matching formal argument be a pointer. In this context, and only in this context, C interprets `int ar[]` to mean the same as `int * ar`; that is, `ar` is type pointer-to-int. Because prototypes allow you to omit a name, all four of the following prototypes are equivalent:

```
int sum(int *ar, int n);
int sum(int *, int);
int sum(int ar[], int n);
int sum(int [], int);
```

You can't omit names in function definitions, so, for definitions, the following two forms are equivalent:

```
int sum(int *ar, int n)
{
    // code goes here
}

int sum(int ar[], int n);
{
    // code goes here
}
```

You should be able to use any of the four prototypes with either of the two definitions shown here.

Listing 10.10 shows a program using the `sum()` function. To point out an interesting fact about array arguments, the program also prints the size of the original array and the size of the function parameter representing the array. (Use `%u` or perhaps `%lu` if your compiler doesn't support the `%zd` specifier for printing `sizeof` quantities.)

LISTING 10.10   The sum_arr1.c Program

```
// sum_arr1.c -- sums the elements of an array
// use %u or %lu if %zd doesn't work
#include <stdio.h>
#define SIZE 10
int sum(int ar[], int n);
```

LISTING 10.10   Continued

```
int main(void)
{
    int marbles[SIZE] = {20,10,5,39,4,16,19,26,31,20};
    long answer;

    answer = sum(marbles, SIZE);
    printf("The total number of marbles is %ld.\n", answer);
    printf("The size of marbles is %zd bytes.\n",
           sizeof marbles);

    return 0;
}

int sum(int ar[], int n)        // how big an array?
{
    int i;
    int total = 0;

    for( i = 0; i < n; i++)
        total += ar[i];
    printf("The size of ar is %zd bytes.\n", sizeof ar);

    return total;
}
```

The output on our system looks like this:

```
The size of ar is 4 bytes.
The total number of marbles is 190.
The size of marbles is 40 bytes.
```

Note that the size of `marbles` is 40 bytes. This makes sense because `marbles` contains 10 `int`s, each 4 bytes, for a total of 40 bytes. But the size of `ar` is just 4 bytes. That's because `ar` is not an array itself; it is a pointer to the first element of `marbles`. Our system uses a 4-byte address, so the size of a pointer variable is 4 bytes. (Other systems might use a different number of bytes.) In short, in Listing 10.10, `marbles` is an array, `ar` is a pointer to the first element of `marbles`, and the C connection between arrays and pointers lets you use array notation with the pointer `ar`.

Using Pointer Parameters

A function working on an array needs to know where to start and stop. The `sum()` function uses a pointer parameter to identify the beginning of the array and an integer parameter to indicate how many elements to process. (The pointer parameter also identifies the type of data in the array.) But this is not the only way to tell a function what it needs to know. Another way to describe the array is by passing two pointers, with the first indicating where the array starts (as before) and the second where the array ends. Listing 10.11 illustrates this approach. It also uses the fact that a pointer parameter is a variable, which means that instead of using an index to indicate which element in the array to access, the function can alter the value of the pointer itself, making it point to each array element in turn.

LISTING 10.11 The sum_arr2.c Program

```c
/* sum_arr2.c -- sums the elements of an array */
#include <stdio.h>
#define SIZE 10
int sump(int * start, int * end);
int main(void)
{
    int marbles[SIZE] = {20,10,5,39,4,16,19,26,31,20};
    long answer;

    answer = sump(marbles, marbles + SIZE);
    printf("The total number of marbles is %ld.\n", answer);

    return 0;
}

/* use pointer arithmetic   */
int sump(int * start, int * end)
{
    int total = 0;

    while (start < end)
    {
        total += *start; /* add value to total                 */
        start++;          /* advance pointer to next element */
    }

    return total;
}
```

The pointer `start` begins by pointing to the first element of `marbles`, so the assignment expression `total +=*start` adds the value of the first element (20) to `total`. Then the expression `start++` increments the pointer variable `start` so that it points to the next element in the array. Because `start` points to type `int`, C increments the value of `start` by the size of `int`.

Note that the `sump()` function uses a different method from `sum()` to end the summation loop. The `sum()` function uses the number of elements as a second argument, and the loop uses that value as part of the loop test:

```c
for( i = 0; i < n; i++)
```

The `sump()` function, however, uses a second pointer to end the loop:

```c
while (start < end)
```

Because the test is for inequality, the last element processed is the one just before the element pointed to by `end`. This means that `end` actually points to the location after the final element in the array. C guarantees that when it allocates space for an array, a pointer to the first location after the end of the array is a valid pointer. That makes constructions such as this one valid, because the final value that `start` gets in the loop is `end`. Note that using this "past-the-end" pointer makes the function call neat:

```c
answer = sump(marbles, marbles + SIZE);
```

Because indexing starts at **0**, `marbles + SIZE` points to the next element after the end. If **end** pointed to the last element instead of to one past the end, you would have to use the following code instead:

```
answer = sump(marbles, marbles + SIZE - 1);
```

Not only is this code less elegant in appearance, it's harder to remember, so it is more likely to lead to programming errors. By the way, although C guarantees that the pointer `marbles + SIZE` is a valid pointer, it makes no guarantees about `marbles[SIZE]`, the value stored at that location.

You can also condense the body of the loop to one line:

```
total += *start++;
```

The unary operators `*` and `++` have the same precedence but associate from right to left. This means the `++` applies to `start`, not to `*start`. That is, the pointer is incremented, not the value pointed to. The use of the postfix form (`start++` rather than `++start`) means that the pointer is not incremented until after the pointed-to value is added to `total`. If the program used `*++start`, the order would be increment the pointer, then use the value pointed to. If the program used `(*start)++`, however, it would use the value of `start` and then increment the value, not the pointer. That would leave the pointer pointing to the same element, but the element would contain a new number. Although the `*start++` notation is commonly used, you should use `*(start++)` for clarity. Listing 10.12 illustrates these "niceties" of precedence.

LISTING 10.12   The `order.c` Program

```
/* order.c -- precedence in pointer operations */
#include <stdio.h>
int data[2] = {100, 200};
int moredata[2] = {300, 400};
int main(void)
{
    int * p1, * p2, * p3;

    p1 = p2 = data;
    p3 = moredata;
    printf("  *p1 = %d,    *p2 = %d,      *p3 = %d\n",
             *p1       ,     *p2    ,       *p3);
    printf("*p1++ = %d, *++p2 = %d, (*p3)++ = %d\n",
            *p1++      ,    *++p2    ,  (*p3)++);
    printf("  *p1 = %d,    *p2 = %d,      *p3 = %d\n",
             *p1      ,     *p2    ,       *p3);

    return 0;
}
```

Here is its output:

```
  *p1 = 100,    *p2 = 100,      *p3 = 300
*p1++ = 100, *++p2 = 200, (*p3)++ = 300
  *p1 = 200,    *p2 = 200,      *p3 = 301
```

The only operation that altered an array value is (*p3)++. The other two operations caused p1 and p2 to advance to point to the next array element.

Comment: Pointers and Arrays

As you have seen, functions that process arrays actually use pointers as arguments, but you do have a choice between array notation and pointer notation for writing array-processing functions. Using array notation, as in Listing 10.10, makes it more obvious that the function is working with arrays. Also, array notation has a more familiar look to programmers versed in other languages, such as FORTRAN, Pascal, Modula-2, or BASIC. Other programmers might be more accustomed to working with pointers and might find the pointer notation, such as that in Listing 10.11, more natural.

As far as C goes, the two expressions ar[i] and *(ar+i) are equivalent in meaning. Both work if ar is the name of an array, and both work if ar is a pointer variable. However, using an expression such as ar++ only works if ar is a pointer variable.

Pointer notation, particularly when used with the increment operator, is closer to machine language and, with some compilers, leads to more efficient code. However, many programmers believe that the programmer's main concerns should be correctness and clarity and that code optimization should be left to the compiler.

Pointer Operations

Just what can you do with pointers? C offers several basic operations you can perform on pointers, and the next program demonstrates eight of these possibilities. To show the results of each operation, the program prints the value of the pointer (which is the address to which it points), the value stored in the pointed-to address, and the address of the pointer itself. (If your compiler doesn't support the %p specifier, try %u or perhaps %lu for printing the addresses.)

Listing 10.13 shows eight basic operations that can be performed with pointer variables. In addition to these operations, you can use the relational operators to compare pointers.

LISTING 10.13   The ptr_ops.c Program

```
// ptr_ops.c -- pointer operations
#include <stdio.h>
int main(void)
{
    int urn[5] = {100,200,300,400,500};
    int * ptr1, * ptr2, *ptr3;

    ptr1 = urn;          // assign an address to a pointer
    ptr2 = &urn[2];      // ditto
                         // dereference a pointer and take
                         // the address of a pointer
```

LISTING 10.13   Continued

```
        printf("pointer value, dereferenced pointer, pointer address:\n");
        printf("ptr1 = %p, *ptr1 =%d, &ptr1 = %p\n",
               ptr1, *ptr1, &ptr1);

        // pointer addition
        ptr3 = ptr1 + 4;
        printf("\nadding an int to a pointer:\n");
        printf("ptr1 + 4 = %p, *(ptr4 + 3) = %d\n",
               ptr1 + 4, *(ptr1 + 3));
        ptr1++;             // increment a pointer
        printf("\nvalues after ptr1++:\n");
        printf("ptr1 = %p, *ptr1 =%d, &ptr1 = %p\n",
               ptr1, *ptr1, &ptr1);
        ptr2--;             // decrement a pointer
        printf("\nvalues after --ptr2:\n");
        printf("ptr2 = %p, *ptr2 = %d, &ptr2 = %p\n",
               ptr2, *ptr2, &ptr2);
        --ptr1;             // restore to original value
        ++ptr2;             // restore to original value
        printf("\nPointers reset to original values:\n");
        printf("ptr1 = %p, ptr2 = %p\n", ptr1, ptr2);
                            // subtract one pointer from another
        printf("\nsubtracting one pointer from another:\n");
        printf("ptr2 = %p, ptr1 = %p, ptr2 - ptr1 = %d\n",
               ptr2, ptr1, ptr2 - ptr1);
                            // subtract an integer from a pointer
        printf("\nsubtracting an int from a pointer:\n");
        printf("ptr3 = %p, ptr3 - 2 = %p\n",
               ptr3,  ptr3 - 2);

        return 0;
}
```

Here is the output:

```
pointer value, dereferenced pointer, pointer address:
ptr1 = 0x0012ff38, *ptr1 =100, &ptr1 = 0x0012ff34

adding an int to a pointer:
ptr1 + 4 = 0x0012ff48, *(ptr4 + 3) = 400

values after ptr1++:
ptr1 = 0x0012ff3c, *ptr1 =200, &ptr1 = 0x0012ff34

values after --ptr2:
ptr2 = 0x0012ff3c, *ptr2 = 200, &ptr2 = 0x0012ff30

Pointers reset to original values:
ptr1 = 0x0012ff38, ptr2 = 0x0012ff40

subtracting one pointer from another:
ptr2 = 0x0012ff40, ptr1 = 0x0012ff38, ptr2 - ptr1 = 2
```

```
subtracting an int from a pointer:
ptr3 = 0x0012ff48, ptr3 - 2 = 0x0012ff40
```

The following list describes the basic operations that can be performed with or on pointer variables:

- **Assignment**—You can assign an address to a pointer. Typically, you do this by using an array name or by using the address operator (&). In the example, ptr1 is assigned the address of the beginning of the array urn. This address happens to be memory cell number 0x0012ff38. The variable ptr2 gets the address of the third and last element, urn[2]. Note that the address should be compatible with the pointer type. That is, you can't assign the address of a **double** to a pointer-to-**int**, at least not without making an ill-advised type cast. C99 enforces this rule.

- **Value finding (dereferencing)**—The * operator gives the value stored in the pointed-to location. Therefore, *ptr1 is initially 100, the value stored at location 0x0012ff38.

- **Taking a pointer address**—Like all variables, pointer variables have an address and a value. The & operator tells you where the pointer itself is stored. In this example, ptr1 is stored in memory location 0x0012ff34. The content of that memory cell is 0x0012ff38, the address of urn.

- **Adding an integer to a pointer**—You can use the + operator to add an integer to a pointer or a pointer to an integer. In either case, the integer is multiplied by the number of bytes in the pointed-to type, and the result is added to the original address. This makes ptr1 + 4 the same as &urn[4]. The result of addition is undefined if it lies outside of the array into which the original pointer points, except that the address one past the end element of the array is guaranteed to be valid.

- **Incrementing a pointer**—Incrementing a pointer to an array element makes it move to the next element of the array. Therefore, ptr1++ increases the numerical value of ptr1 by 4 (4 bytes per **int** on our system) and makes ptr1 point to urn[1] (see Figure 10.4). Now ptr1 has the value 0x0012ff3c (the next array address) and *ptr1 has the value 200 (the value of urn[1]). Note that the address of ptr1 itself remains 0x0012ff34. After all, a variable doesn't move around just because it changes value!

- **Subtracting an integer from a pointer**—You can use the - operator to subtract an integer from a pointer; the pointer has to be the first operand or a pointer to an integer. The integer is multiplied by the number of bytes in the pointed-to type, and the result is subtracted from the original address. This makes ptr3 - 2 the same as &urn[2] because ptr3 points to &urn[4]. The result of subtraction is undefined if it lies outside of the array into which the original pointer points, except that the address one past the end element of the array is guaranteed to be valid.

- **Decrementing a pointer**—Of course, you can also decrement a pointer. In this example, decrementing ptr2 makes it point to the second array element instead of the third. Note that you can use both the prefix and postfix forms of the increment and decrement operators. Also note that both ptr1 and ptr2 wind up pointing to the same element, urn[1], before they get reset.

FIGURE 10.4

Incrementing a type int
pointer.

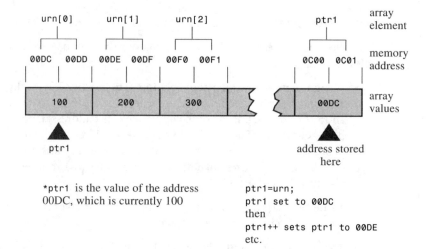

*ptr1 is the value of the address
00DC, which is currently 100

ptr1=urn;
ptr1 set to 00DC
then
ptr1++ sets ptr1 to 00DE
etc.

- **Differencing**—You can find the difference between two pointers. Normally, you do this for two pointers to elements that are in the same array to find out how far apart the elements are. The result is in the same units as the type size. For example, in the output from Listing 10.13, ptr2 - ptr1 has the value 2, meaning that these pointers point to objects separated by two ints, not by 2 bytes. Subtraction is guaranteed to be a valid operation as long as both pointers point into the same array (or possibly to a position one past the end). Applying the operation to pointers to two different arrays might produce a value or could lead to a runtime error.

- **Comparisons**—You can use the relational operators to compare the values of two pointers, provided the pointers are of the same type.

Note that there are two forms of subtraction. You can subtract one pointer from another to get an integer, and you can subtract an integer from a pointer and get a pointer.

There are some cautions to remember when incrementing or decrementing a pointer. The computer does not keep track of whether a pointer still points to an array element. C guarantees that, given an array, a pointer to any array element, or to the position after the last element, is a valid pointer. But the effect of incrementing or decrementing a pointer beyond these limits is undefined. Also, you can dereference a pointer to any array element. However, even though a pointer to one past the end element is valid, it's not guaranteed that such a one-past-the-end pointer can be dereferenced.

Dereferencing an Uninitialized Pointer

Speaking of cautions, there is one rule you should burn into your memory: Do not dereference an uninitialized pointer. For example, consider the following:

```
int * pt;   // an uninitialized pointer
*pt = 5;    // a terrible error
```

Why is this so bad? The second line means store the value 5 in the location to which pt points. But pt, being uninitialized, has a random value, so there is no knowing where the 5 will be placed. It might go somewhere harmless, it might overwrite data or code, or it might cause the program to crash. Remember, creating a pointer only allocates memory to store the pointer itself; it doesn't allocate memory to store data. Therefore, before you use a pointer, it should be assigned a memory location that has already been allocated. For example, you can assign the address of an existing variable to the pointer. (This is what happens when you use a function with a pointer parameter.) Or you can use the `malloc()` function, as discussed in Chapter 12, to allocate memory first. Anyway, to drive the point home, do not dereference an uninitialized pointer!

```
double * pd;  // uninitialized pointer
*pd = 2.4;    // DON'T DO IT
```

Given

```
int urn[3];
int * ptr1, * ptr2;
```

the following are some valid and invalid statements:

Valid	Invalid
ptr1++;	urn++;
ptr2 = ptr1 + 2;	ptr2 = ptr2 + ptr1;
ptr2 = urn + 1;	ptr2 = urn * ptr1;

These operations open many possibilities. C programmers create arrays of pointers, pointers to functions, arrays of pointers to pointers, arrays of pointers to functions, and so on. Relax, though—we'll stick to the basic uses we have already unveiled. The first basic use for pointers is to communicate information to and from functions. You already know that you must use pointers if you want a function to affect variables in the calling function. The second use is in functions designed to manipulate arrays. Let's look at another programming example using functions and arrays.

Protecting Array Contents

When you write a function that processes a fundamental type, such as `int`, you have a choice of passing the `int` by value or of passing a pointer-to-`int`. The usual rule is to pass quantities by value unless the program needs to alter the value, in which case you pass a pointer. Arrays don't give you that choice; you *must* pass a pointer. The reason is efficiency. If a function passed an array by value, it would have to allocate enough space to hold a copy of the original array and then copy all the data from the original array to the new array. It is much quicker to pass the address of the array and have the function work with the original data.

This technique can cause problems. The reason C ordinarily passes data by value is to preserve the integrity of the data. If a function works with a copy of the original data, it won't accidentally modify the original data. But, because array-processing functions do work with the original data, they *can* modify the array. Sometimes that's desirable. For example, here's a function that adds the same value to each member of an array:

```
void add_to(double ar[], int n, double val)
{
    int i;
    for( i = 0; i < n; i++)
        ar[i] += val;
}
```

Therefore, the function call

```
add_to(prices, 100, 2.50);
```

causes each element in the `prices` array to be replaced by a value larger by 2.5; this function modifies the contents of the array. It can do so because, by working with pointers, the function uses the original data.

Other functions, however, do not have the intent of modifying data. The following function, for example, is intended to find the sum of the array's contents; it shouldn't change the array. However, because `ar` is really a pointer, a programming error could lead to the original data being corrupted. Here, for example, the expression `ar[i]++` results in each element having 1 added to its value:

```
int sum(int ar[], int n)  // faulty code
{
    int i;
    int total = 0;

    for( i = 0; i < n; i++)
        total += ar[i]++;   // error increments each element
    return total;
}
```

Using `const` with Formal Parameters

With K&R C, the only way to avoid this sort of error is to be vigilant. With ANSI C, there is an alternative. If a function's intent is that it not change the contents of the array, use the keyword const when declaring the formal parameter in the prototype and in the function definition. For example, the prototype and definition for sum() should look like this:

```
int sum(const int ar[], int n);  /* prototype */

int sum(const int ar[], int n)   /* definition */
{
    int i;
    int total = 0;

    for( i = 0; i < n; i++)
        total += ar[i];
    return total;
}
```

This tells the compiler that the function should treat the array pointed to by ar as though the array contains constant data. Then, if you accidentally use an expression such as ar[i]++, the compiler can catch it and generate an error message, telling you that the function is attempting to alter constant data.

It's important to understand that using const this way does not require that the original array *be* constant; it just says that the function has to treat the array *as though* it were constant. Using const this way provides the protection for arrays that passing by value provides for fundamental types; it prevents a function from modifying data in the calling function. In general, if you write a function intended to modify an array, don't use const when declaring the array parameter. If you write a function not intended to modify an array, do use const when declaring the array parameter.

In the program shown in Listing 10.14, one function displays an array and one function multiplies each element of an array by a given value. Because the first function should not alter the array, it uses const. Because the second function has the intent of modifying the array, it doesn't use const.

LISTING 10.14   The arf.c Program

```
/* arf.c -- array functions */
#include <stdio.h>
#define SIZE 5
void show_array(const double ar[], int n);
void mult_array(double ar[], int n, double mult);
int main(void)
{
    double dip[SIZE] = {20.0, 17.66, 8.2, 15.3, 22.22};

    printf("The original dip array:\n");
    show_array(dip, SIZE);
    mult_array(dip, SIZE, 2.5);
    printf("The dip array after calling mult_array():\n");
    show_array(dip, SIZE);
```

LISTING 10.14   Continued

```
        return 0;
}

/* displays array contents */
void show_array(const double ar[], int n)
{
    int i;

    for (i = 0; i < n; i++)
        printf("%8.3f ", ar[i]);
    putchar('\n');
}

/* multiplies each array member by the same multiplier */
void mult_array(double ar[], int n, double mult)
{
    int i;

    for (i = 0; i < n; i++)
        ar[i] *= mult;
}
```

Here is the output:

```
The original dip array:
  20.000    17.660     8.200    15.300    22.220
The dip array after calling mult_array():
  50.000    44.150    20.500    38.250    55.550
```

Note that both functions are type `void`. The `mult_array()` function does provide new values to the `dip` array, but not by using the `return` mechanism.

More About `const`

Earlier, you saw that you can use `const` to create symbolic constants:

```
const double PI = 3.14159;
```

That was something you could do with the `#define` directive, too, but `const` additionally lets you create constant arrays, constant pointers, and pointers to constants.

Listing 10.4 showed how to use the `const` keyword to protect an array:

```
#define MONTHS 12
...
const int days[MONTHS] = {31,28,31,30,31,30,31,31,30,31,30,31};
```

If the program code subsequently tries to alter the array, you'll get a compile-time error message:

```
days[9] = 44;    /* compile error */
```

Pointers to constants can't be used to change values. Consider the following code:

```
double rates[5] = {88.99, 100.12, 59.45, 183.11, 340.5};
const double * pd = rates;    // pd points to beginning of the array
```

The second line of code declares that the type `double` value to which `pd` points is a `const`. That means you can't use `pd` to change pointed-to values:

```
*pd = 29.89;      // not allowed
pd[2] = 222.22;   // not allowed
rates[0] = 99.99; // allowed because rates is not const
```

Whether you use pointer notation or array notation, you are not allowed to use `pd` to change the value of pointed-to data. Note, however, that because `rates` was not declared as a constant, you can still use `rates` to change values. Also, note that you can make `pd` point somewhere else:

```
pd++;      /* make pd point to rates[1] -- allowed */
```

A pointer-to-constant is normally used as a function parameter to indicate that the function won't use the pointer to change data. For example, the `show_array()` function from Listing 10.14 could have been prototyped as

```
void show_array(const double *ar, int n);
```

There are some rules you should know about pointer assignments and `const`. First, it's valid to assign the address of either constant data or nonconstant data to a pointer-to-constant:

```
double rates[5] = {88.99, 100.12, 59.45, 183.11, 340.5};
const double locked[4] = {0.08, 0.075, 0.0725, 0.07};
const double * pc = rates;    // valid
pc = locked;                  // valid
pc = &rates[3];               // valid
```

However, only the addresses of nonconstant data can be assigned to regular pointers:

```
double rates[5] = {88.99, 100.12, 59.45, 183.11, 340.5};
const double locked[4] = {0.08, 0.075, 0.0725, 0.07};
double * pnc = rates;         // valid
pnc = locked;                 // not valid
pnc = &rates[3];              // valid
```

This is a reasonable rule. Otherwise, you could use the pointer to change data that was supposed to be constant.

A practical consequence of these rules is that a function such as `show_array()` can accept the names of regular arrays *and* of constant arrays as actual arguments, because either can be assigned to a pointer-to-constant:

```
show_array(rates, 5);    // valid
show_array(locked, 4);   // valid
```

A function such as `mult_array()`, however, can't accept the name of a constant array as an argument:

```
mult_array(rates, 5, 1.2);    // valid
mult_array(locked, 4, 1.2);   // not allowed
```

Therefore, using `const` in a function parameter definition not only protects data, it also allows the function to work with arrays that have been declared `const`.

There are more possible uses of `const`. For example, you can declare and initialize a pointer so that it can't be made to point elsewhere. The trick is the placement of the keyword `const`:

```
double rates[5] = {88.99, 100.12, 59.45, 183.11, 340.5};
double * const pc = rates;    // pc points to beginning of the array
pc = &rates[2];               // not allowed
*pc = 92.99;                  // ok -- changes rates[0]
```

Such a pointer can still be used to change values, but it can point only to the location originally assigned to it.

Finally, you can use `const` twice to create a pointer that can neither change where it's pointing nor change the value to which it points:

```
double rates[5] = {88.99, 100.12, 59.45, 183.11, 340.5};
const double * const pc = rates;
pc = &rates[2];               // not allowed
*pc = 92.99;                  // not allowed
```

Pointers and Multidimensional Arrays

How do pointers relate to multidimensional arrays? And why would you want to know? Functions that work with multidimensional arrays do so with pointers, so you need some further pointer background before working with such functions. As to the first question, let's look at some examples now to find the answer. To simplify the discussion, let's use a small array. Suppose you have this declaration:

```
int zippo[4][2];  /* an array of arrays of ints */
```

Then `zippo`, being the name of an array, is the address of the first element of the array. In this case, the first element of `zippo` is itself an array of two `int`s, so `zippo` is the address of an array of two `int`s. Let's analyze that further in terms of pointer properties:

- Because `zippo` is the address of the array's first element, `zippo` has the same value as `&zippo[0]`. Next, `zippo[0]` is itself an array of two integers, so `zippo[0]` has the same value as `&zippo[0][0]`, the address of its first element, an `int`. In short, `zippo[0]` is the address of an `int`-sized object, and `zippo` is the address of a two-`int`-sized object. Because both the integer and the array of two integers begin at the same location, both `zippo` and `zippo[0]` have the same numeric value.

- Adding 1 to a pointer or address yields a value larger by the size of the referred-to object. In this respect, `zippo` and `zippo[0]` differ, because `zippo` refers to an object two `int`s in size, and `zippo[0]` refers to an object one `int` in size. Therefore, `zippo + 1` has a different value from `zippo[0] + 1`.

- Dereferencing a pointer or an address (applying the `*` operator or else the `[ ]` operator with an index) yields the value represented by the referred-to object. Because `zippo[0]` is the address of its first element, (zippo[0][0]), *(zippo[0]) represents the value stored in zippo[0][0], an int value. Similarly, *zippo represents the value of its first element, zippo[0], but zippo[0] itself is the address of an int. It's the address &zippo[0][0], so *zippo is &zippo[0][0]. Applying the dereferencing operator to both expressions implies that **zippo equals *&zippo[0][0], which reduces to zippo[0][0], an int. In short, zippo is the address of an address and must be dereferenced twice to get an ordinary value. An address of an address or a pointer of a pointer is an example of *double indirection*.

Clearly, increasing the number of array dimensions increases the complexity of the pointer view. At this point, most students of C begin realizing why pointers are considered one of the more difficult aspects of the language. You might want to study the preceding points carefully and see how they are illustrated in Listing 10.15, which displays some address values and array contents.

LISTING 10.15   The zippo1.c Program

```
/* zippo1.c -- zippo info */
#include <stdio.h>
int main(void)
{
    int zippo[4][2] = { {2,4}, {6,8}, {1,3}, {5, 7} };

    printf("   zippo = %p,    zippo + 1 = %p\n",
                zippo,           zippo + 1);
    printf("zippo[0] = %p, zippo[0] + 1 = %p\n",
               zippo[0],       zippo[0] + 1);
    printf("  *zippo = %p,    *zippo + 1 = %p\n",
                *zippo,          *zippo + 1);
    printf("zippo[0][0] = %d\n", zippo[0][0]);
    printf("  *zippo[0] = %d\n", *zippo[0]);
    printf("    **zippo = %d\n", **zippo);
    printf("      zippo[2][1] = %d\n", zippo[2][1]);
    printf("*(*(zippo+2) + 1) = %d\n", *(*(zippo+2) + 1));

    return 0;
}
```

Here is the output for one system:

```
   zippo = 0x0064fd38,    zippo + 1 = 0x0064fd40
zippo[0] = 0x0064fd38, zippo[0] + 1 = 0x0064fd3c
  *zippo = 0x0064fd38,    *zippo + 1 = 0x0064fd3c
zippo[0][0] = 2
  *zippo[0] = 2
    **zippo = 2
      zippo[1][2] = 3
*(*(zippo+1) + 2) = 3
```

Other systems might display different address values, but the relationships will be the same as described here. The output shows that the address of the two-dimensional array, zippo, and the address of the one-dimensional array, `zippo[0]`, are the same. Each is the address of the corresponding array's first element, and this is the same numerically as `&zippo[0][0]`.

Nonetheless, there is a difference. On our system, `int` is 4 bytes. As discussed earlier, `zippo[0]` points to a 4-byte data object. Adding 1 to `zippo[0]` should produce a value larger by 4, which it does. The name `zippo` is the address of an array of two `int`s, so it identifies an 8-byte data object. Therefore, adding 1 to `zippo` should produce an address 8 bytes larger, which it does.

The program shows that `zippo[0]` and `*zippo` are identical, and they should be. Next, it shows that the name of a two-dimensional array has to be dereferenced twice to get a value stored in the array. This can be done by using the indirection operator (`*`) twice or by using the bracket operator (`[ ]`) twice. (It also can be done by using one `*` and one set of `[ ]`, but let's not get carried away by all the possibilities.)

In particular, note that the pointer notation equivalent of `zippo[2][1]` is `*(*(zippo+2) + 1)`. You probably should make the effort at least once in your life to break this down. Let's build up the expression in steps:

`zippo`	←the address of the first two-`int` element
`zippo+2`	←the address of the third two-`int` element
`*(zippo+2)`	←the third element, a two-`int` array, hence the address of its first element, an `int`
`*(zippo+2) + 1`	←the address of the second element of the two-`int` array, also an `int`
`*(*(zippo+2) + 1)`	←the value of the second `int` in the third row (`zippo[2][1]`)

The point of the baroque display of pointer notation is not that you can use it instead of the simpler `zippo[2][1]` but that, if you happen to have a pointer to a two-dimensional array and want to extract a value, you can use the simpler array notation rather than pointer notation.

Figure 10.5 provides another view of the relationships among array addresses, array contents, and pointers.

FIGURE 10.5
An array of arrays.

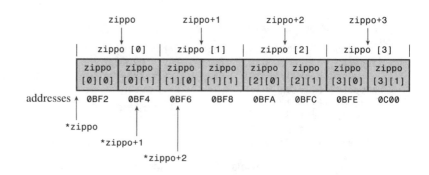

Pointers to Multidimensional Arrays

How would you declare a pointer variable `pz` that can point to a two-dimensional array such as `zippo`? Such a pointer could be used, for example, in writing a function to deal with `zippo`-like arrays. Will the type pointer-to-`int` suffice? No. That type is compatible with `zippo[0]`, which points to a single `int`. But `zippo` is the address of its first element, which is an array of two `int`s. Hence, `pz` must point to an array of two `int`s, not to a single `int`. Here is what you can do:

```
int (* pz)[2];  // pz points to an array of 2 ints
```

This statement says that `pz` is a pointer to an array of two `int`s. Why the parentheses? Well, [ ] has a higher precedence than `*`. Therefore, with a declaration such as

```
int * pax[2];
```

you apply the brackets first, making `pax` an array of two somethings. Next, you apply the `*`, making `pax` an array of two pointers. Finally, use the `int`, making `pax` an array of two pointers to `int`. This declaration creates *two* pointers to single `int`s, but the original version uses parentheses to apply the `*` first, creating *one* pointer to an array of two `int`s. Listing 10.16 shows how you can use such a pointer just like the original array.

LISTING 10.16   The `zippo2.c` Program

```c
/* zippo2.c -- zippo info via a pointer variable */
#include <stdio.h>
int main(void)
{
    int zippo[4][2] = { {2,4}, {6,8}, {1,3}, {5, 7} };
    int (*pz)[2];
    pz = zippo;

    printf("   pz = %p,     pz + 1 = %p\n",
             pz,            pz + 1);
    printf("pz[0] = %p, pz[0] + 1 = %p\n",
           pz[0],       pz[0] + 1);
    printf("  *pz = %p,    *pz + 1 = %p\n",
            *pz,          *pz + 1);
    printf("pz[0][0] = %d\n", pz[0][0]);
    printf("  *pz[0] = %d\n", *pz[0]);
    printf("    **pz = %d\n", **pz);
    printf("     pz[2][1] = %d\n", pz[2][1]);
    printf("*(*(pz+2) + 1) = %d\n", *(*(pz+2) + 1));

    return 0;
}
```

Here is the new output:

```
pz = 0x0064fd38,    pz + 1 = 0x0064fd40
pz[0] = 0x0064fd38, pz[0] + 1 = 0x0064fd3c
  *pz = 0x0064fd38,   *pz + 1 = 0x0064fd3c
pz[0][0] = 2
  *pz[0] = 2
    **pz = 2
      pz[2][1] = 3
*(*(pz+2) + 1) = 3
```

Again, you might get different addresses, but the relationships will be the same. As promised, you can use notation such as `pz[2][1]`, even though `pz` is a pointer, not an array name. More generally, you can represent individual elements by using array notation or pointer notation with either an array name or a pointer:

```
zippo[m][n] == *(*(zippo + m) + n)
pz[m][n] == *(*(pz + m) + n)
```

Pointer Compatibility

The rules for assigning one pointer to another are tighter than the rules for numeric types. For example, you can assign an `int` value to a `double` variable without using a type conversion, but you can't do the same for pointers to these two types:

```
int n = 5;
double x;
int * p1 = &n;
double * pd   = &x;
x = n;                  // implicit type conversion
pd = p1;                // compile-time error
```

These restrictions extend to more complex types. Suppose we have the following declarations:

```
int * pt;
int (*pa)[3];
int ar1[2][3];
int ar2[3][2];
int **p2;               // a pointer to a pointer
```

Then we have the following:

```
pt = &ar1[0][0];      // both pointer-to-int
pt = ar1[0];          // both pointer-to-int
pt = ar1;             // not valid
pa = ar1;             // both pointer-to-int[3]
pa = ar2;             // not valid
p2 = &pt;             // both pointer-to-int *
*p2 = ar2[0];         // both pointer-to-int
p2 = ar2;             // not valid
```

Notice that the nonvalid assignments all involve two pointers that don't point to the same type. For example, `pt` points to a single `int`, but `ar1` points to an array of three `ints`. Similarly, pa points to an array of two ints, so it is compatible with ar1, but not with ar2, which points to an array of two ints.

The last two examples are somewhat tricky. The variable p2 is a pointer-to-pointer-to-int, whereas ar2 is a pointer-to-array-of-two-ints (or, more concisely, pointer-to-int[2]). So p2 and ar2 are of different types, and you can't assign ar2 to p2. But *p2 is type pointer-to-int, making it compatible with ar2[0]. Recall that ar2[0] is a pointer to its first element, ar2[0][0], making ar2[0] type pointer-to-int also.

In general, multiple indirection is tricky. For instance, consider the next snippet of code:

```
int * p1;
const int * p2;
const int ** pp2;
p1 = p2;   // not valid -- assigning const to non-const
p2 = p1;   // valid     -- assigning non-const to const
pp2 = &p1; // not valid -- assigning non-const to const
```

As you saw earlier, assigning a const pointer to a non-const pointer is invalid, because you could use the new pointer to alter const data. But assigning a non-const pointer to a const pointer is okay, provided that you're dealing with just one level of indirection:

```
p2 = p1;   // valid     -- assigning non-const to const
```

But such assignments no longer are safe when you go to two levels of indirection. If it were allowed, you could do something like this:

```
const int **pp2;
int *p1;
const int n = 13;
pp2 = &p1; // not allowed, but suppose it were
*pp2 = &n; // valid, both const, but sets p1 to point at n
*p1 = 10;  // valid, but changes const n
```

Functions and Multidimensional Arrays

If you want to write functions that process two-dimensional arrays, you need to understand pointers well enough to make the proper declarations for function arguments. In the function body itself, you can usually get by with array notation.

Let's write a function to deal with two-dimensional arrays. One possibility is to use a for loop to apply a one-dimensional array function to each row of the two-dimensional array. That is, you could do something like the following:

```
int junk[3][4] = { {2,4,5,8}, {3,5,6,9}, {12,10,8,6} };
int i, j;
int total = 0;
for (i = 0; i < 3 ; i++)
   total += sum(junk[i], 4);  // junk[i] -- one-dimensional array
```

Remember, if junk is a two-dimensional array, junk[i] is a one-dimensional array, which you can visualize as being one row of the two-dimensional array. Here, the sum() function calculates the subtotal of each row of the two-dimensional array, and the for loop adds up these subtotals.

However, this approach loses track of the column-and-row information. In this application (summing all), that information is unimportant, but suppose each row represented a year and each column a month. Then you might want a function to, say, total up individual columns. In that case, the function should have the row and column information available. This can be accomplished by declaring the right kind of formal variable so that the function can pass the array properly. In this case, the array `junk` is an array of three arrays of four `int`s. As the earlier discussion pointed out, that means `junk` is a pointer to an array of four `int`s. You can declare a function parameter of this type like this:

```
void somefunction( int (* pt)[4] );
```

Alternatively, if (and only if) `pt` is a formal parameter to a function, you can declare it as follows:

```
void somefunction( int pt[][4] );
```

Note that the first set of brackets is empty. The empty brackets identify `pt` as being a pointer. Such a variable can then be used in the same way as `junk`. That is what we have done in the next example, shown in Listing 10.17. Notice that the listing exhibits three equivalent alternatives for the prototype syntax.

LISTING 10.17   The `array2d.c` Program

```
// array2d.c -- functions for 2d arrays
#include <stdio.h>
#define ROWS 3
#define COLS 4
void sum_rows(int ar[][COLS], int rows);
void sum_cols(int [][COLS], int );     // ok to omit names
int sum2d(int (*ar)[COLS], int rows); // another syntax
int main(void)
{
    int junk[ROWS][COLS] = {
            {2,4,6,8},
            {3,5,7,9},
            {12,10,8,6}
    };

    sum_rows(junk, ROWS);
    sum_cols(junk, ROWS);
    printf("Sum of all elements = %d\n", sum2d(junk, ROWS));

    return 0;
}

void sum_rows(int ar[][COLS], int rows)
{
    int r;
    int c;
    int tot;
```

LISTING 10.17 Continued

```c
    for (r = 0; r < rows; r++)
    {
        tot = 0;
        for (c = 0; c < COLS; c++)
            tot += ar[r][c];
        printf("row %d: sum = %d\n", r, tot);
    }
}

void sum_cols(int ar[][COLS], int rows)
{
    int r;
    int c;
    int tot;

    for (c = 0; c < COLS; c++)
    {
        tot = 0;
        for (r = 0; r < rows; r++)
            tot += ar[r][c];
        printf("col %d: sum = %d\n", c, tot);
    }
}

int sum2d(int ar[][COLS], int rows)
{
    int r;
    int c;
    int tot = 0;

    for (r = 0; r < rows; r++)
        for (c = 0; c < COLS; c++)
            tot += ar[r][c];

    return tot;
}
```

Here is the output:

```
row 0: sum = 20
row 1: sum = 24
row 2: sum = 36
col 0: sum = 17
col 1: sum = 19
col 2: sum = 21
col 3: sum = 23
Sum of all elements = 80
```

The program in Listing 10.17 passes as arguments the name junk, which is a pointer to the first element, a subarray, and the symbolic constant ROWS, representing 3, the number of rows. Each function then treats ar as an array of arrays of four ints. The number of columns is built in to the function, but the number of rows is left open. The same function will work with, say, a 12×4 array if 12 is passed as the number of rows. That's because `rows` is the number of elements; however, because each element is an array, or row, `rows` becomes the number of rows.

Note that `ar` is used in the same fashion as `junk` is used in `main()`. This is possible because `ar` and `junk` are the same type: pointer-to-array-of-four-`int`s.

Be aware that the following declaration will not work properly:

```
int sum2(int ar[][], int rows); // faulty declaration
```

Recall that the compiler converts array notation to pointer notation. This means, for example, that `ar[1]` will become `ar+1`. For the compiler to evaluate this, it needs to know the size object to which `ar` points. The declaration

```
int sum2(int ar[][4], int rows); // valid declaration
```

says that `ar` points to an array of four `int`s (hence, to an object 16 bytes long on our system), so `ar+1` means "add 16 bytes to the address." With the empty-bracket version, the compiler would not know what to do.

You can also include a size in the other bracket pair, as shown here, but the compiler ignores it:

```
int sum2(int ar[3][4], int rows); // valid declaration, 3 ignored
```

This is convenient for those who use `typedef`s:

```
typedef int arr4[4];            // arr4 array of 4 int
typedef arr4 arr3x4[3];         // arr3x4 array of 3 arr4
int sum2(arr3x4 ar, int rows);     // same as next declaration
int sum2(int ar[3][4], int rows); // same as next declaration
int sum2(int ar[][4], int rows);  // standard form
```

In general, to declare a pointer corresponding to an *N*-dimensional array, you must supply values for all but the leftmost set of brackets:

```
int sum4d(int ar[][12][20][30], int rows);
```

That's because the first set of brackets indicates a pointer, whereas the rest of the brackets describe the type of data object being pointed to, as the following equivalent prototype illustrates:

```
int sum4d(int (*ar)[12][20][30], int rows);  // ar a pointer
```

Here, `ar` points to a 12×20×30 array of `int`s.

Variable-Length Arrays (VLAs)

You might have noticed an oddity about functions dealing with two-dimensional arrays: You can describe the number of rows with a function parameter, but the number of columns is built in to the function. For example, look at this definition:

```
#define COLS 4
int sum2d(int ar[][COLS], int rows)
{
    int r;
    int c;
    int tot = 0;

    for (r = 0; r < rows; r++)
        for (c = 0; c < COLS; c++)
            tot += ar[r][c];
    return tot;
}
```

Next, suppose the following arrays have been declared:

```
int array1[5][4];
int array2[100][4];
int array3[2][4];
```

You can use the `sum2d()` function with any of these arrays:

```
tot = sum2d(array1, 5);   // sum a 5 x 4 array
tot = sum2d(array2, 100); // sum a 100 x 4 array
tot = sum2d(array3, 2);   // sum a 2 x 4 array
```

That's because the number of rows is passed to the `rows` parameter, a variable. But if you wanted to sum a 6×5 array, you would need to use a new function, one for which `COLS` is defined to be **5**. This behavior is a result of the fact that you have to use constants for array dimensions; therefore, you can't replace `COLS` with a variable.

If you really want to create a single function that will work with any size two-dimensional array, you can, but it's awkward to do. (You have to pass the array as a one-dimensional array and have the function calculate where each row starts.) Furthermore, this technique doesn't mesh smoothly with FORTRAN subroutines, which do allow one to specify both dimensions in a function call. FORTRAN might be a hoary old programming language, but over the decades experts in the field of numerical calculations have developed many useful computational libraries in FORTRAN. C is being positioned to take over from FORTRAN, so the ability to convert FORTRAN libraries with a minimum of fuss is useful.

This need was the primary impulse for C99 introducing variable-length arrays, which allow you to use variables when dimensioning an array. For example, you can do this:

```
int quarters = 4;
int regions = 5;
double sales[regions][quarters]; // a VLA
```

As mentioned earlier, VLAs have some restrictions. They need to have the automatic storage class, which means they are declared either in a function or as function parameters. Also, you can't initialize them in a declaration.

VLAs Do Not Change Size

The term *variable* in variable-length array does not mean that you can modify the length of the array after you create it. Once created, a VLA keeps the same size. What the term *variable* does mean is that you can use a variable when specifying the array dimensions.

Because VLAs are a new addition to the language, support for them is spotty at the present. Let's look at a simple example that shows how to write a function that will sum the contents of any two-dimensional array of `int`s.

First, here's how to declare a function with a two-dimensional VLA argument:

```
int sum2d(int rows, int cols, int ar[rows][cols]);   // ar a VLA
```

Note that the first two parameters (`rows` and `cols`) are used as dimensions for declaring the array parameter `ar`. Because the `ar` declaration uses `rows` and `cols`, they have to be declared before `ar` in the parameter list. Therefore, the following prototype is in error:

```
int sum2d(int ar[rows][cols], int rows, int cols); // invalid order
```

The C99 standard says you can omit names from the prototype; but in that case, you need to replace the omitted dimensions with asterisks:

```
int sum2d(int, int, int ar[*][*]);   // ar a VLA, names omitted
```

Second, here's how to define the function:

```
int sum2d(int rows, int cols, int ar[rows][cols])
{
    int r;
    int c;
    int tot = 0;

    for (r = 0; r < rows; r++)
        for (c = 0; c < cols; c++)
            tot += ar[r][c];
    return tot;
}
```

Aside from the new function header, the only difference from the classic C version of this function (Listing 10.17) is that the constant `COLS` has been replaced with the variable `cols`. The VLA in the function header is what makes it possible to make this change. Also, having variables that represent both the number of rows and columns lets you use the new `sum2d()` with any size of two-dimensional array of `int`s. Listing 10.18 illustrates this point. However, it does require a C compiler that implements the new VLA feature. It also demonstrates that this VLA-based function can be used with either traditional C arrays or with a variable-length array.

LISTING 10.18   The vararr2d.c Program

```
//vararr2d.c -- functions using VLAs
#include <stdio.h>
#define ROWS 3
#define COLS 4
int sum2d(int rows, int cols, int ar[rows][cols]);
int main(void)
{
    int i, j;
    int rs = 3;
    int cs = 10;
    int junk[ROWS][COLS] = {
            {2,4,6,8},
            {3,5,7,9},
            {12,10,8,6}
    };

    int morejunk[ROWS-1][COLS+2] = {
            {20,30,40,50,60,70},
            {5,6,7,8,9,10}
    };

    int varr[rs][cs];   // VLA

    for (i = 0; i < rs; i++)
        for (j = 0; j < cs; j++)
            varr[i][j] = i * j + j;

    printf("3x5 array\n");
    printf("Sum of all elements = %d\n",
            sum2d(ROWS, COLS, junk));

    printf("2x6 array\n");
    printf("Sum of all elements = %d\n",
            sum2d(ROWS-1, COLS+2, morejunk));

    printf("3x10 VLA\n");
    printf("Sum of all elements = %d\n",
            sum2d(rs, cs, varr));

    return 0;
}

// function with a VLA parameter
int sum2d(int rows, int cols, int ar[rows][cols])
{
    int r;
    int c;
    int tot = 0;
```

LISTING 10.18   *Continued*

```
        for (r = 0; r < rows; r++)
            for (c = 0; c < cols; c++)
                tot += ar[r][c];

        return tot;
    }
```

Here is the output:

```
3x5 array
Sum of all elements = 80
2x6 array
Sum of all elements = 315
3x10 VLA
Sum of all elements = 270
```

One point to note is that a VLA declaration in a function definition parameter list doesn't actually create an array. Just as with the old syntax, the VLA name really is a pointer. This means a function with a VLA parameter actually works with the data in the original array, and therefore has the ability to modify the array passed as an argument. The following snippet points out when a pointer is declared and when an actual array is declared:

```
    int thing[10][6];
    twoset(10,6,thing);
    ...
}
void twoset (int n, int m, int ar[n][m])   // ar a pointer to
                                           // an array of m ints
{
    int temp[n][m];       // temp an n x m array of int
    temp[0][0] = 2;       // set an element of temp to 2
    ar[0][0] = 2;         // set thing[0][0] to 2
}
```

When `twoset()` is called as shown, `ar` becomes a pointer to `thing[0]`, and `temp` is created as a 10×6 array. Because both `ar` and `thing` are pointers to `thing[0]`, `ar[0][0]` accesses the same data location as `thing[0][0]`.

Variable-length arrays also allow for dynamic memory allocation. This means you can specify the size of the array while the program is running. Regular C arrays have static memory allocation, meaning the size of the array is determined at compile time. That's because the array sizes, being constants, are known to the compiler. Chapter 12 will take a look at dynamic memory allocation.

Compound Literals

Suppose you want to pass a value to a function with an `int` parameter; you can pass an `int` variable, but you also can pass an `int` constant, such as **5**. Before C99, the situation for a function with an array argument was different; you could pass an array, but there was no equivalent to an array constant. C99 changes that with the addition of *compound literals*. Literals are constants that aren't symbolic. For example, 5 is a type `int` literal, 81.3 is a type `double` literal, 'Y' is a type `char` literal, and "elephant" is a string literal. The committee that developed the C99 standard concluded that it would be convenient to have compound literals that could represent the contents of arrays and of structures.

For arrays, a compound literal looks like an array initialization list preceded by a type name that is enclosed in parentheses. For example, here's an ordinary array declaration:

```
int diva[2] = {10, 20};
```

And here's a compound literal that creates a nameless array containing the same two `int` values:

```
(int [2]){10, 20}    // a compound literal
```

Note that the type name is what you would get if you removed `diva` from the earlier declaration, leaving `int [2]` behind.

Just as you can leave out the array size if you initialize a named array, you can omit it from a compound literal, and the compiler will count how many elements are present:

```
(int []){50, 20, 90}    // a compound literal with 3 elements
```

Because these compound literals are nameless, you can't just create them in one statement and then use them later. Instead, you have to use them somehow when you make them. One way is to use a pointer to keep track of the location. That is, you can do something like this:

```
int * pt1;
pt1 = (int [2]) {10, 20};
```

Note that this literal constant is identified as an array of `int`s. Like the name of an array, this translates to the address of the first element, so it can be assigned to a pointer-to-`int`. You then can use the pointer later. For example, `*pt1` would be 10 in this case, and `pt1[1]` would be 20.

Another thing you could do with a compound literal is pass it as an actual argument to a function with a matching formal parameter:

```
int sum(int ar[], int n);
...
int total3;
total3 = sum((int []){4,4,4,5,5,5}, 6);
```

Here, the first argument is a six-element array of `int`s that acts like the address of the first element, just as an array name does. This kind of use, in which you pass information to a function without having to create an array first, is a typical use for compound literals.

You can extend the technique to two-dimensional arrays, and beyond. Here, for example, is how to create a two-dimensional array of `int`s and store the address:

```
int (*pt2)[4];    // declare a pointer to an array of 4-int arrays
pt2 = (int [2][4]) { {1,2,3,-9}, {4,5,6,-8} };
```

Here, the type is `int [2][4]`, a 2×4 array of `int`s.

Listing 10.19 incorporates these examples into a complete program.

LISTING 10.19   The flc.c Program

```c
// flc.c -- funny-looking constants
#include <stdio.h>
#define COLS 4
int sum2d(int ar[][COLS], int rows);
int sum(int ar[], int n);
int main(void)
{
    int total1, total2, total3;
    int * pt1;
    int (*pt2)[COLS];

    pt1 = (int [2]) {10, 20};
    pt2 = (int [2][COLS]) { {1,2,3,-9}, {4,5,6,-8} };

    total1 = sum(pt1, 2);
    total2 = sum2d(pt2, 2);
    total3 = sum((int []){4,4,4,5,5,5}, 6);
    printf("total1 = %d\n", total1);
    printf("total2 = %d\n", total2);
    printf("total3 = %d\n", total3);

    return 0;
}

int sum(int ar[], int n)
{
    int i;
    int total = 0;

    for( i = 0; i < n; i++)
        total += ar[i];

    return total;
}

int sum2d(int ar[][COLS], int rows)
{
    int r;
    int c;
    int tot = 0;

    for (r = 0; r < rows; r++)
        for (c = 0; c < COLS; c++)
            tot += ar[r][c];

    return tot;
}
```

You'll need a compiler that accepts this C99 addition (and, at this time, many compiler's don't). Here is the output:

```
total1 = 30
total2 = 4
total3 = 27
```

Key Concepts

When you need to store many items, all of the same kind, an array might be the answer. C refers to arrays as *derived types* because they are built on other types. That is, you don't simply declare an array. Instead, you declare an array-of-int or an array-of-float, or an array of some other type. That other type can itself be an array type, in which case, you get an array of arrays, or a two-dimensional array.

It's often advantageous to write functions to process arrays; that helps modularize a program by locating specific tasks in specific functions. It's important to realize that when you use an array name as an actual argument, you're not passing the entire array to the function; you are just passing the address of the array (hence, the corresponding formal parameter is a pointer). To process the array, the function has to know where the array is and how many elements the array has. The array address provides the "where"; the "how many" either has to be built in to the function or be passed as a separate argument. The second approach is more general so that the same function can work with arrays of different sizes.

The connection between arrays and pointers is an intimate one, and you can often represent the same operation using either array notation or pointer notation. It's this connection that allows you to use array notation in an array-processing function even though the formal parameter is a pointer, not an array.

You must specify the size of a conventional C array with a constant expression, so the size is determined at compile time. C99 offers the variable-length array alternative for which the size specifier can be a variable. This allows you to delay specifying the size of a VLA until the program is running.

Summary

An *array* is a set of elements that all have the same data type. Array elements are stored sequentially in memory and are accessed by using an integer index (or *offset*). In C, the first element of an array has an index of 0, so the final element in an array of n elements has an index of n - 1. It's your responsibility to use array indices that are valid for the array, because neither the compiler nor the running program checks for this.

To declare a simple *one-dimensional* array, use this form:

```
type name[size];
```

Here, *type* is the data type for each and every element, *name* is the name of the array, and *size* is the number of elements. Traditionally, C has required that *size* be a constant integer expression. C99 allows you to use a nonconstant integer expression; in that case, the array is termed a variable-length array.

C interprets the name of an array to be the address of the first element of the array. In other terms, the name of an array is equivalent to a pointer to the first element. In general, arrays and pointers are closely connected. If `ar` is an array, then the expressions `ar[i]` and `*(ar + i)` are equivalent.

C does not enable entire arrays to be passed as function arguments, but you can pass the address of an array. The function can then use this address to manipulate the original array. If the intent of the function is not to modify the original array, you should use the **const** keyword when declaring the formal parameter representing the array. You can use either array notation or pointer notation in the called function. In either case, you're actually using a pointer variable.

Adding an integer to a pointer or incrementing a pointer changes the value of the pointer by the number of bytes of the object being pointed to. That is, if **pd** points to an 8-byte **double** value in an array, adding 1 to **pd** increases its value by 8 so that it will point to the next element of the array.

Two-dimensional arrays represent an array of arrays. For instance, the declaration

```
double sales[5][12];
```

creates an array called **sales** having five elements, each of which is an array of 12 **double**s. The first of these one-dimensional arrays can be referred to as **sales[0]**, the second as **sales[1]**, and so on, with each being an array of 12 **double**s. Use a second index to access a particular element in these arrays. For example, **sales[2][5]** is the sixth element of **sales[2]**, and **sales[2]** is the third element of **sales**.

The traditional C method for passing a multidimensional array to a function is to pass the array name, which is an address, to a suitably typed pointer parameter. The declaration for this pointer should specify all the dimensions of the array aside from the first; the dimension of the first parameter typically is passed as a second argument. For example, to process the previously mentioned **sales** array, the function prototype and function call would look like this:

```
void display(double ar[][12], int rows);
...
display(sales, 5);
```

Variable-length arrays provide a second syntax in which both array dimensions are passed as arguments. In this case, the function prototype and function call would look like this:

```
void display(int rows, int cols, double ar[rows][cols]);
...
display(5, 12, sales);
```

We've used **int** arrays and **double** arrays in this discussion, but the same concepts apply to other types. Character strings, however, have many special rules. This stems from the fact that the terminal null character in a string provides a way for functions to detect the end of a string without being passed a size. We will look at character strings in detail in Chapter 11, "Character Strings and String Functions."

Review Questions

1. What will this program print?

    ```c
    #include <stdio.h>
    int main(void)
    {
      int ref[] = {8, 4, 0, 2};
      int *ptr;
      int index;

      for (index = 0, ptr = ref; index < 4; index++, ptr++)
         printf("%d %d\n", ref[index], *ptr);
      return 0;
    }
    ```

2. In question 1, how many elements does `ref` have?

3. In question 1, `ref` is the address of what? What about `ref + 1`? What does `++ref` point to?

4. What is the value of `*ptr` and of `*(ptr + 2)` in each case?

    a.

    ```c
    int *ptr;
    int torf[2][2] = {12, 14, 16};
    ptr = torf[0];
    ```

    b.

    ```c
    int * ptr;
    int fort[2][2] = { {12}, {14,16} };
    ptr = fort[0];
    ```

5. What is the value of `**ptr` and of `**(ptr + 1)` in each case?

    a.

    ```c
    int (*ptr)[2];
    int torf[2][2] = {12, 14, 16};
    ptr = torf;
    ```

    b.

    ```c
    int (*ptr)[2];
    int fort[2][2] = { {12}, {14,16} };
    ptr = fort;
    ```

6. Suppose you have the following declaration:

   `int grid[30][100];.`

   a. Express the address of `grid[22][56]` one way.

   b. Express the address of `grid[22][0]` two ways.

   c. Express the address of `grid[0][0]` three ways.

7. Create an appropriate declaration for each of the following variables:

   a. `digits` is an array of 10 `ints`.

   b. `rates` is an array of six `floats`.

   c. `mat` is an array of three arrays of five integers.

   d. `psa` is an array of 20 pointers to `char`.

   e. `pstr` is a pointer to an array of 20 `chars`.

8.   a. Declare an array of six `ints` and initialize it to the values 1, 2, 4, 8, 16, and 32.

   b. Use array notation to represent the third element (the one with the value 4) of the array in part a.

   c. Assuming C99 rules are in effect, declare an array of 100 `ints` and initialize it so that the last element is -1; don't worry about the other elements.

9. What is the index range for a 10-element array?

10. Suppose you have these declarations:

   ```
   float rootbeer[10], things[10][5], *pf, value = 2.2;
   int i = 3;
   ```

   Identify each of the following statements as valid or invalid:

   a. `rootbeer[2] = value;`

   b. `scanf("%f", &rootbeer );`

   c. `rootbeer = value;`

   d. `printf("%f", rootbeer);`

   e. `things[4][4] = rootbeer[3];`

   f. `things[5] = rootbeer;`

   g. `pf = value;`

   h. `pf = rootbeer;`

11. Declare an 800×600 array of `int`.

12. Here are three array declarations:

```
double trots[20];
short clops[10][30];
long shots[5][10][15];
```

   a. Show a function prototype and a function call for a traditional **void** function that processes **trots** and also for a C function using a VLA.

   b. Show a function prototype and a function call for a traditional **void** function that processes **clops** and also for a C function using a VLA.

   c. Show a function prototype and a function call for a traditional **void** function that processes **shots** and also for a C function using a VLA.

13. Here are two function prototypes:

```
void show(double ar[], int n);    // n is number of elements
void show2(double ar2[][3], int n);   // n is number of rows
```

   a. Show a function call that passes a compound literal containing the values **8**, **3**, **9**, and **2** to the **show()** function.

   b. Show a function call that passes a compound literal containing the values **8**, **3**, and **9** as the first row and the values **5**, **4**, and **1** as the second row to the **show2()** function.

Programming Exercises

1. Modify the rain program in Listing 10.7 so that it does the calculations using pointers instead of subscripts. (You still have to declare and initialize the array.)

2. Write a program that initializes an array-of-**double** and then copies the contents of the array into two other arrays. (All three arrays should be declared in the main program.) To make the first copy, use a function with array notation. To make the second copy, use a function with pointer notation and pointer incrementing. Have each function take as arguments the name of the target array and the number of elements to be copied. That is, the function calls would look like this, given the following declarations:

```
double source[5] = {1.1, 2.2, 3.3., 4.4, 5.5};
double target1[5];
double target2[5];
copy_arr(source, target1, 5);
copy_ptr(source, target1, 5);
```

3. Write a function that returns the largest value stored in an array-of-**int**. Test the function in a simple program.

4. Write a function that returns the index of the largest value stored in an array-of-**double**. Test the function in a simple program.

5. Write a function that returns the difference between the largest and smallest elements of an array-of-**double**. Test the function in a simple program.

6. Write a program that initializes a two-dimensional array-of-**double** and uses one of the copy functions from exercise 2 to copy it to a second two-dimensional array. (Because a two-dimensional array is an array of arrays, a one-dimensional copy function can be used with each subarray.)

7. Use a copy function from exercise 2 to copy the third through fifth elements of a seven-element array into a three-element array. The function itself need not be altered; just choose the right actual arguments. (The actual arguments need not be an array name and array size. They only have to be the address of an array element and a number of elements to be processed.)

8. Write a program that initializes a two-dimensional 3×5 array-of-**double** and uses a VLA-based function to copy it to a second two-dimensional array. Also provide a VLA-based function to display the contents of the two arrays. The two functions should be capable, in general, of processing arbitrary N×M arrays. (If you don't have access to a VLA-capable compiler, use the traditional C approach of functions that can process an N×5 array).

9. Write a function that sets each element in an array to the sum of the corresponding elements in two other arrays. That is, if array 1 has the values **2**, **4**, **5**, and **8** and array 2 has the values **1**, **0**, **4**, and **6**, the function assigns array 3 the values **3**, **4**, **9**, and **14**. The function should take three array names and an array size as arguments. Test the function in a simple program.

10. Write a program that declares a 3×5 array and initializes it to some values of your choice. Have the program print the values, double all the values, and then display the new values. Write a function to do the displaying and a second function to do the doubling. Have the functions take the array name and the number of rows as arguments.

11. Rewrite the rain program in Listing 10.7 so that the main tasks are performed by functions instead of in **main()**.

12. Write a program that prompts the user to enter three sets of five **double** numbers each. The program should accomplish all of the following:

    a. Store the information in a 3×5 array.

    b. Compute the average of each set of five values.

    c. Compute the average of all the values.

    d. Determine the largest value of the 15 values.

    e. Report the results.

    Each major task should be handled by a separate function using the traditional C approach to handling arrays. Accomplish task "b" by using a function that computes and returns the average of a one-dimensional array; use a loop to call this function three times. The other tasks should take the entire array as an argument, and the functions performing tasks "c" and "d" should return the answer to the calling program.

13. Do exercise 12, but use variable-length array function parameters.

CHAPTER 11

CHARACTER STRINGS AND STRING FUNCTIONS

You will learn about the following in this chapter:

- Functions:
  gets(), puts(), strcat(),
  strncat(), strcmp(), strncmp(),
  strcpy(), strncpy(), sprintf(),
  strchr()

- Creating and using strings

- Using several string and character
  functions from the C library and
  creating your own string functions

- Using command-line arguments

The character string is one of the most useful and important data types in C. You have been using character strings all along, but there still is much to learn about them. The C library provides a wide range of functions for reading and writing strings, copying strings, comparing strings, combining strings, searching strings, and more. This chapter will add these capabilities to your programming skills.

Representing Strings and String I/O

Of course, you already know the most basic fact: A *character string* is a char array terminated with a null character (\0). Therefore, what you've learned about arrays and pointers carries over to character strings. But because character strings are so commonly used, C provides many functions specifically designed to work with strings. This chapter discusses the nature of strings, how to declare and initialize strings, how to get them into and out of programs, and how to manipulate strings.

Listing 11.1 presents a busy program that illustrates several ways to set up, read, and print strings. It uses two new functions—gets(), which reads a string, and puts(), which prints a string. (You probably notice a family resemblance to getchar() and putchar().) The rest of the program should look fairly familiar.

LISTING 11.1   The `strings.c` Program

```c
// strings.c -- stringing the user along
#include <stdio.h>
#define MSG "You must have many talents. Tell me some."
                         // a symbolic string constant
#define LIM  5
#define LINELEN 81       // maximum string length + 1
int main(void)
{
    char name[LINELEN];
    char talents[LINELEN];
    int i;
                        // initializing a dimensioned
                        // char array
    const char m1[40] = "Limit yourself to one line's worth.";
                        // letting the compiler compute the
                        // array size
    const char m2[] = "If you can't think of anything, fake it.";
                        // initializing a pointer
    const char *m3 = "\nEnough about me -- what's your name?";
                        // initializing an array of
                        // string pointers
    const char *mytal[LIM] = {  // array of 5 pointers
            "Adding numbers swiftly",
            "Multiplying accurately", "Stashing data",
            "Following instructions to the letter",
            "Understanding the C language"
            };

    printf("Hi! I'm Clyde the Computer."
           " I have many talents.\n");
    printf("Let me tell you some of them.\n");
    puts("What were they? Ah, yes, here's a partial list.");
    for (i = 0; i < LIM; i++)
        puts(mytal[i]);    // print list of computer talents
    puts(m3);
    gets(name);
    printf("Well, %s, %s\n", name, MSG);
    printf("%s\n%s\n", m1, m2);
    gets(talents);
    puts("Let's see if I've got that list:");
    puts(talents);
    printf("Thanks for the information, %s.\n", name);

    return 0;
}
```

To show you what this program does, here is a sample run:

```
Hi! I'm Clyde the Computer. I have many talents.
Let me tell you some of them.
What were they? Ah, yes, here's a partial list.
Adding numbers swiftly
```

```
Multiplying accurately
Stashing data
Following instructions to the letter
Understanding the C language

Enough about me -- what's your name?
Nigel Barntwit
Well, Nigel Barntwit, You must have many talents. Tell me some.
Just limit yourself to one line's worth.
If you can't think of anything, fake it.
Fencing, yodeling, malingering, cheese tasting, and sighing.
Let's see if I've got that list:
Fencing, yodeling, malingering, cheese tasting, and sighing.
Thanks for the information, Nigel Barntwit.
```

Rather than going through Listing 11.1 line-by-line, let's take a more encompassing approach. First, you will look at ways of defining a string within a program. Then you will see what is involved in reading a string into a program. Finally, you will study ways to output a string.

Defining Strings Within a Program

As you probably noticed when you read Listing 11.1, there are many ways to define a string. The principal ways are using string constants, using char arrays, using char pointers, and using arrays of character strings. A program should make sure there is a place to store a string, and we will cover that topic, too.

Character String Constants (String Literals)

A *string constant*, also termed a *string literal*, is anything enclosed in double quotation marks. The enclosed characters, plus a terminating \0 character automatically provided by the compiler, are stored in memory as a character string. The program uses several such character string constants, most often as arguments for the printf() and puts() functions. Note, too, that you can use #define to define character string constants.

Recall that ANSI C concatenates string literals if they are separated by nothing or by whitespace. For example,

```
char greeting[50] = "Hello, and"" how are"  " you"
                    " today!";
```

is equivalent to this:

```
char greeting[50] = "Hello, and how are you today!";
```

If you want to use a double quotation mark within a string, precede the quotation mark with a backslash, as follows:

```
printf("\"Run, Spot, run!\" exclaimed Dick.\n");
```

This produces the following output:

```
"Run, Spot, run!" exclaimed Dick.
```

Character string constants are placed in the *static storage* class, which means that if you use a string constant in a function, the string is stored just once and lasts for the duration of the program, even if the function is called several times. The entire quoted phrase acts as a pointer to where the string is stored. This action is analogous to the name of an array acting as a pointer to the array's location. If this is true, what kind of output should the program in Listing 11.2 produce?

LISTING 11.2   The quotes.c Program

```
/* quotes.c -- strings as pointers */
#include <stdio.h>
int main(void)
{
    printf("%s, %p, %c\n", "We", "are", *"space farers");

    return 0;
}
```

The %s format should print the string We. The %p format produces an address. So if the phrase "are" is an address, then %p should print the address of the first character in the string. (Pre-ANSI implementations might have to use %u or %lu instead of %p.) Finally, *"space farers" should produce the value of the address pointed to, which should be the first character of the string "space farers". Does this really happen? Well, here is the output:

```
We, 0x0040c010, s
```

Character String Arrays and Initialization

When you define a character string array, you must let the compiler know how much space is needed. One way is to specify an array size large enough to hold the string. The following declaration initializes the array m1 to the characters of the indicated string:

```
const char m1[40] = "Limit yourself to one line's worth.";
```

The const indicates the intent to not alter this string.

This form of initialization is short for the standard array initialization form:

```
const char m1[40] = { 'L',
'i', 'm', 'i', 't', ' ', 'y', 'o', 'u', 'r', 's', 'e', 'l',
'f', ' ', 't', 'o', ' ', 'o', 'n', 'e', ' ',
'l', 'i', 'n', 'e', '\'', 's', ' ', 'w', 'o', 'r',
't', 'h', '.', '\0'
};
```

Note the closing null character. Without it, you have a character array, but not a string.

When you specify the array size, be sure that the number of elements is at least one more (that null character again) than the string length. Any unused elements are automatically initialized to 0 (which in char form is the null character, not the zero digit character). See Figure 11.1.

FIGURE 11.1
Initializing an array.

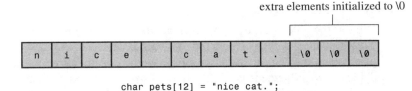

```
char pets[12] = "nice cat.";
```

Often, it is convenient to let the compiler determine the array size; recall that if you omit the size in an initializing declaration, the compiler determines the size for you:

```
const char m2[] = "If you can't think of anything, fake it.";
```

Initializing character arrays is one case when it really does make sense to let the compiler determine the array size. That's because string-processing functions typically don't need to know the size of the array because they can simply look for the null character to mark the end.

Note that the program had to assign a size explicitly for the array **name**:

```
#define LINELEN 81          // maximum string length + 1
...
char name[LINELEN];
```

Because the contents for **name** are to be read when the program runs, the compiler has no way of knowing in advance how much space to set aside unless you tell it. There is no string constant present whose characters the compiler can count, so we gambled that 80 characters would be enough to hold the user's name. When you declare an array, the array size must evaluate to an integer constant. You can't use a variable that gets set at runtime. The array size is locked into the program at compile time. (Actually, with C99 you could use a variable-length array, but you still have no way of knowing in advance how big it has to be.)

```
int n = 8;
char cakes[2 + 5];  /* valid, size is a constant expression
char crumbs[n];     /* invalid prior to C99, a VLA after C99
```

The name of a character array, like any array name, yields the address of the first element of the array. Therefore, the following holds for the array **m1**:

```
m1 == &m1[0] , *m1 == 'L', and *(m1+1) == m1[1] == 'i'
```

Indeed, you can use pointer notation to set up a string. For example, Listing 11.1 uses the following declaration:

```
const char *m3 = "\nEnough about me -- what's your name?";
```

This declaration is very nearly the same as this one:

```
char m3[] = "\nEnough about me -- what's your name?"
```

Both declarations amount to saying that **m3** is a pointer to the indicated string. In both cases, the quoted string itself determines the amount of storage set aside for the string. Nonetheless, the forms are not identical.

Array Versus Pointer

What is the difference, then, between an array and a pointer form? The array form (m3[ ]) causes an array of 38 elements (one for each character plus one for the terminating '\0') to be allocated in the computer memory. Each element is initialized to the corresponding character. Typically, what happens is that the quoted string is stored in a data segment that is part of the executable file; when the program is loaded into memory, so is that string. The quoted string is said to be in *static memory*. But the memory for the array is allocated only after the program begins running. At that time, the quoted string is copied into the array. (Chapter 12, "Storage Classes, Linkage, and Memory Management," will discuss memory management more fully.) Hereafter, the compiler will recognize the name m3 as a synonym for the address of the first array element, &m3[0]. One important point here is that in the array form, m3 is an address *constant*. You can't change m3, because that would mean changing the location (address) where the array is stored. You can use operations such as m3+1 to identify the next element in an array, but ++m3 is not allowed. The increment operator can be used only with the names of variables, not with constants.

The pointer form (*m3) also causes 38 elements in static storage to be set aside for the string. In addition, once the program begins execution, it sets aside one more storage location for the pointer *variable* m3 and stores the address of the string in the pointer variable. This variable initially points to the first character of the string, but the value can be changed. Therefore, you can use the increment operator. For instance, ++m3 would point to the second character (E).

In short, initializing the array copies a string from static storage to the array, whereas initializing the pointer merely copies the address of the string.

Are these differences important? Often they are not, but it depends on what you try to do. See the following discussion for some examples.

Array and Pointer Differences

Let's examine the differences between initializing a character array to hold a string and initializing a pointer to point to a string. (By "pointing to a string," we really mean pointing to the first character of a string.) For example, consider these two declarations:

```
char heart[] = "I love Tillie!";
char *head = "I love Millie!";
```

The chief difference is that the array name heart is a constant, but the pointer head is a variable. What practical difference does this make?

First, both can use array notation:

```
for (i = 0; i < 6; i++)
    putchar(heart[i]);
putchar('\n');
for (i = 0; i < 6; i++)
    putchar(head[i]));
putchar('\n');
```

This is the output:

```
I love
I love
```

Next, both can use pointer addition:

```
for (i = 0; i < 6; i++)
    putchar(*(heart + i));
putchar('\n');
for (i = 0; i < 6; i++)
    putchar(*(head + i));
putchar('\n');
```

Again, the output is as follows:

```
I love
I love
```

Only the pointer version, however, can use the increment operator:

```
while (*(head) != '\0')   /* stop at end of string           */
    putchar(*(head++));   /* print character, advance pointer */
```

This produces the following output:

```
I love Millie!
```

Suppose you want **head** to agree with **heart**. You can say

```
head = heart;   /* head now points to the array heart */
```

This makes the **head** pointer point to the first element of the **heart** array.

However, you cannot say

```
heart = head;   /* illegal construction */
```

The situation is analogous to **x = 3;** versus **3 = x;**. The left side of the assignment statement must be a variable or, more generally, an *lvalue*, such as ***p_int**. Incidentally, **head = heart;** does not make the Millie string vanish; it just changes the address stored in **head**. Unless you've saved the address of **"I love Millie!"** elsewhere, however, you won't be able to access that string when **head** points to another location.

There is a way to alter the **heart** message—go to the individual array elements:

```
heart[7]= 'M';
```

or

```
*(heart + 7) = 'M';
```

The *elements* of an array are variables (unless the array was declared as **const**), but the *name* is not a variable.

Let's go back to a pointer initialization:

```
char * word = "frame";
```

Can you use the pointer to change this string?

```
word[1] = 'l';   // allowed??
```

Your compiler probably will allow this, but, under the current C standard, the behavior for such an action is undefined. Such a statement could, for example, lead to memory access errors. The reason is that a compiler can choose to represent all identical string literals with a single copy in memory. For example, the following statements could all refer to a single memory location of string `"Klingon"`:

```
char * p1 = "Klingon";
p1[0] = 'F';     // ok?
printf("Klingon");
printf(": Beware the %ss!\n", "Klingon");
```

That is, the compiler can replace each instance of `"Klingon"` with the same address. If the compiler uses this single-copy representation and allows changing `p1[0]` to `'F'`, that would affect all uses of the string, so statements printing the string literal `"Klingon"` would actually display `"Flingon"`:

```
Flingon: Beware the Flingons!
```

In fact, several compilers do behave this rather confusing way, whereas others produce programs that abort. Therefore, the recommended practice for initializing a pointer to a string literal is to use the `const` modifier:

```
const char * pl = "Klingon";   // recommended usage
```

Initializing a non-`const` array with a string literal, however, poses no such problems, because the array gets a copy of the original string.

Arrays of Character Strings

It is often convenient to have an array of character strings. Then you can use a subscript to access several different strings. Listing 11.1 used this example:

```
const char *mytal[LIM] = {"Adding numbers swiftly",
        "Multiplying accurately", "Stashing data",
        "Following instructions to the letter",
        "Understanding the C language"};
```

Let's study this declaration. Because `LIM` is `5`, you can say that `mytal` is an array of five pointers-to-`char`. That is, `mytal` is a one-dimensional array, and each element in the array holds the address of a `char`. The first pointer is `mytal[0]`, and it points to the first character of the first string. The second pointer is `mytal[1]`, and it points to the beginning of the second string. In general, each pointer points to the first character of the corresponding string

```
*mytal[0] == 'A', *mytal[1] == 'M', *mytal[2] == 'S'
```

and so on. The `mytal` array doesn't actually hold the strings; it just holds the addresses of the strings. (The strings are in the part of memory the program uses to store constants.) You can think of `mytal[0]` as representing the first string and `*mytal[0]` as the first character of the first string. Because of the relationship between array notation and pointers, you can also use `mytal[0][0]` to represent the first character of the first string, even though `mytal` is not defined as a two-dimensional array.

The initialization follows the rules for arrays. The braced portion is equivalent to

`{{...}, {...},{...},{...} };`

The ellipses indicate the stuff we were too lazy to type. The main point is that the first set of double quotation marks corresponds to a brace-pair and so is used to initialize the first character string pointer. The next set of double quotation marks initializes the second pointer, and so on. A comma separates adjacent strings.

Another approach is to create a two-dimensional array:

`char mytal_2[LIM][LINLIM];`

Here, `mytal_2` is an array of five elements, and each of these elements is itself an array of 81 `char` values. In this case, the strings themselves are stored in the array. One difference is that this second choice sets up a *rectangular* array with all the rows of the same length. That is, 81 elements are used to hold each string. The array of pointers, however, sets up a *ragged* array, with each row's length determined by the string it was initialized t.

`char *mytal[LIM];`

This ragged array doesn't waste any storage space. Figure 11.2 shows the two kinds of arrays. (Actually, the strings pointed to by the `mytal` array elements don't necessarily have to be stored consecutively in memory, but the figure does illustrate the difference in storage requirements.)

Another difference is that `mytal` and `mytal_2` have different types; `mytal` is an array of pointers-to-`char`, but `mytal_2` is an array of arrays of `char`. In short, `mytal` holds five addresses, but `mytal_2` holds five complete character arrays.

Pointers and Strings

Perhaps you noticed an occasional reference to pointers in this discussion of strings. Most C operations for strings actually work with pointers. Consider, for example, the instructive program shown in Listing 11.3.

LISTING 11.3   The `p_and_s.c` Program

```
/* p_and_s.c -- pointers and strings */
#include <stdio.h>
int main(void)
{
    const char * mesg = "Don't be a fool!";
    const char * copy;

    copy = mesg;
    printf("%s\n", copy);
    printf("mesg = %s; &mesg = %p; value = %p\n",
            mesg, &mesg, mesg);
```

LISTING 11.3   Continued

```
        printf("copy = %s; &copy = %p; value = %p\n",
                copy, &copy, copy);

        return 0;
    }
```

FIGURE 11.2
Rectangular versus ragged array.

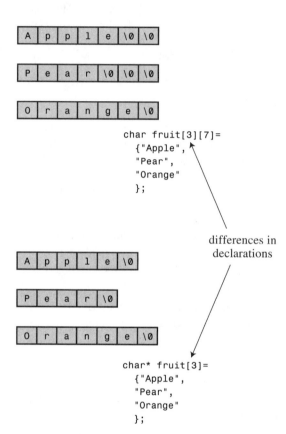

> **Note**
>
> Use %u or %lu instead of %p if your compiler doesn't support %p.

Looking at this program, you might think that it makes a copy of the string "Don't be a fool!", and your first glance at the output might seem to confirm this guess:

```
Don't be a fool!
mesg = Don't be a fool!; &mesg = 0x0012ff48; value = 0x0040a000
copy = Don't be a fool!; &copy = 0x0012ff44; value = 0x0040a000
```

But study the `printf()` output more carefully. First, `mesg` and `copy` are printed as strings (`%s`). No surprises here; all the strings are `"Don't be a fool!"`.

The next item on each line is the address of the specified pointer. The two pointers `mesg` and `copy` are stored in locations `0x0064fd58` and `0x0064fd5c`, respectively.

Now notice the final item, the one we called `value`. It is the value of the specified pointer. The value of the pointer is the address it contains. You can see that `mesg` points to location `0x0040c000`, and so does `copy`. Therefore, the string itself was never copied. All that `copy = mesg;` does is produce a second pointer pointing to the very same string.

Why all this pussyfooting around? Why not just copy the whole string? Well, ask yourself which is more efficient: copying one address or copying, say, 50 separate elements? Often, the address is all that is needed to get the job done. If you truly require a copy that is a duplicate, you can use the `strcpy()` or `strncpy()` function, discussed later in this chapter.

Now that we have discussed defining strings within a program, let's turn to strings provided by keyboard input.

String Input

If you want to read a string into a program, you must first set aside space to store the string and then use an input function to fetch the string.

Creating Space

The first order of business is setting up a place to put the string after it is read. As mentioned earlier, this means you need to allocate enough storage to hold whatever strings you expect to read. Don't expect the computer to count the string length as it is read and then allot space for it. The computer won't (unless you write a function to do so). For example, suppose you try something like this:

```
char *name;

scanf("%s", name);
```

It will probably get by the compiler, but when the name is read, the name might be written over data or code in your program, and it might cause a program abort. That's because `scanf()` copies information to the address given by the argument, and in this case, the argument is an uninitialized pointer; `name` might point anywhere. Most programmers regard this as highly humorous, but only in other people's programs.

The simplest course is to include an explicit array size in the declaration:

```
char name[81];
```

Now `name` is the address of an allocated block of 81 bytes. Another possibility is to use the C library functions that allocate memory, and we'll touch on those in Chapter 12.

After you have set aside space for the string, you can read the string. The C library supplies a trio of functions that can read strings: `scanf()`, `gets()`, and `fgets()`. The most commonly used one is `gets()`, which we discuss first.

The `gets()` Function

The `gets()` (*get* string) function is very handy for interactive programs. It gets a string from your system's standard input device, normally your keyboard. Because a string has no predetermined length, `gets()` needs a way to know when to stop. Its method is to read characters until it reaches a newline (\n) character, which you generate by pressing the Enter key. It takes all the characters up to (but not including) the newline, tacks on a null character (\0), and gives the string to the calling program. The newline character itself is read and discarded so that the next read begins at the start of the next line. Listing 11.4 shows a simple means of using `gets()`.

LISTING 11.4 The name1.c Program

```
/* name1.c -- reads a name */
#include <stdio.h>
#define MAX 81
int main(void)
{
    char name[MAX];  /* allot space                 */

    printf("Hi, what's your name?\n");
    gets(name);      /* place string into name array */
    printf("Nice name, %s.\n", name);

    return 0;
}
```

Here is a sample run:

```
Hi, what's your name?
The Mysterious Davina D'Lema
Nice name, The Mysterious Davina D'Lema
```

Listing 11.4 accepts and stores any name (including spaces) up to 80 characters. (Remember to reserve one space for the \0 in the array.) Note that you want `gets()` to affect something (name) in the calling function. This means you should use an address as an argument, and, of course, the name of an array *is* an address.

The `gets()` function is more sophisticated than this preceding example suggests. Look at Listing 11.5.

LISTING 11.5   The name2.c Program

```c
/* name2.c -- reads a name */
#include <stdio.h>
#define MAX 81
int main(void)
{
    char name[MAX];
    char * ptr;

    printf("Hi, what's your name?\n");
    ptr = gets(name);
    printf("%s? Ah! %s!\n", name, ptr);

    return 0;
}
```

Here is a sample exchange:

```
Hi, what's your name?
Wellington Snackworthy
Wellington Snackworthy? Ah! Wellington Snackworthy!
```

The gets() function gets input in two ways:

- It uses an address to feed the string into name.

- The code for gets() uses the return keyword to return the address of the string, and the program assigns that address to ptr. Notice that ptr is a pointer to char. This means that gets() must return a value that is a pointer to char.

ANSI C mandates that the stdio.h header file include a function prototype for gets(). You need not declare the function yourself, as long as you remember to include that header file. However, some very old versions of C require that you provide your own function declaration for gets().

The design of a gets() function could look something like this:

```c
char *gets(char * s)
{
    ...
    return(s);
}
```

The function header indicates that gets() returns a pointer to a char. Note that gets() returns the same pointer that was passed to it. There is but one copy of the input string; the one placed at the address passed as a function argument, so ptr in Listing 11.5 ends up pointing to the name array. The actual design is slightly more complicated because gets() has two possible returns. If everything goes well, it returns the address of the read string, as we have said. If something goes wrong or if gets() encounters end-of-file, it returns a null, or zero, address. This null address is called the *null pointer* and is represented in stdio.h by the defined constant NULL. Therefore, gets() incorporates a bit of error-checking, making it convenient to use constructions such as this:

```
while (gets(name) != NULL)
```

Such a construction enables you to both check for end-of-file and read a value. If end-of-file is encountered, nothing is read into name. This two-pronged approach is more compact than that of getchar(), which has a return value but no argument:

```
while ((ch = getchar()) != EOF)
```

By the way, don't confuse the null pointer with the null character. The null pointer is an address, and the null character is a type char data object with the value zero. Numerically, both can be represented by 0, but they differ conceptually from each other: NULL is a pointer, \0 is a type char constant.

The fgets() Function

One weakness of gets() is that it doesn't check to see whether the input actually fits into the reserved storage area. Extra characters simply overflow into the adjoining memory. The fgets() function improves on this questionable behavior by enabling you to specify an upper limit for the number of characters to be read. Because fgets() is designed for file I/O, it's slightly more awkward than gets() for keyboard input. It differs from gets() in three respects:

- It takes a second argument indicating the maximum number of characters to read. If this argument has the value n, fgets() reads up to n-1 characters or through the newline character, whichever comes first.

- If fgets() reads the newline, it stores it in the string, unlike gets(), which discards it.

- It takes a third argument indicating which file to read. To read from the keyboard, use stdin (for *standard input*) as the argument; this identifier is defined in stdio.h.

Listing 11.6 modifies Listing 11.5 to use fgets() instead of gets().

LISTING 11.6   The name3.c Program

```
/* name3.c -- reads a name using fgets() */
#include <stdio.h>
#define MAX 81
int main(void)
{
    char name[MAX];
    char * ptr;

    printf("Hi, what's your name?\n");
    ptr = fgets(name, MAX, stdin);
    printf("%s? Ah! %s!\n", name, ptr);

    return 0;
}
```

Here is some sample output, which reveals one of the awkward aspects of `fgets()`:

```
Hi, what's your name?
Jon Dough
Jon Dough
? Ah! Jon Dough
!
```

The problem is that `fgets()` stores the newline in the string, so that a newline gets displayed every time you display the string. Later in this chapter, at the end of the "Other String Functions" section, you'll learn how to use `strchr()` to locate and remove the newline.

Because `gets()` doesn't check whether the input will fit in the destination array, it is considered unsafe. Indeed, a few years ago someone noted that some Unix operating system code used `gets()` and used that weakness by providing long input that overwrote operating system code, creating a "worm" that propagated through the Unix network. That system code has since been replaced by `gets()`-free code. So in serious programming, you should use `fgets()` rather than `gets()`, but this book takes a more relaxed approach.

The `scanf()` Function

You've used `scanf()` with the `%s` format before to read a string. The chief difference between `scanf()` and `gets()` lies in how they decide when they have reached the end of the string: `scanf()` is more of a "get word" than a "get string" function. The `gets()` function, as you've seen, takes in all the characters up to the first newline. The `scanf()` function has two choices for terminating input. For either choice, the string starts at the first non-whitespace character encountered. If you use the `%s` format, the string runs up to (but not including) the next whitespace character (blank, tab, or newline). If you specify a field width, as in `%10s`, the `scanf()` collects up to 10 characters or up to the first whitespace character, whichever comes first (see Figure 11.3).

FIGURE 11.3
Field widths and `scanf()`.

Input Statement	Original Input Queue*	Name Contents	Remaining Queue
`scanf("%s", name);`	Fleebert☐Hup	Fleebert	☐Hup
`scanf("%5s", name);`	Fleebert☐Hup	Fleeb	ert☐Hup
`scanf("%5s", name);`	Ann☐Ular	Ann	☐Ular

*the ☐ represents the space character

Recall that the `scanf()` function returns an integer value that equals the number of items successfully read or returns `EOF` if it encounters the end of file.

Listing 11.7 illustrates how `scanf()` works when you specify a field width.

LISTING 11.7   The scan_str.c Program

```c
/* scan_str.c -- using scanf() */
#include <stdio.h>
int main(void)
{
    char name1[11], name2[11];
    int count;

    printf("Please enter 2 names.\n");
    count = scanf("%5s %10s",name1, name2);
    printf("I read the %d names %s and %s.\n",
            count, name1, name2);

    return 0;
}
```

Here are three runs:

```
Please enter 2 names.
Jesse Jukes
I read the 2 names Jesse and Jukes.

Please enter 2 names.
Liza Applebottham
I read the 2 names Liza and Applebotth.

Please enter 2 names.
Portensia Callowit
I read the 2 names Porte and nsia.
```

In the first example, both names fell within the allowed size limits. In the second example, only the first 10 characters of Applebottham were read because we used a %10s format. In the third example, the last four letters of Portensia went into name2 because the second call to scanf() resumed reading input where the first ended; in this case, that was still inside the word Portensia.

Depending on the nature of the desired input, you may be better off using gets() to read text from the keyboard. It is easier to use, faster, and more compact. The typical use for scanf() is reading and converting a mixture of data types in some standard form. For example, if each input line contains the name of a tool, the number in stock, and the cost of the item, you might use scanf(), or you might throw together a function of your own that does some entry error-checking. If you want to process input a word at a time, you can use scanf().

String Output

Now let's move from string input to string output. Again, we will use library functions. C has three standard library functions for printing strings: puts(), fputs(), and printf().

The `puts()` Function

The `puts()` function is very easy to use. Just give it the address of a string for an argument. Listing 11.8 illustrates some of the many ways to do this.

LISTING 11.8   The `put_out.c` Program

```
/* put_out.c -- using puts() */
#include <stdio.h>
#define DEF "I am a #defined string."
int main(void)
{
    char str1[80] = "An array was initialized to me.";
    const char * str2 = "A pointer was initialized to me.";

    puts("I'm an argument to puts().");
    puts(DEF);
    puts(str1);
    puts(str2);
    puts(&str1[5]);
    puts(str2+4);

    return 0;
}
```

The output is this:

```
I'm an argument to puts().
I am a #defined string.
An array was initialized to me.
A pointer was initialized to me.
ray was initialized to me.
inter was initialized to me.
```

Note that each string appears on its own line. Unlike `printf()`, `puts()` automatically appends a newline when it displays a string.

This example reminds you that phrases in double quotation marks are string constants and are treated as addresses. Also, the names of character array strings are treated as addresses. The expression `&str1[5]` is the address of the sixth element of the array `str1`. That element contains the character `'r'`, and that is what `puts()` uses for its starting point. Similarly, `str2+4` points to the memory cell containing the `'i'` of `"pointer"`, and the printing starts there.

How does `puts()` know when to stop? It stops when it encounters the null character, so there had better be one. Don't emulate the program in Listing 11.9!

LISTING 11.9   The `nono.c` Program

```
/* nono.c -- no! */
#include <stdio.h>
int main(void)
```

LISTING 11.9   Continued

```
{
    char side_a[] = "Side A";
    char dont[] = {'W', 'O', 'W', '!' };
    char side_b[] = "Side B";

    puts(dont);    /* dont is not a string */

    return 0;
}
```

Because dont lacks a closing null character, it is not a string, so puts() won't know where to stop. It will just keep printing from memory following dont until it finds a null somewhere. To ensure that a null character is not too distant, the program stores dont between two true strings. Here's a sample run:

```
WOW!Side A
```

The particular compiler used here stored the side_a array after the dont array in memory, so puts() kept going until hitting the null character in side_a. You may get different results, depending on how your compiler arranges data in memory. What if the program had omitted the arrays side_a and side_b? There are usually lots of nulls in memory, and if you're lucky, puts() might find one soon, but don't count on it.

The fputs() Function

The fputs() function is the file-oriented version of gets(). The main differences are these:

- The fputs() function takes a second argument indicating the file to which to write. You can use stdout (for *standard output*), which is defined in stdio.h, as an argument to output to your display.

- Unlike puts(), fputs() does not automatically append a newline to the output.

Note that gets() discards a newline on input, but puts() adds a newline on output. On the other hand, fgets() stores the newline on input, and fputs() doesn't add a newline on output. Suppose you want to write a loop that reads a line and echoes it on the next line. You can do this:

```
char line[81];
while (gets(line))
    puts(line);
```

Recall that gets() returns the null pointer if it encounters end-of-file. The null pointer evaluates as zero, or false, so that terminates the loop. Or you can do this:

```
char line[81];
while (fgets(line, 81, stdin))
    fputs(line, stdout);
```

With the first loop, the string in the line array is displayed on a line of its own because puts() adds a newline. With the second loop, the string in the line array is displayed on a line of its own because `fgets()` stores a newline. Note that if you mix `fgets()` input with `puts()` output, you'd get two newlines displayed for each string. The point is that `puts()` is designed to work with `gets()`, and `fputs()` is designed to work with `fgets()`.

The `printf()` Function

We discussed `printf()` pretty thoroughly in Chapter 4, "Character Strings and Formatted Input/Output." Like `puts()`, it takes a string address as an argument. The `printf()` function is less convenient to use than `puts()`, but it is more versatile because it formats various data types.

One difference is that `printf()` does not automatically print each string on a new line. Instead, you must indicate where you want new lines. Therefore,

```
printf("%s\n", string);
```

has the same effect as

```
puts(string);
```

As you can see, the first form takes more typing. It also takes longer for the computer to execute (not that you would notice). On the other hand, `printf()` makes it simple to combine strings for one line of printing. For example, the following statement combines `Well,` with the user's name and a `#define`d character string, all on one line:

```
printf("Well, %s, %s\n", name, MSG);
```

The Do-It-Yourself Option

You aren't limited to the standard C library options for input and output. If you don't have these options or don't like them, you can prepare your own versions, building on `getchar()` and `putchar()`. Suppose you want a function like `puts()` that doesn't automatically add a newline. Listing 11.10 shows one way to create it.

LISTING 11.10   The `put1.c` Program

```
/* put1.c -- prints a string  without adding \n */
#include <stdio.h>
void put1(const char * string) /* string not altered */
{
    while (*string != '\0')
        putchar(*string++);
}
```

The `char` pointer `string` initially points to the first element of the called argument. Because this function doesn't change the string, use the `const` modifier. After the contents of that element are printed, the pointer increments and points to the next element. This goes on until the pointer points to an element containing the null character. Remember, the higher precedence of `++` compared to `*` means that `putchar(*string++)` prints the value pointed to by `string` but increments `string` itself, not the character to which it points.

You can regard put1.c as a model for writing string-processing functions. Because each string has a null character marking its end, you don't have to pass a size to the function. Instead, the function processes each character in turn until it encounters the null character.

A somewhat longer way of writing the function is to use array notation:

```
int i = 0;
while (string[i]!= '\0')
        putchar(string[i++]);
```

This involves an additional variable for the index.

Many C programmers would use the following test for the while loop:

```
while (*string)
```

When string points to the null character, *string has the value 0, which terminates the loop. This approach certainly takes less typing than the previous version. If you are not familiar with C practice, it is less obvious. This idiom is widespread, and C programmers are expected to be familiar with it.

Note

Why does Listing 11.10 use const char * string rather than const char string[] as the formal argument? Technically, the two are equivalent, so either form will work. One reason to use bracket notation is to remind the user that the function processes an array. With strings, however, the actual argument can be the name of an array, a quoted string, or a variable that has been declared as type char *. Using const char * string reminds you that the actual argument isn't necessarily an array.

Suppose you want a function like puts() that also tells you how many characters are printed. As Listing 11.11 demonstrates, it's easy to add that feature.

LISTING 11.11   The put2.c Program

```
/* put2.c -- prints a string and counts characters */
#include <stdio.h>
int put2(const char * string)
{
    int count = 0;
    while (*string)          /* common idiom       */
    {
        putchar(*string++);
        count++;
    }
    putchar('\n');           /* newline not counted */

    return(count);
}
```

The following call prints the string `pizza`:

```
put1("pizza");
```

The next call also returns a character count that is assigned to `num` (in this case, the value 5):

```
num = put2("pizza");
```

Listing 11.12 presents a driver using `put1()` and `put2()` and showing nested function calls.

LISTING 11.12   The `put_put.c` Program

```
//put_put.c -- user-defined output functions
#include <stdio.h>
void put1(const char *);
int put2(const char *);

int main(void)
{
    put1("If I'd as much money");
    put1(" as I could spend,\n");
    printf("I count %d characters.\n",
            put2("I never would cry old chairs to mend."));

    return 0;
}

void put1(const char * string)
{
    while (*string)   /* same as *string != '\0' */
        putchar(*string++);
}

int put2(const char * string)
{
    int count = 0;
    while (*string)
    {
        putchar(*string++);
        count++;
    }
    putchar('\n');

    return(count);
}
```

Hmmm, we are using `printf()` to print the value of `put2()`, but in the act of finding the value of `put2()`, the computer first must execute that function, causing the string to be printed. Here's the output:

```
If I'd as much money as I could spend,
I never would cry old chairs to mend.
I count 37 characters.
```

String Functions

The C library supplies several string-handling functions; ANSI C uses the `string.h` header file to provide the prototypes. We'll look at some of the most useful and common ones: `strlen()`, `strcat()`, `strncat()`, `strcmp()`, `strncmp()`, `strcpy()`, and `strncpy()`. We'll also examine `sprintf()`, supported by the `stdio.h` header file. For a complete list of the `string.h` family of functions, see Reference Section V, "The Standard ANSI C Library with C99 Additions."

The `strlen()` Function

The `strlen()` function, as you already know, finds the length of a string. It's used in the next example, a function that shortens lengthy strings:

```c
/* fit.c -- procrustean function */
void fit(char * string, unsigned int size)
{
    if (strlen(string) > size)
        *(string + size) = '\0';
}
```

This function does change the string, so the function header doesn't use `const` in declaring the formal parameter `string`.

Try the `fit()` function in the test program of Listing 11.13. Note that the code uses C's string literal concatenation feature.

LISTING 11.13   The `test_fit.c` Program

```c
/* test_fit.c -- try the string-shrinking function */
#include <stdio.h>
#include <string.h> /* contains string function prototypes */
void fit(char *, unsigned int);

int main(void)
{
    char mesg[] = "Things should be as simple as possible,"
                  " but not simpler.";

    puts(mesg);
    fit(mesg,38);
    puts(mesg);
    puts("Let's look at some more of the string.");
    puts(mesg + 39);

    return 0;
}

void fit(char *string, unsigned int size)
{
    if (strlen(string) > size)
        *(string + size) = '\0';
}
```

The output is this:

```
Things should be as simple as possible, but not simpler.
Things should be as simple as possible
Let's look at some more of the string.
 but not simpler.
```

The `fit()` function placed a `'\0'` character in the 39th element of the array, replacing a comma. The `puts()` function stops at the first null character and ignores the rest of the array. However, the rest of the array is still there, as shown by the following call:

```
puts(mesg + 8);
```

The expression `mesg + 39` is the address of `mesq[39]`, which is a space character. So `puts()` displays that character and keeps going until it runs into the original null character. Figure 11.4 illustrates (with a shorter string) what's happening in this program.

(Variations of this quotation are attributed to Albert Einstein, but it appears more likely to be a representation of his philosophy than a direct quote.)

FIGURE 11.4

The `puts()` function and the null character.

Original string:

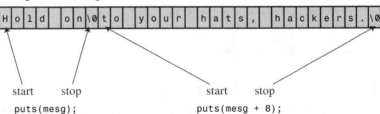

String after fit(mesg, 7):

The ANSI `string.h` file contains function prototypes for the C family of string functions, which is why this example includes it.

> **Note**
>
> Some pre-ANSI systems use `strings.h` instead, and others might lack a string header file entirely.

The `strcat()` Function

The `strcat()` (for *string concatenation*) function takes two strings for arguments. A copy of the second string is tacked onto the end of the first, and this combined version becomes the new first string. The second string is not altered. Function `strcat()` is type `char *` (that is, a pointer-to-`char`). It returns the value of its first argument—the address of the first character of the string to which the second string is appended.

Listing 11.14 illustrates what `strcat()` can do.

LISTING 11.14   The `str_cat.c` Program

```
/* str_cat.c -- joins two strings */
#include <stdio.h>
#include <string.h>  /* declares the strcat() function */
#define SIZE 80
int main(void)
{
    char flower[SIZE];
    char addon[] = "s smell like old shoes.";

    puts("What is your favorite flower?");
    gets(flower);
    strcat(flower, addon);
    puts(flower);
    puts(addon);

    return 0;
}
```

This is the output:

```
What is your favorite flower?
Rose
Roses smell like old shoes.
s smell like old shoes.
```

The `strncat()` Function

The `strcat()` function does not check to see whether the second string will fit in the first array. If you fail to allocate enough space for the first array, you will run into problems as excess characters overflow into adjacent memory locations. Of course, you can use `strlen()` to look before you leap, as shown in Listing 11.15. Note that it adds 1 to the combined lengths to allow space for the null character. Alternatively, you can use `strncat()`, which takes a second argument indicating the maximum number of characters to add. For example, `strncat(bugs, addon, 13)` will add the contents of the `addon` string to `bugs`, stopping when it reaches 13 additional characters or the null character, whichever comes first. Therefore, counting the null character (which is appended in either case), the `bugs` array should be large enough to hold the original string (not counting the null character), a maximum of 13 additional characters, and the terminal null character. Listing 11.15 uses this information to calculate a value for the `available` variable, which is used as the maximum number of additional characters allowed.

LISTING 11.15   The `join_chk.c` Program

```c
/* join_chk.c -- joins two strings, check size first */
#include <stdio.h>
#include <string.h>
#define SIZE 30
#define BUGSIZE 13
int main(void)
{
    char flower[SIZE];
    char addon[] = "s smell like old shoes.";
    char bug[BUGSIZE];
    int available;

    puts("What is your favorite flower?");
    gets(flower);
    if ((strlen(addon) + strlen(flower) + 1) <= SIZE)
        strcat(flower, addon);
    puts(flower);
    puts("What is your favorite bug?");
    gets(bug);
    available = BUGSIZE - strlen(bug) - 1;
    strncat(bug, addon, available);
    puts(bug);

    return 0;
}
```

Here is a sample run:

```
What is your favorite flower?
Rose
Roses smell like old shoes.
What is your favorite bug?
Aphid
Aphids smell
```

The `strcmp()` Function

Suppose you want to compare someone's response to a stored string, as shown in Listing 11.16.

LISTING 11.16   The `nogo.c` Program

```c
/* nogo.c -- will this work? */
#include <stdio.h>
#define ANSWER "Grant"
int main(void)
{
    char try[40];
```

LISTING 11.16 Continued

```
    puts("Who is buried in Grant's tomb?");
    gets(try);
    while (try != ANSWER)
    {
        puts("No, that's wrong. Try again.");
        gets(try);
    }
    puts("That's right!");

    return 0;
}
```

As nice as this program might look, it will not work correctly. ANSWER and try really are pointers, so the comparison try != ANSWER doesn't check to see whether the two strings are the same. Rather, it checks to see whether the two strings have the same address. Because ANSWER and try are stored in different locations, the two addresses are never the same, and the user is forever told that he or she is wrong. Such programs tend to discourage people.

What you need is a function that compares string *contents*, not string *addresses*. You could devise one, but the job has been done for you with strcmp() (for *string comparison*). This function does for strings what relational operators do for numbers. In particular, it returns 0 if its two string arguments are the same. The revised program is shown in Listing 11.17.

LISTING 11.17 The compare.c Program

```
/* compare.c -- this will work */
#include <stdio.h>
#include <string.h>    /* declares strcmp() */
#define ANSWER "Grant"
#define MAX 40
int main(void)
{
    char try[MAX];

    puts("Who is buried in Grant's tomb?");
    gets(try);
    while (strcmp(try,ANSWER) != 0)
    {
        puts("No, that's wrong. Try again.");
        gets(try);
    }
    puts("That's right!");

    return 0;
}
```

Note

Because any nonzero value is "true," most experienced C programmers would abbreviate the while statement to while (strcmp(try,ANSWER)).

One of the nice features of strcmp() is that it compares strings, not arrays. Although the array try occupies 40 memory cells and "Grant" only six (one for the null character), the comparison looks only at the part of try up to its first null character. Therefore, strcmp() can be used to compare strings stored in arrays of different sizes.

What if the user answers "GRANT" or "grant" or "Ulysses S. Grant"? The user is told that he or she is wrong. To make a friendlier program, you have to anticipate all possible correct answers. There are some tricks you can use. For example, you can use #define to define the answer as "GRANT" and write a function that converts all input to uppercase. That eliminates the problem of capitalization, but you still have the other forms to worry about. We leave that as an exercise for you.

The strcmp() Return Value

What value does strcmp() return if the strings are not the same? Listing 11.18 shows an example.

LISTING 11.18   The compback.c Program

```
/* compback.c -- strcmp returns */
#include <stdio.h>
#include <string.h>
int main(void)
{
    printf("strcmp(\"A\", \"A\") is ");
    printf("%d\n", strcmp("A", "A"));

    printf("strcmp(\"A\", \"B\") is ");
    printf("%d\n", strcmp("A", "B"));

    printf("strcmp(\"B\", \"A\") is ");
    printf("%d\n", strcmp("B", "A"));

    printf("strcmp(\"C\", \"A\") is ");
    printf("%d\n", strcmp("C", "A"));

    printf("strcmp(\"Z\", \"a\") is ");
    printf("%d\n", strcmp("Z", "a"));

    printf("strcmp(\"apples\", \"apple\") is ");
    printf("%d\n", strcmp("apples", "apple"));

    return 0;
}
```

Here is the output on one system:

```
strcmp("A", "A") is 0
strcmp("A", "B") is -1
strcmp("B", "A") is 1
strcmp("C", "A") is 1
```

```
strcmp("Z", "a") is -1
strcmp("apples", "apple") is 1
```

Comparing "A" to itself returns 0. Comparing "A" to "B" returns -1, and reversing the comparison returns 1. These results suggest that strcmp() returns a negative number if the first string precedes the second alphabetically and that it returns a positive number if the order is the other way. Therefore, comparing "C" to "A" gives a 1. Other systems might return 2—the difference in ASCII code values. The ANSI standard says that strcmp() returns a negative number if the first string comes before the second alphabetically, returns 0 if they are the same, and returns a positive number if the first string follows the second alphabetically. The exact numerical values, however, are left open to the implementation. Here, for example, is the output for another implementation, one that returns the difference between the character codes:

```
strcmp("A", "A") is 0
strcmp("A", "B") is -1
strcmp("B", "A") is 1
strcmp("C", "A") is 2
strcmp("Z", "a") is -7
strcmp("apples", "apple") is 115
```

What if the initial characters are identical? In general, strcmp() moves along until it finds the first pair of disagreeing characters. It then returns the corresponding code. For instance, in the very last example, "apples" and "apple" agree until the final s of the first string. This matches up with the sixth character in "apple", which is the null character, ASCII 0. Because the null character is the very first character in the ASCII sequence, s comes after it, and the function returns a positive value.

The last comparison points out that strcmp() compares all characters, not just letters, so instead of saying the comparison is alphabetic, we should say that strcmp() goes by the machine *collating sequence*. That means characters are compared according to their numeric representation, typically the ASCII values. In ASCII, the codes for uppercase letters precede those for lowercase letters. Therefore, strcmp("Z", "a") is negative.

Most often, you won't care about the exact value returned. You just want to know if it is zero or nonzero—that is, whether there is a match or not—or you might be trying to sort the strings alphabetically, in which case you want to know if the comparison is positive, negative, or zero.

Note

The strcmp() function is for comparing *strings*, not *characters*. So you can use arguments such as "apples" and "A", but you cannot use character arguments, such as 'A'. However, recall that the char type is an integer type, so you can use the relational operators for character comparisons. Suppose word is a string stored in an array of char and that ch is a char variable. Then the following statements are valid:

```
if (strcmp(word, "quit") == 0)   // use strcmp() for strings
    puts("Bye!");
if (ch == 'q')                   // use == for chars
    puts("Bye!");
```

However, don't use ch or 'q' as arguments for strcmp().

Listing 11.19 uses the `strcmp()` function for checking to see whether a program should stop reading input.

LISTING 11.19   The `quit_chk.c` Program

```
/* quit_chk.c -- beginning of some program */
#include <stdio.h>
#include <string.h>
#define SIZE 81
#define LIM 100
#define STOP "quit"
int main(void)
{
    char input[LIM][SIZE];
    int ct = 0;

    printf("Enter up to %d lines (type quit to quit):\n", LIM);
    while (ct < LIM && gets(input[ct]) != NULL &&
            strcmp(input[ct],STOP) != 0)
    {
        ct++;
    }
    printf("%d strings entered\n", ct);

    return 0;
}
```

This program quits reading input when it encounters an **EOF** character (`gets()` returns null in that case), when you enter the word *quit,* or when you reach the limit **LIM**.

Incidentally, sometimes it is more convenient to terminate input by entering an empty line— that is, by pressing the Enter key or Return key without entering anything else. To do so, you can modify the `while` loop control statement so that it looks like this:

```
while (ct < LIM && gets(input[ct]) != NULL
                && input[ct][0] != '\0')
```

Here, `input[ct]` is the string just entered and `input[ct][0]` is the first character of that string. If the user enters an empty line, `gets()` places the null character in the first element, so the expression

```
input[ct][0] != '\0'
```

tests for an empty input line.

The `strncmp()` Variation

The `strcmp()` function compares strings until it finds corresponding characters that differ, which could take the search to the end of one of the strings. The `strncmp()` function compares the strings until they differ or until it has compared a number of characters specified by a third argument. For example, if you wanted to search for strings that begin with `"astro"`, you could limit the search to the first five characters. Listing 11.20 shows how.

LISTING 11.20 The `starsrch.c` Program

```
/* starsrch.c -- use strncmp() */
#include <stdio.h>
#include <string.h>
#define LISTSIZE 5
int main()
{
    const char * list[LISTSIZE] =
    {
        "astronomy", "astounding",
        "astrophysics", "ostracize",
        "asterism"
    };
    int count = 0;
    int i;

    for (i = 0; i < LISTSIZE; i++)
        if (strncmp(list[i],"astro", 5) == 0)
        {
            printf("Found: %s\n", list[i]);
            count++;
        }
    printf("The list contained %d words beginning"
            " with astro.\n", count);

    return 0;
}
```

Here is the output:

```
Found: astronomy
Found: astrophysics
The list contained 2 words beginning with astro.
```

The `strcpy()` and `strncpy()` Functions

We've said that if **pts1** and **pts2** are both pointers to strings, the expression

```
pts2 = pts1;
```

copies only the address of a string, not the string itself. Suppose, though, that you do want to copy a string. Then you can use the `strcpy()` function. Listing 11.21 asks the user to enter words beginning with *q*. The program copies the input into a temporary array, and if the first letter is a *q*, the program uses `strcpy()` to copy the string from the temporary array to a permanent destination. The `strcpy()` function is the string equivalent of the assignment operator.

LISTING 11.21 The `copy1.c` Program

```
/* copy1.c -- strcpy() demo */
#include <stdio.h>
#include <string.h>  /* declares strcpy() */
```

LISTING 11.21   Continued

```
#define SIZE 40
#define LIM 5

int main(void)
{
    char qwords[LIM][SIZE];
    char temp[SIZE];
    int i = 0;

    printf("Enter %d words beginning with q:\n", LIM);
    while (i < LIM && gets(temp))
    {
        if (temp[0] != 'q')
            printf("%s doesn't begin with q!\n", temp);
        else
        {
            strcpy(qwords[i], temp);
            i++;
        }
    }
    puts("Here are the words accepted:");
    for (i = 0; i < LIM; i++)
        puts(qwords[i]);

    return 0;
}
```

Here is a sample run:

```
Enter 5 words beginning with q:
quackery
quasar
quilt
quotient
no more
no more doesn't begin with q!
quiz
Here are the words accepted:
quackery
quasar
quilt
quotient
quiz
```

Note that the counter i is incremented only when the word entered passes the q test. Also note that the program uses a character-based test:

```
if (temp[0] != 'q')
```

That is, is the first character in the temp array not a q? Another possibility is using a string-based test:

```
if (strncmp(temp, "q", 1) != 0)
```

That is, are the strings `temp` and `"q"` different from each other in the first element?

Note that the string pointed to by the second argument (`temp`) is copied into the array pointed to by the first argument (`qword[i]`). The copy is called the *target*, and the original string is called the *source*. You can remember the order of the arguments by noting that it is the same as the order in an assignment statement (the target string is on the left):

```
char target[20];
int x;
x = 50;                      /* assignment for numbers */
strcpy(target, "Hi ho!");    /* assignment for strings */
target = "So long";          /* syntax error           */
```

It is your responsibility to make sure the destination array has enough room to copy the source. The following is asking for trouble:

```
char * str;
strcpy(str, "The C of Tranquility"); /* a problem */
```

The function will copy the string `"The C of Tranquility"` to the address specified by `str`, but `str` is uninitialized, so the copy might wind up anywhere!

In short, `strcpy()` takes two string pointers as arguments. The second pointer, which points to the original string, can be a declared pointer, an array name, or a string constant. The first pointer, which points to the copy, should point to a data object, such as an array, roomy enough to hold the string. Remember, declaring an array allocates storage space for data; declaring a pointer only allocates storage space for one address.

Further `strcpy()` Properties

The `strcpy()` function has two more properties that you might find useful. First, it is type `char *`. It returns the value of its first argument—the address of a character. Second, the first argument need not point to the beginning of an array; this lets you copy just part of an array. Listing 11.22 illustrates both these points.

LISTING 11.22   The `copy2.c` Program

```
/* copy2.c -- strcpy() demo */
#include <stdio.h>
#include <string.h>       /* declares strcpy() */
#define WORDS  "beast"
#define SIZE 40

int main(void)
{
    const char * orig = WORDS;
    char copy[SIZE] = "Be the best that you can be.";
    char * ps;

    puts(orig);
    puts(copy);
    ps = strcpy(copy + 7, orig);
```

LISTING 11.22   Continued

```
        puts(copy);
        puts(ps);

        return 0;
}
```

Here is the output:

```
beast
Be the best that you can be.
Be the beast
beast
```

Note that `strcpy()` copies the null character from the source string. In this example, the null character overwrites the first *t* in **that** in **copy** so that the new string ends with **beast** (see Figure 11.5). Also note that **ps** points to the eighth element (index of 7) of **copy** because the first argument is **copy + 7**. Therefore, **puts(ps)** prints the string starting at that point.

FIGURE 11.5

The `strcpy()` function uses pointers.

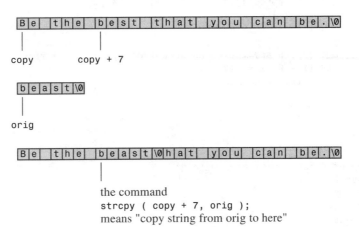

The Careful Choice: `strncpy()`

The `strcpy()` function shares a problem with `gets()`—neither checks to see whether the source string actually fits in the target string. The safer way to copy strings is to use `strncpy()`. It takes a third argument, which is the maximum number of characters to copy. Listing 11.23 is a rewrite of Listing 11.21, using `strncpy()` instead of `strcpy()`. To illustrate what happens if the source string is too large, it uses a rather small size (seven elements, six characters) for the target strings.

LISTING 11.23   The copy3.c Program

```
/* copy3.c -- strncpy() demo */
#include <stdio.h>
#include <string.h>   /* declares strncpy() */
```

LISTING 11.23 *Continued*

```c
#define SIZE 40
#define TARGSIZE 7
#define LIM 5
int main(void)
{
    char qwords[LIM][TARGSIZE];
    char temp[SIZE];
    int i = 0;

    printf("Enter %d words beginning with q:\n", LIM);
    while (i < LIM && gets(temp))
    {
        if (temp[0] != 'q')
            printf("%s doesn't begin with q!\n", temp);
        else
        {
            strncpy(qwords[i], temp, TARGSIZE - 1);
            qwords[i][TARGSIZE - 1] = '\0';
            i++;
        }
    }
    puts("Here are the words accepted:");
    for (i = 0; i < LIM; i++)
        puts(qwords[i]);

    return 0;
}
```

Here is a sample run:

```
Enter 5 words beginning with q:
quack
quadratic
quisling
quota
quagga
Here are the words accepted:
quack
quadra
quisli
quota
quagga
```

The function call `strncpy(target, source, n)` copies up to n characters or up through the null character (whichever comes first) from **source** to **target**. Therefore, if the number of characters in **source** is less than n, the entire string is copied, including the null character. The function never copies more than n characters, so if it reaches the limit before reaching the end of the source string, no null character is added. As a result, the final product may or may not have a null character. For this reason, the program sets n to one less than the size of the target array and then sets the final element in the array to the null character:

```c
strncpy(qwords[i], temp, TARGSIZE - 1);
qwords[i][TARGSIZE - 1] = '\0';
```

This ensures that you've stored a string. If the source string actually fits, the null character copied with it marks the true end of the string. If the source string doesn't fit, this final null character marks the end of the string.

The `sprintf()` Function

The `sprintf()` function is declared in `stdio.h` instead of `string.h`. It works like `printf()`, but it writes to a string instead of writing to a display. Therefore, it provides a way to combine several elements into a single string. The first argument to `sprintf()` is the address of the target string. The remaining arguments are the same as for `printf()`—a conversion specification string followed by a list of items to be written.

Listing 11.24 uses `sprintf()` to combine three items (two strings and a number) into a single string. Note that it uses `sprintf()` the same way you would use `printf()`, except that the resulting string is stored in the array `formal` instead of being displayed onscreen.

LISTING 11.24   The `format.c` Program

```c
/* format.c -- format a string */
#include <stdio.h>
#define MAX 20

int main(void)
{
    char first[MAX];
    char last[MAX];
    char formal[2 * MAX + 10];
    double prize;

    puts("Enter your first name:");
    gets(first);
    puts("Enter your last name:");
    gets(last);
    puts("Enter your prize money:");
    scanf("%lf", &prize);
    sprintf(formal, "%s, %-19s: $%6.2f\n", last, first, prize);
    puts(formal);

    return 0;
}
```

Here's a sample run:

```
Enter your first name:
Teddy
Enter your last name:
Behr
Enter your prize money:
2000
Behr, Teddy           : $2000.00
```

The `sprintf()` command took the input and formatted it into a standard form, which it then stored in the string `formal`.

Other String Functions

The ANSI C library has more than 20 string-handling functions, and the following list summarizes some of the more commonly used ones:

- `char *strcpy(char * s1, const char * s2);`

  This function copies the string (including the null character) pointed to by `s2` to the location pointed to by `s1`. The return value is `s1`.

- `char *strncpy(char * s1, const char * s2, size_t n);`

  This function copies to the location pointed to by `s1` no more than `n` characters from the string pointed to by `s2`. The return value is `s1`. No characters after a null character are copied and, if the source string is shorter than `n` characters, the target string is padded with null characters. If the source string has `n` or more characters, no null character is copied. The return value is `s1`.

- `char *strcat(char * s1, const char * s2);`

  The string pointed to by `s2` is copied to the end of the string pointed to by `s1`. The first character of the `s2` string is copied over the null character of the `s1` string. The return value is `s1`.

- `char *strncat(char * s1, const char * s2, size_t n);`

  No more than the first `n` characters of the `s2` string are appended to the `s1` string, with the first character of the `s2` string being copied over the null character of the `s1` string. The null character and any characters following it in the `s2` string are not copied, and a null character is appended to the result. The return value is `s1`.

- `int strcmp(const char * s1, const char * s2);`

  This function returns a positive value if the `s1` string follows the `s2` string in the machine collating sequence, the value `0` if the two strings are identical, and a negative value if the first string precedes the second string in the machine collating sequence.

- `int strncmp(const char * s1, const char * s2, size_t n);`

  This function works like `strcmp()`, except that the comparison stops after `n` characters or when the first null character is encountered, whichever comes first.

- `char *strchr(const char * s, int c);`

  This function returns a pointer to the first location in the string `s` that holds the character `c`. (The terminating null character is part of the string, so it can be searched for.) The function returns the null pointer if the character is not found.

- `char *strpbrk(const char * s1, const char * s2);`

  This function returns a pointer to the first location in the string s1 that holds any character found in the s2 string. The function returns the null pointer if no character is found.

- `char *strrchr(const char * s, int c);`

  This function returns a pointer to the last occurrence of the character c in the string s. (The terminating null character is part of the string, so it can be searched for.) The function returns the null pointer if the character is not found.

- `char *strstr(const char * s1, const char * s2);`

  This function returns a pointer to the first occurrence of string s2 in string s1. The function returns the null pointer if the string is not found.

- `size_t strlen(const char * s);`

  This function returns the number of characters, not including the terminating null character, found in the string s.

Note that these prototypes use the keyword `const` to indicate which strings are not altered by a function. For example, consider the following:

```
char *strcpy(char * s1, const char * s2);
```

It means s2 points to a string that can't be changed, at least not by the `strcpy()` function, but s1 points to a string that can be changed. This makes sense, because s1 is the target string, which gets altered, and s2 is the source string, which should be left unchanged.

The `size_t` type, as discussed in Chapter 5, "Operators, Expressions, and Statements," is whatever type the `sizeof` operator returns. C states that the `sizeof` operator returns an integer type, but it doesn't specify which integer type, so `size_t` can be `unsigned int` on one system and `unsigned long` on another. Your `string.h` file defines `size_t` for your particular system or else refers to another header file having the definition.

As mentioned earlier, Reference Section V lists all the functions in the `string.h` family. Many implementations provide additional functions beyond those required by the ANSI standard. You should check the documentation for your implementation to see what is available.

Let's look at a simple use of one of these functions. Earlier you saw that `fgets()`, when it reads a line of input, stores the newline in the destination string. You can use `strchr()` to replace the newline with a null character. First, use `strchr()` to find the newline, if any. If the function finds the newline, it returns the address of the newline, and you then can place a null character at that address:

```
char line[80];
char * find;

fgets(line, 80, stdin);
find = strchr(line, '\n');   // look for newline
if (find)                    // if the address is not NULL,
    *find = '\0';            // place a null character there
```

If `strchr()` fails to find a newline, `fgets()` ran into the size limit before reaching the end of the line. You can add an `else` to the `if` to process that circumstance.

Next, let's look at a full program that handles strings.

A String Example: Sorting Strings

Let's tackle the practical problem of sorting strings alphabetically. This task can show up in preparing name lists, in making up an index, and in many other situations. One of the main tools in such a program is `strcmp()`, because it can be used to determine the order of two strings. The general plan will be to read an array of strings, sort them, and print them. Earlier, we presented a scheme for reading strings, and we will start the program that way. Printing the strings is no problem. We'll use a standard sorting algorithm that we'll explain later. We will also do one slightly tricky thing; see whether you can spot it. Listing 11.25 presents the program.

LISTING 11.25   The `sort_str.c` Program

```
/* sort_str.c -- reads in strings and sorts them */
#include <stdio.h>
#include <string.h>
#define SIZE 81        /* string length limit, including \0  */
#define LIM 20         /* maximum number of lines to be read */
#define HALT ""         /* null string to stop input          */
void stsrt(char *strings[], int num);/* string-sort function */

int main(void)
{
    char input[LIM][SIZE];    /* array to store input      */
    char *ptstr[LIM];         /* array of pointer variables */
    int ct = 0;               /* input count               */
    int k;                    /* output count              */

    printf("Input up to %d lines, and I will sort them.\n",LIM);
    printf("To stop, press the Enter key at a line's start.\n");
    while (ct < LIM && gets(input[ct]) != NULL
                    && input[ct][0] != '\0')
    {
        ptstr[ct] = input[ct];  /* set ptrs to strings       */
        ct++;
    }
    stsrt(ptstr, ct);           /* string sorter             */
    puts("\nHere's the sorted list:\n");
    for (k = 0; k < ct; k++)
        puts(ptstr[k]) ;        /* sorted pointers           */

    return 0;
}
```

LISTING 11.25   *Continued*

```
/* string-pointer-sorting function */
void stsrt(char *strings[], int num)
{
    char *temp;
    int top, seek;

    for (top = 0; top < num-1; top++)
        for (seek = top + 1; seek < num; seek++)
            if (strcmp(strings[top],strings[seek]) > 0)
            {
                temp = strings[top];
                strings[top] = strings[seek];
                strings[seek] = temp;
            }
}
```

We fed Listing 11.22 an obscure nursery rhyme to test it:

```
Input up to 20 lines, and I will sort them.
To stop, press the Enter key at a line's start.
O that I was where I would be,
Then would I be where I am not;
But where I am I must be,
And where I would be I can not.

Here's the sorted list:

And where I would be I can not.
But where I am I must be,
O that I was where I would be,
Then would I be where I am not;
```

Hmm, the nursery rhyme doesn't seem to suffer much from being alphabetized.

Sorting Pointers Instead of Strings

The tricky part of the program is that instead of rearranging the strings themselves, we just rearranged *pointers* to the strings. Let us explain. Originally, ptrst[0] is set to input[0], and so on. That means the pointer ptrst[i] points to the first character in the array input[i]. Each input[i] is an array of 81 elements, and each ptrst[i] is a single variable. The sorting procedure rearranges ptrst, leaving input untouched. If, for example, input[1] comes before input[0] alphabetically, the program switches ptrsts, causing ptrst[0] to point to the beginning of input[1] and causing ptrst[1] to point to the beginning of input[0]. This is much easier than using, say, strcpy() to interchange the contents of the two input strings. See Figure 11.6 for another view of this process. It also has the advantage of preserving the original order in the input array.

FIGURE 11.6

Sorting string pointers.

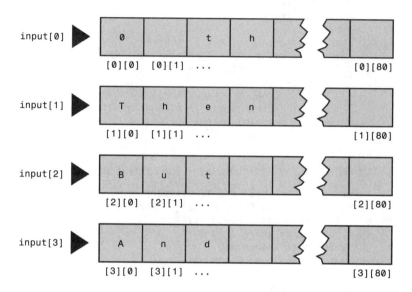

before sorting:

```
ptrst[0] points to input[0]
ptrst[1] points to input[1]
etc
```

input[0]

0		t	h			

[0][0] [0][1] ...   [0][80]

input[1]

T	h	e	n			

[1][0] [1][1] ...   [1][80]

input[2]

B	u	t			

[2][0] [2][1] ...   [2][80]

input[3]

A	n	d			

[3][0] [3][1] ...   [3][80]

after sorting:

```
ptrst[0] points to input[3]
ptrst[1] points to input[2]
etc
```

The Selection Sort Algorithm

To sort the pointers, we use the *selection sort* algorithm. The idea is to use a `for` loop to compare each element in turn with the first element. If the compared element precedes the current first element, the program swaps the two. By the time the program reaches the end of the loop, the first element contains a pointer to whichever string is first in the machine collating sequence. Then the outer `for` loop repeats the process, this time starting with the second element of `input`. When the inner loop completes, the pointer to the second-ranking string ends up in the second element of `ptrst`. The process continues until all the elements have been sorted.

Now let's take a more detailed look at the selection sort. Here is an outline in pseudocode:

```
for n = first to n = next-to-last element,
    find largest remaining number and place it in the nth element
```

The plan works like this: First, start with n = 0. Scan the entire array, find the largest number, and swap it with the first element. Next, set n = 1 and then scan all but the first element of the array. Find the largest remaining number and swap it with the second element. Continue this process until reaching the next-to-last element. Now only two elements are left. Compare them and place the larger in the next-to-last position. This leaves the smallest element of all in the final position.

It looks like a `for` loop task, but we still have to describe the "find and place" process in more detail. One way to select the largest remaining value is to compare the first and second elements of the remaining array. If the second is larger, swap the two values. Now compare the first element with the third. If the third is larger, swap those two. Each swap moves a larger element to the top. Continue this way until you have compared the first with the last element. When you finish, the largest value is now in the first element of the remaining array. You have sorted the array for the first element, but the rest of the array is in a jumble. Here is the procedure in pseudocode:

```
for n - second element to last element,
  compare nth element with first element; if nth is greater, swap values
```

This process looks like another `for` loop. It will be nested in the first `for` loop. The outer loop indicates which array element is to be filled, and the inner loop finds the value to put there. Putting the two parts of the pseudocode together and translating them into C, we get the function in Listing 11.25. Incidentally, the C library includes a more advanced sorting function called `qsort()`. Among other things, it uses a pointer to a function to make the sorting comparison. Chapter 16, "The C Preprocessor and the C Library," gives examples of its use.

The `ctype.h` Character Functions and Strings

Chapter 7, "C Control Statements: Branching and Jumps," introduced the `ctype.h` family of character-related functions. These functions can't be applied to a string as a whole, but they can be applied to the individual characters in a string. Listing 11.26, for example, defines a function that applies the `toupper()` function to each character in a string, thus converting the whole string to uppercase. It also defines a function that uses `ispunct()` to count the number of punctuation characters in a string.

LISTING 11.26   The `mod_str.c` Program

```c
/* mod_str.c -- modifies a string */
#include <stdio.h>
#include <string.h>
#include <ctype.h>
#define LIMIT 80
void ToUpper(char *);
int PunctCount(const char *);

int main(void)
{
    char line[LIMIT];

    puts("Please enter a line:");
    gets(line);
    ToUpper(line);
```

LISTING 11.26   *Continued*

```
    puts(line);
    printf("That line has %d punctuation characters.\n",
            PunctCount(line));

    return 0;
}

void ToUpper(char * str)
{
    while (*str)
    {
        *str = toupper(*str);
        str++;
    }
}

int PunctCount(const char * str)
{
    int ct = 0;
    while (*str)
    {
        if (ispunct(*str))
            ct++;
        str++;
    }

    return ct;
}
```

The `while (*str)` loop processes each character in the string pointed to by `str` until the null character is reached. At that point, the value of `*str` becomes 0 (the code for the null character), or false, and the loop terminates. Here is a sample run:

```
Please enter a line:
Me? You talkin' to me? Get outta here!
ME? YOU TALKIN' TO ME? GET OUTTA HERE!
That line has 4 punctuation characters.
```

The `ToUpper()` function applies `toupper()` to each character in a string. (The fact that C distinguishes between uppercase and lowercase makes these two function names different from one another.) As defined by ANSI C, the `toupper()` function alters only characters that are lowercase. However, very old implementations of C don't do that check automatically, so old code normally does something like this:

```
if (islower(*str))          /* pre-ANSI C -- check before converting */
    *str = toupper(*str);
```

Incidentally, the `ctype.h` functions are usually implemented as *macros*. These are C preprocessor constructions that act much like functions but have some important differences. We'll cover macros in Chapter 16.

Next, let's try to fill an old emptiness in our lives, namely, the void between the parentheses in `main()`.

Command-Line Arguments

Before the modern graphical interface, there was the command-line interface. DOS and Unix are examples. The *command line* is the line you type to run your program in a command-line environment. Suppose you have a program in a file named `fuss`. Then the command line to run it might look like this in Unix:

```
$ fuss
```

Or it might look like this in a Windows command-line mode, such as XP's Command Prompt:

```
C> fuss
```

Command-line arguments are additional items on the same line. Here's an example:

```
% fuss -r Ginger
```

A C program can read those additional items for its own use (see Figure 11.7).

FIGURE 11.7
Command-line arguments.

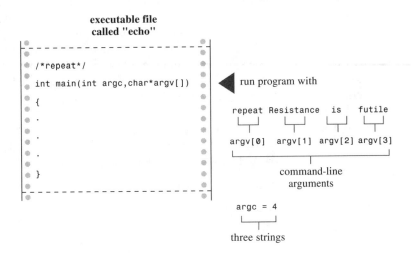

A C program reads these items by using arguments to `main()`. Listing 11.27 shows a typical example.

LISTING 11.27   The `repeat.c` Program

```
/* repeat.c -- main() with arguments */
#include <stdio.h>
int main(int argc, char *argv[])
{
    int count;

    printf("The command line has %d arguments:\n", argc - 1);
    for (count = 1; count < argc; count++)
```

LISTING 11.27 *Continued*

```
        printf("%d: %s\n", count, argv[count]);
    printf("\n");

    return 0;
}
```

Compile this program into an executable file called **repeat**. Here is what happens when you run it from a command line:

```
C>repeat Resistance is futile
The command line has 3 arguments:
1: Resistance
2: is
3: futile
```

You can see why it is called **repeat**, but you might wonder how it works. We'll explain now.

C compilers allow **main()** to have no arguments or else to have two arguments. (Some implementations allow additional arguments, but that would be an extension of the standard.) With two arguments, the first argument is the number of strings in the command line. By tradition (but not by necessity), this **int** argument is called **argc** for *argument count*. The system uses spaces to tell when one string ends and the next begins. Therefore, the **repeat** example has four strings, including the command name, and the **fuss** example has three. The second argument is an array of pointers to strings. Each string on the command line is stored in memory and has a pointer assigned to point to it. By convention, this array of pointers is called **argv**, for *argument values*. When possible (some operating systems don't allow this), **argv[0]** is assigned the name of the program itself. Then **argv[1]** is assigned the first following string, and so on. For our example, we have the following relationships:

argv[0] points to **repeat** (for most systems)

argv[1] points to **Resistance**

argv[2] points to **is**

argv[3] points to **futile**

The program in Listing 11.27 uses a **for** loop to print each string in turn. Recall that the **%s** specifier for **printf()** expects the address of a string to be provided as an argument. Each element—**argv[0]**, **argv[1]**, and so on—is just such an address.

The form is the same as for any other function having formal arguments. Many programmers use a different declaration for **argv**:

```
int main(int argc, char **argv)
```

This alternative declaration for **argv** really is equivalent to **char *argv[]**. It says that **argv** is a pointer to a pointer to **char**. The example comes down to the same thing. It had an array with seven elements. The name of the array is a pointer to the first element, so `argv` points to `argv[0]`, and `argv[0]` is a pointer to `char`. Hence, even with the original definition, `argv` is a pointer to a pointer to `char`. You can use either form, but we think that the first more clearly suggests that `argv` represents a set of strings.

Incidentally, many environments, including Unix and DOS, allow the use of quotation marks to lump several words into a single argument. For example, the command

```
repeat "I am hungry" now
```

would assign the string `"I am hungry"` to `argv[1]` and the string `"now"` to `argv[2]`.

Command-Line Arguments in Integrated Environments

Integrated Windows environments, such as Metrowerks CodeWarrior, Microsoft Visual C++, and Borland C/C++, don't use command lines to run programs. However, some have menu selections that enable you to specify a command-line argument. In other cases, you may be able to compile the program in the IDE and then open an MS-DOS window to run the program in command-line mode.

Command-Line Arguments with the Macintosh

The Macintosh operating system doesn't use command lines, but Metrowerks CodeWarrior enables you to simulate a command-line environment with the `ccommand()` function. Use the `console.h` header file and start your programs like this:

```
#include <stdio.h>
#include <console.h>
int main(int argc, char *argv[])
{
    ...       /* variable declarations */
    argc = ccommand(&argv);
    ...
}
```

When the program reaches the `ccommand()` function call, it puts a dialog box onscreen and provides a box in which you can type a command line. The command then places the command-line words in the `argv` strings and returns the number of words. The current project name will appear as the first word in the command-line box, so you should type the command-line arguments after that name. The `ccommand()` function also enables you to simulate redirection.

Why bother with this on a Mac? About the only reason is to practice the command-line idiom, in case someday you do have to write command-line-based programs. Now that Macintosh has moved to the Unix-based Mac OS X, Mac programmers may get a more intimate acquaintance with command-line programs.

String-to-Number Conversions

Numbers can be stored either as strings or in numeric form. Storing a number as a string means storing the digit characters. For example, the number 213 can be stored in a character string array as the digits '2', '1', '3', '\0'. Storing 213 in numeric form means storing it as, say, an int.

C requires numeric forms for numeric operations, such as addition and comparison, but displaying numbers on your screen requires a string form because a screen displays characters. The printf() and sprintf() functions, through their %d and other specifiers, convert numeric forms to string forms, and vice versa. C also has functions whose sole purpose is to convert string forms to numeric forms.

Suppose, for example, that you want a program to use a numeric command-line argument. Unfortunately, command-line arguments are read as strings. Therefore, to use the numeric value, you must first convert the string to a number. If the number is an integer, you can use the atoi() function (for *alphanumeric to integer*). It takes a string as an argument and returns the corresponding integer value. Listing 11.28 shows a sample use.

LISTING 11.28   The hello.c Program

```
/* hello.c -- converts command-line argument to number */
#include <stdio.h>
#include <stdlib.h>

int main(int argc, char *argv[])
{
    int i, times;

    if (argc < 2 || (times = atoi(argv[1])) < 1)
        printf("Usage: %s positive-number\n", argv[0]);
    else
        for (i = 0; i < times; i++)
            puts("Hello, good looking!");

    return 0;
}
```

Here's a sample run:

```
% hello 3
Hello, good looking!
Hello, good looking!
Hello, good looking!
```

The % is a Unix prompt. The command-line argument of 3 was stored as the string 3\0. The atoi() function converted this string to the integer value 3, which was assigned to times. This then determined the number of for loop cycles executed.

If you run the program without a command-line argument, the `argc < 2` test aborts the program and prints a usage message. The same thing happens if `times` is 0 or negative. C's order-of-evaluation rule for logical operators guarantees that if `argc < 2`, `atoi(argv[1])` is not evaluated.

The `atoi()` function still works if the string only begins with an integer. In that case, it converts characters until it encounters something that is not part of an integer. For example, `atoi("42regular")` returns the integer `42`. What if the command line is something like `hello what`? On the implementations we've used, the `atoi()` function returns a value of `0` if its argument is not recognizable as a number. However, the ANSI standard says the behavior in that case is undefined. The `strtol()` function, discussed shortly, provides error checking that is more reliable.

We include the `stdlib.h` header because, under ANSI C, it contains the function declaration for `atoi()`. That header file also includes declarations for `atof()` and `atol()`. The `atof()` function converts a string to a type `double` value, and the `atol()` function converts a string to a type `long` value. They work analogously to `atoi()`, so they are type `double` and `long`, respectively.

ANSI C has supplied more sophisticated versions of these functions: `strtol()` converts a string to a `long`, `strtoul()` converts a string to an `unsigned long`, and `strtod()` converts a string to `double`. The more sophisticated aspect is that the functions identify and report the first character in the string that is not part of a number. Also, `strtol()` and `strtoul()` allow you to specify a number base.

Let's look at an example involving `strtol()`. It's prototype is as follows:

```
long strtol(const char *nptr, char **endptr, int base);
```

Here, `nptr` is a pointer to the string you want to convert, `endptr` is the address of a pointer that gets set to the address of the character terminating the input number, and `base` is the number base the number is written in. An example, given in Listing 11.29, makes this clearer.

LISTING 11.29   The `strcnvt.c` Program

```
/* strcnvt.c -- try strtol() */
#include <stdio.h>
#include <stdlib.h>

int main()
{
    char number[30];
    char * end;
    long value;

    puts("Enter a number (empty line to quit):");
    while(gets(number) && number[0] != '\0')
    {
        value = strtol(number, &end, 10);  /* base 10 */
        printf("value: %ld, stopped at %s (%d)\n",
```

LISTING 11.29 Continued

```
                         value, end, *end);
          value = strtol(number, &end, 16);   /* base 16 */
          printf("value: %ld, stopped at %s (%d)\n",
                         value, end, *end);
          puts("Next number:");
     }
     puts("Bye!\n");

     return 0;
}
```

Here is some sample output:

```
Enter a number (empty line to quit):
10
value: 10, stopped at  (0)
value: 16, stopped at  (0)
Next number:
10atom
value: 10, stopped at atom (97)
value: 266, stopped at tom (116)
Next number:

Bye!
```

First, note that the string "10" is converted to the number 10 when base is 10 and to 16 when base is 16. Also note that if end points to a character, *end is a character. Therefore, the first conversion ended when the null character was reached, so end pointed to the null character. Printing end displays an empty string, and printing *end with the %d format displays the ASCII code for the null character.

For the second input string (base-10 interpretation), end is given the address of the 'a' character. So printing end displays the string "atom", and printing *end displays the ASCII code for the 'a' character. When the base is changed to 16, however, the 'a' character is recognized as a valid hexadecimal digit, and the function converts the hexadecimal number 10a to 266, base 10.

The strtol() function goes up to base 36, using the letters through 'z' as digits. The strtoul() function does the same, but converts unsigned values. The strtod() function does only base 10, so it uses just two arguments.

Many implementations have itoa() and ftoa() functions for converting integers and floating-point values to strings. However, they are not part of the ANSI C library; use sprintf(), instead, for greater compatibility.

Key Concepts

Many programs deal with text data. A program may ask you to enter your name, a list of corporations, an address, the botanical name for a type of fern, the cast of a musical, or…well, because we interact with the world using words, there's really no end to examples using text. And strings are the means a C program uses to handle strings.

A C *string*—whether it be identified by a character array, a pointer, or a string literal—is stored as a series of bytes containing character codes, and the sequence is terminated by the null character. C recognizes the usefulness of strings by providing a library of functions for manipulating them, searching them, and analyzing them. In particular, keep in mind that you should use `strcmp()` instead of relational operators when comparing strings, and you should use `strcpy()` or `strncpy()` instead of the assignment operator to assign a string to a character array.

Summary

A C *string* is a series of `char`s terminated by the null character, `'\0'`. A string can be stored in a character array. A string can also be represented with a *string constant*, in which the characters, aside from the null character, are enclosed in double quotation marks. The compiler supplies the null character. Therefore, `"joy"` is stored as the four characters `j`, `o`, `y`, and `\0`. The length of a string, as measured by `strlen()`, doesn't count the null character.

String constants, also known as *string literals*, can be used to initialize character arrays. The array size should be at least one greater than the string length to accommodate the terminating null character. String constants can also be used to initialize pointers of type pointer-to-`char`.

Functions use pointers to the first character of a string to identify on which string to act. Typically, the corresponding actual argument is an array name, a pointer variable, or a quoted string. In each case, the address of the first character is passed. In general, it is not necessary to pass the length of the string, because the function can use the terminating null character to locate the end of a string.

The `gets()` and `puts()` functions fetch a line of input and print a line of output, respectively. They are part of the `stdio.h` family of functions.

The C library includes several *string-handling* functions. Under ANSI C, these functions are declared in the `string.h` file. The library also has several *character-processing* functions; they are declared in the `ctype.h` file.

You can give a program access to *command-line arguments* by providing the proper two formal variables to the `main()` function. The first argument, traditionally called `argc`, is an `int` and is assigned the count of command-line words. The second argument, traditionally called `argv`, is a pointer to an array of pointers to `char`. Each pointer-to-`char` points to one of the command-line argument strings, with `argv[0]` pointing to the command name, `argv[1]` pointing to the first command-line argument, and so on.

The `atoi()`, `atol()`, and `atof()` functions convert string representations of numbers to type `int`, `long`, and `double` forms, respectively. The `strtol()`, `strtoul()`, and `strtod()` functions convert string representations of numbers to type `long`, `unsigned long`, and `double` forms, respectively.

Review Questions

1. What's wrong with this attempted declaration of a character string?

```
int main(void)
{
    char name[] = {'F', 'e', 's', 's' };
    ...
}
```

2. What will this program print?

```
#include <stdio.h>
int main(void)
{
    char note[] = "See you at the snack bar.";
    char *ptr;

    ptr = note;
    puts(ptr);
    puts(++ptr);
    note[7] = '\0';
    puts(note);
    puts(++ptr);
    return 0;
}
```

3. What will this program print?

```
#include <stdio.h>
#include <string.h>
int main(void)
{
    char food[] = "Yummy";
    char *ptr;

    ptr = food + strlen(food);
    while (--ptr >= food)
        puts(ptr);
    return 0;
}
```

4. What will the following program print?

```
#include <stdio.h>
#include <string.h>
int main(void)
{
    char goldwyn[40] = "art of it all ";
    char samuel[40] = "I read p";
    const char * quote = "the way through.";

    strcat(goldwyn, quote);
    strcat( samuel, goldwyn);
```

```
        puts(samuel);
        return 0;
}
```

5. The following provides practice with strings, loops, pointers, and pointer incrementing.
   First, suppose you have this function definition:

```
#include <stdio.h>
char *pr (char *str)
{
    char *pc;

    pc = str;
    while (*pc)
        putchar(*pc++);
    do {
        putchar(*--pc);
        } while (pc - str);
    return (pc);
}
```

Consider the following function call:

```
x = pr("Ho Ho Ho!");
```

   a. What is printed?

   b. What type should x be?

   c. What value does x get?

   d. What does the expression *--pc mean, and how is it different from --*pc?

   e. What would be printed if *--pc were replaced with *pc--?

   f. What do the two while expressions test for?

   g. What happens if pr() is supplied with a null string as an argument?

   h. What must be done in the calling function so that pr() can be used as shown?

6. Assume this declaration:

```
char sign = '$';
```

   How many bytes of memory does sign use? What about '$'? What about "$"?

7. What does the following program print?

```
#include <stdio.h>
#include <string.h>
#define M1    "How are ya, sweetie? "
char M2[40] = "Beat the clock.";
char * M3   = "chat";
int main(void)
{
        char words[80];
        printf(M1);
```

```
            puts(M1);
            puts(M2);
            puts(M2 + 1);
            strcpy(words,M2);
            strcat(words, " Win a toy.");
            puts(words);
            words[4] = '\0';
            puts(words);
            while (*M3)
                puts(M3++);
            puts(--M3);
            puts(--M3);
            M3 = M1;
            puts(M3);
            return 0;
    }
```

8. What does the following program print?

```
#include <stdio.h>
int main(void)
{
    char str1[] = "gawsie";
    char str2[] = "bletonism";
    char *ps;
    int i = 0;

    for (ps = str1; *ps != '\0'; ps++) {
        if ( *ps == 'a' || *ps == 'e')
                putchar(*ps);
        else
                (*ps)--;
        putchar(*ps);
        }
    putchar('\n');
    while (str2[i] != '\0' ) {
        printf("%c", i % 3 ? str2[i] : '*');
        ++i;
        }
    return 0;
}
```

9. The strlen() function takes a pointer to a string as an argument and returns the length of the string. Write your own version of this function.

10. Design a function that takes a string pointer as an argument and returns a pointer to the first space character in the string on or after the pointed-to position. Have it return a null pointer if it finds no spaces.

11. Rewrite Listing 11.17 using ctype.h functions so that the program recognizes a correct answer regardless of the user's choice of uppercase or lowercase.

Programming Exercises

1. Design and test a function that fetches the next n characters from input (including blanks, tabs, and newlines), storing the results in an array whose address is passed as an argument.

2. Modify and test the function in exercise 1 so that it stops after n characters or after the first blank, tab, or newline, whichever comes first. (Don't just use scanf().)

3. Design and test a function that reads the first word from a line of input into an array and discards the rest of the line. Define a word as a sequence of characters with no blanks, tabs, or newlines in it.

4. Design and test a function that searches the string specified by the first function parameter for the first occurrence of a character specified by the second function parameter. Have the function return a pointer to the character if successful, and a null if the character is not found in the string. (This duplicates the way that the library strchr() function works.) Test the function in a complete program that uses a loop to provide input values for feeding to the function.

5. Write a function called is_within() that takes a character and a string pointer as its two function parameters. Have the function return a nonzero value (true) if the character is in the string and zero (false) otherwise. Test the function in a complete program that uses a loop to provide input values for feeding to the function.

6. The strncpy(s1,s2,n) function copies exactly n characters from s2 to s1, truncating s2 or padding it with extra null characters as necessary. The target string may not be null-terminated if the length of s2 is n or more. The function returns s1. Write your own version of this function. Test the function in a complete program that uses a loop to provide input values for feeding to the function.

7. Write a function called string_in() that takes two string pointers as arguments. If the second string is contained in the first string, have the function return the address at which the contained string begins. For instance, string_in("hats", "at") would return the address of the a in hats. Otherwise, have the function return the null pointer. Test the function in a complete program that uses a loop to provide input values for feeding to the function.

8. Write a function that replaces the contents of a string with the string reversed. Test the function in a complete program that uses a loop to provide input values for feeding to the function.

9. Write a function that takes a string as an argument and removes the spaces from the string. Test it in a program that uses a loop to read lines until you enter an empty line. The program should apply the function to each input string and display the result.

10. Write a program that reads in up to 10 strings or to EOF, whichever comes first. Have it offer the user a menu with five choices: print the original list of strings, print the strings in ASCII collating sequence, print the strings in order of increasing length, print the strings in order of the length of the first word in the string, and quit. Have the menu recycle until the user enters the quit request. The program, of course, should actually perform the promised tasks.

11. Write a program that reads input up to EOF and reports the number of words, the number of uppercase letters, the number of lowercase letters, the number of punctuation characters, and the number of digits. Use the ctype.h family of functions.

12. Write a program that echoes the command-line arguments in reverse word order. That is, if the command-line arguments are see you later, the program should print later you see.

13. Write a power-law program that works on a command-line basis. The first command-line argument should be the type double number to be raised to a certain power, and the second argument should be the integer power.

14. Use the character classification functions to prepare an implementation of atoi().

15. Write a program that reads input until end-of-file and echoes it to the display. Have the program recognize and implement the following command-line arguments:

-p	Print input as is
-u	Map input to all uppercase
-l	Map input to all lowercase

CHAPTER 12

STORAGE CLASSES, LINKAGE, AND MEMORY MANAGEMENT

You will learn about the following in this chapter:

- Keywords:
  auto, extern, static, register,
  const, volatile, restricted

- Functions:
  rand(), srand(), time(),
  malloc(), calloc(), free()

- How C allows you to determine
  the scope of a variable (how
  widely known it is) and the life-
  time of a variable (how long it
  remains in existence)

- Designing more complex programs

One of C's strengths is that it enables you to control a program's fine points. C's memory management system exemplifies that control by letting you determine which functions know which variables and for how long a variable persists in a program. Using memory storage is one more element of program design.

Storage Classes

C provides five different models, or *storage classes*, for variables. There's also a sixth model, based on pointers, that we'll get to later in this chapter (in the section "Allocated Memory: malloc() and free()"). You can describe a variable (or, more generally, a data object) in terms of its *storage duration*, which is how long it stays in memory, and its *scope* and its *linkage*, which together indicate which parts of a program can use it by name. The different storage classes offer different combinations of scope, linkage, and storage duration. You can have variables that can be shared over several files of source code, variables that can be used by any function in one particular file, variables that can be used only within a particular function, and even variables that can be used only within a subsection of a function. You can have variables that exist for the duration of a program and variables that exist only while the function containing them is executing. You also can store data in memory that is allocated and freed explicitly by means of function calls.

Before examining the five storage classes, we need to investigate the meaning of the terms *scope*, *linkage*, and *storage duration*. After that, we'll return to the specific storage classes.

Scope

Scope describes the region or regions of a program that can access an identifier. A C variable has one of the following scopes: block scope, function prototype scope, or file scope. The program examples to date have used block scope. A *block*, as you'll recall, is a region of code contained within an opening brace and the matching closing brace. For instance, the entire body of a function is a block. Any compound statement within a function also is a block. A variable defined inside a block has *block scope*, and it is visible from the point it is defined until the end of the block containing the definition. Also, formal function parameters, even though they occur before the opening brace of a function, have block scope and belong to the block containing the function body. So the local variables we've used to date, including formal function parameters, have block scope. Therefore, the variables `cleo` and `patrick` in the following code both have block scope extending to the closing brace:

```
double blocky(double cleo)
{
    double patrick = 0.0;
    ...
    return patrick;
}
```

Variables declared in an inner block have scope restricted just to that block:

```
double blocky(double cleo)
{
    double patrick = 0.0;
    int i;
    for (i = 0; i < 10; i++)
    {
        double q = cleo * i; // start of scope for q
        ...
        patrick *= q;
    }                        // end of scope for q
    ...
     return patrick;
}
```

In this example, the scope of q is limited to the inner block, and only code within that block can access q.

Traditionally, variables with block scope had to be declared at the beginning of a block. C99 has relaxed that rule, allowing you to declare variables anywhere in a block. One new possibility is in the control section of a `for` loop. That is, you now can do this:

```
for (int i = 0; i < 10; i++)
    printf("A C99 feature: i = %d", i);
```

As part of this new feature, C99 expands the concept of a block to include the code controlled by a `for` loop, `while` loop, `do while` loop, or `if` statement, even if no brackets are used. So in the previous `for` loop, the variable `i` is considered to be part of the `for` loop block. Therefore, its scope is limited to the `for` loop. After execution leaves the `for` loop, the program will no longer see that `i`.

Function prototype scope applies to variable names used in function prototypes, as in the following:

```
int mighty(int mouse, double large);
```

Function prototype scope runs from the point the variable is defined to the end of the prototype declaration. What this means is that all the compiler cares about when handling a function prototype argument is the types; the names you use, if any, normally don't matter, and they needn't match the names you use in the function definition. One case in which the names matter a little is with variable-length array parameters:

```
void use_a_VLA(int n, int m, ar[n][m]);
```

If you use names in the brackets, they have to be names declared earlier in the prototype.

A variable with its definition placed outside of any function has *file scope*. A variable with file scope is visible from the point it is defined to the end of the file containing the definition. Take a look at this example:

```
#include <stdio.h>
int units = 0;          /* a variable with file scope */
void critic(void);
int main(void)
{
    ...
}

void critic(void)
{
    ...
}
```

Here, the variable `units` has file scope, and it can be used in both `main()` and `critic()`. Because they can be used in more than one function, file scope variables are also called *global variables*.

There is one other type of scope, called *function scope*, but it applies only to labels used by `goto` statements. Function scope means a `goto` label in a particular function is visible to code anywhere in that function, regardless of the block in which it appears.

Linkage

Next, let's look at linkage. A C variable has one of the following linkages: external linkage, internal linkage, or no linkage. Variables with block scope or prototype scope have no linkage. That means they are private to the block or prototype in which they are defined. A variable with file scope can have either internal or external linkage. A variable with external linkage can be used anywhere in a multifile program. A variable with internal linkage can be used anywhere in a single file.

So how can you tell whether a file scope variable has internal or external linkage? You look to see if the storage class specifier `static` is used in the external definition:

```
int giants = 5;         // file scope, external linkage
static int dodgers = 3; // file scope, internal linkage
int main()
{
    ...
}
...
```

The variable `giants` can be used by other files that are part of the same program. The `dodgers` variable is private to this particular file, but can be used by any function in the file.

Storage Duration

A C variable has one of the following two storage durations: static storage duration or automatic storage duration. If a variable has static storage duration, it exists throughout program execution. Variables with file scope have static storage duration. Note that for file scope variables, the keyword `static` indicates the linkage type, not the storage duration. A file scope variable declared using `static` has internal linkage, but all file scope variables, using internal linkage or external linkage, have static storage duration.

Variables with block scope normally have automatic storage duration. These variables have memory allocated for them when the program enters the block in which they are defined, and the memory is freed when the block is exited. The idea is that memory used for automatic variables is a workspace or scratch pad that can be reused. For example, after a function call terminates, the memory it used for its variables can be used to hold variables for the next function that is called.

The local variables we've used so far fall into the automatic category. For example, in the following code, the variables `number` and `index` come into being each time the `bore()` function is called and pass away each time the function completes:

```
void bore(int number)
{
    int index;
    for (index = 0; index < number; index++)
        puts("They don't make them the way they used to.\n");
    return 0;
}
```

C uses scope, linkage, and storage duration to define five storage classes: automatic, register, static with block scope, static with external linkage, and static with internal linkage. Table 12.1 lists the combinations. Now that we've covered scope, linkage, and storage duration, we can discuss these storage classes in more detail.

TABLE 12.1 The Five Storage Classes

Storage Class	Duration	Scope	Linkage	How Declared
`automatic`	Automatic	Block	None	In a block
`register`	Automatic	Block	None	In a block with the keyword `register`
`static` with external linkage	Static	File	External	Outside of all functions
`static` with internal linkage	Static	File	Internal	Outside of all functions with the keyword `static`
`static` with no linkage	Static	Block	None	In a block with the keyword `static`

Automatic Variables

A variable belonging to the automatic storage class has automatic storage duration, block scope, and no linkage. By default, any variable declared in a block or function header belongs to the automatic storage class. You can, however, make your intentions perfectly clear by explicitly using the keyword `auto`, as shown here:

```
int main(void)
{
    auto int plox;
```

You might do this, for example, to document that you are intentionally overriding an external function definition or that it is important not to change the variable to another storage class. The keyword `auto` is termed a *storage class specifier*.

Block scope and no linkage implies that only the block in which the variable is defined can access that variable by name. (Of course, arguments can be used to communicate the variable's value and address to another function, but that is indirect knowledge.) Another function can use a variable with the same name, but it will be an independent variable stored in a different memory location.

Recall that automatic storage duration means that the variable comes into existence when the program enters the block that contains the variable declaration. When the program exits the block, the automatic variable disappears. Its memory location can now be used for something else.

Let's look more closely at nested blocks. A variable is known only to the block in which it is declared and to any block inside that block:

```
int loop(int n)
{
    int m;          // m in scope
    scanf("%d", &m);
    {
```

```
        int i;    // both m and i in scope
        for (i = m; i < n; i++)
            puts("i is local to a sub-block\n");
    }
    return m;    // m in scope, i gone
}
```

In this code, i is visible only within the inner braces. You'd get a compiler error if you tried to use it before or after the inner block. Normally, you wouldn't use this feature when designing a program. Sometimes, however, it is useful to define a variable in a sub-block if it is not used elsewhere. In that way, you can document the meaning of a variable close to where it is used. Also, the variable doesn't sit unused, occupying memory when it is no longer needed. The variables n and m, being defined in the function head and in the outer block, are in scope for the whole function and exist until the function terminates.

What if you declare a variable in an inner block that has the same name as one in the outer block? Then the name defined inside the block is the variable used inside the block. We say it *hides* the outer definition. However, when execution exits the inner block, the outer variable comes back into scope. Listing 12.1 illustrates these points and more.

LISTING 12.1   The hiding.c Program

```
/* hiding.c -- variables in blocks */
#include <stdio.h>
int main()
{
    int x = 30;        /* original x            */

    printf("x in outer block: %d\n", x);
    {
        int x = 77;   /* new x, hides first x */
        printf("x in inner block: %d\n", x);
    }
    printf("x in outer block: %d\n", x);
    while (x++ < 33) /* original x            */
    {
        int x = 100; /* new x, hides first x */
        x++;
        printf("x in while loop: %d\n", x);
    }
    printf("x in outer block: %d\n", x);

    return 0;
}
```

Here's the output:

```
x in outer block: 30
x in inner block: 77
x in outer block: 30
x in while loop: 101
```

LISTING 12.1   Continued

```
x in while loop: 101
x in while loop: 101
x in outer block: 34
```

First, the program creates an x variable with the value **30**, as the first `printf()` statement shows. Then it defines a new x variable with the value **77**, as the second `printf()` statement shows. That it is a new variable hiding the first x is shown by the third `printf()` statement. It is located after the first inner block, and it displays the original x value, showing that the original x variable never went away and never got changed.

Perhaps the most intriguing part of the program is the `while` loop. The `while` loop test uses the original x:

```
while(x++ < 33)
```

Inside the loop, however, the program sees a third x variable, one defined just inside the `while` loop block. So when the code uses x++ in the body of the loop, it is the new x that is incremented to **101** and then displayed. When each loop cycle is completed, that new x disappears. Then the loop test condition uses and increments the original x, the loop block is entered again, and the new x is created again. In this example, that x is created and destroyed three times. Note that, to terminate, this loop had to increment x in the test condition because incrementing x in the body increments a different x than the one used for the test.

The intent of this example is not to encourage you to write code like this. Rather, it is to illustrate what happens when you define variables inside a block.

Blocks Without Braces

A C99 feature, mentioned earlier, is that statements that are part of a loop or `if` statement qualify as a block even if braces (that is, `{ }`) aren't used. More completely, an entire loop is a sub-block to the block containing it, and the loop body is a sub-block to the entire loop block. Similarly, an `if` statement is a block, and its associated substatement is a sub-block to the `if` statement. These rules affect where you can declare a variable and the scope of that variable. Listing 12.2 shows how this works in a `for` loop.

LISTING 12.2   The `forc99.c` Program

```
//forc99.c -- new C99 block rules
#include <stdio.h>
int main()
{
    int n = 10;

    printf("Initially, n = %d\n", n);
    for (int n = 1; n < 3; n++)
        printf("loop 1: n = %d\n", n);
    printf("After loop 1, n = %d\n", n);
    for (int n = 1; n < 3; n++)
    {
```

LISTING 12.2   Continued

```
            printf("loop 2 index n = %d\n", n);
            int n = 30;
            printf("loop 2: n = %d\n", n);
            n++;
        }
        printf("After loop 2, n = %d\n", n);

        return 0;
}
```

Here is the output, assuming the compiler supports this particular C99 feature:

```
Initially, n = 10
loop 1: n = 1
loop 1: n = 2
After loop 1, n = 10
loop 2 index n = 1
loop 2: n = 30
loop 2 index n = 2
loop 2: n = 30
After loop 2, n = 10
```

C99 Support

Some compilers may not support these new C99 scope rules. Others may provide an option for activating these rules. For example, at the time of this writing, gcc supports many C99 features by default but requires using the −std=c99 option to activate these rules:

```
gcc −std=c99 forc99.c
```

The n declared in the control section of the first **for** loop is in scope to the end of the loop and hides the initial n. But after execution leaves the loop, the original n comes into scope.

In the second **for** loop, the n declared as a loop index hides the initial n. Then, the n declared inside the loop body hides the loop index n. When the program finishes executing the body, the n declared in the body disappears, and the loop test uses the index n. When the entire loop terminates, the original n comes back into scope.

Initialization of Automatic Variables

Automatic variables are not initialized unless you do so explicitly. Consider the following declarations:

```
int main(void)
{
  int repid;
  int tents = 5;
```

The **tents** variable is initialized to **5**, but the **repid** variable ends up with whatever value happened to previously occupy the space assigned to **repid**. You cannot rely on this value being **0**.

You can initialize an automatic variable with a nonconstant expression, provided any variables used have been defined previously:

```
int main(void)
{
    int ruth = 1;
    int rance = 5 * ruth;    // use previously defined variable
```

Register Variables

Variables are normally stored in computer memory. With luck, register variables are stored in the CPU registers or, more generally, in the fastest memory available, where they can be accessed and manipulated more rapidly than regular variables. Because a register variable may be in a register rather than in memory, you can't take the address of a register variable. In most other respects, register variables are the same as automatic variables. That is, they have block scope, no linkage, and automatic storage duration. A variable is declared by using the storage class specifier `register`:

```
int main(void)
{
    register int quick;
```

We say "with luck" because declaring a variable as a `register` class is more a request than a direct order. The compiler has to weigh your demands against the number of registers or amount of fast memory available, so you might not get your wish. In that case, the variable becomes an ordinary automatic variable; however, you still can't use the address operator with it.

You can request that formal parameters be register variables. Just use the keyword in the function heading:

```
void macho(register int n)
```

The types that can be declared `register` may be restricted. For example, the registers in a processor might not be large enough to hold type `double`.

Static Variables with Block Scope

The name *static variable* sounds like a contradiction, like a variable that can't vary. Actually, *static* means that the variable stays put. Variables with file scope automatically (and necessarily) have static storage duration. It's also possible to create local variables—that is, variables having block scope that have static storage. These variables have the same scope as automatic variables, but they don't vanish when the containing function ends its job. That is, such variables have block scope, no linkage, but static storage duration. The computer remembers their values from one function call to the next. Such variables are created by declaring them in a block (which provides the block scope and lack of linkage) with the storage class specifier `static` (which provides the static storage duration). The example in Listing 12.3 illustrates this technique.

LISTING 12.3   The `loc_stat.c` Program

```c
/* loc_stat.c -- using a local static variable */
#include <stdio.h>
void trystat(void);

int main(void)
{
    int count;

    for (count = 1; count <= 3; count++)
    {
        printf("Here comes iteration %d:\n", count);
        trystat();
    }

    return 0;
}

void trystat(void)
{
    int fade = 1;
    static int stay = 1;

    printf("fade = %d and stay = %d\n", fade++, stay++);
}
```

Note that `trystat()` increments each variable after printing its value. Running the program returns this output:

```
Here comes iteration 1:
fade = 1 and stay = 1
Here comes iteration 2:
fade = 1 and stay = 2
Here comes iteration 3:
fade = 1 and stay = 3
```

The static variable `stay` remembers that its value was increased by 1, but the `fade` variable starts anew each time. This points out a difference in initialization: `fade` is initialized each time `trystat()` is called, but `stay` is initialized just once, when `trystat()` is compiled. Static variables are initialized to zero if you don't explicitly initialize them to some other value.

The two declarations look similar:

```c
int fade = 1;
static int stay = 1;
```

However, the first statement is really part of the `trystat()` function and is executed each time the function is called. It is a runtime action. The second statement isn't actually part of the `trystat()` function. If you use a debugger to execute the program step-by-step, you'll see that the program seems to skip that step. That's because static variables and external variables are already in place after a program is loaded into memory. Placing the statement in the `trystat()`

function tells the compiler that only the `trystat()` function is allowed to see the variable; it's not a statement that's executed during runtime.

You can't use `static` for function parameters:

```
int wontwork(static int flu);    // not allowed
```

If you read some of the older C literature, you'll find this storage class referred to as the *internal static storage class*. However, the word *internal* was used to indicate internal to a function, not internal linkage.

Static Variables with External Linkage

A static variable with external linkage has file scope, external linkage, and static storage duration. This class is sometimes termed the *external storage class*, and variables of this type are called *external variables*. You create an external variable by placing a defining declaration outside of any function. As a matter of documentation, an external variable can additionally be declared inside a function that uses it by using the `extern` keyword. If the variable is defined in *another* file, declaring the variable with `extern` is mandatory. Declarations look like this:

```
int Errupt;          /* externally defined variable   */
double Up[100];      /* externally defined array       */
extern char Coal;    /* mandatory declaration          */
                     /* Coal defined in another file   */
void next(void);
int main(void)
{
  extern int Errupt;  /* optional declaration           */

  extern double Up[]; /* optional declaration           */
  ...
}
void next(void)
{
  ...
}
```

The two declarations of `Errupt` are examples of linkage because they both refer to the same variable. External variables have external linkage, a point we'll return to later.

Note that you don't have to give the array size in the optional declaration of `double Up`. That's because the original declaration already supplied that information. The group of `extern` declarations inside `main()` can be omitted entirely because external variables have file scope, so they are known from the point of declaration to the end of the file. They do serve, however, to document your intention that `main()` use these variables.

If only `extern` is omitted from the declaration inside a function, a separate automatic variable is set up. That is, replacing

```
extern int Errupt;
```

with

```
int Errupt;
```

in `main()` causes the compiler to create an automatic variable named `Errupt`. It would be a separate, local variable, distinct from the original `Errupt`. The local variable would be in scope while the program executes `main()`, but the external `Errupt` would be in scope for other functions, such as `next()`, in the same file. In short, a variable in block scope "hides" a variable of the same name in file scope while the program executes statements in the block.

External variables have static storage duration. Therefore, the array `Up` maintains its existence and values regardless of whether the program is executing `main()`, `next()`, or some other function.

The following three examples show four possible combinations of external and automatic variables. Example 1 contains one external variable: `Hocus`. It is known to both `main()` and `magic()`.

```
/* Example 1 */
int Hocus;
int magic();
int main(void)
{
    extern int Hocus;   // Hocus declared external
    ...
}
int magic()
{
    extern int Hocus;   // same Hocus as above
    ...
}
```

Example 2 has one external variable, `Hocus`, known to both functions. This time, `magic()` knows it by default.

```
/* Example 2 */
int Hocus;
int magic();
int main(void)
{
    extern int Hocus;   // Hocus declared external
    ...
}
int magic()
{
                        // Hocus not declared but is known
    ...
}
```

In Example 3, four separate variables are created. The `Hocus` variable in `main()` is automatic by default and is local to `main`. The `Hocus` variable in `magic()` is automatic explicitly and is known only to `magic()`. The external `Hocus` variable is not known to `main()` or `magic()` but would be known to any other function in the file that did not have its own local `Hocus`. Finally, `Pocus` is an external variable known to `magic()` but not to `main()` because `Pocus` follows `main()`.

```
/* Example 3 */
int Hocus;
int magic();
int main(void)
{
  int Hocus;          // Hocus declared, is auto by default
   ...
}
int Pocus;
int magic()
{
   auto int Hocus;  // local Hocus declared automatic
   ...
}
```

These examples illustrate the scope of external variables: from the point of declaration to the end of the file. They also illustrate the lifetimes of variables. The external Hocus and Pocus variables persist as long as the program runs, and, because they aren't confined to any one function, they don't fade away when a particular function returns.

Initializing External Variables

Like automatic variables, external variables can be initialized explicitly. Unlike automatic variables, external variables are automatically initialized to zero if you don't initialize them. This rule applies to elements of an externally defined array, too. Unlike the case for automatic variables, you can use only constant expressions to initialize file scope variables:

```
int x = 10;               // ok, 10 is constant
int y = 3 + 20;           // ok, a constant expression
size_t z = sizeof(int);   // ok, a constant expression
int x2 = 2 * x;           // not ok, x is a variable
```

(As long as the type is not a variable array, a sizeof expression is considered a constant expression.)

Using an External Variable

Let's look at a simple example that involves an external variable. Specifically, suppose you want two functions, call them main() and critic(), to have access to the variable units. You can do this by declaring units outside of and above the two functions, as shown in Listing 12.4.

LISTING 12.4   The global.c Program

```
/* global.c  -- uses an external variable */
#include <stdio.h>
int units = 0;          /* an external variable      */
void critic(void);
int main(void)
{
    extern int units;  /* an optional redeclaration */
```

LISTING 12.4 Continued

```
    printf("How many pounds to a firkin of butter?\n");
    scanf("%d", &units);
    while ( units != 56)
        critic();
    printf("You must have looked it up!\n");

    return 0;
}

void critic(void)
{
    /* optional redeclaration omitted */
    printf("No luck, chummy. Try again.\n");
    scanf("%d", &units);
}
```

Here is some sample output:

```
How many pounds to a firkin of butter?
14
No luck, chummy. Try again.
56
You must have looked it up!
```

(We did.)

Note how the second value for `units` was read by the `critic()` function, yet `main()` also knew the new value when it finished the `while` loop. So both the `main()` function and the `critic()` function use the identifier `units` to access the same variable. In C terminology, we say that `units` has file scope, external linkage, and static storage duration.

We made `units` an external variable by defining it outside of (that is, external to) any function definition. That's all you need to do to make `units` available to all the subsequent functions in the file.

Let's look at some of the details. First, declaring `units` where it is declared makes it available to the functions below it without any further action taken. Therefore, `critics()` uses the `units` variable.

Similarly, nothing needed to be done to give `main()` access to `units`. However, `main()` does have the following declaration in it:

```
extern int units;
```

In the example, this declaration is mainly a matter of documentation. The storage class specifier `extern` tells the compiler that any mention of `units` in this particular function refers to a variable defined outside the function, perhaps even outside the file. Again, both `main()` and `critic()` use the externally defined `units`.

External Names

The C99 standard requires compilers to recognize the first 63 characters for local identifiers and the first 31 characters for external identifiers. This revises the previous requirement of recognizing the first 31 characters for local identifiers and the first six characters for external identifiers. Because the C99 standard is relatively new, it's possible that you may be working with the old rules. The reason the rules for names of external variables are more restrictive than for local variables is that external names need to comply with the rules of the local environment, which may be more limiting.

Definitions and Declarations

Let's take a longer look at the difference between defining a variable and declaring it. Consider the following example:

```
int tern = 1;           /* tern defined              */
main()
{
    external int tern;  /* use a tern defined elsewhere */
```

Here, `tern` is declared twice. The first declaration causes storage to be set aside for the variable. It constitutes a definition of the variable. The second declaration merely tells the compiler to use the `tern` variable that has been created previously, so it is not a definition. The first declaration is called a *defining declaration*, and the second is called a *referencing declaration*. The keyword `extern` indicates that a declaration is not a definition because it instructs the compiler to look elsewhere.

Suppose you do this:

```
extern int tern;
int main(void)
{
```

The compiler will assume that the actual definition of `tern` is somewhere else in your program, perhaps in another file. This declaration does not cause space to be allocated. Therefore, don't use the keyword `extern` to create an external definition; use it only to *refer* to an existing external definition.

An external variable can be initialized only once, and that must occur when the variable is defined. A statement such as

```
extern char permis = 'Y';   /* error */
```

is in error because the presence of the keyword `extern` signifies a referencing declaration, not a defining declaration.

Static Variables with Internal Linkage

Variables of this storage class have static storage duration, file scope, and internal linkage. You create one by defining it outside of any function (just as with an external variable) with the storage class specifier `static`:

```
static int svil = 1;   // static variable, internal linkage
int main(void)
{
```

Such variables were once termed *external static* variables, but that's a bit confusing because they have internal linkage. Unfortunately, no new compact term has taken the place of *external static*, so we're left with *static variable with internal linkage*. The ordinary external variable can be used by functions in any file that's part of the program, but the static variable with internal linkage can be used only by functions in the same file. You can redeclare any file scope variable within a function by using the storage class specifier `extern`. Such a declaration doesn't change the linkage. Consider the following code:

```
int traveler = 1;         // external linkage
static int stayhome = 1;  // internal linkage
int main()
{
    extern int traveler;   // use global traveler
    extern int stayhome;   // use global stayhome
    ...
```

Both `traveler` and `stayhome` are global for this particular file, but only `traveler` can be used by code in other files. The two declarations using `extern` document that `main()` is using the two global variables, but `stayhome` continues to have internal linkage.

Multiple Files

The difference between internal linkage and external linkage is important only when you have a program built from multiple files, so let's take a quick look at that topic.

Complex C programs often use several separate files of code. Sometimes these files might need to share an external variable. The ANSI C way to do this is to have a defining declaration in one file and referencing declarations in the other files. That is, all but one declaration (the defining declaration) should use the `extern` keyword, and only the defining declaration can be used to initialize the variable.

Note that an external variable defined in one file is not available to a second file unless it is also declared (by using `extern`) in the second file. An external declaration by itself only makes a variable potentially available to other files.

Historically, however, many compilers have followed different rules in this regard. Many Unix systems, for example, enable you to declare a variable in several files without using the `extern` keyword, provided that no more than one declaration includes an initialization. If there is a declaration with an initialization, it is taken to be the definition.

Storage-Class Specifiers

You may have noticed that the meaning of the keywords `static` and `extern` depends on the context. The C language has five keywords that are grouped together as storage-class specifiers. They are `auto`, `register`, `static`, `extern`, and `typedef`. The `typedef` keyword doesn't say anything about memory storage, but it is thrown in for syntax reasons. In particular, you can use no more than one storage-class specifier in a declaration, so that means you can't use one of the other storage-class specifiers as part of a `typedef`.

The `auto` specifier indicates a variable with automatic storage duration. It can be used only in declarations of variables with block scope, which already have automatic storage duration, so its main use is documenting intent.

The `register` specifier also can be used only with variables of block scope. It puts a variable into the register storage class, which amounts to a request that the variable be stored in a register for faster access. It also prevents you from taking the address of the variable.

The `static` specifier, when used in a declaration for a variable with block scope, gives that variable static storage duration so it exists and retains its value as long as the program is running, even at times the containing block isn't in use. The variable retains block scope and no linkage. When used in a declaration with file scope, it indicates that the variable has internal linkage.

The `extern` specifier indicates that you are declaring a variable that has been defined elsewhere. If the declaration containing `extern` has file scope, the variable referred to must have external linkage. If the declaration containing `extern` has block scope, the referred-to variable can have either external linkage or internal linkage, depending on the defining declaration for that variable.

Summary: Storage Classes

Automatic variables have block scope, no linking, and automatic storage duration. They are local and private to the block (typically a function) where they are defined. Register variables have the same properties as automatic variables, but the compiler may use faster memory or a register to store them. You can't take the address of a register variable.

Variables with static storage duration can have external linkage, internal linkage, or no linkage. When a variable is declared external to any function in a file, it's an external variable and has file scope, external linkage, and static storage duration. If you add the keyword `static` to such a declaration, you get a variable with static storage duration, file scope, and internal linkage. If you declare a variable inside a function and use the keyword `static`, the variable has static storage duration, block scope, and no linkage.

Memory for a variable with automatic storage duration is allocated when program execution enters the block containing the variable declaration and is freed when the block is exited. If uninitialized, such a variable has a garbage value. Memory for a variable with static storage duration is allocated at compile time and lasts as long as the program runs. If uninitialized, such a variable is set to 0.

A variable with block scope is local to the block containing the declaration. A variable with file scope is known to all functions in a file following its declaration. If a file scope variable has external linkage, it can be used by other files in the program. If a file scope variable has internal linkage, it can be used just within the file in which it is declared.

Here's a short program that uses all five storage classes. It's spread over two files (Listing 12.5 and Listing 12.6), so you will have to do a multiple-file compile. (See Chapter 9, "Functions," or your compiler manual for guidance.) Its main goal is to use all five storage types, not to offer a design model; a better design wouldn't need the file-scope variables.

LISTING 12.5   The `parta.c` File

```
// parta.c --- various storage classes
#include <stdio.h>
void report_count();
void accumulate(int k);
int count = 0;        // file scope, external linkage

int main(void)
{
    int value;        // automatic variable
    register int i;   // register variable

    printf("Enter a positive integer (0 to quit): ");
    while (scanf("%d", &value) == 1 && value > 0)
    {
        ++count;      // use file scope variable
        for (i = value; i >= 0; i--)
            accumulate(i);
        printf("Enter a positive integer (0 to quit): ");
    }
    report_count();

    return 0;
}

void report_count()
{
    printf("Loop executed %d times\n", count);
}
```

LISTING 12.6   The `partb.c` File

```
// partb.c -- rest of the program
#include <stdio.h>

extern int count;        // reference declaration, external linkage

static int total = 0;    // static definition, internal linkage
void accumulate(int k);  // prototype


void accumulate(int k)   // k has block scope, no linkage
{
    static int subtotal = 0;  // static, no linkage
```

LISTING 12.6 Continued

```
        if (k <= 0)
        {
            printf("loop cycle: %d\n", count);
            printf("subtotal: %d; total: %d\n", subtotal, total);
            subtotal = 0;
        }
        else
        {
            subtotal += k;
            total += k;
        }
    }
```

In this program, the block scope static variable `subtotal` keeps a running subtotal of the values passed to the `accumulate()` function, and the file scope, internal linkage variable `total` keeps a running total. The `accumulate()` function reports `total` and `subtotal` whenever a nonpositive value is passed to it; when the function reports, it resets `subtotal` to 0. The `accumulate()` prototype in `parta.c` is mandatory because the file contains an `accumulate()` function call. For `partb.c`, the prototype is optional because the function is defined, but not called in that file. The function also uses the external variable `count` to keep track of how many times the `while` loop in `main()` has been executed. (Incidentally, this is a good example of how not to use an external variable, because it unnecessarily intertwines the code of `parta.c` with the code of `partb.c`.) In `parta.c`, `main()` and `report_count()` share access to `count`.

Here's a sample run:

```
Enter a positive integer (0 to quit): 5
loop cycle: 1
subtotal: 15; total: 15
Enter a positive integer (0 to quit): 10
loop cycle: 2
subtotal: 55; total: 70
Enter a positive integer (0 to quit): 2
loop cycle: 3
subtotal: 3; total: 73
Enter a positive integer (0 to quit): 0
Loop executed 3 times
```

Storage Classes and Functions

Functions, too, have storage classes. A function can be either external (the default) or static. (C99 adds a third possibility, the inline function, discussed in Chapter 16, "The C Preprocessor and the C Library.") An external function can be accessed by functions in other files, but a static function can be used only within the defining file. Consider, for example, a file containing these function declarations:

```
double gamma();          /* external by default */
static double beta();
extern double delta();
```

The functions `gamma()` and `delta()` can be used by functions in other files that are part of the program, but `beta()` cannot. Because this `beta()` is restricted to one file, you can use a different function having the same name in the other files. One reason to use the **static** storage class is to create functions that are private to a particular module, thereby avoiding the possibility of name conflicts.

The usual practice is to use the **extern** keyword when declaring functions defined in other files. This practice is mostly a matter of clarity because a function declaration is assumed to be **extern** unless the keyword **static** is used.

Which Storage Class?

The answer to the question "Which storage class?" is most often "automatic." After all, why else was automatic selected as the default? Yes, we know that at first glance external storage is quite alluring. Just make all your variables external, and you never have to worry about using arguments and pointers to communicate between functions. There is a subtle pitfall, however. You will have to worry about function `A()` sneakily altering the variables used in function `B()`, despite your intentions to the contrary. The unquestionable evidence of untold years of collective computer experience is that this one subtle danger far outweighs the superficial attraction of using external storage indiscriminately.

One of the golden rules of protective programming is the "need to know" principle. Keep the inner workings of each function as private to that function as possible, sharing only those variables that need to be shared. The other classes are useful, and they are available. Before using one, though, ask yourself whether it is necessary.

A Random-Number Function and a Static Variable

Now that you have some background on the different storage classes, let's look at a couple programs that use some of them. First, let's look at a function that makes use of a static variable with internal linkage: a random-number function. The ANSI C library provides the `rand()` function to generate random numbers. There are a variety of algorithms for generating random numbers, and ANSI C enables implementations to use the best algorithm for a particular machine. However, the ANSI C standard also supplies a standard, portable algorithm that produces the same random numbers on different systems. Actually, `rand()` is a "pseudorandom number generator," meaning that the actual sequence of numbers is predictable (computers are not known for their spontaneity), but the numbers are spread pretty uniformly over the possible range of values.

Instead of using your compiler's built-in `rand()` function, we'll use the portable ANSI version so that you can see what goes on inside. The scheme starts with a number called the "seed." The function uses the seed to produce a new number, which becomes the new seed. Then the new seed can be used to produce a newer seed, and so on. For this scheme to work, the random-number function must remember the seed it used the last time it was called. Aha! This calls for a static variable. Listing 12.7 is version 0. (Yes, version 1 comes soon.)

LISTING 12.7   The rand0.c Function File

```
/* rand0.c -- produces random numbers          */
/*              uses ANSI C portable algorithm  */
static unsigned long int next = 1;  /* the seed */

int rand0(void)
{
/* magic formula to generate pseudorandom number */
    next = next * 1103515245 + 12345;
    return (unsigned int) (next/65536) % 32768;
}
```

In Listing 12.7, the static variable **next** starts with the value **1** and is altered by the magic formula each time the function is called. The result is a return value somewhere in the range of **0** to **32767**. Note that **next** is static with internal linkage, rather than merely static with no linkage. That's because the example will be expanded later so that **next** is shared between two functions in the same file.

Let's try the rand0() function with the simple driver shown in Listing 12.8.

LISTING 12.8   The r_drive0.c Driver

```
/* r_drive0.c -- test the rand0() function */
/* compile with rand0.c                    */
#include <stdio.h>
extern int rand0(void);

int main(void)
{
    int count;

    for (count = 0; count < 5; count++)
        printf("%hd\n", rand0());

    return 0;
}
```

Here's another chance to practice using multiple files. Use one file for Listing 12.7 and one for Listing 12.8. The **extern** keyword reminds you that rand0() is defined in a separate file.

The output is this:

```
16838
5758
10113
17515
31051
```

The output looks random, but let's run it again. This time the result is as follows:

16838
5758
10113
17515
31051

Hmmm, that looks familiar; this is the "pseudo" aspect. Each time the main program is run, you start with the same seed of 1. You can get around this problem by introducing a second function called srand1() that enables you to reset the seed. The trick is to make next a static variable with internal linkage known only to rand1() and srand1(). (The C library equivalent to srand1() is called srand().) Add srand1() to the file containing rand1(). Listing 12.9 is the modification.

LISTING 12.9   The s_and_r.c Program

```
/* s_and_r.c -- file for rand1() and srand1()    */
/*                  uses ANSI C portable algorithm */
static unsigned long int next = 1;  /* the seed  */

int rand1(void)
{
/* magic formula to generate pseudorandom number */
    next = next * 1103515245 + 12345;
    return (unsigned int) (next/65536) % 32768;
}

void srand1(unsigned int seed)
{
    next = seed;
}
```

Notice that next is a file-scope static variable with internal linkage. That means it can be used by both rand1() and srand1(), but not by functions in other files. To test these functions, use the driver in Listing 12.10.

LISTING 12.10   The r_drive1.c Program

```
/* r_drive1.c -- test rand1() and srand1() */
/* compile with s_and_r.c                  */
#include <stdio.h>
extern void srand1(unsigned int x);
extern int rand1(void);

int main(void)
{
    int count;
    unsigned seed;
```

LISTING 12.10   Continued

```
    printf("Please enter your choice for seed.\n");
    while (scanf("%u", &seed) == 1)
    {
        srand1(seed);    /* reset seed */
        for (count = 0; count < 5; count++)
            printf("%hd\n", rand1());
        printf("Please enter next seed (q to quit):\n");
    }
    printf("Done\n");

    return 0;
}
```

Again, use two files, and run the program.

```
Please enter your choice for seed.
1
16838
5758
10113
17515
31051
Please enter next seed (q to quit):
513
20067
23475
8955
20841
15324
Please enter next seed (q to quit):
q
Done
```

Using a value of 1 for **seed** yields the same values as before, but a **seed** value of 3 gives new results.

Automated Reseeding

If your C implementation gives you access to some changing quantity, such as the system clock, you can use that value (possibly truncated) to initialize the seed value. For instance, ANSI C has a `time()` function that returns the system time. The time units are system dependent, but what matters here is that the return value is an arithmetic type and that its value changes with time. The exact type is system dependent and is given the label `time_t`, but you can use a type cast. Here's the basic setup:

```
#include <time.h>   /* ANSI prototype for time() */
srand1((unsigned int) time(0));   /* initialize seed */
```

In general, `time()` takes an argument that is the address of a type `time_t` object. In that case, the time value is also stored at that address. However, you can pass the null pointer (**0**) as an argument, in which case the value is supplied only through the return value mechanism.

You can use the same technique with the standard ANSI C functions `srand()` and `rand()`. If you do use these functions, include the `stdlib.h` header file. In fact, now that you've seen how `srand1()` and `rand1()` use a static variable with internal linkage, you might as well use the versions your compiler supplies. We'll do that for the next example.

Roll 'Em

We are going to simulate that very popular random activity, dice-rolling. The most popular form of dice-rolling uses two six-sided dice, but there are other possibilities. Many adventure-fantasy games use all of the five geometrically possible dice: 4, 6, 8, 12, and 20 sides. Those clever ancient Greeks proved that there are but five regular solids having all faces the same shape and size, and these solids are the basis for the dice varieties. You could make dice with other numbers of sides, but the faces would not all be the same, so they wouldn't all necessarily have equal odds of turning up.

Computer calculations aren't limited by these geometric considerations, so we can devise an electronic die that has any number of sides. Let's start with six sides and then generalize.

We want a random number from 1 to 6. However, `rand()` produces an integer in the range 0 to `RAND_MAX`; `RAND_MAX` is defined in `stdlib.h`. It is typically `INT_MAX`. Therefore, we have some adjustments to make. Here's one approach:

1. Take the random number modulus 6. It produces an integer in the range 0 through 5.

2. Add 1. The new number is in the range 1 through 6.

3. To generalize, just replace the number 6 in step 1 by the number of sides.

The following code implements these ideas:

```
#include <stdlib.h>    /* for rand() */
int rollem(int sides)
{
    int roll;

    roll = rand() % sides + 1;
    return roll;
}
```

Let's get a bit more ambitious and ask for a function that lets you roll an arbitrary number of dice and returns the total count. Listing 12.11 does this.

LISTING 12.11   The `diceroll.c` File

```
/* diceroll.c -- dice role simulation*/
#include "diceroll.h"
#include <stdio.h>
#include <stdlib.h>                /* for library rand()    */
```

LISTING 12.11   Continued

```
int roll_count = 0;              /* external linkage    */

static int rollem(int sides)   /* private to this file */
{
    int roll;

    roll = rand() % sides + 1;
    ++roll_count;                    /* count function calls */

    return roll;
}

int roll_n_dice(int dice, int sides)
{
    int d;
    int total = 0;
    if (sides < 2)
    {
        printf("Need at least 2 sides.\n");
        return -2;
    }
    if (dice < 1)
    {
        printf("Need at least 1 die.\n");
        return -1;
    }

    for (d = 0; d < dice; d++)
        total += rollem(sides);

    return total;
}
```

This file adds some wrinkles. First, it turns `rollem()` into a function private to this file. It's there as a helper function for `roll_n_dice()`. Second, to illustrate how external linkage works, the file declares an external variable called `roll_count`. This variable keeps track of how many times the `rollem()` function is called. The example is a little contrived, but it shows how the external variable feature works.

Third, the file contains the following statement:

`#include "diceroll.h"`

When you use standard library functions, such as `rand()`, you include the standard header file (`stdlib.h` for `rand()`) instead of declaring the function. That's because the header file already contains the correct declaration. We'll emulate that approach by providing a `diceroll.h` header file to be used with the `roll_n_dice()` function. Enclosing the filename in double quotation marks instead of in angle brackets instructs the compiler to look locally for the file instead of in the standard locations the compiler uses for the standard header files. The meaning of "look locally" depends on the implementation. Some common interpretations are placing the header file in the same directory or folder as the source code files or in the same directory or folder as the project file (if your compiler uses them). Listing 12.12 shows the contents of the header file.

LISTING 12.12   The `diceroll.h` File

```
//diceroll.h
extern int roll_count;

int roll_n_dice(int dice, int sides);
```

This header file contains function prototypes and an `extern` declaration. Because the `diceroll.c` file includes this header, `diceroll.c` actually contains two declarations of `roll_count`:

```
extern int roll_count;   // from header file
int roll_count = 0;      // from source code file
```

This is fine. You can have only one defining declaration of a variable. But the declaration with `extern` is a reference declaration, and you can have as many of those as you want.

The program using `roll_n_dice()` should also include this header file. Not only does this provide the prototype for `roll_n_dice()`, it also makes `roll_count` available to that program. Listing 12.13 illustrates these points.

LISTING 12.13   The `manydice.c` File

```
/* manydice.c -- multiple dice rolls              */
/* compile with diceroll.c                        */
#include <stdio.h>
#include <stdlib.h>              /* for library srand() */
#include <time.h>               /* for time()        */
#include "diceroll.h"           /* for roll_n_dice()   */
                                /* and for roll_count  */
int main(void)
{
  int dice,roll;
  int sides;

  srand((unsigned int) time(0)); /* randomize seed     */
  printf("Enter the number of sides per die, 0 to stop.\n");
  while (scanf("%d", &sides) == 1 && sides > 0)
  {
      printf("How many dice?\n");
      scanf("%d", &dice);
      roll = roll_n_dice(dice, sides);
      printf("You have rolled a %d using %d %d-sided dice.\n",
             roll, dice, sides);
      printf("How many sides? Enter 0 to stop.\n");
  }
  printf("The rollem() function was called %d times.\n",
         roll_count);              /* use extern variable */
```

LISTING 12.13 Continued

```
    printf("GOOD FORTUNE TO YOU!\n");

    return 0;
}
```

Compile Listing 12.13 with the file containing Listing 12.11. To simplify matters, have Listings 12.11, 12.12, and 12.13 all in the same file or directory. Run the resulting program. The output should look something like this:

```
Enter the number of sides per die, 0 to stop.
6
How many dice?
2
You have rolled a 12 using 2 6-sided dice.
How many sides? Enter 0 to stop.
6
How many dice?
2
You have rolled a 4 using 2 6-sided dice.
How many sides? Enter 0 to stop.
6
How many dice?
2
You have rolled a 5 using 2 6-sided dice.
How many sides? Enter 0 to stop.
0
The rollem() function was called 6 times.
GOOD FORTUNE TO YOU!
```

Because the program uses `srand()` to randomize the random-number seed, you most likely won't get the same output even with the same input. Note that `main()` in `manydice.c` does have access to the `roll_count` variable defined in `diceroll.c`.

You can use `roll_n_dice()` in many ways. With `sides` equal to 2, the program simulates a coin toss with "heads" being 2 and "tails" being 1 (or vice versa, if you really prefer it). You can easily modify the program to show the individual results as well as the total, or you can construct a craps simulator. If you require a large number of rolls, as in some role-playing games, you can easily modify the program to produce output like this:

```
Enter the number of sets; enter q to stop.
18
How many sides and how many dice?
6 3
Here are 18 sets of 3 6-sided throws.
   12  10   6   9   8  14   8  15   9  14  12  17  11   7  10
   13   8  14
How many sets? Enter q to stop.
q
```

Another use for `rand1()` or `rand()` (but not of `rollem()`) is creating a number-guessing program so that the computer chooses and you guess. You can try that yourself.

Allocated Memory: `malloc()` and `free()`

The five storage classes have one thing in common. After you decide which storage class to use, the decisions about scope and storage duration follow automatically. Your choices obey the prepackaged memory management rules. There is, however, one more choice, one that gives you more flexibility. That choice is using library functions to allocate and manage memory.

First, let's review some facts about memory allocation. All programs have to set aside enough memory to store the data they use. Some of this memory allocation is done automatically. For example, you can declare

```
float x;
char place[] = "Dancing Oxen Creek";
```

and enough memory to store that `float` or `string` is set aside, or you can be more explicit and ask for a certain amount of memory:

```
int plates[100];
```

This declaration sets aside 100 memory locations, each fit to store an `int` value. In all these cases, the declaration also provides an identifier for the memory, so you can use `x` or `place` to identify data.

C goes beyond this. You can allocate more memory as a program runs. The main tool is the `malloc()` function, which takes one argument: the number of bytes of memory you want. Then `malloc()` finds a suitable block of free memory. The memory is anonymous; that is, `malloc()` allocates memory but it doesn't assign a name to it. However, it does return the address of the first byte of that block. Therefore, you can assign that address to a pointer variable and use the pointer to access the memory. Because `char` represents a byte, `malloc()` has traditionally been defined as type pointer-to-`char`. The ANSI C standard, however, uses a new type: pointer-to-`void`. This type is intended to be a "generic pointer." The `malloc()` function can be used to return pointers to arrays, structures, and so forth, so normally the return value is typecast to the proper value. Under ANSI C, you should still typecast for clarity, but assigning a pointer-to-`void` value to a pointer of another type is not considered a type clash. If `malloc()` fails to find the required space, it returns the null pointer.

Let's apply `malloc()` to the task of creating an array. You can use `malloc()` to request a block of storage as the program is running. You also need a pointer to keep track of where the block is in memory. For example, consider this code:

```
double * ptd;
ptd = (double *) malloc(30 * sizeof(double));
```

This code requests space for 30 type `double` values and sets `ptd` to point to the location. Note that `ptd` is declared as a pointer to a single `double` and not to a block of 30 `double` values. Remember that the name of an array is the address of its first element. Therefore, if you make `ptd` point to the first element of the block, you can use it just like an array name. That is, you can use the expression `ptd[0]` to access the first element of the block, `ptd[1]` to access the second element, and so on. As you've learned earlier, you can use pointer notation with array names, and you can use array notation with pointers.

You now have three ways to create an array:

- Declare an array using constant expressions for the array dimensions and use the array name to access elements.

- Declare a variable-length array using variable expressions for the array dimensions and use the array name to access elements. (Recall that this is a C99 feature.)

- Declare a pointer, call `malloc()`, and use the pointer to access elements.

You can use the second and third methods to do something you can't do with an ordinary declared array—create a *dynamic array*, one that's allocated while the program runs and that you can choose a size for while the program runs. Suppose, for example, that n is an integer variable. Prior to C99, you couldn't do the following:

```
double item[n];    /* pre C99: not allowed if n is a variable */
```

However, you can do the following, even with a pre-C99 compiler:

```
ptd = (double *) malloc(n * sizeof(double)); /* okay */
```

This works, and, as you'll see, it's a bit more flexible than the variable-length array.

Normally, you should balance each use of `malloc()` with a use of `free()`. The `free()` function takes as its argument an address returned earlier by `malloc()` and frees up the memory that had been allocated. Thus, the duration of allocated memory is from when `malloc()` is called to allocate the memory until `free()` is called to free up the memory so that it can be reused. Think of `malloc()` and `free()` as managing a pool of memory. Each call to `malloc()` allocates memory for program use, and each call to `free()` restores memory to the pool so it can be reused. The argument to `free()` should be a pointer to a block of memory allocated by `malloc()`; you can't use `free()` to free memory allocated by other means, such as declaring an array. Both `malloc()` and `free()` have prototypes in the `stdlib.h` header file.

By using `malloc()`, then, a program can decide what size array is needed and create it while the program runs. Listing 12.14 illustrates this possibility. It assigns the address of the block of memory to the pointer `ptd`, and then it uses `ptd` in the same fashion you would use an array name. Also, the `exit()` function, prototyped in `stdlib.h`, is called to terminate the program if memory allocation fails. The value `EXIT_FAILURE` also is defined in that header file. The standard provides for two return values that are guaranteed to work with all operating systems: `EXIT_SUCCESS` (or, equivalently, the value `0`) to indicate normal program termination, and `EXIT_FAILURE` to indicate abnormal termination. Some operating systems, including Unix, Linux, and Windows, can accept additional integer values.

LISTING 12.14   The dyn_arr.c Program

```
/* dyn_arr.c -- dynamically allocated array */
#include <stdio.h>
#include <stdlib.h> /* for malloc(), free() */

int main(void)
{
```

LISTING 12.14 *Continued*

```
        double * ptd;
        int max;
        int number;
        int i = 0;

        puts("What is the maximum number of type double entries?");
        scanf("%d", &max);
        ptd = (double *) malloc(max * sizeof (double));
        if (ptd == NULL)
        {
            puts("Memory allocation failed. Goodbye.");
            exit(EXIT_FAILURE);
        }
        /* ptd now points to an array of max elements */
        puts("Enter the values (q to quit):");
        while (i < max && scanf("%lf", &ptd[i]) == 1)
            ++i;
        printf("Here are your %d entries:\n", number = i);
        for (i = 0; i < number; i++)
        {
            printf("%7.2f ", ptd[i]);
            if (i % 7 == 6)
                putchar('\n');
        }
        if (i % 7 != 0)
            putchar('\n');
        puts("Done.");
        free(ptd);

        return 0;
    }
```

Here's a sample run. In it, we entered six numbers, but the program processes just five of them because we limited the array size to 5.

```
What is the maximum number of entries?
5
Enter the values (q to quit):
20 30 35 25 40 80
Here are your 5 entries:
  20.00   30.00   35.00   25.00   40.00
Done.
```

Let's look at the code. The program finds the desired array size with the following lines:

```
puts("What is the maximum number of type double entries?");
scanf("%d", &max);
```

Next, the following line allocates enough space to hold the requested number of entries and then assigns the address of the block to the pointer ptd:

```
ptd = (double *) malloc(max * sizeof (double));
```

The typecast to `(double *)` is optional in C but required in C++, so using the typecast makes it simpler to move a program from C to C++.

It's possible that `malloc()` can fail to procure the desired amount of memory. In that case, the function returns the null pointer, and the program terminates:

```
if (ptd == NULL)
{
    puts("Memory allocation failed. Goodbye.");
    exit(EXIT_FAILURE);
}
```

If the program clears this hurdle, it can treat `ptd` as though it were the name of an array of `max` elements, and so it does.

Note the `free()` function near the end of the program. It frees memory allocated by `malloc()`. The `free()` function frees only the block of memory to which its argument points. In this particular example, using `free()` isn't really necessary, because any allocated memory automatically is freed when the program terminates. In a more complex program, however, the ability to free and reuse memory can be important.

What have you gained by using a dynamic array? Primarily, you've gained program flexibility. Suppose you know that most of the time the program will need no more than 100 elements, but sometimes it will need 10,000 elements. If you declare an array, you would have to allow for the worst case and declare it with 10,000 elements. Most of the time, that program would be wasting memory. Then, the one time you need 10,001 elements, the program will fail. You can use a dynamic array to adjust the program to fit the circumstances.

The Importance of `free()`

The amount of static memory is fixed at compile time; it does not change while the program is running. The amount of memory used for automatic variables grows and shrinks automatically as the program executes. But the amount of memory used for allocated memory just grows unless you remember to use `free()`. For example, suppose you have a function that creates a temporary copy of an array as sketched in the following code:

```
...
int main()
{
double glad[2000];
int i;
...for (i = 0; i < 1000; i++)
    gobble(glad, 2000);
...}

void gobble(double ar[], int n)
{
    double * temp = (double *) malloc( n * sizeof(double));
...     /* free(temp);  // forgot to use free()  */
}
```

The first time `gobble()` is called, it creates the pointer `temp`, and it uses `malloc()` to allocate 16,000 bytes of memory (assuming `double` is 8 bytes). Suppose, as indicated, we don't use `free()`. When the function terminates, the pointer `temp`, being an automatic variable, disappears. But the 16,000 bytes of memory it pointed to still exists. It can't be accessed because we no longer have the address. It can't be reused because we didn't call `free()`.

The second time `gobble()` is called, it creates `temp` again, and again it uses `malloc()` to allocate 16,000 bytes. The first block of 16,000 bytes is no longer available, so `malloc()` has to find a second block of 16,000 bytes. When the function terminates, this block of memory also becomes inaccessible and not reusable.

But the loop executes 1,000 times, so by the time the loop finishes, 16,000,000 bytes of memory have been removed from the memory pool. In fact, the program may have run out of memory before getting this far. This sort of problem is called a *memory leak*, and it could have been prevented by having a call to `free()` at the end of the function.

The `calloc()` Function

Another option for memory allotment is to use `calloc()`. A typical use looks like this:

```
long * newmem;

newmem = (long *)calloc(100, sizeof (long));
```

Like `malloc()`, `calloc()` returns a pointer-to-char in its pre-ANSI version and a pointer-to-void under ANSI. You should use the cast operator if you want to store a different type. This new function takes two arguments, both of which should be unsigned integers (type `size_t` under ANSI). The first argument is the number of memory cells you want. The second argument is the size of each cell in bytes. In our case, `long` uses 4 bytes, so this instruction sets up 100 4-byte units, using 400 bytes in all for storage.

Using `sizeof (long)` instead of 4 makes this coding more portable. It will work on those systems where `long` is some size other than 4.

The `calloc()` function throws in one more feature: It sets all the bits in the block to zero. (Note, however, that on some hardware systems, a floating-point value of 0 is not represented by all bits set to 0.)

The `free()` function can also be used to free memory allocated by `calloc()`.

Dynamic memory allocation is the key to many advanced programming techniques. We'll examine some in Chapter 17, "Advanced Data Representation." Your own C library probably offers several other memory-management functions—some portable, some not. You might want to take a moment to look them over.

Dynamic Memory Allocation and Variable-Length Arrays

There's some overlap in functionality between variable-length arrays (VLAs) and the use of `malloc()`. Both, for example, can be used to create an array whose size is determined during runtime:

```
int vlamal()
{
    int n;
    int * pi;
    scanf("%d", &n);
    pi = (int *) malloc (n * sizeof(int));
    int ar[n];    // vla
    pi[2] = ar[2] = -5;
...
}
```

One difference is that the VLA is automatic storage. One consequence of automatic storage is that the memory space used by the VLA is freed automatically when the execution leaves the defining block—in this case, when the `vlamal()` function terminates. Therefore, you don't have to worry about using `free()`. On the other hand, the array created using `malloc()` needn't have its access limited to one function. For example, one function could create an array and return the pointer, giving the calling function access. Then the calling function could call `free()` when it is finished. It's okay to use a different pointer variable with `free()` than with `malloc()`; what must agree are the addresses stored in the pointers.

VLAs are more convenient for multidimensional arrays. You can create a two-dimensional array using `malloc()`, but the syntax is awkward. If a compiler doesn't support the VLA feature, one of the dimensions has to be fixed, just like in function calls:

```
int n = 5;
int m = 6;
int ar2[n][m];      // n x m VLA
int (* p2)[6];      // works pre-C99
int (* p3)[m];      // requires VLA support
p2 = (int (*)[6]) malloc(n * 6 * sizeof(int));  // n * 6 array
p3 = (int (*)[m]) malloc(n * m * sizeof(int));  // n * m array
// above expression also requires VLA support
ar2[1][2] = p2[1][2] = 12;
```

It's worth reviewing the pointer declarations. The `malloc()` function returns a pointer, so `p2` has to be a pointer of a suitable type. The declaration

```
int (* p2)[6];      // works pre-C99
```

says that `p2` points to an array of six `int`s. This means that `p2[i]` would be interpreted as an element consisting of six `int`s and that `p2[i][j]` would be a single `int`.

The second pointer declaration uses a variable to specify the size of the array to which `p3` points. This means that `p3` is considered to be a pointer to a VLA, which is why the code won't work with the C90 standard.

Storage Classes and Dynamic Memory Allocation

You might be wondering about the connection between storage classes and dynamic memory allocation. Let's look at an idealized model. You can think of a program as dividing its available memory into three separate sections: one for static variables with external linkage, internal linkage, and no linkage; one for automatic variables; and one for dynamically allocated memory.

The amount of memory needed for the static duration storage classes is known at compile time, and the data stored in this section is available as long as the program runs. Each variable of these classes comes into being when the program starts and expires when the program ends.

An automatic variable, however, comes into existence when a program enters the block of code containing the variable's definition and expires when its block of code is exited. Therefore, as a program calls functions and as functions terminate, the amount of memory used by automatic variables grows and shrinks. This section of memory is typically handled as a stack. That means new variables are added sequentially in memory as they are created and then are removed in the opposite order as they pass away.

Dynamically allocated memory comes into existence when `malloc()` or a related function is called, and it's freed when `free()` is called. Memory persistence is controlled by the programmer, not by a set of rigid rules, so a memory block can be created in one function and disposed of in another function. Because of this, the section of memory used for dynamic memory allocation can end up fragmented—that is, unused chunks could be interspersed among active blocks of memory. Using dynamic memory tends to be a slower process than using stack memory, however.

ANSI C Type Qualifiers

You've seen that a variable is characterized by both its type and its storage class. C90 has added two more properties: constancy and volatility. These properties are declared with the keywords `const` and `volatile`, which create *qualified types*. The C99 standard adds a third qualifier, `restrict`, designed to facilitate compiler optimizations.

C99 grants type qualifiers a new property—they now are idempotent! Although this sounds like a powerful claim, all it really means is that you can use the same qualifier more than once in a declaration, and the superfluous ones are ignored:

```
const const const int n = 6;  // same as const int n = 6;
```

This makes it possible, for example, for the following sequence to be accepted:

```
typedef const int zip;
const zip q = 8;
```

The `const` Type Qualifier

Chapter 4, "Character Strings and Formatted Input/Output," and Chapter 10, "Arrays and Pointers," have already introduced `const`. To review, the `const` keyword in a declaration establishes a variable whose value cannot be modified by assignment or by incrementing or decrementing. On an ANSI-compliant compiler, the code

```
const int nochange;    /* qualifies m as being constant */
nochange = 12;         /* not allowed                   */
```

should produce an error message. You can, however, initialize a `const` variable. Therefore, the following code is fine:

```
const int nochange = 12;   /* ok */
```

The preceding declaration makes `nochange` a read-only variable. After it is initialized, it cannot be changed.

You can use the `const` keyword to, for example, create an array of data that the program can't alter:

```
const int days1[12] = {31,28,31,30,31,30,31,31,30,31,30,31};
```

Using `const` with Pointers and Parameter Declarations

Using the `const` keyword when declaring a simple variable and an array is pretty easy. Pointers are more complicated because you have to distinguish between making the pointer itself `const` and making the value that is pointed to `const`. The declaration

```
const float * pf;  /* pf points to a constant float value */
```

establishes that `pf` points to a value that must remain constant. The value of `pf` itself can be changed. For example, it can be set to point at another `const` value. In contrast, the declaration

```
float * const pt;    /* pt is a const pointer */
```

says that the pointer `pt` itself cannot have its value changed. It must always point to the same address, but the pointed-to value can change. Finally, the declaration

```
const float * const ptr;
```

means both that `ptr` must always point to the same location and that the value stored at the location must not change.

There is a third location in which you can place `const`:

```
float const * pfc;   // same as const float * pfc;
```

As the comment indicates, placing `const` after the type name and before the `*` means that the pointer can't be used to change the pointed-to value. In short, a `const` anywhere to the left of the `*` makes the data constant, and a `const` to the right of the `*` makes the pointer itself constant.

One common use for this new keyword is declaring pointers that serve as formal function parameters. For example, suppose you have a function called `display()` that displays the contents of an array. To use it, you would pass the name of the array as an actual argument, but the name of an array is an address. That would enable the function to alter data in the calling function. But the following prototype prevents this from happening:

```
void display(const int array[], int limit);
```

In a prototype and a function header, the parameter declaration `const int array[]` is the same as `const int * array`, so the declaration says that the data to which `array` points cannot be changed.

The ANSI C library follows this practice. If a pointer is used only to give a function access to values, the pointer is declared as a pointer to a `const`-qualified type. If the pointer is used to alter data in the calling function, the `const` keyword isn't used. For example, the ANSI C declaration for `strcat()` is this:

```
char *strcat(char *, const char *);
```

Recall that `strcat()` adds a copy of the second string to the end of the first string. This modifies the first string, but leaves the second string unchanged. The declaration reflects this.

Using `const` with Global Data

Recall that using global variables is considered a risky approach because it exposes data to being mistakenly altered by any part of a program. That risk disappears if the data is constant, so it is perfectly reasonable to use global variables with the `const` qualifier. You can have `const` variables, `const` arrays, and `const` structures. (Structures are a compound data type discussed in the next chapter.)

One area that requires care, however, is sharing `const` data across files. There are two strategies you can use. The first is to follow the usual rules for external variables—use defining declarations in one file and reference declarations (using the keyword `extern`) in the other files:

```
/* file1.c -- defines some global constants */
const double PI = 3.14159;
const char * MONTHS[12] =
    {"January", "February", "March", "April", "May", "June", "July",
     "August", "September", "October", "November", "December"};

/* file2.c -- use global constants defined elsewhere */
extern const double PI;
extern const * MONTHS[];
```

The second approach is to place the constants in an `include` file. Here, you must take the additional step of using the static external storage class:

```
/* constant.h -- defines some global constants */
static const double PI = 3.14159;
static const char * MONTHS[12] =
    {"January", "February", "March", "April", "May", "June", "July",
     "August", "September", "October", "November", "December"};

/* file1.c -- use global constants defined elsewhere */
#include "constant.h"
```

```
/* file2.c -- use global constants defined elsewhere */
#include "constant.h"
```

If you don't use the keyword `static`, including `constant.h` in `file1.c` and in `file2.c` would result in each file having a defining declaration of the same identifier, which is not supported by the ANSI standard. (Some compilers, however, do allow it.) By making each identifier static external, you actually give each file a separate copy of the data. That wouldn't work if the files are supposed to use the data to communicate with one another because each file would see only its own copy. Because the data is constant (by using the `const` keyword) and identical (by having both files include the same header file), however, that's not a problem.

The advantage of the header file approach is that you don't have to remember to use defining declarations in one file and reference declarations in the next; all files simply include the same header file. The disadvantage is that the data is duplicated. For the preceding examples, that's not a real problem, but it might be one if your constant data includes enormous arrays.

The `volatile` Type Qualifier

The `volatile` qualifier tells the compiler that a variable can have its value altered by agencies other than the program. It is typically used for hardware addresses and for data shared with other programs running simultaneously. For example, an address might hold the current clock time. The value at that address changes as time changes, regardless of what your program is doing. Or an address could be used to receive information transmitted from, say, another computer.

The syntax is the same as for `const`:

```
volatile int loc1;   /* loc1 is a volatile location        */
volatile int * ploc; /* ploc points to a volatile location */
```

These statements declare `loc1` to be a `volatile` value and `ploc` to point to a `volatile` value.

You may think that `volatile` is an interesting concept, but you might be wondering why the ANSI committee felt it necessary to make `volatile` a keyword. The reason is that it facilitates compiler optimization. Suppose, for example, you have code like this:

```
val1 = x;
 /* some code not using x */
val2 = x;
```

A smart (optimizing) compiler might notice that you use `x` twice without changing its value. It would temporarily store the `x` value in a register. Then, when `x` is needed for `val2`, it can save time by reading the value from a register instead of from the original memory location. This procedure is called *caching*. Ordinarily, caching is a good optimization, but not if `x` is changed between the two statements by some other agency. If there were no `volatile` keyword, a compiler would have no way of knowing whether this might happen. Therefore, to be safe, the compiler couldn't cache. That was the pre-ANSI situation. Now, however, if the `volatile` keyword is not used in the declaration, the compiler can assume that a value hasn't changed between uses, and it can then attempt to optimize the code.

A value can be both `const` and `volatile`. For example, the hardware clock setting normally should not be changed by the program, making it `const`, but it is changed by an agency other than the program, making it `volatile`. Just use both qualifiers in the declaration, as shown here; the order doesn't matter:

```
volatile const int loc;
const volatile int * ploc;
```

The `restrict` Type Qualifier

The `restrict` keyword enhances computational support by giving the compiler permission to optimize certain kinds of code. It can be applied only to pointers, and it indicates that a pointer is the sole initial means of accessing a data object. To see why this is useful, we need to look at a few examples. Consider the following:

```
int ar[10];
int * restrict restar = (int *) malloc(10 * sizeof(int));
int * par = ar;
```

Here, the pointer `restar` is the sole initial means of access to the memory allocated by `malloc()`. Therefore, it can be qualified with the keyword `restrict`. The pointer `par`, however, is neither the initial nor the sole means of access to the data in the `ar` array, so it cannot be qualified as `restrict`.

Now consider the following rather artificial example, in which `n` is an `int`:

```
for (n = 0; n < 10; n++)
{
    par[n] += 5;
    restar[n] += 5;
    ar[n] *= 2;
    par[n] += 3;
    restar[n] += 3;
}
```

Knowing that `restar` is the sole initial means of access to the block of data it points to, the compiler can replace the two statements involving `restar` with a single statement having the same effect:

```
restar[n] += 8;    /* ok replacement */
```

It would be a computational error, however, to condense the two statements involving `par` into one:

```
par[n] += 8;    / * gives wrong answer */
```

The reason it gives the wrong answer is that the loop uses `ar` to change the value of the data between the two times `par` accesses the same data.

Without the `restrict` keyword, the compiler has to assume the worse case; namely, that some other identifier might have changed the data in between two uses of a pointer. With the `restrict` keyword used, the compiler is free to look for computational shortcuts.

You can use the `restrict` keyword as a qualifier for function parameters that are pointers. This means that the compiler can assume that no other identifiers modify the pointed-to data within the body of the function and that the compiler can try optimizations it might not otherwise use. For example, the C library has two functions for copying bytes from one location to another. Under C99, they have these prototypes:

```
void * memcpy(void * restrict s1, const void * restrict s2, size_t n);
void * memmove(void * s1, const void * s2, size_t n);
```

Each one copies n bytes from location `s2` to location `s1`. The `memcpy()` function requires that there be no overlap between the two locations, but `memmove()` doesn't have that requirement. Declaring `s1` and `s2` as `restrict` means each pointer is a sole means of access, so they can't access the same block of data. This matches the requirement that there be no overlap. The `memmove()` function, which does allow overlap, has to be more careful about copying data so that it doesn't overwrite data before it is used.

The keyword `restrict` has two audiences. One is the compiler, and it tells the compiler it is free to make certain assumptions concerning optimization. The other audience is the user, and it tells the user to use only arguments that satisfy the `restrict` requirements. In general, the compiler can't check whether you obey this restriction, but you flout it at your own risk.

New Places for Old Keywords

C99 allows you to place the type qualifiers and the storage class qualifier `static` inside the initial brackets of a formal parameter in a function prototype and function header. In the case of the type qualifiers, this provides an alternative syntax for an existing capability. For example, here is a declaration with the older syntax:

```
void ofmouth(int * const a1, int * restrict a2, int n);  // older style
```

It says that `a1` is a `const` pointer to `int`, which, as you'll recall, means that the pointer is constant, not the data to which it points. It also indicates that `a2` is a restricted pointer, as described in the preceding section. The new and equivalent syntax is

```
void ofmouth(int a1[const], int a2[restrict], int n);   // allowed by C99
```

The case for `static` is different because it introduces something brand new. For example, consider this prototype:

```
double stick(double ar[static 20]);
```

This use of `static` indicates that the actual argument in a function call will be a pointer to the first element of an array having at least 20 elements. The purpose of this is to enable the compiler to use that information to optimize its coding of the function.

As with `restrict`, the keyword `static` has two audiences. One is the compiler, and it tells the compiler it is free to make certain assumptions concerning optimization. The other audience is the user, and it tells the user to only use arguments that satisfy the `static` requirements.

Key Concepts

C provides several models for managing memory. You should become familiar with the various choices. You also need to develop a sense of when to choose the various types. Most of the time, the automatic variable is the best choice. If you decide to use another type, you should have a good reason. For communicating between functions, it's usually better to use automatic variables, function parameters, and return values rather than global variables. On the other hand, global variables are particularly useful for constant data.

You should try to understand the properties of static memory, automatic memory, and allocated memory. In particular, be aware that the amount of static memory used is determined at compile time, and that static data is loaded into memory when the program is loaded into memory. Automatic variables are allocated and freed as the program runs, so the amount of memory used by automatic variables changes while a program executes. You can think of automatic memory as a rewriteable workspace. Allocated memory also grows and shrinks, but, in this case, the process is controlled by function calls rather than happening automatically.

Summary

The memory used to store data in a program can be characterized by storage duration, scope, and linkage. Storage duration can be static, automatic, or allocated. If static, memory is allocated at the start of program execution and persists as long as the program is running. If automatic, memory for a variable is allocated when program execution enters the block in which the variable is defined and is freed when the block is exited. If allocated, memory is allocated by calling `malloc()` (or a related function) and freed by calling the `free()` function.

Scope determines which parts of a program can access the data. A variable defined outside of any function has file scope and is visible to any function defined after the variable's declaration. A variable defined inside a block or as a function parameter has block scope and is visible just in that block and any blocks nested in it.

Linkage describes the extent to which a variable defined in one unit of a program can be linked to elsewhere. Variables with block scope, being local, have no linkage. Variables with file scope can have internal linkage or external linkage. Internal linkage means the variable can be used only in the file containing the definition. External linkage means the variable also can be used in other files.

The following are C's five storage classes:

- **Automatic**—A variable declared in a block (or as a parameter in a function header) with no storage class modifier, or with the `auto` storage class modifier, belongs to the automatic storage class. It has automatic storage duration, block scope, and no linkage. Its value, if uninitialized, is not undetermined.

- **Register**—A variable declared in a block (or as a parameter in a function header) with the `register` storage class modifier belongs to the register storage class. It has automatic storage duration, block scope, and no linkage, and its address cannot be taken.

Declaring a variable as a register variable is a hint to the compiler to provide the fastest access possible. Its value, if uninitialized, is not undetermined.

- **Static, no linkage**—A variable declared in a block with the `static` storage class modifier belongs to the "static, no linkage" storage class. It has static storage duration, block scope, and no linkage. It is initialized just once, at compile time. If not initialized explicitly, its bytes are set to 0.

- **Static, external linkage**—A variable defined external to any function and without using the `static` storage class modifier belongs to the "static, external linkage" storage class. It has static storage duration, file scope, and external linkage. It is initialized just once, at compile time. If not initialized explicitly, its bytes are set to 0.

- **Static, internal linkage**—A variable defined external to any function and using the `static` storage class modifier belongs to the "static, internal linkage" storage class. It has static storage duration, file scope, and internal linkage. It is initialized just once, at compile time. If not initialized explicitly, its bytes are set to 0.

Allocated memory is provided by using the `malloc()` (or related) function, which returns a pointer to a block of memory having the requested number of bytes. This memory can be made available for reuse by calling the `free()` function, using the address as the argument.

The type qualifiers are `const`, `volatile`, and `restrict`. The `const` specifier qualifies data as being constant. When used with pointers, `const` can indicate that the pointer itself is constant or that the data it points to is constant, depending on the placement of `const` in the declaration. The `volatile` specifier indicates that data may be altered by processes other than the program. Its purpose is to warn the compiler to avoid optimizations that assume otherwise. The `restrict` specifier is also provided for reasons of optimization. A pointer qualified with `restrict` is identified as providing the only access to a block of data.

Review Questions

1. Which storage classes create variables local to the function containing them?

2. Which storage classes create variables that persist for the duration of the containing program?

3. Which storage class creates variables that can be used across several files? Restricted to just one file?

4. What kind of linkage do block scope variables have?

5. What is the `extern` keyword used for?

6. Consider this code fragment:

```
int * p1 = (int *) malloc(100 * sizeof(int));
```

In terms of the final outcome, how does the following statement differ?

```
int * p1 = (int *) calloc(100, sizeof(int));
```

7. Which functions know each variable in the following? Are there any errors?

```
/* file 1 */
int daisy;
int main(void)
{
  int lily;
  ...;
}
int petal()
{
  extern int daisy, lily;
  ...;
}
/* file 2 */
extern int daisy;
static int lily;
int rose;
int stem()
{
  int rose;
  ...;
}
void root()
{
  ...;
}
```

8. What will the following program print?

```
#include <stdio.h>
char color= 'B';
void first(void);
void second(void);

int main(void)
{
  extern char color;

  printf("color in main() is %c\n", color);
  first();
  printf("color in main() is %c\n", color);
  second();
  printf("color in main() is %c\n", color);
  return 0;
}

void first(void)
{
  char color;

  color = 'R';
```

```
    printf("color in first() is %c\n", color);
}

void second(void)
{
    color = 'G';
    printf("color in second() is %c\n", color);
}
```

9. A file begins with the following declarations:

```
static int plink;
int value_ct(const int arr[], int value, int n);
```

   a. What do these declarations tell you about the programmer's intent?

   b. Will replacing int value and int n with const int value and const int n enhance the protection of values in the calling program?

Programming Exercises

1. Rewrite the program in Listing 12.4 so that it does not use global variables.

2. Gasoline consumption commonly is computed in miles per gallon in the U.S. and in liters per 100 kilometers in Europe. What follows is part of a program that asks the user to choose a mode (metric or U.S.) and then gathers data and computes fuel consumption:

```
// pe12-2b.c
#include <stdio.h>
#include "pe12-2a.h"
int main(void)
{
    int mode;

    printf("Enter 0 for metric mode, 1 for US mode: ");
    scanf("%d", &mode);
    while (mode >= 0)
    {
        set_mode(mode);
        get_info();
        show_info();
        printf("Enter 0 for metric mode, 1 for US mode");
        printf(" (-1 to quit): ");
        scanf("%d", &mode);
    }
    printf("Done.\n");
    return 0;
}
```

Here is some sample output:

```
Enter 0 for metric mode, 1 for US mode: 0
Enter distance traveled in kilometers: 600
Enter fuel consumed in liters: 78.8
Fuel consumption is 13.13 liters per 100 km.
Enter 0 for metric mode, 1 for US mode (-1 to quit): 1
Enter distance traveled in miles: 434
Enter fuel consumed  in gallons: 12.7
Fuel consumption is 34.2 miles per gallon.
Enter 0 for metric mode, 1 for US mode (-1 to quit): 3
Invalid mode specified. Mode 1(US) used.
Enter distance traveled in miles: 388
Enter fuel consumed  in gallons: 15.3
Fuel consumption is 25.4 miles per gallon.
Enter 0 for metric mode, 1 for US mode (-1 to quit): -1
Done.
```

If the user enters an incorrect mode, the program comments on that and uses the most recent mode. Supply a `pe12-2a.h` header file and a `pe12-2a.c` source code file to make this work. The source code file should define three file-scope, internal-linkage variables. One represents the mode, one represents the distance, and one represents the fuel consumed. The `get_info()` function prompts for data according to the mode setting and stores the responses in the file-scope variables. The `show_info()` function calculates and displays the fuel consumption based on the mode setting.

3. Redesign the program described in exercise 2 so that it uses only automatic variables. Have the program offer the same user interface—that is, it should prompt the user to enter a mode, and so on. You'll have to come up with a different set of function calls, however.

4. Write and test in a loop a function that returns the number of times it has been called.

5. Write a program that generates a list of 100 random numbers in the range 1–10 in sorted decreasing order. (You can adapt the sorting algorithm from Chapter 11, "Character Strings and String Functions," to type `int`. In this case, just sort the numbers themselves.)

6. Write a program that generates 1,000 random numbers in the range 1–10. Don't save or print the numbers, but do print how many times each number was produced. Have the program do this for 10 different seed values. Do the numbers appear in equal amounts? You can use the functions from this chapter or the ANSI C `rand()` and `srand()` functions, which follow the same format that our functions do. This is one way to test the randomness of a particular random-number generator.

7. Write a program that behaves like the modification of Listing 12.13, which we discussed after showing the output of Listing 12.13. That is, have the program produce output like the following:

```
Enter the number of sets; enter q to stop.
18
How many sides and how many dice?
6 3
Here are 18 sets of 3 6-sided throws.
   12  10   6   9   8  14   8  15   9  14  12  17  11   7  10
   13   8  14
How many sets? Enter q to stop.
q
```

8. Here's part of a program:

```
// pe12-8.c
#include <stdio.h>
int * make_array(int elem, int val);
void show_array(const int ar[], int n);
int main(void)
{
  int * pa;
  int size;
  int value;

  printf("Enter the number of elements: ");
  scanf("%d", &size);
  while (size > 0)
  {
      printf("Enter the initialization value: ");
      scanf("%d", &value);
      pa = make_array(size, value);
      if (pa)
      {
          show_array(pa, size);
              free(pa);
      }
      printf("Enter the number of elements (<1 to quit): ");
      scanf("%d", &size);
  }
  printf("Done.\n");
  return 0;
}
```

Complete the program by providing function definitions for make_array() and show_array(). The make_array() function takes two arguments. The first is the number of elements of an **int** array, and the second is a value that is to be assigned to each element. The function uses **malloc()** to create an array of a suitable size, sets each element to the indicated value, and returns a pointer to the array. The show_array() function displays the contents, eight numbers to a line.

## CHAPTER 13

FILE INPUT/OUTPUT

You will learn about the following in this chapter:

- Functions:
  `fopen()`, `getc()`, `putc()`, `exit()`,
  `fclose()`

  `fprintf()`, `fscanf()`, `fgets()`,
  `fputs()`

  `rewind()`, `fseek()`, `ftell()`,
  `fflush()`

  `fgetpos()`, `fsetpos()`, `feof()`,
  `ferror()`

  `ungetc()`, `setvbuf()`, `fread()`,
  `fwrite()`

- How to process files using C's
  standard I/O family of functions

- Text modes and binary modes,
  text and binary formats, and
  buffered and nonbuffered I/O

- Using functions that can access
  files both sequentially and
  randomly

F iles are essential to today's computer systems. They are used to store programs, documents, data, correspondence, forms, graphics, and myriad other kinds of information. As a programmer, you will have to write programs that create files, write into files, and read from files. In this chapter, we show you how.

Communicating with Files

Often you need programs that can read information from files or can write results into a file. One such form of program-file communication is file redirection, as you saw in Chapter 8, "Character Input/Output and Input Validation." This method is simple but limited. For example, suppose you want to write an interactive program that asks you for book titles and then saves the complete listing in a file. If you use redirection, as in

```
books > bklist
```

your interactive prompts are redirected into `bklist`. Not only does this put unwanted text into `bklist`, it prevents you from seeing the questions you are supposed to answer.

C, as you might expect, offers more powerful methods of communicating with files. It enables you to open a file from within a program and then use special I/O functions to read from or write to that file. Before investigating these methods, however, let's briefly review the nature of a file.

What Is a File?

A *file* is a named section of storage, usually on a disk. You think of `stdio.h`, for instance, as the name of a file containing some useful information. To the operating system, however, a file is a bit more complicated. A large file, for example, could wind up stored in several scattered fragments, or it might contain additional data that allows the operating system to determine what kind of file it is. However, these are the operating system's concerns, not yours (unless you are writing operating systems). Your concern is how files appear to a C program.

C views a file as a continuous sequence of bytes, each of which can be read individually. This corresponds to the file structure in the Unix environment, where C grew up. Because other environments may not correspond exactly to this model, ANSI C provides two ways to view files: the text view and the binary view.

The Text View and the Binary View

The two ANSI-mandated views of a file are *binary* and *text*. In the binary view, each and every byte of the file is accessible to a program. In the text view, what the program sees can differ from what is in the file. With the text view, the local environment's representation of such things as the end of a line are mapped to the C view when a file is read. Similarly, the C view is mapped to the local representation of output. For example, MS-DOS text files represent the end of a line with the carriage-return/linefeed combination: \r\n. Macintosh text files represent the end of a line with just a carriage-return, \r. C programs represent the end of a line with just \n. Therefore, when a C program takes the text view of an MS-DOS text file, it converts \r\n to \n when reading from a file, and it converts \n to \r\n when writing to a file. When a C program takes the text view of a Macintosh text file, it converts the \r to \n when reading from a file, and it converts \n to \r when writing to a file.

You aren't restricted to using only the text view for an MS-DOS text file. You can also use the binary view of the same file. If you do, your program sees both the \r and the \n characters in the file; no mapping takes place (see Figure 13.1). MS-DOS distinguishes between text and binary *files*, but C provides for text and binary *views*. Normally, you use the text view for text files and the binary view for binary files. However, you can use either view of either type of file, although a text view of a binary file works poorly.

Although ANSI C provides for both a binary view and a text view, these views can be implemented identically. For example, because Unix uses just one file structure, both views are the same for Unix implementations.

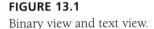

FIGURE 13.1
Binary view and text view.

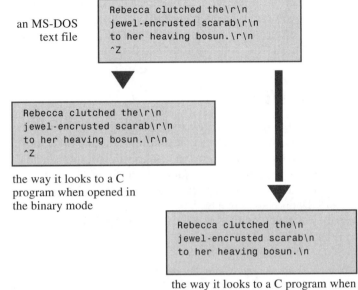

an MS-DOS
text file

```
Rebecca clutched the\r\n
jewel-encrusted scarab\r\n
to her heaving bosun.\r\n
^Z
```

```
Rebecca clutched the\r\n
jewel-encrusted scarab\r\n
to her heaving bosun.\r\n
^Z
```

the way it looks to a C
program when opened in
the binary mode

```
Rebecca clutched the\n
jewel-encrusted scarab\n
to her heaving bosun.\n
```

the way it looks to a C program when
opened in the text mode

Levels of I/O

In addition to selecting the view of a file, you can, in most cases, choose between two levels of
I/O (that is, between two levels of handling access to files). *Low-level I/O* uses the fundamental
I/O services provided by the operating system. *Standard high-level I/O* uses a standard package
of C library functions and `stdio.h` header file definitions. ANSI C supports only the standard
I/O package because there is no way to guarantee that all operating systems can be represented
by the same low-level I/O model. Because ANSI C establishes the portability of the standard
I/O model, we will concentrate on it.

Standard Files

C programs automatically open three files on your behalf. They are termed the *standard input*,
the *standard output*, and the *standard error output*. The standard input, by default, is the normal input device for your system, usually your keyboard. Both the standard output and the
standard error output, by default, are the normal output device for your system, usually your
display screen.

The standard input, naturally, provides input to your program. It's the file that is read by
`getchar()`, `gets()`, and `scanf()`. The standard output is where normal program output goes.
It is used by `putchar()`, `puts()`, and `printf()`. Redirection, as you learned in Chapter 8,
causes other files to be recognized as the standard input or standard output. The purpose of

the standard error output file is to provide a logically distinct place to send error messages. If, for example, you use redirection to send output to a file instead of to the screen, output sent to the standard error output still goes to the screen. This is good because if the error messages were routed to the file, you would not see them until you viewed the file.

Standard I/O

The standard I/O package has two advantages, besides portability, over low-level I/O. First, it has many specialized functions that simplify handling different I/O problems. For example, printf() converts various forms of data to string output suitable for terminals. Second, input and output are *buffered*. That is, information is transferred in large chunks (typically 512 bytes at a time or more) instead of a byte at a time. When a program reads a file, for example, a chunk of data is copied to a buffer—an intermediate storage area. This buffering greatly increases the data transfer rate. The program can then examine individual bytes in the buffer. The buffering is handled behind the scenes, so you have the illusion of character-by-character access. (You can also buffer low-level I/O, but you have to do much of the work yourself.) Listing 13.1 shows how to use standard I/O to read a file and count the number of characters in the file. We'll discuss the features of Listing 13.1 in the next several sections. (This program uses command-line arguments. If you're a Windows user, you might have to run the program in an MS-DOS window after compiling. If you're a Macintosh user, you should use console.h and the ccommand() function as described in Chapter 11, "Character Strings and String Functions," and in the Code Warrior documentation. Alternatively, you can alter the program to use puts() and gets() instead of command-line arguments to get the filename.)

LISTING 13.1   The count.c Program

```
/* count.c -- using standard I/O */
#include <stdio.h>

#include <stdlib.h> // ANSI C exit() prototype
int main(int argc, char *argv[])
{
    int ch;          // place to store each character as read
    FILE *fp;        // "file pointer"
    long count = 0;

    if (argc != 2)
    {
        printf("Usage: %s filename\n", argv[0]);
        exit(1);
    }
    if ((fp = fopen(argv[1], "r")) == NULL)
    {
        printf("Can't open %s\n", argv[1]);
        exit(1);
    }
    while ((ch = getc(fp)) != EOF)
```

LISTING 13.1   Continued

```
    {
        putc(ch,stdout);  // same as putchar(ch);
        count++;
    }
    fclose(fp);
    printf("File %s has %ld characters\n", argv[1], count);

    return 0;
}
```

Checking for Command-Line Arguments

First, the program in Listing 13.1 checks the value of `argc` to see if there is a command-line argument. If there isn't, the program prints a usage message and exits. The string `argv[0]` is the name of the program. Using `argv[0]` instead of the program name explicitly causes the error message to change automatically if you change the name of the executable file. This feature is also handy in environments such as Unix that permit multiple names for a single file. But beware—some operating systems, such as pre–MS-DOS 3.0, don't recognize `argv[0]`, so this usage is not completely portable.

The `exit()` function causes the program to terminate, closing any open files. The argument to `exit()` is passed on to some operating systems, including Unix, Linux, and MS-DOS, where it can be used by other programs. The usual convention is to pass a value of `0` for programs that terminate normally and to pass nonzero values for abnormal termination. Different exit values can be used to distinguish between different causes of failure, and this is the usual practice in Unix and DOS programming. However, not all operating systems recognize the same range of possible return values. Therefore, the ANSI C standard mandates a rather restricted minimum range. In particular, the standard requires that the value `0` or the macro `EXIT_SUCCESS` be used to indicate successful termination, and the macro `EXIT_FAILURE` be used to indicate unsuccessful termination. These macros, along with the `exit()` prototype, are found in the `stdlib.h` header file. This book will follow the common practice of using integer exit values, but for maximum portability, use `EXIT_SUCCESS` and `EXIT_FAILURE`.

Under ANSI C, using `return` in the initial call to `main()` has the same effect as calling `exit()`. Therefore, if in `main()`, the statement

```
return 0;
```

which you've been using all along, is equivalent in effect to this statement:

```
exit(0);
```

Note, however, the qualifying phrase "the initial call." If you make `main()` into a recursive program, `exit()` still terminates the program, but `return` passes control to the previous level of recursion until the original level is reached. Then `return` terminates the program. Another difference between `return` and `exit()` is that `exit()` terminates the program even if called in a function other than `main()`.

The `fopen()` Function

Next, the program uses `fopen()` to open the file. This function is declared in `stdio.h`. Its first argument is the name of the file to be opened; more exactly, it is the address of a string containing that name. The second argument is a string identifying the mode in which the file is to be opened. The C library provides for several possibilities, as shown in Table 13.1.

TABLE 13.1   Mode Strings for `fopen()`

Mode String	Meaning
`"r"`	Open a text file for reading.
`"w"`	Open a text file for writing, truncating an existing file to zero length, or creating the file if it does not exist.
`"a"`	Open a text file for writing, appending to the end of an existing file, or creating the file if it does not exist.
`"r+"`	Open a text file for update (that is, for both reading and writing).
`"w+"`	Open a text file for update (reading and writing), first truncating the file to zero length if it exists or creating the file if it does not exist.
`"a+"`	Open a text file for update (reading and writing), appending to the end of an existing file, or creating the file if it does not yet exist; the whole file can be read, but writing can only be appended.
`"rb"`, `"wb"`, `"ab"`, `"ab+"`, `"a+b"`, `"wb+"`, `"w+b"`, `"ab+"`, `"a+b"`	Like the preceding modes, except it uses binary mode instead of text mode.

For systems such as Unix and Linux that have just one file type, the modes with the **b** are equivalent to the corresponding modes lacking the **b**.

Caution!

If you use any of the `"w"` modes for an existing file, the file contents are truncated so that your program can start with a clean slate.

After your program successfully opens a file, `fopen()` returns a *file pointer*, which the other I/O functions can then use to specify the file. The file pointer (`fp` in this example) is of type pointer-to-`FILE`; `FILE` is a derived type defined in `stdio.h`. The pointer `fp` doesn't point to the actual file. Instead, it points to a data package containing information about the file, including information about the buffer used for the file's I/O. Because the I/O functions in the standard library use a buffer, they need to know where the buffer is. They also need to know how full the buffer is and which file is being used. This enables the functions to refill or empty the buffer when necessary. The data package pointed to by `fp` has all that information. (This data package is an example of a C structure, a topic we discuss in Chapter 14, "Structures and Other Data Forms.")

The `fopen()` function returns the null pointer (also defined in `stdio.h`) if it cannot open the file. The program exits if `fp` is `NULL`. The `fopen()` function can fail because the disk is full, because the name is illegal, because access is restricted, or because of a hardware problem, to name just a few reasons, so check for trouble; a little error-trapping can go a long way.

The `getc()` and `putc()` Functions

The two functions `getc()` and `putc()` work very much like `getchar()` and `putchar()`. The difference is that you must tell these newcomers which file to use. So the following old standby means "get a character from the standard input":

```
ch = getchar();
```

However, this statement means "get a character from the file identified by `fp`":

```
ch = getc(fp);
```

Similarly, this statement means "put the character `ch` into the file identified by the `FILE` pointer `fpout`":

```
putc(ch, fpout);
```

In the `putc()` argument list, the character comes first, and then the file pointer.

Listing 13.1 uses `stdout` for the second argument of `putc()`. It is defined in `stdio.h` as being the file pointer associated with the standard output, so `putc(ch,stdout)` is the same as `putchar(ch)`. Indeed, the latter function is normally defined as being the former. Similarly, `getchar()` is defined as being `getc()` using the standard input.

You may wonder why this example uses `putc()` instead of `putchar()`. One reason is to introduce the `putc()` function. The other is that you can easily convert this program to produce file output by using an argument other than `stdout`.

End-of-File

A program reading data from a file needs to stop when it reaches the end of the file. How can a program tell if it has reached the end? The `getc()` function returns the special value `EOF` if it tries to read a character and discovers it has reached the end of the file. So a C program discovers it has reached the end of a file only after it tries to read past the end of the file. (This is unlike the behavior of some languages, which use a special function to test for end-of-file *before* attempting a read.)

To avoid problems attempting to read an empty file, you should use an entry-condition loop (not a `do while` loop) for file input. Because of the design of `getc()` (and other C input functions), a program should attempt the first read before entering the body of the loop. So the following design is good:

```
// good design #1
int ch;                 // int to hold EOF
FILE * fp;
fp = fopen("wacky.txt", "r");
ch = getc(fp);          // get initial input
while (ch != EOF)
{
    putchar(ch);        // process input
    ch = getc(fp);      // get next input
}
```

This can be condensed to the following design:

```
// good design #2
int ch;
FILE * fp;
fp = fopen("wacky.txt", "r");
while (( ch = getc(fp)) != EOF)
{
    putchar(ch);        // process input
}
```

Because the input statement is part of the `while` test condition, it is executed before the program enters the body of the loop.

You should avoid a design of this sort:

```
// bad design (two problems)
int ch;
FILE * fp;
fp = fopen("wacky.txt", "r");
while (ch != EOF)       // ch undetermined value first use
{
    ch = getc(fp);      // get input
    putchar(ch);        // process input
}
```

The first problem is that the first time `ch` is compared with `EOF`, it has not yet been assigned a value. The second problem is that if `getc()` does return `EOF`, the loop tries to process `EOF` as if it were a valid character. These defects are fixable. For example, you could initialize `ch` to a dummy value and stick an `if` statement inside the loop, but why bother when good designs are already available.

These cautions carry over to the other input functions. They also return an error signal (either `EOF` or the `NULL` pointer) after running into the end of a file.

The `fclose()` Function

The `fclose(fp)` function closes the file identified by `fp`, flushing buffers as needed. For a program less casual than this one, you would check to see whether the file had been closed successfully. The function `fclose()` returns a value of `0` if successful, and `EOF` if not:

```
if (fclose(fp) != 0)
    printf("Error in closing file %s\n", argv[1]);
```

The `fclose()` function can fail if, for example, the disk is full, the floppy disk has been removed, or there has been an I/O error.

Pointers to the Standard Files

The `stdio.h` file associates three file pointers with the three standard files automatically opened by C programs:

Standard File	File Pointer	Normally
Standard input	`stdin`	Your keyboard
Standard output	`stdout`	Your screen
Standard error	`stderr`	Your screen

These pointers are all type pointer-to-`FILE`, so they can be used as arguments to the standard I/O functions, just as `fp` was in the example. Let's move on to an example that creates a new file and writes to it.

A Simple-Minded File-Condensing Program

This next program copies selected data from one file to another. It opens two files simultaneously, using the `"r"` mode for one and the `"w"` mode for the other. The program (shown in Listing 13.2) condenses the contents of the first file by the brutal expedient of retaining only every third character. Finally, it places the condensed text into the second file. The name for the second file is the old name with `.red` (for reduced) appended. Using command-line arguments, opening more than one file simultaneously, and filename appending are generally quite useful techniques. This particular form of condensing is of more limited appeal, but it can have its uses, as you will see. (Again, it is a simple matter to modify this program to use standard I/O techniques instead of command-line arguments to provide filenames.)

LISTING 13.2   The `reducto.c` Program

```
// reducto.c -- reduces your files by two-thirds!
#include <stdio.h>
#include <stdlib.h>     // for exit()
#include <string.h>     // for strcpy(), strcat()
```

LISTING 13.2 Continued

```c
#define LEN 40

int main(int argc, char *argv[])
{
    FILE  *in, *out;    // declare two FILE pointers
    int ch;
    char name[LEN];     // storage for output filename
    int count = 0;

// check for command-line arguments
    if (argc < 2)
    {
        fprintf(stderr, "Usage: %s filename\n", argv[0]);
        exit(1);
    }
// set up input
    if ((in = fopen(argv[1], "r")) == NULL)
    {
        fprintf(stderr, "I couldn't open the file \"%s\"\n",
                argv[1]);
        exit(2);
    }
// set up output
    strncpy(name,argv[1], LEN - 5); // copy filename
    name[LEN - 5] = '\0';
    strcat(name,".red");            // append .red
    if ((out = fopen(name, "w")) == NULL)
    {                               // open file for writing
        fprintf(stderr,"Can't create output file.\n");
        exit(3);
    }
// copy data
    while ((ch = getc(in)) != EOF)
        if (count++ % 3 == 0)
            putc(ch, out);  // print every 3rd char
// clean up
    if (fclose(in) != 0 || fclose(out) != 0)
        fprintf(stderr,"Error in closing files\n");

    return 0;
}
```

The executable file is called `reducto`. We applied it to a file called `eddy`, which contains this single line:

```
So even Eddy came oven ready.
```

The command was as follows:

```
reducto eddy
```

The output was written to a file called `eddy.red`. The program doesn't produce any onscreen output, but displaying the `eddy.red` file reveals the following:

```
Send money
```

This example illustrates several programming techniques. Let's examine some of them now.

The `fprintf()` function is like `printf()`, except that it requires a file pointer as its first argument. We've used the `stderr` pointer to send error messages to the standard error; this is a standard C practice.

To construct the new name for the output file, the program uses `strncpy()` to copy the name `eddy` into the array `name`. The `LEN - 5` argument leaves room for the `.red` suffix and the final null character. No null character is copied if the `argv[2]` string is longer than `LEN - 5`, so the program adds a null character just in case. The first null character in `name` after the `strncpy()` call then is overwritten by the period in `.red` when the `strcat()` function appends that string, producing, in this case, `eddy.red`. We also checked to see whether the program succeeded in opening a file by that name. This is particularly important in some environments because a filename such as, say, `strange.c.red`, may be invalid. For example, you can't add extensions to extensions under traditional DOS. (The proper MS-DOS approach is to replace any existing extension with `.red`, so the reduced version of `strange.c` would be `strange.red`. You could use the `strchr()` function, for example, to locate the period, if any, in a name and copy only the part of the string before the period.)

This program had two files open simultaneously, so we declared two `FILE` pointers. Note that each file is opened and closed independently of the other. There are limits to how many files you can have open at one time. The limit depends on your system and implementation; the range is often 10 to 20. You can use the same file pointer for different files, provided those files are not open at the same time.

File I/O: `fprintf()`, `fscanf()`, `fgets()`, and `fputs()`

For each of the I/O functions in the preceding chapters, there is a similar file I/O function. The main distinction is that you need to use a `FILE` pointer to tell the new functions with which file to work. Like `getc()` and `putc()`, these functions require that you identify a file by using a pointer-to-`FILE`, such as `stdout`, or that you use the return value of `fopen()`.

The `fprintf()` and `fscanf()` Functions

The file I/O functions `fprintf()` and `fscanf()` work just like `printf()` and `scanf()`, except that they require an additional first argument to identify the proper file. You've already used `fprintf()`. Listing 13.3 illustrates both of these file I/O functions, along with the `rewind()` function.

LISTING 13.3   The addaword.c Program

```c
/* addaword.c -- uses fprintf(), fscanf(), and rewind() */
#include <stdio.h>
#include <stdlib.h>
#define MAX 40

int main(void)
{
    FILE *fp;
    char words[MAX];

    if ((fp = fopen("wordy", "a+")) == NULL)
    {
        fprintf(stdout,"Can't open \"words\" file.\n");
        exit(1);
    }

    puts("Enter words to add to the file; press the Enter");
    puts("key at the beginning of a line to terminate.");
    while (gets(words) != NULL  && words[0] != '\0')
        fprintf(fp, "%s ", words);

    puts("File contents:");
    rewind(fp);             /* go back to beginning of file */
    while (fscanf(fp,"%s",words) == 1)
        puts(words);

    if (fclose(fp) != 0)
        fprintf(stderr,"Error closing file\n");

    return 0;
}
```

This program enables you to add words to a file. By using the "a+" mode, the program can both read and write in the file. The first time the program is used, it creates the wordy file and enables you to place words in it. When you use the program subsequently, it enables you to add (append) words to the previous contents. The append mode only enables you to add material to the end of the file, but the "a+" mode does enable you to read the whole file. The rewind() command takes the program to the file beginning so that the final while loop can print the file contents. Note that rewind() takes a file pointer argument.

If you enter an empty line, gets() places a null character in the first element of the array. The program uses that fact to terminate the loop.

Here's a sample run from a DOS environment:

```
C>addaword
Enter words to add to the file; press the Enter
key at the beginning of a line to terminate.
The fabulous programmer[enter]
[enter]
```

```
File contents:
The
fabulous
programmer
C>addaword
Enter words to add to the file; press the Enter
key at the beginning of a line to terminate.
enchanted the[enter]
large[enter]
[enter]
File contents:
The
fabulous
programmer
enchanted
the
large
```

As you can see, `fprintf()` and `fscanf()` work like `printf()` and `scanf()`. Unlike `putc()`, the `fprintf()` and `fscanf()` functions take the `FILE` pointer as the first argument instead of as the last argument.

The `fgets()` and `fputs()` Functions

You met `fgets()` in Chapter 11. The `fgets()` function takes three arguments to the `gets()` function's one. The first argument, as with `gets()`, is the address (type `char *`) where input should be stored. The second argument is an integer representing the maximum size of the input string. The final argument is the file pointer identifying the file to be read. A function call, then, looks like this:

```
fgets(buf, MAX, fp);
```

Here, `buf` is the name of a `char` array, `MAX` is the maximum size of the string, and `fp` is the pointer-to-`FILE`.

The `fgets()` function reads input through the first newline character, until one fewer than the upper limit of characters is read, or until the end-of-file is found; `fgets()` then adds a terminating null character to form a string. Therefore, the upper limit represents the maximum number of characters plus the null character. If `fgets()` reads in a whole line before running into the character limit, it adds the newline character, marking the end of the line into the string, just before the null character. Here it differs from `gets()`, which reads the newline but discards it.

Like `gets()`, `fgets()` returns the value `NULL` when it encounters `EOF`. You can use this to check for the end of a file. Otherwise, it returns the address passed to it.

The `fputs()` function takes two arguments: first, an address of a string, and then a file pointer. It writes the string found at the pointed-to location into the indicated file. Unlike `puts()`, `fputs()` does not append a newline when it prints. A function call looks like this:

```
fputs(buf, fp);
```

Here, buf is the string address, and fp identifies the target file.

Because fgets() keeps the newline and fputs() doesn't add one, they work well in tandem. Listing 13.4 shows an echo program using these two functions.

LISTING 13.4   The parrot.c Program

```
/* parrot.c -- using fgets() and fputs() */
#include <stdio.h>
#define MAXLINE 20
int main(void)
{
    char line[MAXLINE];

    while (fgets(line, MAXLINE, stdin) != NULL &&
            line[0] != '\n')
       fputs(line, stdout);
    return 0;
}
```

When you press the Enter key at the beginning of a line, fgets() reads the newline and places it into the first element of the array line. Use that fact to terminate the input loop. Encountering end-of-file also terminates it. (Listing 13.3 tested for '\0' instead of '\n' because gets() discards the newline.)

Here is a sample run. Do you notice anything odd?

```
The silent knight
The silent knight
strode solemnly down the dank and dark hall.
strode solemnly down the dank and dark hall.
[enter]
```

The program works fine. This should seem surprising because the second line entered contains 44 characters, and the line array holds only 20, including the newline character! What happened? When fgets() read the second line, it read just the first 19 characters, through the w in the word *down*. They were copied into line, which fputs() printed. Because fgets() hadn't reached the end of a line, line did not contain a newline character, so fputs() didn't print a newline. The third call to fgets() resumed where the second call left off. Therefore, it read the next 19 characters into line, beginning with the n after the w in *down*. This next block replaced the previous contents of line and, in turn, was printed on the same line as the output. Remember, the last output didn't have a newline. In short, fgets() read the second line in chunks of 19 characters, and fputs() printed it in the same-size chunks.

This program also terminates input if a line has exactly 19 characters. In that case, fgets() stops reading input after the 19 characters, so the next call to fgets() starts with the newline at the end of the line. This newline becomes the first character read, thus terminating the loop. So although the program worked with the sample input, it doesn't work correctly in all cases. You really should use a storage array big enough to hold entire lines or else use the simpler approach of reading single characters at a time.

You might be wondering why the program didn't print the first 19 characters of the second line as soon as you typed them. That is where screen buffering comes in. The second line wasn't sent to the screen until the newline character had been reached.

Commentary: `gets()` and `fgets()`

Because `fgets()` can be used to prevent storage overflow, it is a better function than `gets()` for serious programming. Because it does read a newline into a string and because `puts()` appends a newline to output, `fgets()` should be used with `fputs()`, not `puts()`. Otherwise, one newline in input can become two upon output.

The six I/O functions we have just discussed should give you tools aplenty for reading and writing text files. So far, we have used them only for sequential access—that is, processing the file contents in order. Next, we look at random access—in other words, accessing the contents in any order you want.

Adventures in Random Access: `fseek()` and `ftell()`

The `fseek()` function enables you to treat a file like an array and move directly to any particular byte in a file opened by `fopen()`. To see how it works, let's create a program (see Listing 13.5) that displays a file in reverse order. Borrowing from the earlier examples, it uses a command-line argument to get the name of the file it will read. Note that `fseek()` has three arguments and returns an `int` value. The `ftell()` function returns the current position in a file as a `long` value.

LISTING 13.5   The `reverse.c` Program

```
/* reverse.c -- displays a file in reverse order */
#include <stdio.h>
#include <stdlib.h>
#define CNTL_Z '\032'    /* eof marker in DOS text files */
#define SLEN 50
int main(void)
{
    char file[SLEN];
    char ch;
    FILE *fp;
    long count, last;

    puts("Enter the name of the file to be processed:");
    gets(file);
    if ((fp = fopen(file,"rb")) == NULL)
    {                        /* read-only and binary modes */
        printf("reverse can't open %s\n", file);
        exit(1);
    }
```

LISTING 13.5   Continued

```
        fseek(fp, 0L, SEEK_END);              /* go to end of file */
        last = ftell(fp);
        for (count = 1L; count <= last; count++)
        {
            fseek(fp, -count, SEEK_END);  /* go backward       */
            ch = getc(fp);
    /* for DOS, works with Unix */
            if (ch != CNTL_Z && ch != '\r')
                putchar(ch);
    /* for Macintosh               */
    /*   if (ch == '\r')
                putchar('\n');
            else
                putchar(ch);          */
        }
        putchar('\n');
        fclose(fp);

        return 0;
    }
```

Here is the output for a sample file:

```
Enter the name of the file to be processed:
cluv

.C ni eno naht ylevol erom margorp a
ees reven llahs I taht kniht I
```

Note

If you run the program from a command-line environment, this program expects the filename to be in the same directory (or folder) as the executable program. If you run the program from an IDE, where the program looks depend on the implementation. For example, Microsoft Visual C++ looks in the directory containing the source code, but Metrowerks CodeWarrior looks in the directory containing the executable file.

We now need to discuss three topics: how `fseek()` and `ftell()` work, how to use a binary stream, and how to make the program portable.

How `fseek()` and `ftell()` Work

The first of the three arguments to `fseek()` is a `FILE` pointer to the file being searched. The file should have been opened by using `fopen()`.

The second argument to `fseek()` is called the *offset*. This argument tells how far to move from the starting point (see the following list of mode starting points). The argument must be a `long` value. It can be positive (move forward), negative (move backward), or zero (stay put).

The third argument is the mode, and it identifies the starting point. Under ANSI, the `stdio.h` header file specifies the following manifest constants for the mode:

Mode	Measures Offset From
SEEK_SET	Beginning of file
SEEK_CUR	Current position
SEEK_END	End of file

Older implementations may lack these definitions and, instead, use the numeric values 0L, 1L, and 2L, respectively, for these modes. Recall that the L suffix identifies type long values. Or the implementation might have the constants defined in a different header file. When in doubt, consult your usage manual or the online manual.

Here are some sample function calls, where `fp` is a file pointer:

```
fseek(fp, 0L, SEEK_SET);    // go to the beginning of the file
fseek(fp, 10L, SEEK_SET);   // go 10 bytes into the file
fseek(fp, 2L, SEEK_CUR);    // advance 2 bytes from the current position
fseek(fp, 0L, SEEK_END);    // go to the end of the file
fseek(fp, -10L, SEEK_END);  // back up 10 bytes from the end of the file
```

There are some possible restrictions on these calls; we'll get back to that topic in a moment or two.

The value returned by `fseek()` is 0 if everything is okay, and -1 if there is an error, such as attempting to move past the bounds of the file.

The `ftell()` function is type long, and it returns the current file location. Under ANSI, it is declared in `stdio.h`. As originally implemented in Unix, `ftell()` specifies the file position by returning the number of bytes from the beginning, with the first byte being byte 0, and so on. Under ANSI C, this definition applies to files opened in the binary mode, but not necessarily to files opened in the text mode. That is one reason Listing 13.5 uses the binary mode.

Now we can examine the basic elements of Listing 13.5. First, the statement

```
fseek(fp, 0L, SEEK_END);
```

sets the position to an offset of 0 bytes from the file end. That is, it sets the position to the end of the file. Next, the statement

```
last = ftell(fp);
```

assigns to `last` the number of bytes from the beginning to the end of the file.

Next is this loop:

```
for (count = 1L; count <= last; count++)
{
  fseek(fp, -count, SEEK_END);    /* go backward */
    ch = getc(fp);
 }
```

The first cycle positions the program at the first character before the end of the file (that is, at the file's final character). Then the program prints that character. The next loop positions the program at the preceding character and prints it. This process continues until the first character is reached and printed.

Binary Versus Text Mode

We designed Listing 13.5 to work in both the Unix and the MS-DOS environments. Unix has only one file format, so no special adjustments are needed. MS-DOS, however, does require extra attention. Many MS-DOS editors mark the end of a text file with the character Ctrl+Z. When such a file is opened in the text mode, C recognizes this character as marking the end of the file. When the same file is opened in the binary mode, however, the Ctrl+Z character is just another character in the file, and the actual end-of-file comes later. It might come immediately after the Ctrl+Z, or the file could be padded with null characters to make the size a multiple of, say, 256. Null characters don't print under DOS, and we included code to prevent the program from trying to print the Ctrl+Z character.

Another difference is one we've mentioned before: MS-DOS represents a text file newline with the \r\n combination. A C program opening the same file in a text mode "sees" \r\n as a simple \n, but, when using the binary mode, the program sees both characters. Therefore, we included coding to suppress printing \r. (Different coding is needed for Macintosh text files because they use the \r as the end-of-line marker. Listing 13.5 shows the Macintosh version as a comment.)

Because a Unix text file normally contains neither Ctrl+Z nor \r, this extra coding does not affect most Unix text files.

The ftell() function may work differently in the text mode than in the binary mode. Many systems have text file formats that are different enough from the Unix model that a byte count from the beginning of the file is not a meaningful quantity. ANSI C states that, for the text mode, ftell() returns a value that can be used as the second argument to fseek(). For MS-DOS, for example, ftell() can return a count that sees \r\n as a single byte.

Portability

Ideally, fseek() and ftell() should conform to the Unix model. However, differences in real systems sometimes make this impossible. Therefore, ANSI provides lowered expectations for these functions. Here are some limitations:

- In the binary mode, implementations need not support the SEEK_END mode. Listing 13.5, then, is not guaranteed to be portable. However, the listing does show an alternative method for locating the end-of-file. Because the alternative method sequentially reads the whole file to find the end, it's slower than simply jumping to the end. The C preprocessor conditional compilation directives, discussed in Chapter 16, "The C Preprocessor and the C Library," provide a more systematic way to handle alternative code choices.

- In the text mode, the only calls to `fseek()` that are guaranteed to work are these:

Function Call	Effect
`fseek(file, 0L, SEEK_SET)`	Go to the beginning of the file.
`fseek(file, 0L, SEEK_CUR)`	Stay at the current position.
`fseek(file, 0L, SEEK_END)`	Go to the file's end.
`fseek(file,ftell-pos, SEEK_SET)`	Go to position `ftell-pos` from the beginning; `ftell-pos` is a value returned by `ftell()`.

Fortunately, many common environments allow stronger implementations of these functions.

The `fgetpos()` and `fsetpos()` Functions

One potential problem with `fseek()` and `ftell()` is that they limit file sizes to values that can be represented by type `long`. Perhaps two-billion bytes seem more than adequate, but the ever-increasing capacities of storage devices makes larger files possible. ANSI C introduced two new positioning functions designed to work with larger file sizes. Instead of using a `long` value to represent a position, it uses a new type, called `fpos_t` (for file position type) for that purpose. The `fpos_t` type is not a fundamental type; rather, it is defined in terms of other types. A variable or data object of `fpos_t` type can specify a location within a file, and it cannot be an array type, but its nature is not specified beyond that. Implementations can then provide a type to meet the needs of a particular platform; the type could, for example, be implemented as a structure.

ANSI C does define how `fpos_t` is used. The `fgetpos()` function has this prototype:

```
int fgetpos(FILE * restrict stream, fpos_t * restrict pos);
```

When called, it places an `fpos_t` value in the location pointed to by `pos`; the value describes a location in the file. The function returns zero if successful, and a nonzero value for failure.

The `fsetpos()` function has this prototype:

```
int fsetpos(FILE *stream, const fpos_t *pos);
```

When called, it uses the `fpos_t` value in the location pointed to by `pos` to set the file pointer to the location indicated by that value. The function returns zero if successful, and a nonzero value for failure. The `fpos_t` value should have been obtained by a previous call to `fgetpos()`.

Behind the Scenes with Standard I/O

Now that you've seen some of the features of the standard I/O package, let's examine a representative conceptual model to see how standard I/O works.

Normally, the first step in using standard I/O is to use `fopen()` to open a file. (Recall, however, that the `stdin`, `stdout`, and `stderr` files are opened automatically.) The `fopen()` function not only opens a file but sets up a buffer (two buffers for read-write modes), and it sets up a data structure containing data about the file and about the buffer. Also, `fopen()` returns a pointer to this structure so that other functions know where to find it. Assume that this value is assigned to a pointer variable named `fp`. The `fopen()` function is said to "open a stream." If the file is opened in the text mode, you get a text stream, and if the file is opened in the binary mode, you get a binary stream.

The data structure typically includes a file position indicator to specify the current position in the stream. It also has indicators for errors and end-of-file, a pointer to the beginning of the buffer, a file identifier, and a count for the number of bytes actually copied into the buffer.

Let's concentrate on file input. Usually, the next step is to call on one of the input functions declared in `stdio.h`, such as `fscanf()`, `getc()`, or `fgets()`. Calling any one of these functions causes a chunk of data to be copied from the file to the buffer. The buffer size is implementation dependent, but it typically is 512 bytes or some multiple thereof, such as 4,096 or 16,384. (As hard drives and computer memories get larger, the choice of buffer size tends to get larger, too.) In addition to filling the buffer, the initial function call sets values in the structure pointed to by `fp`. In particular, the current position in the stream, and the number of bytes copied into the buffer are set. Usually the current position starts at byte 0.

After the data structure and buffer are initialized, the input function reads the requested data from the buffer. As it does so, the file position indicator is set to point to the character following the last character read. Because all the input functions from the `stdio.h` family use the same buffer, a call to any one function resumes where the previous call to any of the functions stopped.

When an input function finds that it has read all the characters in the buffer, it requests that the next buffer-sized chunk of data be copied from the file into the buffer. In this manner, the input functions can read all the file contents up to the end of the file. After a function reads the last character of the final buffer's worth of data, it sets the end-of-file indicator to true. The next call to an input function then returns `EOF`.

In a similar manner, output functions write to a buffer. When the buffer is filled, the data is copied to the file.

Other Standard I/O Functions

The ANSI standard library contains over three dozen functions in the standard I/O family. Although we don't cover them all here, we will briefly describe a few more to give you a better idea of what is available. We'll list each function by its ANSI C prototype to indicate its arguments and return values. Of those functions we discuss here, all but `setvbuf()` are also available in pre-ANSI implementations. Reference Section V, "The Standard ANSI C Library with C99 Additions," lists the full ANSI C standard I/O package.

The `int ungetc(int c, FILE *fp)` Function

The `int ungetc()` function pushes the character specified by `c` back onto the input stream. If you push a character onto the input stream, the next call to a standard input function reads that character (see Figure 13.2). Suppose, for example, that you want a function to read characters up to, but not including, the next colon. You can use `getchar()` or `getc()` to read characters until a colon is read and then use `ungetc()` to place the colon back in the input stream. The ANSI C standard guarantees only one pushback at a time. If an implementation permits you to push back several characters in a row, the input functions read them in the reversed order of pushing.

FIGURE 13.2
The `ungetc()` function.

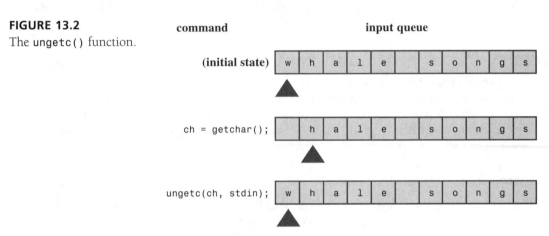

The `int fflush()` Function

The prototype for `fflush()` is this:

```
int fflush(FILE *fp);
```

Calling the `fflush()` function causes any unwritten data in the output buffer to be sent to the output file identified by `fp`. This process is called *flushing a buffer*. If `fp` is the null pointer, all output buffers are flushed. The effect of using `fflush()` on an input stream is undefined. You can use it with an update stream (any of the read-write modes), provided that the most recent operation using the stream was not input.

The `int setvbuf()` Function

The prototype for `setvbuf()` is this:

```
int setvbuf(FILE * restrict fp, char * restrict buf, int mode, size_t size);
```

The `setvbuf()` function sets up an alternative buffer to be used by the standard I/O functions. It is called after the file has been opened and before any other operations have been performed on the stream. The pointer `fp` identifies the stream, and `buf` points to the storage to be used. If the value of `buf` is not `NULL`, you must create the buffer. For instance, you could declare an array of 1,024 `chars` and pass the address of that array. However, if you use `NULL` for the value of `buf`, the function allocates a buffer itself. The `size` variable tells `setvbuf()` how big the array is. (The `size_t` type is a derived integer type; see Chapter 5, "Operators, Expressions, and Statements.") The `mode` is selected from the following choices: `_IOFBF` means fully buffered (buffer flushed when full), `_IOLBF` means line-buffered (buffer flushed when full or when a newline is written), and `_IONBF` means nonbuffered. The function returns zero if successful, nonzero otherwise.

Suppose you have a program that works with stored data objects having, say, a size of 3,000 bytes each. You could use `setvbuf()` to create a buffer whose size matches that of the data object.

Binary I/O: `fread()` and `fwrite()`

The `fread()` and `fwrite()` functions are next on the list, but first some background. The standard I/O functions you've used to this point are text oriented, dealing with characters and strings. What if you want to save numeric data in a file? True, you can use `fprintf()` and the `%f` format to save a floating-point value, but then you are saving it as a string. For example, the sequence

```
double num = 1./3.;
fprintf(fp,"%f", num);
```

saves `num` as a string of eight characters: `0.333333`. Using a `%.2f` specifier saves it as four characters: `0.33`. Using a `%.12f` specifier saves it as 14 characters: `0.333333333333`. Changing the specifier alters the amount of space needed to store the value; it can also result in different values being stored. After the value of `num` is stored as `0.33`, there is no way to get back the full precision when the file is read. In general, `fprintf()` converts numeric values to strings, possibly altering the value.

The most accurate and consistent way to store a number is to use the same pattern of bits that the program does. Therefore, a `double` value should be stored in a size `double` unit. When data is stored in a file using the same representation that the program uses, we say that the data is stored in *binary form*. There is no conversion from numeric forms to strings. For standard I/O, the `fread()` and `fwrite()` functions provide this binary service (see Figure 13.3).

Actually, all data is stored in binary form. Even characters are stored using the binary representation of the character code. However, if all data in the file is interpreted as character codes, we say that the file contains text data. If some or all of the data is interpreted as numeric data in binary form, we say that the file contains binary data. (Also, files in which the data represents machine-language instructions are binary files.)

The uses of the terms *binary* and *text* can get confusing. ANSI C recognizes two modes for opening files: binary and text. Many operating systems recognize two file formats: binary and text. Information can be stored or read as binary data or as text data. These are all related, but not identical. You can open a text format file in the binary mode. You can store text in a binary format file. You can use `getc()` to copy files containing binary data. In general, however, you use the binary mode to store binary data in a binary format file. Similarly, you most often use text data in text files opened in the text format. (Files produced by word processors typically are binary files because they contain a lot of non-text information describing fonts and formatting.)

FIGURE 13.3
Binary and text output.

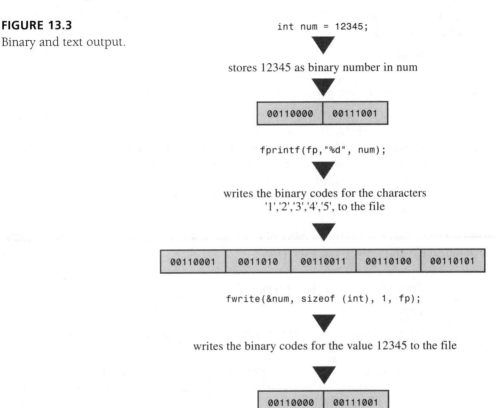

int num = 12345;

stores 12345 as binary number in num

| 00110000 | 00111001 |

fprintf(fp,"%d", num);

writes the binary codes for the characters
'1','2','3','4','5', to the file

| 00110001 | 0011010 | 00110011 | 00110100 | 00110101 |

fwrite(&num, sizeof (int), 1, fp);

writes the binary codes for the value 12345 to the file

| 00110000 | 00111001 |

(this figure assumes an integer size of 16 bits)

The size_t fwrite() Function

The prototype for `fwrite()` is this:

```
size_t fwrite(const void * restrict ptr, size_t size, size_t nmemb,
              FILE * restrict fp);
```

The `fwrite()` function writes binary data to a file. The **size_t** type is defined in terms of the standard C types. It is the type returned by the **sizeof** operator. Typically, it is **unsigned int**, but an implementation can choose another type. The pointer **ptr** is the address of the chunk of data to be written. Also, **size** represents the size, in bytes, of the chunks to be written, and **nmemb** represents the number of chunks to be written. As usual, **fp** identifies the file to be written to. For instance, to save a data object (such as an array) that is 256 bytes in size, you can do this:

```
char buffer[256];
fwrite(buffer, 256, 1, fp);
```

This call writes one chunk of 256 bytes from `buffer` to the file. Or, to save an array of 10 `double` values, you can do this:

```
double earnings[10];
fwrite(earnings, sizeof (double), 10, fp);
```

This call writes data from the `earnings` array to the file in 10 chunks, each of size `double`.

You probably noticed the odd declaration of const `void * restrict ptr` in the `fwrite()` prototype. One problem with `fwrite()` is that its first argument is not a fixed type. For instance, the first example used `buffer`, which is type pointer-to-`char`, and the second example used `earnings`, which is type pointer-to-`double`. Under ANSI C function prototyping, these actual arguments are converted to the pointer-to-`void` type, which acts as a sort of catchall type for pointers. (Pre-ANSI C uses type `char *` for this argument, requiring you to typecast actual arguments to that type.)

The `fwrite()` function returns the number of items successfully written. Normally, this equals `nmemb`, but it can be less if there is a write error.

The `size_t fread()` Function

The prototype for `fread()` is this:

```
size_t fread(void * restrict ptr, size_t size, size_t nmemb,
             FILE * restrict fp);
```

The `fread()` function takes the same set of arguments that `fwrite()` does. This time `ptr` is the address of the memory storage into which file data is read, and `fp` identifies the file to be read. Use this function to read data that was written to a file using `fwrite()`. For example, to recover the array of 10 `doubles` saved in the previous example, use this call:

```
double earnings[10];
fread(earnings, sizeof (double), 10, fp);
```

This call copies 10 size `double` values into the `earnings` array.

The `fread()` function returns the number of items successfully read. Normally, this equals `nmemb`, but it can be less if there is a read error or if the end-of-file is reached.

The `int feof(FILE *fp)` and `int ferror(FILE *fp)` Functions

When the standard input functions return `EOF`, this usually means they have reached the end of a file. However, it can also indicate that a read error has occurred. The `feof()` and `ferror()` functions enable you to distinguish between the two possibilities. The `feof()`

function returns a nonzero value if the last input call detected the end-of-file, and it returns zero otherwise. The `ferror()` function returns a nonzero value if a read or write error has occurred, and it returns zero otherwise.

An `fread()` and `fwrite()` Example

Let's use some of these functions in a program that appends the contents from a list of files to the end of another file. One problem is passing the file information to the program. This can be done interactively or by using command-line arguments. We'll take the first approach, which suggests a plan along the following lines:

- Request a name for the destination file and open it.
- Use a loop to request source files.
- Open each source file in turn in the read mode and add it to the append file.

To illustrate `setvbuf()`, we'll use it to specify a different buffer size. The next stage of refinement examines opening the append file. We will use the following steps:

1. Open the destination file in the append mode.
2. If this cannot be done, quit.
3. Establish a 1,024-byte buffer for this file.
4. If this cannot be done, quit.

Similarly, we can refine the copying portion by doing the following for each file:

- If it is the same as the append file, skip to the next file.
- If it cannot be opened in the read mode, skip to the next file.
- Add the contents of the file to the append file.

For practice, we'll use `fread()` and `fwrite()` for the copying. Listing 13.6 shows the result.

LISTING 13.6   The `append.c` Program
```
/* append.c -- appends files to a file */
#include <stdio.h>
#include <stdlib.h>
#include <string.h>
#define BUFSIZE 1024
#define SLEN 81
void append(FILE *source, FILE *dest);

int main(void)
{
    FILE *fa, *fs; // fa for append file, fs for source file
    int files = 0;  // number of files appended
    char file_app[SLEN];  // name of append file
```

LISTING 13.6 *Continued*

```
        char file_src[SLEN];  // name of source file
        puts("Enter name of destination file:");
        gets(file_app);
        if ((fa = fopen(file_app, "a")) == NULL)
        {
            fprintf(stderr, "Can't open %s\n", file_app);
            exit(2);
        }
        if (setvbuf(fa, NULL, _IOFBF, BUFSIZE) != 0)
        {
            fputs("Can't create output buffer\n", stderr);
            exit(3);
        }
        puts("Enter name of first source file (empty line to quit):");
        while (gets(file_src) && file_src[0] != '\0')
        {
            if (strcmp(file_src, file_app) == 0)
                fputs("Can't append file to itself\n",stderr);
            else if ((fs = fopen(file_src, "r")) == NULL)
                fprintf(stderr, "Can't open %s\n", file_src);
            else
            {
                if (setvbuf(fs, NULL, _IOFBF, BUFSIZE) != 0)
                {
                    fputs("Can't create input buffer\n",stderr);
                    continue;
                }
                append(fs, fa);
                if (ferror(fs) != 0)
                    fprintf(stderr,"Error in reading file %s.\n",
                            file_src);
                if (ferror(fa) != 0)
                    fprintf(stderr,"Error in writing file %s.\n",
                            file_app);
                fclose(fs);
                files++;
                printf("File %s appended.\n", file_src);
                puts("Next file (empty line to quit):");
            }
        }
        printf("Done. %d files appended.\n", files);
        fclose(fa);

        return 0;
    }

    void append(FILE *source, FILE *dest)
    {
        size_t bytes;
        static char temp[BUFSIZE]; // allocate once
```

```
    while ((bytes = fread(temp,sizeof(char),BUFSIZE,source)) > 0)
        fwrite(temp, sizeof (char), bytes, dest);
}
```

The following code creates a buffer 1,024 bytes in size to be used with the append file:

```
if (setvbuf(fa, NULL, _IOFBF, BUFSIZE) != 0)
{
    fputs("Can't create output buffer\n", stderr);
    exit(3);
}
```

If `setvbuf()` is unable to create the buffer, it returns a nonzero value, and the code then terminates the program. Similar coding establishes a 1,024-byte buffer for the file currently being copied. By using `NULL` as the second argument to `setvbuf()`, we let that function allocate storage for the buffer.

This code prevents the program from trying to append a file to itself:

```
if (strcmp(file_src, file_app) == 0)
    fputs("Can't append file to itself\n",stderr);
```

The argument `file_app` represents the name of the destination file, and `file_src` represents the name of the file currently being processed.

The `append()` function does the copying. Instead of copying a byte at a time, it uses `fread()` and `fwrite()` to copy 1,024 bytes at a time:

```
void append(source, dest)
FILE *source, *dest;
{
    size_t bytes;
    static char temp[BUFSIZE]; // allocate once

    while ((bytes = fread(temp,sizeof(char),BUFSIZE,source)) > 0)
        fwrite(temp, sizeof (char), bytes, dest);
}
```

Because the file specified by `dest` is opened in the append mode, each source file is added to the end of the destination file, one after the other. Note that the `temp` array is static duration (meaning it's allocated at compile time, not each time the `append()` function is called) and block scope (meaning that it is private to the function).

The example uses text-mode files; by using the `"ab"` and `"rb"` modes, it could handle binary files.

Random Access with Binary I/O

Random access is most often used with binary files written using binary I/O, so let's look at a short example. The program in Listing 13.7 creates a file of `double` numbers and then lets you access the contents.

LISTING 13.7   The randbin.c Program

```c
/* randbin.c -- random access, binary i/o */
#include <stdio.h>
#include <stdlib.h>
#define ARSIZE 1000

int main()
{
    double numbers[ARSIZE];
    double value;
    const char * file = "numbers.dat";
    int i;
    long pos;
    FILE *iofile;

    // create a set of double values
    for(i = 0; i < ARSIZE; i++)
        numbers[i] = 100.0 * i + 1.0 / (i + 1);
    // attempt to open file
    if ((iofile = fopen(file, "wb")) == NULL)
    {
        fprintf(stderr, "Could not open %s for output.\n", file);
        exit(1);
    }
    // write array in binary format to file
    fwrite(numbers, sizeof (double), ARSIZE, iofile);
    fclose(iofile);
    if ((iofile = fopen(file, "rb")) == NULL)
    {
        fprintf(stderr,
            "Could not open %s for random access.\n", file);
        exit(1);
    }
    // read selected items from file
    printf("Enter an index in the range 0-%d.\n", ARSIZE - 1);
    scanf("%d", &i);
    while (i >= 0 && i < ARSIZE)
    {
        pos = (long) i * sizeof(double); // calculate offset
        fseek(iofile, pos, SEEK_SET);    // go there
        fread(&value, sizeof (double), 1, iofile);
        printf("The value there is %f.\n", value);
        printf("Next index (out of range to quit):\n");
        scanf("%d", &i);
    }
    // finish up
    fclose(iofile);
    puts("Bye!");

    return 0;
}
```

First, the program creates an array and places some values into it. Then it creates a file called `numbers.dat` in binary mode and uses `fwrite()` to copy the array contents to the file. The 64-bit pattern for each `double` value is copied from memory to the file. You can't read the resulting binary file with a text editor because the values are not translated to strings. However, each value is stored in the file precisely as it was stored in memory, so there is no loss of precision. Furthermore, each value occupies exactly 64 bits of storage in the file, so it is a simple matter to calculate the location of each value.

The second part of the program opens the file for reading and asks the user to enter the index for a value. Multiplying the index times the number of bytes per `double` yields the location in the file. The program then uses `fseek()` to go to that location and `fread()` to read the value there. Note that there are no format specifiers. Instead, `fread()` copies the 8 bytes, starting at that location, into the memory location indicated by `&value`. Then it can use `printf()` to display `value`. Here is a sample run:

```
Enter an index in the range 0-999.
500
The value there is 50000.001996.
Next index (out of range to quit):
900
The value there is 90000.001110.
Next index (out of range to quit):
0
The value there is 1.000000.
Next index (out of range to quit):
-1
Bye!
```

Key Concepts

A C program views input as a stream of bytes; the source of this stream could be a file, an input device (such as a keyboard), or even the output of another program. Similarly, a C program views output as a stream of bytes; the destination could be a file, a video display, and so on.

How C interprets an input stream or output stream of bytes depends on which input/output functions you use. A program can read and store the bytes unaltered, or it can interpret the bytes as characters, which, in turn, can be interpreted as ordinary text or as the text representation of numbers. Similarly, on output, the functions you use determine whether binary values are transferred unaltered or converted to text or textual representations of numbers. If you have numeric data that you want to save and recover with no loss of precision, use the binary mode and the `fread()` and `fwrite()` functions. If you're saving text information and want to create files that can be viewed with ordinary text editors, use the text mode and functions such as `getc()` and `fprintf()`.

To access a file, you need to create a file pointer (type `FILE *`) and associate the pointer with a particular filename. Subsequent code then uses the pointer, not the filename, when dealing with the file.

It's important to understand how C handles the end-of-file concept. Typically, a file-reading program uses a loop to read input until reaching the end of file. The C input functions don't detect end-of-file until they attempt to read past the end. This means that testing for end-of-file should occur immediately *after* an attempted read. You can use the two file input models labeled "good design" in the "End-of-File" section of this chapter as a guide.

Summary

Writing to and reading from files is essential for most C programs. Most C implementations offer both low-level I/O services and standard high-level I/O services for these purposes. Because the ANSI C library includes the standard I/O services but not the low-level services, the standard package is more portable.

The standard I/O package automatically creates input and output buffers to speed up data transfer. The `fopen()` function opens a file for standard I/O and creates a data structure designed to hold information about the file and the buffer. The `fopen()` function returns a pointer to that data structure, and this pointer is used by other functions to identify the file to be processed. The `feof()` and `ferror()` functions report the reason an I/O operation failed.

C views input as a stream of bytes. If you use `fread()`, C views the input as binary values to be placed into whichever storage location you indicate. If you use `fscanf()`, `getc()`, `fgets()`, or any of the related functions, C views each byte as being a character code. The `fscanf()` and `scanf()` functions then attempt to translate the character code into other types, as indicated by the format specifiers. For example, the `%f` specifier would translate an input of 23 into a floating-point value, the `%d` specifier would translate the same input into an integer value, and the `%s` specifier would save the character input as a string. The `getc()` and `fgets()` family of functions leave the input as character code and store it either in `char` variables as individual characters or in `char` arrays as strings. Similarly, `fwrite()` places binary data directly into the output stream, whereas the other output functions convert non-character data to character representations before placing it in the output stream.

ANSI C provides two file-opening modes: binary and text. When a file is opened in binary mode, it can be read byte-for-byte. When a file is opened in text mode, its contents may be mapped from the system representation of text to the C representation. For Unix and Linux systems, the two modes are identical.

The input functions `getc()`, `fgets()`, `fscanf()`, and `fread()` normally read a file sequentially, starting at the beginning of the file. However, the `fseek()` and `ftell()` functions let a program move to an arbitrary position in a file, enabling random access. Both `fgetpos()` and `fsetpos()` extend similar capabilities to larger files. Random access works better in the binary mode than in the text mode.

Review Questions

1. What's wrong with this program?

```
int main(void)
{
    int * fp;
    int k;

    fp = fopen("gelatin");
    for (k = 0; k < 30; k++)
        fputs(fp, "Nanette eats gelatin.");
    fclose("gelatin");
    return 0;
}
```

2. What would the following program do? (Macintosh users can assume the program correctly uses `console.h` and the `ccommand()` function.)

```
#include <stdio.h>
#include <stdlib.h>
#include <ctype.h>
int main(int argc, char *argv[])
{
    int ch;
    FILE *fp;

    if (argc < 2)
     exit(2);
    if ( (fp = fopen(argv[1], "r")) == NULL)
         exit(1);
    while ( (ch= getc(fp)) != EOF )
        if( isdigit(ch) )
             putchar(ch);
    fclose (fp);

    return 0;
}
```

3. Suppose you have these statements in a program:

```
#include <stdio.h>
FILE * fp1,* fp2;
char ch;

fp1 = fopen("terky", "r");
fp2 = fopen("jerky", "w");
```

Also, suppose that both files were opened successfully. Supply the missing arguments in the following function calls:

    a. `ch = getc();`

    b. `fprintf( ,"%c\n", );`

    c. `putc( , );`

    d. `fclose(); /* close the terky file */`

4. Write a program that takes zero command-line arguments or one command-line argument. If there is one argument, it is interpreted as the name of a file. If there is no argument, the standard input (`stdin`) is to be used for input. Assume that the input consists entirely of floating-point numbers. Have the program calculate and report the arithmetic mean (the average) of the input numbers.

5. Write a program that takes two command-line arguments. The first is a character, and the second is a filename. The program should print only those lines in the file containing the given character.

Note

Lines in a file are identified by a terminating `'\n'`. Assume that no line is more than 256 characters long. You might want to use `fgets()`.

6. What's the difference between binary files and text files on the one hand versus binary streams and text streams on the other?

7.   a. What is the difference between saving `8238201` by using `fprintf()` and saving it by using `fwrite()`?

    b. What is the difference between saving the character *S* by using `putc()` and saving it by using `fwrite()`?

8. What's the difference among the following?

```
printf("Hello, %s\n", name);
fprintf(stdout, "Hello, %s\n", name);
fprintf(stderr, "Hello, %s\n", name);
```

9. The `"a+"`, `"r+"`, and `"w+"` modes all open files for both reading and writing. Which one is best suited for altering material already present in a file?

Programming Exercises

1. Modify Listing 13.1 so that it solicits the user to enter the filename and reads the user's response instead of using command-line arguments.

2. Write a file-copy program that takes the original filename and the copy file from the command line. Use standard I/O and the binary mode, if possible.

3. Write a file copy program that prompts the user to enter the name of a text file to act as the source file and the name of an output file. The program should use the `toupper()` function from `ctype.h` to convert all text to uppercase as it's written to the output file. Use standard I/O and the text mode.

4. Write a program that sequentially displays onscreen all the files listed in the command line. Use `argc` to control a loop.

5. Modify the program in Listing 13.6 so that it uses a command-line interface instead of an interactive interface.

6. Programs using command-line arguments rely on the user's memory of how to use them correctly. Rewrite the program in Listing 13.2 so that, instead of using command-line arguments, it prompts the user for the required information.

7. Write a program that opens two files. You can obtain the filenames either by using command-line arguments or by soliciting the user to enter them.

   a. Have the program print line 1 of the first file, line 1 of the second file, line 2 of the first file, line 2 of the second file, and so on, until the last line of the longer file (in terms of lines) is printed.

   b. Modify the program so that lines with the same line number are printed on the same line.

8. Write a program that takes as command-line arguments a character and zero or more filenames. If no arguments follow the character, have the program read the standard input. Otherwise, have it open each file in turn and report how many times the character appears in each file. The filename and the character itself should be reported along with the count. Include error-checking to see whether the number of arguments is correct and whether the files can be opened. If a file can't be opened, have the program report that fact and go on to the next file.

9. Modify the program in Listing 13.3 so that each word is numbered according to the order in which it was added to the list, starting with 1. Make sure that, when the program is run a second time, new word numbering resumes where the previous numbering left off.

10. Write a program that opens a text file whose name is obtained interactively. Set up a loop that asks the user to enter a file position. The program then should print the part of the file starting at that position and proceed to the next newline character. Let nonnumeric input terminate the user-input loop.

11. Write a program that takes two command-line arguments. The first is a string; the second is the name of a file. The program should then search the file, printing all lines containing the string. Because this task is line oriented rather than character oriented, use `fgets()` instead of `getc()`. Use the standard C library function `strstr()` (briefly described in exercise 7 of Chapter 11) to search each line for the string.

12. Create a text file consisting of 20 rows of 30 integers. The integers should be in the range 0–9 and be separated by spaces. The file is a digital representation of a picture, with the values **0** through **9** representing increasing levels of darkness. Write a program that reads the contents of the file into a 20-by-30 array of `int`s. In a crude approach toward converting this digital representation to a picture, have the program use the values in this array to initialize a 20-by-31 array of `char`s, with a **0** value corresponding to a space character, a **1** value to the period character, and so on, with each larger number represented by a character that occupies more space. For example, you might use **#** to represent 9. The last character (the 31st) in each row should be a null character, making it an array of 20 strings. Have the program display the resulting picture (that is, print the strings) and also store the result in a text file. For example, suppose you start with this data:

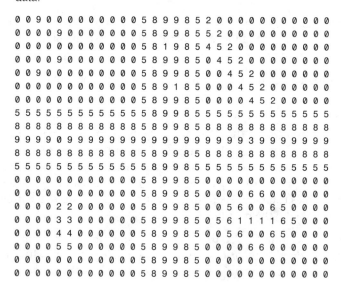

For one particular choice of output characters, the output looks like this:

```
#               *%##%*'
    #           *%##%**'
                *%.#%*~*'
      #         *%##%* ~*'
   #            *%##%*  ~*'
                *%#.%*   ~*'
                *%##%*     ~*'
***************%##%*************
%%%%%%%%%%%%*%##%*%%%%%%%%%%%%%%
#### ################:#######
%%%%%%%%%%%%*%##%*%%%%%%%%%%%%%%
***************%##%*************
                *%##%*
                *%##%*       ==
    ''          *%##%*   *=   =*
    ::          *%##%*  *=....=*
    ~~          *%##%*   *=   =*
    **          *%##%*       ==
                *%##%*
                *%##%*
```

13. Digital images, particularly those radioed back from spacecraft, may have glitches. Add a de-glitching function to programming exercise 12. It should compare each value to its immediate neighbors to the left and right, above and below. If the value differs by more than 1 from each of its neighbors, replace the value with the average of the neighboring values. You should round the average to the nearest integer value. Note that the points along the boundaries have fewer than four neighbors, so they require special handling.

CHAPTER 14

STRUCTURES AND OTHER DATA FORMS

You will learn about the following in this chapter:

- Keywords:
  struct, union, typedef

- Operators:
  . ->

- What C structures are and how to create structure templates and variables

- How to access the members of a structure and how to write functions to handle structures

- C's typedef facility

- Unions and pointers to functions

O ne of the most important steps in designing a program is choosing a good way to represent the data. In many cases, a simple variable or even an array is not enough. C takes your ability to represent data a step further with the C *structure variables*. The C structure is flexible enough in its basic form to represent a diversity of data, and it enables you to invent new forms. If you are familiar with the "records" of Pascal, you should be comfortable with structures. If not, this chapter will introduce you to C structures. Let's study a concrete example to see why a C structure might be needed and how to create and use one.

Sample Problem: Creating an Inventory of Books

Gwen Glenn wants to print an inventory of her books. She would like to print a variety of information for each book: title, author, publisher, copyright date, the number of pages, the number of copies, and the dollar value. Some of these items, such as the titles, can be stored in an array of strings. Other items require an array of ints or an array of floats. With seven different arrays, keeping track of everything can get complicated, especially if Gwen wants to generate several complete lists—one sorted by title, one sorted by author, one sorted by value, and so on. A better solution is to use one array, in which each member contains all the information about one book.

Gwen needs a data form, then, that can contain both strings and numbers and somehow keep the information separate. The C structure meets this need. To see how a structure is set up and how it works, we'll start with a limited example. To simplify the problem, we will impose two restrictions. First, we'll include only title, author, and current market value. Second, we'll limit the inventory to one book. Don't worry about this limitation, however, because we'll extend the program soon.

Look at the program in Listing 14.1 and its output. Then read the explanation of the main points.

LISTING 14.1   The book.c Program

```
/* book.c -- one-book inventory */
#include <stdio.h>
#define MAXTITL  41      /* maximum length of title + 1         */
#define MAXAUTL  31      /* maximum length of author's name + 1 */

struct book {            /* structure template: tag is book     */
    char title[MAXTITL];
    char author[MAXAUTL];
    float value;
};                       /* end of structure template          */

int main(void)
{
    struct book library; /* declare library as a book variable  */

    printf("Please enter the book title.\n");
    gets(library.title); /* access to the title portion        */
    printf("Now enter the author.\n");
    gets(library.author);
    printf("Now enter the value.\n");
    scanf("%f", &library.value);
    printf("%s by %s: $%.2f\n",library.title,
        library.author, library.value);
    printf("%s: \"%s\" ($%.2f)\n", library.author,
        library.title, library.value);
    printf("Done.\n");

    return 0;
}
```

Here is a sample run:

```
Please enter the book title.
Chicken of the Alps
Now enter the author.
Bismo Lapoult
Now enter the value.
14.95
Chicken of the Alps by Bismo Lapoult: $14.95
Bismo Lapoult: "Chicken of the Alps" ($14.95)
```

The structure created in Listing 14.1 has three parts (called *members* or *fields*)—one to store the title, one to store the author, and one to store the value. These are the three main skills you must acquire:

- Setting up a format or layout for a structure
- Declaring a variable to fit that layout
- Gaining access to the individual components of a structure variable

Setting Up the Structure Declaration

A *structure declaration* is the master plan that describes how a structure is put together. The declaration looks like this:

```
struct book {
    char title[MAXTITL];
    char author[MAXAUTL];
    float value;
};
```

This declaration describes a structure made up of two character arrays and one **float** variable. It does not create an actual data object, but it describes what constitutes such an object. (Occasionally, we'll refer to a structure declaration as a *template* because it outlines how data will be stored. If you've heard of templates in C++, that's a different, more ambitious use of the word.) Let's look at the details. First comes the keyword **struct**. It identifies what comes next as a structure. Next comes an optional tag—the word **book**—that is a shorthand label you can use to refer to this structure. Therefore, later we have this declaration:

```
struct book library;
```

It declares **library** to be a structure variable using the **book** structure design.

Next in the structure declaration, the list of structure members are enclosed in a pair of braces. Each member is described by its own declaration, complete with a terminating semicolon. For example, the **title** portion is a **char** array with **MAXTITL** elements. A member can be any C data type—and that includes other structures!

A semicolon after the closing brace ends the definition of the structure design. You can place this declaration outside any function (externally), as we have done, or inside a function definition. If the declaration is placed inside a function, its tag can be used only inside that function. If the declaration is external, it is available to all the functions following the declaration in the file. For example, in a second function, you could define

```
struct book dickens;
```

and that function would have a variable, **dickens**, that follows the form of the **book** design.

The tag name is optional, but you must use one when you set up structures as we did, with the structure design defined one place and the actual variables defined elsewhere. We will return to this point soon, after we look at defining structure variables.

Defining a Structure Variable

The word *structure* is used in two senses. One is the sense "structure plan," which is what we just discussed. The structure plan tells the compiler *how* to represent the data, but it doesn't make the computer *allocate* space for the data. The next step is to create a "structure variable," the second sense of the word. The line in the program that causes a structure variable to be created is this:

```
struct book library;
```

Seeing this instruction, the compiler creates the variable `library`. Using the `book` template, the compiler allots space for a `char` array of `MAXTITL` elements, for a `char` array of `MAXAUTL` elements, and for a `float` variable. This storage is lumped together under the single name `library` (see Figure 14.1). (The next section explains how to unlump it as needed.)

In declaring a structure variable, `struct book` plays the same role that `int` or `float` does in simpler declarations. For example, you could declare two variables of the `struct book` type or even a pointer to that kind of structure:

```
struct book doyle, panshin, * ptbook;
```

The structure variables `doyle` and `panshin` would each have the parts `title`, `author`, and `value`. The pointer `ptbook` could point to `doyle`, `panshin`, or any other `book` structure. In essence, the `book` structure declaration creates a new type called `struct book`.

FIGURE 14.1

Memory allocation for a structure.

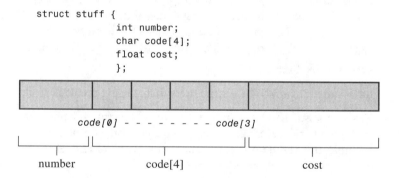

As far as the computer is concerned, the declaration

```
struct book library;
```

is short for

```
struct book {
    char title[MAXTITL];
    char author[AXAUTL];
    float value;
} library;    /* follow declaration with variable name */
```

In other words, the process of declaring a structure and the process of defining a structure variable can be combined into one step. Combining the declaration and the variable definitions, as shown here, is the one circumstance in which a tag need not be used:

```
struct {           /* no tag */
    char title[MAXTITL];
    char author[MAXAUTL];
    float value;
} library;
```

Use the tag form, however, if you plan to use a structure template more than once, or you can use the **typedef** alternative coming up later in this chapter.

There is one aspect of defining a structure variable that did not come up in this example: initialization. We'll look at that now.

Initializing a Structure

You've seen how to initialize variables and arrays:

```
int count = 0;
int fibo[7] = {0,1,1,2,3,5,8};
```

Can a structure variable be initialized, too? Yes, it can. To initialize a structure (any storage class for ANSI C, but excluding automatic variables for pre-ANSI C), you use a syntax similar to that used for arrays:

```
struct book library = {
    "The Pirate and the Devious Damsel",
    "Renee Vivotte",
    1.95
};
```

In short, you use a comma-separated list of initializers enclosed in braces. Each initializer should match the type of structure member being initialized. Therefore, you can initialize the **title** member to a string and the **value** member to a number. To make the associations more obvious, we gave each member its own line of initialization, but all the compiler needs are commas to separate one member's initialization from the next.

Structure Initialization and Storage Class Duration

Chapter 12, "Storage Classes, Linkage, and Memory Management," mentioned that if you initialize a variable with static storage duration (such as static external linkage, static internal linkage, or static with no linkage), you have to use constant values. This applies to structures, too. If you are initializing a structure with static storage duration, the values in the initializer list must be constant expressions. If the storage duration is automatic, the values in the list need not be constants.

Gaining Access to Structure Members

A structure is like a "superarray," in which one element can be `char`, the next element `float`, and the next an `int` array. You can access the individual elements of an array by using a subscript. How do you access individual members of a structure? Use a dot (.), the structure member operator. For example, `library.value` is the `value` portion of `library`. You can use `library.value` exactly as you would use any other `float` variable. Similarly, you can use `library.title` exactly as you would use a `char` array. Therefore, the program uses expressions such as

```
gets(library.title);
```

and

```
scanf("%f", &library.value);
```

In essence, `.title`, `.author`, and `.value` play the role of subscripts for a `book` structure.

Note that although `library` is a structure, `library.value` is a `float` type and is used like any other `float` type. For example, `scanf("%f",...)` requires the address of a `float` location, and that is what `&library.float` is. The dot has higher precedence than the `&` here, so the expression is the same as `&(library.float)`.

If you had a second structure variable of the same type, you would use the same method:

```
struct book bill, newt;
```

```
gets(bill.title);
gets(newt.title);
```

The `.title` refers to the first member of the `book` structure. Notice how the initial program prints the contents of the structure `library` in two different formats. This illustrates the freedom you have in using the members of a structure.

Designated Initializers for Structures

C99 provides designated initializers for structures. The syntax is similar to that for designated initializers for arrays. However, designated initializers for structures use the dot operator and member names instead of brackets and indices to identify particular elements. For example, to initialize just the `value` member of a book structure, you would do this:

```
struct book surprise = { .value = 10.99};
```

You can use designated initializers in any order:

```
struct book gift = { .value = 25.99,
                     .author = "James Broadfool",
                     .title = "Rue for the Toad"};
```

Just as with arrays, a regular initializer following a designated initializer provides a value for the member following the designated member. Also, the last value supplied for a particular member is the value it gets. For example, consider this declaration:

```
struct book gift= { .value = 18.90,
                    .author = "Philionna Pestle",
                    0.25};
```

The value `0.25` is assigned to the `value` member because it is the one immediately listed after the `author` member in the structure declaration. The new value of `0.25` supersedes the value of `18.90` provided earlier. Now that you have these basics in hand, you're ready to expand your horizons and look at several ramifications of structures. You'll see arrays of structures, structures of structures, pointers to structures, and functions that process structures.

Arrays of Structures

Let's extend our book program to handle more books. Clearly, each book can be described by one structure variable of the `book` type. To describe two books, you need to use two such variables, and so on. To handle several books, you can use an array of such structures, and that is what we have created in the next program, shown in Listing 14.2. (If you're using Borland C/C++, see "Borland C and Floating Point.")

Structures and Memory

The `manybook.c` program uses an array of 100 structures. Because the array is an automatic storage class object, the information is typically placed on the stack. Such a large array requires a good-sized chunk of memory, which can cause problems. If you get a runtime error, perhaps complaining about the stack size or stack overflow, your compiler probably uses a default size for the stack that is too small for this example. To fix things, you can use the compiler options to set the stack size to 10,000 to accommodate the array of structures, or you can make the array static or external (so that it isn't placed in the stack), or you can reduce the array size to 16. Why didn't we just make the stack small to begin with? Because you should know about the potential stack size problem so that you can cope with it if you run into it on your own.

LISTING 14.2   The `manybook.c` Program

```
/* manybook.c -- multiple book inventory */
#include <stdio.h>
#define MAXTITL   40
#define MAXAUTL   40
#define MAXBKS    100           /* maximum number of books  */

struct book {                   /* set up book template     */
    char title[MAXTITL];
    char author[MAXAUTL];
    float value;
};
```

LISTING 14.2   Continued

```
int main(void)
{
    struct book library[MAXBKS]; /* array of book structures */
    int count = 0;
    int index;

    printf("Please enter the book title.\n");
    printf("Press [enter] at the start of a line to stop.\n");
    while (count < MAXBKS && gets(library[count].title) != NULL
                       && library[count].title[0] != '\0')
    {
        printf("Now enter the author.\n");
        gets(library[count].author);
        printf("Now enter the value.\n");
        scanf("%f", &library[count++].value);
        while (getchar() != '\n')
            continue;            /* clear input line          */
        if (count < MAXBKS)
        printf("Enter the next title.\n");
    }

    if (count > 0)
    {
        printf("Here is the list of your books:\n");
        for (index = 0; index < count; index++)
        printf("%s by %s: $%.2f\n", library[index].title,
            library[index].author, library[index].value);
    }
    else
        printf("No books? Too bad.\n");

    return 0;
}
```

Borland C and Floating Point

Older Borland C compilers attempt to make programs more compact by using a small version of scanf() if the program doesn't use floating-point values. However, the compilers (through Borland C/C++ 3.1 for DOS, but not Borland C/C++ 4.0) are fooled if the only floating-point values are in an array of structures, as in the case for Listing 14.2. As a result, you get a message like this:

```
scanf : floating point formats not linked
Abnormal program termination
```

One workaround is adding this code to your program:

```
#include <math.h>
double dummy = sin(0.0);
```

This code forces the compiler to load the floating-point version of scanf().

Here is a sample program run:

```
Please enter the book title.
Press [enter] at the start of a line to stop.
My Life as a Budgie
Now enter the author.
Mack Zackles
Now enter the value.
12.95
Enter the next title.
    ...more entries...
Here is the list of your books:
My Life as a Budgie by Mack Zackles: $12.95
Thought and Unthought Rethought by Kindra Schlagmeyer: $43.50
The Business of a Bee by Salome Deschamps: $14.99
The CEO Power Diet by Buster Downsize: $19.25
C++ Primer Plus by Stephen Prata: $40.00
Under a Tofu Moon by Angus Bull: $15.97
Coping with Coping by Dr. Rubin Thonkwacker: $0.00
Delicate Frivolity by Neda McFey: $29.99
Murder Wore a Bikini by Mickey Splats: $18.95
A History of Buvania, Volume 4, by Prince Nikoli Buvan: $50.00
Mastering Your Digital Watch, 2nd Edition, by Miklos Mysz: $18.95
A Foregone Confusion by Phalty Reasoner: $5.99
Outsourcing Government: Selection vs. Election by Ima Pundit: $33.33
```

First, we'll describe how to declare arrays of structures and how to access individual members. Then we will highlight two aspects of the program.

Declaring an Array of Structures

Declaring an array of structures is like declaring any other kind of array. Here's an example:

```
struct book library[MAXBKS];
```

This declares `library` to be an array with `MAXBKS` elements. Each element of this array is a structure of `book` type. Thus, `library[0]` is one `book` structure, `library[1]` is a second `book` structure, and so on. Figure 14.2 may help you visualize this. The name `library` itself is not a structure name; it is the name of the array whose elements are type `struct book` structures.

Identifying Members of an Array of Structures

To identify members of an array of structures, you apply the same rule used for individual structures: Follow the structure name with the dot operator and then with the member name. Here's an example:

```
library[0].value    /* the value associated with the first array element */
library[4].title    /* the title associated with the fifth array element */
```

Note that the array subscript is attached to `library`, not to the end of the name:

```
library.value[2]    // WRONG
library[2].value    // RIGHT
```

FIGURE 14.2
An array of structures.

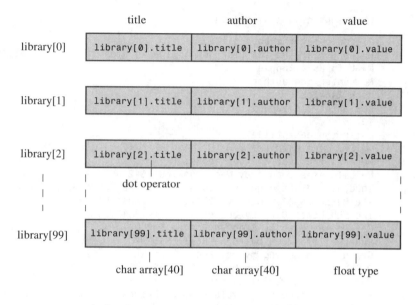

declaration: `struct book library[MAXBKS]`

The reason `library[2].value` is used is that `library[2]` is the structure variable name, just as `library[1]` is another structure variable name.

By the way, what do you suppose the following represents?

`library[2].title[4]`

It's the fifth character in the title (the `title[4]` part) of the book described by the third structure (the `library[2]` part). In the example, it would be the character *B*. This example points out that subscripts found to the right of the dot operator apply to individual members, but subscripts to the left of the dot operator apply to arrays of structures.

In summary, we have this sequence:

```
library              // an array of book structures
library[2]           // an array element, hence a book structure
library[2].title     // a char array (the title member of library[2])
library[2].title[4]  // a char in the title member array
```

Let's finish the program now.

Program Discussion

The main change from the first program is that we inserted a loop to read multiple entries. The loop begins with this `while` condition:

```
while (count < MAXBKS && gets(library[count].title) != NULL
                      && library[count].title[0] != '\0')
```

The expression `gets(library[count].title)` reads a string for the title of a book; the expression evaluates to `NULL` if `gets()` attempts to read past the end-of-file. The expression `library[count].title[0] != '\0'` tests whether the first character in the string is the null character (that is, if the string is empty). If the user presses the Enter key at the beginning of a line, the empty string is transmitted, and the loop ends. We also have a check to keep the number of books entered from exceeding the array's size limit.

Then the program has these lines:

```
while (getchar() != '\n')
    continue;                /* clear input line */
```

As you might recall from earlier chapters, this code compensates for the `scanf()` function ignoring spaces and newlines. When you respond to the request for the book's value, you type something like this:

```
12.50[enter]
```

This statement transmits the following sequence of characters:

```
12.50\n
```

The `scanf()` function collects the 1, the 2, the ., the 5, and the 0, but it leaves the \n sitting there, awaiting whatever read statement comes next. If the precautionary code were missing, the next read statement, `gets(library[count].title)`, would read the leftover newline character as an empty line, and the program would think you had sent a stop signal. The code we inserted will eat up characters until it finds and disposes of the newline. It doesn't do anything with the characters except remove them from the input queue. This gives `gets()` a fresh start.

Now let's return to exploring structures.

Nested Structures

Sometimes it is convenient for one structure to contain, or *nest*, another. For example, Shalala Pirosky is building a structure of information about her friends. One member of the structure, naturally enough, is the friend's name. The name, however, can be represented by a structure itself, with separate entries for first and last name members. Listing 14.3 is a condensed example of Shalala's work.

LISTING 14.3   The `friend.c` Program

```
// friend.c -- example of a nested structure
#include <stdio.h>
#define LEN 20
const char * msgs[5] =
{
    "    Thank you for the wonderful evening, ",
    "You certainly prove that a ",
    "is a special kind of guy. We must get together",
    "over a delicious ",
```

LISTING 14.3   Continued

```
        " and have a few laughs"
};

struct names {                    // first structure
    char first[LEN];
    char last[LEN];
};

struct guy {                      // second structure
    struct names handle;          // nested structure
    char favfood[LEN];
    char job[LEN];
    float income;
};

int main(void)
{
    struct guy fellow = {   // initialize a variable
        { "Ewen", "Villard" },
        "grilled salmon",
        "personality coach",
        58112.00
    };

    printf("Dear %s, \n\n", fellow.handle.first);
    printf("%s%s.\n", msgs[0], fellow.handle.first);
    printf("%s%s\n", msgs[1], fellow.job);
    printf("%s\n", msgs[2]);
    printf("%s%s%s", msgs[3], fellow.favfood, msgs[4]);
    if (fellow.income > 150000.0)
        puts("!!");
    else if (fellow.income > 75000.0)
        puts("!");
    else
        puts(".");
    printf("\n%40s%s\n", " ", "See you soon,");
    printf("%40s%s\n", " ", "Shalala");

    return 0;
}
```

Here is the output:

```
Dear Ewen,

    Thank you for the wonderful evening, Ewen.
You certainly prove that a personality coach
is a special kind of guy. We must get together
over a delicious grilled salmon and have a few laughs.

                                       See you soon,
                                       Shalala
```

First, note how the nested structure is set up in the structure declaration. It is simply declared, just as an **int** variable would be:

```
struct names handle;
```

This declaration says that **handle** is a variable of the **struct names** type. Of course, the file should also include the declaration for the **names** structure.

Second, note how you gain access to a member of a nested structure; you merely use the dot operator twice:

```
printf("Hello, %s!\n", fellow.handle.first);
```

The construction is interpreted this way, going from left to right:

```
(fellow.handle).first
```

That is, find **fellow**, then find the **handle** member of **fellow**, and then find the **first** member of that.

Pointers to Structures

Pointer lovers will be glad to know that you can have pointers to structures. There are at least three reasons why having pointers to structures is a good idea. First, just as pointers to arrays are easier to manipulate (in a sorting problem, say) than the arrays themselves, pointers to structures are often easier to manipulate than structures themselves. Second, in some older implementations, a structure can't be passed as an argument to a function, but a pointer to a structure can. Third, many wondrous data representations use structures containing pointers to other structures.

The next short example (see Listing 14.4) shows how to define a pointer to a structure and how to use it to access the members of a structure.

LISTING 14.4   The `friends.c` Program

```
/* friends.c -- uses pointer to a structure */
#include <stdio.h>
#define LEN 20

struct names {
    char first[LEN];
    char last[LEN];
};

struct guy {
    struct names handle;
    char favfood[LEN];
    char job[LEN];
    float income;
};
```

LISTING 14.4   Continued

```
int main(void)
{
    struct guy fellow[2] = {
        {{ "Ewen", "Villard"},
         "grilled salmon",
         "personality coach",
         58112.00
        },
        {{"Rodney", "Swillbelly"},
         "tripe",
         "tabloid editor",
         232400.00
        }
    };
    struct guy * him;    /* here is a pointer to a structure */

    printf("address #1: %p #2: %p\n", &fellow[0], &fellow[1]);
    him = &fellow[0];    /* tell the pointer where to point  */
    printf("pointer #1: %p #2: %p\n", him, him + 1);
    printf("him->income is $%.2f: (*him).income is $%.2f\n",
        him->income, (*him).income);
    him++;                  /* point to the next structure     */
    printf("him->favfood is %s:  him->handle.last is %s\n",
        him->favfood, him->handle.last);

    return 0;
}
```

The output, please:

```
address #1: 0x0012fea4 #2: 0x0012fef8
pointer #1: 0x0012fea4 #2: 0x0012fef8
him->income is $58112.00: (*him).income is $58112.00
him->favfood is tripe:  him->handle.last is Swillbelly
```

Let's look first at how we created a pointer to a **guy** structure. Then we'll explain how to specify individual structure members by using the pointer.

Declaring and Initializing a Structure Pointer

Declaration is as easy as can be:

```
struct guy * him;
```

First is the keyword **struct**, then the structure tag **guy**, and then an asterisk (*) followed by the pointer name. The syntax is the same as for the other pointer declarations you have seen.

This declaration does not create a new structure, but the pointer **him** can now be made to point to any existing structure of the **guy** type. For instance, if **barney** is a structure of the **guy** type, you could do this:

```
him = &barney;
```

Unlike the case for arrays, the name of a structure is not the address of the structure; you need to use the & operator.

In the example, `fellow` is an array of structures, which means that `fellow[0]` is a structure, so the code initializes `him` by making it point to `fellow[0]`:

```
him = &fellow[0];
```

The first two output lines show the success of this assignment. Comparing the two lines, you see that `him` points to `fellow[0]`, and `him + 1` points to `fellow[1]`. Note that adding 1 to `him` adds 84 to the address. In hexadecimal, ef8 – ea4 = 54 (hex) = 84 (base 10) because each `guy` structure occupies 84 bytes of memory: `names.first` is 20, `names.last` is 20, `favfood` is 20, `job` is 20, and `income` is 4, the size of `float` on our system. Incidentally, on some systems, the size of a structure may be greater than the sum of its parts. That's because a system's alignment requirements for data may cause gaps. For example, a system may have to place each member at an even address or at an address that is a multiple of four. Such structures might end up with unused "holes" in them.

Member Access by Pointer

The pointer `him` is pointing to the structure `fellow[0]`. How can you use `him` to get a value of a member of `fellow[0]`? The third output line shows two methods.

The first method, and the most common, uses a new operator, `->`. This operator is formed by typing a hyphen (-) followed by the greater-than symbol (>). The example helps make the meaning clear:

```
him->income  is  fellow[0].income  if  him == &fellow[0]
```

In other words, a structure pointer followed by the `->` operator works the same way as a structure name followed by the . (dot) operator. (You can't properly say `him.income` because `him` is not a structure name.)

It is important to note that `him` is a pointer, but `him->income` is a member of the pointed-to structure. So in this case, `him->income` is a `float` variable.

The second method for specifying the value of a structure member follows from this sequence: If `him == &fellow[0]`, then `*him == fellow[0]` because & and * are reciprocal operators. Hence, by substitution, you have the following:

```
fellow[0].income == (*him).income
```

The parentheses are required because the . operator has higher precedence than *.

In summary, if `him` is a pointer to a type `guy` structure named `barney`, the following are all equivalent:

```
barney.income == (*him).income == him->income   // assuming him == &barney
```

Now let's look at the interaction between structures and functions.

Telling Functions About Structures

Recall that function arguments pass values to the function. Each value is a number—perhaps `int`, perhaps `float`, perhaps ASCII character code, or perhaps an address. A structure is a bit more complicated than a single value, so it is not surprising that ancient C implementations do not allow a structure to be used as an argument for a function. This limitation was removed in newer implementations, and ANSI C allows structures to be used as arguments. Therefore, modern implementations give you a choice between passing structures as arguments and passing pointers to structures as arguments—or if you are concerned with just part of a structure, you can pass structure members as arguments. We'll examine all three methods, beginning with passing structure members as arguments.

Passing Structure Members

As long as a structure member is a data type with a single value (that is, an `int` or one of its relatives, a `char`, a `float`, a `double`, or a pointer), it can be passed as a function argument to a function that accepts that particular type. The fledgling financial analysis program in Listing 14.5, which adds the client's bank account to his or her savings and loan account, illustrates this point.

LISTING 14.5   The `funds1.c` Program

```
/* funds1.c -- passing structure members as arguments */
#include <stdio.h>
#define FUNDLEN 50

struct funds {
    char    bank[FUNDLEN];
    double bankfund;
    char    save[FUNDLEN];
    double savefund;
};

double sum(double, double);

int main(void)
{
    struct funds stan = {
        "Garlic-Melon Bank",
        3024.72,
        "Lucky's Savings and Loan",
        9237.11
    };

    printf("Stan has a total of $%.2f.\n",
            sum(stan.bankfund, stan.savefund) );
    return 0;
}
```

LISTING 14.5   Continued

```
/* adds two double numbers */
double sum(double x, double y)
{
    return(x + y);
}
```

Here is the result of running this program:

```
Stan has a total of $12261.83.
```

Ah, it works. Notice that the function `sum()` neither knows nor cares whether the actual arguments are members of a structure; it requires only that they be type `double`.

Of course, if you want a called function to affect the value of a member in the calling function, you can transmit the address of the member:

```
modify(&stan.bankfund);
```

This would be a function that alters Stan's bank account.

The next approach to telling a function about a structure involves letting the called function know that it is dealing with a structure.

Using the Structure Address

We will solve the same problem as before, but this time we will use the address of the structure as an argument. Because the function has to work with the `funds` structure, it, too, has to make use of the `funds` declaration. See Listing 14.6 for the program.

LISTING 14.6   The `funds2.c` Program

```
/* funds2.c -- passing a pointer to a structure */
#include <stdio.h>
#define FUNDLEN 50

struct funds {
    char    bank[FUNDLEN];
    double bankfund;
    char    save[FUNDLEN];
    double savefund;
};

double sum(const struct funds *);  /* argument is a pointer */

int main(void)
{
    struct funds stan = {
        "Garlic-Melon Bank",
        3024.72,
        "Lucky's Savings and Loan",
        9237.11
    };
```

LISTING 14.6   Continued

```
    printf("Stan has a total of $%.2f.\n", sum(&stan));

    return 0;
}

double sum(const struct funds * money)
{
    return(money->bankfund + money->savefund);
}
```

This, too, produces the following output:

```
Stan has a total of $12261.83.
```

The `sum()` function uses a pointer (`money`) to a `funds` structure for its single argument. Passing the address `&stan` to the function causes the pointer `money` to point to the structure `stan`. Then the `->` operator is used to gain the values of `stan.bankfund` and `stan.savefund`. Because the function does not alter the contents of the pointed-to value, it declares `money` as a pointer-to-`const`.

This function also has access to the institution names, although it doesn't use them. Note that you must use the `&` operator to get the structure's address. Unlike the array name, the structure name alone is not a synonym for its address.

Passing a Structure as an Argument

For compilers that permit passing structures as arguments, the last example can be rewritten as shown in Listing 14.7.

LISTING 14.7   The `funds3.c` Program

```
/* funds3.c -- passing a structure */
#include <stdio.h>
#define FUNDLEN 50

struct funds {
    char    bank[FUNDLEN];
    double bankfund;
    char    save[FUNDLEN];
    double savefund;
};

double sum(struct funds moolah);  /* argument is a structure */

int main(void)
{
    struct funds stan = {
        "Garlic-Melon Bank",
        3024.72,
        "Lucky's Savings and Loan",
```

LISTING 14.7   Continued

```
            9237.11
    };
    printf("Stan has a total of $%.2f.\n", sum(stan));

    return 0;
}

double sum(struct funds moolah)
{
    return(moolah.bankfund + moolah.savefund);
}
```

Again, the output is this:

```
Stan has a total of $12261.83.
```

We replaced `money`, which was a pointer to `struct funds`, with `moolah`, which is a `struct funds` variable. When `sum()` is called, an automatic variable called `moolah` is created according to the `funds` template. The members of this structure are then initialized to be copies of the values held in the corresponding members of the structure `stan`. Therefore, the computations are done by using a copy of the original structure, whereas the preceding program (the one using a pointer) used the original structure itself. Because `moolah` is a structure, the program uses `moolah.bankfund`, not `moolah->bankfund`. On the other hand, Listing 14.6 used `money->bankfund` because `money` is a pointer, not a structure.

More on Structure Features

Modern C allows you to assign one structure to another, something you can't do with arrays. That is, if `n_data` and `o_data` are both structures of the same type, you can do the following:

```
o_data = n_data;    // assigning one structure to another
```

This causes each member of `n_data` to be assigned the value of the corresponding member of `o_data`. This works even if a member happens to be an array. Also, you can initialize one structure to another of the same type:

```
struct names right_field = {"Ruthie", "George"};
struct names captain = right_field;  // initialize a structure to another
```

Under modern C, including ANSI C, not only can structures be passed as function arguments, they can be returned as function return values. Using structures as function arguments enables you to convey structure information to a function; using functions to return structures enables you to convey structure information from a called function to the calling function. Structure pointers also allow two-way communication, so you can often use either approach to solve programming problems. Let's look at another set of examples illustrating these two approaches.

To contrast the two approaches, we'll write a simple program that handles structures by using pointers; then we'll rewrite it by using structure passing and structure returns. The program itself asks for your first and last names and reports the total number of letters in them. This project hardly requires structures, but it offers a simple framework for seeing how they work. Listing 14.8 presents the pointer form.

LISTING 14.8   The names1.c Program

```c
/* names1.c -- uses pointers to a structure */
#include <stdio.h>
#include <string.h>

struct namect {
    char fname[20];
    char lname[20];
    int letters;
};

void getinfo(struct namect *);
void makeinfo(struct namect *);
void showinfo(const struct namect *);

int main(void)
{
    struct namect person;

    getinfo(&person);
    makeinfo(&person);
    showinfo(&person);
    return 0;
}

void getinfo (struct namect * pst)
{
    printf("Please enter your first name.\n");
    gets(pst->fname);
    printf("Please enter your last name.\n");
    gets(pst->lname);
}

void makeinfo (struct namect * pst)
{
    pst->letters = strlen(pst->fname) +
                    strlen(pst->lname);
}

void showinfo (const struct namect * pst)
{
    printf("%s %s, your name contains %d letters.\n",
        pst->fname, pst->lname, pst->letters);
}
```

Compiling and running the program produces results like the following:

```
Please enter your first name.
Viola
```

Please enter your last name.
Plunderfest
Viola Plunderfest, your name contains 16 letters.

The work of the program is allocated to three functions called from `main()`. In each case, the address of the **person** structure is passed to the function.

The `getinfo()` function transfers information from itself to `main()`. In particular, it gets names from the user and places them in the **person** structure, using the **pst** pointer to locate it. Recall that `pst->lname` means the `lname` member of the structure pointed to by `pst`. This makes `pst->lname` equivalent to the name of a `char` array, hence a suitable argument for `gets()`. Note that although `getinfo()` feeds information to the main program, it does not use the return mechanism, so it is type `void`.

The `makeinfo()` function performs a two-way transfer of information. By using a pointer to **person**, it locates the two names stored in the structure. It uses the C library function `strlen()` to calculate the total number of letters in each name and then uses the address of **person** to stow away the sum. Again, the type is `void`. Finally, the `showinfo()` function uses a pointer to locate the information to be printed. Because this function does not alter the contents of an array, it declares the pointer as `const`.

In all these operations, there has been but one structure variable, **person**, and each of the functions have used the structure address to access it. One function transferred information from itself to the calling program, one transferred information from the calling program to itself, and one did both.

Now let's see how you can program the same task using structure arguments and return values. First, to pass the structure itself, use the argument **person** rather than **&person**. The corresponding formal argument, then, is declared type `struct namect` instead of being a pointer to that type. Second, to provide structure values to `main()`, you can return a structure. Listing 14.9 presents the non-pointer version.

LISTING 14.9 The `names2.c` Program

```
/* names2.c -- passes and returns structures */
#include <stdio.h>
#include <string.h>

struct namect {
    char fname[20];
    char lname[20];
    int letters;
};

struct namect getinfo(void);
struct namect makeinfo(struct namect);
void showinfo(struct namect);

int main(void)
{
```

LISTING 14.9 Continued

```
    struct namect person;

    person = getinfo();
    person = makeinfo(person);
    showinfo(person);

    return 0;
}

struct namect getinfo(void)
{
    struct namect temp;
    printf("Please enter your first name.\n");
    gets(temp.fname);
    printf("Please enter your last name.\n");
    gets(temp.lname);

    return temp;
}

struct namect makeinfo(struct namect info)
{
    info.letters = strlen(info.fname) + strlen(info.lname);

    return info;
}

void showinfo(struct namect info)
{
    printf("%s %s, your name contains %d letters.\n",
        info.fname, info.lname, info.letters);
}
```

This version produces the same final result as the preceding one, but it proceeds in a different manner. Each of the three functions creates its own copy of `person`, so this program uses four distinct structures instead of just one.

Consider the `makeinfo()` function, for example. In the first program, the address of `person` was passed, and the function fiddled with the actual `person` values. In this second version, a new structure called `info` is created. The values stored in `person` are copied to `info`, and the function works with the copy. Therefore, when the number of letters is calculated, it is stored in `info`, but not in `person`. The return mechanism, however, fixes that. The `makeinfo()` line

```
return info;
```

combines with the `main()` line

```
person = makeinfo(person);
```

to copy the values stored in `info` into `person`. Note that the `makeinfo()` function had to be declared type `struct namect` because it returns a structure.

Structures or Pointer to Structures?

Suppose you have to write a structure-related function. Should you use structure pointers as arguments, or should you use structure arguments and return values? Each approach has its strengths and weaknesses.

The two advantages of the pointer argument method are that it works on older as well as newer C implementations and that it is quick; you just pass a single address. The disadvantage is that you have less protection for your data. Some operations in the called function could inadvertently affect data in the original structure. However, the ANSI C addition of the `const` qualifier solves that problem. For example, if you put code into the `showinfo()` function that changes any member of the structure, the compiler will catch it as an error.

One advantage of passing structures as arguments is that the function works with copies of the original data, which is safer than working with the original data. Also, the programming style tends to be clearer. Suppose you define the following structure type:

```
struct vector {double x; double y;};
```

You want to set the vector **ans** to the sum of the vectors **a** and **b**. You could write a structure-passing and returning function that would make the program like this:

```
struct vector ans, a, b;
struct vector sum_vect(vector, vector);
...
ans = sum_vect(a,b);
```

The preceding version is more natural looking to an engineer than a pointer version, which might look like this:

```
struct vector ans, a, b;
void sum_vect(const vector *, const vector *, vector *);
...
sum_vect(&a, &b, &ans);
```

Also, in the pointer version, the user has to remember whether the address for the sum should be the first or the last argument.

The two main disadvantages to passing structures are that older implementations might not handle the code and that it wastes time and space. It's especially wasteful to pass large structures to a function that uses only one or two members of the structure. In that case, passing a pointer or passing just the required members as individual arguments makes more sense.

Typically, programmers use structure pointers as function arguments for reasons of efficiency, using `const` when needed to protect data from unintended changes. Passing structures by value is most often done for structures that are small to begin with.

Character Arrays or Character Pointers in a Structure

The examples so far have used character arrays to store strings in a structure. You might have wondered if you can use pointers-to-char instead. For example, Listing 14.3 had this declaration:

```
#define LEN 20
struct names {
    char first[LEN];
    char last[LEN];
};
```

Can you do this instead?

```
struct pnames {
    char * first;
    char * last;
};
```

The answer is that you can, but you might get into trouble unless you understand the implications. Consider the following code:

```
struct names veep = {"Talia", "Summers"};
struct pnames treas = {"Brad", "Fallingjaw"};
printf("%s and %s\n", veep.first, treas.first);
```

This is valid code, and it works, but consider where the strings are stored. For the **struct names** variable **veep**, the strings are stored inside the structure; the structure has allocated a total of 40 bytes to hold the two names. For the **struct pnames** variable **treas**, however, the strings are stored wherever the compiler stores string constants. All the structure holds are the two addresses, which, on our system, take a total of 8 bytes. In particular, the **struct pnames** structure allocates no space to store strings. It can be used only with strings that have had space allocated for them elsewhere, such as string constants or strings in arrays. In short, the pointers in a **pnames** structure should be used only to manage strings that were created and allocated elsewhere in the program.

Let's see where this restriction is a problem. Consider the following code:

```
struct names accountant;
struct pnames attorney;
puts("Enter the last name of your accountant:");
scanf("%s", accountant.last);
puts("Enter the last name of your attorney:");
scanf("%s", attorney.last);   /* here lies the danger */
```

As far as syntax goes, this code is fine. But where does the input get stored? For the accountant, the name is stored in the last member of the **accountant** variable; this structure has an array to hold the string. For the attorney, **scanf()** is told to place the string at the address given by **attorney.last**. Because this is an uninitialized variable, the address could have any value, and the program could try to put the name anywhere. If you are lucky, the program might work, at least some of the time—or an attempt could bring your program to a crashing halt. Actually, if the program works, you're unlucky, because the program will have a dangerous programming error of which you are unaware.

So if you want a structure to store the strings, use character array members. Storing pointers-to-char has its uses, but it also has the potential for serious misuse.

Structure, Pointers, and `malloc()`

One instance in which it does make sense to use a pointer in a structure to handle a string is if you use `malloc()` to allocate memory and use a pointer to store the address. This approach has the advantage that you can ask `malloc()` to allocate just the amount of space that's needed for a string. You can ask for 4 bytes to store `"Joe"` and 18 bytes for `"Rasolofomasoandro"`. It doesn't take much to adapt Listing 14.9 to this approach. The two main changes are changing the structure definition to use pointers instead of arrays and then providing a new version of the `getinfo()` function.

The new structure definition will look like this:

```
struct namect {
    char * fname;   // using pointers instead of arrays
    char * lname;
    int letters;
};
```

The new version of `getinfo()` will read the input into a temporary array, use `malloc()` to allocate storage space, and copy the string to the newly allocated space. It will do so for each name:

```
void getinfo (struct namect * pst)
{
    char temp[81];
    printf("Please enter your first name.\n");
    gets(temp);
    // allocate memory to hold name
    pst->fname = (char *) malloc(strlen(temp) + 1);
    // copy name to allocated memory
    strcpy(pst->fname, temp);
    printf("Please enter your last name.\n");
    gets(temp);
    pst->lname = (char *) malloc(strlen(temp) + 1);
    strcpy(pst->lname, temp);
}
```

Make sure you understand that the two strings are not stored in the structure. They are stored in the chunk of memory managed by `malloc()`. However, the addresses of the two strings are stored in the structure, and the addresses are what string-handling functions typically work with. Therefore, the remaining functions in the program need not be changed at all.

However, as Chapter 12 suggests, you should balance calls to `malloc()` with calls to `free()`, so the program adds a new function called `cleanup()` to free the memory once the program is done using it. You'll find this new function and the rest of the program in Listing 14.10.

LISTING 14.10   The `names3.c` Program

```c
// names3.c -- use pointers and malloc()
#include <stdio.h>
#include <string.h>   // for strcpy(), strlen()
#include <stdlib.h>    // for malloc(), free()

struct namect {
    char * fname;  // using pointers
    char * lname;
    int letters;
};

void getinfo(struct namect *);          // allocates memory
void makeinfo(struct namect *);
void showinfo(const struct namect *);
void cleanup(struct namect *);          // free memory when done

int main(void)
{
    struct namect person;

    getinfo(&person);
    makeinfo(&person);
    showinfo(&person);
    cleanup(&person);

    return 0;
}

void getinfo (struct namect * pst)
{
    char temp[81];
    printf("Please enter your first name.\n");
    gets(temp);
    // allocate memory to hold name
    pst->fname = (char *) malloc(strlen(temp) + 1);
    // copy name to allocated memory
    strcpy(pst->fname, temp);
    printf("Please enter your last name.\n");
    gets(temp);
    pst->lname = (char *) malloc(strlen(temp) + 1);
    strcpy(pst->lname, temp);
}

void makeinfo (struct namect * pst)
{
    pst->letters = strlen(pst->fname) +
                        strlen(pst->lname);
}

void showinfo (const struct namect * pst)
{
    printf("%s %s, your name contains %d letters.\n",
```

LISTING 14.10   Continued

```
            pst->fname, pst->lname, pst->letters);
}

void cleanup(struct namect * pst)
{
    free(pst->fname);
    free(pst->lname);
}
```

Here is some sample output:

```
Please enter your first name.
Australopithecines
Please enter your last name.
Mann
Australopithecines Mann,  your name contains 22 letters.
```

Compound Literals and Structures (C99)

C99's new compound literal feature is available for structures as well as for arrays. You can use compound literals to create a structure to be used as a function argument or to be assigned to another structure. The syntax is to preface a brace-enclosed initializer list with the type name in parentheses. For example, the following is a compound literal of the **struct book** type:

```
(struct book) {"The Idiot", "Fyodor Dostoyevsky", 6.99}
```

Listing 14.11 shows an example using compound literals to provide two alternative values for a structure variable. (At the time of writing, several, but not all, compilers support this feature, but time should remedy this problem.)

LISTING 14.11   The complit.c Program

```
/* complit.c -- compound literals */
#include <stdio.h>
#define MAXTITL  41
#define MAXAUTL  31

struct book {           // structure template: tag is book
    char title[MAXTITL];
    char author[MAXAUTL];
    float value;
};

int main(void)
{
    struct book readfirst;
    int score;

    printf("Enter test score: ");
    scanf("%d",&score);
```

LISTING 14.11 Continued

```
        if(score >= 84)
            readfirst = (struct book) {"Crime and Punishment",
                                       "Fyodor Dostoyevsky",
                                       9.99};
        else
                readfirst = (struct book) {"Mr. Bouncy's Nice Hat",
                                           "Fred Winsome",
                                           5.99};
        printf("Your assigned reading:\n");
        printf("%s by %s: $%.2f\n",readfirst.title,
               readfirst.author, readfirst.value);

        return 0;
}
```

You also can use compound literals as arguments to functions. If the function expects a structure, you can pass the compound literal as the actual argument:

```
struct rect {double x; double y;};
double rect_area(struct rect r){return r.x * r.y;}
...

double area;
area = rect_area( (struct rect) {10.5, 20.0});
```

This causes **area** to be assigned the value **210.0**.

If a function expects an address, you can pass the address of a compound literal:

```
struct rect {double x; double y;};
double rect_areap(struct rect * rp){return rp->x * rp->y;}
...

double area;
area = rect_areap( &(struct rect) {10.5, 20.0});
```

This causes **area** to be assigned the value **210.0**.

Compound literals occurring outside of any function have static storage duration, and those occurring inside a block have automatic storage duration. The same syntax rules hold for compound literals as hold for regular initializer lists. This means, for example, that you can use designated initializers in a compound literal.

Flexible Array Members (C99)

C99 has a new feature called the *flexible array member*. It lets you declare a structure for which the last member is an array with special properties. One special property is that the array doesn't exist—at least, not immediately. The second special property is that, with the right code, you can use the flexible array member as if it did exist and has whatever number of elements you need. This probably sounds a little peculiar, so let's go through the steps of creating and using a structure with a flexible array member.

First, here are the rules for declaring a flexible array member:

- The flexible array member must be the last member of the structure.

- There must be at least one other member.

- The flexible array is declared like an ordinary array, except that the brackets are empty.

Here's an example illustrating these rules:

```
struct flex
{
    int count;
    double average;
    double scores[];   // flexible array member
};
```

If you declare a variable of type **struct flex**, you can't use **scores** for anything, because no memory space is set aside for it. In fact, it's not intended that you ever declare variables of the **struct flex** type. Instead, you are supposed to declare a *pointer* to the **struct flex** type and then use **malloc()** to allocate enough space for the ordinary contents of **struct flex** *plus* any extra space you want for the flexible array member. For example, suppose you want **scores** to represent an array of five **double** values. Then you would do this:

```
struct flex * pf;  // declare a pointer
// ask for space for a structure and an array
pf = malloc(sizeof(struct flex) + 5 * sizeof(double));
```

Now you have a chunk of memory large enough to store **count**, **average**, and an array of five **double** values. You can use the pointer **pf** to access these members:

```
pf->count = 5;          // set count member
pf->scores[2] = 18.5;   // access an element of the array member
```

Listing 14.12 carries this example a little further, letting the flexible array member represent five values in one case and nine values in a second case. It also illustrates writing a function for processing a structure with a flexible array element. (Support for flexible array members seems more widespread at this time than support for compound structure literals.)

LISTING 14.12   The `flexmemb.c` Program

```
// flexmemb.c -- flexible array member
#include <stdio.h>
#include <stdlib.h>

struct flex
{
    int count;
    double average;
    double scores[];   // flexible array member
};

void showFlex(const struct flex * p);
```

LISTING 14.12   Continued

```
int main(void)
{
    struct flex * pf1, *pf2;
    int n = 5;
    int i;
    int tot = 0;

    // allocate space for structure plus array
    pf1 = malloc(sizeof(struct flex) + n * sizeof(double));
    pf1->count = n;
    for (i = 0; i < n; i++)
    {
        pf1->scores[i] = 20.0 - i;
        tot += pf1->scores[i];
    }
    pf1->average = tot / n;
    showFlex(pf1);

    n = 9;
    tot = 0;
    pf2 = malloc(sizeof(struct flex) + n * sizeof(double));
    pf2->count = n;
    for (i = 0; i < n; i++)
    {
        pf2->scores[i] = 20.0 - i/2.0;
        tot += pf2->scores[i];
    }
    pf2->average = tot / n;
    showFlex(pf2);
    free(pf1);
    free(pf2);

    return 0;
}

void showFlex(const struct flex * p)
{
    int i;
    printf("Scores : ");
    for (i = 0; i < p->count; i++)
        printf("%g ", p->scores[i]);
    printf("\nAverage: %g\n", p->average);
}
```

Here is the output:

```
Scores : 20 19 18 17 16
Average: 18
Scores : 20 19.5 19 18.5 18 17.5 17 16.5 16
Average: 17
```

Functions Using an Array of Structures

Suppose you have an array of structures that you want to process with a function. The name of an array is a synonym for its address, so it can be passed to a function. Again, the function needs access to the structure template. To show how this works, Listing 14.13 expands our monetary program to two people so that it has an array of two `funds` structures.

LISTING 14.13   The `funds4.c` Program

```
/* funds4.c -- passing an array of structures to a function */
#include <stdio.h>
#define FUNDLEN 50
#define N 2

struct funds {
    char    bank[FUNDLEN];
    double bankfund;
    char    save[FUNDLEN];
    double savefund;
};

double sum(const struct funds money[], int n);

int main(void)
{
    struct funds jones[N] = {
        {
            "Garlic-Melon Bank",
            3024.72,
            "Lucky's Savings and Loan",
            9237.11
        },
        {
            "Honest Jack's Bank",
            3534.28,
            "Party Time Savings",
            3203.89
        }
    };

    printf("The Joneses have a total of $%.2f.\n",
            sum(jones,N));

    return 0;
}

double sum(const struct funds money[], int n)
{
    double total;
    int i;

    for (i = 0, total = 0; i < n; i++)
```

LISTING 14.13 *Continued*

```
            total += money[i].bankfund + money[i].savefund;

    return(total);
}
```

The output is this:

```
The Joneses have a total of $19000.00.
```

(What an even sum! One would almost think the figures were contrived.)

The array name `jones` is the address of the array. In particular, it is the address of the first element of the array, which is the structure `jones[0]`. Therefore, initially the pointer `money` is given by this expression:

```
money = &jones[0];
```

Because money points to the first element of the `jones` array, `money[0]` is another name for the first element of that array. Similarly, `money[1]` is the second element. Each element is a funds structure, so each can use the dot (.) operator to access the structure members.

These are the main points:

- You can use the array name to pass the address of the first structure in the array to a function.

- You can then use array bracket notation to access the successive structures in the array. Note that the function call

  ```
  sum(&jones[0], N)
  ```

  would have the same effect as using the array name because both `jones` and `&jones[0]` are the same address. Using the array name is just an indirect way of passing the structure address.

- Because the `sum()` function ought not alter the original data, the function uses the ANSI C `const` qualifier.

Saving the Structure Contents in a File

Because structures can hold a wide variety of information, they are an important tool for constructing databases. For example, you could use a structure to hold all the pertinent information about an employee or an auto part. Ultimately, you would want to be able to save this information in, and retrieve it from, a file. A database file could contain an arbitrary number of such data objects. The entire set of information held in a structure is termed a *record*, and the individual items are *fields*. Let's investigate these topics.

What is perhaps the most obvious way to save a record is the least efficient way, and that is to use `fprintf()`. For example, recall the `book` structure introduced in Listing 14.1:

```
#define MAXTITL    40
#define MAXAUTL    40
struct book {
    char title[MAXTITL];
    char author[MAXAUTL];
    float value;
};
```

If `pbooks` identified a file stream, you could save the information in a `struct book` variable called `primer` with the following statement:

```
fprintf(pbooks, "%s %s %.2f\n", primer.title,
        primer.author, primer.value);
```

This setup becomes unwieldy for structures with, say, 30 members. Also, it poses a retrieval problem because the program would need some way of telling where one field ends and another begins. This problem can be fixed by using a format with fixed-size fields (for example, `"%39s%39s%8.2f"`), but the awkwardness remains.

A better solution is to use `fread()` and `fwrite()` to read and write structure-sized units. Recall that these functions read and write using the same binary representation that the program uses. For example,

```
fwrite(&primer, sizeof (struct book), 1, pbooks);
```

goes to the beginning address of the `primer` structure and copies all the bytes of the structure to the file associated with `pbooks`. The `sizeof (struct book)` term tells the function how large a block to copy, and the `1` indicates that it should copy just one block. The `fread()` function with the same arguments copies a structure-sized chunk of data from the file to the location pointed to by `&primer`. In short, these functions read and write one whole record at a time instead of a field at a time.

A Structure-Saving Example

To show how these functions can be used in a program, we've modified the program in Listing 14.2 so that the book titles are saved in a file called `book.dat`. If the file already exists, the program shows you its current contents and then enables you to add to the file. Listing 14.14 presents the new version. (If you're using an older Borland compiler, review the "Borland C and Floating Point" discussion in the sidebar near Listing 14.2.)

LISTING 14.14   The `booksave.c` Program

```
/* booksave.c -- saves structure contents in a file */
#include <stdio.h>
#include <stdlib.h>
#define MAXTITL    40
#define MAXAUTL    40
#define MAXBKS     10                /* maximum number of books */
```

LISTING 14.14   Continued

```c
struct book {                     /* set up book template   */
    char title[MAXTITL];
    char author[MAXAUTL];
    float value;
};

int main(void)
{
    struct book library[MAXBKS]; /* array of structures     */
    int count = 0;
    int index, filecount;
    FILE * pbooks;
    int size = sizeof (struct book);

    if ((pbooks = fopen("book.dat", "a+b")) == NULL)
    {
        fputs("Can't open book.dat file\n",stderr);
        exit(1);
    }

    rewind(pbooks);               /* go to start of file     */
    while (count < MAXBKS &&  fread(&library[count], size,
                1, pbooks) == 1)
    {
        if (count == 0)
            puts("Current contents of book.dat:");
        printf("%s by %s: $%.2f\n",library[count].title,
            library[count].author, library[count].value);
        count++;
    }
    filecount = count;
    if (count == MAXBKS)
    {
        fputs("The book.dat file is full.", stderr);
        exit(2);
    }

    puts("Please add new book titles.");
    puts("Press [enter] at the start of a line to stop.");
    while (count < MAXBKS && gets(library[count].title) != NULL
                    && library[count].title[0] != '\0')
    {
        puts("Now enter the author.");
        gets(library[count].author);
        puts("Now enter the value.");
        scanf("%f", &library[count++].value);
        while (getchar() != '\n')
            continue;                   /* clear input line  */
         if (count < MAXBKS)
            puts("Enter the next title.");
    }
```

LISTING 14.14   *Continued*

```
    if (count > 0)
    {
        puts("Here is the list of your books:");
        for (index = 0; index < count; index++)
            printf("%s by %s: $%.2f\n",library[index].title,
                    library[index].author, library[index].value);
        fwrite(&library[filecount], size, count - filecount,
                pbooks);
    }
    else
        puts("No books? Too bad.\n");

    puts("Bye.\n");
    fclose(pbooks);

    return 0;
}
```

We'll look at a couple of sample runs and then discuss the main programming points.

```
% booksave
Please add new book titles.
Press [enter] at the start of a line to stop.
Metric Merriment
Now enter the author.
Polly Poetica
Now enter the value.
18.99
Enter the next title.
Deadly Farce
Now enter the author.
Dudley Forse
Now enter the value.
15.99
Enter the next title.
[enter]
Here is the list of your books:
Metric Merriment by Polly Poetica: $18.99
Deadly Farce by Dudley Forse: $15.99
Bye.
% booksave
Current contents of book.dat:
Metric Merriment by Polly Poetica: $18.99
Deadly Farce by Dudley Forse: $15.99
Please add new book titles.
The Third Jar
Now enter the author.
Nellie Nostrum
Now enter the value.
22.99
Enter the next title.
[enter]
```

```
Here is the list of your books:
Metric Merriment by Polly Poetica: $18.99
Deadly Farce by Dudley Forse: $15.99
The Third Jar by Nellie Nostrum: $22.99
Bye.
%
```

Running the `booksave.c` program again would show all three books as current file records.

Program Points

First, the `"a+b"` mode is used for opening the file. The `a+` part lets the program read the whole file and append data to the end of the file. The `b` is the ANSI way of signifying that the program will use the binary file format. For Unix systems that don't accept the `b`, you can omit it because Unix has only one file form anyway. For other pre-ANSI implementations, you might need to find the local equivalent to using `b`.

We chose the binary mode because `fread()` and `fwrite()` are intended for binary files. True, some of the structure contents are text, but the `value` member is not. If you use a text editor to look at `book.dat`, the text part will show up okay, but the numeric part will be unreadable and could even cause your text editor to barf.

The `rewind()` command ensures that the file position pointer is situated at the start of the file, ready for the first read.

The initial `while` loop reads one structure at a time into the array of structures, stopping when the array is full or when the file is exhausted. The variable `filecount` keeps track of how many structures were read.

The next `while` loop prompts for, and takes, user input. As in Listing 14.2, this loop quits when the array is full or when the user presses the Enter key at the beginning of a line. Notice that the `count` variable starts with the value it had after the preceding loop. This causes the new entries to be added to the end of the array.

The `for` loop then prints the data both from the file and from the user. Because the file was opened in the append mode, new writes to the file are appended to the existing contents.

We could have used a loop to add one structure at a time to the end of the file. However, we decided to use the ability of `fwrite()` to write more than one block at a time. The expression `count - filecount` yields the number of new book titles to be added, and the call to `fwrite()` writes that number of structure-sized blocks to the file. The expression `&library[filecount]` is the address of the first new structure in the array, so copying begins from that point.

This example is, perhaps, the simplest way to write structures to a file and to retrieve them, but it can waste space because the unused parts of a structure are saved, too. The size of this structure is `2 x 40 x sizeof (char) + sizeof (float)`, which totals 84 bytes on our system. None of the entries actually need all that space. However, each data chunk being the same size makes retrieving the data easy.

Another approach is to use variably sized records. To facilitate reading such records from a file, each record can begin with a numerical field specifying the record size. This is a bit more complex than what we have done. Normally, this method involves "linked structures," which we describe next, and dynamic memory allocation, which we discuss in Chapter 16, "The C Preprocessor and the C Library."

Structures: What Next?

Before ending our exploration of structures, we would like to mention one of the more important uses of structures: creating new data forms. Computer users have developed data forms much more efficiently for certain problems than the arrays and simple structures we have presented. These forms have names such as queues, binary trees, heaps, hash tables, and graphs. Many such forms are built from linked structures. Typically, each structure contains one or two items of data plus one or two pointers to other structures of the same type. Those pointers link one structure to another and furnish a path to enable you to search through the overall tree of structures. For example, Figure 14.3 shows a binary tree structure, with each individual structure (or node) connected to the two below it.

FIGURE 14.3

A binary tree structure.

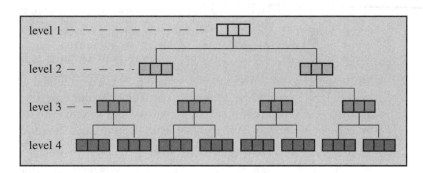

Is the hierarchical, or *tree*, structure shown in Figure 14.3 more efficient than an array? Consider the case of a tree with 10 levels of nodes. It has $2^{10}-1$, or 1,023, nodes in which you could store up to 1,023 words. If the words were arranged according to some sensible plan, you could start at the top level and find any word in at most nine moves as your search moves down one level to the next. If you have the words in an array, you might have to search all 1,023 elements before finding the word you seek.

If you are interested in more advanced concepts such as this, you can consult any number of computer science texts on data structures. With the C structures, you can create and use virtually every form presented in these texts. Also, Chapter 17, "Advanced Data Representation," investigates some of these advanced forms.

That's our final word on structures for this chapter, but we will present examples of linked structures in Chapter 17. Next, we'll look at three other C features for dealing with data: unions, enumerations, and `typedef`.

Unions: A Quick Look

A *union* is a type that enables you to store different data types in the same memory space (but not simultaneously). A typical use is a table designed to hold a mixture of types in some order that is neither regular nor known in advance. By using an array of unions, you can create an array of equal-sized units, each of which can hold a variety of data types.

Unions are set up in much the same way as structures. There is a union template and a union variable. They can be defined in one step or, by using a union tag, in two. Here is an example of a union template with a tag:

```
union hold {
    int digit;
    double bigfl;
    char letter;
};
```

A structure with a similar declaration would be able to hold an `int` value *and* a `double` value *and* a `char` value. This union, however, can hold an `int` value *or* a `double` value *or* a `char` value.

Here is an example of defining three union variables of the `hold` type:

```
union hold fit;       // union variable of hold type
union hold save[10];  // array of 10 union variables
union hold * pu;      // pointer to a variable of hold type
```

The first declaration creates a single variable, `fit`. The compiler allots enough space so that it can hold the largest of the described possibilities. In this case, the biggest possibility listed is `double`, which requires 64 bits, or 8 bytes, on our system. The second declaration creates an array called `save` with 10 elements, each 8 bytes in size. The third declaration creates a pointer that can hold the address of a `hold` union.

You can initialize a union. Because the union holds only one value, the rules are different from those in a structure. In particular, you have three choices: You can initialize a union to another union of the same type, you can initialize the first element of a union, or, with C99, you can use a designated initializer:

```
union hold valA;
valA.letter = 'R';
union hold valB = valA;  // initialize one union to another
union hold valC = {88};  // initialize digit member of union
union hold valD = {.bigfl = 118.2};  // designated initializer
```

Here is how you can use a union:

```
fit.digit = 23;    // 23 is stored in fit; 2 bytes used
fit.bigfl = 2.0;   // 23 cleared, 2.0 stored; 8 bytes used
fit.letter = 'h';  // 2.0 cleared, h stored; 1 byte used
```

The dot operator shows which data type is being used. Only one value is stored at a time. You can't store a `char` and an `int` at the same time, even though there is enough space to do so. It is your responsibility to keep track of the data type currently being stored in a union.

You can use the `->` operator with pointers to unions in the same fashion that you use the operator with pointers to structures:

```
pu = &fit;
x = pu->digit;  // same as x = fit.digit
```

The next sequence shows what *not* to do:

```
fit.letter = 'A';
flnum = 3.02*fit.bigfl;    // ERROR ERROR ERROR
```

This sequence is wrong because a `char` type is stored, but the next line assumes that the content of `fit` is a `double` type.

However, sometimes it can be useful to use one member to place values into a union and to then use a different member for viewing the contents. Listing 15.4 in the next chapter shows an example.

Another place you might use a union is in a structure for which the stored information depends on one of the members. For example, suppose you have a structure representing an automobile. If the automobile is owned by the user, you want a structure member describing the owner. If the automobile is leased, you want the member to describe the leasing company. Then you can do something along the following lines:

```
struct owner {
    char socsecurity[12];
    ...
};

struct leasecompany  {
    char name[40];
    char headquarters[40];
    ...
};

union data {
    struct owner owncar;
    struct leasecompany leasecar;
};

struct car_data {
    char make[15];
    int status; /* 0 = owned, 1 = leased */
    union data ownerinfo;
    ...
};
```

Suppose `flits` is a `car_data` structure. Then if `flits.status` were 0, the program could use `flits.ownerinfo.owncar.socsecurity`, and if `flits.status` were 1, the program could use `flits.ownerinfo.leasecar.name`.

Summary: Structure and Union Operators

The Membership Operator:

.

General Comments:

This operator is used with a structure or union name to specify a member of that structure or union. If `name` is the name of a structure and `member` is a member specified by the structure template, the following identifies that member of the structure:

```
name.member
```

The type of `name.member` is the type specified for `member`. The membership operator can also be used in the same fashion with unions.

Example:

```
struct {
      int code;
      float cost;
} item;

item.code = 1265;
```

The last statement assigns a value to the `code` member of the structure `item`.

The Indirect Membership Operator:

->

General Comments:

This operator is used with a pointer to a structure or union to identify a member of that structure or union. Suppose that `ptrstr` is a pointer to a structure and that `member` is a member specified by the structure template. Then the statement

```
ptrstr->member
```

identifies that member of the pointed-to structure. The indirect membership operator can be used in the same fashion with unions.

Example:

```
struct {
      int code;
      float cost;
} item, * ptrst;
ptrst = &item;
ptrst->code = 3451;
```

The last statement assigns an `int` value to the `code` member of `item`. The following three expressions are equivalent:

```
ptrst->code    item.code    (*ptrst).code
```

Enumerated Types

You can use the *enumerated type* to declare symbolic names to represent integer constants. By using the `enum` keyword, you can create a new "type" and specify the values it may have. (Actually, `enum` constants are type `int`; therefore, they can be used wherever you would use an `int`.) The purpose of enumerated types is to enhance the readability of a program. The syntax is similar to that used for structures. For example, you can make these declarations:

```
enum spectrum {red, orange, yellow, green, blue, violet};
enum spectrum color;
```

The first declaration establishes `spectrum` as a tag name, which allows you to use `enum spectrum` as a type name. The second declaration makes `color` a variable of that type. The identifiers within the braces enumerate the possible values that a `spectrum` variable can have. Therefore, the possible values for `color` are `red`, `orange`, `yellow`, and so on. Then, you can use statements such as the following:

```
int c;
color = blue;
if (color == yellow)
    ...;
for (color = red; color <= violet; coloc++)
    ...;
```

Although enumerated constants are type `int`, enumerated variables are more loosely constrained to be an integral type as long as the type can hold the enumerated constants. For example, the enumerated constants for `spectrum` have the range 0–5, so a compiler could choose to use `unsigned char` to represent the `color` variable.

Incidentally, some C enumeration properties don't carry over to C++. For example, C allows you to apply the ++ operator to an enumeration variable, and C++ doesn't. So if you think your code might be incorporated into a C++ program some day, you should declare `color` as type `int` in the previous example. Then the code will work with either C or C++.

enum Constants

Just what are `blue` and `red`? Technically, they are type `int` constants. For example, given the preceding enumeration declaration, you can try this:

```
printf("red = %d, orange = %d\n", red, orange);
```

Here is the output:

```
red = 0, orange = 1
```

What has happened is that `red` has become a named constant representing the integer 0. Similarly, the other identifiers are named constants representing the integers 1 through 5. You can use an enumerated constant anywhere you can use an integer constant. For example, you can use them as sizes in array declarations, and you can use them as labels in a switch statement.

Default Values

By default, the constants in the enumeration list are assigned the integer values 0, 1, 2, and so on. Therefore, the declaration

```
enum kids {nippy, slats, skippy, nina, liz};
```

results in `nina` having the value `3`.

Assigned Values

You can choose the integer values that you want the constants to have. Just include the desired values in the declaration:

```
enum levels {low = 100, medium = 500, high = 2000};
```

If you assign a value to one constant but not to the following constants, the following constants will be numbered sequentially. For example, suppose you have this declaration:

```
enum feline {cat, lynx = 10, puma, tiger};
```

Then `cat` is `0`, by default, and `lynx`, `puma`, and `tiger` are `10`, `11`, and `12`, respectively.

enum Usage

Recall that the purpose of enumerated types is to enhance a program's readability. If you are dealing with colors, using `red` and `blue` is much more obvious than using `0` and `1`. Note that the enumerated types are for internal use. If you want to enter a value of `orange` for `color`, you have to enter a `1`, not the word `orange`, or you can read in the string `"orange"` and have the program convert it to the value `orange`.

Because the enumerated type is an integer type, `enum` variables can be used in expressions in the same manner as integer variables. They make convenient labels for a `case` statement.

Listing 14.15 shows a short example using `enum`. The example relies on the default value-assignment scheme. This gives `red` the value `0`, which makes it the index for the pointer to the string `"red"`.

LISTING 14.15   The `enum.c` Program

```
/* enum.c -- uses enumerated values */
#include <stdio.h>
#include <string.h>      // for strcmp()
#include <stdbool.h>     // C99 feature

enum spectrum {red, orange, yellow, green, blue, violet};
const char * colors[] = {"red", "orange", "yellow",
                         "green", "blue", "violet"};
#define LEN 30

int main(void)
{
```

LISTING 14.15   Continued

```
        char choice[LEN];
        enum spectrum color;
        bool color_is_found = false;

        puts("Enter a color (empty line to quit):");
        while (gets(choice) != NULL && choice[0] != '\0')
        {
            for (color = red; color <= violet; color++)
            {
                if (strcmp(choice, colors[color]) == 0)
                {
                    color_is_found = true;
                    break;
                }
            }
            if (color_is_found)
                switch(color)
                {
                    case red    : puts("Roses are red.");
                                  break;
                    case orange : puts("Poppies are orange.");
                                  break;
                    case yellow : puts("Sunflowers are yellow.");
                                  break;
                    case green  : puts("Grass is green.");
                                  break;
                    case blue   : puts("Bluebells are blue.");
                                  break;
                    case violet : puts("Violets are violet.");
                                  break;
                }
            else
                printf("I don't know about the color %s.\n", choice);
            color_is_found = false;
            puts("Next color, please (empty line to quit):");
        }
        puts("Goodbye!");

    return 0;
}
```

The code breaks out of the **for** loop if the input string matches one of the strings pointed to by the members of the **colors** array. If the loop finds a matching color, the program then uses the value of the enumeration variable to match an enumeration constant used as a case label. Here is a sample run:

```
Enter a color (empty line to quit):
blue
Bluebells are blue.
Next color, please (empty line to quit):
orange
Poppies are orange.
```

```
Next color, please (empty line to quit):
purple
I don't know about the color purple.
Next color, please (empty line to quit):

Goodbye!
```

Shared Namespaces

C uses the term *namespace* to identify parts of a program in which a name is recognized. Scope is part of the concept: Two variables having the same name but in different scopes don't conflict; two variables having the same name in the same scope do conflict. There also is a category aspect to namespaces. Structure tags, union tags, and enumeration tags in a particular scope all share the same namespace, and that namespace is different from the one used by ordinary variables. What this means is that you can use the same name for one variable and one tag in the same scope without causing an error, but you can't declare two tags of the same name or two variables of the same name in the same scope. For example, the following doesn't cause a conflict in C:

```
struct rect { double x; double y; };
int rect;    // not a conflict in C
```

However, it can be confusing to use the same identifier in two different ways; also, C++ doesn't allow this because it puts tags and variable names into the same namespace.

typedef: A Quick Look

The typedef facility is an advanced data feature that enables you to create your own name for a type. It is similar to #define in that respect, but with three differences:

- Unlike #define, typedef is limited to giving symbolic names to types only and not to values.

- The typedef interpretation is performed by the compiler, not the preprocessor.

- Within its limits, typedef is more flexible than #define.

Let's see how typedef works. Suppose you want to use the term BYTE for one-byte numbers. You simply define BYTE as if it were a char variable and precede the definition by the keyword typedef, like so:

```
typedef unsigned char BYTE;
```

From then on, you can use BYTE to define variables:

```
BYTE x, y[10], * z;
```

The scope of this definition depends on the location of the typedef statement. If the definition is inside a function, the scope is local, confined to that function. If the definition is outside a function, the scope is global.

Often, uppercase letters are used for these definitions to remind the user that the type name is really a symbolic abbreviation, but you can use lowercase, too:

```
typedef unsigned char byte;
```

The same rules that govern the valid names of variables govern the name used for a `typedef`.

Creating a name for an existing type might seem a bit frivolous, but it can be useful. With the preceding example, using BYTE instead of `unsigned char` helps document that you plan to use BYTE variables to represent numbers rather than character codes. Using `typedef` also helps increase portability. For example, we've mentioned the `size_t` type, which represents the type returned by the `sizeof` operator, and the `time_t` type, which represents the type of value returned by the `time()` function. The C standard says `sizeof` and `time()` return integer types but leaves it up to the implementation to determine which type. The reason for this lack of specificity is that the ANSI C committee feels that no one choice is likely to be the best choice for every computer platform. So they make up a new type name, such as `time_t`, and let the implementation use a `typedef` to set that name to some specific type. That way, they can provide a general prototype such as the following:

```
time_t time(time_t *);
```

On one system, `time_t` can be `unsigned int`; on another, it can be `unsigned long`. As long as you include the `time.h` header file, your program can access the appropriate definition, and you can declare `time_t` variables in your code.

Some features of `typedef` can be duplicated with a `#define`. For example,

```
#define BYTE unsigned char
```

causes the preprocessor to replace BYTE with `unsigned char`. Here is one that can't be duplicated with a `#define`:

```
typedef char * STRING;
```

Without the keyword `typedef`, this example would identify STRING itself as a pointer-to-`char`. With the keyword, it makes STRING an identifier for pointers-to-`char`. Therefore,

```
STRING name, sign;
```

means

```
char * name, * sign;
```

Suppose, instead, you did this:

```
#define STRING char *
```

Then

```
STRING name, sign;
```

would translate to the following:

```
char * name, sign;
```

In this case, only `name` would be a pointer.

You can use **typedef** with structures, too:

```
typedef struct complex {
        float real;
        float imag;
} COMPLEX;
```

You can then use the type **COMPLEX** instead of the **struct** called **complex** to represent complex numbers. One reason to use **typedef** is to create convenient, recognizable names for types that turn up often. For instance, many people prefer to use **STRING** or its equivalent, as in the earlier example.

You can omit a tag when using **typedef** to name a structure type:

```
typedef struct {double x; double y;} rect;
```

Suppose you use the **typedef** like this:

```
rect r1 = {3.0, 6.0};
rect r2;
```

This is translated to

```
struct {double x; double y;} r1= {3.0, 6.0};
struct {double x; double y;} r2;
r2 = r1;
```

If two structures are declared without a tag but with identical members (with both member names and types matching), C considers the two structures to be of the same type, so assigning **r1** to **r2** is a valid operation.

A second reason for using **typedef** is that **typedef** names are often used for complicated types. For example, the declaration

```
typedef char (* FRPTC ()) [5];
```

makes **FRPTC** announce a type that is a function that returns a pointer to a five-element array of **char**. (See the upcoming discussion on fancy declarations in the next section.)

When using **typedef**, bear in mind that it does not create new types; instead, it just creates convenient labels. This means, for example, that variables using the **STRING** type we created can be used as arguments for functions expecting type pointer-to-**char**.

With structures, unions, and **typedef**, C gives you the tools for efficient and portable data handling.

Fancy Declarations

C enables you to create elaborate data forms. Although we are sticking to simpler forms, we feel it is our duty to point out the potentialities. When you make a declaration, the name (or identifier) can be modified by tacking on a modifier.

Modifier	Significance
*	Indicates a pointer
()	Indicates a function
[]	Indicates an array

C enables you to use more than one modifier at a time, and that enables you to create a variety of types, as shown in the following examples:

```
int board[8][8];     // an array of arrays of int
int ** ptr;          // a pointer to a pointer to int
int * risks[10];     // a 10-element array of pointers to int
int (* rusks)[10];   // a pointer to an array of 10 ints
int * oof[3][4];     // a 3 x 4 array of pointers to int
int (* uuf)[3][4];   // a pointer to a 3 x 4 array of ints
int (* uof[3])[4];   // a 3-element array of pointers to
                     //    4-element arrays of int
```

The trick to unraveling these declarations is figuring out the order in which to apply the modifiers. These rules should get you through:

1. The [], which indicates an array, and the (), which indicates a function, have the same precedence. This precedence is higher than that of the * indirection operator, which means that the following declaration makes risks an array of pointers rather than a pointer to an array:

   ```
   int * risks[10];
   ```

2. The [] and () associate from left to right. This next declaration makes goods an array of 12 arrays of 50 ints, not an array of 50 arrays of 12 ints:

   ```
   int goods[12][50];
   ```

3. Both [] and () have the same precedence, but because they associate from left to right, the following declaration groups * and rusks together before applying the brackets. This means that the following declaration makes rusks a pointer to an array of 10 ints:

   ```
   int (* rusks)[10];
   ```

Let's apply these rules to this declaration:

```
int * oof[3][4];
```

The [3] has higher precedence than the *, and, because of the left-to-right rule, it has higher precedence than the [4]. Hence, oof is an array with three elements. Next in order is [4], so the elements of oof are arrays of four elements. The * tells us that these elements are pointers. The int completes the picture: oof is a three-element array of four-element arrays of pointers to int, or, for short, a 3×4 array of pointers to int. Storage is set aside for 12 pointers.

Now look at this declaration:

```
int (* uuf)[3][4];
```

The parentheses cause the * modifier to have first priority, making **uuf** a pointer to a 3×4 array of **int**s. Storage is set aside for a single pointer.

These rules also yield the following types:

```
char * fump();        // function returning pointer to char
char (* frump)();     // pointer to a function that returns type char
char (* flump[3])();// array of 3 pointers to functions that
                      //  return type char
```

You can use **typedef** to build a sequence of related types:

```
typdef int arr5[5];
typedef arr5 * p_arr5;
typedef p_arr5 arrp10[10];
arr5 togs; // togs an array of 5 int
p_arr5 p2; // p2 a pointer to an array of 5 int
arrp10 ap; // ap an array of 10 pointers to array-of-5-int
```

When you bring structures into the picture, the possibilities for declarations truly grow baroque. And the applications... well, we'll leave that for more advanced texts.

Functions and Pointers

As the discussion on declarations illustrated, it's possible to declare pointers to functions. You might wonder whether such a beast has any usefulness. Typically, a function pointer is used as an argument to another function, telling the second function which function to use. For instance, sorting an array involves comparing two elements to see which comes first. If the elements are numbers, you can use the > operator. More generally, the elements may be a string or a structure, requiring a function call to do the comparison. The **qsort()** function from the C library is designed to work with arrays of any kind as long as you tell it what function to use to compare elements. For that purpose, it takes a pointer to a function as one of its arguments. The **qsort()** function then uses that function to sort the type—whether it be integer, string, or structure.

Let's take a closer look at function pointers. First, what does it mean? A pointer to, say, an **int** holds the address of a location in memory at which an **int** can be stored. Functions, too, have addresses, because the machine-language implementation of a function consists of code loaded into memory. A pointer to a function can hold the address marking the start of the function code.

Next, when you declare a data pointer, you have to declare the type of data to which it points. When declaring a function pointer, you have to declare the type of function pointed to. To specify the function type, you indicate the return type for the function and the parameter types for a function. For example, consider this prototype:

```
void ToUpper(char *);   // convert string to uppercase
```

The type for the ToUpper() function is "function with char * parameter and return type void." To declare a pointer called pf to this function type, do this:

```
void (*pf)(char *);     // pf a pointer-to-function
```

Reading this declaration, you see the first parentheses pair associates the * operator with pf, meaning that pf is a pointer to a function. This makes (*pf) a function, which makes (char *) the parameter list for the function and void the return type. Probably the simplest way to create this declaration is to note that it replaces the function name ToUpper with the expression (*pf). So if you want to declare a pointer to a specific type of function, you can declare a function of that type and then replace the function name with an expression of the form (*pf) to create a function pointer declaration. As mentioned earlier, the first parentheses are needed because of operator precedence rules. Omitting them leads to something quite different:

```
void *pf(char *);     // pf a function that returns a pointer
```

Tip

To declare a pointer to a particular type of function, first declare a function of the desired type and then replace the function name with an expression of the form (*pf); pf then becomes a pointer to a function of that type.

After you have a function pointer, you can assign to it the addresses of functions of the proper type. In this context, the *name* of a function can be used to represent the address of the function:

```
void ToUpper(char *);
void ToLower(char *);
int round(double);
void (*pf)(char *);
pf = ToUpper;          // valid, ToUpper is address of the function
pf = ToLower;          // valid, ToLower is address of the function
pf = round;            // invalid, round is the wrong type of function
pf = ToLower();        // invalid, ToLower() is not an address
```

The last assignment is also invalid because you can't use a void function in an assignment statement. Note that the pointer pf can point to any function that takes a char * argument and has a return type of void, but not to functions with other characteristics.

Just as you can use a data pointer to access data, you can use a function pointer to access a function. Strangely, there are two logically inconsistent syntax rules for doing so, as the following illustrates:

```
void ToUpper(char *);
void ToLower(char *);
void (*pf)(char *);
char mis[] = "Nina Metier";
pf = ToUpper;
(*pf)(mis);       // apply ToUpper to mis (syntax 1)
pf = ToLower;
pf(mis);          // apply ToLower to mis (syntax 2)
```

Each approach sounds sensible. Here is the first approach: Because pf points to the ToUpper function, *pf is the ToUpper function, so the expression (*pf)(mis) is the same as ToUpper(mis). Just look at the declarations of ToUpper and of pf to see that ToUpper and (*pf) are equivalent. Here is the second approach: Because the name of a function is a pointer, you can use a pointer and a function name interchangeably, hence pf(mis) is the same as ToLower(mis). Just look at the assignment statement for pf to see that pf and ToLower are equivalent. Historically, the developers of C and Unix at Bell Labs took the first view and the extenders of Unix at Berkeley took the second view. K&R C did not allow the second form, but to maintain compatibility with existing code, ANSI C accepts both forms as equivalent.

Just as one of the most common uses of a data pointer is an argument to a function, one of the most common uses of a function pointer is an argument to a function. For example, consider this function prototype:

```
void show(void (* fp)(char *), char * str);
```

It looks messy, but it declares two parameters, fp and str. The fp parameter is a function pointer, and the str is a data pointer. More specifically, fp points to a function that takes a char * parameter and has a void return type, and str points to a char. So, given the declarations we had earlier, you can make function calls such as the following:

```
show(ToLower, mis);  /* show() uses ToLower() function: fp = ToLower   */
show(pf, mis);       /* show() uses function pointed to by pf: fp = pf */
```

And how does show() use the function pointer passed to it? It uses either the fp() or the (*fp)() syntax to invoke the function:

```
void show(void (* fp)(char *), char * str)
{
    (*fp)(str); /* apply chosen function to str */
    puts(str);  /* display result               */
}
```

Here, for example, show() first transforms the string str by applying to it the function pointed to by fp, and then it displays the transformed string.

By the way, functions with return values can be used two different ways as arguments to other functions. For example, consider the following:

```
function1(sqrt);       /* passes address of sqrt function       */
function2(sqrt(4.0)); /* passes return value of sqrt function */
```

The first passes the address of the sqrt() function, and presumably function1() will use that function in its code. The second statement initially calls the sqrt() function, evaluates it, and then passes the return value (2.0, in this case) to function2().

To show the essential ideas, the program in Listing 14.16 uses show() with a variety of transforming functions as arguments. The listing also shows some useful techniques for handling a menu.

LISTING 14.16   The func_ptr.c Program

```c
// func_ptr.c -- uses function pointers
#include <stdio.h>
#include <string.h>
#include <ctype.h>

char showmenu(void);
void eatline(void);      // read through end of line
void show(void (* fp)(char *), char * str);
void ToUpper(char *);    // convert string to uppercase
void ToLower(char *);    // convert string to uppercase
void Transpose(char *); // transpose cases
void Dummy(char *);      // leave string unaltered

int main(void)
{
    char line[81];
    char copy[81];
    char choice;
    void (*pfun)(char *); // points a function having a
                          // char * argument and no
                          // return value
    puts("Enter a string (empty line to quit):");
    while (gets(line) != NULL && line[0] != '\0')
    {
        while ((choice = showmenu()) != 'n')
        {
            switch (choice   )  // switch sets pointer
            {
                case 'u' : pfun = ToUpper;   break;
                case 'l' : pfun = ToLower;   break;
                case 't' : pfun = Transpose; break;
                case 'o' : pfun = Dummy;     break;
            }
            strcpy(copy, line);// make copy for show()
            show(pfun, copy);  // use selected function
        }
        puts("Enter a string (empty line to quit):");
    }
    puts("Bye!");

    return 0;
}

char showmenu(void)
{
    char ans;
    puts("Enter menu choice:");
    puts("u) uppercase        l) lowercase");
    puts("t) transposed case o) original case");
    puts("n) next string");
    ans = getchar();     // get response
    ans = tolower(ans); // convert to lowercase
```

LISTING 14.16 Continued

```
        eatline();              // dispose of rest of line
        while (strchr("ulton", ans) == NULL)
        {
            puts("Please enter a u, l, t, o, or n:");
            ans = tolower(getchar());
            eatline();
        }

        return ans;
    }

    void eatline(void)
    {
        while (getchar() != '\n')
            continue;
    }

    void ToUpper(char * str)
    {
        while (*str)
        {
            *str = toupper(*str);
            str++;
        }
    }

    void ToLower(char * str)
    {
        while (*str)
        {
            *str = tolower(*str);
            str++;
        }
    }
    void Transpose(char * str)
    {
        while (*str)
        {
            if (islower(*str))
                *str = toupper(*str);
            else if (isupper(*str))
                *str = tolower(*str);
            str++;
        }
    }

    void Dummy(char * str)
    {
        // leaves string unchanged
    }
```

LISTING 14.16   Continued

```
void show(void (* fp)(char *), char * str)
{
    (*fp)(str); // apply chosen function to str
    puts(str);  // display result
}
```

Here is a sample run:

```
Enter a string (empty line to quit):
Does C make you feel loopy?
Enter menu choice:
u) uppercase      l) lowercase
t) transposed case o) original case
n) next string
t
dOES c MAKE YOU FEEL LOOPY?
Enter menu choice:
u) uppercase      l) lowercase
t) transposed case o) original case
n) next string
l
does c make you feel loopy?
Enter menu choice:
u) uppercase      l) lowercase
t) transposed case o) original case
n) next string
n
Enter a string (empty line to quit):

Bye!
```

Note that the ToUpper(), ToLower(), Transpose(), and Dummy() functions all have the same type, so all four can be assigned to the pfun pointer. This program uses pfun as the argument to show(), but you can also use any of the four function names directly as arguments, as in show(Transpose, copy).

You can use typedef in situations like these. For example, the program could have done this:

```
typedef void (*V_FP_CHARP)(char *);
void show (V_FP_CHARP fp, char *);
V_FP_CHARP pfun;
```

If you're feeling adventurous, you can declare and initialize an array of such pointers:

```
V_FP_CHARP arpf[4] = {ToUpper, ToLower, Transpose, Dummy};
```

If you then modify the showmenu() function so that it is type int and returns 0 if the user enters u, 1 if the user enters l, 2 if the user enters t, and so on, you could replace the loop holding the switch statement with the following:

```
index = showmenu();
while (index >= 0 && index <= 3)
```

```
{
    strcpy(copy, line);         /* make copy for show()  */
    show(arpf[index], copy);    /* use selected function */
    index = showmenu();
}
```

You can't have an array of functions, but you can have an array of function pointers.

You've now seen all four ways in which a function name can be used: in defining a function, in declaring a function, in calling a function, and as a pointer. Figure 14.4 sums up the uses.

FIGURE 14.4

Uses for a function name.

function name used in a prototype declaration: `int comp(int x, int y);`
function name used in a function call: `status = comp(q,r);`
function name used in a function definition: `int comp(int x, int y)` `{ ...`
function name used as a pointer in assignment: `pfunct = comp;`
function name used as pointer argument: `slowsort(arr,n,comp);`

As far as menu handling goes, the `showmenu()` function shows several techniques. First, the code

```
ans = getchar();     // get response
ans = tolower(ans);  // convert to lowercase
```

and

```
ans = tolower(getchar());
```

show two ways to convert user input to one case so that you don't have to test for both `'u'` and `'U'`, and so on.

The `eatline()` function disposes of the rest of the entry line. This is useful on two accounts. First, to enter a choice, the user types a letter and then presses the Enter key, which generates a newline character. That newline character will be read as the next response unless you get rid of it first. Second, suppose the user responds by typing the entire word *uppercase* instead of the letter *u*. Without the `eatline()` function, the program would treat each character in the word *uppercase* as a separate response. With `eatline()`, the program processes the *u* and discards the rest of the line.

Next, the `showmenu()` function is designed to return only valid choices to the program. To help with that task, the program uses the standard library function `strchr()` from the `string.h` header file:

```
while (strchr("ulton", ans) == NULL)
```

This function looks for the location of the first occurrence of the character `ans` in the string `"ulton"` and returns a pointer to it. If it doesn't find the character, it returns the null pointer. Therefore, this `while` loop test is a more convenient replacement for the following:

```
while (ans != 'u' && ans != 'l' && ans != 't' && ans != 'o' && ans != 'n')
```

The more choices you have to check, the more convenient using `strchr()` becomes.

Key Concepts

The information we need to represent a programming problem often is more involved than a single number or a list of numbers. A program may deal with an entity or collection of entities having several properties. For example, you might represent a client by his or her name, address, phone number, and other information. Or you might describe a movie DVD by its title, distributor, playing time, cost, and so on. A C structure lets you collect all this information in a single unit. This is very helpful in organizing a program. Rather than storing information in a scattered collection of variables, you can store all the related information in one place.

When you design a structure, it's often useful to develop a package of functions to go along with it. For example, rather than write a bunch of `printf()` statements every time you want to display the contents of a structure, you can write a display function that takes the structure (or its address) as an argument. Because all the information is in the structure, you need just one argument. If you had put the information into separate variables, you would have had to use a separate argument for each individual part. Also, if you, say, add a member to the structure, you have to rewrite the functions, but you don't have to change the function calls, which is a great convenience if you modify the design.

A union declaration looks much like a structure declaration. However, the union members share the same memory space and only one member can inhabit the union at a time. In essence, a union allows you to create a variable that can hold one value, but more than one type.

The `enum` facility offers a means of defining symbolic constants, and the `typedef` facility offers a means to create a new identifier for a basic or derived type.

Pointers to functions provide a means to tell one function which function it should use.

Summary

A C structure provides the means to store several data items, usually of different types, in the same data object. You can use a tag to identify a specific structure template and to declare variables of that type. The membership dot operator (`.`) enables you to access the individual members of a structure by using labels from the structure template.

If you have a pointer to a structure, you can use the pointer and the indirect membership operator (->) instead of a name and the dot operator to access individual members. To find the address of a structure, use the & operator. Unlike arrays, the name of a structure does not serve as the address of the structure.

Traditionally, structure-related functions have used pointers to structures as arguments. Modern C permits structures to be passed as arguments, used as return values, and assigned to structures of the same type.

Unions use the same syntax as structures. However, with unions, the members share a common storage space. Instead of storing several data types simultaneously in the manner of a structure, the union stores a single data item type from a list of choices. That is, a structure can hold, say, an `int` and a `double` and a `char`, and the corresponding union can hold an `int` or a `double` or a `char`.

Enumerations allow you to create a group of symbolic integer constants (enumeration constants) and to define an associated enumeration type.

The `typedef` facility enables you to establish aliases or shorthand representations of standard C types.

The name of a function yields the address of that function. Such addresses can be passed as arguments to functions, which then use the pointed-to function. If `pf` is a function pointer that has been assigned the address of a particular function, you can invoke that function in two ways:

```c
#include <math.h>    /* declares double sin(double) function */
...
double (*pdf)(double);
double x;
pdf = sin;
x = (*pdf)(1.2);  // invokes sin(1.2)
x = pdf(1.2);     // also invokes sin(1.2)
```

Review Questions

1. What's wrong with this template?

```c
structure {
        char itable;
        int  num[20];
        char * togs
}
```

2. Here is a portion of a program. What will it print?

```c
#include <stdio.h>
struct house {
    float sqft;
    int rooms;
    int stories;
    char address[40];
};
```

```
int main(void)
{
   struct house fruzt = {1560.0, 6, 1, "22 Spiffo Road"};
   struct house *sign;

   sign = &fruzt;
   printf("%d %d\n", fruzt.rooms, sign->stories);
   printf("%s \n", fruzt.address);
   printf("%c %c\n", sign->address[3], fruzt.address[4]);
   return 0;
}
```

3. Devise a structure template that will hold the name of a month, a three-letter abbreviation for the month, the number of days in the month, and the month number.

4. Define an array of 12 structures of the sort in question 3 and initialize it for a non-leap year.

5. Write a function that, when given the month number, returns the total days in the year up to and including that month. Assume that the structure template of question 3 and an appropriate array of such structures are declared externally.

6.   a. Given the following typedef, declare a 10-element array of the indicated structure. Then, using individual member assignment (or the string equivalent), let the third element describe a Remarkatar lens with a focal length of 500 mm and an aperture of f/2.0.

```
typedef struct lens {      /* lens descriptor  */
     float foclen;         /* focal length,mm */
     float fstop;          /* aperture        */
     char brand[30];       /* brand name      */
   } LENS;
```

   b. Repeat part "a," but use an initialization list with a designated initializer in the declaration rather than using separate assignment statements for each member.

7. Consider the following programming fragment:

```
struct name {
        char first[20];
        char last[20];
};
struct bem {
        int limbs;
        struct name title;
        char type[30];
};
struct bem * pb;
struct bem deb = {
        6,
        {"Berbnazel", "Gwolkapwolk"},
        "Arcturan"

};

pb = &deb;
```

a. What would each of the following statements print?

```
printf("%d\n", deb.limbs);
printf("%s\n", pb->type);
printf("%s\n", pb->type + 2);
```

b. How could you represent "Gwolkapwolk" in structure notation (two ways)?

c. Write a function that takes the address of a bem structure as its argument and prints the contents of that structure in the form shown here (assume that the structure template is in a file called starfolk.h):

Berbnazel Gwolkapwolk is a 6-limbed Arcturan.

8. Consider the following declarations:

```
struct fullname {
                char fname[20];
                char lname[20];
                };
struct bard    {
                struct fullname name;
                int born;
                int died;
                };
struct bard willie;
struct bard *pt = &willie;
```

a. Identify the born member of the willie structure using the willie identifier.

b. Identify the born member of the willie structure using the pt identifier.

c. Use a scanf() call to read in a value for the born member using the willie identifier.

d. Use a scanf() call to read in a value for the born member using the pt identifier.

e. Use a scanf() call to read in a value for the lname member of the name member using the willie identifier.

f. Use a scanf() call to read in a value for the lname member of the name member using the pt identifier.

g. Construct an identifier for the third letter of the first name of someone described by the willie variable.

h. Construct an expression representing the total number of letters in the first and last names of someone described by the willie variable.

9. Define a structure template suitable for holding the following items: the name of an automobile, its horsepower, its EPA city-driving MPG rating, its wheelbase, and its year. Use car as the template tag.

10. Suppose you have this structure:

```
struct gas {
        float distance;
        float gals;
        float mpg;
};
```

    a. Devise a function that takes a `struct gas` argument. Assume that the passed structure contains the `distance` and `gals` information. Have the function calculate the correct value for the `mpg` member and return the now completed structure.

    b. Devise a function that takes the address of a `struct gas` argument. Assume that the passed structure contains the `distance` and `gals` information. Have the function calculate the correct value for the `mpg` member and assign it to the appropriate member.

11. Declare an enumeration with the tag choices that sets the enumeration constants `no`, `yes`, and `maybe` to 0, 1, and 2, respectively.

12. Declare a pointer to a function that returns a pointer-to-`char` and that takes a pointer-to-`char` and a `char` as arguments.

13. Declare four functions and initialize an array of pointers to point to them. Each function should take two `double` arguments and return a `double`.

Programming Exercises

1. Redo review question 3, but make the argument the spelled-out name of the month instead of the month number. (Don't forget about `strcmp()`.)

2. Write a program that prompts the user to enter the day, month, and year. The month can be a month number, a month name, or a month abbreviation. The program then should return the total number of days in the year up through the given day.

3. Revise the book-listing program in Listing 14.2 so that it prints the book descriptions in the order entered, then alphabetized by title, and then in order of increased value.

4. Write a program that creates a structure template with two members according to the following criteria:

    a. The first member is a social security number. The second member is a structure with three members. Its first member contains a first name, its second member contains a middle name, and its final member contains a last name. Create and initialize an array of five such structures. Have the program print the data in this format:

```
Dribble, Flossie M. -- 302039823
```

Only the initial letter of the middle name is printed, and a period is added. Neither the initial (of course) nor the period should be printed if the middle name member is empty. Write a function to do the printing; pass the structure array to the function.

b. Modify part "a" by passing the structure value instead of the address.

5. Write a program that fits the following recipe:

a. Externally define a `name` structure template with two members: a string to hold the first name and a string to hold the second name.

b. Externally define a `student` structure template with three members: a `name` structure, a `grade` array to hold three floating-point scores, and a variable to hold the average of those three scores.

c. Have the `main()` function declare an array of `CSIZE` (with `CSIZE = 4`) student structures and initialize the name portions to names of your choice. Use functions to perform the tasks described in parts "d," "e," "f," and "g."

d. Interactively acquire scores for each student by prompting the user with a student name and a request for scores. Place the scores in the grade array portion of the appropriate structure. The required looping can be done in `main()` or in the function, as you prefer.

e. Calculate the average score value for each structure and assign it to the proper member.

f. Print the information in each structure.

g. Print the class average for each of the numeric structure members.

6. A text file holds information about a softball team. Each line has data arranged as follows:

```
4 Jessie Joybat 5 2 1 1
```

The first item is the player's number, conveniently in the range 0–18. The second item is the player's first name, and the third is the player's last name. Each name is a single word. The next item is the player's official times at bat, followed by the number of hits, walks, and runs batted in (RBIs). The file may contain data for more than one game, so the same player may have more than one line of data, and there may be data for other players between those lines. Write a program that stores the data into an array of structures. The structure should have members to represent the first and last names, the at bats, hits, walks, and RBIs (runs batted in), and the batting average (to be calculated later). You can use the player number as an array index. The program should read to end-of-file, and it should keep cumulative totals for each player.

The world of baseball statistics is an involved one. For example, a walk or reaching base on an error doesn't count as an at-bat but could possibly produce an RBI. But all this program has to do is read and process the data file, as described next, without worrying about how realistic the data is.

The simplest way for the program to proceed is to initialize the structure contents to zeros, read the file data into temporary variables, and then add them to the contents of the corresponding structure. After the program has finished reading the file, it should then calculate the batting average for each player and store it in the corresponding structure member. The batting average is calculated by dividing the cumulative number of hits for a player by the cumulative number of at-bats; it should be a floating-point calculation. The program should then display the cumulative data for each player along with a line showing the combined statistics for the entire team.

7. Modify Listing 14.14 so that as each record is read from the file and shown to you, you are given the chance to delete the record or to modify its contents. If you delete the record, use the vacated array position for the next record to be read. To allow changing the existing contents, you'll need to use the "r+b" mode instead of the "a+b" mode, and you'll have to pay more attention to positioning the file pointer so that appended records don't overwrite existing records. It's simplest to make all changes in the data stored in program memory and then write the final set of information to the file.

8. The Colossus Airlines fleet consists of one plane with a seating capacity of 12. It makes one flight daily. Write a seating reservation program with the following features:

   a. The program uses an array of 12 structures. Each structure should hold a seat identification number, a marker that indicates whether the seat is assigned, the last name of the seat holder, and the first name of the seat holder.

   b. The program displays the following menu:

   ```
   To choose a function, enter its letter label:
   a) Show number of empty seats
   b) Show list of empty seats
   c) Show alphabetical list of seats
   d) Assign a customer to a seat assignment
   e) Delete a seat assignment
   f) Quit
   ```

   c. The program successfully executes the promises of its menu. Choices d) and e) require additional input, and each should enable the user to abort an entry.

   d. After executing a particular function, the program shows the menu again, except for choice f).

   e. Data is saved in a file between runs. When the program is restarted, it first loads in the data, if any, from the file.

9. Colossus Airlines (from exercise 8) acquires a second plane (same capacity) and expands its service to four flights daily (Flights 102, 311, 444, and 519). Expand the program to handle four flights. Have a top-level menu that offers a choice of flights and the option to quit. Selecting a particular flight should then bring up a menu similar to that of exercise 8. However, one new item should be added: confirming a seat assignment. Also, the quit choice should be replaced with the choice of exiting to the top-level menu. Each display should indicate which flight is currently being handled. Also, the seat assignment display should indicate the confirmation status.

10. Write a program that implements a menu by using an array of pointers to functions. For instance, choosing **a** from the menu would activate the function pointed to by the first element of the array.

11. Write a function called `transform()` that takes four arguments: the name of a source array containing type `double` data, the name of a target array of type `double`, an `int` representing the number of array elements, and the name of a function (or, equivalently, a pointer to a function). The `transform()` function should apply the indicated function to each element in the source array, placing the return value in the target array. For example, the call

```
transform(source, target, 100, sin);
```

would set `target[0]` to `sin(source[0])`, and so on, for 100 elements. Test the function in a program that calls `transform()` four times, using two functions from the `math.h` library and two suitable functions of your own devising as arguments to successive calls of the `transform()` function.

## CHAPTER 15

BIT FIDDLING

You will learn about the following in this chapter:

- Operators:

  ~ & |^

  >> <<

  &= |= ^= >>= <<=

- Binary, octal, and hexadecimal number notations (a review)

- Two C facilities for handling the individual bits in a value: bitwise operators and bit fields

W ith C, you can manipulate the individual bits in a variable. Perhaps you are wondering why anyone would want to. Be assured that sometimes this ability is necessary, or at least useful. For example, a hardware device is often controlled by sending it a byte or two in which each bit has a particular meaning. Also, operating system information about files is often stored by using particular bits to indicate particular items. Many compression and encryption operations manipulate individual bits. High-level languages generally don't deal with this level of detail; C's ability to provide high-level language facilities while also being able to work at a level typically reserved for assembly language makes it a preferred language for writing device drivers and embedded code.

We'll investigate C's bit powers in this chapter after we supply you with some background about bits, bytes, binary notation, and other number bases.

Binary Numbers, Bits, and Bytes

The usual way to write numbers is based on the number 10. For example, 2157 has a 2 in the thousands place, a 1 in the hundreds place, a 5 in the tens place, and a 7 in the ones place. This means you can think of 2157 as being the following:

```
2 x 1000 + 1 x 100 + 5 x 10 + 7 x 1
```

However, 1000 is 10 cubed, 100 is 10 squared, 10 is 10 to the first power, and, by convention, 1 is 10 (or any positive number) to the zero power. Therefore, you can also write 2157 as this:

```
2 x 10³ + 1 x 10² + 5 x 10¹ + 7 x 10⁰
```

Because our system of writing numbers is based on powers of 10, we say that 2157 is written in *base 10*.

Presumably, the decimal system evolved because we have 10 fingers. A computer bit, in a sense, has only two fingers because it can be set only to 0 or 1, off or on. Therefore, a *base 2* system is natural for a computer. It uses powers of two instead of powers of 10. Numbers expressed in base 2 are termed *binary numbers*. The number 2 plays the same role for binary numbers that the number 10 does for base 10 numbers. For example, a binary number such as 1101 mean this:

$1 \times 2^3 + 1 \times 2^2 + 0 \times 2^1 + 1 \times 20$

In decimal numbers, it becomes this:

$1 \times 8 + 1 \times 4 + 0 \times 2 + 1 \times 1 = 13$

You can use the binary system to express any integer (if you have enough bits) as a combination of 1s and 0s. This system is very convenient for digital computers, which express information in combinations of on and off states that can be interpreted as 1s and 0s. Let's see how the binary system works for a 1-byte integer.

Binary Integers

Usually, a byte contains 8 bits. C, remember, uses the term *byte* to denote the size used to hold a system's character set, so a C byte could be 8 bits, 9 bits, 16 bits, or some other value. However, the 8-bit byte is the byte used to describe memory chips and the byte used to describe data transfer rates. To keep matters simple, this chapter assumes an 8-bit byte. You can think of these 8 bits as being numbered from 7 to 0, left to right. Bit 7 is called the *high-order bit*, and bit 0 is the *low-order bit* in the byte. Each bit number corresponds to a particular exponent of 2. Imagine the byte as looking like Figure 15.1.

FIGURE 15.1

Bit numbers and bit values.

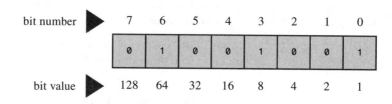

This example shows bits 6, 3, and 0 set to 1.
The value of this byte is 64 + 8 + 1 or 73.

Here, 128 is 2 to the 7th power, and so on. The largest number this byte can hold is 1, with all bits set to 1: 11111111. The value of this binary number is as follows:

$128 + 64 + 32 + 16 + 8 + 4 + 2 + 1 = 255$

The smallest binary number would be 00000000, or a simple 0. A byte can store numbers from 0 to 255, for a total of 256 possible values. Or, by interpreting the bit pattern differently, a program can use a byte to store numbers from −128 to +127, again a total of 256 values. For example, `unsigned char` typically uses a byte to represent the 0-to-255 range, whereas `signed char` typically uses a byte to represent the –128 to +127 range.

Signed Integers

The representation of signed numbers is determined by the hardware, not by C. Probably the simplest way to represent signed numbers is to reserve 1 bit, such as the high-order bit, to represent the sign. In a 1-byte value, this leaves 7 bits for the number itself. In such a *sign-magnitude* representation, 10000001 is –1 and 00000001 is 1. The total range, then, is –127 to +127.

One disadvantage of this approach is that it has two zeros: +0 and –0. This is confusing, and it also uses up two bit patterns for just one value.

The *two's-complement* method avoids that problem and is the most common system used today. We'll discuss this method as it applies to a 1-byte value. In that context, the values 0 through 127 are represented by the last 7 bits, with the high-order bit set to 0. So far, that's the same as the sign-magnitude method. Also, if the high-order bit is 1, the value is negative. The difference comes in determining the value of that negative number. Subtract the bit-pattern for a negative number from the 9-bit pattern 100000000 (256 expressed in binary), and the result is the magnitude of value. For example, suppose the pattern is 10000000. As an unsigned byte, it would be 128. As a signed value, it is negative (bit 7 is 1) and has a value of 100000000–10000000, or 10000000 (128). Therefore, the number is –128. (It would have been –0 in the sign-magnitude system.) Similarly, 10000001 is –127, and 11111111 is –1. The method represents numbers in the range –128 to +127.

The simplest method for reversing the sign of a two's-complement binary number is to invert each bit (convert 0s to 1s and 1s to 0s) and then add 1. Because 1 is 00000001, –1 is 11111110 + 1, or 11111111, just as you saw earlier.

The *one's-complement* method forms the negative of a number by inverting each bit in the pattern. For instance, 00000001 is 1 and 11111110 is –1. This method also has a –0: 11111111. Its range (for a 1-byte value) is –127 to +127.

Binary Floating Point

Floating-point numbers are stored in two parts: a binary fraction and a binary exponent. Let's see how this is done.

Binary Fractions

The ordinary fraction 0.527 represents

`5/10 + 2/100 + 7/1000`

with the denominators representing increasing powers of 10. In a binary fraction, you use powers of two for denominators, so the binary fraction .101 represents

`1/2 + 0/4 + 1/8`

which in decimal notation is

`0.50 + 0.00 + 0.125`

or 0.625.

Many fractions, such as 1/3, cannot be represented exactly in decimal notation. Similarly, many fractions cannot be represented exactly in binary notation. Indeed, the only fractions that can be represented exactly are combinations of multiples of powers of 1/2. Therefore, 3/4 and 7/8 can be represented exactly as binary fractions, but 1/3 and 2/5 cannot be.

Floating-Point Representation

To represent a floating-point number in a computer, a certain number of bits (depending on the system) are set aside to hold a binary fraction. Additional bits hold an exponent. In general terms, the actual value of the number consists of the binary fraction times 2 to the indicated exponent. Multiplying a floating-point number by, say, 4, increases the exponent by 2 and leaves the binary fraction unchanged. Multiplying by a number that is not a power of 2 changes the binary fraction and, if necessary, the exponent.

Other Number Bases

Computer workers often use number systems based on 8 and on 16. Because 8 and 16 are powers of 2, these systems are more closely related to a computer's binary system than the decimal system is.

Octal

Octal refers to a base 8 system. In this system, the different places in a number represent powers of 8. You use the digits 0 to 7. For example, the octal number 451 (written 0451 in C) represents this:

`4 x 8² + 5 x 8¹ + 1 x 8⁰ = 297 (base 10)`

A handy thing to know about octal is that each octal digit corresponds to three binary digits. Table 15.1 shows the correspondence. This correspondence makes it simple to translate between the two systems. For example, the octal number 0377 is 11111111 in binary. We replaced the 3 with 011, dropped the leading 0, and then replaced each 7 with 111. The only awkward part is that a 3-digit octal number might take up to 9 bits in binary form, so an octal value larger than 0377 requires more than a byte. Note that internal 0s are not dropped: 0173 is 01 111 011, not 01 111 11.

TABLE 15.1   Binary Equivalents for Octal Digits

Octal Digit	Binary Equivalent
0	000
1	001
2	010
3	011
4	100
5	101
6	110
7	111

Hexadecimal

Hexadecimal (or *hex*) refers to a base 16 system. It uses powers of 16 and the digits 0 to 15, but because base 10 doesn't have single digits to represent the values 10 to 15, hexadecimal uses the letters A to F for that purpose. For instance, the hex number A3F (written 0xA3F in C) represents

```
10 x 16² + 3 x 16¹ + 15 x 16⁰ = 2623 (base 10)
```

because A represents 10 and F represents 15. In C, you can use either lowercase or uppercase letters for the additional hex digits. Therefore, you can also write 2623 as `0xa3f`.

Each hexadecimal digit corresponds to a 4-digit binary number, so two hexadecimal digits correspond exactly to an 8-bit byte. The first digit represents the upper 4 bits, and the second digit the last 4 bits. This makes hexadecimal a natural choice for representing byte values. Table 15.2 shows the correspondence. For example, the hex value 0xC2 translates to 11000010. Going the other direction, the binary value 11010101 can be viewed as 1101 0101, which translates to 0xD5.

TABLE 15.2   Decimal, Hexadecimal, and Binary Equivalents

Decimal Digit	Hexadecimal Digit	Binary Equivalent	Decimal Digit	Hexadecimal Digit	Binary Equivalent
0	0	0000	8	8	1000
1	1	0001	9	9	1001
2	2	0010	10	A	1010

TABLE 15.2   Continued

Decimal Digit	Hexadecimal Digit	Binary Equivalent	Decimal Digit	Hexadecimal Digit	Binary Equivalent
3	3	0011	11	B	1011
4	4	0100	12	C	1100
5	5	0101	13	D	1101
6	6	0110	14	E	1110
7	7	0111	15	F	1111

Now that you've seen what bits and bytes are, let's examine what C can do with them. C has two facilities to help you manipulate bits. The first is a set of six bitwise operators that act on bits. The second is the *field* data form, which gives you access to bits within an int. The following discussion outlines these C features.

C's Bitwise Operators

C offers bitwise logical operators and shift operators. In the following examples, we will write out values in binary notation so that you can see what happens to the bits. In an actual program, you would use integer variables or constants written in the usual forms. For example, instead of **00011001**, you would use **25** or **031** or **0x19**. For our examples, we will use 8-bit numbers, with the bits numbered 7 to 0, left to right.

Bitwise Logical Operators

The four bitwise logical operators work on integer-type data, including `char`. They are called *bitwise* because they operate on each bit independently of the bit to the left or right. Don't confuse them with the regular logical operators (`&&`, `||`, and `!`), which operate on values as a whole.

One's Complement, or Bitwise Negation: ~

The unary operator ~ changes each 1 to a 0 and each 0 to a 1, as in the following example:

```
~(10011010)  // expression
 (01100101)  // resulting value
```

Suppose that `val` is an `unsigned char` assigned the value 2. In binary, 2 is **00000010**. Then `~val` has the value **11111101**, or 253. Note that the operator does not change the value of `val`, just as **3 * val** does not change the value of `val`; `val` is still **2**, but it does create a new value that can be used or assigned elsewhere:

```
newval = ~val;
printf("%d", ~val);
```

If you want to change the value of `val` to `~val`, use this simple assignment:

```
val = ~val;
```

Bitwise AND: &

The binary operator `&` produces a new value by making a bit-by-bit comparison between two operands. For each bit position, the resulting bit is 1 only if both corresponding bits in the operands are 1. (In terms of true/false, the result is true only if each of the two bit operands is true.) Therefore, the expression

```
(10010011) & (00111101)  // expression
```

evaluates to the following value:

```
(00010001)               // resulting value
```

The reason is that only bits 4 and 0 are 1 in both operands.

C also has a combined bitwise AND-assignment operator: `&=`. The statement

```
val &= 0377;
```

produces the same final result as the following:

```
val = val & 0377;
```

Bitwise OR: |

The binary operator `|` produces a new value by making a bit-by-bit comparison between two operands. For each bit position, the resulting bit is 1 if either of the corresponding bits in the operands is 1. (In terms of true/false, the result is true if one or the other bit operands are true or if both are true.) Therefore, the expression

```
(10010011) | (00111101)  // expression
```

evaluates to the following value:

```
(10111111)               // resulting value
```

The reason is that all bit positions but bit 6 have the value 1 in one or the other operand (or both).

C also has a combined bitwise OR-assignment operator: `|=`. The statement

```
val |= 0377;
```

produces the same final result as this:

```
val = val | 0377;
```

Bitwise EXCLUSIVE OR: ^

The binary operator `^` makes a bit-by-bit comparison between two operands. For each bit position, the resulting bit is 1 if one or the other (but not both) of the corresponding bits in the operands is 1. (In terms of true/false, the result is true if one or the other bit operands—but not both— is true.) Therefore, the expression

```
(10010011) ^ (00111101)  // expression
```

evaluates the following:

```
(10101110)               // resulting value
```

Note that because bit position 0 has the value 1 in both operands, the resulting 0 bit has value 0.

C also has a combined bitwise OR-assignment operator: ^=. The statement

```
val ^= 0377;
```

produces the same final result as this:

```
val = val ^ 0377;
```

Usage: Masks

The bitwise AND operator is often used with a mask. A *mask* is a bit pattern with some bits set to on (1) and some bits to off (0). To see why a mask is called a mask, let's see what happens when a quantity is combined with a mask by using &. For example, suppose you define the symbolic constant MASK as 2 (that is, binary 00000010), with only bit number 1 being nonzero. Then the statement

```
flags = flags & MASK;
```

would cause all the bits of flags (except bit 1) to be set to 0 because any bit combined with 0 using the & operator yields 0. Bit number 1 will be left unchanged. (If the bit is 1, 1 & 1 is 1; if the bit is 0, 0 & 1 is 0.) This process is called "using a mask" because the zeros in the mask hide the corresponding bits in flags.

Extending the analogy, you can think of the 0s in the mask as being opaque and the 1s as being transparent. The expression flags & MASK is like covering the flags bit pattern with the mask; only the bits under MASK's 1s are visible (see Figure 15.2).

FIGURE 15.2
A mask.

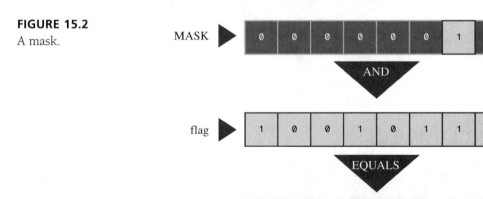

You can shorten the code by using the AND-assignment operator, as shown here:

```
flags &= MASK;
```

One common C usage is this statement:

```
ch &= 0xff;   /* or ch &= 0377; */
```

The value `0xff`, recall, is `11111111` in binary, as is the value `0377`. This mask leaves the final 8 bits of `ch` alone and sets the rest to 0. Regardless of whether the original `ch` is 8 bits, 16 bits, or more, the final value is trimmed to something that fits into a single byte. In this case, the mask is 8 bits wide.

Usage: Turning Bits On

Sometimes you might need to turn on particular bits in a value while leaving the remaining bits unchanged. For instance, an IBM PC controls hardware through values sent to ports. To turn on, say, the speaker, you might have to turn on the 1 bit while leaving the others unchanged. You can do this with the bitwise OR operator.

For example, consider the `MASK`, which has bit 1 set to 1. The statement

```
flags = flags | MASK;
```

sets bit number 1 in `flags` to 1 and leaves all the other bits unchanged. This follows because any bit combined with 0 by using the | operator is itself, and any bit combined with 1 by using the | operator is 1.

For short, you can use the bitwise OR-assignment operator:

```
flags |= MASK;
```

This, too, sets to 1 those bits in `flags` that are also on in `MASK`, leaving the other bits unchanged.

Usage: Turning Bits Off

Just as it's useful to be able to turn on particular bits without disturbing the other bits, it's useful to be able to turn them off. Suppose you want to turn off bit 1 in the variable `flags`. Once again, `MASK` has only the 1 bit turned on. You can do this:

```
flags = flags & ~MASK;
```

Because `MASK` is all 0s except for bit 1, `~MASK` is all 1s except for bit 1. A 1 combined with any bit using & is that bit, so the statement leaves all the bits other than bit 1 unchanged. Also, a 0 combined with any bit using & is 0, so bit 1 is set to 0 regardless of its original value.

You can use this short form instead:

```
flags &= ~MASK;
```

Usage: Toggling Bits

Toggling a bit means turning it off if it is on, and turning it on if it is off. You can use the bit-wise EXCLUSIVE OR operator to toggle a bit. The idea is that if **b** is a bit setting (1 or 0), then 1 ^ **b** is **0** if **b** is **1** and is **1** if **b** is **0**. Also **0** ^ **b** is **b**, regardless of its value. Therefore, if you combine a value with a mask by using ^, values corresponding to 1s in the mask are toggled, and values corresponding to 0s in the mask are unaltered. To toggle bit 1 in **flag**, you can do either of the following:

```
flag = flag ^ MASK;
flag ^= MASK;
```

Usage: Checking the Value of a Bit

You've seen how to change the values of bits. Suppose, instead, that you want to check the value of a bit. For example, does **flag** have bit 1 set to 1? You shouldn't simply compare **flag** to MASK:

```
if (flag == MASK)
  puts("Wow!");    /* doesn't work right */
```

Even if bit 1 in **flag** is set to 1, the other bit setting in **flag** can make the comparison untrue. Instead, you must first mask the other bits in **flag** so that you compare only bit 1 of **flag** with MASK:

```
if ((flag & MASK) == MASK)
  puts("Wow!");
```

The bitwise operators have lower precedence than ==, so the parentheses around **flag & MASK** are needed.

To avoid information peeking around the edges, a bit mask should be at least as wide as the value it's masking.

Bitwise Shift Operators

Now let's look at C's shift operators. The bitwise shift operators shift bits to the left or right. Again, we will write binary numbers explicitly to show the mechanics.

Left Shift: <<

The left shift operator (<<) shifts the bits of the value of the left operand to the left by the number of places given by the right operand. The vacated positions are filled with 0s, and bits moved past the end of the left operand are lost. In the following example, then, each bit is moved two places to the left:

```
(10001010) << 2  // expression
(00101000)       // resulting value
```

This operation produces a new bit value, but it doesn't change its operands. For example, suppose `stonk` is 1. Then `stonk<<2` is 4, but `stonk` is still 1. You can use the left-shift assignment operator (`<<=`) to actually change a variable's value. This operator shifts the bit in the variable to its left by the number of places given by the right-hand value. Here's an example:

```
int stonk = 1;
int onkoo;
onkoo = stonk << 2;    /* assigns 4 to onkoo */
stonk <<= 2;           /* changes stonk to 4 */
```

Right Shift: >>

The right shift operator (`>>`) shifts the bits of the value of the left operand to the right by the number of places given by the right operand. Bits moved past the right end of the left operand are lost. For `unsigned` types, the places vacated at the left end are replaced by 0s. For signed types, the result is machine dependent. The vacated places may be filled with 0s, or they may be filled with copies of the sign (leftmost) bit:

```
(10001010) >> 2  // expression, signed value
(00100010)       // resulting value, some systems
(10001010) >> 2  // expression, signed value
(11100010)       // resulting value, other systems
```

For an unsigned value, you have the following:

```
(10001010) >> 2  // expression, unsigned value
(00100010)       // resulting value, all system
```

Each bit is moved two places to the right, and the vacated places are filled with 0s.

The right-shift assignment operator (`>>=`) shifts the bits in the left-hand variable to the right by the indicated number of places, as shown here:

```
int sweet = 16;
int ooosw;

ooosw = sweet >> 3;    /* ooosw = 2, sweet still 16 */
sweet >>=3;            /* sweet changed to 2          */
```

Usage: Bitwise Shift Operators

The bitwise shift operators can provide swift, efficient (depending on the hardware) multiplication and division by powers of 2:

number << n	Multiplies number by 2 to the nth power
number >> n	Divides number by 2 to the nth power if number is not negative

These shift operations are analogous to the decimal system procedure of shifting the decimal point to multiply or divide by 10.

The shift operators can also be used to extract groups of bits from larger units. Suppose, for example, you use an unsigned long value to represent color values, with the low-order byte holding the red intensity, the next byte holding the green intensity, and the third byte holding the blue intensity. Supposed you then wanted to store the intensity of each color in its own unsigned char variable. Then you could do something like this:

```
#define BYTE_MASK 0xff
unsigned long color = 0x002a162f;
unsigned char blue, green, red;
red = color & BYTE_MASK;
green = (color >> 8) & BYTE_MASK;
blue = (color >> 16) & BYTE_MASK;
```

The code uses the right-shift operator to move the 8-bit color value to the low-order byte, and then uses the mask technique to assign the low-order byte to the desired variable.

Programming Example

In Chapter 9, "Functions," we used recursion to write a program to convert numbers to a binary representation. Now we'll solve the same problem by using the bitwise operators. The program in Listing 15.1 reads an integer from the keyboard and passes it and a string address to a function called itobs() (for *integer-to-binary string*, of course). This function then uses the bitwise operators to figure out the correct pattern of 1s and 0s to put into the string.

LISTING 15.1   The binbit.c Program

```
/* binbit.c -- using bit operations to display binary */
#include <stdio.h>
char * itobs(int, char *);
void show_bstr(const char *);

int main(void)
{
    char bin_str[8 * sizeof(int) + 1];
    int number;

    puts("Enter integers and see them in binary.");
    puts("Non-numeric input terminates program.");
    while (scanf("%d", &number) == 1)
    {
        itobs(number,bin_str);
        printf("%d is ", number);
        show_bstr(bin_str);
        putchar('\n');
    }
    puts("Bye!");

    return 0;
}
```

LISTING 15.1   *Continued*

```
char * itobs(int n, char * ps)
{
    int i;
    static int size = 8 * sizeof(int);

    for (i = size - 1; i >= 0; i--, n >>= 1)
        ps[i] = (01 & n) + '0';
    ps[size] = '\0';

    return ps;
}

/* show binary string in blocks of 4 */
void show_bstr(const char * str)
{
    int i = 0;

    while (str[i])   /* not the null character */
    {
        putchar(str[i]);
        if(++i % 4 == 0 && str[i])
            putchar(' ');
    }
}
```

Listing 15.1 assumes that the system uses 8 bits to a byte. Therefore, the expression **8 * sizeof(int)** is the number of bits in an **int**. The **bin_str** array has that many elements plus 1 to allow for the terminating null character.

The **itobs()** function returns the same address passed to it, so you can use the function as, say, an argument to **printf()**. The first time through the **for** loop, the function evaluates the quantity **01 & n**. The term **01** is the octal representation of a mask with all but the zero bit set to 0. Therefore, **01 & n** is just the value of the final bit in **n**. This value is **0** or 1, but for the array, you need the *character* '**0**' or the *character* '**1**'. Adding the ASCII code for '**0**' accomplishes that conversion. The result is placed in the next-to-last element of the array. (The last element is reserved for the null character.)

By the way, you can just as well use **1 & n** as **01 & n**. Using octal 1 instead of decimal 1 just makes the mood a bit more computeresque.

Then the loop executes the statements **i--** and **n >>= 1**. The first statement moves to one element earlier in the array, and the second shifts the bits in **n** over one position to the right. The next time through the loop, then, the code finds the value of the new rightmost bit. The corresponding digit character is then placed in the element preceding the final digit. In this fashion, the function fills the array from right to left.

You can use **printf()** or **puts()** to display the resulting string, but Listing 15.1 defines the **show_bstr()** function, which breaks up the bits into groups of four to make the string easier to read.

Here is a sample run:

```
Enter integers and see them in binary.
Non-numeric input terminates program.
7
7 is 0000 0000 0000 0000 0000 0000 0000 0111
2005
2005 is 0000 0000 0000 0000 0000 0111 1101 0101
-1
-1 is 1111 1111 1111 1111 1111 1111 1111 1111
32123
32123 is 0000 0000 0000 0000 0111 1101 0111 1011
q
Bye!
```

Another Example

Let's work through one more example. The goal this time is to write a function that inverts the last n bits in a value, with both n and the value being function arguments.

The ~ operator inverts bits, but it inverts all the bits in a byte, not just a select few. However, the ^ operator (EXCLUSIVE OR), as you have seen, can be used to toggle individual bits. Suppose you create a mask with the last n bits set to 1 and the remaining bits set to 0. Then applying ^ to that mask and a value toggles, or *inverts*, the last n bits, leaving the other bits unchanged. That's the approach used here:

```c
int invert_end(int num, int bits)
{
    int mask = 0;
    int bitval = 1;

    while (bits-- > 0)
    {
        mask |= bitval;
        bitval <<= 1;
    }
    return num ^ mask;
}
```

The while loop creates the mask. Initially, mask has all its bits set to 0. The first pass through the loop sets bit 0 to 1 and then increases the value of bitval to 2; that is, it sets bit 0 to 0 and bit 1 to 1. The next pass through then sets bit 1 of mask to 1, and so on. Finally, the num ^ mask operation produces the desired result.

To test the function, you can slip it into the preceding program, as shown in Listing 15.2.

LISTING 15.2   The invert4.c Program

```c
/* invert4.c -- using bit operations to display binary */
#include <stdio.h>
char * itobs(int, char *);
void show_bstr(const char *);
```

LISTING 15.2   Continued

```c
int invert_end(int num, int bits);

int main(void)
{
    char bin_str[8 * sizeof(int) + 1];
    int number;

    puts("Enter integers and see them in binary.");
    puts("Non-numeric input terminates program.");
    while (scanf("%d", &number) == 1)
    {
        itobs(number,bin_str);
        printf("%d is\n", number);
        show_bstr(bin_str);
        putchar('\n');
        number = invert_end(number, 4);
        printf("Inverting the last 4 bits gives\n");
        show_bstr(itobs(number,bin_str));
        putchar('\n');
    }
    puts("Bye!");

    return 0;
}

char * itobs(int n, char * ps)
{
    int i;
    static int size = 8 * sizeof(int);

    for (i = size - 1; i >= 0; i--, n >>= 1)
        ps[i] = (01 & n) + '0';
    ps[size] = '\0';

    return ps;
}

/* show binary string in blocks of 4 */
void show_bstr(const char * str)
{
    int i = 0;

    while (str[i])   /* not the null character */
    {
        putchar(str[i]);
        if(++i % 4 == 0 && str[i])
            putchar(' ');
    }
}

int invert_end(int num, int bits)
{
```

LISTING 15.2   *Continued*

```
        int mask = 0;
        int bitval = 1;

        while (bits-- > 0)
        {
            mask |= bitval;
            bitval <<= 1;
        }

        return num ^ mask;
}
```

Here's a sample run:

```
Enter integers and see them in binary.
Non-numeric input terminates program.
7
7 is
0000 0000 0000 0000 0000 0000 0000 0111
Inverting the last 4 bits gives
0000 0000 0000 0000 0000 0000 0000 1000
12541
12541 is
0000 0000 0000 0000 0011 0000 1111 1101
Inverting the last 4 bits gives
0000 0000 0000 0000 0011 0000 1111 0010
q
Bye!
```

Bit Fields

The second method of manipulating bits is to use a *bit field*, which is just a set of neighboring bits within a `signed int` or an `unsigned int`. (C99 additionally allows type `_Bool` bit fields.) A bit field is set up with a structure declaration that labels each field and determines its width. For example, the following declaration sets up four 1-bit fields:

```
struct   {
    unsigned int autfd    : 1;
    unsigned int bldfc    : 1;
    unsigned int undln    : 1;
    unsigned int itals    : 1;
} prnt;
```

This definition causes `prnt` to contain four 1-bit fields. Now you can use the usual structure membership operator to assign values to individual fields:

```
prnt.itals = 0;
prnt.undln = 1;
```

Because each of these particular fields is just 1 bit, 1 and 0 are the only values you can use for assignment. The variable `prnt` is stored in an `int`-sized memory cell, but only 4 bits are used in this example.

Structures with bit fields provide a handy way to keep track of settings. Many settings, such as boldface and italics for fonts, are simply a matter specifying one of two choices, such as on or off, yes or no, or true or false. There's no need to use a whole variable when all you need is a single bit. A structure with bit fields allows you to store several settings in a single unit.

Sometimes there are more than two choices for a setting, so you need more than a single bit to represent all the choices. That's not a problem because fields aren't limited to 1-bit sizes. You can also do this:

```
struct {
    unsigned int code1 : 2;
    unsigned int code2 : 2;
    unsigned int code3 : 8;
} prcode;
```

This code creates two 2-bit fields and one 8-bit field. You can now make assignments such as the following:

```
prcode.code1 = 0;
prcode.code2 = 3;
prcode.code3 = 102;
```

Just make sure the value doesn't exceed the capacity of the field.

What if the total number of bits you declare exceeds the size of an `unsigned int`? Then the next `unsigned int` storage location is used. A single field is not allowed to overlap the boundary between two `unsigned int`s. The compiler automatically shifts an overlapping field definition so that the field is aligned with the `unsigned int` boundary. When this occurs, it leaves an unnamed hole in the first `unsigned int`.

You can "pad" a field structure with unnamed holes by using unnamed field widths. Using an unnamed field width of 0 forces the next field to align with the next integer:

```
struct {
    unsigned int field1 : 1;
    unsigned int        : 2;
    unsigned int field2 : 1;
    unsigned int        : 0;
    unsigned int field3 : 1;
} stuff;
```

Here, there is a 2-bit gap between `stuff.field1` and `stuff.field2`, and `stuff.field3` is stored in the next `int`.

One important machine dependency is the order in which fields are placed into an `int`. On some machines, the order is left to right; on others, it is right to left. Also, machines differ in the location of boundaries between fields. For these reasons, bit fields tend not to be very portable. Typically, however, they are used for nonportable purposes, such as putting data in the exact form used by a particular hardware device.

Bit-Field Example

Often bit fields are used as a more compact way of storing data. Suppose, for example, you decided to represent the properties of an onscreen box. Let's keep the graphics simple and suppose the box has the following properties:

- The box is opaque or transparent.
- The fill color is selected from the following palette of colors: black, red, green, yellow, blue, magenta, cyan, or white.
- The border can be shown or hidden.
- The border color is selected from the same palette used for the fill color.
- The border can use one of three line styles—solid, dotted, or dashed.

You could use a separate variable or a full-sized structure member for each property, but that is a bit wasteful of bits. For example, you need only a single bit to indicate whether the box is opaque or transparent, and you need only a single bit to indicate if the border is shown or hidden. The eight possible color values can be represented by the eight possible values of a 3-bit unit, and a 2-bit unit is more than enough to represent the three possible border styles. A total of 10 bits, then, is enough to represent the possible settings for all five properties.

One possible representation of the information is to use padding to place the fill-related information in one byte and the border-related information in a second byte. The `struct box_props` declaration does this:

```
struct box_props {
    unsigned int opaque          : 1;
    unsigned int fill_color      : 3;
    unsigned int                 : 4;
    unsigned int show_border     : 1;
    unsigned int border_color    : 3;
    unsigned int border_style    : 2;
    unsigned int                 : 2;
};
```

The padding brings the structure up to 16 bits. Without padding, the structure would be 10 bits. Keep in mind, however, that C uses `unsigned int` as the basic layout unit for structures with bit fields. So even if the sole member of a structure is a single 1-bit field, the structure will have the same size as an `unsigned int`, which is 32 bits on our system.

You can use a value of `1` for the `opaque` member to indicate that the box is opaque and a `0` value to indicate transparency. You can do the same for the `show_border` member. For colors, you can use a simple RGB (red-green-blue) representation. These are the primary colors for mixing light. A monitor blends red, green, and blue pixels to reproduce different colors. In the early days of computer color, each pixel could be either on or off, so you could use one bit to represent the intensity of each of the three binary colors. The usual order is for the left bit to represent blue intensity, the middle bit green intensity, and the right bit red intensity. Table 15.3 shows the eight possible combinations. They can be used as values for the `fill_color` and `border_color` members. Finally, you can choose to let 0, 1, and 2 represent the solid, dotted, and dashed styles; they can be used as values for the `border_style` member.

TABLE 15.3 Simple Color Representation

Bit Pattern	Decimal	Color
000	0	Black
001	1	Red
010	2	Green
011	3	Yellow
100	4	Blue
101	5	Magenta
110	6	Cyan
111	7	White

Listing 15.3 uses the `box_props` structure in a simple example. It uses `#define` to create symbolic constants for the possible member values. Note that the primary colors are represented by a single bit being on. The other colors can be represented by combinations of the primary colors. For example, magenta consists of the blue bit and the red bit being on, so it can be represented by the combination `BLUE | RED`.

LISTING 15.3 The `fields.c` Program

```
/* fields.c -- define and use fields */
#include <stdio.h>
/* opaque and show */
#define YES      1
#define NO       0
/* line styles     */
#define SOLID    0
#define DOTTED   1
#define DASHED   2
/* primary colors  */
#define BLUE     4
#define GREEN    2
#define RED      1
/* mixed colors    */
#define BLACK    0
#define YELLOW   (RED | GREEN)
#define MAGENTA  (RED | BLUE)
#define CYAN     (GREEN | BLUE)
#define WHITE    (RED | GREEN | BLUE)
```

LISTING 15.3   *Continued*

```c
const char * colors[8] = {"black", "red", "green", "yellow",
            "blue", "magenta", "cyan", "white"};

struct box_props {
    unsigned int opaque        : 1;
    unsigned int fill_color    : 3;
    unsigned int               : 4;
    unsigned int show_border   : 1;
    unsigned int border_color  : 3;
    unsigned int border_style  : 2;
    unsigned int               : 2;
};

void show_settings(const struct box_props * pb);

int main(void)
{
    /* create and initialize box_props structure */
    struct box_props box = {YES, YELLOW , YES, GREEN, DASHED};

    printf("Original box settings:\n");
    show_settings(&box);

    box.opaque = NO;
    box.fill_color = WHITE;
    box.border_color = MAGENTA;
    box.border_style = SOLID;
    printf("\nModified box settings:\n");
    show_settings(&box);

    return 0;
}

void show_settings(const struct box_props * pb)
{
    printf("Box is %s.\n",
            pb->opaque == YES? "opaque": "transparent");
    printf("The fill color is %s.\n", colors[pb->fill_color]);
    printf("Border %s.\n",
            pb->show_border == YES? "shown" : "not shown");
    printf("The border color is %s.\n", colors[pb->border_color]);
    printf ("The border style is ");
    switch(pb->border_style)
    {
        case SOLID  : printf("solid.\n"); break;
        case DOTTED : printf("dotted.\n"); break;
        case DASHED : printf("dashed.\n"); break;
        default     : printf("unknown type.\n");
    }
}
```

Here is the output:

```
Original box settings:
Box is opaque.
The fill color is yellow.
Border shown.
The border color is green.
The border style is dashed.

Modified box settings:
Box is transparent.
The fill color is white.
Border shown.
The border color is magenta.
The border style is solid.
```

There are some points to note. First, you can initialize a bit-field structure by using the same syntax regular structures use:

```
struct box_props box = {YES, YELLOW , YES, GREEN, DASHED};
```

Similarly, you can assign to bit-field members:

```
box.fill_color = WHITE;
```

Also, you can use a bit-field member as the value expression for a `switch` statement. You can even use a bit-field member as an array index:

```
printf("The fill color is %s.\n", colors[pb->fill_color]);
```

Notice that the `colors` array was defined so that each index value corresponds to a string representing the name of the color having the index value as its numeric color value. For example, an index of 1 corresponds to the string `"red"`, and the enumeration constant `red` has the value of 1.

Bit Fields and Bitwise Operators

Bit fields and bitwise operators are two alternative approaches to the same type of programming problem. That is, often you could use either approach. For instance, the previous example used a structure the same size as `unsigned int` to hold information about a graphics box. Instead, you could use an `unsigned int` variable to hold the same information. Then, instead of using structure member notation to access different parts, you could use the bitwise operators for that purpose. Typically, this is a bit more awkward to do. Let's look at an example that takes both approaches. (The reason for taking both approaches is to illustrate the differences, not to suggest that taking both approaches simultaneously is a good idea!)

You can use a union as a means of combining the structure approach with the bitwise approach. Given the existing declaration of the `struct box_props` type, you can declare the following union:

```
union Views      /* look at data as struct or as unsigned short */
{
    struct box_props st_view;
```

```
     unsigned int      ui_view;
};
```

On some systems, an `unsigned int` and a `box_props` structure both occupy 16 bits of memory. On others, such as ours, `unsigned int` and `box_props` are 32 bits. In either case, with this union, you can use the `st_view` member to look at that memory as a structure or use the `sh_view` member to look at the same block of memory as an `unsigned int`. Which bit fields of the structure correspond to which bits in the `unsigned int`? That depends on the implementation and the hardware. On an IBM PC using Microsoft Visual C/C++ 7.1, structures are loaded into memory from the low-bit end to the high-bit end of a byte. That is, the first bit field in the structure goes into bit 0 of the word. (For simplicity, Figure 15.3 illustrates this idea with a 16-bit unit.)

FIGURE 15.3

A union as an integer and as a structure.

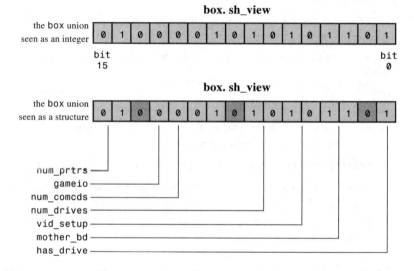

Listing 15.4 uses the `Views` union to let you compare the bit field and bitwise approaches. In it, `box` is a `Views` union, so `box.st_view` is a `box_props` structure using bit fields, and `box.ui_view` is the same data viewed as an `unsigned int`. Recall that a union can have its first member initialized, so the initialization values match the structure view. The program displays box properties using a function based on the structure view and also with a function based on the `unsigned int` view. Either approach lets you access the data, but the techniques differ. The program also uses the `itobs()` function defined earlier in this chapter to display the data as a binary string so that you can see which bits are on and which are off.

LISTING 15.4   The `dualview.c` Program

```
/* dualview.c -- bit fields and bitwise operators */
#include <stdio.h>
/* BIT-FIELD CONSTANTS */
/* opaque and show */
```

LISTING 15.4   Continued

```
#define YES      1
#define NO       0
/* line styles    */
#define SOLID   0
#define DOTTED  1
#define DASHED  2
/* primary colors */
#define BLUE     4
#define GREEN    2
#define RED      1
/* mixed colors    */
#define BLACK    0
#define YELLOW  (RED | GREEN)
#define MAGENTA (RED | BLUE)
#define CYAN    (GREEN | BLUE)
#define WHITE   (RED | GREEN | BLUE)

/* BITWISE CONSTANTS   */
#define OPAQUE          0x1
#define FILL_BLUE       0x8
#define FILL_GREEN      0x4
#define FILL_RED        0x2
#define FILL_MASK       0xE
#define BORDER          0x100
#define BORDER_BLUE     0x800
#define BORDER_GREEN    0x400
#define BORDER_RED      0x200
#define BORDER_MASK     0xE00
#define B_SOLID         0
#define B_DOTTED        0x1000
#define B_DASHED        0x2000
#define STYLE_MASK      0x3000

const char * colors[8] = {"black", "red", "green", "yellow",
            "blue", "magenta", "cyan", "white"};
struct box_props {

    unsigned int opaque         : 1;
    unsigned int fill_color     : 3;
    unsigned int                : 4;
    unsigned int show_border    : 1;
    unsigned int border_color   : 3;
    unsigned int border_style   : 2;
    unsigned int                : 2;
  };

union Views     /* look at data as struct or as unsigned short */
{
    struct box_props st_view;
    unsigned int    ui_view;
};
```

LISTING 15.4   Continued

```
void show_settings(const struct box_props * pb);
void show_settings1(unsigned short);
char * itobs(unsigned int n, char * ps);

int main(void)
{
    /* create Views object, initialize struct box view */
    union Views box = {{YES, YELLOW , YES, GREEN, DASHED}};
    char bin_str[8 * sizeof(unsigned int) + 1];

    printf("Original box settings:\n");
    show_settings(&box.st_view);
    printf("\nBox settings using unsigned int view:\n");
    show_settings1(box.ui_view);

    printf("bits are %s\n",
        itobs(box.ui_view,bin_str));
    box.ui_view &= ~FILL_MASK;              /* clear fill bits */
    box.ui_view |= (FILL_BLUE | FILL_GREEN); /* reset fill */
    box.ui_view ^= OPAQUE;                  /* toggle opacity */
    box.ui_view |= BORDER_RED;              /* wrong approach */
    box.ui_view &= ~STYLE_MASK;             /* clear style bits */
    box.ui_view |= B_DOTTED;                /* set style to dotted*/
    printf("\nModified box settings:\n");
    show_settings(&box.st_view);
    printf("\nBox settings using unsigned int view:\n");
    show_settings1(box.ui_view);
    printf("bits are %s\n",
    itobs(box.ui_view,bin_str));

    return 0;
}

void show_settings(const struct box_props * pb)
{
    printf("Box is %s.\n",
            pb->opaque == YES? "opaque": "transparent");
    printf("The fill color is %s.\n", colors[pb->fill_color]);
    printf("Border %s.\n",
            pb->show_border == YES? "shown" : "not shown");
    printf("The border color is %s.\n", colors[pb->border_color]);
    printf ("The border style is ");
    switch(pb->border_style)
    {
        case SOLID  : printf("solid.\n"); break;
        case DOTTED : printf("dotted.\n"); break;
        case DASHED : printf("dashed.\n"); break;
        default     : printf("unknown type.\n");
    }
}
```

LISTING 15.4   Continued

```
void show_settings1(unsigned short us)
{
    printf("box is %s.\n",
            us & OPAQUE == OPAQUE? "opaque": "transparent");
    printf("The fill color is %s.\n",
            colors[(us >> 1) & 07]);
    printf("Border %s.\n",
            us & BORDER == BORDER? "shown" : "not shown");
    printf ("The border style is ");
    switch(us & STYLE_MASK)
    {
        case B_SOLID  : printf("solid.\n"); break;
        case B_DOTTED : printf("dotted.\n"); break;
        case B_DASHED : printf("dashed.\n"); break;
        default       : printf("unknown type.\n");
    }
    printf("The border color is %s.\n",
            colors[(us >> 9) & 07]);

}

/* convert int to binary string */
char * itobs(unsigned int n, char * ps)
{
    int i;
    static int size = 8 * sizeof(unsigned int);

    for (i = size - 1; i >= 0; i--, n >>= 1)
        ps[i] = (01 & n) + '0';
    ps[size] = '\0';

    return ps;
}
```

Here is the output:

```
Original box settings:
Box is opaque.
The fill color is yellow.
Border shown.
The border color is green.
The border style is dashed.

Box settings using unsigned int view:
box is opaque.
The fill color is yellow.
Border shown.
The border style is dashed.
The border color is green.
bits are 00000000000000000010010100000111
```

LISTING 15.4   *Continued*

```
Modified box settings:
Box is transparent.
The fill color is cyan.
Border shown.
The border color is yellow.
The border style is dotted.

Box settings using unsigned int view:
box is transparent.
The fill color is cyan.
Border not shown.
The border style is dotted.
The border color is yellow.
bits are 00000000000000000001011100001100
```

There are several points to discuss. One difference between the bit-field and bitwise views is that the bitwise view needs positional information. For example, we've used **BLUE** to represent the color blue. This constant has the numerical value of **4**. But, because of the way the data is arranged in the structure, the actual bit holding the blue setting for the fill color is bit 3 (remember, numbering starts at 0—refer to Figure 15.1), and the bit holding the blue setting for the border color is bit 11. Therefore, the program defines some new constants:

```
#define FILL_BLUE        0x8
#define BORDER_BLUE      0x800
```

Here, **0x8** is the value if just bit 3 is set to 1, and **0x800** is the value if just bit 11 is set to 1. You can use the first constant to set the blue bit for the fill color and the second constant to set the blue bit for the border color. Using hexadecimal notation makes it easier to see which bits are involved. Recall that each hexadecimal digit represents four bits. Thus, **0x800** is the same bit pattern as **0x8**, but with eight 0-bits tagged on. This relationship is much less obvious with 2048 and 8, the base 10 equivalents.

If the values are powers of two, you can use the left-shift operator to supply values. For example, you could replace the last #define statements with these:

```
#define FILL_BLUE        1<<3
#define BORDER_BLUE      1<<11
```

Here, the second operand is the power to be used with 2. That is, **0x8** is 2^3 and **0x800** is 2^{11}. Equivalently, the expression 1<<n is the value of an integer with just the nth bit set to 1. Expressions such as 1<<11 are constant expressions and are evaluated at compile time.

You can use an enumeration instead of #define to create symbolic constants. For example, you can do this:

```
enum { OPAQUE = 0x1, FILL_BLUE = 0x8, FILL_GREEN = 0x4, FILL_RED = 0x2,
       FILL_MASK = 0xE, BORDER = 0x100, BORDER_BLUE = 0x800,
       BORDER_GREEN = 0x400, BORDER_RED = 0x200, BORDER_MASK = 0xE00,
       B_DOTTED = 0x1000, B_DASHED = 0x2000, STYLE_MASK = 0x3000};
```

If you don't intend to create enumerated variables, you don't need to use a tag in the declaration.

Note that using bitwise operators to change settings is more complicated. For example, consider setting the fill color to cyan. It is not enough just to turn the blue bit and the green bit on:

```
box.ui_view |= (FILL_BLUE | FILL_GREEN); /* reset fill */
```

The problem is that the color also depends on the red bit setting. If that bit is already set (as it is for the color yellow), this code leaves the red bit set and sets the blue and green bits, resulting in the color white. The simplest way around this problem is to turn all the color bits off first, before setting the new values. That is why the program uses the following code:

```
box.ui_view &= ~FILL_MASK;            /* clear fill bits */
box.ui_view |= (FILL_BLUE | FILL_GREEN); /* reset fill */
```

To show what can happen if you don't first clear the relevant bits, the program also does this:

```
box.ui_view |= BORDER_RED;            /* wrong approach */
```

Because the **BORDER_GREEN** bit already was set, the resulting color is **BORDER_GREEN | BORDER_RED**, which translates to yellow.

In cases like this, the bit-field versions are simpler:

```
box.st_view.fill_color = CYAN;  /*bit field equivalent */
```

You don't need to clear the bits first. Also, with the bit-field members, you can use the same color values for the border as for the fill, but you need to use different values (values reflecting the actual bit positions) for the bitwise operator approach.

Next, compare the following two print statements:

```
printf("The border color is %s.\n", colors[pb->border_color]);
printf("The border color is %s.\n", colors[(us >> 9) & 07]);
```

In the first statement, the expression **pb->border_color** has a value in the range 0–7, so it can be used as an index for the **colors** array. Getting the same information with bitwise operators is more complex. One approach is to use **ui >> 9** to right-shift the border-color bits to the rightmost position in the value (bits 0–2) and then combine this value with a mask of **07** so that all bits but the rightmost three are turned off. Then what is left is in the range 0–7 and can be used as an index for the **colors** array.

Caution

The correspondence between bit fields and bit positions is implementation dependent. For example, running Listing 15.4 on a Macintosh produces the following output:

```
Original box settings:
Box is opaque.
The fill color is yellow.
Border shown.
The border color is green.
The border style is dashed.
```

```
Box settings using unsigned int view:
box is transparent.
The fill color is black.
Border not shown.
The border style is solid.
The border color is black.
bits are 10110000101010000000000000000000

Modified box settings:
Box is opaque.
The fill color is yellow.
Border shown.
The border color is green.
The border style is dashed.

Box settings using unsigned int view:
box is opaque.
The fill color is cyan.
Border shown.
The border style is dotted.
The border color is red.
bits are 10110000101010000001001000001101
```

The code changed the same bits as before, but the Macintosh loads the structure into memory differently. In particular, it loads the first bit field into the highest-order bit instead of the lowest-order bit. So the structure representation winds up in the first 16 bits (and in different order from the PC version) whereas the `unsigned int` representation winds up in the last 16 bits. Therefore, the assumptions that Listing 15.4 makes about the location of bits is incorrect for the Macintosh, and using bitwise operators to change the opacity and fill color settings alters the wrong bits.

Key Concepts

One of the features that sets C apart from most high-level languages is its ability to access individual bits in an integer. This often is the key to interfacing with hardware devices and with operating systems.

C has two main facilities for accessing bits. One is the family of bitwise operators, and the other is the ability to create bit fields in a structure.

Typically, but not always, programs using these features are tied to particular hardware platforms or operating systems and aren't intended to be portable.

Summary

Computing hardware is closely tied to the binary number system because the 1s and 0s of binary numbers can be used to represent the on and off states of bits in computer memory and registers. Although C does not allow you to write numbers in binary form, it does recognize the related octal and hexadecimal notations. Just as each binary digit represents 1 bit, each octal digit represents 3 bits, and each hexadecimal digit represents 4 bits. This relationship makes it relatively simple to convert binary numbers to octal or hexadecimal form.

C features several bitwise operators, so called because they operate independently on each bit within a value. The bitwise negation operator (~) inverts each bit in its operand, converting 1s to 0s, and vice versa. The bitwise AND operator (&) forms a value from two operands. Each bit in the value is set to 1 if both corresponding bits in the operands are 1. Otherwise, the bit is set to 0. The bitwise OR operator (|) also forms a value from two operands. Each bit in the value is set to 1 if either or both corresponding bits in the operands are 1; otherwise, the bit is set to 0. The bitwise EXCLUSIVE OR operator (^) acts similarly, except that the resulting bit is set to 1 only if one or the other, but not both, of the corresponding bits in the operands is 1.

C also has left-shift (<<) and right-shift (>>) operators. Each produces a value formed by shifting the bits in a pattern the indicated number of bits to the left or right. For the left-shift operator, the vacated bits are set to 0. For the right-shift operator, the vacated bits are set to 0 if the value is unsigned. The behavior of the right-shift operator is implementation dependent for signed values.

You can use bit fields in a structure to address individual bits or groups of bits in a value. The details are implementation independent.

These bit tools help C programs deal with hardware matters, so they most often appear in implementation-dependent contexts.

Review Questions

1. Convert the following decimal values to binary:

    a. 3

    b. 13

    c. 59

    d. 119

2. Convert the following binary values to decimal, octal, and hexadecimal:

    a. 00010101

    b. 01010101

    c. 01001100

    d. 10011101

3. Evaluate the following expressions; assume each value is 8 bits:

   a. ~3

   b. 3 & 6

   c. 3 | 6

   d. 1 | 6

   e. 3 ^ 6

   f. 7 >> 1

   g. 7 << 2

4. Evaluate the following expressions; assume each value is 8 bits:

   a. ~0

   b. !0

   c. 2 & 4

   d. 2 && 4

   e. 2 | 4

   f. 2 || 4

   g. 5 << 3

5. Because the ASCII code uses only the final 7 bits, sometimes it is desirable to mask off the other bits. What's the appropriate mask in binary? In decimal? In octal? In hexadecimal?

6. In Listing 15.2, you can replace

```
while (bits-- > 0)
    {
        mask |= bitval;
        bitval <<= 1;
    }
```

with

```
while (bits-- > 0)
    {
        mask += bitval;
        bitval *= 2;
    }
```

and the program still works. Does this mean the operation *= 2 is equivalent to <<= 1? What about |= and +=?

7. a. The Tinkerbell computer has a hardware byte that can be read into a program. This byte contains the following information:

Bit(s)	Meaning
0–1	Number of 1.4MB floppy drives
2	Not used
3–4	Number of CD-ROM drives
5	Not used
6–7	Number of hard drives

Like the IBM PC, the Tinkerbell fills in structure bit fields from right to left. Create a bit-field template suitable for holding the information.

   b. The Klinkerbell, a near Tinkerbell clone, fills in structures from left to right. Create the corresponding bit-field template for the Klinkerbell.

Programming Exercises

1. Write a function that converts a binary string to a numeric value. That is, if you have

```
char * pbin = "01001001";
```

you can pass `pbin` as an argument to the function and have the function return an `int` value of **25**.

2. Write a program that reads two binary strings as command-line arguments and prints the results of applying the ~ operator to each number and the results of applying the &, |, and ^ operators to the pair. Show the results as binary strings.

3. Write a function that takes an `int` argument and returns the number of "on" bits in the argument. Test the function in a program.

4. Write a function that takes two `int` arguments: a value and a bit position. Have the function return 1 if that particular bit position is 1, and have it return 0 otherwise. Test the function in a program.

5. Write a function that rotates the bits of an `unsigned int` by a specified number of bits to the left. For instance, `rotate_l(x,4)` would move the bits in `x` four places to the left, and the bits lost from the left end would reappear at the right end. That is, the bit moved out of the high-order position is placed in the low-order position. Test the function in a program.

6. Design a bit-field structure that holds the following information:

Font ID: A number in the range 0–255

Font Size: A number in the range 0–127

Alignment: A number in the range 0–2 represented the choices Left, Center, and Right

Bold: Off (0) or on (1)

Italic: Off (0) or on (1)

Underline: Off (0) or on (1)

Use this structure in a program that displays the font parameters and uses a looped menu to let the user change parameters. For example, a sample run might look like this:

```
ID SIZE ALIGNMENT   B   I   U
 1   12   left      off off off

f)change font    s)change size    a)change alignment
b)toggle bold    i)toggle italic  u)toggle underline
q)quit
s
Enter font size (0-127): 36

ID SIZE ALIGNMENT   B   I   U
 1   36   left      off off off

f)change font    s)change size    a)change alignment
b)toggle bold    i)toggle italic  u)toggle underline
q)quit
a
Select alignment:
l)left   c)center   r)right
r

ID SIZE ALIGNMENT   B   I   U
 1   36   right     off off off

f)change font    s)change size    a)change alignment
b)toggle bold    i)toggle italic  u)toggle underline
q)quit
i

ID SIZE ALIGNMENT   B   I   U
 1   36   right     off  on off

f)change font    s)change size    a)change alignment
b)toggle bold    i)toggle italic  u)toggle underline
q)quit
q
Bye!
```

The program should use the **&** operator and suitable masks to ensure that the ID and size entries are converted to the specified range.

7. Write a program with the same behavior as described in Programming Exercise 6, but use an **unsigned long** variable to hold the font information and use the bitwise operators instead of bit members to manage the information.

## CHAPTER 16

THE C PREPROCESSOR AND THE C LIBRARY

You will learn about the following in this chapter:

- Preprocessor directives:
  `#define`, `#include`, `#ifdef`
  `#else`, `#endif`, `#ifndef`
  `#if`, `#elif`, `#line`, `#error`, `#pragma`

- Functions:
  `sqrt()`, `atan()`, `atan2()`
  `exit()`, `atexit()`
  `assert()`
  `memcpy()`, `memmove()`
  `va_start()`, `va_arg()`, `va_copy()`,
  `va_end()`

- More capabilities of the C preprocessor

- Function-like macros and conditional compilation

- Inline functions

- The C library in general and some of its handy functions in particular

The C language proper is built on the C keywords, expressions, and statements as well as the rules for using them. The ANSI C standard, however, goes beyond describing just the C language. It also describes how the C preprocessor should perform, establishes which functions form the standard C library, and details how these functions work. We'll explore the C preprocessor and the C library in this chapter, beginning with the preprocessor.

The preprocessor looks at your program before it is compiled (hence the term *pre*processor). Following your preprocessor directives, the preprocessor replaces the symbolic abbreviations in your program with the directions they represent. The preprocessor can include other files at your request, and it can select which code the compiler sees. The preprocessor doesn't know about C. Basically, it takes some text and converts it to other text. This description does not do justice to its true utility and value, so let's turn to examples. You've encountered examples of `#define` and `#include` all along. Now we can gather what you have learned in one place and add to it.

First Steps in Translating a Program

The compiler has to put a program through some translation phases before jumping into pre-processing. The compiler starts its work by mapping characters appearing in the source code to the source character set. This takes care of multibyte characters and trigraphs—character extensions that make the outer face of C more international. (XB "Reference Section VII, Expanded Character Support," gives an overview of these extensions.)

Second, the compiler locates each instance of a backslash followed by a newline character and deletes them. That is, two physical lines such as

```
printf("That's wond\
erful!\n");
```

are converted to a single *logical line*:

```
printf("That's wonderful\n!");
```

Note that in this context, "newline character" means the character produced by pressing the Enter key to start a new line in your source code file; it doesn't mean the symbolic representation \n.

This feature is useful as a preparation for preprocessing because preprocessing expressions are required to be one logical line long, but that one logical line can be more than one physical line.

Next, the compiler breaks the text into a sequence of preprocessing tokens and sequences of whitespace and comments. (In basic terms, tokens are groups separated from each other by spaces; this chapter will look at tokens in more detail later.) One point of interest now is that each comment is replaced by one space character. So something such as

```
int/* this doesn't look like a space*/fox;
```

becomes

```
int fox;
```

Also, an implementation may choose to replace each sequence of whitespace characters (other than a newline) with a single space. Finally, the program is ready for the preprocessing phase, and the preprocessor looks for potential preprocessing directives, indicated by a # symbol at the beginning of a line.

Manifest Constants: #define

The #define preprocessor directive, like all preprocessor directives, begins with the # symbol at the beginning of a line. The ANSI standard permits the # symbol to be preceded by spaces or tabs, and it allows for space between the # and the remainder of the directive. However, older versions of C typically require that the directive begin in the leftmost column and that there be no spaces between the # and the remainder of the directive. A directive can appear anywhere in the source file, and the definition holds from its place of appearance to the end of the file. We have used directives heavily to define symbolic, or *manifest*, constants in our programs, but they have more range than that, as we will show. Listing 16.1 illustrates some of the possibilities and properties of the #define directive.

Preprocessor directives run until the first newline following the #. That is, a directive is limited to one line in length. However, as mentioned earlier, the combination backslash/newline is deleted before preprocessing begins, so you can spread the directive over several physical lines. These lines, however, constitute a single logical line.

LISTING 16.1   The preproc.c Program

```
/* preproc.c -- simple preprocessor examples */
#include <stdio.h>
#define TWO 2          /* you can use comments if you like    */
#define OW "Consistency is the last refuge of the unimagina\
tive. - Oscar Wilde" /* a backslash continues a definition */
                       /* to the next line                    */
#define FOUR   TWO*TWO
#define PX printf("X is %d.\n", x)
#define FMT   "X is %d.\n"

int main(void)
{
    int x = TWO;

    PX;
    x = FOUR;
    printf(FMT, x);
    printf("%s\n", OW);
    printf("TWO: OW\n");

    return 0;
}
```

Each #define line (logical line, that is) has three parts. The first part is the #define directive itself. The second part is your chosen abbreviation, known as a *macro*. Some macros, like these examples, represent values; they are called *object-like macros*. (C also has *function-like macros*, and we'll get to them later.) The macro name must have no spaces in it, and it must conform to the same rules that C variables follow: Only letters, digits, and the underscore (_) character can be used, and the first character cannot be a digit. The third part (the remainder of the line) is termed the *replacement list* or *body* (see Figure 16.1). When the preprocessor finds an example of one of your macros within your program, it almost always replaces it with the body. (There is one exception, as we will show you in just a moment.) This process of going from a macro to a final replacement is called *macro expansion*. Note that you can use standard C comments on a #define line; as mentioned earlier, each is replaced by a space before the preprocessor sees it.

FIGURE 16.1

Parts of an object-like macro definition.

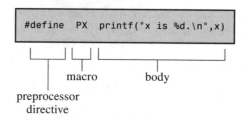

Let's run the example and see how it works:

```
X is 2.
X is 4.
Consistency is the last refuge of the unimaginative. - Oscar Wilde
TWO: OW
```

Here's what happened. The statement

```
int x = TWO;
```

becomes

```
int x = 2;
```

as 2 is substituted for TWO. Then the statement

```
PX;
```

becomes

```
printf("X is %d.\n", x);
```

as that wholesale substitution is made. This is a new wrinkle, because up to now we've used macros only to represent constants. Here you see that a macro can express any string, even a whole C expression. Note, though, that this is a constant string; PX will print only a variable named x.

The next line also represents something new. You might think that FOUR is replaced by 4, but the actual process is this:

```
x = FOUR;
```

becomes

```
x = TWO*TWO;
```

which then becomes

```
x = 2*2;
```

The macro expansion process ends there. The actual multiplication takes place not while the preprocessor works, but during compilation, because the C compiler evaluates all constant expressions (expressions with just constants) at compile time. The preprocessor does no calculation; it just makes the suggested substitutions very literally.

Note that a macro definition can include other macros. (Some compilers do not support this nesting feature.)

In the next line

```
printf (FMT, x);
```

becomes

```
printf("X is %d.\n",x);
```

as `FMT` is replaced by the corresponding string. This approach could be handy if you had a lengthy control string that you had to use several times. Alternatively, you can do the following:

```
const char * fmt = "X is %d.\n";
```

Then you can use `fmt` as the `printf()` control string.

In the next line, `OW` is replaced by the corresponding string. The double quotation marks make the replacement string a character string constant. The compiler will store it in an array terminated with a null character. Therefore,

```
#define HAL 'Z'
```

defines a character constant, but

```
#define HAP "Z"
```

defines a character string: `Z\0`.

In the example, we used a backslash immediately before the end of the line to extend the string to the next line:

```
#define OW "Consistency is the last refuge of the unimagina\
tive. - Oscar Wilde"
```

Note that the second line is flush left. Suppose, instead, we did this:

```
#define OW "Consistency is the last refuge of the unimagina\
    tive. - Oscar Wilde"
```

Then the output would be this:

```
Consistency is the last refuge of the unimagina     tive. - Oscar Wilde
```

The space between the beginning of the line and `tive` counts as part of the string.

In general, wherever the preprocessor finds one of your macros in your program, it replaces it literally with the equivalent replacement text. If that string also contains macros, they, too, are replaced. The one exception to replacement is a macro found within double quotation marks. Therefore,

```
printf("TWO: OW");
```

prints `TWO: OW` literally instead of printing

```
2: Consistency is the last refuge of the unimaginative. - Oscar Wilde
```

To print this last line, you would use this:

```
printf("%d: %s\n", TWO, OW);
```

Here, the macros are outside the double quotation marks.

When should you use symbolic constants? You should use them for most numeric constants. If the number is some constant used in a calculation, a symbolic name makes its meaning clearer. If the number is an array size, a symbolic name makes it simpler to change the array size and loop limits later. If the number is a system code for, say, EOF, a symbolic representation makes your program much more portable; just change one EOF definition. Mnemonic value, easy alterability, portability—these features all make symbolic constants worthwhile.

It is true that the **const** keyword now supported by C allows for a more flexible way of creating constants. With **const** you can create global constants and local constants, numeric constants, array constants, and structure constants. On the other hand, macro constants can be used to specify the sizes of standard arrays and as initialization values for **const** values:

```
#define LIMIT 20
const int LIM = 50;
static int data1[LIMIT];    // valid
static int data2[LIM];      // invalid
const int LIM2 = 2 * LIMIT; // valid
const int LIM3 = 2 * LIM;   // invalid
```

Tokens

Technically, the body of a macro is considered to be a string of *tokens* rather than a string of characters. C preprocessor tokens are the separate "words" in the body of a macro definition. They are separated from one another by whitespace. For example, the definition

```
#define FOUR 2*2
```

has one token—the sequence **2*2**—but the definition

```
#define SIX 2 * 3
```

has three tokens in it: **2**, *****, and **3**.

Character strings and token strings differ in how multiple spaces in a body are treated. Consider this definition:

```
#define EIGHT 4    *    8
```

A preprocessor that interprets the body as a character string would replace EIGHT with **4   *   8**. That is, the extra spaces would be part of the replacement, but a preprocessor that interprets the body as tokens will replace EIGHT with three tokens separated by single spaces: **4 * 8**. In other words, the character string interpretation views the spaces as part of the body, but the token interpretation views the spaces as separators between the tokens of the body. In practice, some C compilers have viewed macro bodies as strings rather than as tokens. The difference is of practical importance only for usages more intricate than what we're attempting here.

Incidentally, the C compiler takes a more complex view of tokens than the preprocessor does. The compiler understands the rules of C and doesn't necessarily require spaces to separate tokens. For example, the C compiler would view 2*2 as three tokens because it recognizes that each 2 is a constant and that * is an operator.

Redefining Constants

Suppose you define `LIMIT` to be 20, and then later in the same file you define it again as 25. This process is called *redefining a constant*. Implementations differ on redefinition policy. Some consider it an error unless the new definition is the same as the old. Others allow redefinition, perhaps issuing a warning. The ANSI standard takes the first view, allowing redefinition only if the new definition duplicates the old.

Having the same definition means the bodies must have the same tokens in the same order. Therefore, these two definitions agree:

```
#define SIX 2 * 3
#define SIX 2      *    3
```

Both have the same three tokens, and the extra spaces are not part of the body. The next definition is considered different:

```
#define SIX 2*3
```

It has just one token, not three, so it doesn't match. If you want to redefine a macro, use the `#undef` directive, which we discuss later.

If you do have constants that you need to redefine, it might be easier to use the `const` keyword and scope rules to accomplish that end.

Using Arguments with #define

By using arguments, you can create *function-like macros* that look and act much like functions. A macro with arguments looks very similar to a function because the arguments are enclosed within parentheses. Function-like macro definitions have one or more arguments in parentheses, and these arguments then appear in the replacement portion, as shown in Figure 16.2.

FIGURE 16.2
Parts of a function-like macro definition.

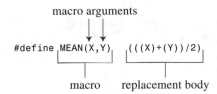

Here's a sample definition:

```
#define SQUARE(X) X *X
```

It can be used in program like this:

```
z = SQUARE(2);
```

This looks like a function call, but it doesn't necessarily behave identically. Listing 16.2 illustrates using this and a second macro. Some of the examples also point out possible pitfalls, so read them carefully.

LISTING 16.2   The `mac_arg.c` Program

```
/* mac_arg.c -- macros with arguments */
#include <stdio.h>
#define SQUARE(X) X*X
#define PR(X)    printf("The result is %d.\n", X)
int main(void)
{
    int x = 4;
    int z;

    printf("x = %d\n", x);
    z = SQUARE(x);
    printf("Evaluating SQUARE(x): ");
    PR(z);
    z = SQUARE(2);
    printf("Evaluating SQUARE(2): ");
    PR(z);
    printf("Evaluating SQUARE(x+2): ");
    PR(SQUARE(x+2));
    printf("Evaluating 100/SQUARE(2): ");
    PR(100/SQUARE(2));
    printf("x is %d.\n", x);
    printf("Evaluating SQUARE(++x): ");
    PR(SQUARE(++x));
    printf("After incrementing, x is %x.\n", x);

    return 0;
}
```

The **SQUARE** macro has this definition:

```
#define SQUARE(X) X*X
```

Here, **SQUARE** is the macro identifier, the **X** in **SQUARE(X)** is the macro argument, and **X*X** is the replacement list. Wherever **SQUARE(x)** appears in Listing 16.2, it is replaced by **x*x**. This differs from the earlier examples in that you are free to use symbols other than x when you use this macro. The x in the macro definition is replaced by the symbol used in the macro call in the program. Therefore, **SQUARE(2)** is replaced by **2*2**, so the x really does act as an argument.

However, as you will soon see, a macro argument does not work exactly like a function argument. Here are the results of running the program. Note that some of the answers are different from what you might expect. Indeed, your compiler might not even give the same answer as what's shown here for the next-to-last line:

```
x = 4
Evaluating SQUARE(x): The result is 16.
Evaluating SQUARE(2): The result is 4.
Evaluating SQUARE(x+2): The result is 14.
Evaluating 100/SQUARE(2): The result is 100.
x is 4.
Evaluating SQUARE(++x): The result is 30.
After incrementing, x is 6.
```

The first two lines are predictable, but then you come to some peculiar results. Recall that x has the value 4. This might lead you to expect that SQUARE(x+2) would be 6*6, or 36, but the printout says it is 14, which sure doesn't look like a square to us! The simple reason for this misleading output is the one we have already stated—the preprocessor doesn't make calculations; it just substitutes strings. Wherever the definition shows an x, the preprocessor substitutes the string x+2. Therefore,

```
x*x
```

becomes

```
x+2*x+2
```

The only multiplication is 2*x. If x is 4, this is the value of this expression:

```
4+2*4+2 = 4 + 8 + 2 = 14
```

This example pinpoints an important difference between a function call and a macro call. A function call passes the value of the argument to the function while the program is running. A macro call passes the argument token to the program before compilation; it's a different process at a different time. Can the definition be fixed to make SQUARE(x+2) yield 36? Sure. You simply need more parentheses:

```
#define SQUARE(x)   (x)*(x)
```

Now SQUARE(x+2) becomes (x+2)*(x+2), and you get the desired multiplication as the parentheses carry over in the replacement string.

This doesn't solve all the problems, however. Consider the events leading to the next output line:

```
100/SQUARE(2)
```

becomes

```
100/2*2
```

By the laws of precedence, the expression is evaluated from left to right: (100/2)*2 or 50*2 or 100. This mix-up can be cured by defining SQUARE(x) as follows:

```
#define SQUARE(x)   (x*x)
```

This produces 100/(2*2), which eventually evaluates to 100/4, or 25.

To handle both of the previous two examples, you need this definition:

```
#define SQUARE(x)  ((x)*(x))
```

The lesson here is to use as many parentheses as necessary to ensure that operations and associations are done in the right order.

Even these precautions fail to save the final example from grief:

```
SQUARE(++x)
```

becomes

```
++x*++x
```

and x gets incremented twice, once before the multiplication and once afterward:

```
++x*++x = 5*6 = 30
```

Because the order of operations is left open, some compilers render the product 6*5. Yet other compilers might increment both terms before multiplication, yielding 6*6. In all these cases, however, x starts with the value 4 and ends up with the value 6, even though the code looks as though x was incremented just once.

The simplest remedy for this problem is to avoid using ++x as a macro argument. In general, don't use increment or decrement operators with macros. Note that ++x would work as a function argument because it would be evaluated to 5, and then the value 5 would be sent to the function.

Creating Strings from Macro Arguments: The # Operator

Here's a function-like macro:

```
#define PSQR(X)  printf("The square of X is %d.\n", ((X)*(X)));
```

Suppose you used the macro like this:

```
PSQR(8);
```

Here's the output:

```
The square of X is 64.
```

Note that the X in the quoted string is treated as ordinary text, not as a token that can be replaced.

Suppose you do want to include the macro argument in a string. ANSI C enables you to do that. Within the replacement part of a function-like macro, the # symbol becomes a preprocessing operator that converts tokens into strings. For example, say that x is a macro parameter, and then #x is that parameter name converted to the string "x". This process is called *stringizing*. Listing 16.3 illustrates how this process works.

LISTING 16.3   The subst.c Program

```
/* subst.c -- substitute in string */
#include <stdio.h>
#define PSQR(x) printf("The square of " #x " is %d.\n",((x)*(x)))

int main(void)
{
    int y = 5;

    PSQR(y);
    PSQR(2 + 4);

    return 0;
}
```

Here's the output:

```
The square of y is 25.
The square of 2 + 4 is 36.
```

In the first call to the macro, #x was replaced by "y", and in the second call #x was replaced by "2 + 4". ANSI C string concatenation then combined these strings with the other strings in the printf() statement to produce the final strings that were used. For example, the first invocation becomes this:

```
printf("The square of " "y" " is %d.\n",((y)*(y)));
```

Then string concatenation converts the three adjacent strings to one string:

```
"The square of y is %d.\n"
```

Preprocessor Glue: The ## Operator

Like the # operator, the ## operator can be used in the replacement section of a function-like macro. Additionally, it can be used in the replacement section of an object-like macro. The ## operator combines two tokens into a single token. For example, you could do this:

```
#define XNAME(n) x ## n
```

Then the macro

```
XNAME(4)
```

would expand to the following:

```
x4
```

Listing 16.4 uses this and another macro using ## to do a bit of token gluing.

LISTING 16.4   The glue.c Program

```
// glue.c -- use the ## operator
#include <stdio.h>
#define XNAME(n) x ## n
```

LISTING 16.4   *Continued*

```
#define PRINT_XN(n) printf("x" #n " = %d\n", x ## n);

int main(void)
{
    int XNAME(1) = 14;   // becomes int x1 = 14;
    int XNAME(2) = 20;   // becomes int x2 = 20;
    PRINT_XN(1);         // becomes printf("x1 = %d\n", x1);
    PRINT_XN(2);         // becomes printf("x2 = %d\n", x2);

    return 0;
}
```

Here's the output:

```
x1 = 14
x2 = 20
```

Note how the `PRINT_XN()` macro uses the `#` operator to combine strings and the `##` operator to combine tokens into a new identifier.

Variadic Macros: ... and _ _VA_ARGS_ _

Some functions, such as `printf()`, accept a variable number of arguments. The `stdvar.h` header file, discussed later in this chapter, provides tools for creating user-defined functions with a variable number of arguments. And C99 does the same thing for macros. Although not used in the standard, the word *variadic* has come into currency to label this facility. (However, the process that has added *stringizing* and *variadic* to the C vocabulary has not yet led to labeling functions or macros with a fixed number of arguments as fixadic functions and normadic macros.)

The idea is that the final argument in an argument list for a macro definition can be ellipses (that is, three periods). If so, the predefined macro _ _VA_ARGS_ _ can be used in the substitution part to indicate what will be substituted for the ellipses. For example, consider this definition:

```
#define PR(...) printf(_ _VA_ARGS_ _)
```

Suppose you later invoke the macro like this:

```
PR("Howdy");
PR("weight = %d, shipping = $%.2f\n", wt, sp);
```

For the first invocation, _ _VA_ARGS_ _ expands to one argument:

```
"Howdy"
```

For the second invocation, it expands to three arguments:

```
"weight = %d, shipping = $%.2f\n", wt, sp
```

Thus, the resulting code is this:

```
printf("Howdy");
printf("weight = %d, shipping = $%.2f\n", wt, sp);
```

Listing 16.5 shows a slightly more ambitious example that uses string concatenation and the # operator:

LISTING 16.5   The `variadic.c` Program

```
// variadic.c -- variadic macros
#include <stdio.h>
#include <math.h>
#define PR(X, ...) printf("Message " #X ": " _ _VA_ARGS_ _)

int main(void)
{
    double x = 48;
    double y;

    y = sqrt(x);
    PR(1, "x = %g\n", x);
    PR(2, "x = %.2f, y = %.4f\n", x, y);

    return 0;
}
```

In the first macro call, `X` has the value `1`, so `#X` becomes `"1"`. That makes the expansion look like this:

```
print("Message " "1" ": " "x = %g\n", x);
```

Then the four strings are concatenated, reducing the call to this:

```
print("Message 1: x = %g\n", x);
```

Here's the output:

```
Message 1: x = 48
Message 2: x = 48.00, y = 6.9282
```

Don't forget, the ellipses have to be the last macro argument:

```
#define WRONG(X, ..., Y)   #X #_ _VA_ARGS_ _ #y
```

Macro or Function?

Many tasks can be done by using a macro with arguments or by using a function. Which one should you use? There is no hard-and-fast rule, but here are some considerations.

Macros are somewhat trickier to use than regular functions because they can have odd side effects if you are unwary. Some compilers limit the macro definition to one line, and it is probably best to observe that limit, even if your compiler does not.

The macro-versus-function choice represents a trade-off between time and space. A macro produces inline code; that is, you get a statement in your program. If you use the macro 20 times, you get 20 lines of code inserted into your program. If you use a function 20 times, you have just one copy of the function statements in your program, so less space is used. On the other hand, program control must shift to where the function is and then return to the calling program, and this takes longer than inline code.

Macros have an advantage in that they don't worry about variable types. (This is because they deal with character strings, not with actual values.) Therefore, the `SQUARE(x)` macro can be used equally well with `int` or `float`.

C99 provides a third alternative—inline functions. We'll look at them later in this chapter.

Programmers typically use macros for simple functions such as the following:

```
#define MAX(X,Y)     ((X) > (Y) ? (X) : (Y))
#define ABS(X)        ((X) < 0 ? -(X) : (X))
#define ISSIGN(X)    ((X) == '+' || (X) == '-' ? 1 : 0)
```

(The last macro has the value 1, or true, if x is an algebraic sign character.)

Here are some points to note:

- Remember that there are no spaces in the macro name, but that spaces can appear in the replacement string. ANSI C permits spaces in the argument list.

- Use parentheses around each argument and around the definition as a whole. This ensures that the enclosed terms are grouped properly in an expression such as

  ```
  forks = 2 * MAX(guests + 3, last);
  ```

- Use capital letters for macro function names. This convention is not as widespread as that of using capitals for macro constants. However, one good reason for using capitals is to remind yourself to be alert to possible macro side effects.

- If you intend to use a macro instead of a function primarily to speed up a program, first try to determine whether it is likely to make a significant difference. A macro that is used once in a program probably won't make any noticeable improvement in running time. A macro inside a nested loop is a much better candidate for speed improvements. Many systems offer program profilers to help you pin down where a program spends the most time.

Suppose you have developed some macro functions you like. Do you have to retype them each time you write a new program? Not if you remember the `#include` directive, reviewed in the following section.

File Inclusion: `#include`

When the preprocessor spots an `#include` directive, it looks for the following filename and includes the contents of that file within the current file. The `#include` directive in your source code file is replaced with the text from the included file. It's as though you sat down and typed in the entire contents of the included file at that particular location in your source file. The `#include` directive comes in two varieties:

`#include <stdio.h>`	←Filename in angle brackets
`#include "mystuff.h"`	←Filename in double quotation marks

On a Unix system, the angle brackets tell the preprocessor to look for the file in one or more standard system directories. The double quotation marks tell it to first look in your current directory (or some other directory that you have specified in the filename) and then look in the standard places:

`#include <stdio.h>`	←Searches system directories
`#include "hot.h"`	←Searches your current working directory
`#include "/usr/biff/p.h"`	←Searches the `/usr/biff` directory

Integrated development environments (IDEs) also have a standard location or locations for the system header files. Many provide menu choices for specifying additional locations to be searched when angle brackets are used. As with Unix, using double quotes means to search a local directory first, but the exact directory searched depends on the compiler. Some search the same directory as that holding the source code; some search the current working directory; and some search the same directory as that holding the project file.

ANSI C doesn't demand adherence to the directory model for files because not all computer systems are organized similarly. In general, the method used to name files is system dependent, but the use of the angle brackets and double quotation marks is not.

Why include files? Because they have information the compiler needs. The `stdio.h` file, for example, typically includes definitions of `EOF`, `NULL`, `getchar()`, and `putchar()`. The last two are defined as macro functions. It also contains function prototypes for the C I/O functions.

The `.h` suffix is conventionally used for *header files*—files with information that are placed at the head of your program. Header files often contain preprocessor statements. Some, such as `stdio.h`, come with the system, but you are free to create your own.

Including a large header file doesn't necessarily add much to the size of your program. The content of header files, for the most part, is information used by the compiler to generate the final code, not material to be added to the final code.

Header Files: An Example

Suppose you developed a structure for holding a person's name and also wrote some functions for using the structure. You could gather together the various declarations in a header file. Listing 16.6 shows an example of this.

LISTING 16.6 The names_st.h Header File

```
// names_st.h -- names_st structure header file
// constants
#define SLEN 32

// structure declarations
struct names_st
{
    char first[SLEN];
    char last[SLEN];
};

// typedefs
typedef struct names_st names;

// function prototypes
void get_names(names *);
void show_names(const names *);
```

This header file includes many of the kinds of things commonly found in header files: `#define` directives, structure declarations, `typedef` statements, and function prototypes. Note that none of these things are executable code; rather, they are information that the compiler uses when it creates executable code.

Executable code normally goes into a source code file, not a header file. For example, Listing 16.7 shows the function definitions for those functions prototyped in the header file. It includes the header file so that the compiler will know about `names` type.

LISTING 16.7 The name_st.c Source File

```
// names_st.c -- define names_st functions
#include <stdio.h>
#include "names_st.h"       // include the header file

// function definitions
void get_names(names * pn)
{
    int i;

    printf("Please enter your first name: ");
    fgets(pn->first, SLEN, stdin);
    i = 0;
    while (pn->first[i] != '\n' && pn->first[i] != '\0')
        i++;
    if (pn->first[i] == '\n')
        pn->first[i] = '\0';
    else
        while (getchar() != '\n')
            continue;

    printf("Please enter your last name: ");
```

LISTING 16.7   Continued

```
        fgets(pn->last, SLEN, stdin);
        i = 0;
        while (pn->last[i] != '\n' && pn->last[i] != '\0')
            i++;
        if (pn->last[i] == '\n')
            pn->last[i] = '\0';
        else
            while (getchar() != '\n')
                continue;
}

void show_names(const names * pn)
{
    printf("%s %s", pn->first, pn->last);
}
```

The `get_names()` function uses `fgets()` so as not to overflow the destination arrays. If there is a newline in the saved string, it replaces it with a null character. If there isn't a newline, `fgets()` is stopped before reaching the end of the line, and the code then disposes of the remaining input on that line.

Listing 16.8 is an example of a program that use this header and source code file.

LISTING 16.8   The `useheader.c` Program

```
// useheader.c -- use the names_st structure
#include <stdio.h>
#include "names_st.h"
// remember to link with names_st.c

int main(void)
{
    names candidate;

    get_names(&candidate);
    printf("Let's welcome ");
    show_names(&candidate);
    printf(" to this program!\n");
    return 0;
}
```

Here is a sample run:

```
Please enter your first name: Ian
Please enter your last name: Smersh
Let's welcome Ian Smersh to this program!
```

Note the following points about this program:

- Both source code files use the `names_st` structure, so both have to include the `names_st.h` header file.

- You need to compile and link the `names_st.c` and the `useheader.c` source code files.
- Declarations and the like go into the `names_st.h` header file; function definitions go into the `names_st.c` source code file.

Uses for Header Files

A look through any of the standard header files can give you a good idea of the sort of information found in them. The most common forms of header contents include the following:

- **Manifest constants**—A typical `stdio.h` file, for instance, defines `EOF`, `NULL`, and `BUFSIZ` (the size of the standard I/O buffer).

- **Macro functions**—For example, `getchar()` is usually defined as `getc(stdin)`, `getc()` is usually defined as a rather complex macro, and the `ctype.h` header typically contains macro definitions for the `ctype` functions.

- **Function declarations**—The `string.h` header (`strings.h` on some older systems), for example, contains function declarations for the family of string functions. Under ANSI C, the declarations are in function prototype form.

- **Structure template definitions**—The standard I/O functions make use of a `FILE` structure containing information about a file and its associated buffer. The `stdio.h` file holds the declaration for this structure.

- **Type definitions**—You might recall that the standard I/O functions use a pointer-to-`FILE` argument. Typically, `stdio.h` uses a `#define` or a `typedef` to make `FILE` represent a pointer to a structure. Similarly, the `size_t` and `time_t` types are defined in header files.

Many programmers develop their own standard header files to use with their programs. This is particularly valuable if you develop a family of related functions and/or structures.

Also, you can use header files to declare external variables to be shared by several files. This makes sense, for example, if you've developed a family of functions that share a variable for reporting a status of some kind, such as an error condition. In that case, you could define a file-scope, external-linkage variable in the source code file containing the function declarations:

```
int status = 0;    // file scope, source code file
```

Then, in the header file associated with the source code file, you could place a reference declaration:

```
extern int status;  // in header file
```

This code would then appear in any file in which you included the header file, making the variable available to those files that use that family of functions. This declaration also would appear, through inclusion, in the function source code file, but it's okay to have both a defining declaration and a reference declaration in the same file, as long as the declarations agree in type.

Another candidate for inclusion in a header file is a variable or array with file scope, internal linkage, and `const` qualification. The `const` part protects against accidental changes, and the `static` part means that each file including the header gets its own copy of the constants so that there isn't the problem of needing one file with a defining declaration and the rest with reference declarations.

The `#include` and `#define` directives are the most heavily used C preprocessor features. We'll look at the other directives in less detail.

Other Directives

Programmers may have to prepare C programs or C library packages that have to work in a variety of environments. The choices of types of code can vary from one environment to another. The preprocessor provides several directives that help the programmer produce code that can be moved from one system to another by changing the values of some `#define` macros. The `#undef` directive cancels an earlier `#define` definition. The `#if`, `#ifdef`, `#ifndef`, `#else`, `#elif`, and `#endif` directives allow you to specify different alternatives for which code is compiled. The `#line` directive lets you reset line and file information, the `#error` directive lets you issue error messages, and the `#pragma` directive lets you give instructions to the compiler.

The `#undef` Directive

The `#undef` directive "undefines" a given `#define`. That is, suppose you have this definition:

```
#define LIMIT 400
```

Then the directive

```
#undef LIMIT
```

removes that definition. Now, if you like, you can redefine `LIMIT` so that it has a new value. Even if `LIMIT` is not defined in the first place, it is still valid to undefine it. If you want to use a particular name and you are unsure whether it has been used previously, you can undefine it to be on the safe side.

Being Defined—The C Preprocessor Perspective

The preprocessor follows the same rules as C about what constitutes an identifier: an identifier can consist only of uppercase letters, lowercase letters, digits, and underscore characters. When the preprocessor encounters an identifier in a preprocessor directive, it considers it to be either defined or undefined. Here, *defined* means defined by the preprocessor. If the identifier is a macro name created by a prior `#define` directive in the same file and it hasn't been turned off by an `#undef` directive, it's defined. If the identifier is not a macro but is, say, a file-scope C variable, it's not defined as far as the preprocessor is concerned.

A defined macro can be an object-like macro, including an empty macro, or a function-like macro:

```
#define LIMIT 1000        // LIMIT is defined
#define GOOD              // GOOD is defined
#define A(X)   ((-(X))*(X)) // A is defined
int q;                    // q not a macro, hence not defined
#undef GOOD               // GOOD not defined
```

Note that the scope of a #define macro extends from the point it is declared in a file until it is the subject of an #undef directive or until the end of the file, whichever comes first. Also note that the position of the #define in a file will depend on the position of an #include directive if the macro is brought in via a header file.

A few predefined macros, such as _ _DATE_ _ and _ _FILE_ _ (discussed later this chapter), are always considered defined and cannot be undefined.

Conditional Compilation

You can use the other directives mentioned to set up conditional compilations. That is, you can use them to tell the compiler to accept or ignore blocks of information or code according to conditions at the time of compilation.

The #ifdef, #else, and #endif Directives

A short example will clarify what conditional compilation does. Consider the following:

```
#ifdef MAVIS
    #include "horse.h"  // gets done if MAVIS is #defined
    #define STABLES    5
#else
    #include "cow.h"    // gets done if MAVIS isn't #defined
    #define STABLES  15
#endif
```

Here we've used the indentation allowed by newer implementations and by the ANSI standard. If you have an older implementation, you might have to move all the directives, or at least the # symbols (see the next example), to flush left:

```
#ifdef MAVIS
#   include "horse.h"  /* gets done if MAVIS is #defined     */
#   define STABLES    5
#else
#   include "cow.h"    /* gets done if MAVIS isn't #defined */
#   define STABLES  15
#endif
```

The #ifdef directive says that if the following identifier (MAVIS) has been defined by the pre-processor, follow all the directives and compile all the C code up to the next #else or #endif, whichever comes first. If there is an #else, everything from the #else to the #endif is done if the identifier isn't defined.

The form #ifdef #else is much like that of the C if else. The main difference is that the preprocessor doesn't recognize the braces ({}) method of marking a block, so it uses the #else (if any) and the #endif (which must be present) to mark blocks of directives. These conditional structures can be nested. You can use these directives to mark blocks of C statements, too, as Listing 16.9 illustrates.

LISTING 16.9   The ifdef.c Program

```
/* ifdef.c -- uses conditional compilation */
#include <stdio.h>
#define JUST_CHECKING
#define LIMIT 4

int main(void)
{
    int i;
    int total = 0;

    for (i = 1; i <= LIMIT; i++)
    {
        total += 2*i*i + 1;
#ifdef JUST_CHECKING
        printf("i=%d, running total = %d\n", i, total);
#endif
    }
    printf("Grand total = %d\n", total);

    return 0;
}
```

Compiling and running the program as shown produces this output:

```
i=1, running total = 3
i=2, running total = 12
i=3, running total = 31
i=4, running total = 64
Grand total = 64
```

If you omit the JUST_CHECKING definition (or enclose it inside a C comment, or use #undef to undefine it) and recompile the program, only the final line is displayed. You can use this approach, for example, to help in program debugging. Define JUST_CHECKING and use a judicious selection of #ifdefs, and the compiler will include program code for printing intermediate values for debugging. After everything is working, you can remove the definition and recompile. If, later, you find that you need the information again, you can reinsert the definition and avoid having to retype all the extra print statements. Another possibility is using #ifdef to select among alternative chunks of codes suited for different C implementations.

The #ifndef Directive

The #ifndef directive can be used with #else and #endif in the same way that #ifdef is. The #ifndef asks whether the following identifier is *not* defined; #ifndef is the negative of

`#ifdef`. This directive is often used to define a constant if it is not already defined. Here's an example:

```
/* arrays.h */
#ifndef SIZE
    #define SIZE 100
#endif
```

(Older implementations might not permit indenting the `#define` directive.)

Typically, this idiom is used to prevent multiple definitions of the same macro when you include several header files, each of which may contain a definition. In this case, the definition in the first header file included becomes the active definition and subsequent definitions in other header files are ignored.

Here's another use. Suppose we place the line

```
#include "arrays.h"
```

at the head of a file. This results in `SIZE` being defined as 100. But placing

```
#define SIZE 10
#include "arrays.h"
```

at the head sets `SIZE` to 10. Here, `SIZE` is defined by the time the lines in `arrays.h` are processed, so the `#define SIZE 100` line is skipped. You might do this, for example, to test a program using a smaller array size. When it works to your satisfaction, you can remove the `#define SIZE 10` statement and recompile. That way, you never have to worry about modifying the header array itself.

The `#ifndef` directive is commonly used to prevent multiple inclusions of a file. That is, header files usually are set up along the following lines:

```
/* things.h */
#ifndef THINGS_ _H_
    #define THINGS_H_
    /* rest of include file */
#endif
```

Suppose this file somehow got included several times. The first time the preprocessor encounters this include file, `THINGS_H_` is undefined, so the program proceeds to define `THINGS_H_` and to process the rest of the file. The next time the preprocessor encounters this file, `THINGS_H_` is defined, so the preprocessor skips the rest of the file.

Why would you include a file more than once? The most common reason is that many include files include other files, so you may include a file explicitly that another include file has already included. Why is this a problem? Some items that appear in include files, such as declarations of structure types, can appear only once in a file. The standard C header files use the `#ifndef` technique to avoid multiple inclusions. One problem is to make sure the identifier you are testing hasn't been defined elsewhere. Vendors typically solve this by using the filename as the identifier, using uppercase, replacing periods with an underscore, and using an underscore (or, perhaps, two underscores) as a prefix and a suffix. If you check your `stdio.h` header file, for example, you'll probably find something similar to this:

```
#ifndef _STDIO_H
#define _STDIO_H
// contents of file
#endif
```

You can do something similar. However, you should avoid using the underscore as a prefix because the standard says such usage is reserved. You wouldn't want to accidentally define a macro that conflicts with something in the standard header files. Listing 16.10 uses `#ifndef` to provide multiple-inclusion protection for the header file from Listing 16.6.

LISTING 16.10   The `names_st.h` Header File

```
// names_st.h --revised with include protection

#ifndef NAMES_H_
#define NAMES_H_

// constants
#define SLEN 32

// structure declarations
struct names_st
{
    char first[SLEN];
    char last[SLEN];
};

// typedefs
typedef struct names_st names;

// function prototypes
void get_names(names *);
void show_names(const names *);

#endif
```

You can test this header file with the program shown in Listing 16.11. This program should work correctly when using the header file shown in Listing 16.10, and it should fail to compile if you remove the `#ifndef` protection from Listing 16.10.

LISTING 16.11   The `doubincl.c` Program

```
// doubincl.c -- include header twice
#include <stdio.h>
#include "names.h"
#include "names.h"    // accidental second inclusion

int main()
```

LISTING 16.11   Continued

```
{
    names winner = {"Less", "Ismoor"};
    printf("The winner is %s %s.\n", winner.first,
            winner.last);
    return 0;
}
```

The #if and #elif Directives

The #if directive is more like the regular C if. It is followed by a constant integer expression that is considered true if nonzero, and you can use C's relational and logical operators with it:

```
#if SYS == 1
#include "ibm.h"
#endif
```

You can use the #elif directive (not available in some older implementations) to extend an if-else sequence. For example, you could do this:

```
#if SYS == 1
    #include "ibmpc.h"
#elif SYS == 2
    #include "vax.h"
#elif SYS == 3
    #include "mac.h"
#else
    #include "general.h"
#endif
```

Many newer implementations offer a second way to test whether a name is defined. Instead of using

```
#ifdef VAX
```

you can use this form:

```
#if defined (VAX)
```

Here, defined is a preprocessor operator that returns 1 if its argument is #defined and 0 otherwise. The advantage of this newer form is that it can be used with #elif. Using it, you can rewrite the previous example this way:

```
#if defined (IBMPC)
    #include "ibmpc.h"
#elif defined (VAX)
    #include "vax.h"
#elif defined (MAC)
    #include "mac.h"
#else
    #include "general.h"
#endif
```

If you were using these lines on, say, a VAX, you would have defined VAX somewhere earlier in the file with this line:

```
#define VAX
```

One use for these conditional compilation features is to make a program more portable. By changing a few key definitions at the beginning of a file, you can set up different values and include different files for different systems.

Predefined Macros

The C standard specifies several predefined macros, which Table 16.1 lists.

TABLE 16.1 Predefined Macros

Macro	Meaning
__DATE__	A character string literal in the form "Mmm dd yyyy" representing the date of preprocessing
__FILE__	A character string literal representing the name of the current source code file
__LINE__	An integer constant representing the line number in the current source code file
__STDC__	Set to 1 to indicate the implementation conforms to the C Standard
__STDC_HOSTED__	Set to 1 for a hosted environment; 0 otherwise
__STDC_VERSION__	For C99, set to 199901L
__TIME__	The time of translation in the form "hh:mm:ss"

While we're discussing predefined identifiers, the C99 standard provides for one called __func__. It expands to a string representing the name of the function containing the identifier. For this reason, the identifier has to have function scope, whereas macros essentially have file scope. Therefore, __func__ is a C language predefined identifier rather than a predefined macro.

Listing 16.12 shows several of these predefined identifiers in use. Note that some of them are C99 additions, so a pre-C99 compiler might not accept them.

LISTING 16.12 The predef.c Program

```
// predef.c -- predefined identifiers
#include <stdio.h>
void why_me();
```

LISTING 16.12 Continued

```
int main()
{
    printf("The file is %s.\n", __FILE__);
    printf("The date is %s.\n", __DATE__);
    printf("The time is %s.\n", __TIME__);
    printf("The version is %ld.\n", __STDC_VERSION__);
    printf("This is line %d.\n", __LINE__);
    printf("This function is %s\n", __func__);
    why_me();

    return 0;
}

void why_me()
{
    printf("This function is %s\n", __func__);
    printf("This is line %d.\n", __LINE__);
}
```

Here's a sample run:

```
The file is predef.c.
The date is Jul 19 2004.
The time is 10:00:30.
The version is 199901.
This is line 11.
This function is main
This function is why_me
This is line 21.
```

#line and #error

The #line directive lets you reset the line numbering and the filename as reported by the __LINE__ and __FILE__ macros. You can use #line like this:

```
#line 1000    // reset current line number to 1000
#line 10 "cool.c" // reset line number to 10, file name to cool.c
```

The #error directive causes the preprocessor to issue an error message that includes any text in the directive. If possible, the compilation process should halt. You could use the directive like this:

```
#if __STDC_VERSION__ != 199901L
    #error Not C99
#endif
```

#pragma

Modern compilers have several settings that can be modified by command-line arguments or by using an IDE menu. The #pragma lets you place compiler instructions in the source code.

For example, while C99 was being developed, it was referred to as C9X, and one compiler used the following pragma to turn on C9X support:

```
#pragma c9x on
```

Generally, each compiler has its own set of pragmas. They might be used, for example, to control the amount of memory set aside for automatic variables or to set the strictness of error checking or to enable nonstandard language features. The C99 standard does provide for three standard pragmas of rather technical nature that we won't discuss here.

C99 also provides the `_Pragma` preprocessor operator. It converts a string into a regular pragma. For example,

```
_Pragma("nonstandardtreatmenttypeB on")
```

is equivalent to the following:

```
#pragma nonstandardtreatmenttypeB on
```

Because the operator doesn't use the # symbol, you can use it as part of a macro expansion:

```
#define PRAGMA(X) _Pragma(#X)
#define LIMRG(X) PRAGMA(STDC CX_LIMITED_RANGE  X)
```

Then you can use code like this:

```
LIMRG ( ON )
```

Incidentally, the following definition doesn't work, although it looks as if it might:

```
#define LIMRG(X) _Pragma(STDC CX_LIMITED_RANGE  #X)
```

The problem is that it relies on string concatenation, but the compiler doesn't concatenate strings until after preprocessing is complete.

The `_Pragma` operator does a complete job of "destringizing"; that is, escape sequences in a string are converted to the character represented. Thus,

```
_Pragma("use_bool \"true \"false")
```

becomes

```
#pragma use_bool "true "false
```

Inline Functions

Normally, a function call has overhead. That means it takes execution time to set up the call, pass arguments, jump to the function code, and return. Reducing that time is one of the justifications for using function-like macros. C99 has an alternative, *inline functions*. The C99 standard has this to say: "Making a function an inline function suggests that calls to the function be as fast as possible. The extent to which such suggestions are effective is implementation-defined." So making a function an inline function may shortcut the usual function call mechanism, or it may do nothing at all.

The way to create an inline function is to use the function specifier `inline` in the function declaration. Usually, inline functions are defined before the first use in a file, so the definition also acts as a prototype. That is, the code would look like this:

```
#include <stdio.h>
inline void eatline()          // inline definition/prototype
{
    while (getchar() != '\n')
        continue;
}

int main()
{
...
    eatline();                 // function call
...
}
```

Seeing the inline declaration, the compiler could choose, for example, to replace the `eatline()` function call with the function body. That is, the effect could end up the same as if you had written this code instead:

```
#include <stdio.h>
inline void eatline()          // inline definition/prototype
{
    while (getchar() != '\n')
        continue;
}

int main()
{
...
    while (getchar() != '\n')    // function call replaced
        continue;
...
}
```

Because an inline function doesn't have a separate block of code set aside for it, you can't take its address. (Actually, you can take the address, but then the compiler will generate a non-inline function.) Also, an inline function may not show up in a debugger.

An inline function should be short. For a long function, the time consumed in calling the function is short compared to the time spent executing the body of the function, so there is no great savings in time using an inline version.

For the compiler to make inline optimizations, it has to know the contents of the function definition. This means the inline function definition has to be in the same file as the function call. For this reason, an inline function ordinarily has internal linkage. Therefore, if you have a multifile program, you need an inline definition in each file that calls the function. The simplest way to accomplish this is to put the inline function definition in a header file and then include the header file in those files that use the function. An inline function is an exception to the rule of not placing executable code in a header file. Because the inline function has internal linkage, defining one in several files doesn't cause problems.

C provides several ways to use inline functions in multiple-file programs. Normally, C allows only one definition of a function, but it relaxes that restriction for inline functions. Therefore, the simplest approach is to place the inline definition in each file that needs to use the function. An easy way to do this is to place the inline definition in a header file and then include the header file in the source code files using the function.

C, unlike C++, also allows a mixture of inline definitions with external definitions (function definitions with external linkage). For example, consider this setup:

```
//file1a.c
...
inline double square(double);
double square(double x) { return x * x; }

int main()
{
    double q = square(1.3);
...
//file2a.c
...
extern double square(double);
double square(double x) { int y; y = x*x; return y; }
void spam(double v)
{
    double kv = square(v);
...
//file3a.c
...
extern double square(double);
void masp(double w)
{
    double kw = square(w);
...
```

Here, file1a.c would use the inline version of square() defined in file1a.c. However, file2a.c and file3a.c both would use the external function definition from file2a.c.

C even lets you place an external declaration in a file with an inline definition:

```
//file1b.c -- careful!
...
extern double square(double);      // declare square() as external
inline double square(double);      // declare square() as inline
double square(double x) { return x * x; }

int main()
{
    double q = square(1.3) + square(1.5);  // which square()?
...
//file2b.c
...
```

```
extern double square(double);
double square(double x) { int y; y = x*x; return y; }
...
```

In this case, the compiler is free to use either definition for `square()` for the call in `file1b.c`. It doesn't even have to be consistent. For example, in the previous code, it could use the inline version for `square(1.3)` and the external version for `square(1.5)`. The standard warns that you should not write code that depends on which version gets chosen. As mentioned earlier, if any file with an inline function definition uses code that takes the address of the function (for example, by passing the function name as an actual argument), the compiler generates an external function definition.

The C Library

Originally, there was no official C library. Later, a de facto standard emerged based on the Unix implementation of C. The ANSI C committee, in turn, developed an official standard library, largely based on the de facto standard. Recognizing the expanded C universe, the committee then sought to redefine the library so that it could be implemented on a wide variety of systems.

We've already discussed some I/O functions, character functions, and string functions from the library. In this chapter, we'll browse through several more. First, however, let's talk about how to use a library.

Gaining Access to the C Library

How you gain access to the C library depends on your implementation, so you need to see how the more general statements apply to your system. First, there are often several different places to find library functions. For example, `getchar()` is usually defined as a macro in the file `stdio.h`, but `strlen()` is usually kept in a library file. Second, different systems have different ways to reach these functions. The following sections outline three possibilities.

Automatic Access

On many systems, you just compile the program and the more common library functions are made available automatically.

Keep in mind that you should declare the function type for functions you use. Usually you can do that by including the appropriate header file. User manuals describing library functions tell you which files to include. On some older systems, however, you might have to enter the function declarations yourself. Again, the user manual indicates the function type. Also, Appendix B, "Reference Section," summarizes the ANSI C library, grouping functions by header file.

In the past, header filenames have not been consistent among different implementations. The ANSI C standard groups the library functions into families, with each family having a specific header file for its function prototypes.

File Inclusion

If a function is defined as a macro, you can include the file containing its definition by using the `#include` directive. Often, similar macros are collected in an appropriately named header file. For example, many systems, including all ANSI C systems, have a `ctype.h` file containing several macros that determine the nature of a character: uppercase, digit, and so forth.

Library Inclusion

At some stage in compiling or linking a program, you might have to specify a library option. Even a system that automatically checks its standard library can have other libraries of functions less frequently used. These libraries have to be requested explicitly by using a compile-time option. Note that this process is distinct from including a header file. A header file provides a function declaration or prototype. The library option tells the system where to find the function code. Clearly, we can't go through all the specifics for all systems, but these discussions should alert you to what you should look for.

Using the Library Descriptions

We haven't the space to discuss the complete library, but we will look at some representative examples. First, though, let's take a look at documentation.

You can find function documentation in several places. Your system might have an online manual, and integrated environments often have online help. C vendors may supply printed user's guides describing library functions, or they might place equivalent material on a reference CD-ROM. Several publishers have issued reference manuals for C library functions. Some are generic in nature, and some are targeted toward specific implementations. And, as mentioned earlier, Appendix B in this book provides a summary.

The key skill you need in reading the documentation is interpreting function headings. The idiom has changed with time. Here, for instance, is how `fread()` is listed in older Unix documentation:

```
#include <stdio.h>

fread(ptr, sizeof(*ptr), nitems, stream)
FILE *stream;
```

First, the proper `include` file is given. No type is given for `fread()`, `ptr`, `sizeof(*ptr)`, or `nitems`. By default, in the old days, they were taken to be type `int`, but the context makes it clear that `ptr` is a pointer. (In C's early days, pointers were handled as integers.) The `stream` argument is declared as a pointer to `FILE`. The declaration makes it look as though you are supposed to use the `sizeof` operator as the second argument. Actually, it's saying that the value of this argument should be the size of the object pointed to by `ptr`. Often, you would use `sizeof` as illustrated, but any type `int` value satisfies the syntax.

Later, the form changed to this:

```
#include <stdio.h>
```

```
int fread(ptr, size, nitems, stream;)
char *ptr;
int size, nitems;
FILE *stream;
```

Now all types are given explicitly, and `ptr` is treated as a pointer-to-`char`.

The ANSI C90 standard provides the following description:

```
#include <stdio.h>
size_t fread(void *ptr, size_t size, size_t nmemb, FILE *stream);
```

First, it uses the new prototype format. Second, it changes some types. The `size_t` type is defined as the unsigned integer type that the `sizeof` operator returns. Usually, it is either `unsigned int` or `unsigned long`. The `stddef.h` file contains a `typedef` or a `#define` for `size_t`, as do several other files, including `stdio.h`, typically by including `stddef.h`. Many functions, including `fread()`, often incorporate the `sizeof` operator as part of an actual argument. The `size_t` type makes that formal argument match this common usage.

Also, ANSI C uses pointer-to-`void` as a kind of generic pointer for situations in which pointers to different types may be used. For example, the actual first argument to `fread()` may be a pointer to an array of `double` or to a structure of some sort. If the actual argument is, say, a pointer-to-array-of-20-`double` and the formal argument is pointer-to-`void`, the compiler makes the appropriate type version without complaining about type clashes.

More recently, the C99 standard incorporates the new keyword `restrict` into the description:

```
#include <stdio.h>
size_t fread(void * restrict ptr, size_t size,
             size_t nmemb, FILE * restrict stream);
```

Now let's turn to some specific functions.

The Math Library

The math library contains many useful mathematical functions. The `math.h` header file provides the function declarations or prototypes for these functions. Table 16.2 lists several functions declared in `math.h`. Note that all angles are measured in radians (one radian = $180/\pi$ = 57.296 degrees). Reference Section V, "The Standard ANSI C Library with C99 Additions," supplies a complete list of the functions specified by the C99 standard.

TABLE 16.2 ANSI C Standard Math Functions

Prototype	Description
`double acos(double x)`	Returns the angle (0 to π radians) whose cosine is x
`double asin(double x)`	Returns the angle ($-\pi/2$ to $\pi/2$ radians) whose sine is x
`double atan(double x)`	Returns the angle ($-\pi/2$ to $\pi/2$ radians) whose tangent is x

Prototype	Description
`double atan2(double y, double x)`	Returns the angle ($-\pi$ to π radians) whose tangent is y / x
`double cos(double x)`	Returns the cosine of x (x in radians)
`double sin(double x)`	Returns the sine of x (x in radians)
`double tan(double x)`	Returns the tangent of x (x in radians)
`double exp(double x)`	Returns the exponential function of x (e^x)
`double log(double x)`	Returns the natural logarithm of x
`double log10(double x)`	Returns the base 10 logarithm of x
`double pow(double x, double y)`	Returns x to the y power
`double sqrt(double x)`	Returns the square root of x
`double ceil(double x)`	Returns the smallest integral value not less than x
`double fabs(double x)`	Returns the absolute value of x
`double floor(double x)`	Returns the largest integral value not greater than x

Let's use the math library to solve a common problem: converting from x/y coordinates to magnitudes and angles. For example, suppose you draw, on a grid work, a line that transverses 4 units horizontally (the x value) and 3 units vertically (the y value). What is the length (magnitude) of the line and what is its direction? Trigonometry tells us the following:

```
magnitude = square root (x² + y²)
```

and

```
angle = arctangent (y/x)
```

The math library provides a square root function and a couple arctangent functions, so you can express this solution in a C program. The square root function, called `sqrt()`, takes a **double** argument and returns the argument's square root, also as a type **double** value.

The `atan()` function takes a double argument—the tangent—and returns the angle having that value as its tangent. Unfortunately, the `atan()` function is confused by, say, a line with x and y values of **-5** and **-5**. Because (–5)/(–5) is 1, `atan()` would report 45°, the same as it does for a line with x and y values of **5** and **5**. In other words, `atan()` doesn't distinguish between a line of a given angle and one 180° in the opposite direction. (Actually, `atan()` reports in radians, not degrees; we'll discuss that conversion soon.)

Fortunately, the C library also provides the `atan2()` function. It takes two arguments: the x value and the y value. That way, the function can examine the signs of x and y and figure out the correct angle. Like `atan()`, `atan2()` returns the angle in radians. To convert to degrees, multiply the resulting angle by 180 and divide by pi. You can have the computer calculate pi by using the expression **4 * atan(1)**. Listing 16.13 illustrates these steps. It also gives you a chance to review structures and the **typedef** facility.

LISTING 16.13   The rect_pol.c Program

```c
/* rect_pol.c -- converts rectangular coordinates to polar */
#include <stdio.h>
#include <math.h>

#define RAD_TO_DEG (180/(4 * atan(1)))

typedef struct polar_v {
    double magnitude;
    double angle;
} POLAR_V;

typedef struct rect_v {
    double x;
    double y;
} RECT_V;

POLAR_V rect_to_polar(RECT_V);

int main(void)
{
    RECT_V input;
    POLAR_V result;

    puts("Enter x,y coordinates; enter q to quit:");
    while (scanf("%lf %lf", &input.x, &input.y) == 2)
    {
        result = rect_to_polar(input);
        printf("magnitude = %0.2f, angle = %0.2f\n",
                result.magnitude, result.angle);
    }
    puts("Bye.");

    return 0;
}

POLAR_V rect_to_polar(RECT_V rv)
{
    POLAR_V pv;

    pv.magnitude = sqrt(rv.x * rv.x + rv.y * rv.y);
    if (pv.magnitude == 0)
        pv.angle = 0.0;
    else
        pv.angle = RAD_TO_DEG * atan2(rv.y, rv.x);

    return pv;
}
```

Here's a sample run:

```
Enter x,y coordinates; enter q to quit:
10 10
magnitude = 14.14, angle = 45.00
-12 -5
magnitude = 13.00, angle = -157.38
q
Bye.
```

If, when you compile, you get a message such as

```
Undefined:    _sqrt
```

or

```
'sqrt': unresolved external
```

or something similar, your compiler-linker is not finding the math library. Unix systems require that you instruct the linker to search the math library by using the `-lm` flag:

```
cc rect_pol.c -lm
```

The gnu compiler on Linux behaves in the same fashion:

```
gcc rect_pol.c -lm
```

The General Utilities Library

The general utilities library contains a grab bag of functions, including a random-number generator, searching and sorting functions, conversion functions, and memory-management functions. You've already seen `rand()`, `srand()`, `malloc()`, and `free()` in Chapter 12, "Storage Classes, Linkage, and Memory Management." Under ANSI C, prototypes for these functions exist in the `stdlib.h` header file. Reference Section V lists all the functions in this family; we'll take a closer look at a few of them now.

The `exit()` and `atexit()` Functions

We've already used `exit()` explicitly in several examples. In addition, the `exit()` function is invoked automatically upon return from `main()`. The ANSI standard has added a couple nice features that we haven't used yet. The most important addition is that you can specify particular functions to be called when `exit()` executes. The `atexit()` function provides this feature by registering the functions to be called on exit; the `atexit()` function takes a function pointer as its argument. Listing 16.14 shows how this works.

LISTING 16.14   The `byebye.c` Program

```
/* byebye.c -- atexit() example */
#include <stdio.h>
#include <stdlib.h>
void sign_off(void);
```

LISTING 16.14   Continued

```
void too_bad(void);

int main(void)
{
    int n;

    atexit(sign_off);     /* register the sign_off() function */
    puts("Enter an integer:");
    if (scanf("%d",&n) != 1)
    {
        puts("That's no integer!");
        atexit(too_bad); /* register the too_bad()  function */
        exit(EXIT_FAILURE);
    }
    printf("%d is %s.\n", n,  (n % 2 == 0)? "even" : "odd");

    return 0;
}

void sign_off(void)
{
    puts("Thus terminates another magnificent program from");
    puts("SeeSaw Software!");
}

void too_bad(void)
{
    puts("SeeSaw Software extends its heartfelt condolences");
    puts("to you upon the failure of your program.");
}
```

Here's one sample run:

```
Enter an integer:
212
212 is even.
Thus terminates another magnificent program from
SeeSaw Software!
```

You might not see the final two lines if you are running in an IDE.

Here's a second run:

```
Enter an integer:
what?
That's no integer!
SeeSaw Software extends its heartfelt condolences
to you upon the failure of your program.
Thus terminates another magnificent program from
SeeSaw Software!
```

You might not see the final four lines if you are running in an IDE.

Let's look at two main areas: the use of the `atexit()` and `exit()` arguments.

Using `atexit()`

Here's a function that uses function pointers! To use the `atexit()` function, simply pass it the address of the function you want called on exit. Because the name of a function acts as an address when used as a function argument, use `sign_off` or `too_bad` as the argument. Then `atexit()` registers that function in a list of functions to be executed when `exit()` is called. ANSI guarantees that you can place at least 32 functions on the list. Each function is added with a separate call to `atexit()`. When the `exit()` function is finally called, it executes these functions, with the last function added being executed first.

Notice that both `sign_off()` and `too_bad()` were called when input failed, but only `sign_off()` was called when input worked. That's because the `if` statement registers `too_bad()` only if input fails. Also note that the last function registered was the first called.

The functions registered by `atexit()` should, like `sign_off()` and `too_bad()`, be type `void` functions taking no arguments. Typically, they would perform housekeeping tasks, such as updating a program-monitoring file or resetting environmental variables.

Note that `sign_off()` is called even when `exit()` is not called explicitly; that's because `exit()` is called implicitly when `main()` terminates.

Using `exit()`

After `exit()` executes the functions specified by `atexit()`, it does some tidying of its own. It flushes all output streams, closes all open streams, and closes temporary files created by calls to the standard I/O function `tmpfile()`. Then `exit()` returns control to the host environment and, if possible, reports a termination status to the environment. Traditionally, Unix programs have used 0 to indicate successful termination and nonzero to report failure. Unix return codes don't necessarily work with all systems, so ANSI C defined a macro called `EXIT_FAILURE` that can be used portably to indicate failure. Similarly, it defined `EXIT_SUCCESS` to indicate success, but `exit()` also accepts 0 for that purpose. Under ANSI C, using the `exit()` function in a nonrecursive `main()` function is equivalent to using the keyword `return`. However, `exit()` also terminates programs when used in functions other than `main()`.

The `qsort()` Function

The "quick sort" method is one of the most effective sorting algorithms, particularly for larger arrays. Developed by C. A. R. Hoare in 1962, it partitions arrays into ever smaller sizes until the element level is reached. First, the array is divided into two parts, with every value in one partition being less than every value in the other partition. This process continues until the array is fully sorted.

The name for the C implementation of the quick sort algorithm is `qsort()`. The `qsort()` function sorts an array of data objects. It has the following ANSI prototype:

```
void qsort (void *base, size_t nmemb, size_t size,
        int (*compar)(const void *, const void *));
```

The first argument is a pointer to the beginning of the array to be sorted. ANSI C permits any data pointer type to be typecast to a pointer-to-**void**, thus permitting the first actual argument to qsort() to refer to any kind of array.

The second argument is the number of items to be sorted. The prototype converts this value to type **size_t**. As you may recall from several previous mentions, **size_t** is the integer type returned by the **sizeof** operator and is defined in the standard header files.

Because qsort() converts its first argument to a **void** pointer, qsort() loses track of how big each array element is. To compensate, you must tell qsort() explicitly the size of the data object. That's what the third argument is for. For example, if you are sorting an array of type **double**, you would use **sizeof(double)** for this argument.

Finally, qsort() requires a pointer to the function to be used to determine the sorting order. The comparison function should take two arguments: pointers to the two items being compared. It should return a positive integer if the first item should follow the second value, zero if the two items are the same, and a negative integer if the second item should follow the first. The qsort() will use this function, passing it pointer values that it calculates from the other information given to it.

The form the comparison function must take is set forth in the qsort() prototype for the final argument:

```
int (*compar)(const void *, const void *)
```

This states that the final argument is a pointer to a function that returns an **int** and that takes two arguments, each of which is a pointer to type **const void**. These two pointers point to the items being compared.

Listing 16.15 and the discussion following it illustrate how to define a comparison function and how to use qsort(). The program creates an array of random floating-point values and sorts the array.

LISTING 16.15   The qsorter.c Program

```
/* qsorter.c -- using qsort to sort groups of numbers */
#include <stdio.h>
#include <stdlib.h>

#define NUM 40
void fillarray(double ar[], int n);
void showarray(const double ar[], int n);
int mycomp(const void * p1, const void * p2);

int main(void)
{
    double vals[NUM];
    fillarray(vals, NUM);
    puts("Random list:");
    showarray(vals, NUM);
    qsort(vals, NUM, sizeof(double), mycomp);
```

LISTING 16.15 Continued

```
        puts("\nSorted list:");
        showarray(vals, NUM);
        return 0;
    }

    void fillarray(double ar[], int n)
    {
        int index;

        for( index = 0; index < n; index++)
            ar[index] = (double)rand()/((double) rand() + 0.1);
    }

    void showarray(const double ar[], int n)
    {
        int index;

        for( index = 0; index < n; index++)
        {
            printf("%9.4f ", ar[index]);
            if (index % 6 == 5)
                putchar('\n');
        }
        if (index % 6 != 0)
            putchar('\n');
    }

    /* sort by increasing value */
    int mycomp(const void * p1, const void * p2)
    {
        /* need to use pointers to double to access values    */
        const double * a1 = (const double *) p1;
        const double * a2 = (const double *) p2;

        if (*a1 < *a2)
            return -1;
        else if (*a1 == *a2)
            return 0;
        else
            return 1;
    }
```

Here is a sample run:

```
Random list:
    0.0022     0.2390     1.2191     0.3910     1.1021     0.2027
    1.3836    20.2872     0.2508     0.8880     2.2180    25.5033
    0.0236     0.9308     0.9911     0.2507     1.2802     0.0939
    0.9760     1.7218     1.2055     1.0326     3.7892     1.9636
    4.1137     0.9241     0.9971     1.5582     0.8955    35.3843
    4.0580    12.0467     0.0096     1.0110     0.8506     1.1530
    2.3614     1.5876     0.4825     6.8751
```

```
Sorted list:
    0.0022    0.0096    0.0236    0.0939    0.2027    0.2390
    0.2507    0.2508    0.3910    0.4825    0.8506    0.8880
    0.8955    0.9241    0.9308    0.9760    0.9911    0.9971
    1.0110    1.0326    1.1021    1.1530    1.2055    1.2191
    1.2802    1.3836    1.5582    1.5876    1.7218    1.9636
    2.2180    2.3614    3.7892    4.0580    4.1137    6.8751
   12.0467   20.2872   25.5033   35.3843
```

Let's look at two main areas: the use of `qsort()` and the definition of `mycomp()`.

Using `qsort()`

The `qsort()` function sorts an array of data objects. The ANSI prototype, again, is this:

```
void qsort (void *base, size_t nmemb, size_t size,
        int (*compar)(const void *, const void *));
```

The first argument is a pointer to the beginning of the array to be sorted. In this program, the actual argument is `vals`, the name of an array of `double`, hence a pointer to the first element of the array. The ANSI prototype causes the `vals` argument to be typecast to type pointer-to-`void`. That's because ANSI C permits any data pointer type to be typecast to a pointer-to-`void`, thus permitting the first actual argument to `qsort()` to refer to any kind of array.

The second argument is the number of items to be sorted. In Listing 16.15, it is `N`, the number of array elements. The prototype converts this value to type `size_t`.

The third argument is the size of each element—`sizeof(double)`, in this case.

The final argument is `mycomp`, the address of the function to be used for comparing elements.

Defining `mycomp()`

As mentioned before, the `qsort()` prototype mandates the form of the comparison function:

```
int (*compar)(const void *, const void *)
```

This states that the final argument is a pointer to a function that returns an `int` and that takes two arguments, each of which is a pointer to type `const void`. We made the prototype for the `mycomp()` function agree with this prototype:

```
int mycomp(const void * p1, const void * p2);
```

Remember that the name of the function is a pointer to the function when used as argument, so `mycomp` matches the `compar` prototype.

The `qsort()` function passes the addresses of the two elements to be compared to the comparison function. In this program, then, `p1` and `p2` are assigned the addresses of two type `double` values to be compared. Note that the first argument to `qsort()` refers to the whole array, and the two arguments in the comparison function refer to two elements in the array. There is a problem. To compare the pointed-to values, you need to dereference a pointer. Because the values are type `double`, you need to dereference a pointer to type `double`. However, `qsort()` requires pointers to type `void`. The way to get around this problem is to declare pointers of the proper type inside the function and initialize them to the values passed as arguments:

```
/* sort by increasing value */
int mycomp(const void * p1, const void * p2)
{
    /* need to use pointers to double to access values    */
    const double * a1 = (const double *) p1;
    const double * a2 = (const double *) p2;

    if (*a1 < *a2)
        return -1;
    else if (*a1 == *a2)
        return 0;
    else
        return 1;
}
```

In short, `qsort()` and the comparison function use `void` pointers for generality. As a consequence, you have to tell `qsort()` explicitly how large each element of the array is, and within the definition of the comparison function, you have to convert its pointer arguments to pointers of the proper type for your application.

void * in C and in C++

C and C++ treat pointer-to-`void` differently. In both languages, you can assign a pointer of any type to type `void *`. The function call to `qsort()` in Listing 16.15, for example, assigns type `double *` to a type `double *` pointer. But C++ requires a type cast when assigning a `void *` pointer to a pointer of another type, whereas C doesn't have that requirement. For instance, the `mycomp()` function in Listing 16.15 has this type cast for the type `void *` pointer p1:

```
const double * a1 = (const double *) p1;
```

In C, this type cast is optional; in C++ it is mandatory. Because the type cast version works in both languages, it makes sense to use it. Then, if you convert the program to C++, you won't have to remember to change that part.

Let's look at one more example of a comparison function. Suppose you have these declarations:

```
struct names {
    char first[40];
    char last[40];
};
struct names staff[100];
```

What should a call to `qsort()` look like? Following the model in Listing 16.15, a call could look like this:

```
qsort(staff, 100, sizeof(struct names), comp);
```

Here, `comp` is the name of the comparison function. What should this function look like?

Suppose you want to sort by last name, then by first name. You could write the function this way:

```
#include <string.h>
int comp(const void * p1, const void * p2)    /* mandatory form */
{
    /* get right type of pointer */
    const struct names *ps1 = (const struct names *) p1;
    const struct names *ps2 = (const struct names *) p2;
    int res;

    res = strcmp(ps1->last, ps2->last);   /* compare last names */
    if (res != 0)
        return res;
    else        /* last names identical, so compare first names */
        return strcmp(ps1->first, ps2->first);
}
```

This function uses the `strcmp()` function to do the comparison; its possible return values match the requirements for the comparison function. Note that you need a pointer to a structure to use the `->` operator.

The Assert Library

The assert library, supported by the `assert.h` header file, is a small one designed to help with debugging programs. It consists of a macro named `assert()`. It takes as its argument an integer expression. If the expression evaluates as false (nonzero), the `assert()` macro writes an error message to the standard error stream (`stderr`) and calls the `abort()` function, which terminates the program. (The `abort()` function is prototyped in the `stdlib.h` header file.) The idea is to identify critical locations in a program where certain conditions should be true and to use the `assert()` statement to terminate the program if one of the specified conditions is not true. Typically, the argument is a relational or logical expression. If `assert()` does abort the program, it first displays the test that failed, the name of the file containing the test, and a line number. Listing 16.16 shows a short example. It asserts that `z` is greater than or equal to `0` before attempting to take its square root. It also mistakenly subtracts a value instead of adding it, making it possible for `z` to obtain forbidden values.

LISTING 16.16   The `assert.c` Program

```
/* assert.c -- use assert() */
#include <stdio.h>
#include <math.h>
#include <assert.h>
int main()
{
    double x, y, z;

    puts("Enter a pair of numbers (0 0 to quit): ");
```

LISTING 16.16   *Continued*

```
    while (scanf("%lf%lf", &x, &y) == 2
            && (x != 0 || y != 0))
    {
        z = x * x - y * y;   /* should be + */
        assert(z >= 0);
        printf("answer is %f\n", sqrt(z));
        puts("Next pair of numbers: ");
    }
    puts("Done");

    return 0;
}
```

Here is a sample run:

```
Enter a pair of numbers (0 0 to quit):
4 3
answer is 2.645751
Next pair of numbers:
5 3
answer is 4.000000
Next pair of numbers:
3 5
Assertion failed:  z >= 0, file C:\assert.c, line 14
```

The exact wording will depend on the compiler. One potentially confusing point to note is that the message is not saying that z >= 0; instead, it's saying that the claim z >= 0 failed.

You could accomplish something similar with an `if` statement:

```
if (z < 0)
{
    puts("z less than 0");
    abort();
}
```

The `assert()` approach has several advantages, however. It identifies the file automatically. It identifies the line number where the problem occurs automatically. Finally, there's a mechanism for turning the `assert()` macro on and off without changing code. If you think you've eliminated the program bugs, place the macro definition

```
#define NDEBUG
```

before the location where `assert.h` is included and then recompile the program, and the compiler will deactivate all `assert()` statements in the file. If problems pop up again, you can remove the `#define` directive (or comment it out) and then recompile, thus reactivating all the `assert()` statements.

`memcpy()` and `memmove()` from the `string.h` Library

You can't assign one array to another, so we've been using loops to copy one array to another, element by element. The one exception is that we've used the `strcpy()` and `strncpy()` functions for character arrays. The `memcpy()` and `memmove()` functions offer you almost the same convenience for other kinds of arrays. Here are the prototypes for these two functions:

```
void *memcpy(void * restrict s1, const void * restrict s2, size_t n);
void *memmove(void *s1, const void *s2, size_t n);
```

Both of these functions copy n bytes from the location pointed to by **s2** to the location pointed to by **s1**, and both return the value of **s1**. The difference between the two, as indicated by the keyword `restrict`, is that `memcpy()` is free to assume that there is no overlap between the two memory ranges. The `memmove()` function doesn't make that assumption, so copying takes place as if all the bytes are first copied to a temporary buffer before being copied to the final destination. What if you use `memcpy()` when there are overlapping ranges? The behavior is undefined, meaning it might work or it might not. The compiler won't stop you from using the `memcpy()` function when you shouldn't, so it's your responsibility to make sure the ranges aren't overlapping when you use it. It's just another part of the programmer's burden.

Because these functions are designed to work with any data type, the two pointer arguments are type pointer-to-**void**. C allows you to assign any pointer type to pointers of the **void *** type. The other side of this tolerant acceptance is that these functions have no way of knowing what type of data is being copied. Therefore, they use the third argument to indicate the number of bytes to be copied. Note that for an array, the number of bytes is not, in general, the number of elements. So if you were copying an array of 10 **double** values, you would use `10*sizeof(double)`, not `10`, as the third argument.

Listing 16.17 shows some examples using these two functions.

LISTING 16.17   The `mems.c` Program

```c
// mems.c -- using memcpy() and memmove()
#include <stdio.h>
#include <string.h>
#include <stdlib.h>
#define SIZE 10
void show_array(const int ar[], int n);

int main()
{
    int values[SIZE] = {1,2,3,4,5,6,7,8,9,10};
    int target[SIZE];
    double curious[SIZE / 2] = {1.0, 2.0, 3.0, 4.0, 5.0};

    puts("memcpy() used:");
    puts("values (original data): ");
```

LISTING 16.17   *Continued*

```
    show_array(values, SIZE);
    memcpy(target, values, SIZE * sizeof(int));
    puts("target (copy of values):");
    show_array(target, SIZE);

    puts("\nUsing memmove() with overlapping ranges:");
    memmove(values + 2, values, 5 * sizeof(int));
    puts("values -- elements 0-5 copied to 2-7:");
    show_array(values, SIZE);

    puts("\nUsing memcpy() to copy double to int:");
    memcpy(target, curious, (SIZE / 2) * sizeof(double));
    puts("target -- 5 doubles into 10 int positions:");
    show_array(target, SIZE);

    return 0;
}

void show_array(const int ar[], int n)
{
    int i;

    for (i = 0; i < n; i++)
        printf("%d ", ar[i]);
    putchar('\n');
}
```

Here is the output:

```
memcpy() used:
values (original data):
1 2 3 4 5 6 7 8 9 10
target (copy of values):
1 2 3 4 5 6 7 8 9 10

Using memmove() with overlapping ranges:
values -- elements 0-5 copied to 2-7:
1 2 1 2 3 4 5 8 9 10

Using memcpy() to copy double to int:
target -- 5 doubles into 10 int positions:
0 1072693248 0 1073741824 0 1074266112 0 1074790400 0 1075052544
```

The last call to memcpy() copies data from a type double array to a type int array. This shows that memcpy() doesn't know or care about data types; it just copies bytes from one location to another. (You could, for example, copy bytes from a structure to a character array.) Also, there is no data conversion. If you had a loop doing element-by-element assignment, the type double values would be converted to type int during assignment. In this case, the bytes are copied over "as is," and the program then interprets the bit patterns as if they were type int.

Variable Arguments: `stdarg.h`

Earlier, this chapter discussed variadic macros—macros that can accept a variable number of arguments. The `stdarg.h` header file provides a similar capability for functions. But the usage is a bit more involved. You have to do the following:

1. Provide a function prototype using ellipses.

2. Create a `va_list` type variable in the function definition.

3. Use a macro to initialize the variable to an argument list.

4. Use a macro to access the argument list.

5. Use a macro to clean up.

Let's look at these steps in more detail. The prototype for such a function should have a parameter list with at least one parameter followed by ellipses:

```
void f1(int n, ...);              // valid
int f2(const char * s, int k, ...);  // valid
char f3(char c1, ..., char c2);   // invalid, ellipses not last
double f3(...);                   // invalid, no parameter
```

The rightmost parameter (the one just before the ellipses) plays a special role; the standard uses the term `parmN` as a name to use in discussion. In the preceding examples, `parmN` would be `n` for the first case and `k` for the second case. The actual argument passed to this parameter will be the number of arguments represented by the ellipses section. For example, the `f1()` function prototyped earlier could be used this way:

```
f1(2, 200, 400);        // 2 additional arguments
f1(4, 13, 117, 18, 23);  // 4 additional arguments
```

Next, the `va_list` type, which is declared in the `stdargs.h` header file, represents a data object used to hold the parameters corresponding to the ellipses part of the parameter list. The beginning of a definition of a variadic function would look something like this:

```
double sum(int lim,...)
{
    va_list ap;                   // declare object to hold arguments
```

In this example, `lim` is the `parmN` parameter, and it will indicate the number of arguments in the variable-argument list.

After this, the function will use the `va_start()` macro, also defined in `stdargs.h`, to copy the argument list to the `va_list` variable. The macro has two arguments: the `va_list` variable and the `parmN` parameter. Continuing with the previous example, the `va_list` variable is called `ap` and the `parmN` parameter is call `lim`, so the call would look like this:

```
va_start(ap, lim);        // initialize ap to argument list
```

The next step is gaining access to the contents of the argument list. This involves using `va_arg()`, another macro. It takes two arguments: a type `va_list` variable and a type name.

The first time it's called, it returns the first item in the list; the next time it's called, it returns the next item, and so on. The type argument specifies the type of value returned. For example, if the first argument in the list were a `double` and the second were an `int`, you could do this:

```
double tic;
int toc;
...
tic = va_arg(ap, double);    // retrieve first argument
toc = va_arg(ap, int);       // retrieve second argument
```

Be careful. The argument type really has to match the specification. If the first argument is 10.0, the previous code for `tic` works fine. But if the argument is 10, the code may not work; the automatic conversion of `double` to `int` that works for assignment doesn't take place here.

Finally, you should clean up by using the `va_end()` macro. It may, for example, free memory dynamically allocated to hold the arguments. This macro takes a `va_list` variable as its argument:

```
va_end(ap);                  // clean up
```

After you do this, the variable `ap` may not be usable unless you use `va_start` to reinitialize it.

Because `va_arg()` doesn't provide a way to back up to previous arguments, it may be useful to preserve a copy of the `va_list` type variable. C99 has added a macro for that purpose. It's called `va_copy()`. Its two arguments are both type `va_list` variables, and it copies the second argument to the first:

```
va_list ap;
va_list apcopy;
double
double tic;
int toc;
...
va_start(ap, lim);           // initialize ap to argument list
va_copy(apcopy, ap);         // apcopy a copy of ap
tic = va_arg(ap, double);    // retrieve first argument
toc = va_arg(ap, int);       // retrieve second argument
```

At this point, you could still retrieve the first two items from `apcopy`, even though they have been removed from `ap`.

Listing 16.18 is a short example of how the facilities can be used to create a function that sums a variable number of arguments; here, the first argument to `sum()` is the number of items to be summed.

LISTING 16.18 The `varargs.c` Program

```
//varargs.c -- use variable number of arguments
#include <stdio.h>
#include <stdarg.h>
double sum(int, ...);
```

LISTING 16.18   Continued

```c
int main(void)
{
    double s,t;

    s = sum(3, 1.1, 2.5, 13.3);
    t = sum(6, 1.1, 2.1, 13.1, 4.1, 5.1, 6.1);
    printf("return value for "
           "sum(3, 1.1, 2.5, 13.3):                %g\n", s);
    printf("return value for "
           "sum(6, 1.1, 2.1, 13.1, 4.1, 5.1, 6.1): %g\n", t);

    return 0;
}

double sum(int lim,...)
{
    va_list ap;                  // declare object to hold arguments
    double tot = 0;
    int i;

    va_start(ap, lim);           // initialize ap to argument list
    for (i = 0; i < lim; i++)
        tot += va_arg(ap, double); // access each item in argument list
    va_end(ap);                  // clean up

    return tot;
}
```

Here is the output:

```
return value for sum(3, 1.1, 2.5, 13.3):                16.9
return value for sum(6, 1.1, 2.1, 13.1, 4.1, 5.1, 6.1): 31.6
```

If you check the arithmetic, you'll find that `sum()` did add three numbers the first function call and six numbers to the second.

All in all, using variadic functions is more involved than using variadic macros, but the functions have a greater range of application.

Key Concepts

The C standard doesn't just describe the C language; it describes a package consisting of the C language, the C preprocessor, and the standard C library. The preprocessor lets you shape the compiling process, listing substitutions to be made, indicating which lines of code should be compiled, and other aspects of compiler behavior. The C library extends the reach of the language and provides prepackaged solutions to many programming problems.

Summary

The C preprocessor and the C library are two important adjuncts to the C language. The C preprocessor, following preprocessor directives, adjusts your source code before it is compiled. The C library provides many functions designed to help with tasks such as input, output, file handling, memory management, sorting and searching, mathematical calculations, and string processing, to name a few. Reference Section V lists the complete ANSI C library.

Review Questions

1. Here are groups of one or more macros followed by a source code line that uses them. What code results in each case? Is it valid code? (Assume C variables have been declared.)

   a.
   ```
   #define FPM  5280     /* feet per mile */
   dist = FPM * miles;
   ```

   b.
   ```
   #define FEET 4
   #define POD FEET + FEET
   plort = FEET * POD;
   ```

   c.
   ```
   #define SIX = 6;
   nex = SIX;
   ```

   d.
   ```
   #define NEW(X) X + 5
   y = NEW(y);
   berg = NEW(berg) * lob;
   est = NEW(berg) / NEW(y);
   nilp = lob * NEW(-berg);
   ```

2. Fix the definition in part "d" of question 1 to make it more reliable.

3. Define a macro function that returns the minimum of two values.

4. Define the EVEN_GT(X,Y) macro, which returns 1 if X is even and also greater than Y.

5. Define a macro function that prints the representations and the values of two integer expressions. For example, it might print

   ```
   3+4 is 7 and 4*12 is 48
   ```

   if its arguments are 3+4 and 4*12.

6. Create **#define** statements to accomplish the following goals:

   a. Create a named constant of value **25**.

   b. Have **SPACE** represent the space character.

   c. Have **PS()** represent printing the space character.

   d. Have **BIG(X)** represent adding 3 to **X**.

   e. Have **SUMSQ(X,Y)** represent the sums of the squares of **X** and **Y**.

7. Define a macro that prints the name, value, and address of an **int** variable in the following format:

   ```
   name: fop;  value: 23;  address: ff464016
   ```

8. Suppose you have a block of code you want to skip over temporarily while testing a program. How can you do so without actually removing the code from the file?

9. Show a code fragment that prints out the date of preprocessing if the macro **PR_DATE** is defined.

10. What's wrong with this program?

    ```
    #include <stdio.h>
    int main(int argc, char argv[])
    {
        printf("The square root of %f is %f\n", argv[1],
               sqrt(argv[1]) );
    }
    ```

11. Suppose **scores** is an array of 1000 **int** values that you want to sort into descending order. You will use **qsort()** and a comparison function called **comp()**.

    a. What is a suitable call to **qsort()**?

    b. What is a suitable definition for **comp()**?

12. Suppose **data1** is an array of 100 **double** values and **data2** is an array of 300 **double** values.

    a. Write a **memcpy()** function call that copies the first 100 elements of **data2** to **data1**.

    b. Write a **memcpy()** function call that copies the last 100 elements of **data2** to **data1**.

Programming Exercises

1. Start developing a header file of preprocessor definitions that you want to use.

2. The harmonic mean of two numbers is obtained by taking the inverses of the two numbers, averaging them, and taking the inverse of the result. Use a **#define** directive to

define a macro "function" that performs this operation. Write a simple program that tests the macro.

3. Polar coordinates describe a vector in terms of magnitude and the counterclockwise angle from the x-axis to the vector. Rectangular coordinates describe the same vector in terms of x and y components (see Figure 16.3). Write a program that reads the magnitude and angle (in degrees) of a vector and then displays the x and y components. The relevant equations are these:

```
x = r cos A     y = r sin A
```

To do the conversion, use a function that takes a structure containing the polar coordinates and returns a structure containing the rectangular coordinates (or use pointers to such structures, if you prefer).

FIGURE 16.3
Rectangular and polar
coordinates.

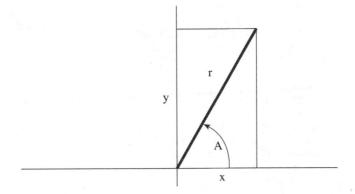

4. The ANSI library features a `clock()` function with this description:

```
#include <time.h>
clock_t clock (void);
```

Here, `clock_t` is a type defined in `time.h`. The function returns the processor time, which is given in some implementation-dependent units. (If the processor time is unavailable or cannot be represented, the function returns a value of -1.) However, `CLOCKS_PER_SEC`, also defined in `time.h`, is the number of processor time units per second. Therefore, dividing the difference between two return values of `clock()` by `CLOCKS_PER_SEC` gives you the number of seconds elapsed between the two calls. Typecasting the values to `double` before division enables you to get fractions of a second. Write a function that takes a `double` argument representing a desired time delay and then runs a loop until that amount of time has passed. Write a simple program that tests the function.

5. Write a function that takes as arguments the name of an array of type `int` elements, the size of an array, and a value representing the number of picks. The function then should select the indicated number of items at random from the array and prints them. No array element is to be picked more than once. (This simulates picking lottery numbers or jury members.) Also, if your implementation has `time()` (discussed in Chapter 12) or a similar function available, use its output with `srand()` to initialize the `rand()` random-number generator. Write a simple program that tests the function.

6. Modify Listing 16.15 so that it uses an array of `struct names` elements (as defined after the listing) instead of an array of `double`. Use fewer elements, and initialize the array explicitly to a suitable selection of names.

7. Here's a partial program using a variadic function:

```c
#include <stdio.h>
#include <stdlib.h>
#include <stdarg.h>
void show_array(const double ar[], int n);
double * new_d_array(int n, ...);
int main()
{
    double * p1;
    double * p2;

    p1 = new_d_array(5, 1.2, 2.3, 3.4, 4.5, 5.6);
    p2 = new_d_array(4, 100.0, 20.00, 8.08, -1890.0);
    show_array(p1, 5);
    show_array(p2, 4);
    free(p1);
    free(p2);

    return 0;
}
```

The `new_d_array()` function takes an `int` argument and a variable number of `double` arguments. The function returns a pointer to a block of memory allocated by `malloc()`. The `int` argument indicates the number of elements to be in the dynamic array, and the `double` values are used to initialize the elements, with the first value being assigned to the first element, and so on. Complete the program by providing the code for `show_array()` and `new_d_array()`.

CHAPTER 17

ADVANCED DATA REPRESENTATION

L earning a computer language is like learning music, carpentry, or engineering. At first, you work with the tools of the trade, playing scales, learning which end of the hammer to hold and which end to avoid, solving countless problems involving falling, sliding, and balanced objects. Acquiring and practicing skills is what you've been doing so far in this book, learning to create variables, structures, functions, and the like. Eventually, however, you move to a higher level in which using the tools is second nature and the real challenge is designing and creating a project. You develop an ability to see the project as a coherent whole. This chapter concentrates on that higher level. You may find the material covered here a little more challenging than the preceding chapters, but you may also find it more rewarding because it helps you move from the role of apprentice to the role of crafts-person.

We'll start by examining a vital aspect of program design: the way a program represents data. Often the most important aspect of program development is finding a good representation of the data manipulated by that program. Getting data representation right can make writing the rest of the program simple. By now you've seen C's built-in data types: simple variables, arrays, pointers, structures, and unions.

Finding the right data representation, however, often goes beyond simply selecting a type. You should also think about what operations will be necessary. That is, you should decide how to store the data, and you should define what operations are valid for the data type. For example, C implementations typically store both the C `int` type and the C pointer type as integers, but the two types have different sets of valid operations. You can multiply one integer by another, for example, but you can't multiply a pointer by a pointer. You can use the `*` operator to deref-erence a pointer, but that operation is meaningless for an integer. The C language defines the valid operations for its fundamental types. However, when you design a scheme to represent data, you might need to define the valid operations yourself. In C, you can do so by designing C functions to represent the desired operations. In short, then, designing a data type consists of deciding on how to store the data and of designing a set of functions to manage the data.

You will also look at some *algorithms*, recipes for manipulating data. As a programmer, you will acquire a repertoire of such recipes that you apply over and over again to similar problems.

This chapter looks into the process of designing data types, a process that matches algorithms to data representations. In it, you'll meet some common data forms, such as the queue, the list, and the binary search tree.

You'll also be introduced to the concept of the abstract data type (ADT). An ADT packages methods and data representations in a way that is problem oriented rather than language oriented. After you've designed an ADT, you can easily reuse it in different circumstances. Understanding ADTs prepares you conceptually for entering the world of object-oriented programming (OOP) and the C++ language.

Exploring Data Representation

Let's begin by thinking about data. Suppose you had to create an address book program. What data form would you use to store information? Because there's a variety of information associated with each entry, it makes sense to represent each entry with a structure. How do you represent several entries? With a standard array of structures? With a dynamic array? With some other form? Should the entries be alphabetized? Should you be able to search through the entries by ZIP Code? By area code? The actions you want to perform might affect how you decide to store the information. In short, you have a lot of design decisions to make before plunging into coding.

How would you represent a bitmapped graphics image that you want to store in memory? A bitmapped image is one in which each pixel on the screen is set individually. In the days of black-and-white screens, you could use one computer bit (1 or 0) to represent one pixel (on or off), hence the name *bitmapped*. With color monitors, it takes more than one bit to describe a single pixel. For example, you can get 256 colors if you dedicate 8 bits to each pixel. Now the industry has moved to 65,536 colors (16 bits per pixel), 16,777,216 colors (24 bits per pixel), 2,147,483,648 colors (32 bits per pixel), and even beyond. If you have 16 million colors and if your monitor has a resolution of 1024×768, you'll need 18.9 million bits (2.25MB) to represent a single screen of bitmapped graphics. Is this the way to go, or can you develop a way of compressing the information? Should this compression be *lossless* (no data lost) or *lossy* (relatively unimportant data lost)? Again, you have a lot of design decisions to make before diving into coding.

Let's tackle a particular case of representing data. Suppose you want to write a program that enables you to enter a list of all the movies (including videotapes and DVDs) you've seen in a year. For each movie, you'd like to record a variety of information, such as the title, the year it was released, the director, the lead actors, the length, the kind of film (comedy, science fiction, romance, drivel, and so forth), your evaluation, and so on. That suggests using a structure for each film and an array of structures for the list. To simplify matters, let's limit the structure to two members: the film title and your evaluation, a ranking on a 0-to-10 scale. Listing 17.1 shows a bare-bones implementation using this approach.

LISTING 17.1   The `films1.c` Program

```
/* films1.c -- using an array of structures */
#include <stdio.h>
#define TSIZE        45        /* size of array to hold title   */
#define FMAX          5        /* maximum number of film titles */

struct film {
    char title[TSIZE];
    int rating;
};

int main(void)
{
    struct film movies[FMAX];
    int i = 0;
    int j;

    puts("Enter first movie title:");
    while (i < FMAX && gets(movies[i].title) != NULL &&
            movies[i].title[0] != '\0')
    {
        puts("Enter your rating <0-10>:");
        scanf("%d", &movies[i++].rating);
        while(getchar() != '\n')
            continue;
        puts("Enter next movie title (empty line to stop):");
    }
    if (i == 0)
        printf("No data entered. ");
    else
        printf ("Here is the movie list:\n");

    for (j = 0; j < i; j++)
        printf("Movie: %s  Rating: %d\n", movies[j].title,
                movies[j].rating);
    printf("Bye!\n");

    return 0;
}
```

The program creates an array of structures and then fills the array with data entered by the user. Entry continues until the array is full (the **FMAX** test), until end-of-file (the **NULL** test) is reached, or until the user presses the Enter key at the beginning of a line (the '**\0**' test).

This formulation has some problems. First, the program will most likely waste a lot of space because most movies don't have titles 40 characters long, but some movies do have long titles, such as *The Discreet Charm of the Bourgeoisie* and *Won Ton Ton, The Dog Who Saved Hollywood*. Second, many people will find the limit of five movies a year too restrictive. Of course, you can increase that limit, but what would be a good value? Some people see 500 movies a year, so you could increase FMAX to 500, but that still might be too small for some, yet it might waste enormous amounts of memory for others. Also, some compilers set a default limit for the amount of memory available for automatic storage class variables such as movies, and such a large array could exceed that value. You can fix that by making the array a static or external array or by instructing the compiler to use a larger stack, but that's not fixing the real problem.

The real problem here is that the data representation is too inflexible. You have to make decisions at compile time that are better made at runtime. This suggests switching to a data representation that uses dynamic memory allocation. You could try something like this:

```
#define TSIZE  45          /* size of array to hold title  */
struct film {
    char title[TSIZE];
    int rating;
};
...
    int n, i;
    struct film * movies;   /* pointer to a structure       */
    ...
    printf("Enter the maximum number of movies you'll enter:\n");
    scanf("%d", &n);
    movies = (struct film *) malloc(n * sizeof(struct film));
```

Here, as in Chapter 12, "Storage Classes, Linkage, and Memory Management," you can use the pointer movies just as though it were an array name:

```
while (i < FMAX && gets(movies[i].title) != NULL &&
        movies[i].title[0] != '\0')
```

By using malloc(), you can postpone determining the number of elements until the program runs, so the program need not allocate 500 elements if only 20 are needed. However, it puts the burden on the user to supply a correct value for the number of entries.

Beyond the Array to the Linked List

Ideally, you'd like to be able to add data indefinitely (or until the program runs out of memory) without specifying in advance how many entries you'll make and without committing the program to allocating huge chunks of memory unnecessarily. You can do this by calling malloc() after each entry and allocating just enough space to hold the new entry. If the user enters three films, the program calls malloc() three times. If the user enters 300 films, the program calls malloc() 300 times.

This fine idea raises a new problem. To see what it is, compare calling malloc() once, asking for enough space for 300 film structures, and calling malloc() 300 times, each time asking for enough space for one film structure. The first case allocates the memory as one contiguous memory block and all you need to keep track of the contents is a single pointer-to-**struct** variable (**film**) that points to the first structure in the block. Simple array notation lets the pointer access each structure in the block, as shown in the preceding code segment. The problem with the second approach is that there is no guarantee that consecutive calls to **malloc()** yield adjacent blocks of memory. This means the structures won't necessarily be stored contiguously (see Figure 17.1). Therefore, instead of storing one pointer to a block of 300 structures, you need to store 300 pointers, one for each independently allocated structure!

FIGURE 17.1

Allocating structures in a block versus allocating them individually.

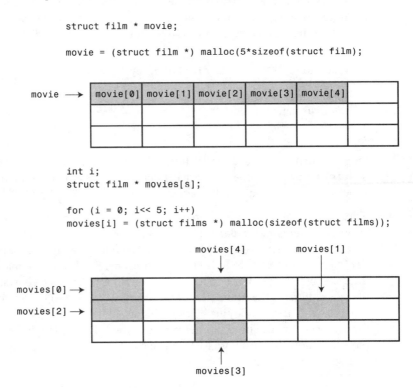

One solution, which we won't use, is to create a large array of pointers and assign values to the pointers, one by one, as new structures are allocated:

```
#define TSIZE   45        /* size of array to hold titles   */
#define FMAX   500        /* maximum number of film titles  */
struct film {
    char title[TSIZE];
    int rating;
};
...
    struct film * movies[FMAX]; /* array of pointers to structures */
    int i;
    ...
    movies[i] = (struct film *) malloc (sizeof (struct film));
```

This approach saves a lot of memory if you don't use the full allotment of pointers, because an array of 500 pointers takes much less memory than an array of 500 structures. It still wastes the space occupied by unused pointers, however, and it still imposes a 500-structure limit.

There's a better way. Each time you use `malloc()` to allocate space for a new structure, you can also allocate space for a new pointer. "But," you say, "then I need another pointer to keep track of the newly allocated pointer, and that needs a pointer to keep track of it, and so on." The trick to avoiding this potential problem is to redefine the structure so that each structure includes a pointer to the *next* structure. Then, each time you create a new structure, you can store its address in the preceding structure. In short, you need to redefine the `film` structure this way:

```
#define TSIZE   45      /* size of array to hold titles  */
struct film {
    char title[TSIZE];
    int rating;
    struct film * next;
};
```

True, a structure can't contain in itself a structure of the same type, but it can contain a pointer to a structure of the same type. Such a definition is the basis for defining a *linked list*—a list in which each item contains information describing where to find the next item.

Before looking at C code for a linked list, let's take a conceptual walk through such a list. Suppose a user enters `Modern Times` as a title and `10` as a rating. The program would allocate space for a `film` structure, copy the string `Modern Times` into the `title` member, and set the `rating` member to `10`. To indicate that no structure follows this one, the program would set the `next` member pointer to `NULL`. (`NULL`, recall, is a symbolic constant defined in the `stdio.h` file and represents the null pointer.) Of course, you need to keep track of where the first structure is stored. You can do this by assigning its address to a separate pointer that we'll refer to as the *head pointer*. The head pointer points to the first item in a linked list of items. Figure 17.2 represents how this structure looks. (The empty space in the `title` member is suppressed to save space in the figure.)

FIGURE 17.2

First item in a linked list.

```
#define TSIZE 45
struct film {
    char title[TSIZE]
    int rating;
    struct film * next;
};
struct film * head;
```

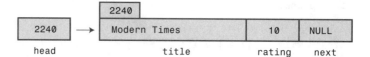

Now suppose the user enters a second movie and rating—for example, `Titanic` and `8`. The program allocates space for a second `film` structure, storing the address of the new structure in the `next` member of the first structure (overwriting the `NULL` previously stored there) so that the `next` pointer of one structure points to the following structure in the linked list. Then the program copies `Titanic` and `8` to the new structure and sets its `next` member to `NULL`, indicating that it is now the last structure in the list. Figure 17.3 shows this list of two items.

FIGURE 17.3

Linked list with two items.

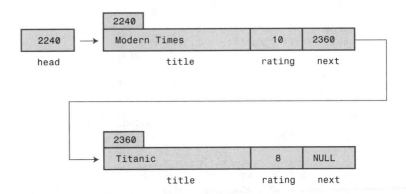

Each new movie will be handled the same way. Its address will be stored in the preceding structure, the new information goes into the new structure, and its `next` member is set to `NULL`, setting up a linked list like that shown in Figure 17.4.

Suppose you want to display the list. Each time you display an item, you can use the address stored in the corresponding structure to locate the next item to be displayed. For this scheme to work, however, you need a pointer to keep track of the very first item in the list because no structure in the list stores the address of the first item. Fortunately, you've already accomplished this with the head pointer.

Using a Linked List

Now that you have a picture of how a linked list works, let's implement it. Listing 17.2 modifies Listing 17.1 so that it uses a linked list instead of an array to hold the movie information.

LISTING 17.2   The `films2.c` Program

```
/* films2.c -- using a linked list of structures */
#include <stdio.h>
#include <stdlib.h>      /* has the malloc prototype    */
#include <string.h>      /* has the strcpy prototype    */
#define TSIZE    45      /* size of array to hold title */

struct film {
    char title[TSIZE];
    int rating;
    struct film * next;  /* points to next struct in list */
```

LISTING 17.2   Continued

```
    };

    int main(void)
    {
        struct film * head = NULL;
        struct film * prev, * current;
        char input[TSIZE];

/* Gather  and store information         */
        puts("Enter first movie title:");
        while (gets(input) != NULL && input[0] != '\0')
        {
            current = (struct film *) malloc(sizeof(struct film));
            if (head == NULL)        /* first structure       */
                head = current;
            else                     /* subsequent structures */
                prev->next = current;
            current->next = NULL;
            strcpy(current->title, input);
            puts("Enter your rating <0-10>:");
            scanf("%d", &current->rating);
            while(getchar() != '\n')
                continue;
            puts("Enter next movie title (empty line to stop):");
            prev = current;
        }

/* Show list of movies                   */
        if (head == NULL)
            printf("No data entered. ");
        else
            printf ("Here is the movie list:\n");
        current = head;
        while (current != NULL)
        {
            printf("Movie: %s  Rating: %d\n",
                    current->title, current->rating);
            current = current->next;
        }

/* Program done, so free allocated memory */
        current = head;
        while (current != NULL)
        {
            free(current);
            current = current->next;
        }
        printf("Bye!\n");

        return 0;
    }
```

FIGURE 17.4
Linked list with several items.

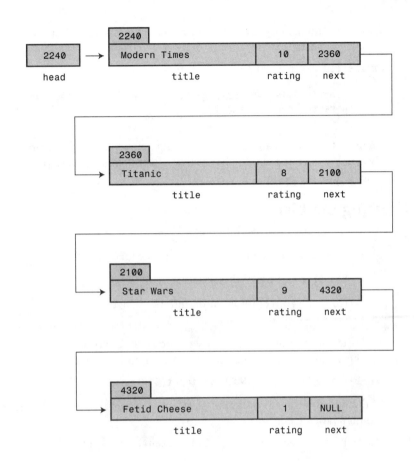

The program performs two tasks using the linked list. First, it constructs the list and fills it with the incoming data. Second, it displays the list. Displaying is the simpler task, so let's look at it first.

Displaying a List

The idea is to begin by setting a pointer (call it **current**) to point to the first structure. Because the head pointer (call it **head**) already points there, this code suffices:

```
current = head;
```

Then you can use pointer notation to access the members of that structure:

```
printf("Movie: %s  Rating: %d\n", current->title, current->rating);
```

The next step is to reset the **current** pointer to point to the next structure in the list. That information is stored in the **next** member of the structure, so this code accomplishes the task:

```
current = current->next;
```

After this is accomplished, repeat the whole process. When the last item in the list is displayed, **current** will be set to NULL, because that's the value of the **next** member of the final structure. You can use that fact to terminate the printing. Here's all the code `films2.c` uses to display the list:

```
while (current != NULL)
{
    printf("Movie: %s  Rating: %d\n", current->title, current->rating);
    current = current->next;
}
```

Why not just use **head** instead of creating a new pointer (**current**) to march through the list? Because using **head** would change the value of **head**, and the program would no longer have a way to find the beginning of the list.

Creating the List

Creating the list involves three steps:

1. Use `malloc()` to allocate enough space for a structure.

2. Store the address of the structure.

3. Copy the correct information into the structure.

There's no point in creating a structure if none is needed, so the program uses temporary storage (the **input** array) to get the user's choice for a movie name. If the user simulates **EOF** from the keyboard or enters an empty line, the input loop quits:

```
while (gets(input) != NULL && input[0] != '\0')
```

If there is input, the program requests space for a structure and assigns its address to the pointer variable **current**:

```
current = (struct film *) malloc(sizeof(struct film));
```

The address of the very first structure should be stored in the pointer variable **head**. The address of each subsequent structure should be stored in the **next** member of the structure that precedes it. Therefore, the program needs a way to know whether it's dealing with the first structure or not. A simple way is to initialize the **head** pointer to **NULL** when the program starts. Then the program can use the value of **head** to decide what to do:

```
if (head == NULL)        /* first structure     */
    head = current;
else                     /* subsequent structures */
    prev->next = current;
```

In this code, **prev** is a pointer that points to the structure allocated the previous time.

Next, you have to set the structure members to the proper values. In particular, you should set the **next** member to **NULL** to indicate that the current structure is the last one in the list. You should copy the film title from the **input** array to the **title** member, and you should get a value for the **rating** member. The following code does these things:

```
current->next = NULL;
strcpy(current->title, input);
```

```
puts("Enter your rating <0-10>:");
scanf("%d", &current->rating);
```

Finally, you should prepare the program for the next cycle of the input loop. In particular, you need to set **prev** to point to the current structure, because it will become the previous structure after the next movie name is entered and the next structure is allocated. The program sets this pointer at the end of the loop:

```
prev = current;
```

Does it work? Here is a sample run:

```
Enter first movie title:
Spirited Away
Enter your rating <0-10>:
8
Enter next movie title (empty line to stop):
The Duelists
Enter your rating <0-10>:
7
Enter next movie title (empty line to stop):
Devil Dog: The Mound of Hound
Enter your rating <0-10>:
1
Enter next movie title (empty line to stop):

Here is the movie list:
Movie: Spirited Away  Rating: 8
Movie: The Duelists  Rating: 7
Movie: Devil Dog: The Mound of Hound  Rating: 1
Bye!
```

Freeing List Memory

The program should free the memory used by `malloc()` when the program terminates, but it's best to get into the habit of balancing calls to `malloc()` with calls to `free()`. Therefore, the program cleans up its memory use by applying `free()` to each of the allocated structures:

```
current = head;
while (current != NULL)
{
    free(current);
    current = current->next;
}
```

Afterthoughts

The `films2.c` program is a bit skimpy. For example, it fails to check whether `malloc()` finds the requested memory, and it doesn't have any provisions for deleting items from the list. These failings can be fixed, however. For example, you can add code that checks whether `malloc()`'s return value is `NULL` (the sign it failed to obtain the memory you wanted). If the program needs to delete entries, you can write some more code to do that.

This ad hoc approach to solving problems and adding features as the need arises isn't always the best programming method. On the other hand, you usually can't anticipate everything a program needs to do. As programming projects get larger, the model of a programmer or programming team planning everything in advance becomes more and more unrealistic. It has been observed that the most successful large programs are those that evolved step-by-step from successful small programs.

Given that you may have to revise your plans, it's a good idea to develop your original ideas in a way that simplifies modification. The example in Listing 17.2 doesn't follow this precept. In particular, it tends to intermingle coding details and the conceptual model. For example, in the sample program, the conceptual model is that you add items to a list. The program obscures that interface by pushing details such as `malloc()` and the `current->next` pointer into the foreground. It would be nice if you could write a program in a way that made it obvious you're adding something to a list and in which bookkeeping details, such as calling memory-management functions and setting pointers, were hidden. Separating the user interface from the details will make the program easier to understand and to update. By making a fresh start, you can meet these goals. Let's see how.

Abstract Data Types (ADTs)

In programming, you try to match the data type to the needs of a programming problem. For example, you would use the `int` type to represent the number of shoes you own and the `float` or `double` type to represent your average cost per pair of shoes. In the movie examples, the data formed a list of items, each of which consisted of a movie name (a C string) and rating (an `int`). No basic C type matches that description, so we defined a structure to represent individual items, and then we devised a couple methods for tying together a series of structures to form a list. In essence, we used C's capabilities to design a new data type that matched our needs, but we did so unsystematically. Now we'll take a more systematic approach to defining types.

What constitutes a type? A *type* specifies two kinds of information: a set of properties and a set of operations. For example, the `int` type's property is that it represents an integer value and, therefore, shares the properties of integers. The allowed arithmetic operations are changing the sign, adding two `int`s, subtracting two `int`s, multiplying two `int`s, dividing one `int` by another, and taking the modulus of one `int` with respect to another. When you declare a variable to be an `int`, you're saying that these and only these operations can affect it.

Integer Properties

Behind the C `int` type is a more abstract concept, that of the *integer*. Mathematicians can, and do, define the properties of integers in a formal abstract manner. For example, if N and M are integers, N + M = M + N, or for every two integers N and M, there is an integer S, such that N + M = S. If N + M = S and if N + Q = S, then M = Q. You can think of mathematics as supplying the abstract concept of the integer and of C as supplying an implementation of that concept. For example, C provides a means of storing an integer and of performing integer operations such as addition and multiplication. Note that providing support for arithmetic operations is an essential part of representing integers. The int type would be much less useful if all you could do was store a value but not use it in arithmetic expressions. Note also that the implementation doesn't do a perfect job of representing integers. For example, there is an infinite number of integers, but a 2-byte int can represent only 65,536 of them; don't confuse the abstract idea with a particular implementation.

Suppose you want to define a new data type. First, you have to provide a way to store the data, perhaps by designing a structure. Second, you have to provide ways of manipulating the data. For example, consider the `films2.c` program (Listing 17.2). It has a linked set of structures to hold the information and supplies code for adding information and displaying information. This program, however, doesn't do these things in a way that makes it clear we were creating a new type. What should we have done?

Computer science has developed a very successful way to define new data types. It's a three-step process that moves from the abstract to the concrete:

1. Provide an abstract description of the type's properties and of the operations you can perform on the type. This description shouldn't be tied to any particular implementation. It shouldn't even be tied to a particular programming language. Such a formal abstract description is called an *abstract data type* (ADT).

2. Develop a programming interface that implements the ADT. That is, indicate how to store the data and describe a set of functions that perform the desired operations. In C, for example, you might supply a structure definition along with prototypes for functions to manipulate the structures. These functions play the same role for the user-defined type that C's built-in operators play for the fundamental C types. Someone who wants to use the new type will use this interface for her or his programming.

3. Write code to implement the interface. This step is essential, of course, but the programmer using the new type need not be aware of the details of the implementation.

Let's work through an example to see how this process works. Because we've already invested some effort into the movie listing example, let's redo it using the new approach.

Getting Abstract

Basically, all you need for the movie project is a list of items. Each item contains a movie name and a rating. You need to be able to add new items to the end of the list, and you need to be able to display the contents of the list. Let's call the abstract type that will handle these needs a *list*. What properties should a list have? Clearly, a list should be able to hold a sequence of items. That is, a list can hold several items, and these items are arranged in some kind of order, so you can speak of the first item in a list or of the second item or of the last item. Next, the list type should support operations such as adding an item to the list. Here are some useful operations:

- Initializing a list to empty

- Adding an item to the end of a list

- Determining whether the list is empty

- Determining whether the list is full

- Determining how many items are in the list

- Visiting each item in a list to perform some action, such as displaying the item

You don't need any further operations for this project, but a more general list of operations for lists might include the following:

- Inserting an item anywhere in the list

- Removing an item from the list

- Retrieving an item from the list (list left unaltered)

- Replacing one item in the list with another

- Searching for an item in the list

The informal, but abstract, definition of a list, then, is that it is a data object capable of holding a sequence of items and to which you can apply any of the preceding operations. This definition doesn't state what kind of items can be stored in the list. It doesn't specify whether an array or a linked set of structures or some other data form should be used to hold the items. It doesn't dictate what method to use, for example, to find the number of elements in a list. These matters are all details left to the implementation.

To keep the example simple, let's adopt a simplified list as the abstract data type, one that embodies only the features needed for the movie project. Here's a summary of the type:

Type Name:	Simple List
Type Properties:	Can hold a sequence of items.
Type Operations:	Initialize list to empty.
	Determine whether list is empty.
	Determine whether list is full.
	Determine number of items in the list.
	Add item to end of list.
	Traverse list, processing each item in list.
	Empty the list.

The next step is to develop a C-language interface for the simple list ADT.

Building an Interface

The interface for the simple list has two parts. The first part describes how the data will be represented, and the second part describes functions that implement the ADT operations. For example, there will be functions for adding an item to a list and for reporting the number of items in the list. The interface design should parallel the ADT description as closely as possible. Therefore, it should be expressed in terms of some general Item type instead of in terms of some specific type, such as int or struct film. One way to do this is to use C's typedef facility to define Item as the needed type:

```
#define TSIZE  45       /* size of array to hold title   */
struct film
{
    char title[TSIZE];
    int rating;
};

typedef struct film Item;
```

Then you can use the Item type for the rest of the definitions. If you later want a list of some other form of data, you can redefine the Item type and leave the rest of the interface definition unchanged.

Having defined Item, you now have to decide how to store items of that type. This step really belongs to the implementation stage, but making a decision now makes the example easier to follow. The linked structure approach worked pretty well in the films2.c program, so let's adapt it as shown here:

```
typedef struct node
{
    Item item;
    struct node * next;
} Node;
typedef Node * List;
```

In a linked list implementation, each link is called a *node*. Each node contains information that forms the contents of the list along with a pointer to the next node. To emphasize this terminology, we've used the tag name node for a node structure, and we've used typedef to make Node the type name for a struct node structure. Finally, to manage a linked list, we need a pointer to its beginning, and we've used typedef to make List the name for a pointer of this type. Therefore, the declaration

```
List movies;
```

establishes movies as a pointer suitable for referring to a linked list.

Is this the only way to define the List type? No. For example, you could incorporate a variable to keep track of the number of entries:

```
typedef struct list
{
    Node * head;    /* pointer to head of list       */
    int size;       /* number of entries in list     */
} List;             /* alternative definition of list */
```

You could add a second pointer to keep track of the end of the list. Later, you'll see an example that does that. For now, let's stick to the first definition of a `List` type. The important point is that you should think of the declaration

```
List movies;
```

as establishing a list, not as establishing a pointer to a node or as establishing a structure. The exact data representation of `movies` is an implementation detail that should be invisible at the interface level.

For example, a program should initialize the head pointer to `NULL` when starting out, but you should not use code like this:

```
movies = NULL;
```

Why not? Because later you might find you like the structure implementation of a `List` type better, and that would require the following initializations:

```
movies.next = NULL;
movies.size = 0;
```

Anyone using the `List` type shouldn't have to worry about such details. Instead, they should be able do something along the following lines:

```
InitializeList(movies);
```

Programmers need to know only that they should use the `InitializeList()` function to initialize a list. They don't have to know the exact data implementation of a `List` variable. This is an example of *data hiding*, the art of concealing details of data representation from the higher levels of programming.

To guide the user, you can supply a function prototype along these lines:

```
/* operation:       initialize a list                    */
/* preconditions:   plist points to a list               */
/* postconditions:  the list is initialized to empty     */
void InitializeList(List * plist);
```

There are three points you should notice. First, the comments outline *preconditions*—that is, conditions that should hold before the function is called. Here, for example, you need a list to initialize. Second, the comments outline *postconditions*—that is, conditions that should hold after the function executes. Finally, the function uses a pointer to a list instead of a list as its argument, so this would be the function call:

```
InitializeList(&movies);
```

The reason is that C passes arguments by value, so the only way a C function can alter a variable in the calling program is by using a pointer to that variable. Here the restrictions of the language make the interface deviate slightly from the abstract description.

The C way to tie all the type and function information into a single package is to place the type definitions and function prototypes (including precondition and postcondition comments) in a header file. This file should supply all the information a programmer needs to use the type. Listing 17.3 shows a header file for the simple `list` type. It defines a particular structure as the `Item` type, and then it defines `Node` in terms of `Item` and it defines `List` in terms of `Node`. The functions representing list operations then use `Item` types and `List` types as arguments. If the function needs to modify an argument, it uses a pointer to the corresponding type instead of using the type directly. The file capitalizes each function name as a way of marking it as part of an interface package. Also, the file uses the `#ifndef` technique discussed in Chapter 16, "The C Preprocessor and the C Library," to protect against multiple inclusions of a file. If your compiler doesn't support the C99 `bool` type, you can replace

```
#include <stdbool.h>      /* C99 feature          */
```

with this in the header file:

```
enum bool {false, true}; /* define bool as type, false, true as values */
```

LISTING 17.3   The `list.h` Interface Header File

```
/* list.h -- header file for a simple list type */
#ifndef LIST_H_
#define LIST_H_
#include <stdbool.h>      /* C99 feature          */

/* program-specific declarations */

#define TSIZE     45    /* size of array to hold title  */
struct film
{
    char title[TSIZE];
    int rating;
};

/* general type definitions */

typedef struct film Item;

typedef struct node
{
    Item item;
    struct node * next;
} Node;

typedef Node * List;

/* function prototypes */

/* operation:       initialize a list                   */
/* preconditions:   plist points to a list              */
/* postconditions:  the list is initialized to empty    */
void InitializeList(List * plist);

/* operation:       determine if list is empty          */
/*                  plist points to an initialized list */
/* postconditions:  function returns True if list is empty */
```

LISTING 17.3   Continued

```
/*                    and returns False otherwise            */
bool ListIsEmpty(const List *plist);

/* operation:        determine if list is full              */
/*                    plist points to an initialized list     */
/* postconditions:   function returns True if list is full   */
/*                    and returns False otherwise            */
bool ListIsFull(const List *plist);

/* operation:        determine number of items in list       */
/*                    plist points to an initialized list     */
/* postconditions:   function returns number of items in list */
unsigned int ListItemCount(const List *plist);

/* operation:        add item to end of list                */
/* preconditions:    item is an item to be added to list     */
/*                    plist points to an initialized list     */
/* postconditions:   if possible, function adds item to end  */
/*                    of list and returns True; otherwise the */
/*                    function returns False                 */
bool AddItem(Item item, List * plist);

/* operation:        apply a function to each item in list    */
/*                    plist points to an initialized list     */
/*                    pfun points to a function that takes an */
/*                    Item argument and has no return value   */
/* postcondition:    the function pointed to by pfun is       */
/*                    executed once for each item in the list */
void Traverse (const List *plist, void (* pfun)(Item item) );

/* operation:        free allocated memory, if any           */
/*                    plist points to an initialized list     */
/* postconditions:   any memory allocated for the list is freed */
/*                    and the list is set to empty           */
void EmptyTheList(List * plist);

#endif
```

Only the `InitializeList()`, `AddItem()`, and `EmptyTheList()` functions modify the list, so, technically, they are the only methods requiring a pointer argument. However, it can get confusing if the user has to remember to pass a `List` argument to some functions and an address of a `List` as the argument to others. So, to simplify the user's responsibilities, all the functions use pointer arguments.

One of the prototypes in the header file is a bit more complex than the others:

```
/* operation:        apply a function to each item in list    */
/*                    plist points to an initialized list     */
/*                    pfun points to a function that takes an */
/*                    Item argument and has no return value   */
/* postcondition:    the function pointed to by pfun is       */
/*                    executed once for each item in the list */
void Traverse (const List *plist, void (* pfun)(Item item) );
```

The argument **pfun** is a pointer to a function. In particular, it is a pointer to a function that takes an item as an argument and that has no return value. As you might recall from Chapter 14, "Structures and Other Data Forms," you can pass a pointer to a function as an argument to a second function, and the second function can then use the pointed-to function. Here, for example, you can let **pfun** point to a function that displays an item. The **Traverse()** function would then apply this function to each item in the list, thus displaying the whole list.

Using the Interface

Our claim is that you should be able to use this interface to write a program without knowing any further details—for example, without knowing how the functions are written. Let's write a new version of the movie program right now before we write the supporting functions. Because the interface is in terms of **List** and **Item** types, the program should be phrased in those terms. Here's a pseudocode representation of one possible plan:

```
Create a List variable.
Create an Item variable.
Initialize the list to empty.
While the list isn't full and while there's more input:
    Read the input into the Item variable.
    Add the item to the end of the list.
Visit each item in the list and display it.
```

The program shown in Listing 17.4 follows this basic plan, with some error-checking. Note how it makes use of the interface described in the **list.h** file (Listing 17.3). Also note that the listing has code for the **showmovies()** function, which conforms to the prototype required by **Traverse()**. Therefore, the program can pass the pointer **showmovies** to **Traverse()** so that **Traverse()** can apply the **showmovies()** function to each item in the list. (Recall that the name of a function is a pointer to the function.)

LISTING 17.4   The `films3.c` Program

```c
/* films3.c -- using an ADT-style linked list */
/* compile with list.c                        */
#include <stdio.h>
#include <stdlib.h>    /* prototype for exit() */
#include "list.h"      /* defines List, Item   */
void showmovies(Item item);

int main(void)
{
    List movies;
    Item temp;


/* initialize       */
    InitializeList(&movies);
    if (ListIsFull(&movies))
    {
        fprintf(stderr,"No memory available! Bye!\n");
```

LISTING 17.4 *Continued*

```
            exit(1);
        }

    /* gather and store */
        puts("Enter first movie title:");
        while (gets(temp.title) != NULL && temp.title[0] != '\0')
        {
            puts("Enter your rating <0-10>:");
            scanf("%d", &temp.rating);
            while(getchar() != '\n')
                continue;
            if (AddItem(temp, &movies)==false)
            {
                fprintf(stderr,"Problem allocating memory\n");
                break;
            }
            if (ListIsFull(&movies))
            {
                puts("The list is now full.");
                break;
            }
            puts("Enter next movie title (empty line to stop):");
        }

    /* display          */
        if (ListIsEmpty(&movies))
            printf("No data entered. ");
        else
        {
            printf ("Here is the movie list:\n");
            Traverse(&movies, showmovies);
        }
        printf("You entered %d movies.\n", ListItemCount(&movies));


    /* clean up          */
        EmptyTheList(&movies);
        printf("Bye!\n");

        return 0;
    }

    void showmovies(Item item)
    {
        printf("Movie: %s  Rating: %d\n", item.title,
                item.rating);
    }
```

Implementing the Interface

Of course, you still have to implement the List interface. The C approach is to collect the function definitions in a file called list.c. The complete program, then, consists of three files: list.h, which defines the data structures and provides prototypes for the user interface, list.c, which provides the function code to implement the interface, and films3.c, which is a source code file that applies the list interface to a particular programming problem. Listing 17.5 shows one possible implementation of list.c. To run the program, you must compile both films3.c and list.c and link them. (You might want to review the discussion in Chapter 9, "Functions," on compiling multiple-file programs.) Together, the files list.h, list.c, and films3.c constitute a complete program (see Figure 17.5).

FIGURE 17.5

The three parts of a program package.

```
                        list.h

/* list.h--header file for a simple list type */

/* program-specific declarations */

#define TSIZE 45 /* size of array to hold title */
struct film
{
  char title[TSIZE];
  int rating;
};
  .
  .
  .

void Traverse (List 1, void (* pfun)(Item item) );
```

```
                                    list.c

/* list.c--functions supporting list operations */
#include<stdio.h>
#include<stdlib.h>
#include "list.h"


  .
  .
  .

/* copies an item into node */
static void CopyToNode (Item item, Node * pnode)
{
pnode->item = item; /* structure copy */
}
```

```
                    films3.c

/* films3.c -- using and ADT-style linked list */
#include <stdio.h>
#include <stdlib.h> /* prototype for exit() */
#include "list.h"
void showmovies(Item item);

int main(void)
{
  .
  .
  .
}
```

LISTING 17.5   The `list.c` Implementation File

```c
/* list.c -- functions supporting list operations */
#include <stdio.h>
#include <stdlib.h>
#include "list.h"

/* local function prototype */
static void CopyToNode(Item item, Node * pnode);

/* interface functions    */
/* set the list to empty */
void InitializeList(List * plist)
{
    * plist = NULL;
}

/* returns true if list is empty */
bool ListIsEmpty(const List * plist)
{
    if (*plist == NULL)
        return true;
    else
        return false;
}

/* returns true if list is full */
bool ListIsFull(const List * plist)
{
    Node * pt;
    bool full;

    pt = (Node *) malloc(sizeof(Node));
    if (pt == NULL)
        full = true;
    else
        full = false;
    free(pt);

    return full;
}

/* returns number of nodes */
unsigned int ListItemCount(const List * plist)
{
    unsigned int count = 0;
    Node * pnode = *plist;      /* set to start of list */

    while (pnode != NULL)
    {
        ++count;
        pnode = pnode->next; /* set to next node      */
    }
```

LISTING 17.5 Continued

```
        return count;
}

/* creates node to hold item and adds it to the end of */
/* the list pointed to by plist (slow implementation)  */
bool AddItem(Item item, List * plist)
{
    Node * pnew;
    Node * scan = *plist;

    pnew = (Node *) malloc(sizeof(Node));
    if (pnew == NULL)
        return false;      /* quit function on failure  */

    CopyToNode(item, pnew);
    pnew->next = NULL;
    if (scan == NULL)          /* empty list, so place */
        *plist = pnew;         /* pnew at head of list */
    else
    {
        while (scan->next != NULL)
            scan = scan->next; /* find end of list    */
        scan->next = pnew;     /* add pnew to end      */
    }

    return true;
}

/* visit each node and execute function pointed to by pfun */
void Traverse  (const List * plist, void (* pfun)(Item item) )
{
    Node * pnode = *plist;     /* set to start of list    */

    while (pnode != NULL)
    {
        (*pfun)(pnode->item); /* apply function to item */
        pnode = pnode->next;  /* advance to next item    */
    }
}

/* free memory allocated by malloc() */
/* set list pointer to NULL          */
void EmptyTheList(List * plist)
{
    Node * psave;

    while (*plist != NULL)
    {
        psave = (*plist)->next; /* save address of next node */
        free(*plist);           /* free current node         */
        *plist = psave;         /* advance to next node      */
```

LISTING 17.5   Continued

```
        }
    }

    /* local function definition  */
    /* copies an item into a node */
    static void CopyToNode(Item item, Node * pnode)
    {
        pnode->item = item;  /* structure copy */
    }
```

Program Notes

The `list.c` file has many interesting points. For one, it illustrates when you might use functions with internal linkage. As described in Chapter 12, functions with internal linkage are known only in the file where they are defined. When implementing an interface, you might find it convenient sometimes to write auxiliary functions that aren't part of the official interface. For example, the example uses the function `CopyToNode()` to copy a type `Item` value to a type `Item` variable. Because this function is part of the implementation but not part of the interface, we hid it in the `list.c` file by using the `static` storage class qualifier. Now, let's examine the other functions.

The `InitializeList()` function initializes a list to empty. In our implementation, that means setting a type `List` variable to `NULL`. As mentioned earlier, this requires passing a pointer to the `List` variable to the function.

The `ListIsEmpty()` function is quite simple, but it does depend on the list variable being set to `NULL` when the list is empty. Therefore, it's important to initialize a list before first using the `ListIsEmpty()` function. Also, if you were to extend the interface to include deleting items, you should make sure the deletion function resets the list to empty when the last item is deleted. With a linked list, the size of the list is limited by the amount of memory available. The `ListIsFull()` function tries to allocate enough space for a new item. If it fails, the list is full. If it succeeds, it has to free the memory it just allocated so that it is available for a real item.

The `ListItemCount()` function uses the usual linked-list algorithm to traverse the list, counting items as it goes:

```
unsigned int ListItemCount(const List * plist)
{
    unsigned int count = 0;
    Node * pnode = *plist;    /* set to start of list */

    while (pnode != NULL)
    {
        ++count;
        pnode = pnode->next; /* set to next node     */
    }

    return count;
}
```

The `AddItem()` function is the most elaborate of the group:

```
bool AddItem(Item item, List * plist)
{
    Node * pnew;
    Node * scan = *plist;

    pnew = (Node *) malloc(sizeof(Node));
    if (pnew == NULL)
        return false;      /* quit function on failure  */

    CopyToNode(item, pnew);
    pnew->next = NULL;
    if (scan == NULL)              /* empty list, so place */
        *plist = pnew;             /* pnew at head of list */
    else
    {
        while (scan->next != NULL)
            scan = scan->next; /* find end of list   */
        scan->next = pnew;         /* add pnew to end    */
    }

    return true;
}
```

The first thing the `AddItem()` function does is allocate space for a new node. If this succeeds, the function uses `CopyToNode()` to copy the item to the node. Then it sets the `next` member of the node to `NULL`. This, as you'll recall, indicates that the node is the last node in the linked list. Finally, after creating the node and assigning the correct values to its members, the function attaches the node to the end of the list. If the item is the first item added to the list, the program sets the head pointer to the first item. (Remember, `AddItem()` is called with the address of the head pointer as its second argument, so `* plist` is the value of the head pointer.) Otherwise, the code marches through the linked list until it finds the item having its `next` member set to `NULL`. That node is currently the last node, so the function resets its `next` member to point to the new node.

Good programming practice dictates that you call `ListIsFull()` before trying to add an item to the list. However, a user might fail to observe this dictate, so `AddItem()` checks for itself whether `malloc()` has succeeded. Also, it's possible a user might do something else to allocate memory between calling `ListIsFull()` and calling `AddItem()`, so it's best to check whether `malloc()` worked.

The `Traverse()` function is similar to the `ListItemCount()` function with the addition of applying a function to each item in the list:

```
void Traverse  (const List * plist, void (* pfun)(Item item) )
{
    Node * pnode = *plist;     /* set to start of list   */

    while (pnode != NULL)
    {
        (*pfun)(pnode->item); /* apply function to item */
```

```
        pnode = pnode->next;  /* advance to next item   */
    }
}
```

Recall that `pnode->item` represents the data stored in a node and that `pnode->next` identifies the next node in the linked list. For example, the function call

```
Traverse(movies, showmovies);
```

applies the `showmovies()` function to each item in the list.

Finally, the `EmptyTheList()` function frees the memory previously allocated using `malloc()`:

```
void EmptyTheList(List * plist)
{
    Node * psave;

    while (*plist != NULL)
    {
        psave = (*plist)->next; /* save address of next node */
        free(*plist);           /* free current node         */
        *plist = psave;         /* advance to next node      */
    }
}
```

The implementation indicates an empty list by having the `List` variable being set to `NULL`. Therefore, this function needs to be passed the address of the `List` variable to be able to reset it. Because `List` already is a pointer, `plist` is a pointer to a pointer. Thus, within the code, the expression `*plist` is type pointer-to-Node. When the list terminates, `*plist` is `NULL`, meaning the original actual argument is now set to `NULL`.

The code saves the address of the next node because the call to `free()`, in principle, may make the contents of the current node (the one pointed to by `*plist`) no longer available.

The Limitations of const

Several of the list-handling functions have `const List * plist` for a parameter. This indicates the intent that these functions don't alter the list. Here, `const` does provide some protection. It prevents `*plist` (the quantity to which `plist` points) from being changed. In this program, `plist` points to `movies`, so `const` prevents those functions from changing `movies`, which, in turn, points to the first link in the list. Therefore, code such as this is not allowed in, say, `ListItemCount()`:

```
*plist = (*plist)->next;   // not allowed if *plist is const
```

This is good, because changing `*plist`, and, hence, `movies`, would cause the program to lose track of the data. However, the fact that `*plist` and `movies` are treated as `const` doesn't mean that data pointed to by `*plist` or `movies` is `const`. For example, code such as this is allowed:

```
(*plist)->item.rating = 3; // allowed even if *plist is const
```

That's because this code doesn't change `*plist`; it changes data that `*plist` points to. The moral is that you can't necessarily rely on `const` to catch programming errors that accidentally modify data.

Contemplating Your Work

Take a little time now to evaluate what the ADT approach has done for you. First, compare Listing 17.2 with Listing 17.4. Both programs use the same fundamental method (dynamic allocation of linked structures) to solve the movie listing problem, but Listing 17.2 exposes all the programming plumbing, putting `malloc()` and `prev->next` into public view. Listing 17.4, on the other hand, hides these details and expresses the program in a language that relates directly to the tasks. That is, it talks about creating a list and adding items to the list, not about calling memory functions or resetting pointers. In short, Listing 17.4 expresses the program in terms of the problem to be solved, not in terms of the low-level tools needed to solve the problem. The ADT version is oriented to the end user's concerns and is much easier to read.

Next, the `list.h` and `list.c` files together constitute a reusable resource. If you need another simple list, just haul out these files. Suppose you need to store an inventory of your relatives: names, relationships, addresses, and phone numbers. First, you would go to the `list.h` file and redefine the `Item` type:

```
typedef struct itemtag
{
    char fname[14];
    char lname [24];
    char relationship[36];
    char address [60];
    char phonenum[20];
}   Item;
```

Next... well, that's all you have to do in this case because all the simple list functions are defined in terms of the `Item` type. In some cases, you would also have to redefine the `CopyToNode()` function. For example, if an item were an array, you couldn't copy it by assignment.

Another important point is that the user interface is defined in terms of abstract list operations, not in terms of some particular set of data representations and algorithms. This leaves you free to fiddle with the implementation without having to redo the final program. For example, the current `AddItem()` function is a bit inefficient because it always starts at the beginning of the list and then searches for the end. You can fix this problem by keeping track of the end of the list. For example, you can redefine the `List` type this way:

```
typedef struct list
{
    Node * head;       /* points to head of list */
    Node * end;        /* points to end of list  */
} List;
```

Of course, you would then have to rewrite the list-processing functions using this new definition, but you wouldn't have to change a thing in Listing 17.4. This sort of isolating implementation from the final interface is particularly useful for large programming projects. It's called *data hiding* because the detailed data representation is hidden from the final user.

Note that this particular ADT doesn't even force you to implement the simple list as a linked list. Here's another possibility:

```
#define MAXSIZE 100
typedef struct list
{
    Item entries[MAXSIZE];   /* array of items          */
    int items;               /* number of items in list */
} List;
```

Again, this would require rewriting the list.c file, but the program using the list doesn't need to be changed.

Finally, think of the benefits this approach provides for the program-development process. If something is not working right, you probably can localize the problem to a single function. If you think of a better way to do one of the tasks, such as adding an item, you just have to rewrite that one function. If you need a new feature, you can think in terms of adding a new function to the package. If you think that an array or double-linked list would be better, you can rewrite the implementation without having to modify the programs that use the implementation.

Getting Queued with an ADT

The abstract data type approach to programming in C, as you've seen, involves the following three steps:

1. Describing a type, including its operations, in an abstract, general fashion

2. Devising a function interface to represent the new type

3. Writing detailed code to implement the interface

You've seen this approach applied to a simple list. Now, apply it to something slightly more complex: the queue.

Defining the Queue Abstract Data Type

A *queue* is a list with two special properties. First, new items can be added only to the end of the list. In this respect, the queue is like the simple list. Second, items can be removed from the list only at the beginning. You can visualize a queue as a line of people buying tickets to a theater. You join the line at the end, and you leave the line at the front, after purchasing your tickets. A queue is a *first in, first out* (FIFO) data form, just the way a movie line is (if no one cuts into the line). Once again, let's frame an informal, abstract definition, as shown here:

Type Name:	Queue
Type Properties:	Can hold an ordered sequence of items.

Type Operations:	Initialize queue to empty.
	Determine whether queue is empty.
	Determine whether queue is full.
	Determine number of items in the queue.
	Add item to rear of queue.
	Remove and recover item from front of queue.
	Empty the queue.

Defining an Interface

The interface definition will go into a file called `queue.h`. We'll use C's `typedef` facility to create names for two types: `Item` and `Queue`. The exact implementation for the corresponding structures should be part of the `queue.h` file, but conceptually, designing the structures is part of the detailed implementation stage. For the moment, just assume that the types have been defined and concentrate on the function prototypes.

First, consider initialization. It involves altering a `Queue` type, so the function should take the address of a `Queue` as an argument:

```
void InitializeQueue (Queue * pq);
```

Next, determining whether the queue is empty or full involves a function that should return a true or false value. Here we assume that the C99 `stdbool.h` header file is available. If it's not, you can use type `int` or define a `bool` type yourself. Because the function doesn't alter the queue, it can take a `Queue` argument. On the other hand, it can be faster and less memory intensive to just pass the address of a `Queue`, depending on how large a `Queue`-type object is. Let's try that approach. Another advantage is that this way all the functions will take an address as an argument. To indicate that these functions don't change a queue, you can, and should, use the `const` qualifier:

```
bool QueueIsFull(const Queue * pq);
bool QueueIsEmpty (const Queue * pq);
```

Paraphrasing, the pointer `pq` points to a `Queue` data object that cannot be altered through the agency of `pq`. You can define a similar prototype for a function that returns the number of items in a queue:

```
int QueueItemCount(const Queue * pq);
```

Adding an item to the end of the queue involves identifying the item and the queue. This time the queue is altered, so using a pointer is necessary, not optional. The function could be type `void`, or you can use the return value to indicate whether the operation of adding an item succeeded. Let's take the second approach:

```
bool EnQueue(Item item, Queue * pq);
```

Finally, removing an item can be done several ways. If the item is defined as a structure or as one of the fundamental types, it could be returned by the function. The function argument could be either a `Queue` or a pointer to a `Queue`. Therefore, one possible prototype is this:

```
Item DeQueue(Queue q);
```

However, the following prototype is a bit more general:

```
bool DeQueue(Item * pitem, Queue * pq);
```

The item removed from the queue goes to the location pointed to by the `pitem` pointer, and the return value indicates whether the operation succeeded.

The only argument that should be needed for a function to empty the queue is the queue's address, suggesting this prototype:

```
void EmptyTheQueue(Queue * pq);
```

Implementing the Interface Data Representation

The first step is deciding what C data form to use for a queue. One possibility is an array. The advantages to arrays are that they're easy to use and that adding an item to the end of an array's filled portion is easy. The problem comes with removing an item from the front of the queue. In the analogy of people in a ticket line, removing an item from the front of the queue consists of copying the value of the first element of the array (simple) and then moving each item left in the array one element toward the front. Although this is easy to program, it wastes a lot of computer time (see Figure 17.6).

FIGURE 17.6

Using an array as a queue.

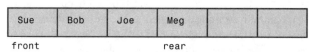

A second way to handle the removal problem in an array implementation is to leave the remaining elements where they are and, instead, change which element you call the front (see

Figure 17.7). This method's problem is that the vacated elements become dead space, so the available space in the queue keeps decreasing.

FIGURE 17.7
Redefining the front element.

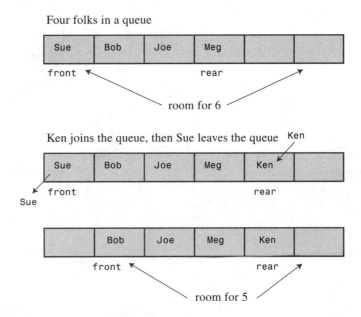

Four folks in a queue

Ken joins the queue, then Sue leaves the queue

A clever solution to the dead space problem is to make the queue *circular*. This means wrapping around from the end of the array to the beginning. That is, consider the first element of the array as immediately following the last element so that when you reach the end of the array, you can start adding items to the beginning elements if they have been vacated (see Figure 17.8). You can imagine drawing the array on a strip of paper, and then pasting one end of the array to the other to form a band. Of course, you now have to do some fancy bookkeeping to make sure the end of the queue doesn't pass the front.

Yet another solution is to use a linked list. This has the advantage that removing the front item doesn't require moving all the other items. Instead, you just reset the front pointer to point to the new first element. Because we've already been working with linked lists, we'll take this track. To test our ideas, we'll start with a queue of integers:

```
typedef int Item;
```

A linked list is built from nodes, so let's define a node next:

```
typedef struct node
{
    Item item;
    struct node * next;
} Node;
```

FIGURE 17.8
A circular queue.

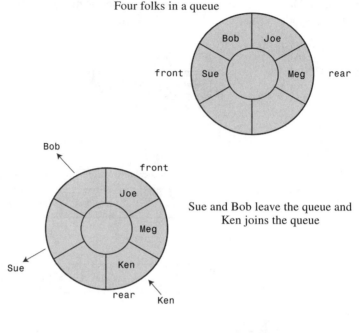

Four folks in a queue

Sue and Bob leave the queue and
Ken joins the queue

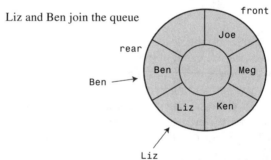

Liz and Ben join the queue

Circular queue wraps around to front of array

For the queue, you need to keep track of the front and rear items. You can use pointers to do this. Also, you can use a counter to keep track of the number of items in a queue. Thus, the structure will have two pointer members and one type **int** member:

```
typedef struct queue
{
    Node * front;   /* pointer to front of queue */
    Node * rear;    /* pointer to rear of queue  */
    int items;      /* number of items in queue  */
} Queue;
```

Note that a `Queue` is a structure with three members, so the earlier decision to use pointers to queues instead of entire queues as arguments is a time and space saver.

Next, think about the size of a queue. With a linked list, the amount of available memory sets the limit, but often a much smaller size is more appropriate. For example, you might use a queue to simulate airplanes waiting to land at an airport. If the number of waiting planes gets too large, new arrivals might be rerouted to other airports. We'll set a maximum queue size of 10. Listing 17.6 contains the definitions and prototypes for the queue interface. It leaves open the exact definition of the `Item` type. When using the interface, you would insert the appropriate definition for your particular program.

LISTING 17.6   The `queue.h` Interface Header File

```c
/* queue.h -- interface for a queue */
#ifndef _QUEUE_H_
#define _QUEUE_H_
#include <stdbool.h>

/* INSERT ITEM TYPE HERE */
/* FOR EXAMPLE, */
typedef int Item;
/* OR typedef struct item {int gumption; int charisma;} Item; */

#define MAXQUEUE 10

typedef struct node
{
    Item item;
    struct node * next;
} Node;

typedef struct queue
{
    Node * front;   /* pointer to front of queue  */
    Node * rear;    /* pointer to rear of queue   */
    int items;      /* number of items in queue   */
} Queue;

/* operation:       initialize the queue                    */
/* precondition:    pq points to a queue                    */
/* postcondition:   queue is initialized to being empty     */
void InitializeQueue(Queue * pq);

/* operation:       check if queue is full                  */
/* precondition:    pq points to previously initialized queue */
/* postcondition:   returns True if queue is full, else False */
bool QueueIsFull(const Queue * pq);

/* operation:       check if queue is empty                 */
/* precondition:    pq points to previously initialized queue */
/* postcondition:   returns True if queue is empty, else False */
bool QueueIsEmpty(const Queue *pq);
```

LISTING 17.6   *Continued*

```
/* operation:        determine number of items in queue    */
/* precondition:     pq points to previously initialized queue  */
/* postcondition:    returns number of items in queue      */
int QueueItemCount(const Queue * pq);

/* operation:        add item to rear of queue             */
/* precondition:     pq points to previously initialized queue */
/*                   item is to be placed at rear of queue   */
/* postcondition:    if queue is not empty, item is placed at  */
/*                   rear of queue and function returns       */
/*                   True; otherwise, queue is unchanged and   */
/*                   function returns False                  */
bool EnQueue(Item item, Queue * pq);

/* operation:        remove item from front of queue        */
/* precondition:     pq points to previously initialized queue  */
/* postcondition:    if queue is not empty, item at head of   */
/*                   queue is copied to *pitem and deleted from */
/*                   queue, and function returns True; if the  */
/*                   operation empties the queue, the queue is  */
/*                   reset to empty. If the queue is empty to   */
/*                   begin with, queue is unchanged and the    */
/*                   function returns False                  */
bool DeQueue(Item *pitem, Queue * pq);

/* operation:        empty the queue                        */
/* precondition:     pq points to previously initialized queue  */
/* postconditions:   the queue is empty                     */
void EmptyTheQueue(Queue * pq);

#endif
```

Implementing the Interface Functions

Now we can get down to writing the interface code. First, initializing a queue to "empty" means setting the front and rear pointers to NULL and setting the item count (the items member) to 0:

```
void InitializeQueue(Queue * pq)
{
    pq->front = pq->rear = NULL;
    pq->items = 0;
}
```

Next, the items member makes it easy to check for a full queue or empty queue and to return the number of items in a queue:

```
bool QueueIsFull(const Queue * pq)
{
    return pq->items == MAXQUEUE;
}
```

```
bool QueueIsEmpty(const Queue * pq)
{
    return pq->items == 0;
}

int QueueItemCount(const Queue * pq)
{
    return pq->items;
}
```

Adding an item to the queue involves the following steps:

1. Creating a new node.

2. Copying the item to the node.

3. Setting the node's **next** pointer to **NULL**, identifying the node as the last in the list.

4. Setting the current rear node's **next** pointer to point to the new node, linking the new node to the queue.

5. Setting the **rear** pointer to the new node, making it easy to find the last node.

6. Adding 1 to the item count.

Also, the function has to handle two special cases. First, if the queue is empty, the **front** pointer should be set to point to the new node. That's because when there is just one node, that node is both the front and the rear of the queue. Second, if the function is unable to obtain memory for the node, it should do something. Because we envision using small queues, such failure should be rare, so we'll simply have the function terminate the program if the program runs out of memory. Here's the code for **EnQueue()**:

```
bool EnQueue(Item item, Queue * pq)
{
    Node * pnew;

    if (QueueIsFull(pq))
        return false;
    pnew = (Node *) malloc( sizeof(Node));
    if (pnew == NULL)
    {
        fprintf(stderr,"Unable to allocate memory!\n");
        exit(1);
    }
    CopyToNode(item, pnew);
    pnew->next = NULL;
    if (QueueIsEmpty(pq))
        pq->front = pnew;            /* item goes to front     */
    else
        pq->rear->next = pnew;       /* link at end of queue   */
    pq->rear = pnew;                 /* record location of end */
    pq->items++;                     /* one more item in queue */

    return true;
}
```

The `CopyToNode()` function is a static function to handle copying the item to a node:

```
static void CopyToNode(Item item, Node * pn)
{
    pn->item = item;
}
```

Removing an item from the front of the queue involves the following steps:

1. Copying the item to a waiting variable

2. Freeing the memory used by the vacated node

3. Resetting the front pointer to the next item in the queue

4. Resetting the front and rear pointers to NULL if the last item is removed

5. Decrementing the item count

Here's code that does all these things:

```
bool DeQueue(Item * pitem, Queue * pq)
{
    Node * pt;

    if (QueueIsEmpty(pq))
        return false;
    CopyToItem(pq->front, pitem);
    pt = pq->front;
    pq->front = pq->front->next;
    free(pt);
    pq->items--;
    if (pq->items == 0)
        pq->rear = NULL;

    return true;
}
```

There are a couple of pointer facts you should note. First, the code doesn't explicitly set the `front` pointer to NULL when the last item is deleted. That's because it already sets the `front` pointer to the `next` pointer of the node being deleted. If that node is the last node, its `next` pointer is NULL, so the `front` pointer gets set to NULL. Second, the code uses a temporary pointer (`pt`) to keep track of the deleted node's location. That's because the official pointer to the first node (`pq->front`) gets reset to point to the next node, so without the temporary pointer, the program would lose track of which block of memory to free.

We can use the `DeQueue()` function to empty a queue. Just use a loop calling `DeQueue()` until the queue is empty:

```
void EmptyTheQueue(Queue * pq)
{
    Item dummy;
    while (!QueueIsEmpty(pq))
        DeQueue(&dummy, pq);
}
```

Keeping Your ADT Pure

After you've defined an ADT interface, you should use only the functions of the interface to handle the data type. Note, for example, that Dequeue() depends on the EnQueue() function doing its job of setting pointers correctly and setting the next pointer of the rear node to NULL. If, in a program using the ADT, you decided to manipulate parts of the queue directly, you might mess up the coordination between the functions in the interface package.

Listing 17.7 shows all the functions of the interface, including the CopyToItem() function used in EnQueue().

LISTING 17.7   The queue.c Implementation File

```c
/* queue.c -- the Queue type implementation*/
#include <stdio.h>
#include <stdlib.h>
#include "queue.h"

/* local functions */
static void CopyToNode(Item item, Node * pn);
static void CopyToItem(Node * pn, Item * pi);

void InitializeQueue(Queue * pq)
{
    pq->front = pq->rear = NULL;
    pq->items = 0;
}

bool QueueIsFull(const Queue * pq)
{
    return pq->items == MAXQUEUE;
}

bool QueueIsEmpty(const Queue * pq)
{
    return pq->items == 0;
}

int QueueItemCount(const Queue * pq)
{
    return pq->items;
}

bool EnQueue(Item item, Queue * pq)
{
    Node * pnew;

    if (QueueIsFull(pq))
        return false;
    pnew = (Node *) malloc( sizeof(Node));
    if (pnew == NULL)
```

LISTING 17.7 Continued

```c
    {
        fprintf(stderr,"Unable to allocate memory!\n");
        exit(1);
    }
    CopyToNode(item, pnew);
    pnew->next = NULL;
    if (QueueIsEmpty(pq))
        pq->front = pnew;           /* item goes to front    */
    else
        pq->rear->next = pnew;      /* link at end of queue   */
    pq->rear = pnew;                /* record location of end */
    pq->items++;                    /* one more item in queue */

    return true;
}

bool DeQueue(Item * pitem, Queue * pq)
{
    Node * pt;

    if (QueueIsEmpty(pq))
        return false;
    CopyToItem(pq->front, pitem);
    pt = pq->front;
    pq->front = pq->front->next;
    free(pt);
    pq->items--;
    if (pq->items == 0)
        pq->rear = NULL;

    return true;
}

/* empty the queue                */
void EmptyTheQueue(Queue * pq)
{
    Item dummy;
    while (!QueueIsEmpty(pq))
        DeQueue(&dummy, pq);
}

/* Local functions                */

static void CopyToNode(Item item, Node * pn)
{
    pn->item = item;
}

static void CopyToItem(Node * pn, Item * pi)
{
    *pi = pn->item;
}
```

Testing the Queue

It's a good idea to test a new design, such as the queue package, before inserting it into a critical program. One approach to testing is writing a short program, sometimes called a *driver*, whose sole purpose is to test the package. For example, Listing 17.8 uses a queue that enables you to add and delete integers. Before using the program, make sure the following line is present in `queue.h`:

```
typedef int item;
```

Remember, too, that you have to link **queue.c** and **use_q.c**.

LISTING 17.8   The use_q.c Program

```c
/* use_q.c -- driver testing the Queue interface */
/* compile with queue.c                          */
#include <stdio.h>
#include "queue.h"  /* defines Queue, Item        */

int main(void)
{
    Queue line;
    Item temp;
    char ch;

    InitializeQueue(&line);
    puts("Testing the Queue interface. Type a to add a value,");
    puts("type d to delete a value, and type q to quit.");
    while ((ch = getchar()) != 'q')
    {
        if (ch != 'a' && ch != 'd')   /* ignore other input */
            continue;
        if ( ch == 'a')
        {
            printf("Integer to add: ");
            scanf("%d", &temp);
            if (!QueueIsFull(&line))
            {
                printf("Putting %d into queue\n", temp);
                EnQueue(temp,&line);
            }
            else
                puts("Queue is full!");
        }
        else
        {
            if (QueueIsEmpty(&line))
                puts("Nothing to delete!");
            else
            {
                DeQueue(&temp,&line);
                printf("Removing %d from queue\n", temp);
```

LISTING 17.8   Continued

```
            }
        }
        printf("%d items in queue\n", QueueItemCount(&line));
        puts("Type a to add, d to delete, q to quit:");
    }
    EmptyTheQueue(&line);
    puts("Bye!");

    return 0;
}
```

Here is a sample run. You should also test to see that the implementation behaves correctly when the queue is full.

```
Testing the Queue interface. Type a to add a value,
type d to delete a value, and type q to quit.
a
Integer to add: 40
Putting 40 into queue
1 items in queue
Type a to add, d to delete, q to quit:
a
Integer to add: 20
Putting 20 into queue
2 items in queue
Type a to add, d to delete, q to quit:
a
Integer to add: 55
Putting 55 into queue
3 items in queue
Type a to add, d to delete, q to quit:
d
Removing 40 from queue
2 items in queue
Type a to add, d to delete, q to quit:
d
Removing 20 from queue
1 items in queue
Type a to add, d to delete, q to quit:
d
Removing 55 from queue
0 items in queue
Type a to add, d to delete, q to quit:
d
Nothing to delete!
0 items in queue
Type a to add, d to delete, q to quit:
q
Bye!
```

Simulating with a Queue

Well, the queue works! Now let's do something more interesting with it. Many real-life situations involve queues. For example, customers queue in banks and in supermarkets, airplanes queue at airports, and tasks queue in multitasking computer systems. You can use the queue package to simulate such situations.

Suppose, for example, that Sigmund Landers has set up an advice booth in a mall. Customers can purchase one, two, or three minutes of advice. To ensure a free flow of foot traffic, mall regulations limit the number of customers waiting in line to 10 (conveniently equal to the program's maximum queue size). Suppose people show up randomly and that the time they want to spend in consultation is spread randomly over the three choices (one, two, or three minutes). How many customers, on average, will Sigmund handle in an hour? How long, on average, will customers have to wait? How long, on average, will the line be? These are the sort of questions a queue simulation can answer.

First, let's decide what to put in the queue. You can describe each customer in terms of the time when he or she joins the queue and in terms of how many minutes of consultation he or she wants. This suggests the following definition for the `Item` type:

```
typedef struct item
{
    long arrive;        /* the time when a customer joins the queue   */
    int processtime;    /* the number of consultation minutes desired */
} Item;
```

To convert the queue package to handle this structure, instead of the `int` type the last example used, all you have to do is replace the former `typedef` for `Item` with the one shown here. After that's done, you don't have to worry about the detailed mechanics of a queue. Instead, you can proceed to the real problem—simulating Sigmund's waiting line.

Here's one approach. Let time move in one-minute increments. Each minute, check to see whether a new customer has arrived. If a customer arrives and the queue isn't full, add the customer to the queue. This involves recording in an `Item` structure the customer's arrival time and the amount of consultation time the customer wants, and then adding the item to the queue. If the queue is full, however, turn the customer away. For bookkeeping, keep track of the total number of customers and the total number of "turnaways" (people who can't get in line because it is full).

Next, process the front of the queue. That is, if the queue isn't empty and if Sigmund isn't occupied with a previous customer, remove the item at the front of the queue. The item, recall, contains the time when the customer joined the queue. By comparing this time with the current time, you get the number of minutes the customer has been in the queue. The item also contains the number of consultation minutes the customer wants, which determines how long Sigmund will be occupied with the new customer. Use a variable to keep track of this waiting time. If Sigmund is busy, no one is "dequeued." However, the variable keeping track of the waiting time should be decremented.

The core code can look like this, with each cycle corresponding to one minute of activity:

```
for (cycle = 0; cycle < cyclelimit; cycle++)
{
    if (newcustomer(min_per_cust))
    {
        if (QueueIsFull(&line))
            turnaways++;
        else
        {
            customers++;
            temp = customertime(cycle);
            EnQueue(temp, &line);
        }
    }
    if (wait_time <= 0 && !QueueIsEmpty(&line))
    {
        DeQueue (&temp, &line);
        wait_time = temp.processtime;
        line_wait += cycle - temp.arrive;
        served++;
    }
    if (wait_time > 0)
        wait_time--;
    sum_line += QueueItemCount(&line);
}
```

Here are the meanings of some of the variables and functions:

- `min_per_cust` is the average number of minutes between customer arrivals.
- `newcustomer()` uses the C `rand()` function to determine whether a customer shows up during this particular minute.
- `turnaways` is the number of arrivals turned away.
- `customers` is the number of arrivals who join the queue.
- `temp` is an `Item` variable describing the new customer.
- `customertime()` sets the `arrive` and `processtime` members of the `temp` structure.
- `wait_time` is the number of minutes remaining until Sigmund finishes with the current client.
- `line_wait` is the cumulative time spent in line by all customers to date.
- `served` is the number of clients actually served.
- `sum_line` is the cumulative length of the line to date.

Think of how much messier and more obscure this code would look if it were sprinkled with `malloc()` and `free()` functions and pointers to nodes. Having the queue package enables you to concentrate on the simulation problem, not on programming details.

Listing 17.9 shows the complete code for the mall advice booth simulation. It uses the standard `rand()`, `srand()`, and `time()` functions to generate random values, following the method suggested in Chapter 12. To use the program, remember to update the `Item` definition in `queue.h` with the following:

```
typedef struct item
{
    long arrive;        /* the time when a customer joins the queue   */
    int processtime;  /* the number of consultation minutes desired */
} Item;
```

Also remember to link the code for `mall.c` with `queue.c`.

LISTING 17.9   The `mall.c` Program

```
/* mall.c -- use the Queue interface */
/* compile with queue.c            */
#include <stdio.h>
#include <stdlib.h>    /* for rand() and srand() */
#include <time.h>      /* for time()             */
#include "queue.h"     /* change Item typedef    */
#define MIN_PER_HR 60.0

bool newcustomer(double x);   /* is there a new customer? */
Item customertime(long when); /* set customer parameters  */

int main(void)
{
    Queue line;
    Item temp;                 /* new customer data              */
    int hours;                 /* hours of simulation            */
    int perhour;               /* average # of arrivals per hour */
    long cycle, cyclelimit;    /* loop counter, limit            */
    long turnaways = 0;        /* turned away by full queue      */
    long customers = 0;        /* joined the queue               */
    long served = 0;           /* served during the simulation   */
    long sum_line = 0;         /* cumulative line length         */
    int wait_time = 0;         /* time until Sigmund is free     */
    double min_per_cust;       /* average time between arrivals  */
    long line_wait = 0;        /* cumulative time in line        */

    InitializeQueue(&line);
    srand(time(0));            /* random initializing of rand() */
    puts("Case Study: Sigmund Lander's Advice Booth");
    puts("Enter the number of simulation hours:");
    scanf("%d", &hours);
    cyclelimit = MIN_PER_HR * hours;
    puts("Enter the average number of customers per hour:");
    scanf("%d", &perhour);
    min_per_cust = MIN_PER_HR / perhour;

    for (cycle = 0; cycle < cyclelimit; cycle++)
```

LISTING 17.9 Continued

```
    {
        if (newcustomer(min_per_cust))
        {
            if (QueueIsFull(&line))
                turnaways++;
            else
            {
                customers++;
                temp = customertime(cycle);
                EnQueue(temp, &line);
            }
        }
        if (wait_time <= 0 && !QueueIsEmpty(&line))
        {
            DeQueue (&temp, &line);
            wait_time = temp.processtime;
            line_wait += cycle - temp.arrive;
            served++;
        }
        if (wait_time > 0)
            wait_time--;
        sum_line += QueueItemCount(&line);
    }

    if (customers > 0)
    {
        printf("customers accepted: %ld\n", customers);
        printf("  customers served: %ld\n", served);
        printf("         turnaways: %ld\n", turnaways);
        printf("average queue size: %.2f\n",
              (double) sum_line / cyclelimit);
        printf(" average wait time: %.2f minutes\n",
              (double) line_wait / served);
    }
    else
        puts("No customers!");
    EmptyTheQueue(&line);
    puts("Bye!");

    return 0;
}

/* x = average time, in minutes, between customers      */
/* return value is true if customer shows up this minute */
bool newcustomer(double x)
{
    if (rand() * x / RAND_MAX < 1)
        return true;
    else
        return false;
}
```

LISTING 17.9   Continued

```
/* when is the time at which the customer arrives        */
/* function returns an Item structure with the arrival time  */
/* set to when and the processing time set to a random value */
/* in the range 1 - 3                                    */
Item customertime(long when)
{
    Item cust;

    cust.processtime = rand() % 3 + 1;
    cust.arrive = when;

    return cust;
}
```

The program enables you to specify the number of hours to simulate and the average number of customers per hour. Choosing a large number of hours gives you good average values, and choosing a small number of hours shows the sort of random variation you can get from hour to hour. The following runs illustrate these points. Note that the average queue sizes and wait times for 80 hours are about the same as for 800 hours, but that the two one-hour samples differ quite a bit from each other and from the long-term averages. That's because smaller statistical samples tend to have larger relative variations.

```
Case Study: Sigmund Lander's Advice Booth
Enter the number of simulation hours:
80
Enter the average number of customers per hour:
20
customers accepted: 1633
  customers served: 1633
        turnaways: 0
average queue size: 0.46
average wait time: 1.35 minutes

Case Study: Sigmund Lander's Advice Booth
Enter the number of simulation hours:
800
Enter the average number of customers per hour:
20
customers accepted: 16020
  customers served: 16019
        turnaways: 0
average queue size: 0.44
average wait time: 1.32 minutes

Case Study: Sigmund Lander's Advice Booth
Enter the number of simulation hours:
1
Enter the average number of customers per hour:
20
customers accepted: 20
  customers served: 20
        turnaways: 0
```

```
average queue size: 0.23
average wait time: 0.70 minutes

Case Study: Sigmund Lander's Advice Booth
Enter the number of simulation hours:
1
Enter the average number of customers per hour:
20
customers accepted: 22
  customers served: 22
       turnaways: 0
average queue size: 0.75
average wait time: 2.05 minutes
```

Another way to use the program is to keep the numbers of hours constant but to try different average numbers of customers per hour. Here are two sample runs exploring this variation:

```
Case Study: Sigmund Lander's Advice Booth
Enter the number of simulation hours:
80
Enter the average number of customers per hour:
25
customers accepted: 1960
  customers served: 1959
       turnaways: 3
average queue size: 1.43
average wait time: 3.50 minutes

Case Study: Sigmund Lander's Advice Booth
Enter the number of simulation hours:
80
Enter the average number of customers per hour:
30
customers accepted: 2376
  customers served: 2373
       turnaways: 94
average queue size: 5.85
average wait time: 11.83 minutes
```

Note how the average wait time takes a sharp upturn as the frequency of customers increases. The average wait for 20 customers per hour (80-hour simulation) was 1.35 minutes. It climbs to 3.50 minutes at 25 customers per hour and soars to 11.83 minutes at 30 customers an hour. Also, the number of turnaways climbs from 0 to 3 to 94. Sigmund could use this sort of analysis to decide whether he needs a second booth.

The Linked List Versus the Array

Many programming problems, such as creating a list or a queue, can be handled with a linked list—by which we mean a linked sequence of dynamically allocated structures—or with an array. Each form has its strengths and weaknesses, so the choice of which to use depends on the particular requirements of a problem. Table 17.1 summarizes the qualities of linked lists and arrays.

TABLE 17.1   Comparing Arrays to Linked Lists

Data Form	Pros	Cons
Array	Directly supported by C. Provides random access.	Size determined at compile time. Inserting and deleting elements is time consuming
Linked list	Size determined during runtime. Inserting and deleting elements is quick.	No random access. User must provide programming support.

Take a closer look at the process of inserting and deleting elements. To insert an element in an array, you have to move elements to make way for the new element, as shown in Figure 17.9. The closer to the front the new element goes, the more elements have to be moved. To insert a node in a linked list, however, you just have to assign values to two pointers, as shown in Figure 17.10. Similarly, removing an element from an array involves a wholesale relocation of elements, but removing a node from a linked list involves resetting a pointer and freeing the memory used by the deleted node.

FIGURE 17.9

Inserting an element into an array.

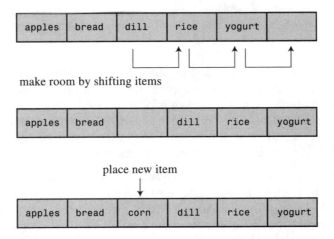

make room by shifting items

place new item

Next, consider how to access the members of a list. With an array, you can use the array index to access any element immediately. This is called *random access*. With a linked list, you have to start at the top of the list and then move from node to node until you get to the node you want, which is termed *sequential access*. You can have sequential access with an array, too. Just increment the array index by one step each to move through the array in order. For some situations, sequential access is sufficient. For example, if you want to display every item in a list, sequential access is fine. Other situations greatly favor random access, as you will see next.

Suppose you want to search a list for a particular item. One algorithm is to start at the beginning of the list and search through it in sequence, called a *sequential search*. If the items aren't arranged in some sort of order, a sequential search is about all you can do. If the sought-for item isn't in the list, you'll have to look at every item in the list before concluding the item isn't there.

FIGURE 17.10
Inserting an element into
a linked list.

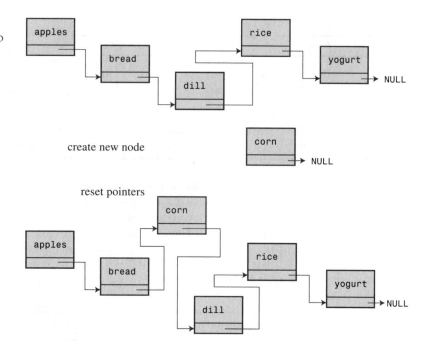

You can improve the sequential search by sorting the list first. That way, you can terminate a search if you haven't found an item by the time you reach an item that would come later. For example, suppose you're seeking *Susan* in an alphabetical list. Starting from the top of the list, you look at each item and eventually encounter *Sylvia* without finding *Susan*. At that point you can quit searching because *Susan*, if in the list, would precede *Sylvia*. On average, this method would cut search times in half for attempting to find items not in the list.

With an ordered list, you can do much better than a sequential search by using the *binary search* method. Here's how it works. First, call the list item you want to find the *goal* and assume the list is in alphabetical order. Next, pick the item halfway down the list and compare it to the goal. If the two are the same, the search is over. If the list item comes before the goal alphabetically, the goal, if it's in the list, must be in the second half. If the list item follows the goal alphabetically, the goal must be in the first half. Either way, the comparison rules out half the list as a place to search. Next, apply the method again. That is, choose an item midway in the half of the list that remains. Again, this method either finds the item or rules out half the remaining list. Proceed in this fashion until you find the item or until you've eliminated the whole list (see Figure 17.11). This method is quite efficient. Suppose, for example, that the list is 127 items long. A sequential search, on the average, would take 64 comparisons before finding an item or ruling out its presence. The binary search method, on the other hand, will take at most seven comparisons. The first comparison prunes the possible matches to 63, the second comparison cuts the possible matches to 31, and so on, until the sixth comparison cuts down the possibilities to 1. The seventh comparison then determines whether the one remaining choice is the goal. In general, n comparisons let you process an array with $2^n - 1$ members, so the advantage of a binary search over a sequential search gets greater the longer the list is.

FIGURE 17.11

A binary search for *Susan*.

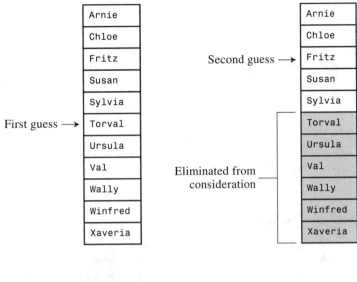

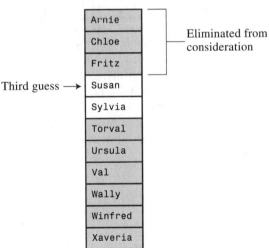

It's simple to implement a binary search with an array, because you can use the array index to determine the midpoint of any list or subdivision of a list. Add the subscripts of the initial and final elements of the subdivision and divide by 2. For example, in a list of 100 elements, the first index is 0, the final index is 99, and the initial guess would be (0 + 99) / 2, or 49 (integer division). If the element having index 49 were too far down the alphabet, the correct choice must be in the range 0–48, so the next guess would be (0 + 48) / 2, or 24. If element 24 were too early in the alphabet, the next guess would be (25 + 48) / 2, or 36. This is where the random access feature of the array comes into play. It enables you to jump from one location to another without visiting every location in between. Linked lists, which support only sequential access, don't provide a means to jump to the midpoint of a list, so you can't use the binary search technique with linked lists.

You can see, then, that the choice of data type depends on the problem. If the situation calls for a list that is continuously resized with frequent insertions and deletions but that isn't searched often, the linked list is the better choice. If the situation calls for a stable list with only occasional insertions and deletions but that has to be searched often, an array is the better choice.

What if you need a data form that supports frequent insertions and deletions and frequent searches? Neither a linked list nor an array is ideal for that set of purposes. Another form—the binary search tree—may be just what you need.

Binary Search Trees

The *binary search tree* is a linked structure that incorporates the binary search strategy. Each node in the tree contains an item and two pointers to other nodes, called *child nodes*. Figure 17.12 shows how the nodes in a binary search tree are linked. The idea is that each node has two child nodes—a left node and a right node. The ordering comes from the fact that the item in a left node precedes the item in the parent node, and the item in the right node follows the item in the parent node. This relationship holds for every node with children. Furthermore, all items that can trace their ancestry back to a left node of a parent contain items that precede the parent item in order, and every item descended from the right node contains items that follow the parent item in order. The tree in Figure 17.12 stores words in this fashion. The top of the tree, in an interesting inversion of botany, is called the *root*. A tree is a *hierarchical* organization, meaning that the data is organized in ranks, or levels, with each rank, in general, having ranks above and below it. If a binary search tree is fully populated, each level has twice as many nodes as the level above it.

FIGURE 17.12

A binary search tree storing words.

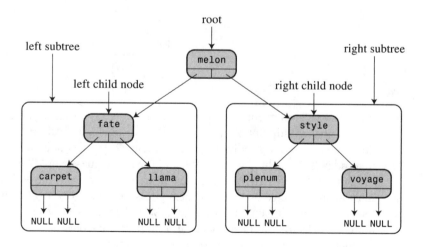

Each node in the binary search tree is itself the root of the nodes descending from it, making the node and its descendants a *subtree*. In Figure 17.12, for example, the nodes containing the words *fate*, *carpet*, and *llama* form the left subtree of the whole tree, and the word *voyage* is the right subtree of the *style-plenum-voyage* subtree.

Suppose you want to find an item—call it the *goal*—in such a tree. If the item precedes the root item, you need to search only the left half of the tree, and if the goal follows the root item, you need to search only the right subtree of the root node. Therefore, one comparison eliminates half the tree. Suppose you search the left half. That means comparing the goal with the item in the left child. If the goal precedes the left-child item, you need to search only the left half of its descendants, and so on. As with the binary search, each comparison cuts the number of potential matches in half.

Let's apply this method to see whether the word *puppy* is in the tree shown in Figure 17.12. Comparing *puppy* to *melon* (the root node item), you see that *puppy*, if present, must be in the right half of the tree. Therefore, you go to the right child and compare *puppy* to *style*. In this case, *puppy* precedes the node item, so you must follow the link to the left node. There you find *plenum*, which precedes *puppy*. You now have to follow the right branch, but it is empty, so three comparisons show you that *puppy* is not in the tree.

A binary search tree, then, combines a linked structure with binary search efficiency. The programming price is that putting a tree together is more involved than creating a linked list. Let's make a binary tree for the next, and final, ADT project.

A Binary Tree ADT

As usual, we'll start by defining a binary tree in general terms. This particular definition assumes the tree contains no duplicate items. Many of the operations are the same as list operations. The difference is in the hierarchical arrangement of data. Here is an informal summary of this ADT:

Type Name:	Binary Search Tree
Type Properties:	A binary tree is either an empty set of nodes (an empty tree) or a set of nodes with one node designated the root.
	Each node has exactly two trees, called the *left subtree* and the *right subtree*, descending from it.
	Each subtree is itself a binary tree, which includes the possibility of being an empty tree.
	A binary search tree is an ordered binary tree in which each node contains an item, in which all items in the left subtree precede the root item, and in which the root item precedes all items in the right subtree.

Type Operations: Initializing tree to empty.

Determining whether tree is empty.

Determining whether tree is full.

Determining the number of items in the tree.

Adding an item to the tree.

Removing an item from the tree.

Searching the tree for an item.

Visiting each item in the tree.

Emptying the tree.

The Binary Search Tree Interface

In principle, you can implement a binary search tree in a variety of ways. You can even implement one as an array by manipulating array indices. But the most direct way to implement a binary search tree is by using dynamically allocated nodes linked together by using pointers, so we'll start with definitions like these:

```
typedef SOMETHING Item;

typedef struct node
{
    Item item;
    struct node * left;
    struct node * right;
} Node;

typedef struct tree
{
    Node * root;
    int size;
} Tree;
```

Each node contains an item, a pointer to the left child node, and a pointer to the right child node. You could define a `Tree` to be type pointer-to-`Node`, because you only need to know the location of the root node to access the entire tree. Using a structure with a size member, however, makes it simpler to keep track of the size of the tree.

The example we'll be developing is maintaining the roster of the Nerfville Pet Club, with each item consisting of a pet name and a pet kind. With that in mind, we can set up the interface shown in Listing 17.10. We've limited the tree size to 10. The small size makes it easier to test whether the program behaves correctly when the tree fills. You can always set `MAXITEMS` to a larger value, if necessary.

LISTING 17.10   The `tree.h` Interface Header File

```
/* tree.h -- binary search tree                          */
/*            no duplicate items are allowed in this tree */
#ifndef _TREE_H_
#define _TREE_H_
#include <stdbool.h>

/* redefine Item as appropriate */
typedef struct item
{
    char petname[20];
    char petkind[20];
} Item;

#define MAXITEMS 10

typedef struct node
{
    Item item;
    struct node * left;    /* pointer to right branch  */
    struct node * right;   /* pointer to left branch   */
} Node;

typedef struct tree
{
    Node * root;           /* pointer to root of tree  */
    int size;              /* number of items in tree  */
} Tree;

/* function prototypes */

/* operation:      initialize a tree to empty       */
/* preconditions:  ptree points to a tree           */
/* postconditions: the tree is initialized to empty */
void InitializeTree(Tree * ptree);

/* operation:      determine if tree is empty        */
/* preconditions:  ptree points to a tree            */
/* postconditions: function returns true if tree is  */
/*                 empty and returns false otherwise */
bool TreeIsEmpty(const Tree * ptree);

/* operation:      determine if tree is full        */
/* preconditions:  ptree points to a tree           */
/* postconditions: function returns true if tree is */
/*                 full and returns false otherwise */
bool TreeIsFull(const Tree * ptree);

/* operation:      determine number of items in tree  */
/* preconditions:  ptree points to a tree             */
/* postconditions: function returns number of items in */
/*                 tree                                */
int TreeItemCount(const Tree * ptree);
```

LISTING 17.10 Continued

```
/* operation:      add an item to a tree         */
/* preconditions:  pi is address of item to be added  */
/*                 ptree points to an initialized tree */
/* postconditions: if possible, function adds item to */
/*                 tree and returns true; otherwise,   */
/*                 the function returns false       */
bool AddItem(const Item * pi, Tree * ptree);

/* operation: find an item in a tree              */
/* preconditions:  pi points to an item            */
/*                 ptree points to an initialized tree */
/* postconditions: function returns true if item is in */
/*                 tree and returns false otherwise   */
bool InTree(const Item * pi, const Tree * ptree);

/* operation:      delete an item from a tree       */
/* preconditions:  pi is address of item to be deleted */
/*                 ptree points to an initialized tree */
/* postconditions: if possible, function deletes item  */
/*                 from tree and returns true;       */
/*                 otherwise, the function returns false*/
bool DeleteItem(const Item * pi, Tree * ptree);

/* operation:      apply a function to each item in  */
/*                 the tree                        */
/* preconditions:  ptree points to a tree           */
/*                 pfun points to a function that takes*/
/*                 an Item argument and has no return */
/*                 value                           */
/* postcondition:  the function pointed to by pfun is */
/*                 executed once for each item in tree */
void Traverse (const Tree * ptree, void (* pfun)(Item item));

/* operation:      delete everything from a tree     */
/* preconditions:  ptree points to an initialized tree */
/* postconditions: tree is empty                    */
void DeleteAll(Tree * ptree);

#endif
```

The Binary Tree Implementation

Next, proceed to the task of implementing the splendid functions outlined in `tree.h`. The `InitializeTree()`, `EmptyTree()`, `FullTree()`, and `TreeItems()` functions are pretty simple, working like their counterparts for the list and queue ADTs, so we'll concentrate on the remaining ones.

Adding an Item

When adding an item to the tree, you should first check whether the tree has room for a new node. Then, because the binary search tree is defined so that it has no duplicate items, you should check that the item is not already in the tree. If the new item clears these first two hurdles, you create a new node, copy the item to the node, and set the node's left and right pointers to NULL. This indicates that the node has no children. Then you should update the size member of the Tree structure to mark the adding of a new item. Next, you have to find where the node should be located in the tree. If the tree is empty, you should set the root pointer to point to the new node. Otherwise, look through the tree for a place to add the node. The AddItem() function follows this recipe, offloading some of the work to functions not yet defined: SeekItem(), MakeNode(), and AddNode().

```
bool AddItem(const Item * pi, Tree * ptree)
{
    Node * new_node;

    if  (TreeIsFull(ptree))
    {
        fprintf(stderr,"Tree is full\n");
        return false;              /* early return         */
    }
    if (SeekItem(pi, ptree).child != NULL)
    {
        fprintf(stderr, "Attempted to add duplicate item\n");
        return false;              /* early return         */
    }
    new_node = MakeNode(pi);       /* points to new node   */
    if (new_node == NULL)
    {
        fprintf(stderr, "Couldn't create node\n");
        return false;              /* early return         */
    }
    /* succeeded in creating a new node */
    ptree->size++;

    if (ptree->root == NULL)       /* case 1: tree is empty  */
        ptree->root = new_node;    /* new node is tree root  */
    else                           /* case 2: not empty      */
        AddNode(new_node,ptree->root); /* add node to tree   */

    return true;                   /* successful return    */
}
```

The SeekItem(), MakeNode(), and AddNode() functions are not part of the public interface for the Tree type. Instead, they are static functions hidden in the tree.c file. They deal with implementation details, such as nodes, pointers, and structures, that don't belong in the public interface.

The MakeNode() function is pretty simple. It handles the dynamic memory allocation and the initialization of the node. The function argument is a pointer to the new item, and the function's return value is a pointer to the new node. Recall that malloc() returns the null pointer if it can't make the requested allocation. The `MakeNode()` function initializes the new node only if memory allocation succeeds. Here is the code for `MakeNode()`:

```
static Node * MakeNode(const Item * pi)
{
    Node * new_node;

    new_node = (Node *) malloc(sizeof(Node));
    if (new_node != NULL)
    {
        new_node->item = *pi;
        new_node->left = NULL;
        new_node->right = NULL;
    }

    return new_node;
}
```

The `AddNode()` function is the second most difficult function in the binary search tree package. It has to determine where the new node goes and then has to add it. In particular, it needs to compare the new item with the root item to see whether the new item goes into the left subtree or the right subtree. If the item were a number, you could use < and > to make comparisons. If the item were a string, you could use `strcmp()` to make comparisons. But the item is a structure containing two strings, so you'll have to define your own functions for making comparisons. The `ToLeft()` function, to be defined later, returns `True` if the new item should be in the left subtree, and the `ToRight()` function returns `True` if the new item should be in the right subtree. These two functions are analogous to < and >, respectively. Suppose the new item goes to the left subtree. It could be that the left subtree is empty. In that case, the function just makes the left child pointer point to the new node. What if the left subtree isn't empty? Then the function should compare the new item to the item in the left child node, deciding whether the new item should go in the left subtree or right subtree of the child node. This process should continue until the function arrives at an empty subtree, at which point the new node can be added. One way to implement this search is to use recursion—that is, apply the `AddNode()` function to a child node instead of to the root node. The recursive series of function calls ends when a left or right subtree is empty—that is, when `root->left` or `root->right` is NULL. Keep in mind that `root` is a pointer to the top of the current subtree, so it points to a new, and lower-level, subtree each recursive call. (You might want to review the discussion of recursion in Chapter 9.)

```
static void AddNode (Node * new_node, Node * root)
{
    if (ToLeft(&new_node->item, &root->item))
    {
        if (root->left == NULL)      /* empty subtree     */
            root->left = new_node;   /* so add node here  */
        else
            AddNode(new_node, root->left);/* else process subtree*/
    }
    else if (ToRight(&new_node->item, &root->item))
    {
```

```
        if (root->right == NULL)
            root->right = new_node;
        else
            AddNode(new_node, root->right);
    }
    else                          /* should be no duplicates */
    {
        fprintf(stderr,"location error in AddNode()\n");
        exit(1);
    }
}
```

The `ToLeft()` and `ToRight()`functions depend on the nature of the `Item` type. The members of the Nerfville Pet Club will be ordered alphabetically by name. If two pets have the same name, order them by kind. If they are also the same kind, then the two items are duplicates, which aren't allowed in the basic search tree. Recall that the standard C library function `strcmp()` returns a negative number if the string represented by the first argument precedes the second string, returns zero if the two strings are the same, and returns a positive number if the first string follows the second. The `ToRight()` function has similar code. Using these two functions instead of making comparisons directly in `AddNode()` makes the code easier to adapt to new requirements. Instead of rewriting `AddNode()` when a different form of comparison is needed, you rewrite `ToLeft()`and `ToRight()`.

```
static bool ToLeft(const Item * i1, const Item * i2)
{
    int comp1;

    if ((comp1 = strcmp(i1->petname, i2->petname)) < 0)
        return true;
    else if (comp1 == 0 &&
                 strcmp(i1->petkind, i2->petkind) < 0 )
        return true;
    else
        return false;
}
```

Finding an Item

Three of the interface functions involve searching the tree for a particular item: `AddItem()`, `InTree()`, and `DeleteItem()`. This implementation uses a `SeekItem()` function to provide that service. The `DeleteItem()` function has an additional requirement: It needs to know the parent node of the deleted item so that the parent's child pointer can be updated when the child is deleted. Therefore, we designed `SeekItem()` to return a structure containing two pointers: one pointing to the node containing the item (`NULL` if the item isn't found) and one pointing to the parent node (`NULL` if the node is the root and has no parent). The structure type is defined as follows:

```
typedef struct pair {
    Node * parent;
    Node * child;
} Pair;
```

The `SeekItem()` function can be implemented recursively. However, to expose you to a variety of programming techniques, we'll use a `while` loop to handle descending through the tree. Like `AddNode()`, `SeekItem()` uses `ToLeft()` and `ToRight()` to navigate through the tree. `SeekItem()` initially sets the `look.child` pointer to point to the root of the tree, and then it resets `look.child` to successive subtrees as it traces the path to where the item should be found. Meanwhile, `look.parent` is set to point to successive parent nodes. If no matching item is found, `look.child` will be `NULL`. If the matching item is in the root node, `look.parent` is `NULL` because the root node has no parent. Here is the code for `SeekItem()`:

```
static Pair SeekItem(const Item * pi, const Tree * ptree)
{
    Pair look;
    look.parent = NULL;
    look.child = ptree->root;

    if (look.child == NULL)
        return look;                              /* early return   */

    while (look.child != NULL)
    {
        if (ToLeft(pi, &(look.child->item)))
        {
            look.parent = look.child;
            look.child = look.child->left;
        }
        else if (ToRight(pi, &(look.child->item)))
        {
            look.parent = look.child;
            look.child = look.child->right;
        }
        else        /* must be same if not to left or right   */
            break; /* look.child is address of node with item */
    }

    return look;                              /* successful return   */
}
```

Note that because the `SeekItem()` function returns a structure, it can be used with the structure membership operator. For example, the `AddItem()` function used the following code:

```
if (SeekItem(pi, ptree).child != NULL)
```

After you have `SeekItem()`, it's simple to code the `InTree()` public interface function:

```
bool InTree(const Item * pi, const Tree * ptree)
{
    return (SeekItem(pi, ptree).child == NULL) ? false : true;
}
```

Considerations in Deleting an Item

Removing an item is the most difficult of the tasks because you have to reconnect the remaining subtrees to form a valid tree. Before attempting to program this task, it's a good idea to develop a visual picture of what has to be done.

Figure 17.13 illustrates the simplest case. Here the node to be deleted has no children. Such a node is called a *leaf*. All that has to be done in this case is to reset a pointer in the parent node to NULL and to use the free() function to reclaim the memory used by the deleted node.

FIGURE 17.13

Deleting a leaf.

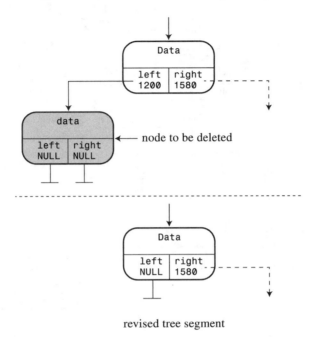

revised tree segment

Next in complexity is deleting a node with one child. Deleting the node leaves the child subtree separate from the rest of the tree. To fix this, the address of the child subtree needs to be stored in the parent node at the location formerly occupied by the address of the deleted node (see Figure 17.14).

The final case is deleting a node with two subtrees. One subtree, say the left, can be attached to where the deleted node was formerly attached. But where should the remaining subtree go? Keep in mind the basic design of a tree. Every item in a left subtree precedes the item in the parent node, and every item in a right subtree follows the item in the parent node. This means that every item in the right subtree comes after every item in the left subtree. Also, because the right subtree once was part of the subtree headed by the deleted node, every item in the right subtree comes before the parent node of the deleted node. Imagine coming down the tree looking for where to place the head of the right subtree. It comes before the parent node, so you have to go down the left subtree from there. However, it comes after every item in the left subtree, so you have to take the right branch of the left subtree and see whether it has an opening for a new node. If not, you must go down the right side of the left subtree until you do find an opening. Figure 17.15 illustrates the approach.

FIGURE 17.14
Deleting a one-child
node.

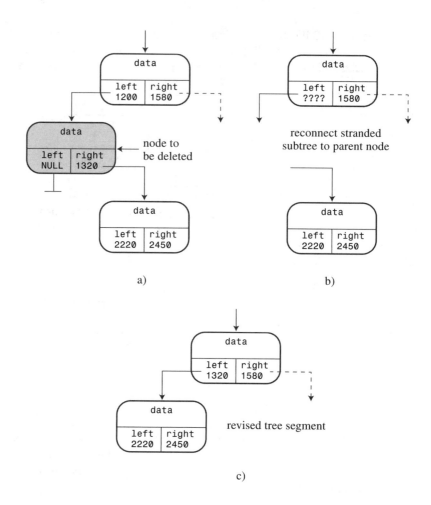

a)

b)

c)

Deleting a Node

Now you can begin to plan the necessary functions, separating the job into two tasks. One is associating a particular item with the node to be deleted, and the second is actually deleting the node. One point to note is that all the cases involve modifying a pointer in the parent node, which has two important consequences:

- The program has to identify the parent node of the node to be deleted.

- To modify the pointer, the code must pass the *address* of that pointer to the deleting function.

FIGURE 17.15
Deleting a two-child
node.

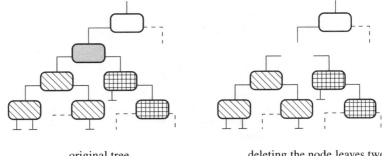

original tree

deleting the node leaves two
unconnected subtrees

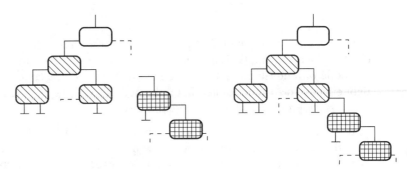

attach left subtree to original
parent node

attach right subtree to first open
location along the rightmost
branches of first subtree

We'll come back to the first point later. Meanwhile, the pointer to be modified is itself of type
Node *, or pointer-to-**Node**. Because the function argument is the address of that pointer, the
argument will be of type **Node ****, or pointer-to-pointer-to-**Node**. Assuming you have the
proper address available, you can write the deletion function as the following:

```
static void DeleteNode(Node **ptr)
/* ptr is address of parent member pointing to target node   */
{
    Node * temp;

    puts((*ptr)->item.petname);
    if ( (*ptr)->left == NULL)
    {
        temp = *ptr;
        *ptr = (*ptr)->right;
        free(temp);
    }
    else if ( (*ptr)->right == NULL)
```

```
        {
            temp = *ptr;
            *ptr = (*ptr)->left;
            free(temp);
        }
        else    /* deleted node has two children */
        {
            /* find where to reattach right subtree */
            for (temp = (*ptr)->left; temp->right != NULL;
                    temp = temp->right)
                continue;
            temp->right = (*ptr)->right;
            temp = *ptr;
            *ptr =(*ptr)->left;
            free(temp);
        }
    }
}
```

This function explicitly handles three cases: a node with no left child, a node with no right child, and a node with two children. A node with no children can be considered a special case of a node with no left child. If the node has no left child, the code assigns the address of the right child to the parent pointer. But if the node also has no right child, that pointer is NULL, which is the proper value for the no-child case.

Notice that the code uses a temporary pointer to keep track of the address of the deleted node. After the parent pointer (*ptr) is reset, the program would lose track of where the deleted node is, but you need that information for the free() function. So the program stores the original value of *ptr in temp and then uses temp to free the memory used for the deleted node.

The code for the two-child case first uses the temp pointer in a for loop to search down the right side of the left subtree for an empty spot. When it finds an empty spot, it attaches the right subtree there. Then it reuses temp to keep track of where the deleted node is. Next, it attaches the left subtree to the parent and then frees the node pointed to by temp.

Note that because ptr is type Node **, *ptr is of type Node *, making it the same type as temp.

Deleting an Item

The remaining part of the problem is associating a node with a particular item. You can use the SeekItem() function to do so. Recall that it returns a structure containing a pointer to the parent node and a pointer to the node containing the item. Then you can use the parent node pointer to get the proper address to pass to the DeleteNode() function. The DeleteItem() function, shown here, follows this plan:

```
bool DeleteItem(const Item * pi, Tree * ptree)
{
    Pair look;

    look = SeekItem(pi, ptree);
```

```
    if (look.child == NULL)
        return false;

    if (look.parent == NULL)        /* delete root item      */
        DeleteNode(&ptree->root);
    else if (look.parent->left == look.child)
        DeleteNode(&look.parent->left);
    else
        DeleteNode(&look.parent->right);
    ptree->size--;

    return true;
}
```

First, the return value of the `SeekItem()` function is assigned to the `look` structure variable. If `look.child` is `NULL`, the search failed to find the item, and the `DeleteItem()` function quits, returning `false`. If the `Item` is found, the function handles three cases. First, a `NULL` value for `look.parent` means the item was found in the root node. In this case, there is no parent node to update. Instead, the program has to update the root pointer in the `Tree` structure. Therefore, the function passes the address of that pointer to the `DeleteNode()` function. Otherwise, the program determines whether the node to be deleted is the left child or the right child of the parent, and then it passes the address of the appropriate pointer.

Note that the public interface function (`DeleteItem()`) speaks in terms of end-user concerns (items and trees), and the hidden `DeleteNode()` function handles the nitty-gritty of pointer shuffling.

Traversing the Tree

Traversing a tree is more involved than traversing a linked list because each node has two branches to follow. This branching nature makes divide-and-conquer recursion (Chapter 9) a natural choice for handling the problem. At each node, the function should do the following:

- Process the item in the node.

- Process the left subtree (a recursive call).

- Process the right subtree (a recursive call).

You can break this process down into two functions: `Traverse()` and `InOrder()`. Note that the `InOrder()` function processes the left subtree, then processes the item, and then processes the right subtree. This order results in traversing the tree in alphabetic order. If you have the time, you might want to see what happens if you use different orders, such as item-left-right and left-right-item.

```
void Traverse (const Tree * ptree, void (* pfun)(Item item))
{

    if (ptree != NULL)
        InOrder(ptree->root, pfun);
}
```

```
static void InOrder(const Node * root, void (* pfun)(Item item))
{
    if (root != NULL)
    {
        InOrder(root->left, pfun);
        (*pfun)(root->item);
        InOrder(root->right, pfun);
    }
}
```

Emptying the Tree

Emptying the tree is basically the same process as traversing it. That is, the code needs to visit each node and apply `free()` to it. It also needs to reset the members of the `Tree` structure to indicate an empty `Tree`. The `DeleteAll()` function takes care of the `Tree` structure and passes off the task of freeing memory to `DeleteAllNodes()`. The latter function has the same design as `InOrder()`. It does save the pointer value `root->right` so that it is still available after the root is freed. Here is the code for these two functions:

```
void DeleteAll(Tree * ptree)
{
    if (ptree != NULL)
        DeleteAllNodes(ptree->root);
    ptree->root = NULL;
    ptree->size = 0;
}


static void DeleteAllNodes(Node * root)
{
    Node * pright;

    if (root != NULL)
    {
        pright = root->right;
        DeleteAllNodes(root->left);
        free(root);
        DeleteAllNodes(pright);
    }
}
```

The Complete Package

Listing 17.11 shows the entire `tree.c` code. Together, `tree.h` and `tree.c` constitute a tree programming package.

LISTING 17.11 The `tree.c` Implementation File

```
/* tree.c -- tree support functions */
#include <string.h>
#include <stdio.h>
#include <stdlib.h>
```

LISTING 17.11   Continued

```
#include "tree.h"

/* local data type */
typedef struct pair {
    Node * parent;
    Node * child;
} Pair;

/* prototypes for local functions */
static Node * MakeNode(const Item * pi);
static bool ToLeft(const Item * i1, const Item * i2);
static bool ToRight(const Item * i1, const Item * i2);
static void AddNode (Node * new_node, Node * root);
static void InOrder(const Node * root, void (* pfun)(Item item));
static Pair SeekItem(const Item * pi, const Tree * ptree);
static void DeleteNode(Node **ptr);
static void DeleteAllNodes(Node * ptr);

/* function definitions */
void InitializeTree(Tree * ptree)
{
    ptree->root = NULL;
    ptree->size = 0;
}

bool TreeIsEmpty(const Tree * ptree)
{
    if (ptree->root == NULL)
        return true;
    else
        return false;
}

bool TreeIsFull(const Tree * ptree)
{
    if (ptree->size == MAXITEMS)
        return true;
    else
        return false;
}

int TreeItemCount(const Tree * ptree)
{
    return ptree->size;
}

bool AddItem(const Item * pi, Tree * ptree)
{
    Node * new_node;

    if  (TreeIsFull(ptree))
```

LISTING 17.11   Continued

```
    {
        fprintf(stderr,"Tree is full\n");
        return false;                 /* early return          */
    }
    if (SeekItem(pi, ptree).child != NULL)
    {
        fprintf(stderr, "Attempted to add duplicate item\n");
        return false;                 /* early return          */
    }
    new_node = MakeNode(pi);          /* points to new node    */
    if (new_node == NULL)
    {
        fprintf(stderr, "Couldn't create node\n");
        return false;                 /* early return          */
    }
    /* succeeded in creating a new node */
    ptree->size++;

    if (ptree->root == NULL)          /* case 1: tree is empty */
        ptree->root = new_node;       /* new node is tree root */
    else                              /* case 2: not empty     */
        AddNode(new_node,ptree->root); /* add node to tree     */

    return true;                      /* successful return     */
}

bool InTree(const Item * pi, const Tree * ptree)
{
    return (SeekItem(pi, ptree).child == NULL) ? false : true;
}

bool DeleteItem(const Item * pi, Tree * ptree)
{
    Pair look;

    look = SeekItem(pi, ptree);
    if (look.child == NULL)
        return false;

    if (look.parent == NULL)          /* delete root item      */
        DeleteNode(&ptree->root);
    else if (look.parent->left == look.child)
        DeleteNode(&look.parent->left);
    else
        DeleteNode(&look.parent->right);
    ptree->size--;

    return true;
}

void Traverse (const Tree * ptree, void (* pfun)(Item item))
```

LISTING 17.11   Continued

```
{
    if (ptree != NULL)
        InOrder(ptree->root, pfun);
}

void DeleteAll(Tree * ptree)
{
    if (ptree != NULL)
        DeleteAllNodes(ptree->root);
    ptree->root = NULL;
    ptree->size = 0;
}


/* local functions */
static void InOrder(const Node * root, void (* pfun)(Item item))
{
    if (root != NULL)
    {
        InOrder(root->left, pfun);
        (*pfun)(root->item);
        InOrder(root->right, pfun);
    }
}

static void DeleteAllNodes(Node * root)
{
    Node * pright;

    if (root != NULL)
    {
        pright = root->right;
        DeleteAllNodes(root->left);
        free(root);
        DeleteAllNodes(pright);
    }
}

static void AddNode (Node * new_node, Node * root)
{
    if (ToLeft(&new_node->item, &root->item))
    {
        if (root->left == NULL)      /* empty subtree        */
            root->left = new_node;   /* so add node here     */
        else
            AddNode(new_node, root->left);/* else process subtree*/
    }
    else if (ToRight(&new_node->item, &root->item))
    {
        if (root->right == NULL)
            root->right = new_node;
```

LISTING 17.11 *Continued*

```
            else
                AddNode(new_node, root->right);
        }
        else                        /* should be no duplicates */
        {
            fprintf(stderr,"location error in AddNode()\n");
            exit(1);
        }
    }

    static bool ToLeft(const Item * i1, const Item * i2)
    {
        int comp1;

        if ((comp1 = strcmp(i1->petname, i2->petname)) < 0)
            return true;
        else if (comp1 == 0 &&
                    strcmp(i1->petkind, i2->petkind) < 0 )
            return true;
        else
            return false;
    }

    static bool ToRight(const Item * i1, const Item * i2)
    {
        int comp1;

        if ((comp1 = strcmp(i1->petname, i2->petname)) > 0)
            return true;
        else if (comp1 == 0 &&
                    strcmp(i1->petkind, i2->petkind) > 0 )
            return true;
        else
            return false;
    }

    static Node * MakeNode(const Item * pi)
    {
        Node * new_node;

        new_node = (Node *) malloc(sizeof(Node));
        if (new_node != NULL)
        {
            new_node->item = *pi;
            new_node->left = NULL;
            new_node->right = NULL;
        }

        return new_node;
    }

    static Pair SeekItem(const Item * pi, const Tree * ptree)
```

LISTING 17.11   Continued

```
{
    Pair look;
    look.parent = NULL;
    look.child = ptree->root;

    if (look.child == NULL)
        return look;                            /* early return   */

    while (look.child != NULL)
    {
        if (ToLeft(pi, &(look.child->item)))
        {
            look.parent = look.child;
            look.child = look.child->left;
        }
        else if (ToRight(pi, &(look.child->item)))
        {
            look.parent = look.child;
            look.child = look.child->right;
        }
        else        /* must be same if not to left or right    */
            break; /* look.child is address of node with item */
    }

    return look;                            /* successful return    */
}

static void DeleteNode(Node **ptr)
/* ptr is address of parent member pointing to target node  */
{
    Node * temp;

    puts((*ptr)->item.petname);
    if ( (*ptr)->left == NULL)
    {
        temp = *ptr;
        *ptr = (*ptr)->right;
        free(temp);
    }
    else if ( (*ptr)->right == NULL)
    {
        temp = *ptr;
        *ptr = (*ptr)->left;
        free(temp);
    }
    else    /* deleted node has two children */
    {
        /* find where to reattach right subtree */
        for (temp = (*ptr)->left; temp->right != NULL;
                temp = temp->right)
            continue;
        temp->right = (*ptr)->right;
```

LISTING 17.11   Continued

```
            temp = *ptr;
            *ptr =(*ptr)->left;
            free(temp);
        }
    }
```

Trying the Tree

Now that you have the interface and the function implementations, let's use them. The program in Listing 17.12 uses a menu to offer a choice of adding pets to the club membership roster, listing members, reporting the number of members, checking for membership, and quitting. The brief `main()` function concentrates on the essential program outline. Supporting functions do most of the work.

LISTING 17.12   The `petclub.c` Program

```
/* petclub.c -- use a binary search tree */
#include <stdio.h>
#include <string.h>
#include <ctype.h>
#include "tree.h"

char menu(void);
void addpet(Tree * pt);
void droppet(Tree * pt);
void showpets(const Tree * pt);
void findpet(const Tree * pt);
void printitem(Item item);
void uppercase(char * str);

int main(void)
{
    Tree pets;
    char choice;

    InitializeTree(&pets);
    while ((choice = menu()) != 'q')
    {
        switch (choice)
        {
            case 'a' :  addpet(&pets);
                        break;
            case 'l' :  showpets(&pets);
                        break;
            case 'f' :  findpet(&pets);
                        break;
            case 'n' :  printf("%d pets in club\n",
                               TreeItemCount(&pets));
                        break;
```

LISTING 17.12   Continued

```
                case 'd' :  droppet(&pets);
                            break;
                default  :  puts("Switching error");
        }
    }
    DeleteAll(&pets);
    puts("Bye.");

    return 0;
}

char menu(void)
{
    int ch;

    puts("Nerfville Pet Club Membership Program");
    puts("Enter the letter corresponding to your choice:");
    puts("a) add a pet          l) show list of pets");
    puts("n) number of pets     f) find pets");
    puts("d) delete a pet       q) quit");
    while ((ch = getchar()) != EOF)
    {
        while (getchar() != '\n')   /* discard rest of line */
            continue;
        ch = tolower(ch);
        if (strchr("alrfndq",ch) == NULL)
            puts("Please enter an a, l, f, n, d, or q:");
        else
            break;
    }
    if (ch == EOF)          /* make EOF cause program to quit */
        ch = 'q';

    return ch;
}

void addpet(Tree * pt)
{
    Item temp;

    if (TreeIsFull(pt))
        puts("No room in the club!");
    else
    {
        puts("Please enter name of pet:");
        gets(temp.petname);
        puts("Please enter pet kind:");
        gets(temp.petkind);
        uppercase(temp.petname);
        uppercase(temp.petkind);
        AddItem(&temp, pt);
    }
}
```

LISTING 17.12   Continued

```c
void showpets(const Tree * pt)
{
    if (TreeIsEmpty(pt))
        puts("No entries!");
    else
        Traverse(pt, printitem);
}

void printitem(Item item)
{
    printf("Pet: %-19s  Kind: %-19s\n", item.petname,
           item.petkind);
}

void findpet(const Tree * pt)
{
    Item temp;

    if (TreeIsEmpty(pt))
    {
        puts("No entries!");
        return;      /* quit function if tree is empty */
    }

    puts("Please enter name of pet you wish to find:");
    gets(temp.petname);
    puts("Please enter pet kind:");
    gets(temp.petkind);
    uppercase(temp.petname);
    uppercase(temp.petkind);
    printf("%s the %s ", temp.petname, temp.petkind);
    if (InTree(&temp, pt))
        printf("is a member.\n");
    else
        printf("is not a member.\n");
}

void droppet(Tree * pt)
{
    Item temp;

    if (TreeIsEmpty(pt))
    {
        puts("No entries!");
        return;      /* quit function if tree is empty */
    }

    puts("Please enter name of pet you wish to delete:");
    gets(temp.petname);
    puts("Please enter pet kind:");
    gets(temp.petkind);
    uppercase(temp.petname);
```

LISTING 17.12   Continued

```
        uppercase(temp.petkind);
        printf("%s the %s ", temp.petname, temp.petkind);
        if (DeleteItem(&temp, pt))
            printf("is dropped from the club.\n");
        else
            printf("is not a member.\n");
}

void uppercase(char * str)
{
    while (*str)
    {
        *str = toupper(*str);
        str++;
    }
}
```

The program converts all letters to uppercase so that *SNUFFY*, *Snuffy*, and *snuffy* are not considered distinct names. Here is a sample run:

```
Nerfville Pet Club Membership Program
Enter the letter corresponding to your choice:
a) add a pet          l) show list of pets
n) number of pets     f) find pets
q) quit
a
Please enter name of pet:
Quincy
Please enter pet kind:
pig
Nerfville Pet Club Membership Program
Enter the letter corresponding to your choice:
a) add a pet          l) show list of pets
n) number of pets     f) find pets
q) quit
a
Please enter name of pet:
Betty
Please enter pet kind:
Boa
Nerfville Pet Club Membership Program
Enter the letter corresponding to your choice:
a) add a pet          l) show list of pets
n) number of pets     f) find pets
q) quit
a
Please enter name of pet:
Hiram Jinx
Please enter pet kind:
domestic cat
Nerfville Pet Club Membership Program
```

LISTING 17.12   Continued

```
Enter the letter corresponding to your choice:
a) add a pet        l) show list of pets
n) number of pets   f) find pets
q) quit
n
3 pets in club
Nerfville Pet Club Membership Program
Enter the letter corresponding to your choice:
a) add a pet        l) show list of pets
n) number of pets   f) find pets
q) quit
l
Pet: BETTY              Kind: BOA
Pet: HIRAM JINX         Kind: DOMESTIC CAT
Pet: QUINCY             Kind: PIG
Nerfville Pet Club Membership Program
Enter the letter corresponding to your choice:
a) add a pet        l) show list of pets
n) number of pets   f) find pets
q)  quit
q
Bye.
```

Tree Thoughts

The binary search tree has some drawbacks. For example, the binary search tree is efficient only if it is fully populated, or *balanced*. Suppose you're storing words that are entered randomly. Chances are the tree will have a fairly bushy look, as in Figure 17.12. Now suppose you enter data in alphabetical order. Then each new node would be added to the right, and the tree might look like Figure 17.16. The Figure 17.12 tree is said to be *balanced*, and the Figure 17.16 tree is *unbalanced*. Searching this tree is no more effective than sequentially searching a linked list.

One way to avoid stringy trees is use more care when building a tree. If a tree or subtree begins to get too unbalanced on one side or the other, rearrange the nodes to restore a better balance. Similarly, you might need to rearrange the tree after a deletion. The Russian mathematicians Adel'son-Vel'skii and Landis developed an algorithm to do this. Trees built with their method are called *AVL trees*. It takes longer to build a balanced tree because of the extra restructuring, but you ensure maximum, or nearly maximum, search efficiency.

You might want a binary search tree that does allow duplicate items. Suppose, for example, that you wanted to analyze some text by tracking how many times each word in the text appears. One approach is to define `Item` as a structure that holds one word and a number. The first time a word is encountered, it's added to the tree, and the number is set to 1. The next time the same word is encountered, the program finds the node containing the word and increments the number. It doesn't take much work to modify the basic binary search tree to behave in this fashion.

FIGURE 17.16
A badly unbalanced
binary search tree.

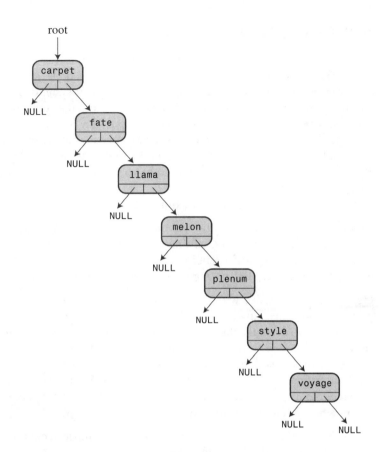

For another possible variation, consider the Nerfville Pet Club. The example ordered the tree by both name and kind, so it could hold Sam the cat in one node, Sam the dog in another node, and Sam the goat in a third node. You couldn't have two cats called Sam, however. Another approach is to order the tree just by name. Making that change alone would allow for only one Sam, regardless of kind, but you could then define `Item` to be a list of structures instead of being a single structure. The first time a Sally shows up, the program would create a new node, then create a new list, and then add Sally and her kind to the list. The next Sally that shows up would be directed to the same node and added to the list.

Add-On Libraries

You've probably concluded that implementing an ADT such as a linked list or a tree is hard work with many, many opportunities to err. Add-on libraries provide an alternative approach: Let someone else do the work and testing. Having gone through the two relatively simple examples in this chapter, you are in a better position to understand and appreciate such libraries.

Other Directions

In this book, we've covered the essential features of C, but we've only touched upon the library. The ANSI C library contains scores of useful functions. Most implementations also offer extensive libraries of functions specific to particular systems. DOS compilers offer functions to facilitate hardware control, keyboard input, and the generation of graphics for IBM PCs and clones. Windows-based compilers support the Windows graphic interface. Macintosh C compilers provide functions to access the Macintosh toolbox to facilitate producing programs with the standard Macintosh interface. Take the time to explore what your system has to offer. If it doesn't have what you want, make your own functions. That's part of C. If you think you can do a better job on, say, an input function, do it! And as you refine and polish your programming technique, you will go from C to shining C.

If you've found the concepts of lists, queues, and trees exciting and useful, you might want to read a book or take a course on advanced programming techniques. Computer scientists have invested a lot of energy and talent into developing and analyzing algorithms and ways of representing data. You may find that someone has already developed exactly the tool you need.

After you are comfortable with C, you might want to investigate C++, Objective C, or Java. These *object-oriented* languages have their roots in C. C already has data objects ranging in complexity from a simple `char` variable to large and intricate structures. Object-oriented languages carry the idea of the object even further. For example, the properties of an object include not only what kinds of information it can hold, but also what kinds of operations can be performed on it. The ADTs in this chapter follow that pattern. Also, objects can inherit properties from other objects. OOP carries modularizing to a higher level of abstraction than does C, and it facilitates writing large programs.

You might want to check out the bibliography in Reference Section I, "Additional Reading," for books that might further your interests.

Key Concepts

A data type is characterized by how the data is structured and stored and also by what operations are possible. An abstract data type (ADT) specifies in an abstract manner the properties and operations characterizing a type. Conceptually, you can translate an ADT to a particular programming language in two steps. The first step is defining the programming interface. In C, you can do this by using a header file to define type names and to provide function prototypes that correspond to the allowed operations. The second step is implementing the interface. In C, you can do this with a source code file that supplies the function definitions corresponding to the prototypes.

Summary

The list, the queue, and the binary tree are examples of ADTs commonly used in computer programming. Often they are implemented using dynamic memory allocation and linked structures, but sometimes implementing them with an array is a better choice.

When you program using a particular type (say, a queue or a tree), you should write the program in terms of the type interface. That way, you can modify and improve the implementation without having to alter programs by using the interface.

Review Questions

1. What's involved in defining a data type?

2. Why can the linked list in Listing 17.2 be traversed in only one direction? How could you modify the **struct film** definition so that the list could be traversed in both directions?

3. What's an ADT?

4. The **QueueIsEmpty()** function took a pointer to a **queue** structure as an argument, but it could have been written so that it took a **queue** structure rather than a pointer as an argument. What are the advantages and disadvantages of each approach?

5. The *stack* is another data form from the list family. In a stack, additions and deletions can be made from only one end of the list. Items are said to be "pushed onto" the top of the stack and to be "popped off" the stack. Therefore, the stack is a LIFO structure (that is, *last in, first out*).

    a. Devise an ADT for a stack.

    b. Devise a C programming interface for a stack.

6. What is the maximum number of comparisons a sequential search and a binary search would need to determine that a particular item is not in a sorted list of three items? 1,023 items? 65,535 items?

7. Suppose a program constructs a binary search tree of words, using the algorithm developed in this chapter. Draw the tree, assuming words are entered in the following orders:

    a. nice food roam dodge gate office wave

    b. wave roam office nice gate food dodge

    c. food dodge roam wave office gate nice

    d. nice roam office food wave gate dodge

8. Consider the binary trees constructed in Review Question 7. What would each one look like after the word *food* is removed from each tree using the algorithm from this chapter?

Programming Exercises

1. Modify Listing 17.2 so that it displays the movie list both in the original order and in reverse order. One approach is to modify the linked-list definition so that the list can be traversed in both directions. Another approach is to use recursion.

2. Suppose `list.h` (Listing 17.3) uses the following definition of a list:

```
typedef struct list
{
    Node * head;    /* points to head of list */
    Node * end;     /* points to end of list  */
} List;
```

Rewrite the `list.c` (Listing 17.5) functions to fit this definition and test the resulting code with the `films3.c` (Listing 17.4) program.

3. Suppose `list.h` (Listing 17.3) uses the following definition of a list:

```
#define MAXSIZE 100
typedef struct list
{
    Item entries[MAXSIZE];    /* array of items            */
    int items;                /* number of items in list */
} List;
```

Rewrite the `list.c` (Listing 17.5) functions to fit this definition and test the resulting code with the `films3.c` (Listing 17.4) program.

4. Rewrite `mall.c` (Listing 17.7) so that it simulates a double booth having two queues.

5. Write a program that lets you input a string. The program then should push the characters of the string onto a stack, one by one (see review question 5), and then pop the characters from the stack and display them. This results in displaying the string in reverse order.

6. Write a function that takes three arguments: the name of an array of sorted integers, the number of elements of the array, and an integer to seek. The function returns the value 1 if the integer is in the array, and 0 if it isn't. Have the function use the binary search technique.

7. Write a program that opens and reads a text file and records how many times each word occurs in the file. Use a binary search tree modified to store both a word and the number of times it occurs. After the program has read the file, it should offer a menu with three choices. The first is to list all the words along with the number of occurrences. The second is to let you enter a word, with the program reporting how many times the word occurred in the file. The third choice is to quit.

8. Modify the Pet Club program so that all pets with the same name are stored in a list in the same node. When the user chooses to find a pet, the program should request the pet name and then list all pets (along with their kinds) having that name.

APPENDIX A

ANSWERS TO THE REVIEW QUESIONS

Answers to Review Questions for Chapter 1

1. A perfectly portable program is one whose source code can, without modification, be compiled to a successful program on a variety of different computer systems.

2. A source code file contains code as written in whatever language the programmer is using. An object code file contains machine language code; it need not be the code for a complete program. An executable file contains the complete code, in machine language, constituting an executable program.

3.   a. Defining program objectives.

   b. Designing the program.

   c. Coding the program.

   d. Compiling the program.

   e. Running the program.

   f. Testing and debugging the program.

   g. Maintaining and modifying the program.

4. A compiler translates source code (for example, code written in C) to the equivalent machine language code, also termed *object code*.

5. The linker combines translated source code with library code and start-up code to produce an executable program.

Answers to Review Questions for Chapter 2

1. They are called functions.

2. A syntax error is a violation of the rules governing how sentences or programs are put together. Here's an example in English: "Me speak English good." Here's an example in C:

```
printf"Where are the parentheses?";.
```

3. A semantic error is one of meaning. Here's an example in English: "This sentence is excellent Italian." Here's a C example:

```
thrice_n = 3 + n;
```

4. Line 1: Begin the line with a #; spell the file **stdio.h**; place the filename within angle brackets.

Line 2: Use (), not {}; end the comment with */, not /*.

Line 3: Use {, not (.

Line 4: Complete the statement with a semicolon.

Line 5: Indiana got this one (the blank line) right!

Line 6: Use =, not := for assignment. (Apparently, Indiana knows a little Pascal.) Use 52, not 56, weeks per year.

Line 7: Should be

```
printf("There are %d weeks in a year.\n", s);
```

Line 9: There isn't a line 9, but there should be, and it should consist of the closing brace, }.

Here's how the code looks after these changes:

```
#include <stdio.h>
int main(void) /* this prints the number of weeks in a year */
{
    int s;

    s = 52;
    printf("There are %d weeks in a year.\n", s);
    return 0;
}
```

5.   a. `Baa Baa Black Sheep.Have you any wool?`

(Note that there is no space after the period. You could have had a space by using " Have instead of "`Have`.)

b.

`Begone!`
`O creature of lard!`

(Note that the cursor is left at the end of the second line.)

c.

`What?`
`No/nBonzo?`

(Note that the slash [/] does not have the same effect as the backslash [\]; it simply prints as a slash.)

d. `2 + 2 = 4`

(Note how each `%d` is replaced by the corresponding variable value from the list. Note, too, that + means addition and that calculation can be done inside a `printf()` statement.)

6. `int` and `char` (`main` is a function name, function is a technical term for describing C, and = is an operator).

7. `printf("There were %d words and %d lines.\n", words, lines);`

8. After line 7, `a` is 5 and `b` is 2. After line 8, both `a` and `b` are 5. After line 9, both `a` and `b` are still 5. (Note that `a` can't be 2 because by the time you say `a = b;`, `b` has already been changed to 5.)

Answers to Review Questions for Chapter 3

1.   a. `int`, possibly `short` or `unsigned` or `unsigned short`; population is a whole number.

b. `float`; it's unlikely the cost will be an exact integer. (You could use `double` but don't really need the extra precision.)

c. `char`.

d. `int`, possibly `unsigned`.

2. One reason is that `long` may accommodate larger numbers than `int` on your system; another reason is that if you do need to handle larger values, you improve portability by using a type guaranteed to be at least 32 bits on all systems.

3. To get exactly 32 bits, you could use `int32_t`, provided it was defined for your system. To get the smallest type that could store at least 32 bits, use `int_least32_t`. And to get the type that would provide the fastest computations for 32 bits, choose `int_fast32_t`.

4.   a. `char` constant (but stored as type `int`)

       b. `int` constant

       c. `double` constant

       d. `unsigned int` constant, hexadecimal format

       e. `double` constant

5. Line 1: Should be `#include <stdio.h>`.

Line 2: Should be `int main(void)`.

Line 3: Use `{`, not `(`.

Line 4: Should be a comma, not a semicolon, between `g` and `h`.

Line 5: Fine.

Line 6 (the blank line): Fine.

Line 7: There should be at least one digit before the `e`. Either `1e21` or `1.0e21` is okay, although rather large.

Line 8: Fine, at least in terms of syntax.

Line 9: Use `}`, not `)`.

Missing lines: First, `rate` is never assigned a value. Second, the variable `h` is never used. Also, the program never informs you of the results of its calculation. None of these errors will stop the program from running (although you might be given a warning about the unused variable), but they do detract from its already limited usefulness. Also, there should be a `return` statement at the end.

Here is one possible correct version:

```
#include <stdio.h>
int main(void)
{
    float g, h;
    float tax, rate;

    rate = 0.08;
    g = 1.0e5;
    tax = rate*g;
    h = g + tax;
    printf("You owe $%f plus $%f in taxes for a total of $%f.\n", g, tax, h);
    return 0;
}
```

6.

	Constant	Type	Specifier
a.	12	int	%d
b.	0X3	unsigned int	%#X
c.	'C'	char (really int)	%c
d.	2.34E07	double	%e
e.	'\040'	char (really int)	%c
f.	7.0	double	%f
g.	6L	long	%ld
h.	6.0f	float	%f

7.

	Constant	Type	Specifier
a.	012	unsigned int	%#o
b.	2.9e05L	long double	%Le
c.	's'	char (really int)	%c
d.	100000	long	%ld
e.	'\n'	char (really int)	%c
f.	20.0f	float	%f
g.	0x44	unsigned int	%x

8.

```
printf("The odds against the %d were %ld to 1.\n", imate, shot);
printf("A score of %f is not an %c grade.\n", log, grade);
```

9.

```
ch = '\r';
ch = 13;
ch = '\015'
ch = '\xd'
```

10. Line 0: Should have `#include <stdio.h>`.

Line 1: Use `/*` and `*/` or else `//`

Line 3: `int cows, legs;`

Line 4: `count?\n");`

Line 5: `%d`, not `%c`; replace `legs` with `&legs`

Line 7: `%d`, not `%f`

Also, add a `return` statement.

Here's one correct version:

```
#include <stdio.h>
int main(void) /* this program is perfect */
{
    int cows, legs;
    printf("How many cow legs did you count?\n");
    scanf("%d", &legs);
    cows = legs / 4;
    printf("That implies there are %d cows.\n", cows);
    return 0;
}
```

11. a. A newline character

b. A backslash character

c. A double quotation mark

d. A tab character

Answers to Review Questions for Chapter 4

1. The program malfunctions. The first `scanf()` statement reads just your first name, leaving your last name untouched but still stored in the input "buffer." (This buffer is just a temporary storage area used to store the input.) When the next `scanf()` statement comes along looking for your weight, it picks up where the last reading attempt ended, and it tries to read your last name as your weight. This frustrates `scanf()`. On the other hand, if you respond to the name request with something such as `Lasha 144`, it uses 144 as your weight, even though you typed it before your weight was requested.

2. a.

`He sold the painting for $234.50.`

b.

`Hi!`

(Note: The first character is a character constant, the second is a decimal integer converted to a character, and the third is an ASCII representation, in octal, of a character constant.)

c.

His Hamlet was funny without being vulgar.
has 42 characters.

d.

Is 1.20e+003 the same as 1201.00?

3. Use \", as in the following:

```
printf("\"%s\"\nhas %d characters.\n", Q, strlen(Q));
```

4. Here is a corrected version:

```
#include <stdio.h>    /* don't forget this    */
#define B "booboo"    /* add #, quotes        */
#define X 10          /* add #                */
int main(void)        /* instead of main(int) */
{
    int age;
    int xp;           /* declare all variables */
    char name[40];    /* make into an array    */

    printf("Please enter your first name.\n"); /* \n for readability */
    scanf("%s", name);
    printf("All right, %s, what's your age?\n", name); /* %s for string */
    scanf("%d", &age);          /* %d, not %f, &age, not age */
    xp = age + X;
    printf("That's a %s! You must be at least %d.\n", B, xp);
    return 0;                   /* not rerun                 */
}
```

5. Recall the %% construction for printing %.

```
printf("This copy of \"%s\" sells for $%0.2f.\n", BOOK, cost);

printf("That is %0.0f%% of list.\n", percent);
```

6.   a. %d

    b. %4X

    c. %10.3f

    d. %12.2e

    e. %-30s

7.   a. %15lu

    b. %#4x

    c. %-12.2E

    d. %+10.3f

    e. %8.8s

8. a. `%6.4d`

    b. `%*o`

    c. `%2c`

    d. `%+0.2f`

    e. `%-7.5s`

9. a.
```
int dalmations;
    scanf("%d", &dalmations);
```
    b.
```
float kgs, share;
    scanf("%f%f", &kgs, &share);
```
    (Note: For input, e, f, and g can be used interchangeably. Also, for all but %c, it makes no difference if you leave spaces between the conversion specifiers.)

    c.
```
char pasta[20];
    scanf("%s", pasta);
```
    d.
```
char action[20];
    int value;
    scanf("%s %d", action, &value);
```
    e.
```
int value;
    scanf("%*s %d", &value);
```

10. Whitespace consists of spaces, tabs, and newlines. C uses whitespace to separate tokens from one another; `scanf()` uses whitespace to separate consecutive input items from each other.

11. The substitutions would take place. Unfortunately, the preprocessor cannot discriminate between those parentheses that should be replaced with braces and those that should not. Therefore,
```
#define ( {
#define ) }
int main(void)

(
    printf("Hello, O Great One!\n");
)
```
    becomes
```
int main{void}
{
    printf{"Hello, O Great One!\n"};
}
```

Answers to Review Questions for Chapter 5

1.   a. `30`.

   b. `27` (not 3). `(12 + 6)/(2*3)` would give `3`.

   c. `x = 1, y = 1` (integer division).

   d. `x = 3` (integer division) and `y = 9`.

2.   a. `6` (reduces to `3 + 3.3`)

   b. `52`

   c. `0` (reduces to `0 * 22.0`)

   d. `13` (reduces to `66.0 / 5` or `13.2` and is then assigned to `int`)

3. **Line 0**: Should include `<stdio.h>`.

   Line 3: Should end in a semicolon, not a comma.

   Line 6: The `while` statement sets up an infinite loop because the value of i remains `1` and is always less than `30`. Presumably, we meant to write `while(i++ < 30)`.

   Lines 6–8: The indentation implies that we wanted lines 7 and 8 to form a block, but the lack of braces means that the `while` loop includes only line 7. Braces should be added.

   Line 7: Because `1` and `i` are both integers, the result of the division will be `1` when `i` is `1`, and `0` for all larger values. Using `n = 1.0/i;` would cause `i` to be converted to floating point before division and would yield nonzero answers.

   Line 8: We omitted a newline character (`\n`) in the control statement. This causes the numbers to be printed on one line, if possible.

   Line 10: Should be `return 0;`.

   Here is a corrected version:

```
#include <stdio.h>
int main(void)
{
  int i = 1;
  float n;
  printf("Watch out! Here come a bunch of fractions!\n");
  while (i++ < 30)
  {
    n = 1.0/i;
    printf(" %f\n", n);
  }
  printf("That's all, folks!\n");
  return 0;
}
```

4. The main problem lies in the relationship between the test statement (is **sec** greater than 0?) and the **scanf()** statement that fetches the value of **sec**. In particular, the first time the test is made, the program hasn't had a chance to even get a value for **sec**, and the comparison will be made to some garbage value that happens to be at that memory location. One solution, albeit an inelegant one, is to initialize **sec** to, say, **1** so that the test is passed the first time through. This uncovers a second problem. When you finally type **0** to halt the program, **sec** doesn't get checked until *after* the loop is finished, and the results for 0 seconds are printed out. What you really want is to have a **scanf()** statement just before the **while** test is made. You can accomplish that by altering the central part of the program to read this way:

```
scanf("%d", &sec);
while ( sec > 0 ) {
  min = sec/S_TO_M;
  left = sec % S_TO_M;
  printf("%d sec is %d min, %d sec. \n", sec, min, left);
  printf("Next input?\n");
  scanf("%d", &sec);
}
```

The first time through, the **scanf()** outside the loop is used. Thereafter, the **scanf()** at the end of the loop (and hence just before the loop begins again) is used. This is a common method for handling problems of this sort, which is why Listing 5.9 used it.

5. Here is the output:

```
%s! C is cool!
! C is cool!
11
11
12
11
```

Let's explain. The first **printf()** statement is the same as this:

```
printf("%s! C is cool!\n","%s! C is cool!\n");
```

The second print statement first increments **num** to **11** and then prints the value. The third print statement prints **num**, which is **11**, and then increments it to **12**. The fourth print statement prints the current value of **n**, which still is **12**, and then decrements **n** to **11**. The final print statement prints the current value of **num**, which is **11**.

6. Here is the output:

```
SOS:4 4.00
```

The expression **c1** - **c2** has the same value as **'S'** - **'0'**, which in ASCII is **83** - **79**.

7. It prints on one line the digits 1 through 10 in fields that are five columns wide and then starts a new line:

```
    1    2    3    4    5    6    7    8    9   10
```

8. Here is one possibility, which assumes that the letters are coded consecutively, as is the case for ASCII:

```
#include <stdio.h>

int main(void)
{
    char c = 'a';
    while (c <= 'g')
        printf("%5c", c++);
    printf("\n");
    return 0;
}
```

9. Here is the output for each example:

    a.   1   2

    Note that x is incremented and then compared. The cursor is left on the same line.

    b.

    ```
    101
    102
    103
    104
    ```

    Note that this time x is compared and then incremented. In both this case and in example a, x is incremented before printing takes place. Note, too, that indenting the second `printf()` statement does not make it part of the `while` loop. Therefore, it is called only once, after the `while` loop ends.

    c. stuvw

    Here, there is no incrementing until after the first `printf()`.

10. This is an ill-constructed program. Because the `while` statement doesn't use braces, only the `printf()` statement is part of the loop, so the program prints the message COMPUTER BYTES DOG indefinitely until you can kill the program.

11.   a. x = x + 10;

        b. x++;   or ++x;   or x = x + 1;

        c. c = 2 * (a + b);

        d. c = a + 2* b;

12.   a. x--;   or --x;   or x = x - 1;

        b. m = n % k;

        c. p = q / (b - a);

        d. x = (a + b) / (c * d);

Answers to Review Questions for Chapter 6

1. 2, 7, 70, 64, 8, 2

2. It would produce the following output:

   36 18 9 4 2 1

   If `value` were `double`, the test would remain true even when `value` became less than 1. The loop would continue until floating-point underflow yielded a value of 0. Also, the `%3d` specifier would be the wrong choice.

3.   a. `x > 5`

      b. `scanf("%lf",&x) != 1`

      c. `x == 5`

4.   a. `scanf("%d", &x) == 1`

      b. `x != 5`

      c. `x >= 20`

5. Line 4: Should be `list[10]`.

   Line 6: Commas should be semicolons.

   Line 6: The range for `i` should be from 0 to 9, not 1 to 10.

   Line 9: Commas should be semicolons.

   Line 9: >= should be <=. Otherwise, when `i` is `1`, the loop runs for quite a while.

   Line 10: There should be another closing brace between lines 9 and 10. One brace closes the compound statement, and one closes the program. In between should be a `return 0;` line.

   Here's a corrected version:

```
#include <stdio.h>
int main(void)
{                                        /* line 3  */
    int i, j, list[10];                  /* line 4  */

    for (i = 0; i <  10;  i++)           /* line 6  */
    {                                    /* line 7  */
        list[i] = 2*i + 3;               /* line 8  */
        for (j = 1; j <= i; j++)         /* line 9  */
            printf(" %d", list[j]);      /* line 10 */
        printf("\n");                    /* line 11 */
    }
    return 0;
}
```

6. Here's one way:

```c
#include <stdio.h>
int main(void)
{
    int col, row;

    for (row = 1; row <= 4; row++)
    {
        for (col = 1; col <= 8; col++)
            printf("$");
        printf("\n");
    }
    return 0;
}
```

7.   a. It would produce the following output:

Hi! Hi! Hi! Bye! Bye! Bye! Bye! Bye!

b. It would produce the following output:

ACGM

8.   a. It would produce the following output:

Go west, youn

b. It would produce the following output:

Hp!xftu-!zpvo

c. It would produce the following output:

Go west, young

d. It would produce the following output:

Go west, youn

9. Here is the output you should get:

31|32|33|30|31|32|33|
***
1
5
9
13

***
2 6
4 8
8 10

***
======
=====
====
===
==

10.   a. `mint`

   b. 10 elements

   c. Type `double` values

   d. Line ii is correct; `mint[2]` is a type `double` value and `&mint[2]` is its location.

11. Because the first element has index `0`, the loop range should be `1` to `SIZE` - `1`, not `1` to `SIZE`. Making that change, however, causes the first element to be assigned the value `0` instead of `2`. So rewrite the loop this way:

```
for (index = 0; index < SIZE; index++)
    by_twos[index] = 2 * (index + 1);
```

Similarly, the limits for the second loop should be changed. Also, an array index should be used with the array name:

```
for( index = 0; index < SIZE; index++)
    printf("%d ", by_twos[index]);
```

One dangerous aspect of bad loop limits is that the program may work; however, because it is placing data where it shouldn't, it might not work at some time in the future, forming sort of a programming time bomb.

12. It should declare the return type as `long`, and it should have a `return` statement that returns a `long` value.

13. Typecasting `num` to `long` makes sure the calculation is done as a `long` calculation, not an `int` calculation. On a system with a 16-bit `int`, multiplying two `int`s produces a result that is truncated to an `int` before the value is returned, possibly losing data.

```
long square(int num)

{

    return ((long) num) * num;

}
```

14. Here is the output:

```
1: Hi!
k = 1
k is 1 in the loop
Now k is 3
k = 3
k is 3 in the loop
Now k is 5
k = 5
k is 5 in the loop
Now k is 7
k = 7
```

Answers to Review Questions for Chapter 7

1. True: b.

2.   a. `number >= 90 && number < 100`

   b. `ch != 'q' && ch != 'k'`

   c. `(number >= 1 && number <= 9) && number != 5`

   d. `!(number >= 1 && number <= 9)` is one choice, but

      `number < 1 || number > 9` is simpler to understand

3. Line 5: Should be `scanf("%d %d", &weight, &height);`. Don't forget those `&`s for `scanf()`. Also, this line should be preceded by a line prompting input.

   Line 9: What is meant is `(height < 72 && height > 64)`. However, the first part of the expression is unnecessary because height must be less than 72 for the `else if` to be reached in the first place. Therefore, a simple `(height > 64)` will serve. But line 6 already guarantees that `height > 64`, so no test at all is needed, and the `if else` should just be an `else`.

   Line 11: The condition is redundant; the second subexpression (`weight` not less than or equal to 300) means the same as the first. A simple `(weight > 300)` is all that is needed. But there is more trouble. Line 11 gets attached to the wrong `if`! Clearly, this `else` is meant to go along with line 6. By the most recent `if` rule, however, it will be associated with the `if` of line 9. Therefore, line 11 is reached when `weight` is less than 100 and `height` is 64 or under. This makes it impossible for `weight` to exceed 300 when this statement is reached.

   Lines 7 through 9: Should be enclosed in braces. Then line 11 will become an alternative to line 6, not to line 9. Alternatively, if the `if else` on line 9 is replaced with a simple `else`, no braces are needed.

   Line 13: Simplify to `if (height > 48)`. Actually, you can omit this line entirely because line 12 already makes this test.

   Line 15: This `else` associates with the last `if`, the one on line 13. Enclose lines 13 and 14 in braces to force this `else` to associate with the `if` of line 11. Or, as suggested, simply eliminate line 13.

   Here's a corrected version:

```
#include <stdio.h>
int main(void)
{
    int weight, height;  /* weight in lbs, height in inches */

    printf("Enter your weight in pounds and ");
    printf("your height in inches.\n");
    scanf("%d %d", &weight, &height);
```

```
    if (weight < 100 && height > 64)
        if (height >= 72)
            printf("You are very tall for your weight.\n");
        else
            printf("You are tall for your weight.\n");
    else if (weight > 300 && height < 48)
            printf(" You are quite short for your weight.\n");
    else
          printf("Your weight is ideal.\n");

    return 0;
}
```

4.   a.   1. The assertion is true, which numerically is a 1.

       b.   0. 3 is not less than 2.

       c.   1. If the first expression is false, the second is true, and vice versa; just one true expression is needed.

       d.   6, because the value of 6 > 2 is 1.

       e.   10, because the test condition is true.

       f.   0. If x > y is true, the value of the expression is y > x, which is false in that case, or 0. If x > y is false, the value of the expression is x > y, which is false in that case.

5. The program prints the following:

#%#%$#%*#%*#%$#%*#%*#%$#%*#%*#%

Despite what the indentation suggests, the # is printed during every loop because it is not part of a compound statement.

6. The program prints the following:

```
fat hat cat Oh no!
hat cat Oh no!
cat Oh no!
```

7. The comments on lines 5 through 7 should be terminated with */, or else you can replace /* with //. The expression 'a' <= ch >= 'z' should be replaced with this:

ch >= 'a' && ch <= 'z'

Or, more simply and more portably, you can include ctype.h and use islower(). Incidentally, 'a' <= ch >= 'z' is valid C; it just doesn't have the right meaning. Because relational operators associate left to right, the expression is interpreted as ('a' <= ch) >= 'z'. The expression in parentheses has the value 1 or 0 (true or false), and this value is checked to see whether it is equal to or greater than the numeric code for 'z'. Neither 0 nor 1 satisfies that test, so the whole expression always evaluates to 0 (false). In the second test expression, || should be &&. Also, although !(ch < 'A') is both valid and correct in meaning, `ch >= 'A'` is simpler. The `'Z'` should be followed by two closing parentheses, not one. Again, more simply, use `isupper()`. The `oc++;` statement should be preceded by an `else`. Otherwise, it is incremented every character. The control expression in the `printf()` call should be enclosed in double quotes.

Here is a corrected version:

```
#include <stdio.h>
#include <ctype.h>
int main(void)
{
  char ch;
  int lc = 0;     /* lowercase char count */
  int uc = 0;     /* uppercase char count */
  int oc = 0;     /* other char count     */

  while ((ch = getchar()) != '#')
  {
      if (islower(ch))
            lc++;
      else if (isupper(ch))
            uc++;
      else
            oc++;
  }
  printf("%d lowercase, %d uppercase, %d other", lc, uc, oc);
  return 0;
}
```

8. Unhappily, it prints the same line indefinitely:

    `You are 65. Here is your gold watch.`

    The problem is that the line

    `if (age = 65)`

    sets `age` to `65`, which tests as true every loop cycle.

9. Here is the resulting run using the given input:

```
q
Step 1
Step 2
Step 3
c
Step 1
g
Step 1
Step 3
b
Step 1
Done
```

    Note that both **b** and **#** terminate the loop, but that entering **b** elicits the printing of step 1, and entering **#** doesn't.

10. Here is one solution:

```c
#include <stdio.h>
int main(void)
{
  char ch;

  while ((ch = getchar()) != '#')
  {
    if (ch != '\n')
    {
      printf("Step 1\n");
      if (ch == 'b')
        break;
      else if (ch != 'c')
      {
          if (ch != 'g')
              printf("Step 2\n");
          printf("Step 3\n");
      }
    }
  }
  printf("Done\n");
  return 0;
}
```

Answers to Review Questions for Chapter 8

1. The expression `putchar(getchar())` causes the program to read the next input character and to print it; the return value from `getchar()` is the argument to `putchar()`. No, `getchar(putchar())` is invalid because `getchar()` doesn't use an argument and `putchar()` needs one.

2.   a. Display the H character.

     b. Sound the alert if the system uses ASCII.

     c. Move the cursor to the beginning of the next line.

     d. Backspace.

3. `count <essay >essayct` or else `count >essayct <essay`

4. Just c. is valid.

5. It's a signal (a special value) returned by `getchar()` and `scanf()` to indicate that they have detected the end of a file.

6.   a. The output is as follows:

```
If you qu
```

Note that the character I is distinct from the character i. Also note that the i is not printed because the loop quits upon detecting it.

    b. The output for ASCII is as follows:

```
HJacrthjacrt
```

The first time through, ch has the value H. The ch++ causes the value to be used (printed) and then incremented (to I). Then the ++ch causes the value to be incremented (to J) and then used (printed). After that, the next character (a) is read, and the process is repeated. An important point to note here is that the incrementations affect the value of ch after it has been assigned a value; they don't somehow cause the program to move through the input queue.

7. C's standard I/O library maps diverse file forms to uniform streams that can be handled equivalently.

8. Numeric input skips over spaces and newlines, but character input does not. Suppose you have code like this:

```
int score;
char grade;
printf("Enter the score.\n");
scanf("%s", %score);
printf("Enter the letter grade.\n");
grade = getchar();
```

If you enter 98 for the score and then press the Enter key to send the score to the program, you also sent a newline character, which becomes the next input character and is read into grade as the grade value. If you precede character input with numeric input, you should add code to dispose of the newline character before the character input takes place.

Answers to Review Questions for Chapter 9

1. A formal parameter is a variable that is defined in the function being called. The actual argument is the value appearing in the function call; this value is assigned to the formal argument. You can think of the actual argument as being the value to which the formal parameter is initialized when the function is called.

2.   a. `void donut(int n)`

    b. `int gear(int t1, int t2)`

    c. `void stuff_it(double d, double *pd)`

3. a. `char n_to_char(int n)`

    b. `int digits(double x, int n)`

    c. `int random(void)`

4.

```
int sum(int a, int b)
{
    return a + b;
}
```

5. Replace `int` with `double` throughout:

```
double sum(double a, double b)

{

    return a + b;

}
```

6. This function needs to use pointers:

```
void alter(int * pa, int * pb)
{
    int temp;
    temp = *pa + *pb;
    *pb = *pa - *pb;
    *pa = temp;
}
```

or

```
void alter(int * pa, int * pb)
{
    *pa += *pb;
    *pb = *pa - 2 * *pb;
}
```

7. Yes; num should be declared in the `salami()` argument list, not after the brace. Also, it should be `count++`, not `num++`.

8. Here is one solution:

```
int largest(int a, int b, int c)
{
    int max = a;
    if (b > max)
        max = b;
    if (c > max)
        max = c;
    return max;
}
```

9. Here is the minimal program; the showmenu() and getchoice() functions are possible solutions to parts a and b.

```
#include <stdio.h>
void showmenu(void);      /* declare functions used */
int getchoice(int, int);
main()
{
    int res;

    showmenu();
    while ((res = getchoice(1,4)) != 4)
        printf("I like choice %d.\n", res);
    printf("Bye!\n");
    return 0;
}
void showmenu(void)
{
    printf("Please choose one of the following:\n");
    printf("1) copy files          2) move files\n");
    printf("3) remove files        4) quit\n");
    printf("Enter the number of your choice:\n");
}

int getchoice(int low, int high)
{
    int ans;
    scanf("%d", &ans);
    while (ans < low || ans  > high)
    {
        printf("%d is not a valid choice; try again\n", ans);
        showmenu();
        scanf("%d", &ans);
    }
    return ans;
}
```

Answers to Review Questions for Chapter 10

1. The printout is this:

```
8 8
4 4
0 0
2 2
```

2. The array ref has four elements because that is the number of values in the initialization list.

3. The array name ref points to the first element of the array, the integer 8. The expression ref + 1 points to the second element, the integer 4. The construction ++ref is not a valid C expression; ref is a constant, not a variable.

4. `ptr` points to the first element, and `ptr + 2` points to the third element, which would be the first element of the second row.

   a. 12 and 16.

   b. 12 and 14 (just the 12 goes in the first row because of the braces).

5. `ptr` points to the first row and `ptr+1` points to the second row; `*ptr` points to the first element in the first row, and `*(ptr + 1)` points to the first element of the second row.

   a. 12 and 16.

   b. 12 and 14 (just the 12 goes in the first row because of the braces).

6.   a. `&grid[22][56]`

   b. `&grid[22][0]` or `grid[22]`

   (The latter is the name of a one-dimensional array of 100 elements, hence the address of its first element, which is the element `grid[22][0]`.)

   c. `&grid[0][0]` or `grid[0]` or `(int *) grid`

   (Here, `grid[0]` is the address of the `int` element `grid[0][0]`, and `grid` is the address of the 100-element array `grid[0]`. The two addresses have the same numeric value but different types; the typecast makes the types the same.)

7.   a. `int digits[10];`

   b. `float rates[6];`

   c. `int mat[3][5];`

   d. `char * psa[20];`

   Note that `[ ]` has higher precedence than `*`, so in the absence of parentheses, the array descriptor is applied first, and then the pointer descriptor. Hence, this declaration is the same as `char *(psa[20]);`.

   e. `char (*pstr)[20];`

Note

char `*pstr[20];` is incorrect for e. This would make `pstr` an array of pointers instead of a pointer to an array. In particular, `pstr` would point to a single `char`, the first member of the array; `pstr + 1` would point to the next byte. With the correct declaration, `pstr` is a variable rather than an array name, and `pstr + 1` points 20 bytes beyond the initial byte.

8.   a. `int sextet[6] = {1, 2, 4, 8, 16, 32};`

   b. `sextet[2]`

   c. `int lots[100] = { [99] = -1};`

9. 0 through 9

10.   a. `rootbeer[2] = value;`

Valid.

b. `scanf("%f", &rootbeer );`

Invalid; `rootbeer` is not a `float`.

c. `rootbeer = value;`

Invalid; `rootbeer` is not a `float`.

d. `printf("%f", rootbeer);`

Invalid; `rootbeer` is not a `float`.

e. `things[4][4] = rootbeer[3];`

Valid.

f. `things[5] = rootbeer;`

Invalid; can't assign arrays.

g. `pf = value;`

Invalid; `value` is not an address.

h. `pf = rootbeer;`

Valid.

11. `int screen[800][600];`

12.   a.

```
void process(double ar[], int n);
void processvla(int n, double ar[n]);
process(trots, 20);
processvla(20, trots);
```

b.

```
void process2(short ar2[30], int n);
void process2vla(int n, int m, short ar2[n][m]);
process2(clops, 10);
process2vla(10, 30, clops);
```

c.

```
void process3(long ar3[10][15], int n);
void process3vla(int n, int m,int k, long ar3[n][m][k]);
process3(shots, 5);
process3vla(5, 10, 15, shots);
```

13.   a.
```
show( (int [4]) {8,3,9,2}, 4);
```
   b.
```
show2( (int [][3]){{8,3,9}, {5,4,1}}, 2);
```

Answers to Review Questions for Chapter 11

1. The initialization should include a '\0' if you want the result to be a string. Of course, the alternative syntax adds the null character automatically:
```
char name[] = "Fess";
```

2.
```
See you at the snack bar.
ee you at the snack bar.
See you
e you
```

3.
```
y

my

mmy

ummy

Yummy
```

4. `I read part of it all the way through.`

5.   a. `Ho Ho Ho!!oH oH oH`

   b. Pointer-to-char (that is, `char *`).

   c. The address of the initial *H*.

   d. `*--pc` means to decrement the pointer by 1 and use the value found there. `--*pc` means to take the value pointed to by `pc` and decrement that value by 1 (for example, H becomes G).

   e. `Ho Ho Ho!!oH oH o`

Note

A null character comes between ! and !, but it produces no printing effect.

f. `while(*pc)` checks to see that `pc` does not point to a null character (that is, to the end of the string). The expression uses the value at the pointed-to location.

`while(pc - str)` checks to see that `pc` does not point to the same location that `str` does (the beginning of the string). The expression uses the values of the pointers themselves.

g. After the first `while` loop, `pc` points to the null character. Upon entering the second loop, it is made to point to the storage location before the null character (that is, to the location just before the one that `str` points to). That byte is interpreted as a character and is printed. The pointer then backs up to the preceding byte. The terminating condition (`pc == str`) never occurs, and the process continues until you, or the system, tire.

h. `pr()` must be declared in the calling program:

```
char * pr(char *);
```

6. Character variables occupy a byte, so `sign` occupies a byte. But a character constant is stored in an `int`, meaning the `'$'` typically would use 2 or 4 bytes; however, only 1 byte of the `int` is actually used to store the code for `'$'`. The string `"$"` uses 2 bytes: one to hold the code for `'$'`, and one to hold the code for `'\0'`.

7. Here is what you get:

```
How are ya, sweetie? How are ya, sweetie?
Beat the clock.
eat the clock.
Beat the clock. Win a toy.
Beat
chat
hat
at
t
t
at
How are ya, sweetie?
```

8. Here is what you get:

```
faavrhee
*le*on*sm
```

9. Here is one solution:

```
int strlen(const char * s)
{
    int ct = 0;

    while (*s++)       // or while (*s++ != '\0')
        ct++;

    return(ct);
}
```

10. Here is one solution:

```
#include <stdio.h>        /* for NULL definition          */
char * strblk(char * string)
{
  while (*string != ' ' && *string != '\0')
    string++;              /* stops at first blank or null */
  if (*string == '\0')
    return NULL;           /* NULL is the null pointer     */
  else
    return string;
}
```

Here is a second solution that prevents the function from modifying the string but that allows the return value to be used to change the string. The expression (char *) string is called "casting away const."

```
#include <stdio.h>        /* for NULL definition          */
char * strblk(const char * string)
{
  while (*string != ' ' && *string != '\0')
    string++;              /* stops at first blank or null */
  if (*string == '\0')
    return NULL;           /* NULL is the null pointer     */
  else
    return (char *) string;
}
```

11. Here is one solution:

```
/* compare.c -- this will work */
#include <stdio.h>
#include <string.h>    /* declares strcmp() */
#include <ctype.h>
#define ANSWER "GRANT"
#define MAX 40
void ToUpper(char * str);
int main(void)
{
    char try[MAX];

    puts("Who is buried in Grant's tomb?");
    gets(try);
    ToUpper(try);
    while (strcmp(try,ANSWER) != 0)
    {
        puts("No, that's wrong. Try again.");
        gets(try);
        ToUpper(try);
    }
    puts("That's right!");
    return 0;
}
```

```
void ToUpper(char * str)
{
    while (*str != '\0')
    {
        *str = toupper(*str);
        str++;
    }
}
```

Answers to Review Questions for Chapter 12

1. The automatic storage class, the register storage class, and the static, no linkage storage class.

2. The static, no linkage storage class, the static, internal linkage storage class, and the static, external linkage storage class.

3. The static, external linkage storage class. The static, internal linkage storage class.

4. No linkage.

5. The keyword extern is used in declarations to indicate a variable or function that has been defined elsewhere.

6. Both allocate an array of 100 int values. The statement using calloc() additionally sets each element to 0.

7. daisy is known to main(), by default, and to petal(), stem(), and root() because of the extern declaration. The extern int daisy; declaration in file 2 makes daisy known to all the functions in file 2. The first lily is local to main(). The reference to lily in petal() is an error because there is no external lily in either file. There is an external static lily, but it is known just to functions in the second file. The first external rose is known to root(), but stem() has overridden it with its own local rose.

8. Here is the output:

```
color in main() is B
color in first() is R
color in main() is B
color in second() is G
color in main() is G
```

9.   a. It tells you that the program will use the variable plink, which is local to the file containing the function. The first argument to value_ct() is a pointer to an integer, presumably the first element of an array of n members. The important point here is that the program will not be allowed to use the pointer arr to modify values in the original array.

b. No. Already, `value` and `n` are copies of original data, so there is no way for the function to alter the corresponding values in the calling program. What these declarations do accomplish is to prevent the function from altering `value` and `n` within the function. For example, the function couldn't use the expression `n++` if `n` were qualified as `const`.

Answers to Review Questions for Chapter 13

1. It should have `#include <stdio.h>` for its file definitions. It should declare `fp` a file pointer: `FILE *fp;`. The function `fopen()` requires a mode: `fopen("gelatin", "w")`, or perhaps the `"a"` mode. The order of the arguments to `fputs()` should be reversed. For clarity, the output string should have a newline because `fputs()` doesn't add one automatically. The `fclose()` function requires a file pointer, not a filename: `fclose(fp);`. Here is a corrected version:

```
#include <stdio.h>
int main(void)
{
    FILE * fp;
    int k;

    fp = fopen("gelatin", "w");
    for (k = 0; k < 30; k++)
        fputs("Nanette eats gelatin.\n", fp);
    fclose(fp);
    return 0;
}
```

2. It would open, if possible, the file whose name is the first command-line argument, and it would display onscreen each digit character in the file.

3.   a. `ch = getc(fp1);`

b. `fprintf(fp2,"%c"\n",ch);`

c. `putc(ch,fp2);`

d. `fclose(fp1); /* close the terky file */`

Note

fp1 is used for input operations because it identifies the file opened in the read mode. Similarly, fp2 was opened in the write mode, so it is used with output functions.

4. Here is one approach:

```c
#include <stdio.h>
#include <stdlib.h>
/* #include <console.h> */   /* for Macs */

int main(int argc,char * argv[])
{
    FILE * fp;
    double n;
    double sum = 0.0;
    int ct = 0;

/*   argc = ccommand(&argv);   */   /* For Macs */
    if (argc == 1)
        fp = stdin;
    else if (argc == 2)
    {
        if ((fp = fopen(argv[1], "r")) == NULL)
        {
            fprintf(stderr, "Can't open %s\n", argv[1]);
            exit(EXIT_FAILURE);
        }
    }
    else
    {
        fprintf(stderr, "Usage: %s [filename]\n", argv[0]);
        exit(EXIT_FAILURE);
    }
    while (fscanf(fp, "%lf", &n) == 1)
    {
        sum += n;
            ++ct;
    }
    if (ct > 0)
            printf("Average of %d values = %f\n", ct, sum / ct);
    else
            printf("No valid data.\n");

    return 0;
}
```

Macintosh C users, remember to use `console.h` and `ccommand()`.

5. Here is one approach. (Macintosh C users, remember to use `console.h` and `ccommand()`.)

```c
#include <stdio.h>
#include <stdlib.h>
/* #include <console.h>   */   /* for Mac */
#define BUF 256
int has_ch(char ch, const char * line);
int main(int argc,char * argv[])
```

```
{
    FILE * fp;
    char ch;
    char line [BUF];

 /* argc = ccommand(&argv); */  /* for Mac */
    if (argc != 3)
    {
        printf("Usage: %s character filename\n", argv[0]);
        exit(1);
    }
    ch = argv[1][0];
    if ((fp = fopen(argv[2], "r")) == NULL)
    {
        printf("Can't open %s\n", argv[2]);
        exit(1);
    }
    while (fgets(line,BUF,fp) != NULL)
    {
        if (has_ch(ch,line))
            fputs(line,stdout);
    }
    fclose(fp);
    return 0;
}

int has_ch(char ch, const char * line)
{
    while (*line)
        if (ch == *line++)
            return(1);
    return 0;
}
```

The `fgets()` and `fputs()` functions work together because `fgets()` leaves the \n produced by Enter in the string, and `fputs()` does not add a \n the way that `puts()` does.

6. The distinction between a binary file and a text file is a system-dependent difference between file formats. The distinction between a binary stream and a text stream consists of translations performed by the program as it reads or writes streams. (A binary stream has no translations; a text stream may convert newline and other characters.)

7. a. When 8238201 is saved using `fprintf()`, it's saved as seven characters stored in 7 bytes. When `fwrite()` is used, it's saved as a 4-byte integer using the binary representation of that numeric value.

   b. No difference; in each case it's saved as a 1-byte binary code.

8. The first is just a shorthand notation for the second; the third writes to the standard error. Normally, the standard error is directed to the same place as the standard output, but the standard error is not affected by standard output redirection.

9. The "r+" mode lets you read and write anywhere in a file, so it's best suited. The "a+" mode only lets you append material to the end of the file, and the "w+" mode starts with a clean slate, discarding previous file contents.

Answers to Review Questions for Chapter 14

1. The proper keyword is `struct`, not `structure`. The template requires either a tag before the opening brace or a variable name after the closing brace. Also, there should be a semicolon after `*` `togs` and at the end of the template.

2. Here is the output:

```
6 1
22 Spiffo Road
S p
```

3.

```
struct month {
    char name[10];
    char abbrev[4];
    int days;
    int monumb;
};
```

4.

```
struct month months[12] =
{
    {"January", "jan", 31, 1},
    {"February", "feb", 28, 2},
    {"March", "mar", 31, 3},
    {"April", "apr", 30, 4},
    {"May", "may", 31, 5},
    {"June", "jun", 30, 6},
    {"July", "jul", 31, 7},
    {"August", "aug", 31, 8},
    {"September", "sep", 30, 9},
    {"October", "oct", 31, 10},
    {"November", "nov", 30, 11},
    {"December", "dec", 31, 12}
};
```

5.

```
extern struct month months[];
int days(int month)
{
    int index, total;

    if (month < 1 || month > 12)
        return(-1);  /* error signal */
    else
```

```
    {
        for (index = 0, total = 0; index < month; index ++)
            total += months[index].days;
        return( total);
    }
}
```

Note that `index` is one less than the month number because arrays start with subscript 0. Therefore, use `index < month` instead of `index <= month`.

6. a. Include `string.h` to provide `strcpy()`:

```
typedef struct lens {      /* lens descriptor */
    float foclen;          /* focal length,mm */
    float fstop;           /* aperture        */
    char brand[30];        /* brand name      */
} LENS;

LENS bigEye[10];
bigEye[2].foclen = 500;
bigEye[2] fstop = 2.0;
strcpy(bigEye[2].brand, "Remarkatar");
```

b.

```
LENS bigEye[10] = { [2] = {500, 2, "Remarkatar"} };
```

7. a.

```
6
Arcturan
cturan
```

b. Use the structure name and use the pointer:

```
deb.title.last
```

```
pb->title.last
```

c. Here is one version:

```
#include <stdio.h>

#include "starfolk.h"    /* make struct defs available */

void prbem (const struct bem * pbem )
{
    printf("%s %s is a %d-limbed %s.\n", pbem->title.first,
            pbem->title.last, pbem->limbs, pbem->type);
}
```

8.   a. `willie.born`

    b. `pt->born`

    c. `scanf("%d", &willie.born);`

    d. `scanf("%d", &pt->born);`

    e. `scanf("%s", willie.name.lname);`

    f. `scanf("%s", pt->name.lname);`

    g. `willie.name.fname[2]`

    h. `strlen(willie.name.fname) + strlen(willie.name.lname)`

9. Here is one possibility:

```
struct car {

    char name[20];
    float hp;
    float epampg;
    float wbase;
    int year;
};
```

10. The functions could be set up like this:

```
struct gas {
    float distance;
    float gals;
    float mpg;
};

struct gas mpgs(struct gas trip)
{
  if (trip.gals > 0)
     trip.mpg = trip.distance / trip.gals ;
  else
     trip.mpg = -1.0;
  return trip;
}

void set_mpgs(struct gas &ptrip)
{
  if (ptrip->gals > 0)
     ptrip->mpg = ptrip->distance / ptrip->gals ;
  else
     ptrip->mpg = -1.0;
}
```

Note that the first function cannot directly alter values in the calling program, so you must use the return value to convey the information:

```
struct gas idaho = {430.0, 14.8};  // set first two members
idaho = mpgs(idaho);               // reset structure
```

The second function, however, accesses the original structure directly:

```
struct gas ohio = {583, 17.6};    // set first two members
set_mpgs(ohio);                    // set third member
```

11. `enum choices {no, yes, maybe};`

12. `char * (*pfun)(char *, char);`

13.

```
double sum(double, double);
double diff(double, double);
double times(double, double);
double divide(double, double);
double (*pf1[4])(double, double) = {sum, diff, times, divide};
```

Or, more simply, replace the last line of code with these lines:

```
typedef double (*ptype)(double, double);
ptype pf[4] = {sum, diff, times, divide};
```

Answers to Review Questions for Chapter 15

1. a. 00000011

   b. 00001101

   c. 00111011

   d. 01110111

2. a. 21, 025, 0x15

   b. 85, 0125, 0x55

   c. 76, 0114, 0x4C

   d. 157, 0235, 0x9D

3. a. 252

   b. 2

   c. 7

   d. 7

   e. 5

   f. 3

   g. 28

4.　a. 255

　　b. 1 (not false is true)

　　c. 0

　　d. 1 (true and true is true)

　　e. 6

　　f. 1 (true or true is true)

　　g. 40

5. In binary, the mask is `1111111`. In decimal, it's `127`. In octal, it's `0177`. In hexadecimal, it's `0x7F`.

6. Both `bitvbal *= 2` and `bitval << 1` double the current value of `bitval`, so they are equivalent. However, `mask += bitval` and `mask |= bitval` have the same effect only if `bitval` and `mask` have no bits set to "on" in common. For example, `2 | 4` is `6`, but so is `3 | 6`.

7.　a.

```
struct tb_drives {
    unsigned int diskdrives  : 2;
    unsigned int             : 1;
    unsigned int cdromdrives : 2;
    unsigned int             : 1;
    unsigned int harddrives  : 2;
};
```

　　b.

```
struct kb_drives {
    unsigned int harddrives  : 2;
    unsigned int             : 1;
    unsigned int cdromdrives : 2;
    unsigned int             : 1;
    unsigned int diskdrives  : 2;
};
```

Answers to Review Questions for Chapter 16

1.　a. `dist = 5280 * miles;` is valid.

　　b. `plort = 4 * 4 + 4;` is valid. But if the user really wanted `4 * (4 + 4)`, he or she should have used `#define POD  (FEET + FEET)`.

　　c. `nex = = 6;;` is invalid. Apparently, the user forgot that he or she was writing for the preprocessor, not writing in C.

　　d. `y = y + 5;` is valid. `berg = berg + 5 * lob;` is valid, but this is probably not the desired result. `est = berg + 5/ y + 5;` is valid, but this is probably not the desired result. `nilp = lob *-berg + 5;` is valid, but this is probably not the desired result.

2. `#define NEW(X) ((X) + 5)`

3. `#define MIN(X,Y) ( (X) < (Y) ? (X) : (Y) )`

4. `#define EVEN_GT(X,Y) ( (X) > (Y) && (X) % 2 == 0 ? 1 : 0 )`

5. `#define PR(X,Y) printf(#X " is %d and " #Y " is %d\n", X,Y)`

   Because X and Y are never exposed to any other operations (such as multiplication) in this macro, you don't have to cocoon everything in parentheses.

6. a. `#define QUARTERCENTURY 25`

    b. `#define SPACE ' '`

    c. `#define PS() putchar(' ')`

       or

       `#define PS() putchar(SPACE)`

    d. `#define BIG(X) ((X) + 3)`

    e. `#define SUMSQ(X,Y)  ((X)*(X) + (Y)*(Y))`

7. Try this:

   `#define P(X) printf("name: "#X"; value: %d; address: %p\n", X, &X)`

   Or, if your implementation doesn't recognize the `%p` specification for the address, try `%u` or `%lu`.

8. Use the conditional compilation directives. One way is to use `#ifndef`:

   ```
   #define _SKIP_   /* remove when you don't want to skip code */
   #ifndef _SKIP_
       /* code to be skipped */
   #endif
   ```

9.

   ```
   #ifdef PR_DATE
       printf("Date = %s\n", __DATE__);
   #endif
   ```

10. The `argv` argument should be declared as type `char *argv[]`. Command-line arguments are stored as strings, so the program should first convert the string in `argv[1]` to a type `double` value—for example, by using `atof()` from the `stdlib.h` library. The `math.h` header file should be included for the `sqrt()` function. The program should check for negative values before taking a square root.

11.   a. The function call should look like this:

```
qsort( (void *)scores, (size_t) 1000, sizeof (double), comp);
```

b. Here's a suitable comparison function:

```
int comp(const void * p1, const void * p2)
{
    /* need to use pointers to int to access values       */
    /* the type casts are optional in C, required in C++ */
    const int * a1 = (const int *) p1;    const int * a2 = (const int *)
p2;

    if (*a1 > *a2)
        return -1;
    else if (*a1 == *a2)
        return 0;
    else
        return 1;
}
```

12.   a. The function call should look like this:

```
memcpy(data1, data2, 100 * sizeof(double));
```

b. The function call should look like this:

```
memcpy(data1, data2 + 200 , 100 * sizeof(double));
```

Answers to Review Questions for Chapter 17

1. Defining a data type consists of deciding how to store the data and designing a set of functions to manage the data.

2. The list can be traversed in only one direction because each structure contains the address of the next structure, but not of the preceding structure. You could modify the structure definition so that each structure contains two pointers—one to the preceding structure and one to the next structure. The program, of course, would have to assign proper addresses to these pointers each time a new structure is added.

3. An ADT is an *abstract data type*, a formal definition of the properties of a type and of the operations that can be performed with the type. An ADT should be expressed in general terms, not in terms of some specific computer language or implementation details.

4. **Advantages of passing a variable directly:** This function inspects a queue, but should not alter it. Passing a queue variable directly means the function works with a copy of the original, guaranteeing that the function does not alter the original data. When passing a variable directly, you don't have to remember to use the address operator or a pointer.

Disadvantages of passing a variable directly: The program has to allocate enough space to hold the variable and then copy information from the original to the copy. If the variable is a large structure, using it has a time and space penalty.

Advantages of passing the address of a variable: Passing an address and accessing the original data is faster and requires less memory than passing a variable if the variable is a large structure.

Disadvantages of passing the address of a variable: You have to remember to use the address operator or a pointer. Under K&R C, the function could inadvertently alter the original data, but you can overcome this objection with the ANSI C **const** qualifier.

5. a.

Type Name:	Stack.
Type Properties:	Can hold an ordered sequence of items.
Type Operations:	Initialize stack to empty.
	Determine whether stack is empty.
	Determine whether stack is full.
	Add item to top of stack (pushing an item).
	Remove and recover item from top of stack (popping an item).

b. The following implements the stack as an array, but that information affects only the structure definition and the details of the function definitions; it doesn't affect the interface described by the function prototypes.

```
/* stack.h -- interface for a stack */
#include <stdbool.h>
/* INSERT ITEM TYPE HERE */
/* FOR EXAMPLE, typedef int Item; */

#define MAXSTACK 100

typedef struct stack
{
    Item items[MAXSTACK];   /* holds info                  */
    int top;                /* index of first empty slot */
} Stack;

/* operation:      initialize the stack                  */
/* precondition:   ps points to a stack                  */
/* postcondition
:    stack is initialized to being empty        */
void InitializeStack(Stack * ps);
/* operation:      check if stack is full                */
/* precondition:   ps points to previously initialized stack */
/* postcondition:  returns true if stack is full, else false */
bool FullStack(const Stack * ps);
```

```
/* operation:        check if stack is empty                  */
/* precondition:     ps points to previously initialized stack */
/* postcondition:    returns true if stack is empty, else false */
bool EmptyStack(const Stack *ps);

/* operation:        push item onto top of stack               */
/* precondition:     ps points to previously initialized stack */
/*                   item is to be placed on top of stack      */
/* postcondition:    if stack is not full, item is placed at   */
/*                   top of stack and function returns         */
/*                   true; otherwise, stack is unchanged and   */
/*                   function returns false                    */
bool Push(Item item, Stack * ps);

/* operation:        remove item from top of stack             */
/* precondition:     ps points to previously initialized stack */
/* postcondition:    if stack is not empty, item at top of     */
/*                   stack is copied to *pitem and deleted from */
/*                   stack, and function returns true; if the  */
/*                   operation empties the stack, the stack is */
/*                   reset to empty. If the stack is empty to  */
/*                   begin with, stack is unchanged and the    */
/*                   function returns false                    */
bool Pop(Item *pitem, Stack * ps);
```

6. Maximum number of comparisons required:

Items	Sequential Search	Binary Search
3	3	2
1,023	1,023	10
65,535	65,535	16

7. See Figure A.1.

8. See Figure A.2.

FIGURE A.1
Binary search tree of words.

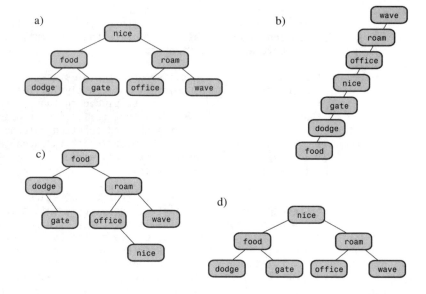

FIGURE A.2
Binary search tree of words after removal.

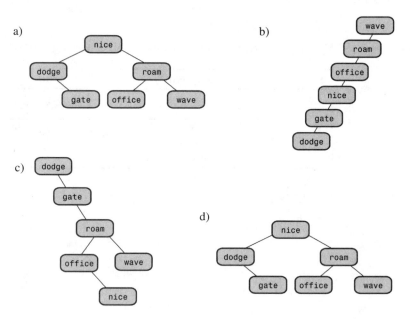

APPENDIX B

REFERENCE SECTION

This portion of the book provides summaries of basic C features along with a more detailed look at particular topics. Here are the sections:

- Section I: Additional Reading
- Section II: C Operators
- Section III: Basic Types and Storage Classes
- Section IV: Expressions, Statements, and Program Flow
- Section V: The Standard ANSI C Library with C99 Additions
- Section VI: Extended Integer Types
- Section VII: Expanded Character Support
- Section VIII: C99 Numeric Computational Enhancements
- Section IX: Differences Between C and C++

Section I: Additional Reading

If you want to learn more about C and programming, you will find the following references useful.

Magazine

C/C++ Users Journal

This monthly magazine (subtitled *Advanced Solutions for C/C++ Programmers*) is a useful resource for C and C++ programmers.

Online Resources

C programmers helped create the Internet, and the Internet can help you with C. The Internet is always growing and changing; the resources listed here are a sample of what you can find.

Probably the place to start, if you have a specific question about C or just want to expand your knowledge, is to visit the C FAQ (Frequently Asked Questions) site:

http://www.eskimo.com/~scs/C-faq/top.html

If you have questions about the C library, you can get information from the following site:

http://www.dinkumware.com/htm_cl/index.html

The next site provides a comprehensive discussion of pointers:

http://pweb.netcom.com/~tjensen/ptr/pointers.htm

You also can use search engines such as Google and Yahoo! Search to find articles and sites about specific topics:

http://www.google.com

http://search.yahoo.com

You can use the advanced search features of these sites to tune your searches more finely.

Many online tutorials are also available. Here are a couple:

http://www-h.eng.cam.ac.uk/help/tpl/languages/C/teaching_C/teaching_C.html

http://www.strath.ac.uk/CC/Courses/NewCcourse/ccourse.html

Newsgroups give you the opportunity to ask questions on the Net. Newsgroups typically are accessed through newsreader programs accessing an account provided by your Internet provider service. Another means of access is via web browser at the following address:

http://groups.google.com

You should take the time to read the newsgroups first to get an idea of what topics are covered. For example, if you have a question about how to do something in C, try this news group:

comp.lang.c

Here you'll find people willing and able to help. The questions should be about the standard C language. Don't ask here about how to get unbuffered input on a Unix system; there are specialized newsgroups for platform-specific questions. And above all, don't ask them how to do homework problems!

If you have a question about interpreting the C standard, try this group:

comp.std.c

But don't ask here how to declare a pointer to a three-dimensional array; that's the sort of question to address to the comp.lang.c group.

Finally, if you're interested in the history of C, Dennis Ritchie, the creator of C, describes the genesis and development of C in an article at the following site.

http://cm.bell-labs.com/cm/cs/who/dmr/chist.html

C Language Books

Feuer, Alan R. *The C Puzzle Book, Second Edition*. Englewood Cliffs, NJ: Prentice Hall, 1989

This book contains many programs whose output you are supposed to predict. Predicting the output gives you a good opportunity to test and expand your understanding of C. The book includes answers and explanations.

Kernighan, Brian W. and Dennis M. Ritchie. *The C Programming Language, Second Edition*. Englewood Cliffs, NJ: Prentice Hall, 1988

This is the second edition of the first book on C. (Note that the creator of C, Dennis Ritchie, is one of the authors.) The first edition constituted the definition of "K&R" C, the unofficial standard for many years. This edition incorporates ANSI changes based on the ANSI draft that was standard at the time the book was written. The book includes many interesting examples. It does, however, assume that the reader is familiar with systems programming.

Koenig, Andrew. *C Traps and Pitfalls*. Reading, MA: Addison-Wesley, 1988

The title says it all.

Summit, Steve. *C Programming FAQs*. Reading, MA: Addison-Wesley, 1995

This is an expanded book version of the Internet FAQ.

Programming Books

Kernighan, Brian W. and P.J. Plauger. *The Elements of Programming Style, Second Edition*. New York: McGraw-Hill, 1978

This slim, out-of-print classic draws on examples from other texts to illustrate the do's and don'ts of clear, effective programming.

Knuth, Donald E. *The Art of Computer Programming, Volume 1 (Fundamental Algorithms), Third Edition*. Reading, MA: Addison-Wesley, 1997

This non-slim classic standard reference examines data representation and algorithm analysis in great detail. It is advanced and mathematical in nature. Volume 2 (Seminumerical Algorithms, 1997) includes an extensive discussion of pseudorandom numbers. Volume 3 (Sorting and Searching, 1998), as the name suggests, examines sorting and searching. Examples are given in pseudocode and assembly language.

Sedgewick, Robert. *Algorithms in C: Fundamentals, Data Structures, Sorting, Searching*. Reading, MA: Addison-Wesley, 1995

Not surprisingly, this book covers data structures, sorting, and searching.

Reference Books

Harbison, Samuel P. and Steele, Guy L. *C: A Reference Manual, Fifth Edition*. Englewood Cliffs, NJ: Prentice Hall, 2002

This reference manual presents the rules of the C language and describes most of the standard library functions. It incorporates discussion of C99 and provides many examples.

Plauger, P.J. *The Standard C Library*. Englewood Cliffs, NJ: Prentice Hall, 1992

This large reference manual describes the standard library functions, with more explanation than you would find in a typical compiler manual.

The International C Standard. ISO/IEC 9899:1999

At the time of this writing, the standard is available as an $18 electronic download from www.ansi.org. Do not expect to learn C from this document because it is not intended as a tutorial. Here is a representative sentence: "If more than one declaration of a particular identifier is visible at any point in a translation unit, the syntactic context disambiguates uses that refer to different entities."

C++ Books

Prata, Stephen. *C++ Primer Plus, Fifth Edition*. Indianapolis, IN: Sams Publishing, 2005

This book introduces you to the C++ language and to the philosophy of object-oriented programming.

Stroustrup, Bjarne. *The C++ Programming Language, Third Edition*. Reading, MA: Addison-Wesley, 1997

This book, by the creator of C++, presents the C++ language and includes the Reference Manual for C++.

Section II: C Operators

C is rich in operators. Table RS.II.1 lists the C operators in order of decreasing precedence and indicates how they associate. All operators are binary (two operands) unless otherwise indicated. Note that some binary and unary operators, such as * (multiplication) and * (indirection), share the same symbol but have different precedence. Following the table are summaries of each operator.

TABLE RS.II.1 The C Operators

Operators (from High to Low Precedence)	Associativity
++ *(postfix)* -- *(postfix)* ( ) *(function call)* [ ] {} *(compound literal)* . ->	L–R
++ *(prefix)* -- *(prefix)* - + ~ ! sizeof * *(dereference)* & *(address)* (type) *(all unary)*	R–L

Operators (from High to Low Precedence)	Associativity
(type name)	R–L
* / %	L–R
+ - (both binary)	L–R
<< >>	L–R
< > <= >=	L–R
== !=	L–R
&	L–R
^	L–R
|	L–R
&&	L–R
||	L–R
? : (conditional expression)	R–L
= *= /= %= += -= <<= >>= &= |= ^=	R–L
, (comma operator)	L–R

Arithmetic Operators

+ adds the value at its right to the value at its left.

+, as a unary operator, produces a value equal in magnitude (and of the same sign) to the operand to the right.

- subtracts the value at its right from the value at its left.

-, as a unary operator, produces a value equal in magnitude (but opposite in sign) to the operand to the right.

* multiplies the value at its right by the value at its left.

/ divides the value at its left by the value at its right. The answer is truncated if both operands are integers.

% yields the remainder when the value at its left is divided by the value to its right (integers only).

++ adds 1 to the value of the variable to its right (prefix mode) or adds 1 to the value of the variable to its left (postfix mode).

- - is like ++, but subtracts 1.

Relational Operators

Each of the following operators compares the value at its left to the value at its right:

<	Less than
<=	Less than or equal to
==	Equal to
>=	Greater than or equal to
>	Greater than
!=	Unequal to

Relational Expressions

A simple relational expression consists of a relational operator with an operand on each side. If the relation is true, the relational expression has the value 1. If the relation is false, the relational expression has the value 0. Here are two examples:

5 > 2 is true and has the value 1.
(2 + a) == a is false and has the value 0.

Assignment Operators

C has one basic assignment operator and several combination assignment operators. The = operator is the basic form:

= assigns the value at its right to the lvalue on its left.

Each of the following assignment operators updates the lvalue at its left by the value at its right, using the indicated operation (we use R–H for right-hand and L–H for left-hand):

+= adds the R–H quantity to the L–H variable and places the result in the L–H variable.
-= subtracts the R–H quantity from the L–H variable and places the result in the L–H variable.
*= multiplies the L–H variable by the R–H quantity and places the result in the L–H variable.
/= divides the L–H variable by the R–H quantity and places the result in the L–H variable.
%= gives the remainder from dividing the L–H quantity by the R–H quantity and places the result in the L–H variable.
&= assigns L–H & R–H to the L–H quantity and places the result in the L–H variable.
|= assigns L–H | R–H to the L–H quantity and places the result in the L–H variable.

^= assigns L–H ^ R–H to the L–H quantity and places the result in the L–H variable.
>>= assigns L–H >> R–H to the L–H quantity and places the result in the L–H variable.
<<= assigns L–H << R–H to the L–H quantity and places the result in the L–H variable.

Example

`rabbits *= 1.6;` has the same effect as `rabbits = rabbits * 1.6;`.

Logical Operators

Logical operators normally take relational expressions as operands. The `!` operator takes one operand. The rest take two: one to the left, and one to the right.

&&	AND
||	OR
!	NOT

Logical Expressions

`expression1 && expression2` is true if, and only if, both expressions are true.

`expression1 || expression2` is true if either one or both expressions are true.

`!expression` is true if the expression is false, and vice versa.

Order of Evaluation for Logical Expressions

Logical expressions are evaluated from left to right. Evaluation stops as soon as something is discovered that renders the expression false.

Examples

`6 > 2 && 3 == 3` is true.
`! ( 6 > 2 && 3 == 3 )` is false.
`x != 0 && 20/x < 5`. The second expression is evaluated only if x is nonzero.

The Conditional Operator

`? :` takes three operands, each of which is an expression. They are arranged this way:

`expression1 ? expression2 : expression3`

The value of the whole expression equals the value of *expression2* if *expression1* is true, and equals the value of *expression3* otherwise.

Examples

(5 > 3) ? 1 : 2 has the value 1.
(3 > 5) ? 1 : 2 has the value 2.
(a > b) ? a : b has the value of the larger of a or b.

Pointer-Related Operators

& is the address operator. When followed by a variable name, & gives the address of that variable.

* is the indirection or dereferencing operator. When followed by a pointer, * gives the value stored at the pointed-to address.

Example

Here, &nurse is the address of the variable nurse:

```
nurse = 22;
ptr = &nurse; /* pointer to nurse */
val = *ptr;
```

The net effect is to assign the value 22 to val.

Sign Operators

– is the minus sign and reverses the sign of the operand.

+ is the plus sign and leaves the sign unchanged.

Structure and Union Operators

Structures and unions use operators to identify individual members. The membership operator is used with structures and unions, and the indirect membership operator is used with pointers to structures or unions.

The Membership Operator

The membership operator (.) is used with a structure or union name to specify a member of that structure or union. If name is the name of a structure and member is a member specified by the structure template, name.member identifies that member of the structure. The type of name.member is the type specified for member. The membership operator can also be used in the same fashion with unions.

Example

```
struct {
        int code;
        float cost;
} item;

item.code = 1265;
```

This statement assigns a value to the `code` member of the structure `item`.

The Indirect Membership Operator (or Structure Pointer Operator)

The indirect membership operator (->) is used with a pointer to a structure or union to identify a member of that structure or union. Suppose that `ptrstr` is a pointer to a structure and that `member` is a member specified by the structure template. Then `ptrstr->member` identifies that member of the pointed-to structure. The indirect membership operator can be used in the same fashion with unions.

Example

```
struct {
        int code;
        float cost;
} item, * ptrst;
ptrst = &item;
ptrst->code = 3451;
```

This program fragment assigns a value to the `code` member of `item`. The following three expressions are equivalent:

```
ptrst->code   item.code   (*ptrst).code
```

Bitwise Operators

All the following bitwise operators, except ~, are binary operators:

~ is the unary operator and produces a value with each bit of the operand inverted.
& is AND and produces a value in which each bit is set to 1 only if both corresponding bits in the two operands are 1.
| is OR and produces a value in which each bit is set to 1 if either, or both, corresponding bits of the two operands are 1.
^ is EXCLUSIVE OR and produces a value in which each bit is set to 1 only if one or the other (but not both) of the corresponding bits of the two operands is 1.
<< is left-shift and produces a value obtained by shifting the bits of the left-hand operand to the left by the number of places given by the right-hand operand. Vacated slots are filled with zeros.
>> is right-shift and produces a value obtained by shifting the bits of the left-hand operand to the right by the number of places given by the right-hand operand. For unsigned integers, the vacated slots are filled with zeros. The behavior for signed values is implementation dependent.

Examples

Suppose you have the following:

```
int x = 2;
int y = 3;
```

Then x & y has the value 2 because only bit 1 is "on" for both x and y. Also, y<<x has the value 12 because that is the value obtained when the bit pattern for 3 is shifted two bits to the left.

Miscellaneous Operators

sizeof yields the size, in units the size of a char value, of the operand to its right. Typically, a char value is 1 byte in size. The operand can be a type-specifier in parentheses, as in sizeof (float), or it can be the name of a particular variable, array, or so on, as in sizeof foo. A sizeof expression is of type size_t.

(type) is the cast operator and converts the value that follows it to the type specified by the enclosed keyword(s). For example, (float) 9 converts the integer 9 to the floating-point number 9.0.

, is the comma operator; it links two expressions into one and guarantees that the leftmost expression is evaluated first. The value of the whole expression is the value of the right-hand expression. This operator is typically used to include more information in a for loop control expression.

Example

```
for (step = 2, fargo = 0; fargo < 1000; step *= 2)
        fargo += step;
```

Section III: Basic Types and Storage Classes

Summary: The Basic Data Types

C's basic types fall into two categories: integers and floating-point numbers. The different varieties give you choices for range and precision.

Keywords

The basic data types are set up using the following eight keywords: int, long, short, unsigned, char, float, double, and signed (ANSI C).

Signed Integers

Signed integers can have positive or negative values:

`int` is the basic integer type for a given system.

`long` or `long int` can hold an integer at least as large as the largest `int` and possibly larger; `long` is at least 32 bits.

The largest `short` or `short int` integer is no larger than the largest `int`, and may be smaller. A `short` is at least 16 bits. Typically, `long` is bigger than `short`, and `int` is the same as one of the two. For example, C DOS compilers for the PC provide 16-bit `short` and `int` and 32-bit `long`. It all depends on the system.

The `long long` type, provided by the C99 standard, is at least as big as `long` and is at least 64 bits.

Unsigned Integers

Unsigned integers have zero or positive values only, which extends the range of the largest possible positive number. Use the keyword `unsigned` before the desired type: `unsigned int`, `unsigned long`, `unsigned short`, or `unsigned long long`. A lone `unsigned` is the same as `unsigned int`.

Characters

Characters are typographic symbols such as `A`, `&`, and `+`. By definition, one byte of memory is used for a `char` variable. In the past, 8 bits has been the most typical size for `char`. However, the ability of C to cope with larger character sets can lead to 16-bit or even 32-bit bytes.

`char` is the keyword for this type. Some implementations use a signed `char`, but others use an unsigned `char`. ANSI C allows you to use the keywords `signed` and `unsigned` to specify which form you want. Technically, `char`, `unsigned char`, and `signed char` are three distinct types, with the `char` type having the same representation as one of the other two.

Boolean Type (C99)

The C99 Boolean type is `_Bool`. It's an unsigned integer type that can hold one of two values: `0` for false and `1` for true. Including the `stdbool.h` header file allows you to use `bool` for `_Bool`, `true` for `1`, and `false` for `0`, making code compatible with C++.

Real and Complex Floating Types

C99 recognizes two domains of floating types: real floating and complex floating types. Collectively, the two domains constitute the floating types.

Real floating-point numbers can have positive or negative values. C recognizes three real floating types:

`float` is the basic floating-point type for the system. It can represent at least six significant digits accurately. Typically, `float` uses 32 bits.

`double` is a (possibly) larger unit for holding floating-point numbers. It may allow more significant figures and perhaps larger exponents than `float`. It can represent at least 10 significant digits accurately. Typically, `double` uses 64 bits.

`long double` is a (possibly) even larger unit for holding floating-point numbers. It may allow more significant figures and perhaps larger exponents than `double`.

Complex numbers have two components: a real part and an imaginary part. C99 represents a complex number internally with a two-element array, with the first component being the real part and the second component being the imaginary part. There are three complex types:

`float _Complex` represents the real and imaginary parts with type `float` values.

`double _Complex` represents the real and imaginary parts with type `double` values.

`long double _Complex` represents the real and imaginary parts with type `long double` values.

In each case, the prefix type is termed the *corresponding real type*. For example, `double` is the corresponding real type for `double _Complex`.

The complex types are optional in a freestanding environment, in which C programs can run without an operating system.

There also are three imaginary types; these are optional in both freestanding environments and hosted environments (environments in which C programs run under an operating system). An imaginary number has just an imaginary part. The three types are listed here:

`float _Imaginary` represents the imaginary part with a type `float` value.

`double _Imaginary` represents the imaginary part with a type `double` value.

`long double _Imaginary` represents the imaginary part with a type `long double` value.

Complex numbers can be initialized using real numbers and the value I, defined in `complex.h` and representing i, the square root of -1:

```
#include <complex.h>  // for I
double _Complex z = 3.0;       // real part = 3.0, imaginary part = 0
double _Complex w = 4.0 * I;   // real part = 0.0, imaginary part = 4.0
double Complex u = 6.0 - 8.0 * I; // real part = 6.0, imaginary part = -8.0
```

Summary: How to Declare a Simple Variable

1. Choose the type you need.

2. Choose a name for the variable.

3. Use this format for a declaration statement:

   ```
   type-specifier variable-name;
   ```

   The *type-specifier* is formed from one or more of the type keywords. Here are some examples:

   ```
   int erest;
   unsigned short cash;
   ```

4. To declare more than one variable of the same type, separate the variable names with commas:

   ```
   char ch, init, ans;
   ```

5. You can initialize a variable in a declaration statement:

   ```
   float mass = 6.0E24;
   ```

Summary: Storage Classes

Keywords:

```
auto, extern, static,
register
```

General Comments:

The storage class of a variable determines its scope, its linkage, and its storage duration. A storage class is determined both by where the variable is defined and by its associated keyword. Variables defined outside all functions are external, have file scope, external linkage, and static storage duration. Variables declared inside a function are automatic unless one of the other keywords is used. They have block scope, no linkage, and automatic storage duration. Variables defined with the keyword `static` inside a function have block scope, no linkage, and static storage duration. Variables defined with the keyword `static` outside a function have file scope, internal linkage, and static storage duration.

Properties:

The following summarizes properties of the storage classes:

Storage Class	Duration	Scope	Linkage	How Declared
Automatic	Automatic	Block	None	In a block
Register	Automatic	Block	None	In a block with the keyword `register`
Static with external linkage	Static	File	External	Outside of all functions

Storage Class	Duration	Scope	Linkage	How Declared
Static with internal linkage	Static	File	Internal	Outside of all functions with `static`
Static with no linkage	static	Block	None	In a block with the keyword `static`

Note that the keyword `extern` is used only to redeclare variables that have been defined externally elsewhere. The act of defining the variable outside a function makes it external.

In addition to these storage classes, C provides allocated memory. This memory is allocated by calling one of the `malloc()` family of functions, which returns a pointer that can be used to access the memory. The memory remains allocated until a call to `free()` or until the program terminates. Access to the memory can be from any function that has access to a pointer to the memory. For example, a function can return the pointer value to another function, which then can access the memory.

Summary: Qualifiers

Keywords

Use the following keywords to qualify variables:

`const`, `volatile`, `restrict`

General Comments

A qualifier constrains a variable's use in some way. A `const` variable, after it's initialized, can't be altered. The compiler can't assume that a `volatile` variable hasn't been changed by some outside agency, such as a hardware update. A pointer qualified with `restrict` is understood to provide the only access (in a particular scope) to a block of memory.

Properties

The declaration

`const int joy = 101;`

establishes that the value of `joy` is fixed at `101`.

The declaration

`volatile unsigned int incoming;`

establishes that the value of `incoming` might change between one occurrence of `incoming` in a program and its next occurrence.

The declaration

```
const int * ptr = &joy;
```

establishes that the pointer **ptr** can't be used to alter the value of the variable **joy**. The pointer can, however, be made to point to another location.

The declaration

```
int * const ptr = &joy;
```

establishes that the pointer **ptr** can't have its value changed; that is, it can point only to **joy**. However, it can be used to alter **joy**.

The prototype

```
void simple (const char * s);
```

establishes that after the formal argument **s** is initialized to whatever value is passed to **simple()** in a function call, **simple()** may not alter the value to which **s** points.

The prototype

```
void supple(int * const pi);
```

and the equivalent prototype

```
void supple(int pi[const]);
```

establish that the function **supple()** will not alter the value of the parameter **pi**.

The prototype

```
void interleave(int * restrict p1, int * restrict p2, int n);
```

indicates that **p1** and **p2** are each the sole access to the respective blocks of memory to which they point; this implies that there is no overlap between the two blocks.

Section IV: Expressions, Statements, and Program Flow

Summary: Expressions and Statements

In C, expressions represent values, and statements represent instructions to the computer.

Expressions

An *expression* is a combination of operators and operands. The simplest expression is just a constant or a variable with no operator, such as **22** or **beebop**. More complex examples are **55 + 22** and **vap = 2 * (vip + (vup = 4))**.

Statements

A *statement* is a command to the computer. Any expression followed by a semicolon forms a statement, although not necessarily a meaningful one. Statements can be simple or compound. *Simple statements* terminate in a semicolon, as shown in these examples:

Declaration statement:	`int toes;`
Assignment statement:	`toes = 12;`
Function call statement:	`printf ("%d\n", toes);`
Control statement:	`while (toes < 20) toes = toes + 2;`
Null statement:	`; /* does nothing */`

(Technically, the Standard assigns declarations their own category rather than grouping them with statements.)

Compound statements, or *blocks*, consist of one or more statements (which themselves can be compound) enclosed in braces. The following `while` statement is an example:

```
while (years < 100)
{
    wisdom = wisdom + 1;
    printf("%d %d\n", years, wisdom);
    years = years + 1;
}
```

Summary: The `while` Statement

Keyword

The keyword for the `while` statement is `while`.

General Comments

The `while` statement creates a loop that repeats until the test *expression* becomes false, or zero. The `while` statement is an *entry-condition* loop; the decision to go through one more pass of the loop is made *before* the loop has been traversed. Therefore, it is possible that the loop is never traversed. The *statement* part of the form can be a simple statement or a compound statement.

Form

```
while (expression)
        statement
```

The *statement* portion is repeated until the *expression* becomes false or zero.

Examples

```
while (n++ < 100)
        printf(" %d %d\n",n, 2*n+1);

while (fargo < 1000)
{
        fargo = fargo + step;
        step = 2 * step;
}
```

Summary: The `for` Statement

Keyword

The `for` statement keyword is `for`.

General Comments

The `for` statement uses three control expressions, separated by semicolons, to control a looping process. The *initialize* expression is executed once, before any of the loop statements are executed. If the *test* expression is true (or nonzero), the loop is cycled through once. Then the *update* expression is evaluated, and it is time to check the *test* expression again. The `for` statement is an *entry-condition* loop; the decision to go through one more pass of the loop is made *before* the loop has been traversed. Therefore, it is possible that the loop is never traversed. The *statement* part of the form can be a simple statement or a compound statement.

Form

```
for (initialize ; test ; update)
        statement
```

The loop is repeated until *test* becomes false or zero.

C99 allows the initialization part to include a declaration. The scope and duration of the variable is restricted to the `for` loop.

Examples

```
for (n = 0;  n < 10 ; ++n)
     printf("%d %d\n", n, 2 * n+1);
for (int k = 0;  k < 10 ; ++k)          // C99
     printf("%d %d\n", k, 2 * k+1);
```

Summary: The `do while` Statement

Keywords

The keywords for the `do while` statement are `do` and `while`.

General Comments

The `do while` statement creates a loop that repeats until the test *expression* becomes false or zero. The `do while` statement is an *exit-condition* loop; the decision to go through one more pass of the loop is made *after* the loop has been traversed. Therefore, the loop must be executed at least once. The *statement* part of the form can be a simple statement or a compound statement.

Form

```
do
     statement
while (expression);
```

The *statement* portion is repeated until *expression* becomes false or zero.

Example

```
do
     scanf("%d", &number)
while(number != 20);
```

Summary: Using `if` Statements for Making Choices

Keywords

The keywords for `if` statements are `if` and `else`.

General Comments

In each of the following forms, the *statement* can be either a simple statement or a compound statement. A "true" expression, more generally, means one with a nonzero value.

Form 1

```
if (expression)
     statement
```

The *statement* is executed if *expression* is true.

Form 2

```
if (expression)
     statement1
else
     statement2
```

If the *expression* is true, *statement1* is executed. Otherwise, *statement2* is executed.

Form 3

```
if (expression1)
     statement1
```

```
else if (expression2)
    statement2
else
    statement3
```

If *expression1* is true, *statement1* is executed. If *expression1* is false but *expression2* is true, *statement2* is executed. Otherwise, if both expressions are false, *statement3* is executed.

Example

```
if (legs == 4)
    printf("It might be a horse.\n");
 else if (legs > 4)
     printf("It is not a horse.\n");
 else    /* case of legs < 4 */
 {
     legs++;
     printf("Now it has one more leg.\n");
 }
```

Summary: Multiple Choice with `switch`

Keyword

The keyword for the `switch` statement is `switch`.

General Comments

Program control jumps to the statement bearing the value of *expression* as a label. Program flow then proceeds through the remaining statements unless redirected again. Both *expression* and labels must have integer values (type `char` is included), and the labels must be constants or expressions formed solely from constants. If no label matches the expression value, control goes to the statement labeled `default`, if present. Otherwise, control passes to the next statement following the `switch` statement. After control goes to a particular label, all the subsequent statements in the `switch` are executed until the end of the `switch`, or a `break` statement, is encountered, whichever comes first.

Form

```
switch (expression)
{
    case label1 : statement1
    case label2 : statement2
    default     : statement3
}
```

There can be more than two labeled statements, and the `default` case is optional.

Examples

```
switch (value)
    case 1  : find_sum(ar, n);
              break;
    case 2  : show_array(ar, n);
              break;
    case 3  : puts("Goodbye!");
              break;
    default : puts("Invalid choice, try again.");
              break;
}

switch (letter)
{
    case 'a' :
    case 'e' : printf("%d is a vowel\n", letter);
    case 'c' :
    case 'n' : printf("%d is in \"cane\"\n", letter);
    default  : printf("Have a nice day.\n");
}
```

If `letter` has the value `'a'` or `'e'`, all three messages are printed; `'c'` and `'n'` cause the last two to be printed. Other values print only the last message.

Summary: Program Jumps

Keywords

The keywords for program jumps are `break`, `continue`, and `goto`.

General Comments

The three instructions `break`, `continue`, and `goto` cause program flow to jump from one location of a program to another location.

The `break` Command

The `break` command can be used with any of the three loop forms and with the `switch` statement. It causes program control to skip the rest of the loop or `switch` containing it, and to resume with the next command following the loop or `switch`.

Example

```
while ((ch = getchar())  != EOF)
{
    putchar(ch);
    if (ch == ' ')
          break;        // terminate loop
    chcount++;
}
```

The `continue` Command

The `continue` command can be used with any of the three loop forms, but not with `switch`. It causes program control to skip the remaining statements in a loop. For a `while` or `for` loop, the next loop cycle is started. For a `do while` loop, the exit condition is tested and then, if necessary, the next loop cycle is started.

Example

```
while ((ch = getchar())  != EOF)
{
    if (ch == ' ')
        continue;      // go to test condition
    putchar(ch);
    chcount++;
}
```

This fragment echoes and counts nonspace characters.

The `goto` Command

A `goto` statement causes program control to jump to a statement bearing the indicated label. A colon is used to separate a labeled statement from its label. Label names follow the rules for variable names. The labeled statement can come either before or after the `goto`.

Form

```
goto label;
    label : statement
```

Example

```
top : ch = getchar();
      if (ch != 'y')
        goto top;
```

Section V: The Standard ANSI C Library with C99 Additions

The ANSI C library classifies functions into several groups, with each group having an associated header file. This appendix gives you an overview of the library, listing the header files and briefly describing their associated functions. Some of these functions (for example, several I/O functions) are discussed in much greater detail in the text. More generally, for complete descriptions, consult the documentation for your implementation, or a reference manual, or try an online reference such as the following:

http://www.dinkumware.com/htm_cl/index.html

Diagnostics: `assert.h`

This header file defines `assert()` as a macro. Defining the macro identifier **NDEBUG** before including the `assert.h` header file deactivates the `assert()` macro. The expression used as an argument is typically a relational or logical expression that should be true at that point in the program if the program is functioning properly. Table RS.V.1 describes the `assert()` macro.

TABLE RS.V.1   Diagnostic Macro

Prototype	Description
`void assert(int exprs);`	If `exprs` evaluates to nonzero (or true), the macro does nothing. If it evaluates to zero (false), `assert()` displays expression, the line number for the `assert()` statement, and the name of the file containing the statement. Then it calls `abort()`.

Complex Numbers: `complex.h` (C99)

The C99 standards add extensive support for complex number calculations. Implementations may choose to provide an `_Imaginary` type in addition to the `_Complex` type. The header file defines the following macros listed in Table RS.V.2.

TABLE RS.V.2   The `complex.h` Macros

Macro	Description
`complex`	Expands to the type keyword `_Complex`
`_Complex_I`	Expands to an expression of type `const float _Complex`, whose value, when squared, is −1
`imaginary`	If imaginary types are supported, expands to the type keyword `_Imaginary`
`_Imaginary_I`	If imaginary types are supported, expands to an expression of type `const float _Imaginary`, whose value, when squared, is −1
`I`	Expands to either `_Complex_I` or `_Imaginary_I`

The C implementation of complex numbers, supported by the `complex.h` header file, is quite different from the C++ implementation, supported by the `complex` header file. C++ uses classes to define a complex type.

The STDC CX_LIMITED_RANGE pragma can be used to indicate whether the usual mathematical formulas can be used (the on setting) or if special attention has to be paid for extreme values (the off setting):

```
#include <complex.h>
#pragma STDC CX_LIMITED_RANGE on
```

The library functions come in three flavors: double, float, and long double. Table RS.V.3 lists the double version. The float and long double versions append an f and an l, respectively, to the function names. Thus, csinf() is the float version of csin(), and csinl() is the long double version.

Angles are measured in radians.

TABLE RS.V.3   Complex Number Functions

Prototype	Description
double complex cacos(double complex z);	Returns the complex arc cosine of z
double complex casin(double complex z);	Returns the complex arcsine of z
double complex catan(double complex z);	Returns the complex arctangent of z
double complex ccos(double complex z);	Returns the complex cosine of z
double complex csin(double complex z);	Returns the complex sine of z
double complex ctan(double complex z);	Returns the complex tangent of z
double complex cacosh(double complex z);	Returns the complex arc hyperbolic cosine of z
double complex casinh(double complex z);	Returns the complex arc hyperbolic sine of z
double complex catanh(double complex z);	Returns the complex arc hyperbolic tangent of z
double complex ccosh(double complex z);	Returns the complex hyperbolic cosine of z
double complex csinh(double complex z);	Returns the complex hyperbolic sine of z

TABLE RS.V.3   Continued

Prototype	Description
`double complex` `ctanh(double complex z);`	Returns the complex hyperbolic tangent of z
`double complex` `cexp(double complex z);`	Returns the complex value of *e* to the z power
`double complex` `clog(double complex z);`	Returns the complex natural (base *e*) logarithm of z
`double` `cabs(double complex z);`	Returns absolute value (or magnitude) of z

`double complex`
`cpows(double complex z,`
`double complex y);`
	Returns the value of z raised to the y power

`double complex` `csqrt(double complex z);`	Returns the complex square root of z
`double` `carg(double complex z);`	Returns the phase angle (or argument), in radians, of z
`double` `cimag(double complex z);`	Returns the imaginary part of z as a real number
`double complex` `conj(double complex z);`	Returns the complex conjugate of z
`double complex` `cproj(double complex z);`	Returns the projection of z onto the Riemann sphere
`double` `creal(double complex z);`	Returns the real part of z as a real number

Character Handling: `ctype.h`

These functions take `int` arguments, which should be able to be represented as either `unsigned char` values or as `EOF`; the effect of supplying other values is undefined. In Table RS.V.4, "true" is used as shorthand for "a nonzero value." Interpretation of some definitions depends on the current locale setting, which is controlled by the functions of `locale.h`; the table shows the interpretations for the "C" locale.

TABLE RS.V.4 Character-Handling Functions

Prototype	Description
`int isalnum(int c);`	Returns true if c is alphanumeric (alphabetic or numeric).
`int isalpha(int c);`	Returns true if c is alphabetic.
`int isblank(int c);`	Returns true if c is a space or a horizontal tab. (C99)
`int iscntrl(int c);`	Returns true if c is a control character, such as Ctrl+B.
`int isdigit(int c);`	Returns true if c is a digit.
`int isgraph(int c);`	Returns true if c is any printing character other than a space.
`int islower(int c);`	Returns true if c is a lowercase character.
`int isprint(int c);`	Returns true if c is a printing character.
`int ispunct(int c);`	Returns true if c is a punctuation character (any printing character other than a space or an alphanumeric character).
`int isspace(int c);`	Returns true if c is a whitespace character: space, newline, formfeed, carriage return, vertical tab, horizontal tab, or, possibly, another implementation-defined character.
`int isupper(int c);`	Returns true if c is an uppercase character.
`int isxdigit(int c);`	Returns true if c is a hexadecimal-digit character.
`int tolower(int c);`	If the argument is an uppercase character, returns the lowercase version; otherwise, just returns the original argument.
`int toupper(int c);`	If the argument is a lowercase character, returns the uppercase version; otherwise, just returns the original argument.

Error Reporting: `errno.h`

The `errno.h` header file supports an older error-reporting mechanism. The mechanism provides an external static memory location that can be accessed by the identifier (or, possibly, the macro) ERRNO. Some library functions place a value in this location to support an error. A program including this header file then can check the value of ERRNO to see whether error has been reported. The ERRNO mechanism is regarded as less than state of the art, and math functions no longer are required to set ERRNO values. The standard provides for three macro values representing particular errors, but an implementation can provide more. Table RS.V.5 lists the standard macros.

TABLE RS.V.5 The errno.h Macros

Macro	Meaning
EDOM	A domain error in a function call (the argument is out of range)
ERANGE	A range error in a function return (the return value is out of range)
EILSEQ	A wide-character translation error

Floating-Point Environment: fenv.h (C99)

The C99 standard provides access to and control of the floating-point environment through the fenv.h header file. This feature supports a more aggressive approach to numeric calculations, but it may be a while before it is commonly implemented.

The *floating-point environment* consists of a set of status flags and control modes. An exceptional circumstance that occurs during floating-point calculation, such as dividing by zero, can "raise an exception." This means the event sets one of the floating-environment flags. The control mode value can control, for example, the direction of rounding. The fenv.h header defines a set of macros representing several exceptions and control modes, and it provides prototypes for functions that interact with the environment. The header also provides a pragma for enabling or disabling access to the floating-point environment.

The directive

```
#pragma STDC FENV_ACCESS on
```

turns on access to the environment, and the directive

```
#pragma STDC FENV_ACCESS off
```

turns it off. If external, the pragma should be given before any outside declarations, or at the beginning of a compound block. It remains in effect until superseded by another occurrence of the pragma, or until the end of the file (external directive) or the end of the compound statement (block directive).

The header file defines two types, shown in Table RS.V.6.

TABLE RS.V.6 The fenv.h Types

Type	Represents
fenv_t	The entire floating-point environment
fexcept_t	The collection of floating-point status flags

The header file defines macros representing several possible floating-point exceptions and control states. The implementation may define additional macros, provided they begin with FE_ followed by an uppercase character. Table RS.V.7 shows the standard exception macros.

TABLE RS.V.7   The fenv.h Types

Macro	Represents
FE_DIVBYZERO	Division-by-zero exception raised
FE_INEXACT	Inexact value exception raised
FE_INVALID	Invalid value exception raised
FE_OVERFLOW	Overflow exception raised
FE_UNDERFLOW	Underflow exception raised
FE_ALL_EXCEPT	The bitwise OR of all the floating-point exceptions supported by the implementation
FE_DOWNWARD	Rounds downward
FE_TONEAREST	Rounds to the nearest value
FE_TOWARDZERO	Rounds toward zero
FE_UPWARD	Rounds upward
FE_DFL_ENV	Represents the default environment and has the type const fenv_t *.

Table RS.V.8 shows the standard function prototypes in the fenv.h header file. Note that often argument values and return values correspond to the macros in Table RS.V.7. For example, FE_UPWARD is an appropriate argument for fesetround().

TABLE RS.V.8   The fenv.h Types

Prototype	Description
void feclearexcept(int excepts);	Clears the exceptions represented by excepts.
void fegetexceptflag(fexcept_t *flagp, int excepts);	Stores the states of the floating-point status flags indicated by excepts in the object pointed to by flagp.
void feraiseexcept(int excepts);	Raises the exceptions specified by excepts.
void fesetexceptflag(const fexcept_t *flagp, int excepts);	Sets those floating-point status flags indicated by excepts to the values provided by flagp; flagp should have been set by a previous call to fegetexceptflag().

TABLE RS.V.8   Continued

Prototype	Description
`int fetestexcept(int excepts);`	`excepts` specifies the status flags to be queried; the function returns the bitwise OR of those specified status flags.
`int fegetround(void);`	Returns the current rounding direction.
`int fesetround(int round);`	Sets the rounding direction to the value provided by `round`; returns 0 if and only if successful.
`void fegetenv(fenv_t *envp);`	Stores the current environment in the location pointed to by `envp`.
`int feholdexcept(fenv_t *envp);`	Saves the current floating-point environment in the location pointed to by `envp`, clears the floating-point status flags, and then, if possible, installs a nonstop mode, in which execution continues despite exceptions; returns 0 if and only if successful.
`void fesetenv(const fenv_t *envp);`	Installs the floating-point environment represented by `envp`; `envp` should point to a data object set by a prior call to `fegetenv()` or `feholdexcept()`, or to a floating-point environment macro.
`void feupdateenv(const fenv_t *envp);`	Function saves the currently raised floating-point exceptions in automatic storage, installs the floating-point environment represented by the object pointed to by `envp`, and then raises the saved floating-point exceptions; `envp` should point to a data object set by a prior call to `fegetenv()` or `feholdexcept()`, or to a floating-point environment macro.

Format Conversion of Integer Types: `inttypes.h` (C99)

This header file defines several macros that can be used as format specifiers for the expanded integer types. Reference Section VI, "Extended Integer Types," discusses these further. This header file also declares the following type:

`imaxdiv_t`

This is a structure type representing the return value of the `idivmax()` function.

This header file also includes `stdint.h` and declares several functions that use the greatest-width integer type, which is declared as `intmax` in `stdint.h`. Table RS.V.9 lists these functions.

TABLE RS.V.9   Greatest-Width Integer Functions

Prototype	Description
`intmax_t imaxabs(intmax_t j);`	Returns the absolute value of j
`imaxdiv_t imaxdiv(intmax_t numer, intmax_t denom);`	Computes the quotient and remainder of numer/denom in a single operation and stores the two values in the returned structure
`intmax_t strtoimax(const char * restrict nptr, char ** restrict endptr, int base);`	Equivalent to the `strtol()` function, except that it converts the string to type `intmax_t` and returns that value
`uintmax_t strtoumax(const char * restrict nptr, char ** restrict endptr, int base);`	Equivalent to the `strtoul()` function, except that it converts the string to type `uintmax_t` and returns that value
`intmax_t wcstoimax(const wchar_t * restrict nptr, wchar_t ** restrict endptr, int base);`	The `wchar_t` version of `strtoimax()`
`uintmax_t wcstoumax(const wchar_t * restrict nptr, wchar_t ** restrict endptr, int base);`	The `wchar_t` version of `strtoumax()`

Localization: `locale.h`

A *locale* is a group of settings that controls items such as the symbol used as a decimal point. Locale values are stored in a structure of type `struct lconv`, defined in the `locale.h` header file. A locale can be specified by a string, which acts to specify a particular set of values for the structure members. The default locale is designated by the string `"C"`. Table RS.V.10 lists the localization functions, and a brief discussion follows.

TABLE RS.V.10   Localization Functions

Prototype	Description
`char * setlocale(int category, const char * locale);`	The function sets certain locale values to the values specified by the locale and indicated by `locale`. The `category` value controls which locale values get set (see Table RS.V.11). The function returns the null pointer if it cannot honor the request. Otherwise, it returns a pointer associated with the specified category in the new locale.
`struct lconv * localeconv(void);`	Returns a pointer to a `struct lconv` structure filled in with the values of the current locale.

The required possible values for the `locale` parameter to `setlocale()` are `"C"`, which is the default, and `""`, which represents the implementation-defined native environment. An implementation can define additional locales. The possible values for the `category` parameter to `setlocale()` are represented by the macros listed in Table RS.V.11.

TABLE RS.V.11   Category Macros

Macro	Description
NULL	Leave the locale unchanged and return a pointer to the current locale.
LC_ALL	Change all locale values.
LC_COLLATE	Change locale values for the collating sequence used by `strcoll()` and `strxfrm()`.
LC_CTYPE	Change locale values for the character-handling functions and the multibyte functions.
LC_MONETARY	Change locale values for monetary-formatting information.
LC_NUMERIC	Change locale values for the decimal point symbol and non-monetary formatting used by formatted I/O and by string-conversion functions.
LC_TIME	Change locale values for the time formatting used by `strftime()`.

Table RS.V.12 lists the required members of a `struct lconv` structure.

TABLE RS.V.12   Required `struct lconv` Members

Macro	Description
char *decimal_point	Decimal-point character for non-monetary values.
char *thousands_sep	Character used to separate groups of digits before the decimal point for non-monetary quantities.
char *grouping	A string whose elements indicate the size of each group of digits for non-monetary quantities.
char *int_curr_symbol	The international currency symbol.
char *currency_symbol	The local currency symbol.
char *mon_decimal_point	Decimal-point character for monetary values.
char *mon_thousands_sep	Character used to separate groups of digits before the decimal point for monetary quantities.
char *mon_grouping	A string whose elements indicate the size of each group of digits for monetary quantities.

Macro	Description
`char *positive_sign`	String used to indicate a non-negative formatted monetary value.
`char *negative_sign`	String used to indicate a negative formatted monetary value.
`char int_frac_digits`	Number of digits displayed after the decimal point for an internationally formatted monetary quantity.
`char frac_digits`	Number of digits displayed after the decimal point for a locally formatted monetary quantity.
`char p_cs_precedes`	Set to 1 or 0 depending on whether `currency_symbol` precedes or follows the value of a non-negative formatted monetary quantity.
`char p_sep_by_space`	Set to 1 or 0 depending on whether `currency_symbol` is separated by a space from the value of a non-negative formatted monetary quantity.
`char n_cs_precedes`	Set to 1 or 0 depending on whether `currency_symbol` precedes or follows the value of a negative formatted monetary quantity.
`char n_sep_by_space`	Set to 1 or 0 depending on whether `currency_symbol` is separated by a space from the value of a negative formatted monetary quantity.
`char p_sign_posn`	Set to a value indicating the positioning of a `positive_sign` string; 0 means parentheses surround the quantity and currency symbol, 1 means the string precedes the quantity and currency symbol, 2 means the string follows the quantity and currency symbol, 3 means the string immediately precedes the currency symbol, and 4 means the string immediately follows the currency symbol.
`char n_sign_posn`	Set to a value indicating the positioning of a `negative_sign` string; the meaning is the same as for `char p_sign_posn`.
`char int_p_cs_precedes`	Set to 1 or 0 depending on whether `int_currency_symbol` precedes or follows the value of a non-negative formatted monetary quantity.
`char int_p_sep_by_space`	Set to 1 or 0 depending on whether `int_currency_symbol` is separated by a space from the value of a non-negative formatted monetary quantity.
`char int_n_cs_precedes`	Set to 1 or 0 depending on whether `int_currency_symbol` precedes or follows the value of a negative formatted monetary quantity.
`char int_n_sep_by_space`	Set to 1 or 0 depending on whether `int_currency_symbol` is separated by a space from the value of a negative formatted monetary quantity.
`char int_p_sign_posn`	Set to a value indicating the positioning of the `positive_sign` for a non-negative internationally formatted monetary quantity.
`char int_n_sign_posn`	Set to a value indicating the positioning of `negative_sign` for a negative internationally formatted monetary quantity.

Math Library: math.h

With C99, the math.h header file defines two types:

```
float_t
double_t
```

These types are at least as wide as float and double, respectively, and double_t is at least as wide as float_t. These are intended to be the most efficient types for doing float and double calculations, respectively.

This header file also defines several macros, as described in Table RS.V.13; all but HUGE_VAL are C99 additions. Some of these are discussed in more detail in Section VIII, "C99 Numeric Computational Enhancements."

TABLE RS.V.13   The math.h Macros

Macro	Description
HUGE_VAL	A positive double constant not necessarily expressible as a float; in the past, it was used as the return value for functions when the magnitude of the result exceeded the largest representable value.
HUGE_VALF	The type float counterpart of HUGE_VAL.
HUGE_VALL	The type long double counterpart of HUGE_VAL.
INFINITY	Expands to a constant float expression representing positive or unsigned infinity, if available; otherwise, expands to a positive float constant that overflows during compile time.
NAN	Defined, if and only if, the implementation supports quiet NaNs (a value signifying Not-a-Number) for float.
FP_INFINITE	Classification number indicating an infinite floating-point value.
FP_NAN	Classification number indicating a floating-point value that is not a number.
FP_NORMAL	Classification number indicating a normal floating-point value.
FP_SUBNORMAL	Classification number indicating a subnormal (lowered precision) floating-point value.
FP_ZERO	Classification number indicating a floating-point value representing 0.
FP_FAST_FMA	(Optional) If defined, this macro indicates that the fma() function works about as fast, or faster than, a multiply and add of double operands.
FP_FAST_FMAF	(Optional) If defined, this macro indicates that the fmaf() function works about as fast, or faster than, a multiply and add of float operands.

Macro	Description
FP_FAST_FMAL	(Optional) If defined, this macro indicates that the `fmal()` function works about as fast, or faster than, a multiply and add of `long double` operands.
FP_ILOGB0	An integer constant expression representing the value returned by `ilogb(0)`.
FP_ILOGBNAN	An integer constant expression representing the value returned by `ilogb(NaN)`.
MATH_ERRNO	Expands to the integer constant 1.
MATH_ERREXCEPT	Expands to the integer constant 2.
math_errhandling	Has the value `MATH_ERRNO` or `MATH_ERREXCEPT` or the bitwise OR of those two values.

The math functions typically work with type `double` values. C99 has added `float` and `long double` versions of these functions, which are indicated by adding an `f` suffix and an `l` suffix, respectively, to the function name. For example, the language now provides these prototypes:

```
double sin(double);
float sinf(float);
long double sinl(long double);
```

For brevity, Table RS.V.14 lists just the `double` versions of the functions of the math library. The table refers to `FLT_RADIX`. This constant, defined in `float.h`, is the base used for exponentiation in the internal floating-point representation. The most common value is `2`.

TABLE RS.V.14   ANSI C Standard Math Functions.

Prototype	Description
`int classify(real-floating x);`	A C99 macro that returns the floating-point classification value appropriate for x.
`int isfinite(real-floating x);`	A C99 macro that returns a nonzero value if, and only if, x is finite.
`int isfin(real-floating x);`	A C99 macro that returns a nonzero value if, and only if, x is infinite.
`int isnan(real-floating x);`	A C99 macro that returns a nonzero value if, and only if, x is a NaN.
`int isnormal(real-floating x);`	A C99 macro that returns a nonzero value if, and only if, x is normal.
`int signbit(real-floating x);`	A C99 macro that returns a nonzero value if, and only if, the sign of x is negative.

TABLE RS.V.14   Continued

Prototype	Description
`double acos(double x);`	Returns the angle (0 to π radians) whose cosine is x.
`double asin(double x);`	Returns the angle ($-\pi/2$ to $\pi/2$ radians) whose sine is x.
`double atan(double x);`	Returns the angle ($-\pi/2$ to $\pi/2$ radians) whose tangent is x.
`double atan2(double y, double x);`	Returns the angle ($-\pi$ to π radians) whose tangent is y / x.
`double cos(double x);`	Returns the cosine of x (x in radians).
`double sin(double x);`	Returns the sine of x (x in radians).
`double tan(double x);`	Returns the tangent of x (x in radians).
`double cosh(double x);`	Returns the hyperbolic cosine of x.
`double sinh(double x);`	Returns the hyperbolic sine of x.
`double tanh(double x);`	Returns the hyperbolic tangent of x.
`double exp(double x);`	Returns the exponential function of x (e^x).
`double exp2(double x);`	Returns 2 to the x power (C99).
`double expm1(double x);`	Returns e^x - 1 (C99).
`double frexp(double v, int *pt_e);`	Breaks a value, v, into a normalized fraction, which is returned, and a power of 2, which is placed in the location pointed to by `pt_e`.
`int ilogb(double x);`	Returns the exponent of x as a signed `int` (C99).
`double ldexp(double x, int p);`	Returns 2 to the p power times x.
`double log(double x);`	Returns the natural logarithm of x.
`double log10(double x);`	Returns the base 10 logarithm of x.
`double log1p(double x);`	Returns `log(1 + x)` (C99).
`double log2(double x);`	Returns the base 2 logarithm of x (C99).
`double logb(double x);`	Returns the signed exponent of its argument for the underlying base used to represent floating-point values on the system (`FLT_RADIX`) (C99).
`double modf(double x, double *p);`	Breaks x into an integral part and a fraction part, both of the same sign, returns the fractional part, and stores the integral part in the location pointed to by p.

Prototype	Description
`double scalbn(double x, int n);`	Returns x × FLT_RADIX^n (C99).
`double scalbln(double x, long n);`	Returns x × FLT_RADIX^n (C99).
`double cbrt(double x);`	Returns the cube root of x (C99).
`double hypot(double x, double y);`	Returns the square root of the sums of the squares of x and y (C99).
`double pow(double x, double y);`	Returns x to the y power.
`double sqrt(double x);`	Returns the square root of x.
`double erf(double x);`	Returns the error function of x (C99).
`double erfc(double x);`	Returns the complementary error function of x (C99).
`double lgamma(double x);`	Returns the natural logarithm of the absolute value of the gamma function of x (C99).
`double tgamma(double x);`	Returns the gamma function of x (C99).
`double ceil(double x);`	Returns the smallest integral value not less than x.
`double fabs(double x);`	Returns the absolute value of x.
`double floor(double x);`	Returns the largest integral value not greater than x.
`double nearbyint(double x);`	Rounds x to the nearest integer in floating-point format; it uses the rounding direction specified by the floating-point environment, if available. The "inexact" exception is not raised. (C99).
`double rint(double x);`	Like `nearbyint()`, except it may raise the "inexact" exception (C99).
`long int lrint(double x);`	Rounds x to the nearest integer in `long int` format; it uses the rounding direction specified by the floating-point environment, if available (C99).
`long long int llrint(double x);`	Rounds x to the nearest integer in `long long int` format; it uses the rounding direction specified by the floating-point environment, if available (C99).
`double round(double x);`	Rounds x to the nearest integer in floating-point format; it always rounds halfway values away from zero (C99).
`long int lround(double x);`	Like `round()`, but the answer is returned as type `long int` (C99).

TABLE RS.V.14 Continued

Prototype	Description
`long long int llround(double x);`	Like `round()`, but the answer is returned as type `long long int` (C99).
`double trunc(double x);`	Rounds x to the nearest integer in floating-point format that is no greater in magnitude than x (C99).
`int fmod(double x, double y);`	Returns the fractional part of x/y; if y is nonzero, the result has the same sign as x and is smaller in magnitude than y.
`double remainder(double x, double y);`	Returns x REM y, which IEC 60559 defines as x - n*y, where n is the integer nearest the value of x/y; n is even if the absolute value of (n - x/y) is 1/2. (C99).
`double remquo(double x, double y, int *quo);`	Returns the same value as `remainder()` and places in the location pointed to by `quo` a value having the same sign as x/y and having the value the integer magnitude of x/y modulus 2^k, where k is an implementation-dependent integer whose value is at least 3 (C99).
`double copysign(double x, double y);`	Returns a value with the magnitude of x and the sign of y (C99).
`double nan(const char *tagp);`	Returns the type `double` representation of a quiet NaN; `nan("n-char-seq")` is equivalent to `strtod("NAN(n-char-seq)", (char **)NULL)`; `nan("")` is equivalent to `strtod("NAN()", (char **)NULL)`; for other argument strings, the call is equivalent to `strtod("NAN", (char **)NULL)`. Returns 0 if quiet NaNs are not supported (C99).
`double nextafter(double x, double y);`	Returns the next representable type `double` value after x in the direction of y; returns x if x equals y (C99).
`double nexttoward(double x, long double y);`	The same as `nextafter()`, except the second argument is `long double` and, if x equals y, the function returns y converted to `double` (C99).
`double fdim(double x, double y);`	Returns the positive difference of the arguments (C99).
`double fmax(double x, double y);`	Returns the maximum numeric value of the arguments; if one argument is a NaN and the other numeric, the numeric value is returned (C99).

Prototype	Description
`double fmin(double x, double y);`	Returns the minimum numeric value of the arguments. If one argument is a NaN and the other numeric, the numeric value is returned (C99).
`double fma(double x, double y, double z);`	Returns the quantity `(x*y)+z` as a ternary operation, rounding once at the end (C99).
`int isgreater(real-floating x, real-floating y);`	A C99 macro that returns the value of `(x) > (y)` without raising the "invalid" floating-point exception if one or both arguments are NaNs.
`int isgreaterequal(real-floating x, real-floating y);`	A C99 macro that returns the value of `(x) >= (y)` without raising the "invalid" floating-point exception if one or both arguments are NaNs.
`int isless(real-floating x, real-floating y);`	A C99 macro that returns the value of `(x) < (y)` without raising the "invalid" floating-point exception if one or both arguments are NaNs.
`int islessequal(real-floating x, real-floating y);`	A C99 macro that returns the value of `(x) <= (y)` without raising the "invalid" floating-point exception if one or both arguments are NaNs.
`int islessgreater(real-floating x, real-floating y);`	A C99 macro that returns the value of `(x) < (y) || (x) > (y)` without raising the "invalid" floating-point exception if one or both arguments are NaNs.
`int isunordered(real-floating x, real-floating y);`	Returns one if the arguments are unordered (at least one being a Nan) and zero otherwise.

Non-Local Jumps: `setjmp.h`

The `setjmp.h` header file enables you to bypass the usual function-call, function-return sequence. The `setjmp()` function stores information about the current execution environment (for example, a pointer to the current instruction) in a type `jmp_buf` variable (an array type defined in this header file), and the `longjmp()` function transfers execution to such an environment. The functions are intended to help handle error conditions, not to be used as part of normal program flow control. Table RS.V.15 lists the functions.

TABLE RS.V.15 The `setjmp.h` Functions

Prototype	Description
`int setjmp(jmp_buf env);`	Saves the calling environment in the array `env` and returns `0` if called directly and nonzero if the return is from a call to `longjmp()`.
`void longjmp(jmp_buf env, int val);`	Restores the environment saved by the most recent evocation of `setjmp()` that set the `env` array; after completing this change, the program continues as though that evocation of `setjmp()` had returned `val`, except that a return value of `0` is not allowed and is converted to `1`.

Signal Handling: `signal.h`

A *signal* is a condition that can be reported during program execution. It is represented by a positive integer. The `raise()` function sends, or *raises*, a signal, and the `signal()` function sets the response to a particular signal.

The standard provides the macros listed in Table RS.V.16 to represent possible signals; an implementation can add further values. They can be used as arguments to `raise()` and `signal()`.

TABLE RS.V.16 Signal Macros

Macro	Description
SIGABRT	Abnormal termination, such as initiated by a call to `abort()`.
SIGFPE	Erroneous arithmetic operation.
SIGILL	Invalid function image (such as illegal instruction) detected.
SIGINT	Interactive attention signal received (such as a DOS interrupt).
SIGSEGV	Invalid access to storage.
SIGTERM	Termination request sent to program.

The `signal()` function takes as its second argument a pointer to a `void` function that takes an `int` argument. It also returns a pointer of the same type. A function invoked in response to a signal is termed a *signal handler*. The standard defines three macros fitting this prototype:

```
void  (*funct)(int);
```

Table RS.V.17 lists these macros.

TABLE RS.V.17   Type `void (*f)(int)` Macros

Macro	Description
SIG_DFL	When used as an argument to `signal()`, along with a signal value, this macro indicates that the default handling for that signal will occur.
SIG_ERR	Used as a return value for `signal()` if it cannot return its second argument.
SIG_IGN	When used as an argument to `signal()`, along with a signal value, this macro indicates that the signal will be ignored.

If the signal `sig` is raised and `func` points to a function (see the `signal()` prototype in Table RS.V.18), first, under most circumstances, `signal(sig, SIG_DFL)` is called to reset signal handling to the default, and then `(*func)(sig)` is called. The signal-handling function pointed to by `func` can terminate by executing a return statement or by calling `abort()`, `exit()`, or `longjmp()`. Table RS.V.18 lists the signal functions.

TABLE RS.V.18   Signal Functions

Prototype	Description
`void (*signal(int sig, void (*func)(int)))(int);`	Causes the function pointed to by `func` to be executed if signal `sig` is raised. If possible, returns `func`; otherwise, returns `SIG_ERR`.
`int raise(int sig);`	Sends the signal `sig` to the executing program; returns zero if successful and nonzero otherwise.

Variable Arguments: `stdarg.h`

The `stdarg.h` header file provides a means for defining a function having a variable number of arguments. The prototype for such a function should have a parameter list with at least one parameter followed by ellipses:

```
void f1(int n, ...);                /* valid   */
int f2(int n, float x, int k, ...); /* valid   */
double  f3(...);                    /* invalid */
```

In the following table, the term *parmN* is the identifier used for the last parameter preceding the ellipses. In the preceding examples, *parmN* would be n for the first case and k for the second case.

The header file declares a `va_list` type to represent a data object used to hold the parameters corresponding to the ellipses part of the parameter list. Table RS.V.19 lists three macros to be used in the function with the variable parameter list. An object of type `va_list` should be declared before using these macros.

TABLE RS.V.19 Variable Argument List Macros

Prototype	Description
void va_start(va_list ap, *parmN*);	This macro initializes ap before use by va_arg () and va_end(); *parmN* is the identifier for the last named parameter in the argument list.
void va_copy(va_list dest, va_list src);	This macro initializes dest as a copy of the current state of src (C99).
type va_arg(va_list ap, *type*);	This macro expands to an expression having the same value and type as the next item in the argument list represented by ap; *type* is the type for that item. Each call advances to the next item in ap.
void va_end(va_list ap);	This macro closes out the process and may render ap unusable without another call to va_start().

Boolean Support: `stdbool.h` (C99)

This header file defines the four macros shown in Table RS.V.20.

TABLE RS.V.20 The `stdbool.h` Macros

Macro	Description
bool	Expands to _Bool
false	Expands to the integer constant 0
true	Expands to the integer constant 1
__bool_true_false_are_defined	Expands to the integer constant 1

Common Definitions: `stddef.h`

This header file defines some types and macros, as shown in Tables RS.V.21 and RS.V.22.

TABLE RS.V.21 The `stddef.h` Types

Type	Description
ptrdiff_t	A signed integer type for representing the result of subtracting one pointer from another
size_t	An unsigned integer type representing the result of the sizeof operator
wchar_t	An integer type that can represent the largest extended character set specified by supported locales

TABLE RS.V.22   The `stddef.h` Macros

Macro	Description
NULL	An implementation-defined constant representing the null pointer.
offsetof(type, *member-designator*)	Expands to a `size_t` value representing the offset, in bytes, of the indicated member from the beginning of a structure having type *type*; the behavior is undefined if the member is a bit field.

Example

```
#include <stddef.h>

struct car
{
    char brand[30];
    char model[30];
    double hp;
    double price;
};
int main(void)
{
    size_t into = offsetof(struct car, hp);  /* offset of hp member */
    ...
```

Integer Types: `stdint.h`

This header file uses the **typedef** facility to create integer type names that specify the properties of the integers. This header file is included by the **inttypes.h** header file, which provides macros for use in input/output function calls.

Exact-Width Types

One set of **typedef**s identify types with precise sizes. Table RS.V.23 lists the names and sizes. Note, however, that not all systems may be able to support all the types.

TABLE RS.V.23   Exact-Width Types

typedef Name	Properties
int8_t	8 bits signed
int16_t	16 bits signed
int32_t	32 bits signed
int64_t	64 bits signed
uint8_t	8 bits unsigned

TABLE RS.V.23 Continued

typedef Name	Properties
uint16_t	16 bits unsigned
uint32_t	32 bits unsigned
uint64_t	64 bits unsigned

Minimum-Width Types

The minimum-width types guarantee a type that is at least a certain number of bits in size. Table RS.V.24 lists the minimum-width types. These types always exist.

TABLE RS.V.24 Minimum Width Types

typedef Name	Properties
int_least8_t	At least 8 bits signed
int_least16_t	At least 16 bits signed
int_least32_t	At least 32 bits signed
int_least64_t	At least 64 bits signed
uint_least8_t	At least 8 bits unsigned
uint_least16_t	At least 16 bits unsigned
uint_least32_t	At least 32 bits unsigned
uint_least64_t	At least 64 bits unsigned

Fastest Minimum-Width Types

For a particular system, some integer representations can be faster than others. So `stdint.h` also defines the fastest type for representing at least a certain number of bits. Table RS.V.25 lists the fastest minimum-width types. These types always exist. In some cases, there might be no clear-cut choice for fastest; in that case, the system simply specifies one of the choices.

TABLE RS.V.25 Fastest Minimum-Width Types

typedef Name	Properties
int_fast8_t	At least 8 bits signed
int_fast16_t	At least 16 bits signed

typedef Name	Properties
int_fast32_t	At least 32 bits signed
int_fast64_t	At least 64 bits signed
uint_fast8_t	At least 8 bits unsigned
uint_fast16_t	At least 16 bits unsigned
uint_fast32_t	At least 32 bits unsigned
uint_fast64_t	At least 64 bits unsigned

Maximum-Width Types

The `stdint.h` header file also defines maximum-width types. A variable of this type can hold any integer value possible for the system, taking the sign into account. Table RS.V.26 lists the types.

TABLE RS.V.26   Maximum-Width Types

typedef Name	Properties
intmax_t	The widest signed type
uintmax_t	The widest unsigned type

Integers That Can Hold Pointer Values

The header file also has two integer types, listed in Table RS.V.27, that can hold pointer values accurately. That is, if you assign a type `void *` value to one of these types, and then assign the integer type back to the pointer, no information is lost. Either or both types might not exist.

TABLE RS.V.27   Integer Types for Holding Pointer Values

typedef Name	Properties
intptr_t	Signed type can hold a pointer value.
uintptr_t	Unsigned type can hold a pointer value.

Defined Constants

The `stdint.h` header file defines constants representing limiting values for the types defined in that header file. The constants are named after the type. Take the type name, replace the _t with _MIN or _MAX, and make all the characters uppercase to get the name of the constant representing the minimum or maximum value for the type. For example, the smallest value for the int32_t type is INT32_MIN, and the largest value for the uint_fast16_t type is UINT_FAST16_MAX. Table RS.V.28 summarizes these constants, with N standing for the number of bits, along with defined constants relating to the intptr_t, uintptr_t, intmax_t, and uintmax_t types. The magnitude of these constants will equal or exceed (unless "exactly" is specified) the listed amount.

TABLE RS.V.28   Integer Constants

Constant Identifier	Minimum (in Magnitude) Value
INTN_MIN	Exactly $-(2^{N-1}-1)$
INTN_MAX	Exactly $2^{N-1}-1$
UINTN_MAX	Exactly $2^{N}-1$
INT_LEASTN_MIN	$-(2^{N-1}-1)$
INT_LEASTN_MAX	$2^{N-1}-1$
UINT_LEASTN_MAX	$2^{N-1}-1$
INT_FASTN_MIN	$-(2^{N-1}-1)$
INT_FASTN_MAX	$2^{N-1}-1$
UINT_FASTN_MAX	$2^{N-1}-1$
INTPTR_MIN	$-(2^{15}-1)$
INTPTR_MAX	$2^{15}-1$
UINTPTR_MAX	$2^{16}-1$
INTMAX_MIN	$-(2^{15}-1)$
INTMAX_MAX	$2^{63}-1$
UINTMAX_MAX	$2^{64}-1$

The header file also defines some constants for types defined elsewhere. Table RS.V.29 lists them.

TABLE RS.V.29   Further Integer Constants

Constant Identifier	Meaning
PTRDIFF_MIN	Minimum value of the ptrdiff_t type
PTRDIFF_MAX	Maximum value of the ptrdiff_t type
SIG_ATOMIC_MIN	Minimum value of the sig_atomic_t type
SIG_ATOMIC_MAX	Maximum value of the sig_atomic_t type
WCHAR_MIN	Minimum value of the wchar_t type
WCHAR_MAX	Maximum value of the wchar_t type
WINT_MIN	Minimum value of the wint_t type
WINT_MAX	Maximum value of the wint_t type
SIZE_MAX	Maximum value of the size_t type

Extended Integer Constants

The `stdint.h` header file defines macros for specifying constants of the various extended integer types. Essentially, the macro is a type cast to the underlying type—that is, to the fundamental type that represents the extended type in a particular implementation.

The macro names are formed by taking the type name, replacing the _t with _C, and making all the letters uppercase. For example, to make `1000` a type `uint_least64_t` constant, use the expression `UINT_LEAST64_C(1000)`.

Standard I/O Library: `stdio.h`

The ANSI C standard library includes several standard I/O functions associated with streams and the `stdio.h` file. Table RS.V.30 presents the ANSI prototypes for these functions, along with a brief explanation of what they do. (Many are described more fully in Chapter 13, "File Input/Output.") The header file also defines the `FILE` type, the values `EOF` and `NULL`, and the standard I/O streams `stdin`, `stdout`, and `stderr`, along with several constants used by the functions in this library.

TABLE RS.V.30   ANSI C Standard I/O Functions

Prototype	Description
void clearerr(FILE *);	Clears end-of-file and error indicators
int fclose(FILE *);	Closes the indicated file
int feof(FILE *);	Tests for end-of-file

TABLE RS.V.30   Continued

Prototype	Description
`int ferror(FILE *);`	Tests error indicator
`int fflush(FILE *);`	Flushes the indicated file
`int fgetc(FILE *);`	Gets the next character from the indicated input stream
`int fgetpos(FILE * restrict, fpos_t * restrict);`	Stores the current value of the file position indicator
`char * fgets(char * restrict, FILE * restrict);`	Gets the next line (or `int`, indicated number of characters) from the indicated stream
`FILE * fopen(const char * restrict, const char *restrict);`	Opens the indicated file
`int fprintf(FILE * restrict, const char * restrict, ...);`	Writes the formatted output to the indicated stream
`int fputc(int, FILE *);`	Writes the indicated character to the indicated stream
`int fputs(const char * restrict, FILE * restrict);`	Writes the character string pointed to by the first argument to the indicated stream
`size_t fread(void * restrict, size_t, size_t, FILE * restrict);`	Reads binary data from the indicated stream
`FILE * freopen( const char * restrict, const char * restrict, FILE * restrict);`	Opens the indicated file and associates it with the indicated stream
`int fscanf(FILE * restrict, const char * restrict, ...);`	Reads formatted input from the indicated stream
`int fsetpos(FILE *, const fpos_t *);`	Sets the file-position pointer to the indicated value
`int fseek(FILE *, long, int);`	Sets the file-position pointer to the indicated value
`long ftell(FILE *);`	Gets the current file position
`size_t fwrite( const void * restrict, size_t, size_t, FILE * restrict);`	Writes binary data to the indicated stream
`int getc(FILE *);`	Reads the next character from the indicated input
`int getchar();`	Reads the next character from the standard input

Prototype	Description
`char * gets(char *);`	Gets the next line from the standard input
`void perror(const char *);`	Writes system error messages to the standard error
`int printf(` `const char * restrict, ...);`	Writes formatted output to the standard output
`int putc(int, FILE *);`	Writes the indicated character to the indicated output
`int putchar(int);`	Writes the indicated character to the standard output
`int puts(const char *);`	Writes the string to the standard output
`int remove(const char *);`	Removes the named file
`int rename(const char *,` `constchar *);`	Renames the named file
`void rewind(FILE *);`	Sets the file-position pointer to the start of the file
`int scanf(const char * restrict,` ` ...);`	Reads formatted input from the standard input
`void setbuf(FILE * restrict,` ` char *  restrict);`	Sets the buffer size and location
`int setvbuf(FILE * restrict,` ` char *restrict, int, size_t);`	Sets the buffer size, location, and mode

`int snprintf(char * restrict,`
`size_t n,`
`const char * restrict, ...);`
	Writes formatted output up to n characters to the indicated string

`int sprintf(char * restrict,` `const char * restrict, ...);`	Writes formatted output to the indicated string
`int sscanf(const char *restrict,` `const char * restrict, ...);`	Reads formatted input from the indicated string
`FILE * tmpfile(void);`	Creates a temporary file
`char * tmpnam(char *);`	Generates a unique name for a temporary file
`int ungetc(int, FILE *);`	Pushes the indicated character back onto the input stream
`int vfprintf(FILE * restrict,` `const char * restrict, va_list);`	Like `fprintf();`, except uses a single list argument of type `va_list`, initialized by `va_start`, instead of a variable argument list
`int vprintf(const char * restrict,`	Like `printf();`, except uses a single list argument

TABLE RS.V.30   Continued

Prototype	Description
`va_list);`	of type `va_list`, initialized by `va_start`, instead of a variable argument list

`int vsprintf(char * restrict,`
`size_t n);`
`const char * restrict, va_list);`
	Like `snprintf();`, except uses a single list argument of type `va_list` initialized by `va_start` instead of a variable argument list

`int vsprintf(char * restrict,` `const char * restrict, va_list);`	Like `sprintf();`, except uses a single list argument of type `va_list` initialized by `va_start` instead of a variable argument list

General Utilities: `stdlib.h`

The ANSI C standard library includes a variety of utility functions defined in `stdlib.h`. The header file defines the types shown in Table RS.V.31.

TABLE RS.V.31   Types Defined in `stdlib.h`

Type	Description
`size_t`	The integer type returned by the `sizeof` operator.
`wchar_t`	The integer type used to represent wide characters.
`div_t`	The structure type returned by `div()`; it has a `quot` and a `rem` member, both of type `int`.
`ldiv_t`	The structure type returned by `ldiv()`; it has a `quot` and a `rem` member, both of type `long`.
`lldiv_t`	The structure type returned by `lldiv()`; it has a `quot` and a `rem` member, both of type `long long`. (C99)

The header file defines the constants listed in Table RS.V.32.

TABLE RS.V.32   Constants Defined in `stdlib.h`

Type	Description
`NULL`	The null pointer (equivalent to 0)
`EXIT_FAILURE`	Can be used as an argument to `exit()` to indicate unsuccessful execution of a program
`EXIT_SUCCESS`	Can be used as an argument to `exit()` to indicate successful execution of a program

Type	Description
RAND_MAX	The maximum value (an integer) returned by rand()
MB_CUR_MAX	The maximum number of bytes for a multibyte character for the extended character set corresponding to the current locale

Table RS.V.33 lists the functions whose prototypes are found in stdlib.h.

TABLE RS.V.33   General Utilities

Prototype	Description
double atof(const char * nptr);	Returns the initial portion of the string nptr converted to a type double value; conversion ends upon reaching the first character that is not part of the number; initial whitespace is skipped; zero is returned if no number is found.
int atoi(const char * nptr);	Returns the initial portion of the string nptr converted to a type int value; conversion ends upon reaching the first character that is not part of the number; initial whitespace is skipped; zero is returned if no number is found.
int atol(const char * nptr);	Returns the initial portion of the string nptr converted to a type long value; conversion ends upon reaching the first character that is not part of the number; initial whitespace is skipped; zero is returned if no number is found.
double strtod(char * restrict npt, char ** restrict ept);	Returns the initial const portion of the string nptr converted to a type double value; conversion ends upon reaching the first character that is not part of the number; initial whitespace is skipped; zero is returned if no number is found. If conversion is successful, the address of the first character after the number is assigned to the location pointed to by ept; if conversion fails, npt is assigned to the location pointed to by ept.
float strtof(const char * restrict npt, char ** restrict ept);	Same as strtod(), but converts the string pointed to by nptr to a type float value (C99).

TABLE RS.V.33 Continued

Prototype	Description

`long double strtols(`
`const char * restrict npt,`
`char ** restrict ept);`
	Same as `strtod()`, but converts the string pointed to by `nptr` to a type `long double` value (C99).

`long strtol(`
`const char * restrict npt`
`char ** restrict ept, int base);`
	Returns the initial portion of the string `nptr` converted to a type `long` value; conversion ends upon reaching the first character that is not part of the number; initial whitespace is skipped; zero is returned if no number is found. If conversion is successful, the address of the first character after the number is assigned to the location pointed to by `ept`; if conversion fails, `npt` is assigned to the location pointed to by `ept`. The number in the string is assumed to be written in a base specified by `base`.

`long long strtoll(`
`const char * restrict npt,`
`char ** restrict ept, int base);`
	Same as `strtol()`, but converts the string pointed to by `nptr` to a type `long long` value (C99).

`unsigned long strtoul(`
`const char * restrict npt,`
`char ** restrict ept, int base);`
	Returns the initial portion of the string `nptr` converted to a type `unsigned long` value; conversion ends upon reaching the first character that is not part of the number; initial whitespace is skipped; zero is returned if no number is found. If conversion is successful, the address of the first character after the number is assigned to the location pointed to by `ept`; if conversion fails, `npt` is assigned to the location pointed to by `ept`. The number in the string is assumed to be written in a base specified by `base`.

`unsigned long long strtoull(`
`const char * restrict npt,`
`char ** restrict ept, int base);`
	Same as `strtoul()`, but converts the string pointed to by `nptr` to a type `unsigned long long` value (C99).

`int rand(void);`	Returns a pseudorandom integer in the range `0` to `RAND_MAX`.
`void srand(unsigned int seed);`	Sets the random-number generator seed to `seed`; if `rand()` is called before a call to `srand()`, the seed is `1`.

Prototype	Description
`void *calloc(size_t nmem, size_t size);`	Allocates space for an array of `nmem` members, each element of which is `size` bytes in size; all bits in the space are initialized to `0`. The function returns the address of the array if successful, and `NULL` otherwise.
`void free(void *ptr);`	Deallocates the space pointed to by `ptr`; `ptr` should be a value previously returned by a call to `calloc()`, `malloc()`, or `realloc()`, or `ptr` can be the null pointer, in which case no action is taken. The behavior is undefined for other pointer values.
`void *malloc(size_t size);`	Allocates an uninitialized block of memory of `size` bytes; the function returns the address of the array if successful, and `NULL` otherwise.
`void *realloc(void *ptr, size_t size);`	Changes the size of the block of memory pointed to by `ptr` to `size` bytes; the contents of the block up to the lesser of the old and new sizes are unaltered; the function returns the location of the block, which may have been moved; if space cannot be reallocated, the function returns `NULL` and leaves the original block unchanged. If `ptr` is `NULL`, the behavior is the same as calling `malloc()` with an argument of `size`; if `size` is zero and `ptr` is not `NULL`, the behavior is the same as calling `free()` with `ptr` as an argument.
`void abort(void);`	Causes abnormal program termination unless the signal `SIGABRT` is caught and the corresponding signal handler does not return; closing of I/O streams and temporary files is implementation dependent; the function executes `raise(SIGABRT)`.
`int atexit(void (*func)(void));`	Registers the function pointed to by `func` to be called upon normal program termination; the implementation should support registration of at least 32 functions, which will be called opposite the order in which they are registered; the function returns zero if registration succeeds, and nonzero otherwise.

TABLE RS.V.33   Continued

Prototype	Description
`void exit(int status);`	Causes normal program termination to occur, first invoking the functions registered by `atexit()`, then flushing all open output streams, and then closing all I/O streams, then closing all files created by `tmpfile()`, and then returning control to the host environment. If `status` is `0` or `EXIT_SUCCESS`, an implementation-defined value indicating successful termination is returned to the host environment; if `status` is `EXIT_FAILURE`, an implementation-defined value indicating unsuccessful termination is returned to the host environment. The effects of other values of `status` are implementation defined.
`void _Exit(int status);`	Similar to `exit()` except that the functions registered by `atexit()` are not called, signal handlers registered by `signal()` are not called, and the handling of open streams is implementation defined (C99).
`char *getenv(const char * name);`	Returns a pointer to a string representing the value of the environmental variable pointed to by `name`; returns `NULL` if it cannot match the specified `name`.
`int system(const char *str);`	Passes the string pointed to by `str` to the host environment to be executed by a command processor, such as DOS or UNIX. If `str` is the `NULL` pointer, the function returns nonzero if a command processor is available, and zero otherwise; if `str` is not `NULL`, the return value is implementation dependent.
`void *bsearch(const void *key, const void *base, size_t nmem, size_t size, int (*comp)(const void *, const void *));`	Searches an array pointed to by `base` having `nmem` members of size `size` for an element matching the object pointed to by `key`; items are compared by the function pointed to by `comp`; the comparison function will return a value less than zero if the key object is less than an array element, zero if they are equivalent, or a value greater than zero if the key object is greater. The function returns a pointer to a matching element, or `NULL` if no element matches; if two or more elements match the key, it is unspecified which of the matching elements will be selected.

Prototype	Description
`void qsort(void *base, size_t nmem, size_t size, int (*comp) (const void *, const void *));`	Sorts the array pointed to by `base` in the order provided by the function pointed to by `comp`; the array has `nmem` elements, each of `size` bytes; the comparison function will return a value less than zero if the object pointed to by the first argument is less than the object pointed to by the second argument, zero if the objects are equivalent, or a value greater than zero if the first object is greater.
`int abs(int n);`	Returns the absolute value of n; the return value may be undefined if n is a negative value with no positive counterpart, which can happen if n is `INT_MIN` in two's complement representation.
`div_t div(int numer, int denom);`	Computes the quotient and remainder from dividing `numer` by `denom`, placing the quotient in the `quot` member of a `div_t` structure and the remainder in the `rem` member; for inexact division, the quotient is the integer of lesser magnitude that is nearest the algebraic quotient (that is, truncate toward zero).
`long labs(int n);`	Returns the absolute value of n; the return value may be undefined if n is a negative value with no positive counterpart, which can happen if n is `LONG_MIN` in two's complement representation.
`ldiv_t ldiv(long numer, long denom);`	Computes the quotient and remainder from dividing `numer` by `denom`, placing the quotient in the `quot` member of an `ldiv_t` structure and the remainder in the `rem` member; for inexact division, the quotient is the integer of lesser magnitude that is nearest the algebraic quotient (that is, truncate toward zero).
`long long llabs(int n);`	Returns the absolute value of n; the return value may be undefined if n is a negative value with no positive counterpart, which can happen if n is `LONG_LONG_MIN` in two's complement representation (C99).

TABLE RS.V.33   Continued

Prototype	Description
`lldiv_t lldiv(long numer, long denom);`	Computes the quotient and remainder from dividing `numer` by `denom`, placing the quotient in the `quot` member of an `lldiv_t` structure and the remainder in the `rem` member; for inexact division, the quotient is the integer of lesser magnitude that is nearest the algebraic quotient—that is, truncate toward zero (C99).
`int mblen(const char *s, size_t n);`	Returns the number of bytes (up to n) constituting the multibyte character pointed to by s, returns 0 if s points to the null character, returns -1 if s does not point to a multibyte character; if s is NULL, returns nonzero if multibyte characters have state-dependent encoding, and zero otherwise.
`int mbtowc(wchar_t *pw, const char *s, size_t n);`	If s is not NULL, determines the number of bytes (up to n) constituting the multibyte character pointed to by s and determines the type wchar_t code for that character; if pw is not NULL, assigns the code to the location pointed to by pw; returns the same value as `mblen(s, n)`.
`int wctomb(char *s, wchar_t wc);`	Converts the character code in wc to the corresponding multibyte character representation and stores it in the array pointed to by s, unless s is NULL; if s is not NULL, it returns -1 if wc does not correspond to a valid multibyte character. If wc is valid, it returns the number of bytes constituting the multibyte character. If s is NULL, it returns nonzero if multibyte characters have state-dependent encoding, and it returns zero otherwise.
`size_t mbstowcs( wchar_t * restrict pwcs, const char *s restrict , size_t n);`	Converts the array of multibyte characters pointed to by s to an array of wide character codes stored at the location beginning at pwcs; conversion proceeds up to n elements in the pwcs array or a null byte in the s array, whichever occurs first. If an invalid multibyte character is encountered, it returns `(size_t) (-1)`; otherwise, it returns the number of array elements filled (excluding a null character, if any).

Prototype	Description
`size_t wcstombs(char * restrict s, const wchart_t * restrict pwcs, size_t n);`	Converts the sequence of wide-character codes stored in the array pointed to by `pwcs` into a multibyte character sequence copied to the location pointed to by `s`, stopping after storing n bytes or a null character, whichever comes first. If an invalid wide-character code is encountered, it returns `(size_t) (-1)`; otherwise, it returns the number of array bytes filled (excluding a null character, if any).

String Handling: `string.h`

The `string.h` library defines the `size_t` type and the `NULL` macro for the null pointer. It provides several functions for analyzing and manipulating character strings and a few that deal with memory more generally. Table RS.V.34 lists the functions.

TABLE RS.V.34   String Functions

Prototype	Description
`void *memchr(const void *s, int c, size_t n);`	Searches for the first occurrence of c (converted to `unsigned char`) in the initial n characters of the object pointed to by `s`; returns a pointer to the first occurrence, `NULL` if none is found.
`int memcmp(const void *s1, const void *s2, size_t n);`	Compares the first n characters of the object pointed to by `s1` to the first n characters of the object pointed to by `s2`, interpreting each value as `unsigned char`. The two objects are identical if all n pairs match; otherwise, the objects compare as the first unmatching pair. Returns zero if the objects are the same, less than zero if the first object is numerically less than the second, and greater than zero if the first object is greater.
`void *memcpy(void * restrict s1, const void * restrict s2, size_t n);`	Copies n bytes from the location pointed to by `s2` to the location pointed to by `s1`; behavior is undefined if the two locations overlap; returns the value of `s1`.
`void *memmove(void *s1, const void *s2, size_t n);`	Copies n bytes from the location pointed to by `s2` to the location pointed to by `s1`; behaves as if copying. First uses a temporary location so that copying to an overlapping location works; returns the value of `s1`.

TABLE RS.V.34 Continued

Prototype	Description
`void *memset(void *s, int v, size_t n);`	Copies the value v (converted to type `unsigned char`) to the first n bytes pointed to by s; returns s.
`char *strcat(char * restrict s1, const char * restrict s2);`	Appends a copy of the string pointed to by s2 (including the null character) to the location pointed to by s1; the first character of the s2 string overwrites the null character of the s1 string; returns s1.
`char *strncat(char * restrict s1, const char * restrict s2, size_t n);`	Appends a copy up to n characters or up to the null character from the string pointed to by s2 to the location pointed to by s1, with the first character of s2 overwriting the null character of s1; a null character is always appended; the function returns s1.
`char *strcpy(char * restrict s1, const char * restrict s2);`	Copies the string pointed to by s2 (including the null character) to the location pointed to by s1; returns s1.
`char *strncpy(char * restrict s1, const char * restrict s2, size_t n);`	Copies up to n characters or up to the null character from the string pointed to by s2 to the location pointed to by s1; if the null character in s2 occurs before n characters are copied, null characters are appended to bring the total to n; if n characters are copied before reaching a null character, no null character is appended; the function returns s1.
`int strcmp(const char *s1, const char *s2);`	Compares the strings pointed to by s1 and s2; two strings are identical if all pairs match; otherwise, the strings compare as the first unmatching pair. Characters are compared using the character code values; the function returns zero if the strings are the same, less than zero if the first string is less than the second, and greater than zero if the string array is greater.
`int strcoll(const char *s1, const char *s2);`	Works like `strcmp()` except that it uses the collating sequence specified by the `LC_COLLATE` category of the current locale as set by the `setlocale()` function.

Prototype	Description
`int strncmp(const char *s1, const char *s2, size_t n);`	Compares up to the first n characters or up to the first null character of the arrays pointed to by s1 and s2; two arrays are identical if all tested pairs match; otherwise, the arrays compare as the first unmatching pair. Characters are compared using the character code values; the function returns zero if the arrays are the same, less than zero if the first array is less than the second, and greater than zero if the first array is greater.
`size_t strxfrm(char * restrict s1, const char * restrict s2, size_t n);`	Transforms the string in s2 and copies up to n characters, including a terminating null character, to the array pointed to by s1; the criterion for the transformation is that two transformed strings will be placed in the same order by `strcmp()` as `strcoll()` would place the untransformed strings; the function returns the length of the transformed string (not including the terminal null character).
`char *strchr(const char *s, int c);`	Searches for the first occurrence of c (converted to char) in the string pointed to by s; the null character is part of the string; returns a pointer to the first occurrence, or NULL if none is found.
`size_t strcspn(const char *s1, const char *s2);`	Returns the length of the maximum initial segment of s1 that does not contain any of the characters found in s2.
`char *strpbrk(const char *s1, const char *s2);`	Returns a pointer to the location of the first character in s1 to match any of the characters in s2; returns NULL if no match is found.
`char *strrchr(const char *s, int c);`	Searches for the last occurrence of c (converted to char) in the string pointed to by s; the null character is part of the string; returns a pointer to the first occurrence, or NULL if none is found.
`size_t strspn(const char *s1, const char *s2);`	Returns the length of the maximum initial segment of s1 that consists entirely of characters from s2.
`char *strstr(const char *s1, const char *s2);`	Returns a pointer to the location of the first occurrence in s1 of the sequence of characters in s2 (excluding the terminating null character); returns NULL if no match is found.

TABLE RS.V.34   Continued

Prototype	Description
```char *strtok(char * restrict s1, const char * restrict s2);```	This function decomposes the string s1 into separate tokens; the string s2 contains the characters that are recognized as token separators. The function is called sequentially. For the initial call, s1 should point to the string to be separated into tokens. The function locates the first token separator that follows a non-separator character and replaces it with a null character. It returns a pointer to a string holding the first token. If no tokens are found, it returns NULL. To find further tokens in the string, call strtok() again, but with NULL as the first argument. Each subsequent call returns a pointer to the next token or to NULL if no further tokens are found. (See the example following this table.)
```char * strerror(int errnum);```	Returns a pointer to an implementation-dependent error message string corresponding to the error number stored in errnum.
```int strlen(const char * s);```	Returns the number of characters (excluding the terminating null character) in the string s.

The `strtok()` function is a bit unusual in how it is used, so here is a short example:

```
#include <stdio.h>
#include <string.h>

int main(void)
{
    char data[] = "  C is\t   too#much\nfun!";
    const char tokseps[] = " \t\n#"; /* separators  */
    char * pt;

    puts(data);
    pt = strtok(data,tokseps);       /* intial call  */
    while (pt)                       /* quit on NULL */
    {
        puts (pt);                   /* show token    */
        pt = strtok(NULL, tokseps);  /* next token    */
    }
    return 0;
}
```

Here is the output:

```
  C is     too#much
fun!
```

```
C
is
too
much
fun!
```

Type-Generic Math: `tgmath.h` (C99)

The `math.h` and `complex.h` libraries provide many instances of functions that differ in type only. For example, the following six functions all compute sines:

```
double sin(double);
float sinf(float);
long double sinl(long double);
double complex csin(double complex);
float csinf(float complex);
long double csinl(long double complex);
```

The `tgmath.h` header file defines macros that expand a generic call to the appropriate function as indicated by the argument type. The following code illustrates using the `sin()` macro, which expands into various forms of the sine function:

```
#include <tgmath.h>
...
double dx, dy;
float fx, fy;
long double complex clx, cly;
dy = sin(dx);   // expands to dy = sin(dx)   (the function)
fy = sin(fx);   // expands to fy = sinf(fx)
cly = sin(clx); // expands to cly = csinl(clyx)
```

The header defines generic macros for three classes of functions. The first class consists of `math.h` and `complex.h` functions defined with six variations, using `l` and `f` suffixes and the `c` prefix, as with the previous `sin()` example. In this case, the generic macro has the same name as the type `double` version of the function.

The second class consists of `math.h` functions defined with three variations, using the `l` and `f` suffixes and having no complex counterparts, such as `erf()`. In this case, the macro name is the same as the suffix-free function, `erf()`, in this example. The effect of using such a macro with a complex argument is undefined.

The third class consists of `complex.h` functions defined with three variations, using the `l` and `f` suffixes and having no real counterparts, such as `cimag()`. In this case, the macro name is the same as the suffix-free function, `cimag()`, in this example. The effect of using such a macro with a real argument is undefined.

Date and Time: `time.h`

The `time.h` header file defines two macros. The first, also defined in many other header files, is `NULL`, representing the null pointer. The second macro is `CLOCKS_PER_SEC`; dividing the value returned by `clock()` by this macro yields time in seconds.

The header file defines the types listed in Table RS.V.35.

TABLE RS.V.35 Types Defined in `time.h`

Type	Description
`size_t`	The integer type returned by the `sizeof` operator
`clock_t`	An arithmetic type suitable to represent time
`time_t`	An arithmetic type suitable to represent time
`struct tm`	A structure type for holding components of calendar time

The components of the calendar type are referred to as *broken-down time*. Table RS.V.36 lists the required members of a **struct tm** structure.

TABLE RS.V.36 Members of a **struct tm** Structure

Member	Description
`int tm_sec`	Seconds after the minute (0–61)
`int tm_min`	Minutes after the hour (0–59)
`int tm_hour`	Hours after midnight (0–23)
`int tm_mday`	Day of the month (0–31)
`int tm_mon`	Months since January (0–11)
`int tm_year`	Years since 1900
`int tm_wday`	Days since Sunday (0–6)
`int tm_yday`	Days since January 1 (0–365)
`int tm_isdst`	Daylight Savings Time flag (greater than zero value means DST is in effect; zero means not in effect; negative means information not available)

The term *calendar time* represents the current date and time; for example, it could be the number of seconds elapsed since the first second of 1900. The term *local time* is the calendar time expressed for a local time zone. Table RS.V.37 lists the time functions.

TABLE RS.V.37 Time Functions

Prototype	Description
`clock_t clock(void);`	Returns the implementation's best approximation of the processor time elapsed since the program was invoked; divide by `CLOCKS_PER_SEC` to get the time in seconds. Returns `(clock_t)(-1)` if the time is not available or representable.

Prototype	Description
`double difftime(time_t t1, time_t t0);`	Calculates the difference (`t1 - t0`) between two calendar times; expresses the result in seconds and returns the result.
`time_t mktime(struct tm *tmptr);`	Converts the broken-down time in the structure pointed to by `tmptr` into a calendar time; having the same encoding used by the `time()` function, the structure is altered in that out-of-range values are adjusted (for example, 2 minutes, 100 seconds becomes 3 minutes, 40 seconds) and `tm_wday` and `tm_yday` are set to the values implied by the other members. Returns `(time_t)(-1)` if the calendar time cannot be represented; otherwise, returns the calendar time in `time_t` format.
`time_t time(time_t *ptm)`	Returns the current calendar time and also places it in the location pointed to by `ptm`, provided `ptm` is not `NULL`. Returns `(time_t)(-1)` if the calendar time is not available.
`char *asctime(const struct tm *tmpt);`	Converts the broken-down time in the structure pointed to by `tmpt` into a string of the form `Thu Feb 26 13:14:33 1998\n\0` and returns a pointer to that string.
`char *ctime(const time_t *ptm);`	Converts the calendar time pointed to by `ptm` into a string in the form `Wed Aug 11 10:48:24 1999\n\0` and returns a pointer to that string.
`struct tm *gmtime(const time_t *ptm);`	Converts the calendar time pointed to by `ptm` into a broken-down time, expressed as Coordinated Universal Time (UTC), formerly known as Greenwich Mean Time (GMT), and returns a pointer to a structure holding that information. Returns `NULL` if UTC is not available.
`struct tm *localtime(const time_t *ptm);`	Converts the calendar time pointed to by `ptm` into a broken-down time, expressed as local time. Stores a `tm` structure and returns a pointer to that structure.

TABLE RS.V.37   Continued

Prototype	Description
`size_t strftime(char * restrict s, size_t max const char * restrict fmt, const struct tm * restrict tmpt);`	Copies string `fmt` to string, `s`, replacing format specifiers (see Table RS.V.38) in `fmt` with appropriate data derived from the contents of the broken-down time structure pointed to by `tmpt`; no more than `max` characters are placed into `s`. The function returns the number of characters placed (excluding the null character); if the resulting string (including null character) is larger than `max` characters, the function returns 0 and the contents of `s` are indeterminate.

Table RS.V.38 shows the format specifiers used by the `strftime()` function. Many replacement values, such as month names, depend on the current locale.

TABLE RS.V.38   Format Specifiers Used by the `strftime()` Function

Format Specifier	Replaced By
%a	Locale's abbreviated weekday name
%A	Locale's full weekday name
%b	Locale's abbreviated month name
%B	Locale's full month name
%c	Locale's appropriate date and time designation
%d	Day of the month as a decimal number (01–31)
%D	Equivalent to "%m/%d%y"
%e	Day of the month as a decimal number, with single digits preceded by a space
%F	Equivalent to "%Y-%m-%d"
%g	The last two digits of the week-based year (00–99)
%G	The week-based year as a decimal number
%h	Equivalent to "%b"
%H	The hour (24-hour clock) as a decimal number (00–23)
%I	The hour (12-hour clock) as a decimal number (01–12)
%j	The day of the year as a decimal number (001–366)
%m	The month as a decimal number (01–12)

Format Specifier	Replaced By
%n	The newline character
%M	The minute as a decimal number (00–59)
%p	Locale's equivalent of a.m./p.m. for 12-hour clock
%r	Locale's 12-hour clock time
%R	Equivalent to "%H:%M"
%S	The second as a decimal number (00–61)
%t	The horizontal tab character
%T	Equivalent to "%H:%M:%S"
%u	ISO 8601 weekday number (1–7), with Monday being 1
%U	Week number of the year, counting Sunday as the first day of week 1 (00–53)
%V	ISO 8601 week number of the year, counting Sunday as the first day of week 1 (00–53)
%w	Weekday as a decimal, beginning with Sunday (0–6)
%W	Week number of the year, counting Monday as the first day of week 1 (00–53)
%x	The locale's date representation
%X	The locale's time representation
%y	The year without century as a decimal number (00–99)
%Y	The year with century as a decimal number
%z	Offset from UTC in ISO 8601 format ("−800" meaning eight hours behind Greenwich, thus eight hours west); no characters are substituted if the information is not available
%Z	The time zone name; no characters are substituted if the information is not available
%%	% (that is, the percent sign)

Extended Multibyte and Wide-Character Utilities: wchar.h (C99)

Each implementation has a basic character set, and the C char type is required to be wide enough to handle that set. An implementation may also support an extended character set, and these characters may have a representation that requires more than one byte per character. Multibyte characters can be stored along with single-byte characters in an ordinary array of char, with particular byte values indicating the presence and size of a multibyte character. The interpretation of multibyte characters can depend on a *shift state*. In the initial shift state, single-byte characters retain their usual interpretation. Specific multibyte characters can then change the shift state. A particular shift state stays in effect until explicitly changed.

The `wchar_t` type provides a second way of representing extended characters, with the type being wide enough to represent the encoding of any member of the extended character set. This wide-character representation allows single characters to be stored in a `wchar_t` variable and strings of wide characters to be stored in an array of `wchar_t`. The wide character representation of a character need not be the same as the multibyte representation, because the latter may use shift states whereas the former does not.

The `wchar.h` header file provides facilities for handling both representations of extended characters. It defines the types shown in Table RS.V.39. (Some of these types are also defined in other header files.)

TABLE RS.V.39   Types Defined in `wchar.h`

Type	Description
wchar_t	An integer type that can represent the largest extended character set specified by supported locales
wint_t	An integer type that can hold any value of the extended character set plus at least one value not a member of the extended character set
size_t	The integer type returned by the `sizeof` operator
mbstate_t	A non-array type that can hold the conversion state information needed to convert between sequences of multibyte character and of wide characters
struct tm	A structure type for holding components of calendar time

The header file also defines some macros, as shown in Table RS.V.40.

TABLE RS.V.40   Macros Defined in `wchar.h`

Macro	Description
NULL	The null pointer.
WCHAR_MAX	The maximum value for `wchar_t`.
WCHAR_MIN	The minimum value for `wchar_t`.
WEOF	A constant expression of type `wint_t` that does not correspond to any member of the extended character set; the wide character equivalent of `EOF`, it's used to indicate end-of-file for wide-character input.

The library provides input/output functions that are analogs to the standard I/O functions described in `stdio.h`. In those cases that a standard I/O function returns `EOF`, the corresponding wide-character function returns `WEOF`. Table RS.V.41 lists these functions.

TABLE RS.V.41   Wide-Character I/O Functions

Function Prototype
`int fwprintf(FILE * restrict stream,const wchar_t * restrict format, ...);`
`int fwscanf(FILE * restrict stream,const wchar_t * restrict format, ...);`
`int swprintf(wchar_t * restrict s, size_t n,const wchar_t * restrict format, ...);`
`int swscanf(const wchar_t * restrict s,const wchar_t * restrict format, ...);`
`int vfwprintf(FILE * restrict stream,` `const wchar_t * restrict format, va_list arg);`
`int vfwscanf(FILE * restrict stream,` `const wchar_t * restrict format, va_list arg);`
`int vswprintf(wchar_t * restrict s, size_t n,` `const wchar_t * restrict format, va_list arg);`
`int vswscanf(const wchar_t * restrict s,` `const wchar_t * restrict format, va_list arg);`
`int vwprintf(const wchar_t * restrict format,va_list arg);`
`int vwscanf(const wchar_t * restrict format,va_list arg);`
`int wprintf(const wchar_t * restrict format, ...);`
`int wscanf(const wchar_t * restrict format, ...);`
`wint_t fgetwc(FILE *stream);`
`wchar_t *fgetws(wchar_t * restrict s, int n,FILE * restrict stream);`
`wint_t fputwc(wchar_t c, FILE *stream);`
`int fputws(const wchar_t * restrict s,FILE * restrict stream);`
`int fwide(FILE *stream, int mode);`
`wint_t getwc(FILE *stream);`

TABLE RS.V.41 *Continued*

Function Prototype
`wint_t getwchar(void);`
`wint_t putwc(wchar_t c, FILE *stream);`
`wint_t putwchar(wchar_t c);`
`wint_t ungetwc(wint_t c, FILE *stream);`

There is one wide-character I/O function without a standard I/O counterpart:

`int fwide(FILE *stream, int mode);`

If `mode` is positive, it first attempts to make the stream represented by the parameter `stream` *wide-character oriented*; if `mode` is negative, it first attempts to make the stream *byte oriented*; if `mode` is 0, it doesn't attempt to change the stream orientation. It attempts to change the orientation only if the stream initially has none. In all cases, it returns a positive value if the stream is wide-character oriented, a negative value if the stream is byte oriented, and zero if the stream has no orientation.

The header provides several string conversion and manipulation functions modeled on those in `string.h`. In general, `str` in the `string.h` identifier is replaced with `wcs`, so `wcstod()` is the wide character version of the `strtod()` function. Table RS.V.42 lists these functions.

TABLE RS.V.42 Wide-Character String Utilities

Function Prototype
`double wcstod(const wchar_t * restrict nptr,` `wchar_t ** restrict endptr);`
`float wcstof(const wchar_t * restrict nptr,` `wchar_t ** restrict endptr);`
`long double wcstold(const wchar_t * restrict nptr,` `wchar_t ** restrict endptr);`
`long int wcstol(const wchar_t * restrict nptr,` `wchar_t ** restrict endptr, int base);`
`long long int wcstoll(const wchar_t * restrict nptr,` `wchar_t ** restrict endptr, int base);`
`unsigned long int wcstoul(const wchar_t * restrict nptr,` `wchar_t ** restrict endptr, int base);`

`unsigned long long int wcstoull(`
`const wchar_t * restrict nptr,`
`wchar_t ** restrict endptr, int base);`

Function Prototype

```
wchar_t *wcscpy(wchar_t * restrict s1,
const wchar_t * restrict s2);
```

```
wchar_t *wcsncpy(wchar_t * restrict s1,
const wchar_t * restrict s2, size_t n);
```

```
wchar_t *wcscat(wchar_t * restrict s1,
const wchar_t * restrict s2);
```

```
wchar_t *wcsncat(wchar_t * restrict s1,
const wchar_t * restrict s2, size_t n);
```

```
int wcscmp(const wchar_t *s1, const wchar_t *s2);
```

```
int wcscoll(const wchar_t *s1, const wchar_t *s2);
```

```
int wcsncmp(const wchar_t *s1, const wchar_t *s2,
size_t n);
```

```
size_t wcsxfrm(wchar_t * restrict s1,
const wchar_t * restrict s2, size_t n);
```

```
wchar_t *wcschr(const wchar_t *s, wchar_t c);
```

```
size_t wcscspn(const wchar_t *s1, const wchar_t *s2);
```

```
size_t wcslen(const wchar_t *s);
```

```
wchar_t *wcspbrk(const wchar_t *s1, const wchar_t *s2);
```

```
wchar_t *wcsrchr(const wchar_t *s, wchar_t c);
```

```
size_t wcsspn(const wchar_t *s1, const wchar_t *s2);
```

```
wchar_t *wcsstr(const wchar_t *s1, const wchar_t *s2);
```

```
wchar_t *wcstok(wchar_t * restrict s1,
const wchar_t * restrict s2, wchar_t ** restrict ptr);
```

```
wchar_t *wmemchr(const wchar_t *s, wchar_t c, size_t n);
```

```
int wmemcmp(wchar_t * restrict s1,
const wchar_t * restrict s2, size_t n);
```

```
wchar_t *wmemcpy(wchar_t * restrict s1,
const wchar_t * restrict s2, size_t n);
```

```
wchar_t *wmemmove(wchar_t *s1, const wchar_t *s2,
size_t n);
```

```
wchar_t *wmemset(wchar_t *s, wchar_t c, size_t n);
```

The header file also declares a one-time function modeled on the `strftime()` function from the `time.h` header file:

```
size_t wcsftime(wchar_t * restrict s, size_t maxsize,
const wchar_t * restrict format,
const struct tm * restrict timeptr);
```

Finally, the header file declares several functions for converting wide-character strings to multibyte strings, and vice versa, as shown in Table RS.V.43.

TABLE RS.V.43   Wide-Character, Multibyte Conversion Functions

Prototype	Description
`wint_t btowc(int c);`	If `(unsigned char)` c is a valid single-byte character in the initial shift state, the function returns the wide-character representation; otherwise, the function returns WEOF.
`int wctob(wint_t c);`	If c is a member of the extended character set whose multibyte character's representation in the initial shift state is a single byte, the function returns the single-byte representation as an `unsigned char` converted to an `int`; otherwise, the function returns EOF.
`int mbsinit(const mbstate_t *ps);`	The function returns nonzero if ps is the null pointer, or points to a data object that specifies an initial conversion state; otherwise, the function returns zero.

`size_t mbrlen(`
`const char * restrict s,`
`size_t n,`
`mbstate_t * restrict ps);`
	The `mbrlen()` function is equivalent to the call `mbrtowc(NULL, s, n, ps != NULL ? ps : &internal)`, where `internal` is the `mbstate_t` object for the `mbrlen()` function, except that the expression designated by ps is evaluated only once.

`size_t mbrtowc(`
`wchar_t * restrict pwc,`
`const char * restrict s, size_t n,`
`mbstate_t * restrict ps);`
	If s is the null pointer, the call is equivalent to setting pwc to the null pointer and n to 1. If s is not null, the function inspects at most n bytes to determine the number of bytes needed to complete the next multibyte character (including any shift sequences). If the function determines that the next multibyte character is complete and valid, it determines the value of the corresponding wide character and then, if pwc is not a null pointer, stores that value in the object pointed to by pwc. If the corresponding wide character is the null wide character, the resulting state described is the initial conversion state. The function returns 0 if the null wide character is detected. If it detects another valid wide character, it returns the number of bytes needed to complete the character. If n bytes

Prototype	Description
	aren't enough to specify a valid wide character but appear to potentially represent part of one, the function returns −2. If there is a coding error, the function returns −1, stores `EILSEQ` in `errno`, and stores no value.

`size_t wcrtomb(char * restrict s,`
`wchar_t wc,`
`mbstate_t * restrict ps);`
	If `s` is the null pointer, the call is equivalent to setting `wc` to the null wide character and using an internal buffer for the first argument. If `s` is not a null pointer, the `wcrtomb()` function determines the number of bytes needed to represent the multibyte character that corresponds to the wide character given by `wc` (including any shift sequences), and stores the multibyte character representation in the array whose first element is pointed to by `s`. At most, `MB_CUR_MAX` bytes are stored. If `wc` is a null wide character, a null byte is stored, preceded by any shift sequence needed to restore the initial shift state; the resulting state described is the initial conversion state. If `wc` is a valid wide character, the function returns the number of bytes to store the multibyte version, include bytes, if any, specifying a shift state. If `wc` is not valid, the function stores `EILSEQ` in `errno`, and returns −1.

`size_t mbsrtowcs(`
`wchar_t * restrict dst,`
`const char ** restrict src,`
`size_t len,`
`mbstate_t * restrict ps);`
	The `mbstrtowcs()` function converts a sequence of multibyte characters that begins in the conversion state described by the object pointed to by `ps`, from the array indirectly pointed to by `src`, into a sequence of corresponding wide characters. If `dst` is not a null pointer, the converted characters are stored in the array pointed to by `dst`. Conversion continues up to and including a terminating null character, which is also stored. Conversion stops earlier in two cases: when a sequence of bytes is encountered that does not form a valid multibyte character, and (if `dst` is not a null pointer) when `len` wide characters have been stored into the array pointed to by `dst`. Each conversion takes place as if by a call to the `mbrtowc()` function. If `dst` is not a null pointer, the pointer object pointed to by `src` is assigned either a null pointer (if conversion stopped due to reaching a terminating null character) or the address just past the last multibyte character converted (if any). If conversion stopped due to reaching a terminating null character and if `dst` is not a null pointer, the resulting state described is the initial conversion state. If successful, the function returns the number of multibyte characters successfully converted (excluding the null character, if any); otherwise it returns −1.

TABLE RS.V.43   Continued

Prototype	Description
| ```
size_t wcsrtombs(
char * restrict dst,
const wchar_t ** restrict src,
size_t len,
mbstate_t * restrict ps);
``` | The wcsrtombs() function converts a sequence of wide characters from the array indirectly pointed to by src into a sequence of corresponding multibyte characters that begins in the conversion state described by the object pointed to by ps. If dst is not a null pointer, the converted characters are then stored into the array pointed to by dst. Conversion continues up to and including a terminating null wide character, which is also stored. Conversion stops earlier in two cases: when a wide character is reached that does not correspond to a valid multibyte character, and (if dst is not a null pointer) when the next multibyte character would exceed the limit of len total bytes to be stored into the array pointed to by dst. Each conversion takes place as if by a call to the wcrtomb function. If dst is not a null pointer, the pointer object pointed to by src is assigned either a null pointer (if conversion stopped due to reaching a terminating null wide character) or the address just past the last wide character converted (if any). If conversion stopped due to reaching a terminating null wide character, the resulting state described is the initial conversion state. If successful, the function returns the number of multibyte characters in the resulting multibyte sequence (excluding the null character, if any); otherwise it returns −1. |

Wide Character Classification and Mapping Utilities: wctype.h (C99)

The wctype.h library provides wide character analogs to the character functions of ctype.h along with a few additional functions. It also defines the three types and the macro shown in Table RS.V.44.

TABLE RS.V.44   wctype.h Types and Macros

Macro	Description
wint_t	An integer type that can hold any value of the extended character set plus at least one value not a member of the extended character set.
wctrans_t	A scalar type that can represent locale-specific character mappings.
```

Macro	Description
wctype_t	A scalar type that can represent locale-specific character classifications.
WEOF	A constant expression of type wint_t that does not correspond to any member of the extended character set; the wide character equivalent of EOF, it's used to indicate end-of-file for wide-character input.

The character classifications in this library return true (nonzero) if the wide-character argument satisfies the conditions described by the function. In general, the wide-character function returns true if the corresponding ctype.h function returns true for the single-byte character corresponding to the wide character. Table RS.V.45 lists these functions.

TABLE RS.V.45 Wide-Character Classification Functions

Prototype	Description
int iswalnum(wint_t wc);	Returns true if wc represents an alphanumeric (alphabetic or numeric) character
int iswalpha(wint_t wc);	Returns true if wc represents an alphabetic character
int iswblank(wint_t wc);	Returns true if wc represents a blank
int iswcntrl(wint_t wc);	Returns true if wc represents a control character
int iswdigit(wint_t wc);	Returns true if wc represents a digit
int iswgraph(wint_t wc);	Returns true if iswprint(wc) is true and iswspace(wc) is false
int iswlower(wint_t wc);	Returns true if wc represents a lowercase character
int iswprint(wint_t wc);	Returns true if wc represents a printable character
int iswpunct(wint_t wc);	Returns true if wc represents a punctuation character
int iswspace(wint_t wc);	Returns true if wc represents a tab, space, or newline
int iswupper(wint_t wc);	Returns true if wc corresponds to a uppercase character
int iswxdigit(wint_t wc);	Returns true if wc represents a hexadecimal digit

The library also includes two classification functions that are termed extensible because they use the LC_CTYPE value of the current locale to classify characters. Table RS.V.46 lists these functions.

TABLE RS.V.46   Extensible Wide-Character Classification Functions

Prototype	Description
`int iswctype(wint_t wc, wctype_t desc);`	Returns true if `wc` has the property described by `desc`. (See discussion in the accompanying text.)
`wctype_t wctype(const char *property);`	The `wctype` function constructs a value with type `wctype_t` that describes a class of wide characters identified by the string argument property. If the property identifies a valid class of wide characters according to the `LC_CTYPE` category of the current locale, the `wctype()` function returns a nonzero value that is valid as the second argument to the `iswctype()` function; otherwise, it returns zero.

The valid arguments for `wctype()` consist of the names of the wide-character classification functions stripped of the `isw` prefix and expressed as strings. For example, `wctype("alpha")` characterizes the class of characters tested by the `iswalpha()` function. Therefore, the call

`iswctype(wc, wctype("alpha"))`

is equivalent to the call

`iswalpha(wc)`

except that characters are classified using the `LC_CTYPE` categories.

The library provides four conversion-related functions. Two are wide-character equivalents to `toupper()` and `tolower()` from the `ctype.h` library. The third is an extensible version that uses the `LC_CTYPE` setting from the locale to determine which characters are considered uppercase or lowercase. The fourth provides suitable classification arguments for the third. Table RS.V.47 lists these functions.

TABLE RS.V.47   Wide-Character Transformation Functions

Prototype	Description
`wint_t towlower(wint_t wc);`	Returns the uppercase version of `wc` if `wc` is lowercase; otherwise, returns `wc`.
`wint_t towupper(wint_t wc);`	Returns the lowercase version of `wc` if `wc` is uppercase; otherwise, returns `wc`.
`wint_t towctrans(wint_t wc, wctrans_t desc);`	Returns the lowercase version of `wc` (as determined by the `LC_CTYPE` setting) if `desc` is equal to the return value of `wctrans("lower")`; returns the uppercase version of `wc` (as determined by the `LC_CTYPE` setting) if `desc` is equal to the return value of `wctrans("upper")`.

Prototype	Description
`wctrans_t wctrans(const char *property);`	If the argument is `"upper"` or `"lower"`, the function returns a `wctrans_t` value usable as an argument to `towctrans()` and reflecting the `LC_CTYPE` setting; otherwise, returns 0.

Section VI: Extended Integer Types

As described in Chapter 3, "Data and C," the C99 header file `inttypes.h` provides a systematic set of alternative names for the various integer types. These names describe the properties of the type more clearly than do the standard names. For example, type `int` might be 16 bits, 32 bits, or 64 bits, but the `int32_t` type always is 32 bits.

More precisely, the `inttypes.h` header file defines macros that can be used with `scanf()` and `printf()` to read and write integers of these types. This header file includes the `stdlib.h` header file, which provides the actual type definitions. The formatting macros are strings that can be concatenated with other strings to produce the proper formatting directions.

The types are defined using `typedef`. For example, a system with a 32-bit `int` might use this definition:

```
typedef int int32_t;
```

The format specifiers are defined using the `#define` directive. For example, a system using the previous definition for `int32_t` might have this definition:

```
#define PRId32 "d"    // output specifier
#define SCNd32 "d"    // input specifier
```

Using these definitions, you could declare an extended integer variable, input a value, and display it as follows:

```
int32_t cd_sales;  // 32-bit integer
scanf("%" SCNd32, &cd_sales);
printf("CD sales = %10" PRId32 " units\n", cd_sales);
```

String concatenation then combines strings, if needed, to get the final control string. Thus, the previous code gets converted to the following:

```
int cd_sales;  // 32-bit integer
scanf("%d", &cd_sales);
printf("CD sales = %10d units\n", cd_sales);
```

If you moved the original code to a system with a 16-bit `int`, that system might define `int32_t` as `long`, `PRId32` as `"ld"`, and `SCNd32` as `"ld"`. But you could use the same code, knowing that it uses a 32-bit integer.

The rest of this reference section lists the extended types along with the format specifiers and macros representing the type limits.

Exact-Width Types

One set of `typedef`s identify types with precise sizes. The general form is `intN_t` for signed types and `uintN_t` for unsigned types, with *N* indicating the number of bits. Note, however, that not all systems can support all the types. For example, there could be a system for which the smallest usable memory size is 16 bits; such a system would not support the `int8_t` and `uint8_t` types. The format macros can use either `d` or `i` for the signed types, so `PRIi8` and `SCNi8` also work. For the unsigned types, you can substitute `o`, `x`, or `X` for `u` to obtain the `%o`, `%x`, or `%X` specifier instead of `%u`. For example, you can use `PRIX32` to print a `uint32_t` type value in hexadecimal format. Table RS.VI.1 lists the exact-width types, format specifiers, and value limits.

TABLE RS.VI.1   Exact-Width Types

Type Name	printf() Specifier	scanf() Specifier	Minimum Value	Maximum Value
int8_t	PRId8	SCNd8	INT8_MIN	INT8_MAX
int16_t	PRId16	SCNd16	INT16_MIN	INT16_MAX
int32_t	PRId32	SCNd32	INT32_MIN	INT32_MAX
int64_t	PRId64	SCNd64	INT64_MIN	INT64_MAX
uint8_t	PRIu8	SCNu8	0	UINT8_MAX
uint16_t	PRIu16	SCNu16	0	UINT16_MAX
uint32_t	PRIu32	SCNu32	0	UINT32_MAX
uint64_t	PRIu64	SCNu64	0	UINT64_MAX

Minimum-Width Types

The minimum-width types guarantee a type that is at least a certain number of bits in size. These types always exist. For example, a system that does not support 8-bit units could define `int_least_8` as a 16-bit type. Table RS.VI.2 lists minimum-width types, format specifiers, and value limits.

TABLE RS.VI.2   Minimum-Width Types

Type Name	printf() Specifier	scanf() Specifier	Minimum Value	Maximum Value
int_least8_t	PRILEASTd8	SCNLEASTd8	INT_LEAST8_MIN	INT_LEAST8_MAX
int_least16_t	PRILEASTd16	SCNLEASTd16	INT_LEAST16_MIN	INT_LEAST16_MAX

Type Name	printf() Specifier	scanf() Specifier	Minimum Value	Maximum Value
int_least32_t	PRILEASTd32	SCNLEASTd32	INT_LEAST32_MIN	INT_LEAST32_MAX
int_least 64_t	PRILEASTd64	SCNLEASTd64	INT_LEAST64_MIN	INT_LEAST64_MAX
uint_least 8_t	PRILEASTu8	SCNLEASTu8	0	UINT_LEAST8_MAX
uint_least 16_t	PRILEASTu16	SCNLEASTu16	0	UINT_LEAST16_MAX
uint_least 32_t	PRILEASTu32	SCNLEASTu32	0	UINT_LEAST32_MAX
uint_least 64_t	PRILEASTu64	SCNLEASTu64	0	UINT_LEAST64_MAX

Fastest Minimum-Width Types

For a particular system, some integer representations can be faster than others. For example, int_least16_t might be implemented as short, but the system might do arithmetic faster using type int. So inttypes.h also defines the fastest type for representing at least a certain number of bits. These types always exist. In some cases, there might be no clear-cut choice for fastest; in that case, the system simply specifies one of the choices. Table RS.VI.3 lists fastest minimum-width types, format specifiers, and value limits.

TABLE RS.VI.3   Fastest Minimum-Width Types

Type Name	printf() Specifier	scanf() Specifier	Minimum Value	Maximum Value
int_fast8_t	PRIFASTd8	SCNFASTd8	INT_FAST8_MIN	INT_FAST8_MAX
int_fast16_t	PRIFASTd16	SCNFASTd16	INT_FAST16_MIN	INT_FAST16_MAX
int_fast32_t	PRIFASTd32	SCNFASTd32	INT_FAST32_MIN	INT_FAST32_MAX
int_fast 64_t	PRIFASTd64	SCNFASTd64	INT_FAST64_MIN	INT_FAST64_MAX
uint_fast 8_t	PRIFASTu8	SCNFASTu8	0	UINT_FAST8_MAX
uint_fast 16_t	PRIFASTu16	SCNFASTu16	0	UINT_FAST16_MAX
uint_fast 32_t	PRIFASTu32	SCNFASTu32	0	UINT_FAST32_MAX
uint_fast 64_t	PRIFASTu64	SCNFASTu64	0	UINT_FAST64_MAX

Maximum-Width Types

Sometimes you may want the largest integer type available. Table RS.VI.4 lists these types. They may, in fact, be wider than `long long` or `unsigned long long`, because a system may provide additional types wider than the required types.

TABLE RS.VI.4   Maximum-Width Types

Type Name	printf() Specifier	scanf() Specifier	Minimum Value	Maximum Value
intmax_t	PRIdMAX	SCNdMAX	INTMAX_MIN	INTMAX_MAX
uintmax_t	PRIuMAX	SCBuMAX	0	UINTMAX_MAX

Integers That Can Hold Pointer Values

The `inttypes.h` header file (via the included `stdint.h` header file) defines two integer types, listed in Table RS.VI.5, that can hold pointer values accurately. That is, if you assign a type `void *` value to one of these types, and then assign the integer type back to the pointer, no information is lost. Either or both types might not exist.

TABLE RS.VI.5   Integer Types for Holding Pointer Values

Type Name	printf() Specifier	scanf() Specifier	Minimum Value	Maximum Value
intptr_t	PRIdPTR	SCNdPTR	INTPTR_MIN	INTPTR_MAX
uintptr_t	PRIuPTR	SCBuPTR	0	UINTPTR_MAX

Extended Integer Constants

You can indicate a long constant with the `L` suffix, as in `445566L`. How do you indicate that a constant is type `int32_t`? Use macros defined in `inttypes.h`. For example, the expression `INT32_C(445566)` expands to a type `int32_t` constant. Essentially, the macro is a type cast to the underlying type—that is, to the fundamental type that represents `int32_t` in a particular implementation.

The macro names are formed by taking the type name, replacing the `_t` with `_C`, and making all the letters uppercase. For example, to make `1000` a type `uint_least64_t` constant, use the expression `UINT_LEAST64_C(1000)`.

Section VII: Expanded Character Support

C wasn't designed originally as an international programming language. Its choice of characters was based on the more or less standard U.S. keyboard. The international popularity of C, however, has led to several extensions supporting different and larger character sets. This section of the reference provides an overview of these additions.

Trigraph Sequences

Some keyboards don't provide all the symbols used in C. Therefore, C provides alternative representations of several symbols with a set of three-character sequences, called *trigraph sequences*. Table RS.VII.1 lists these trigraphs.

TABLE RS.VII.1 Trigraph Sequences

Trigraph	Symbol	Trigraph	Symbol	Trigraph	Symbol
??=	#	??(	[	??/	\
??)	]	??'	^	??<	{
??!	|	??>	}	??-	~

C replaces all occurrences of these trigraphs in a source code file, even in a quoted string, with the corresponding symbol. Thus,

```
??=include <stdio.h>
??=define LIM 100
int main()
??<
    int q??(LIM??);
    printf("More to come.??/n");
    ...
??>
```

becomes the following:

```
#include <stdio.h>
#define LIM 100
int main()
{
    int q[LIM];
    printf("More to come.\n");
    ...
}
```

You may have to turn on a compiler flag to activate this feature.

Digraphs

Recognizing the clumsiness of the trigraph system, C99 provides two-character tokens, called *digraphs*, that can be used instead of certain standard C punctuators. Table RS.VII.2 lists these digraphs.

TABLE RS.VII.2 Digraphs

Digraph	Symbol	Digraph	Symbol	Digraph	Symbol
<:	[	:>	]	<%	{
%>	}	%:	#	%:%:	##

Unlike trigraphs, digraphs within a quoted string have no special meaning. Thus,

```
%:include <stdio.h>
%:define LIM 100
int main()
<%
    int q<:LIM:>;
    printf("More to come.:>");
    ...
%>
```

behaves the same as the following:

```
#include <stdio.h>
#define LIM 100
int main()
{
    int q[LIM];
 printf("More to come.:>");   // :> just part of string
    ...
}                             // :> same as }
```

Alternative Spellings: `iso646.h`

Using trigraph sequences, you can write the || operator as ??!??!, which is a bit unappealing. C99, via the `iso646.h` header, provides macros that expand into operators, as shown in Table RS.VII.3. The standard refers to these macros as *alternative spellings*.

TABLE RS.VII.3 Alternative Spellings

Macro	Operator	Macro	Operator	Macro	Operator
and	&&	and_eq	&=	bitand	&
bitor	|	compl	~	not	!

Macro	Operator	Macro	Operator	Macro	Operator
not_eq	!=	or	||	or_eq	|=
xor	^	xor_eq	^=		

If you include the `iso646.h` header file, a statement such as

```
if(x == M1 or x == M2)
    x and_eq 0XFF;
```

is expanded to the following:

```
if(x == M1 || x == M2)
    x &= 0XFF;
```

Multibyte Characters

The standard describes a multibyte character as a sequence of one or more bytes representing a member of the extended character set of either the source or execution environment. The source environment is the one in which you prepare the source code; the execution environment is the one in which you run the compiled program. The two can be different. For example, you could develop a program in one environment with the intent of running in another environment. The extended character set is a superset of the basic character set that C requires.

An implementation may provide an extended character set that allows you, for example, to enter keyboard characters not corresponding to the basic character set. These can be used in string literals and character constants and can appear in files. An implementation may also provide multibyte equivalents of characters in the basic character set that can be used instead of trigraphs or digraphs.

A German implementation, for example, might allow you to use an umlauted character in a string:

```
puts("eins zwei drei vier fünf");
```

Universal Character Names (UCNs)

Multibyte characters can be used in strings but not in identifiers. Universal character names (UCNs) are a C99 addition that allows you to use characters from an extended character set as part of identifier names. The system extends the escape sequence concept to allow encoding of characters from the ISO/IEC 10646 standard. This standard is the joint work of the International Organization for Standardization (ISO) and the International Electrotechnical Commission (IEC) and provides numeric codes for a vast list of characters.

There are two forms of UCN sequences. The first is `\u` *hexquad*, where *hexquad* is a sequence of four hexadecimal digits; `\u00F6` is an example. The second is `\U` *hexquad* *hexquad*; `\U0000AC01` is an example. Because each hexadecimal digit corresponds to four bits, the `\u` form can be used for codes representable by a 16-bit integer, and the `\U` form can be used for codes representable by a 32-bit integer.

If your system implements UCNs and includes the desired characters in the extended character set, UCNs can be used in strings, character constants, and identifiers:

```
wchar_t value\u00F6\u00F8 = '\u00f6';
```

Wide Characters

C99, through the `wchar.h` and `wctype.h` libraries, provides yet more support for larger character sets through the use of wide characters. These header files define `wchar_t` as an integer type; the exact type is implementation dependent. Its intended use is to hold characters from an extended character set that is a superset of the basic character set. By definition, the `char` type is sufficient to handle the basic character set. The `wchar_t` type may need more bits to handle a greater range of code values. For example, `char` might be an 8-bit byte and `wchar_t` might be a 16-bit `unsigned short`.

Wide-character constants and string literals are indicated with an `L` prefix, and you can use the `%lc` and `%ls` modifiers to display wide-character data:

```
wchar_t wch = L'I';
wchar_t w_arr[20] = L"am wide!";
printf("%lc %ls\n", wch, w_arr);
```

If, for example, `wchar_t` is implemented as a 2-byte unit, the 1-byte code for `'I'` would be stored in the low-order byte of `wch`. Characters not from the standard set might require both bytes to hold the character code. You could use universal character codes, for example, to indicate characters whose code values exceed the `char` range:

```
wchar_t w = L'\u00E2'; /* 16-bit code value */
```

An array of `wchar_t` values can hold a wide-character string, with each element holding a single wide-character code. A `wchar_t` value with a code value of `0` is the `wchar_t` equivalent of the null character, and it is termed a *null wide character*. It is used to terminate wide-character strings.

You can use the `%lc` and `%ls` specifiers to read wide characters:

```
wchar_t wch;
wchar_t w_arr[20];
puts("Enter your grade:");
scanf("%lc", &wch);
puts("Enter your first name:");
scanff("%ls",w_arr);
```

The `wchar.h` header file offers further wide-character support. In particular, it provides wide-character I/O functions, wide-character conversion functions, and wide-character string-manipulation functions. For the most part, they are wide-character equivalents of existing functions. For example, you can use `fwprintf()` and `wprintf()` for output and `fwscanf()` and `wscanf()` for input. The main differences are that these functions require a wide-character control string and they deal with input and output streams of wide characters. For example, the following displays information as a sequence of wide characters:

```
wchar_t * pw = L"Points to a wide-character string";
int dozen = 12;
wprintf(L"Item %d: %ls\n", dozen, pw);
```

Similarly, there are `getwchar()`, `putwchar()`, `fgetws()`, and `fputws()` functions. The header defines a `WEOF` macro that plays the same role that `EOF` does for byte-oriented I/O. It's required to be a value that does not correspond to a valid character. Because it is possible that all values of `wchar_t` type are valid characters, the library defines a `wint_t` type that can encompass all `wchar_t` values plus `WEOF`.

There are equivalents to the `string.h` library functions. For example, `wcscpy(ws2, ws1)` copies the wide-character string pointed to by `ws1` to the wide-character array pointed to by `ws2`. Similarly, there is a `wcscmp()` function for comparing wide strings, and so on.

The `wctype.h` header file adds character-classification functions to the mix. For example, `iswdigit()` returns true if its wide-character argument is a digit, and the `iswblank()` function returns true if its argument is a blank. The standard values for a blank are a space, written as `L' '`, and a horizontal tab, written as `L'\t'`.

Wide Characters and Multibyte Characters

Wide characters and multibyte characters are two different approaches to dealing with extended character sets. A multibyte character, for example, might be a single byte, two bytes, three bytes, or more. All wide characters will have just one width. Multibyte characters might use a shift state (that is, a byte that determines how subsequent bytes are interpreted); wide characters don't have a shift state. A file of multibyte characters would be read into an ordinary array of `char` using the standard input functions; a file of wide characters would be read into a wide-character array using one of the wide-character input functions.

C99, through the `wchar.h` library, provides functions for converting between these two representations. The `mbrtowc()` function converts a multibyte character to a wide character, and the `wcrtomb()` function converts a wide character to a multibyte character. Similarly, the `mbstrtowcs()` function converts a multibyte string to a wide character string, and the `wcstrtombs()` function converts a wide character string to a multibyte string.

Section VIII: C99 Numeric Computational Enhancements

Historically, FORTRAN has been the premier language for numerical scientific and engineering computation. C90 brought C computational methods into closer agreement with FORTRAN. For example, the specification of floating-point characteristics used in `float.h` is based on the model developed by the FORTRAN standardization committee. The C99 standard continues the work of enhancing C's appropriateness for computational work.

The IEC Floating-Point Standard

The International Electotechnical Committee (IEC) has published a standard for floating-point calculations (IEC 60559). The standard includes discussion of floating-point formats, precision, NaNs, infinities, rounding practices, conversions, exceptions, recommended functions and algorithms, and so on. C99 accepts this standard as a guide to the C implementation of floating-point calculations. Most of the C99 additions to floating-point facilities are part of this effort, such as the `fenv.h` header file and several of the new math functions.

However, it could be that an implementation doesn't meet all the requirements of IEC 60559; for example, the underlying hardware may not be up to the task. Therefore, C99 defines two macros that can be used in preprocessor directives to check for compliance. First, the macro

```
__STDC_IEC_559__
```

is conditionally defined as the constant 1 if the implementation conforms to IEC 60559 floating-point specifications. Second, the macro

```
__STDC_IEC_559_COMPLEX__
```

is conditionally defined as the constant 1 if the implementation adheres to IEC 60559–compatible complex arithmetic.

If an implementation doesn't define these macros, there is no guarantee of IEC60559 compliance.

The `fenv.h` Header File

The `fenv.h` header file provides a means of interacting with the floating-point environment. That is, it allows you to set floating-point *control mode values* that govern how floating-point calculations take place, and it allows you to determine the value of floating-point status flags, or *exceptions*, that report information about the effects of an arithmetic calculation. An example of a control mode setting is specifying the method used to round numbers. An example of a status flag is a flag that is set if an operation produces floating-point overflow. An operation that sets a status flag is described as *raising an exception*.

The status flags and control modes are meaningful only if the hardware supports them. For example, you can't change the rounding method if the hardware doesn't have that option.

You use a preprocessor directive to turn support on:

```
#pragma STDC FENV_ACCESS ON
```

Support stays on until the program reaches the end of the block containing the pragma, or, if the pragma is external, to the end of the file or translation unit. Alternatively, you can use the following directive to turn off support:

```
#pragma STDC FENV_ACCESS OFF
```

You also can issue the following pragma:

```
#pragma STDC FENV_ACCESS DEFAULT
```

This restores the default state for the compiler, which is implementation dependent.

This facility is important for those involved in critical floating-point calculations, but of limited interest to the general user, so this appendix doesn't go into the details.

The `STDC FP_CONTRACT` Pragma

Some floating-point processors can contract a multiple-operator floating-expression into a single operation. For example, a processor might be able to evaluate the following expression in one step:

```
x*y - z
```

This increases the speed of the calculation, but it can decrease the predictability of the calculation. The `STDC FP_CONTRACT` pragma allows you to turn this feature on or off. The default state is implementation dependent.

To turn the contraction feature off for a particular calculation, and then turn it back on again, you can do this:

```
#pragma STDC FP_CONTRACT OFF
val = x * y - z;
#pragma STDC FP_CONTRACT ON
```

Additions to the `math.h` Library

The C90 math library, for the most part, declares functions with type **double** arguments and type **double** return values, such as the following

```
double sin(double);
double sqrt(double);
```

The C99 library provides type **float** and type **long double** versions of all these functions. These functions use an **f** or an **l** suffix in the name, as follows:

```
float sinf(float);              /* float version of sin()       */
long double sinl(long double);  /* long double version of sin() */
```

Having function families with different levels of precision allows you to choose the most efficient combination of types and functions needed for a particular purpose.

C99 also adds several functions commonly used in scientific, engineering, and mathematical computations. Table RS.V.14, which lists the type **double** versions of all the math functions, identifies the C99 additions. In many cases, the functions return values that could be calculated using existing functions, but the new functions do so faster or more accurately. For instance, `log1p(x)` represents the same value as `log(1 + x)`, but `log1p(x)` uses a different algorithm, one that is more accurate for small values of **x**. So you would use the `log()` function for calculations in general, but you would use `log1p()` for small values of **x** if high accuracy were critical.

In addition to these functions, the math library defines several constants and functions related to classifying numbers and rounding them. For example, a value can be classified as being infinite, not a number (NaN), normal, subnormal, and true zero. (NaN is a special value indicating that a value is not a number; for example, asin(2.0) returns NaN because asin() is defined only for arguments in the range -1 to 1. A subnormal number is one whose magnitude is smaller than the smallest value that can be represented to full precision.) There are also specialized comparison functions that behave differently from the standard relational operators when one or more arguments are abnormal values.

You can use C99's classification schemes to detect computational irregularities. For example, the isnormal() macro from math.h returns true if its argument is a normal number. Here is code using that function to terminate a loop when a number becomes subnormal:

```
#include <math.h>  // for isnormal()
...
float num = 1.7e-19;
float numprev = num;

while (isnormal(num))  // while num has full float precision
{
    numprev = num;
    num /= 13.7f;
}
```

In short, there is expanded support for detailed control of how floating-point calculations are handled.

Support for Complex Numbers

A *complex number* is a number with a real part and an imaginary part. The real part is an ordinary real number, such as what's represented by the floating-point types. The imaginary part represents an imaginary number. An imaginary number, in turn, is a multiple of the square root of −1. In mathematics, complex numbers are often written in the form 4.2 + 2.0i; i symbolically represents the square root of −1.

C99 supports three complex types:

- float _Complex
- double _Complex
- long double _Complex

A float _Complex value, for example, would be stored using the same memory layout as a two-element array of float, with the real value stored in the first element and the imaginary value in the second element.

C99 implementations may also support three imaginary types:

- float _Imaginary
- double _Imaginary
- long double _Imaginary

Including the `complex.h` header file lets you use `complex` for `_Complex` and `imaginary` for `_Imaginary`.

Arithmetic operations are defined for complex types following the usual rules of mathematics. For example, the value of `(a+b*I)*(c+d*I)` is `(a*c-b*d)+(b*c+a*d)*I`.

The `complex.h` header file defines some macros and several functions that accept complex numbers and return complex numbers. In particular, the macro `I` represents the square root of −1. It enables you do the following:

```
double complex c1 = 4.2 + 2.0 * I;
float imaginary c2= -3.0 * I;
```

The `complex.h` header file prototypes several complex functions. Many are complex equivalents of `math.h` functions, using a `c` prefix. For example, `csin()` returns the complex sine of its complex argument. Others relate specifically to the features of complex numbers. For example, `creal()` returns the real part of a complex number, and `cimag()` returns the imaginary part as a real number. That is, given that `z` is type `double complex`, the following is true:

```
z = creal(z) + cimag(z) * I;
```

If you are familiar with complex numbers and need to use them, you'll want to peruse the contents of `complex.h`.

If you use C++, you should be aware that the C++ `complex` header file provides a different way, based on classes, of handling complex numbers than does the C `complex.h` header file.

Section IX: Differences Between C and C++

For the most part, C++ is a superset of C, meaning that a valid C program is also a valid C++ program. The main differences between C++ and C are the many additional features that C++ supports. However, there are a few areas in which the C++ rules are slightly different from the C equivalents. These are the differences that might cause a C program to work a little differently, or perhaps, not at all, if you compile it as a C++ program. And these are the differences this appendix discusses. If you compile your C programs using a compiler that does just C++ and not C, you need to know about these differences. Although they affect very few of the examples in this book, the differences can cause some instances of valid C code to lead to error messages if the code is compiled as a C++ program.

The release of the C99 standard complicates issues because in some places it brings C closer to C++. For example, it allows interspersing declarations throughout the body of the code and recognizes the `//` comment indicator. In other ways, C99 increases the separation from C++—for example, by adding variable arrays and the `restrict` keyword. With C99 still in its infancy, we're faced with differences between C90 and C99, C90 and C++, and C99 and C++. But eventually, C99 will completely replace C90, so this section will face the future and discuss some of differences between C99 and C++.

Function Prototypes

In C++, function prototyping is mandatory, but it is optional in C. This difference shows up if you leave the parentheses empty when declaring a function. In C, empty parentheses mean you are foregoing prototyping, but in C++ they mean the function has no parameters. That is, in C++, the prototype

```
int slice();
```

means the same as the following:

```
int slice(void);
```

For example, the following sequence is acceptable, if old-fashioned, in C but an error in C++:

```
int slice();
int main()
{
...
   slice(20, 50);
...
}
int slice(int a, int b)
{
...
}
```

In C, the compiler assumes you used the older form for declaring functions. In C++, the compiler assumes that `slice()` is the same as `slice(void)` and that you failed to declare the `slice(int, int)` function.

Also, C++ allows you to declare more than one function of the same name, provided they have different argument lists.

char Constants

C treats `char` constants as type `int`, and C++ treats them as type `char`. For instance, consider this statement:

```
char ch = 'A';
```

In C, the constant `'A'` is stored in an `int`-sized chunk of memory; more precisely, the character code is stored in the `int`. The same numeric value is also stored in the variable `ch`, but here it occupies just one byte of memory.

C++, on the other hand, uses one byte for `'A'`, as well as for `ch`. This distinction doesn't affect any of the examples in this text. However, some C programs do make use of `char` constants being type `int` by using character notation to represent integer values. For instance, if a system has a 4-byte `int`, you can do this in C:

```
int x = 'ABCD';  /* ok in C for 4-byte int but not for C++ */
```

The meaning of `'ABCD'` is a 4-byte `int` in which the first byte stores the character code for the letter A, the second byte stores the character code of B, and so on. Note that `'ABCD'` is something quite different from `"ABCD"`. The former is just a funny way of writing an `int` value, but the latter is a string and corresponds to the address of a 5-byte chunk of memory.

Consider the following code:

```
int x = 'ABCD';
char c = 'ABCD';
printf("%d %d %c %c\n", x, 'ABCD', c, 'ABCD');
```

On our system, it produces this output:

```
1094861636 1094861636 D D
```

This example illustrates that if you treat `'ABCD'` as an `int`, it is a 4-byte integer value, but if you treat it as type `char`, the program looks only at the final byte. Attempting to print `'ABCD'` by using the `%s` specifier caused the program to crash on our system, because the numeric value of `'ABCD'` (`1094861636`) was an out-of-bounds address.

The rationale for using values such as `'ABCD'` is that it provides a means to set each byte in the `int` independently, because each character corresponds exactly to one byte. However, a better approach, because it doesn't depend on particular character codes, is to use hexadecimal values for integer constants, using the fact that each two-digit hexadecimal group corresponds to one byte. Chapter 15, "Bit Fiddling," discusses this technique. (Early versions of C didn't provide hexadecimal notation, which probably is why the multicharacter character constant technique was developed in the first place.)

The `const` Modifier

In C, a global `const` has external linkage, but in C++, it has internal linkage. That is, the C++ declaration

```
const double PI = 3.14159;
```

is equivalent to the C declaration

```
static const double PI = 3.14159;
```

provided both declarations are outside of any function. The C++ rule has the goal of making it simpler to use `const` in header files. If the constant has internal linkage, each file that includes the header file gets its own copy of the constant. If a constant has external linkage, one file has to have a defining declaration and the other files have to have a reference declaration, one that uses the keyword `extern`.

Incidentally, C++ can use the keyword `extern` to make a `const` value have external linkage, so both languages can create constants with internal linkage and external linkage. The difference is just in which kind of linkage is used by default.

One additional property of the C++ `const` is that it can be used to declare the size of an ordinary array:

```
const int ARSIZE = 100;
double loons[ARSIZE];  /* in C++, same as double loons[100];  */
```

You can make the same declarations in C99, but in C99, the declaration creates a variable array.

In C++, but not in C, you can use const values to initialize other const values:

```
const double RATE = 0.06;            // valid C++, C
const double STEP = 24.5;            // valid C++, C
const double LEVEL = RATE * STEP;    // valid C++, invalid C
```

Structures and Unions

After you declare a structure or union having a tag, you can use the tag as a type name in C++:

```
struct duo
{
    int a;
    int b;
};
struct duo m;   /* valid C, C++ */
duo n;          /* invalid C, valid C++ */
```

As a result, a structure name can conflict with a variable name. For example, the following program compiles as a C program, but it fails as a C++ program because C++ interprets duo in the printf() statement as a structure type rather than as the external variable:

```
#include <stdio.h>
float duo = 100.3;
int main(void)
{
    struct duo { int a; int b;};
    struct duo y = { 2, 4};
    printf ("%f\n", duo);   /* ok in C, not in C++ */
    return 0;
}
```

In C and in C++, you can declare one structure inside another:

```
struct box
{
    struct point {int x; int y; } upperleft;
    struct point lowerright;
};
```

In C, you can use either structure later, but C++ requires a special notation for the nested structure:

```
struct box ad;      /* valid C, C++          */
struct point dot;   /* valid C, invalid C++ */
box::point dot;   /* invalid C, valid C++ */
```

Enumerations

C++ is stricter about using enumerations than C is. In particular, about the only useful things you can do with an enum variable are assign an enum constant to it and compare it to other values. You can't assign `int`s to an `enum` without an explicit type cast, and you can't increment an `enum` variable. The following code illustrates these points:

```
enum sample {sage, thyme, salt, pepper};
enum sample season;
season = sage;            /* ok in C, C++           */
season = 2;               /* warning in C, error in C++ */
season = (enum sample) 3; /* ok in C, C++           */
season++;                 /* ok in C, error in C++   */
```

Also, C++ lets you drop the keyword `enum` when declaring a variable:

```
enum sample {sage, thyme, salt, pepper};
sample season;    /* invalid C, valid C++ */
```

As was the case with structures and unions, this can lead to conflicts if a variable and an `enum` type have the same name.

Pointer-to-`void`

In C++, as in C, you can assign a pointer of any type to a pointer-to-`void`, but, unlike in C, you cannot assign a pointer-to-`void` to another type unless you use an explicit type cast. The following code illustrates these points:

```
int ar[5] = {4, 5, 6,7, 8};
int * pi;
void * pv;
pv = ar;            /* ok in C, C++           */
pi = pv;            /* ok in C, invalid in C++ */
pi = (int * ) pv;   /* ok in C, C++           */
```

Another difference in C++ is that you can assign the address of a derived-class object to a base-class pointer, but that relates to features that don't even exist in C.

Boolean Types

In C++, the Boolean type is `bool`, and `true` and `false` are keywords. In C, the Boolean type is `_Bool`, but including the header file `stdbool.h` makes `bool`, `true`, and `false` available.

Alternative Spellings

In C++, the alternative spellings of `or` for `||`, and so on, are keywords. In C99, they are defined as macros, and you need to include `iso646.h` to make them available.

Wide-Character Support

In C++, `wchar_t` is a built-int type, and `wchar_t` is a keyword. In C99, the `wchar_t` type is defined in several header files (`stddef.h`, `stdlib.h`, `wchar.h`, `wctype.h`).

C++ provides wide-character I/O support through the `iostream` header file, whereas C99 provides a completely different package of I/O support through the `wchar.h` header file. Also,

C99 supports multibyte characters and multibyte-wide character conversions, and C++ doesn't.

Complex Types

C++ supports complex types through a complex class provided by the `complex` header file. C has built-in complex types and supports them through the `complex.h` header file. The two approaches are quite different and are not compatible with one another. The C version reflects a greater concern with the needs and practices of the numerical computation community.

Inline Functions

C99 has added inline function support, a feature C++ already had. However, the C99 implementation is more flexible. In C++, an inline function has internal linkage by default. If a C++ inline function appears in more than one file, it has to have the same definition, using the same tokens. For example, one file can't have a definition using a type `int` parameter and another file have a definition using a type `int32_t` parameter, even if `int32_t` is a `typedef` for `int`. C, however, allows that arrangement. Also, C, as described in Chapter 15, allows a mixture of inline and external definitions that C++ doesn't allow.

C99 Features Not Found in C++

Although C traditionally is more or less a subset of C++, the C99 standard adds several features missing in C++. Here are some of the more prominent C99-only features:

- Designated initializers
- Compound initializers
- Restricted pointers
- Variable-length arrays
- Flexible array members
- `long long` and `unsigned long long` types
- Portable integer types (`inttypes.h` and `stdint.h`)
- Universal character names
- Additional math library functions
- Floating-point environment access via `fenv.h`
- Predefined identifiers, such as `__func__`
- Macros with a variable number of arguments

Probably some of these, such as the `long long` type, will become common C++ extensions, and some may become incorporated into the next edition of the C++ standard.

INDEX

How can we make this index more useful? Email us at indexes@samspublishing.com

C

D

F

How can we make this index more useful? Email us at indexes@samspublishing.com

H

M

N

P

T

U

W - Z

RELATED TITLES

Visual Basic .NET Primer Plus
Jack Purdum
0-672-32485-7
$44.99 USA / $64.99 C

XML Primer Plus
Nicholas Chase
0-672-32422-9
$44.99 USA / $64.99 CAN

Sams Teach Yourself C++ in 24 Hours, Complete Starter Kit, Fourth Edition
Jesse Liberty, David B. Horvath, CCP
0-672-32681-7
$29.99 USA / $42.99 CAN

Borland C++ Builder 6 Developer's Guide
Bob Swart, Mark Cashman, Paul Gustavson, and Jarrod Hollingworth
0-672-32480-6
$59.99 USA / $86.99 CAN

Sams Teach Yourself Visual C++ .NET in 21 Days, Second Edition
Davis Chapman
0-672-32197-1
$39.99 USA / $57.99 CAN

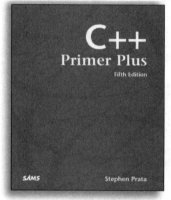

C++ Primer Plus, Fift Edition
Stephen Prata
0-672-32697-3
$44.99 USA / $64.99 CA

Java 2 Primer Plus
Steven Haines and Steve Potts
0-672-32415-6
$44.99 USA / $64.99 CA

SAMS

www.samspublishing.com

All prices are subject to change.